# Wales

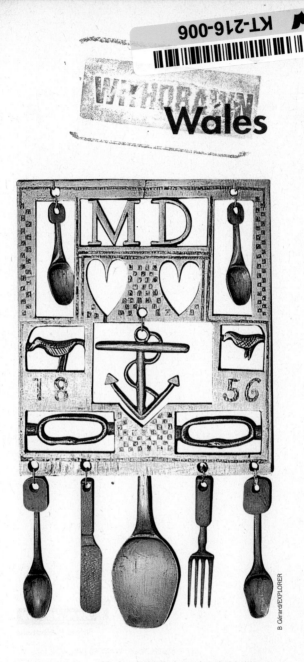

B Gérard/EXPLORER

Mae'n wlad i ti ac mae'n wlad i tithau;
O gopau'r Wyddfa i lawr i'r traethau.
O'r De i'r Gogledd, o Fôn i Fynwy,
Mae'r hen wlad hon yn eiddo i ti a mi.
It's a country for you and a country for me;
from the summit of Snowdon, down to the beaches.
from the South to the North,
from Anglesey to Monmouthshire,
This old country belongs to you and me.

Traditional

30/4/09

914
.29
GRE

Travel Publications

38 Clarendon Road - WATFORD Herts WD1 1SX - U.K.
☏ (01923) 415 000
www.michelin-travel.com
TheGreenGuide-uk@uk.michelin.com

## Manufacture française des pneumatiques Michelin

Société en commandite par actions au capital de 2 000 000 000 de francs
Place des Carmes-Déchaux – 63 Clermont-Ferrand (France)
R.C.S. Clermont-Fd B 855 200 507

Dépôt légal Mars 2001 – ISBN 2-06-000152-8 – ISSN 0763-1383
Printed in France 03-01/2.1

Typesetting: APS/Chromostyle, Tours
Printing-binding: MAME Imprimeur-Relieur, Tours

Cover design: Carré Noir, Paris 17ᵉ arr.

# THE GREEN GUIDE:
## The Spirit of Discovery

The exhilaration of new horizons, the fun
of seeing the world, the excitement
of discovery: this is what we seek to share
with you. To help you make the most
of your travel experience, we offer first-hand
knowledge and turn a discerning eye
on places to visit.

This wealth of information gives you
the expertise to plan your own enriching
adventure. With THE GREEN GUIDE
showing you the way, you can explore new
destinations with confidence or rediscover
old ones.

Leisure time spent with THE GREEN GUIDE
is also a time for refreshing your spirit
and enjoying yourself.

So turn the page and open a window
on the world. Join THE GREEN GUIDE
in the spirit of discovery.

# Contents

Ph Montigny/VANDYSTADT

R Manin/HOA QUI

# Sights 73

# Maps and Plans

## COMPANION PUBLICATIONS

A map reference to the appropriate Michelin map is given for each chapter in the Sights section of this guide.

## Regional maps:

The Michelin map 403 (Scale 1: 400 000 – 1cm = 4km – 1in: 6.30miles), on one sheet, covers Wales, the West Country and the Midlands, the network of motorways and major roads and some secondary roads. It provides information on shipping routes, distances in miles and kilometres, major town plans, services, sporting and tourist attractions, a list of the Unitary Authorities of Wales and an index of places; the key and text are printed in four languages.

## Country maps:

The Michelin Tourist and Motoring Atlas – Great Britain & Ireland (Scale 1: 300 000 – 1cm = 3km – 1in: 4.75 miles - based on 1: 400 000) covers the whole of the United Kingdom and the Republic of Ireland, the national networks of motorways and major roads. It provides information on route planning, shipping routes, distances in miles and kilometres, over 60 town plans, services, sporting and tourist attractions and an index of places; the key and text are printed in six languages.

The Michelin map 986 – Great Britain & Ireland (Scale 1: 1 000 000 – 1cm = 10km – 1inch: 15.8 miles), on one sheet, covers the whole of the United Kingdom and the Republic of Ireland, the national networks of motorways and major roads. It provides information on shipping routes, distances in miles and kilometres, a list of Unitary Authorities for Wales and Scotland; the key and text are printed in four languages.

## Internet:

Users can access personalised route plans, Michelin mapping on line, addresses of hotels and restaurants listed in The Red Guides and practical and tourist information through the internet:
www.michelin-travel.com

# LIST OF MAPS AND PLANS

## Plans of monuments

## Local maps

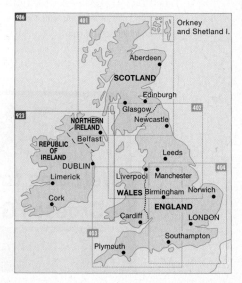

# Using this Guide

● The summary maps on pages 10-15 are designed to assist at the planning stage: the **Map of Principal Sights** identifies the major attractions according to their star ratings; the **Map of Touring Programmes** outlines regional motoring itineraries; the **Map of Activities** shows a range of leisure and sporting activities and several categories of places to stay.

● The **Practical Information** section provides useful travel advice, addresses, services, information on recreational facilities, a calendar of events and bibliography.

● It is worth reading the **Introduction** before setting out as it gives background information on history, the arts and traditional culture.

● The main natural and cultural attractions are presented in alphabetical order in the **Sights** section; excursions to places in the surrounding district are attached to many of the town chapters. Place names often have two versions – the English and the Welsh; the official version has been adopted in this guide. There is a glossary of Welsh place names and expressions in the Introduction.

● The clock symbol ⊙ placed after the name of a sight refers to the Admission Times and Charges chapter.

● This guide is designed to be used in conjunction with the Michelin road **Map 403** (Wales, West Country, Midlands), **Map 986** (Great Britain and Ireland) and the Michelin Tourist and Motoring **Atlas Great Britain and Ireland**. Cross-references to these maps (except map 986) appear under the chapter headings in the Sights section.

● For a selection of hotels and restaurants, consult the **Wales section** in the **Michelin Red Guide Great Britain and Ireland**, which also contains town plans.

● To find a particular place or historic figure or event or practical information, consult the **Index**.

● We greatly appreciate comments and suggestions from our readers. Contact us at

Michelin Travel Publications,

38 Clarendon Road, Watford WD1 1SX, UK

☎ 01923 415 000 - Fax 01923 415 250

thegreenguide-uk@uk.michelin.com

www.michelin-travel.com

# Key

## Tourism

| | | | |
|---|---|---|---|
| Admission Times and Charges listed at the end of the guide | | ►► | Visit if time permits |
| Sightseeing route with departure point indicated | | AZ B | Map co-ordinates locating sights |
| Ecclesiastical building | | | Tourist information |
| Synagogue – Mosque | | | Historic house, castle – Ruins |
| Building (with main entrance) | | | Dam – Factory or power station |
| Statue, small building | | | Fort – Cave |
| Wayside cross | | | Prehistoric site |
| Fountain | | | Viewing table – View |
| Fortified walls – Tower – Gate | | | Miscellaneous sight |

## Recreation

| | | |
|---|---|---|
| Racecourse | | Waymarked footpath |
| Skating rink | | Outdoor leisure park/centre |
| Outdoor, indoor swimming pool | | Theme/Amusement park |
| Marina, moorings | | Wildlife/Safari park, zoo |
| Mountain refuge hut | | Gardens, park, arboretum |
| Overhead cable-car | | Aviary, bird sanctuary |
| Tourist or steam railway | | |

## Additional symbols

| | | |
|---|---|---|
| Motorway (unclassified) | | Post office – Telephone centre |
| Junction: complete, limited | | Covered market |
| Pedestrian street | | Barracks |
| Unsuitable for traffic, street subject to restrictions | | Swing bridge |
| Steps – Footpath | | Quarry – Mine |
| Railway – Coach station | | Ferry (river and lake crossings) |
| Funicular – Rack-railway | | Ferry services: Passengers and cars |
| Tram – Metro, Underground | | Foot passengers only |
| Bert (R.)... Main shopping street | | Access route number common to MICHELIN maps and town plans |

## Abbreviations and special symbols

| | | | | |
|---|---|---|---|---|
| C | County council offices | | T | Theatre |
| H | Town hall | | U | University |
| J | Law courts | | P R | Park and Ride |
| M | Museum | | M 3 | Motorway |
| POL. | Police | | A 2 | Primary route |

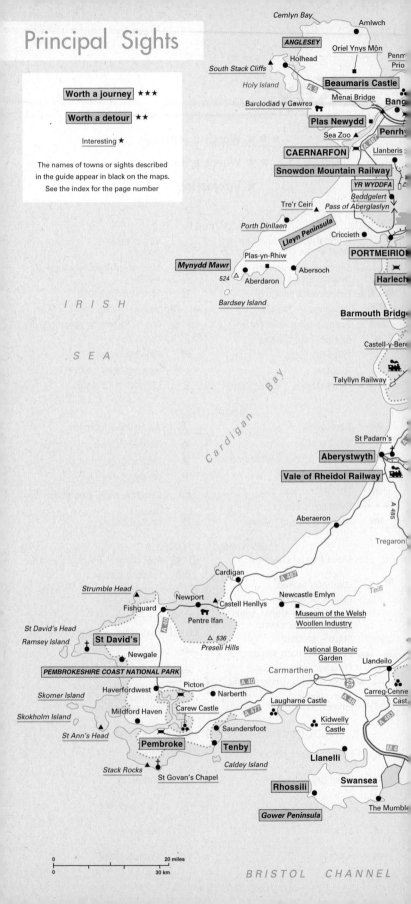

# Principal Sights

**Worth a journey** ★★★

**Worth a detour** ★★

Interesting ★

The names of towns or sights described
in the guide appear in black on the maps.
See the index for the page number

*Cemlyn Bay*
Amlwch
*ANGLESEY*
Oriel Ynys Môn
Penr
Prio
Holhead
*South Stack Cliffs*
Holyhead
**Beaumaris Castle**
*Holy Island*
Menai Bridge
Bang
Barclodiad y Gawres
**Plas Newydd**
**Penr**
Sea Zoo ▲
**CAERNARFON**
Llanberis
**Snowdon Mountain Railway**
*YR WYDDFA*
*Beddgelert*
Tre'r Ceiri
*Pass of Aberglaslyn*
*Porth Dinllaen*
*Lleyn Peninsula*
Criccieth
**PORTMEIRIO**
Plas-yn-Rhiw
*Mynydd Mawr*
Abersoch
**Harlech**
524
Aberdaron
○
*Bardsey Island*
**Barmouth Bridg**
*Castell-y-Ber*

*I R I S H*

*S E A*

*Talyllyn Railway*

*Cardigan Bay*

St Padarn's
**Aberystwyth**
**Vale of Rheidol Railway**

Aberaeron
A 485
Tregaron

Cardigan
A 487
Newcastle Emlyn
*Teifi*
*Strumble Head*
Newport
Fishguard
Castell Henllys
Pentre Ifan
**Museum of the Welsh
Woollen Industry**
*St David's Head*
**St David's**
*Ramsey Island*
△ 536
Newgale
*Preseli Hills*
National Botanic
Garden
Llandeilo
Carmarthen
**PEMBROKESHIRE COAST NATIONAL PARK**
Picton
A 40
*Skomer Island*
Haverfordwest
Narberth
Carreg Cenne
Cast
*Skokholm Island*
Mildford Haven
Carew Castle
Laugharne Castle
A 48
A 477
A 485
*St Ann's Head*
Saundersfoot
Kidwelly
Castle
**Pembroke**
**Tenby**
*Stack Rocks*
*Caldey Island*
**Llanelli**
M 4
St Govan's Chapel
**Rhossili**
**Swansea**
*Gower Peninsula*
The Mumble

0          20 miles
0        30 km

*B R I S T O L   C H A N N E L*

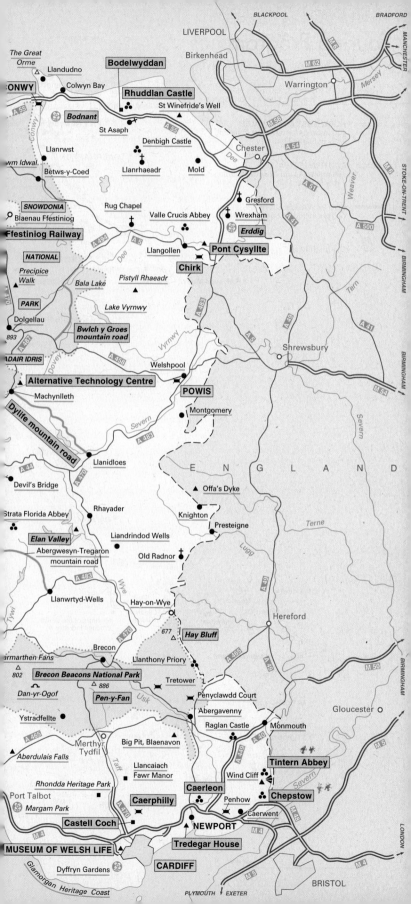

# Touring Programmes

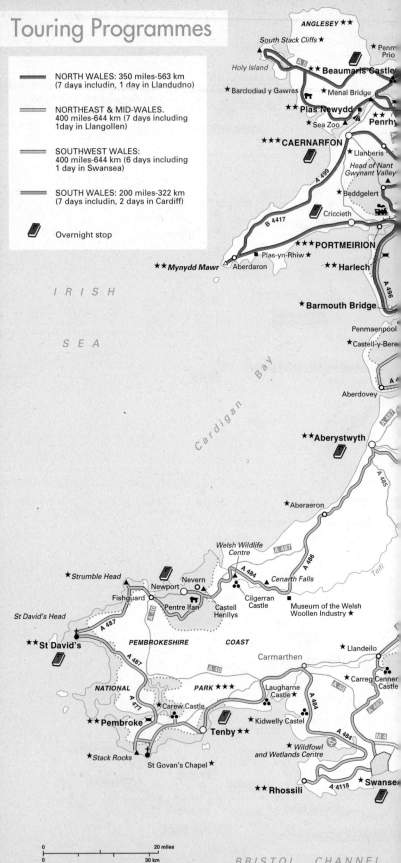

**NORTH WALES: 350 miles-563 km**
(7 days includin, 1 day in Llandudno)

**NORTHEAST & MID-WALES.**
400 miles-644 km (7 days including
1day in Llangollen)

**SOUTHWEST WALES:**
400 miles-644 km (6 days including
1 day in Swansea)

**SOUTH WALES: 200 miles-322 km**
(7 days includin, 2 days in Cardiff)

Overnight stop

*ANGLESEY* ★★
South Stack Cliffs ★
Penm Prio
*Holy Island*
★★ **Beaumaris Castle**
★ Barclodiad y Gawres
★ Menal Bridge
★★ **Plas Newydd**
★ Sea Zoo
**Penrhy**
★★★ **CAERNARFON**
Llanberis
*Head of Nant Gwynant Valley*
A 499
★ Beddgelert
Criccieth
B 4417
★★★ **PORTMEIRION**
★ Plas-yn-Rhiw ★
★★ **Harlech**
★★ *Mynydd Mawr*
Aberdaron
A 496
★ **Barmouth Bridge**
Penmaenpool
★Castell-y-Bere
A
Aberdovey
A 487
★★**Aberystwyth**
A 485
★ Aberaeron

*I R I S H*

*S E A*

*Cardigan Bay*

*Telfi*

*Welsh Wildlife Centre*
A 484
Cenarth Falls
★ Strumble Head
Newport
Fishguard
Pentre Ifan
A 487
Castell Henllys
Cilgerran Castle
Museum of the Welsh Woollen Industry ★
St David's Head
★★ **St David's**
A 487
*PEMBROKESHIRE*    *COAST*
Carmarthen
★ Llandeilo
★ Carreg Cennen Castle
A 48
A 40
*NATIONAL*    *PARK* ★★★
A 471
★ Carew Castle
Laugharne Castle ★
A 484
A 483
★★ **Pembroke**
★ Kidwelly Castel
A 484
**Tenby** ★★
M 4
★ *Stack Rocks*
St Govan's Chapel ★
★ *Wildfowl and Wetlands Centre*
A 484
★★ **Rhossili**
A 4118
★ **Swanse**

0  20 miles
0  30 km

*BRISTOL   CHANNEL*

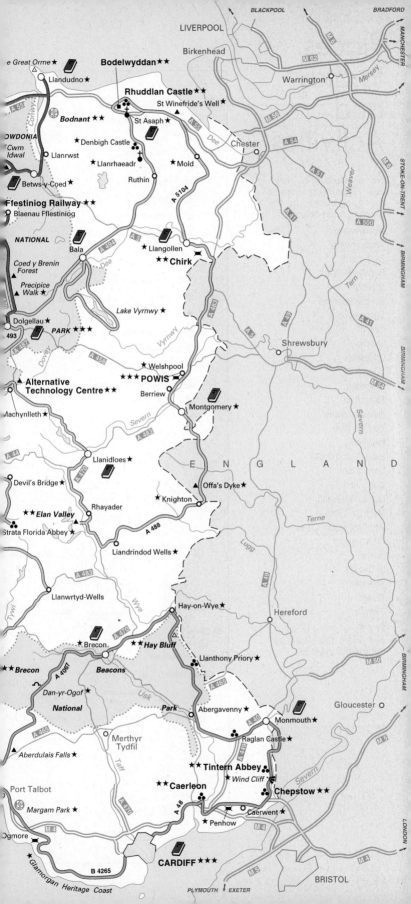

# Places to Stay and Activities

For a selection of hotels and restaurants consult the blue panels in the chapters listed below

Abergavenny
Aberystwyth
Beaumaris
Betwys-y-Coed
Brecon
Brecon Beacons
Caernarfon
Cardiff
Cardigan
Chepstow
Conwy
Dolgellau
Fishguard
Haverfordwest
Hay-on-Wye
Holyhead
Llandrindod Wells
Llandudno
Llangollen
LLeyn Peninsula
Merthyr Tydfil
Pembrokeshire Coast
Portmeirion
Ruthin
St David's
Swansea
Tenby
Tintern
Twywn

*See also the Practical Information page 23.*

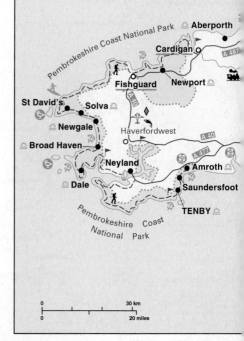

|  | Overnight stop |
|---|---|
|  | Sightseeing centre |
| ● | Resort |
|  | Seaside resort |
|  | Marina |
|  | Beach |
|  | Surf |
|  | Nature reserve |
|  | Garden |
|  | Golf |
|  | Racecourse |
|  | Waymarked footpath |
|  | Wildlife/Safari park, zoo |
|  | Country park |
|  | Forest, Forest park |
|  | Airfield |
|  | Airport |
|  | Tourist or steam railway |
|  | Canal cruises |
|  | Fishing |

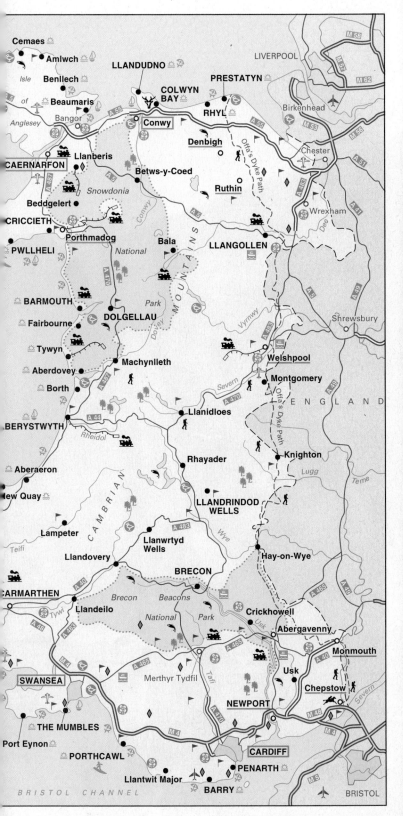

*Penrhyn Quarry* by Henry Hawkins (1822-80)

# Practical
# Information

# Planning your Trip

**Seasons** – Summer is the best time for visiting Wales and enjoying its natural attractions on the coast or in the mountains. Spring and autumn are good seasons for visiting parks and gardens when the flowers are in bloom or the leaves are turning colour. The tourist season, when the main festivals are held *(see p 34)*, runs from Easter to October. At any time of year there is the possibility of rain, owing to the mountains and the prevailing westerly wind; in winter there may be snow, especially on the high ground.

**Standard Time** – In winter standard time throughout the British Isles is Greenwich Mean Time (GMT). In summer clocks are advanced by an hour to give British Summer Time (BST). The actual dates are announced annually but always occur at the weekend in March and October.

Time may be expressed according to the 24-hour clock or the 12-hour clock.

| | | | |
|---|---|---|---|
| 12.00 | noon | 19.00 | 7pm |
| 13.001 | pm | 20.00 | 8pm |
| 14.002 | pm | 21.00 | 9pm |
| 15.00 | 3pm | 22.00 | 10pm |
| 16.00 | 4pm | 23.00 | 11pm |
| 17.00 | 5pm | 24.00 | midnight |
| 18.00 | 6pm | | |

**Public Holidays** – The list below gives the public (bank) holidays in England and Wales, when most shops and municipal museums are closed.

1 January
Good Friday (Friday before Easter Day)
Easter Monday (Monday after Easter Day)
First Monday in May (May Day)
Last Monday in May (Spring Bank Holiday)
Last Monday in August
25 December (Christmas Day)
26 December (Boxing Day)

In addition to the usual school holidays in the spring and summer and at Christmas, there are mid-term breaks in February, May and October.

**Documents** – Despite the law, which came into force on 1 January 1993, authorising the free flow of goods and people within the European Union, it is nonetheless advisable for EU nationals to hold some means of identification, such as a **passport**. Non-EU nationals must be in possession of a valid national passport. Loss or theft should be reported to the appropriate embassy or consulate and to the local police.

A **visa** to visit the United Kingdom is not required by nationals of the member states of the European Union and of the Commonwealth (including Australia, Canada, New Zealand, and South Africa) and the USA. Nationals of other countries should check with the British Embassy and apply for a visa if necessary in good time.

The brochure *Safe Trip Abroad* (US$1.25) provides useful information for US nationals on obtaining a passport, visa requirements, customs regulations, medical care etc for international travel; it is published by the government printing office and can be ordered by telephone ☎ 1-202-512-1800 and ordered or consulted via the Internet on www.access.gpo.gov

**Customs** – Tax free allowances for various commodities are governed by EU legislation. Details of these allowances and restrictions are available at most ports of entry to Great Britain.

The UK Customs Office produces a leaflet on customs regulations and the full range of "duty free" allowances; available from HM Customs and Excise, Dorset House, Stamford Street, London SE1 9PY; ☎ 020 7620 1313 (HQ); 020 7928 3344 (central switchboard); 020 7202 4227 (Advice centre).

Domestic animals (dogs, cats) are allowed into the country only if they have been vaccinated in accordance with the regulations and have vaccination documents. It is against the law to bring into the United Kingdom drugs, firearms and ammunition, obscene material featuring children, counterfeit merchandise, unlicensed livestock (birds or animals), anything related to endangered species (furs, ivory, horn, leather) and certain plants (potatoes, bulbs, seeds, trees).

A booklet *Know before you go* is published by the US Customs Service; its offices are listed in the phone book in the Federal Government section under the US Department of the Treasury or can be obtained by consulting www.customs.ustreas.gov

**Medical treatment** – Visitors from EU countries should apply to their own National Social Security Offices for Form E111 which entitles them to medical treatment under an EU Reciprocal Medical Treatment arrangement.

Nationals of non-EU countries should take out comprehensive insurance. American Express offers a service, **Global Assist**, for any medical, legal or personal emergency – freephone 0800 892 333; ☎ 02920 66 55 55 (UK); ☎ 800 554 2639 (tollfree in the USA).

## Tourist Information Centres

The **Wales Tourist Board** provides assistance in planning a trip to Wales and an excellent range of brochures and maps.

**Wales Tourist Board**: Brunel House, 2 Fitzalan Road, Cardiff CF24 0UY; ☎ 029 2047 5226 (brochures); ☎ 029 2049 9909 (switchboard); Fax 029 2047 5345; info@tourism.wales.gov.uk; www.visitwales.com

**North Wales Tourism**: 77 Conway Road, Colwyn Bay LL29 7LN; ☎ 01492 531 731; Fax 01492 530 059; croeso@nwt.co.uk; www. nwt.co.uk

**Mid-Wales Tourism**: The Station, Machynlleth SY20 8TG; ☎ 0800 273 747 (free-phone); ☎ 01654 702 653; Fax 01654 703 235; mwt@mid-wales-tourism.org.uk; www.mid-wales-tourism.org.uk

**Tourism South and West Wales**: Charter Court, Enterprise Park, Swansea SA7 9DB; ☎ 01792 781 212; Fax 01792 781 300; croeso@tsww.com; www.tsww.org.uk

**Wales Information Bureau**: British Visitor Centre, 1 Lower Regent Street, London SW1 4XT; ☎ 020 8846 9000 (British Tourist Authority); 020 7808 3838 (Enquiries about Wales).

There are **Tourist Information Centres** in all parts of the country with information on sightseeing, accommodation, places to eat, transport, entertainment, sports and local events. They are usually well signed but some are open only during the summer season; addresses and telephone numbers are given in the chapters in the Sights section.

The **British Tourist Authority** (BTA) also provides information about Wales from its offices in Belgium, Brazil, Denmark, Germany, Hong Kong, Ireland, Italy, Japan, the Netherlands, Norway, Spain, Sweden and Switzerland as well as those listed below.

**United States** – 625 North Michigan Avenue, Suite 1001, **Chicago**, Illinois 60611, ☎ 1 800 462 2748 (toll free); travelinfo@bta.org.uk; www.travelbritain.org
7th Floor, 551 Fifth Avenue, **New York**, NY 10176-0799, ☎ 00 1 (212) 986 2266; 1 800 GO 2 BRITAIN (toll free); travelinfo@bta.org.uk; www.travelbritain.org

**Canada** – 5915 Airport Road, Suite 120, **Mississauga**, Ontario, L4V 1T1, ☎ 1 888 VISIT UK (toll free); Fax 00 1 (905) 45 1835; travelinfo@bta.org.uk; www.visitbritain.com/ca

**France** – Maison de la Grande Bretagne, 19 rue des Mathurins, 75009 **Paris**, ☎ 00 33 (1) 4451 5620 (information).

**Australia** – Level 16, Gateway, 1 Macquarie Place, **Sydney**, NSW 2000, ☎ 00 61 (2) 9377 4400; Fax 00 61 (2) 9377 4499; visitbritainaus@bta.org.uk; www.visitbritain.com/au

**New Zealand** – 17th Floor, NZI House, 151 Queen Street, **Auckland 1**, ☎ 00 64 (9) 303 1446; Fax 00 64 (9) 377 6965; bta.nz@bta.org.uk; www.visitbritain.uk

**Tourism for the Disabled** – Many of the sights described in this guide are accessible to disabled people *(see Admission Times and Charges at the end of the guide)*.
The Wales Tourist Board issues a pamphlet *Discovering Accessible Wales* which gives advice for disabled people on holiday in Wales.
Organisations such as the British Tourist Authority, National Trust and the Department of Transport publish booklets for the disabled.
The *Michelin Red Guide Great Britain and Ireland* indicates hotels with facilities suitable for disabled people; it is advisable to book in advance.
The Royal Association for Disability and Rehabilitation (RADAR) publishes an annual guide with detailed information on hotels and holiday centres as well as on transport, accommodation for children and activity holidays.
Specialised information and assistance with travel planning, access, transport and accommodation, for which a charge may be made, is provided by

**RADAR**, 12 City Forum, 250 City Road, London ECIV 8AF, ☎ 020 7250 3222; Fax 020 7250 0212; minicom 020 7250 4119; radar@radar.org.uk; www.radar.org.uk

**Holiday Care**, 2nd Floor, Imperial Buildings, Victoria Road, Horley RH6 7PZ ☎ 01293 774 535

**Disability Wales**, Llys Ifor, Crescent Road, Caerphilly CF83 1XL ☎ 029 2088 7325; Fax 029 2088 8702; info@dwac.demon.co.uk

**Euramp**, National Mobility Centre, Unit 2, Atcham Estate, Shrewsbury SY4 4UG ☎ 01743 761 181; Fax 01743 761 149; euramp@nmcshropshire.freeserve.co.uk; www.mis.org.uk

**Tripscope**, Tripscope@cableinet.co.uk; www.justmobility.couk/tripscope

# Getting there

For comprehensive public transport information in the UK: www.pti.org.uk

**By Air** – Cardiff-Wales airport (12mi/19km west of Cardiff city centre) at Rhoose in the Vale of Glamorgan has daily scheduled flights to a number of cities in the UK, Ireland and continental Europe with world-wide connections via Manchester and Amsterdam. The international airports at Manchester and Birmingham are accessible from many parts of Wales and London Heathrow is 140mi/225km from Cardiff via the M 4 motorway.
Information, brochures and timetables are available from the airlines and from travel agents. Many airlines organise fly-drive facilities.
Three major airports serve passengers travelling to Wales; two are just over the border in England; Cardiff and Birmingham offer long-term parking
- Cardiff Airport ☎ 01446 711 111;
- Birmingham International Airport ☎ 0121 767 5511;
- Manchester Airport ☎ 0161 489 3000;
- Fairwood Airport near Swansea (a smaller airport for light aircraft)
☎ 01792 468 321 (Swansea TIC).

**By Sea** – There are five permanent ferry services between the major Welsh ports and the major east and south coast ports in Ireland, operated by three ferry companies.
**Irish Ferries UK Ltd** – www.irishferries.com
  **Holyhead-Dublin** – Salt Island, Holyhead, Gwynedd LL65 1DR; ☎ 0990 329 129, 08705 171717; Fax 01407 760 340; info@irishferries.com
  **Pembroke Dock-Rosslare** – Irish Ferries UK Ltd, Ferryport, Pembroke Dock, Pembroke, Dyfed SA72 6TW; ☎ 0990 329 543, 08705 171717; Fax 01646 621 125; info@irishferries.com; www.irishferries.com
**Stena Line** – www.stenaline.co.uk
  **Holyhead-Dun Laoghaire** – Stena Line; ☎ 08705 707070; Fax 01233 202 231;
  **Fishguard-Rosslare** – Stena Line; ☎ 08705 707070; Fax 01233 202 231;
**Swansea-Cork Ferries** – www.swansea-cork.ie
  **Swansea-Cork** – Harbour Office, Kings Dock, Swansea SA1 1SF; ☎ 01792 456 116; Fax 01792 644 356; scf@iol.ie

It is also possible to drive into Wales from the ports in England.
  **Hoverspeed**, International Hoverport, Marine Parade, Dover, Kent CT17 9TG. ☎ 08705 240 241; Fax 01304 240 088; info@hoverspeed.co.uk; www.hoverspeed.co.uk
  **P&O European Ferries**, Channel House, Channel View Road, Dover, Kent CT17 9TJ. ☎ 0990 980 980, 01304 863 000 (Switchboard); Fax 01304 223 464; www. p-and-o.com
  **Stena Line**, Charter House, Park Street, Ashford, Kent TN24 8EX. ☎ 0990 707 070; www.stenaline.co.uk

**By Rail** – Fast rail services link major towns in South and North Wales with London and other English cities and also connect with ferry services to and from Fishguard and Holyhead. Other trains serve west Wales and operate on the mid-Wales, Conwy Valley and Cambrian Coast lines while a dense local network serves Cardiff and the Valleys. The rail network also provides a link with the Channel Tunnel service; details available from travel agencies and from
  **Eurostar** – ☎ 0990 186 186; www.eurostar.com
Eurotunnel Customer Service, St Martin's Lane, Cheriton, Folkestone CT19 4QD; ☎ 0990 353 535; Fax 01303 288 784; ☎ 08000 969 992 (free 24-hr information service); www.eurotunnel.com

There are no sleeper or motorail services in Wales.

Wales has a large number of preserved, mostly **narrow-gauge railways**, nine of which are grouped under the title "Great Little Trains" (see pp 30 and 47).

**Freedom of Wales Flexi-Passes** offer unlimited travel on all mainline rail services in Wales and most scheduled bus services, and also free or discount tickets on some of the narrow-gauge railways. 15-day Flexi-Pass in summer £92, £60.70 (child/railcard holder); in winter £75, £49.50 (child). 8-day Flexi-Pass in summer £49, £32.35 (child); in winter £39, £25.75 (child).
Regional Flexi-Rover passes offer unlimited travel by train or bus in south, north or mid Wales. 7-day South Wales Rover in summer £32, £21.10 (child); in winter £27, £17.80 (child). 7-day North and mid Wales Rover all year £26.30, £17.35 (child). For details and credit card bookings ☎ 08457 125 625, 01766 512 340; www. travelwales-flexipass.co.uk

**BritRail Passes** or **Flexipasses** are available to visitors from North America, South Africa and certain Asia-Pacific countries including Australia and New Zealand. BritRail Passes allow travel on consecutive days for various periods and Flexipasses allow travel on a number of days within a given month. As these concessions cannot be obtained in Britain, they should be purchased before the beginning of the journey in question. Information available in the USA on ☎ 00 1-888-667-9731; Fax 1-519-645-0682 www.eurail.on.ca or from Rail Europe 2100 Central Avenue Boulder CO 80301 ☎ 00 1 800 4 EURAIL, 00 1 888 BRITRAIL and 00 1 888 EUROSTAR; www.raileurope.com.us

For information on rail services within Wales and on other concessionary tickets, including combined train and bus tickets ☎ 0345 484 950 (National Rail Enquiries); ☎ 029 2043 0090 (Wales and West Trains); ☎ 08457 484 950 (timetables); ☎ 0870 9000 773 (for ticket sales); www.railtrack.co.uk

Combined train and bus tickets are available allowing unlimited travel by bus and train in mid-Wales and North Wales. ☎ 029 2043 0090 (Wales and West Trains).

**By Bus and Coach** – A network of express coach services run by a number of operators covers most of Wales. North and South Wales are linked by the Traws-Cambria line between Cardiff, Aberystwyth and Bangor. Details available from Tourist Information Centres and local bus stations. Connections to the rest of Great Britain are run by National Express.

**National Express**, Birmingham; ☎ 08705 808 080 (National call centre); ☎ 0121 625 1122; Fax 0121 456 1397 (Head Office); www.gobycoach.com

Local councils publish timetables giving comprehensive details of local bus services which are often provided by a variety of operators. The special bus services in the National Parks are particularly useful to those who would like to explore the parks on foot.

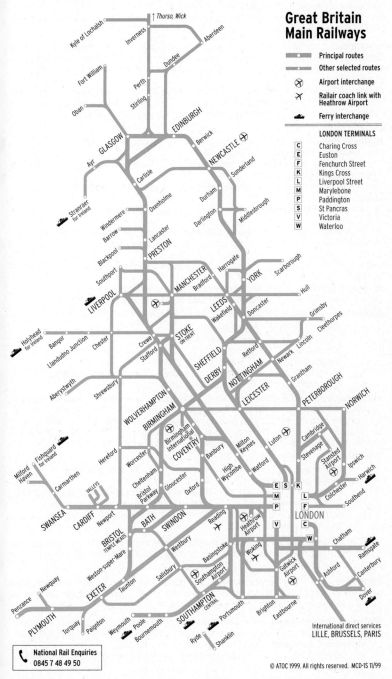

# Great Britain
# Main Railways

| | |
|---|---|
| ▭▭▭ | Principal routes |
| ▭▭▭ | Other selected routes |
| ⊗ | Airport interchange |
| ✕ | Railair coach link with Heathrow Airport |
| ⛴ | Ferry interchange |

**LONDON TERMINALS**

| | |
|---|---|
| C | Charing Cross |
| E | Euston |
| F | Fenchurch Street |
| K | Kings Cross |
| L | Liverpool Street |
| M | Marylebone |
| P | Paddington |
| S | St Pancras |
| V | Victoria |
| W | Waterloo |

International direct services
LILLE, BRUSSELS, PARIS

📞 **National Rail Enquiries**
**0845 7 48 49 50**

# Motoring in Wales

South Wales is linked to the national motorway network by the M 4 motorway while a highway of near-motorway standard, the North Wales Expressway, connects the towns and resorts of the north coast to the north of England. Main roads generally are well engineered and relatively uncrowded, though the nature of the country imposes many bends and steep gradients. Special care needs to be taken on minor roads, especially in mountainous areas and in other places where grazing animals may be a hazard.

**Documents** – Nationals of EU countries require a valid **national driving licence**; US driving licence valid for 12 months; a permit (US$10) is available from the National Auto Club, Touring Department, 188 The Embarcardero, Suite 300, San Francisco CA 94105 or from the local branch of the American Automobile Association. Other nationals require an international driving licence.
For the vehicle it is necessary to have the **registration papers** (log-book) and a **nationality plate** of the approved size.

**Insurance** – Insurance cover is compulsory and although an **International Insurance Certificate** (Green Card) is no longer a legal requirement in the United Kingdom, it is the most effective proof of insurance cover and is internationally recognised by the police and other authorities.
Certain UK motoring organisations *(see below)* run accident insurance and breakdown service schemes for members. Europ-Assistance has special schemes for members. The American Automobile Association publishes a free brochure *Offices to Serve You Abroad* for its members.

**Highway Code** – Traffic drives on the left and overtakes on the right.
The minimum driving age is 17 years old.
The compulsory wearing of seat belts includes rear seat passengers, when belts are fitted, and all children under 14.
Vehicles must give way to pedestrians on zebra crossings and when traffic lights flash amber.
In the case of a **breakdown** a red warning triangle or hazard warning lights are obligatory.
On single track roads drivers should take extra care and use the passing places.
Headlights must be used at night even in built-up areas and at other times when visibility is poor.
There are severe penalties for driving after drinking more than the legal limit of alcohol.
In general important traffic signs correspond to international norms.
Do not leave anything of value in unattended vehicles at any time.

**Speed limits** – The maximum speed limits are as follows:

| | |
|---|---|
| 70mph/112kph | on motorways |
| 60mph/96kph | on dual carriageways |
| 50mph/80kph | on other roads |
| 40mph/56kph | in outer built-up areas |
| 30mph/48kph | in built-up areas where there is street lighting |
| 20mph/28kph | in inner built-up areas |

**Parking Regulations** – Off-street parking is indicated by blue signs with white lettering (Parking or P); payment is made on leaving or in advance for a certain period. There are also parking meters, disc systems and paying parking zones; in the last case tickets must be obtained from ticket machines (small change necessary) and displayed inside the windscreen. Illegal parking is liable to fines and also in certain cases to the vehicle being clamped or towed away. The usual restrictions are as follows:

| | |
|---|---|
| Double red line | No stopping at any time (freeway) |
| Double yellow line | No parking at any time |
| Single yellow line | No parking for set periods indicated on panel |
| Dotted yellow line | Parking limited to certain times only |
| White zigzag lines before and after a zebra crossing | No stopping or parking at any time. |

**Tolls** – Tolls are rare in the United Kingdom; they are levied only on road tunnels (Dartford, Tyne) and on the most recent bridges (Severn, Humber and Skye) and a few minor rural bridges.

**Petrol/Gas** – In many service stations dual-pumps are the rule with **unleaded pumps** being identified by green pump handles or a green stripe. Leaded two-star petrol is no longer available in Britain, only unleaded two-star.

**Motoring Organisations** – The two major motoring organisations provide services in varying degrees for their own members and non-resident members of affiliated clubs.
**Automobile Association**, Fanum House, Basingstoke, Hants, RG21 4EA; ☎ 0990 500 600 (information centre); ☎ 0990 448 866 (administration); www.theaa.co.uk/theaa

**Royal Automobile Club**, RAC House, 1 Forest Road, Feltham, Middlesex TW13 7RR; ☏ 020 8917 2500 (motoring services); 09068 347 333 (domestic travel information); ☏ 0860 550055 (international travel information); Fax 020 8917 2525; www.rac.co.uk

**Europ-Assistance**, Sussex House, Perrymount Road, Haywards Heath, West Sussex, RH16 1DN, ☏ 01444 442 442 (Customer Services).

**Route Planning** – Wales is covered by the *Michelin Road Atlas of Great Britain and Ireland* (scale 1:300 000) and by *Michelin Map 403* (scale: 1:400 000). In addition to the usual detailed road information they show tourist features such as beaches and bathing areas, swimming pools, golf courses, racecourses, scenic routes, tourist sights, country parks etc. These publications are an essential complement to the annual *Michelin Red Guide Great Britain and Ireland*, which offers an up-to-date selection of hotels and restaurants.

**Car Rental** – There are car rental agencies at Cardiff-Wales airport, at railway stations and in larger towns and resorts throughout Wales. European cars usually have manual transmission but automatic cars are available on demand. An international driving licence is required for non-EU nationals. Most companies will not rent to those aged under 21 or 25. The following firms operate on a national basis:

| | |
|---|---|
| Avis | 0990 900 500; www.avis.com |
| Budget | 0800 181 181, 0541 565 656; www.budget.co.uk |
| National Car Rental | 0870 600 6666, 08705 565 656; www.nationalcar.co.uk |
| Europcar | 0345 222 525, 0870 607 5000; www.europcar.co.uk |
| Hertz | 020 8679 1799, 0990 99 66 99; www.hertz.com |

# Places to Stay

The long Welsh coastline offers a chain of major and minor resorts, including the two major cities – Cardiff, the capital, and Swansea. Inland resorts are to be found in the valleys and spa towns – Llandrindod Wells, Llanwrtyd Wells – of mid-Wales and in the National Parks – Snowdonia, the Brecon Beacons and the Pembrokeshire Coast.

*To find a place to stay turn to the Places to Stay Map (p 15) and to the blue pages in selected chapters in the Sights section and consult the list of addresses – hotels, guesthouses, pubs with rooms – chosen to suit a variety of tastes and budgets.*

*It is advisable to book well in advance for the holiday season.*

**Hotels and Guesthouses** – The **Michelin Red Guide Great Britain and Ireland** is an annual publication, which presents a selection of hotels and restaurants. All are classified according to the standard of their amenities and their selection is based on regular on-the-spot visits and enquiries. Pleasant settings, attractive decor, quiet or secluded locations and a warm welcome are identified by special symbols.

The places listed in the Michelin Red Guide **Great Britain and Ireland** are underlined in red on the **Michelin map 403** (scale 1:400 000 – 1in:6.30mi) which covers Wales.

**Bed and Breakfast (B&B)** – Many private individuals take in a limited number of guests. Prices include bed and cooked breakfast. Some offer full board or an evening meal but meals tend to be at a set time and the menu may be limited. Local Tourist Information Centres usually have a list of the bed and breakfast establishments in the area and will make a booking if necessary for a fee. Many houses advertise with a B&B sign.

**Rural Accommodation** – In this largely rural country staying on a farm can be a particularly rewarding experience. There are many different types of working farm – arable, livestock, hill or mixed – set in the heart of glorious countryside. For information apply for the booklet **Stay on a Farm** supplied by the British Tourist Authority or by The Farm Holiday Bureau based at the National Agricultural Centre, Stoneleigh Park, Warwickshire CV8 2LZ, ☏ 02476 696 909.

**University Residences** – During student vacations many universities and colleges offer low-cost accommodation in the student halls of residence. Apply to the British Universities Accommodation Consortium Ltd, Box 1385, University Park, Nottingham NG7 2RD, ☏ 0115 846 6444, Fax 0115 846 6333; buac@nottingham.ac.uk; www.buac.co.uk

**Youth Hostels** – There are youth hostels in all parts of Wales. Visitors must hold an international membership card or be members of the British Youth Hostels Association - www.yha.org.uk

**Youth Hostels Association**, 1 Cathedral Road, Cardiff, CF11 9HA; ☏ 029 2039 6766; Fax 029 2023 7817; wales@yha.org.uk

**British Youth Hostels Association**, Trevelyan House, 8 St Stephen's Hill, St Albans, Herts, AL1 2DY; ☎ 01727 855 215; Fax 01727 844 126; customerservices@yha. org.uk

**Camping** – There are many officially graded caravan and camping sites in Wales. The hire of a static caravan is usually very economical. Details of inspected caravan parks and camp sites are listed in a free brochure published by the Wales Tourist Board – *Wales Touring Caravan and Camping; Freedom Holidays Parks Wales.*
The following clubs also publish guides for members:
> **The Camping and Caravanning Club of Great Britain and Ireland**, Greenfields House, Westwood Way, Coventry CV4 8JH, ☎ 02476 694 995;
> **The Caravan Club**, East Grinstead House, London Road, East Grinstead, West Sussex, RH19 IVA, ☎ 01342 326 944.

**Booking service** – Most Tourist Information Centres will arrange accommodation for a small fee. Room prices, even for a double room, may be quoted per person.

**Publications** – Most Tourist Information Centres provide, free of charge, an information booklet listing hotels, bed and breakfast and other accommodation in their area. The **Wales Tourist Board** *(see p 19)* publishes a number of magazines (free of charge) which provide a selection of hotels, guesthouses, farmhouse accommodation, self-catering properties and caravan parks:
*Wales Countryside Holidays* and *Wales Farm Holidays.*

**Places to Stay and Activities Map** – This map *(see p 15)* classifies places to stay in four categories – overnight stop, sightseeing centres, seaside and inland resorts.
It also shows leisure facilities – beaches, marinas, tourist railways, long-distance footpaths, golf courses, national and regional parks, bird sanctuaries, scenic routes, mountain peaks and passes, racecourses, airports, aerodromes etc.

# Services

**Currency** – The currency is Sterling (£1 = 100 pence) and is issued in notes – £50, £20, £10 and £5 – and coins – £2, £1, 50p, 20p, 10p, 5p, 2p and 1p.

**Banking** – Banks are open from Monday to Friday (except public holidays – *see below*), 9.30am to 3.30pm or 4.30pm or 5pm or 5.30pm. Some branches offer a limited service on Saturdays from 9.30am to 12.30pm. Some banks may close for an hour at lunchtime; all banks are closed on Sundays and bank holidays.
Exchange facilities outside these hours are available at airports, bureaux de change, travel agencies and hotels.
Some form of identification is necessary when cashing travellers cheques or Eurocheques in banks. Commission charges vary; hotels usually charge more than banks.

**Credit Cards** – The major credit cards – Visa/Barclaycard (Carte Bleue), Eurocard (Mastercard/Access), American Express and Diners Club – are widely accepted in shops, hotels and restaurants and petrol stations. Most banks have cash dispensers which accept international credit cards.
In case of loss or theft, phone:

| | |
|---|---|
| Amex | 020 7222 9633 |
| Access/Eurocard | 01702 364 364 |
| Barclaycard | 01604 230 230 |

**Post** – Postage stamps are available from post offices and some shops (newsagents, tobacconists etc).
Post offices are open Mondays to Fridays, 9am to 5.30pm, and Saturdays, 9am to 12.30pm; sub-post offices close at 1pm on Wednesdays or Thursdays.
Poste Restante items are held for 14 days; proof of identity is required.
Airmail delivery usually takes 3 to 4 days in Europe and 4 to 7 days elsewhere in the world.

| | |
|---|---|
| Within UK | first class post 27p; second class post 19p |
| Within EU | letter 36p (20g; additional charge for extra weight) |
| | postcard 36p |
| Non-EU Europe | letter 40p (20g; additional charge for extra weight) |
| | postcard 40p |
| Elsewhere | letter 66p (20g; additional charge for extra weight) |
| | postcard 40p |
| | air letters 40-49p |

**Telephoning** – Prepaid **British Telecom** phonecards, of varying value, are available from post offices and some shops (newsagents, tobacconists etc). They can be used in booths with phonecard facilities for national and international calls. Some public telephones accept credit cards.

Rates vary; the cheaper rate period is Mon-Fri, before 8am and after 6pm; weekends, midnight Friday to midnight Sunday.

| | |
|---|---|
| 100 | Operator |
| 192 | Directory Enquiries within the UK |
| 999 | **Emergency** number (free nationwide); ask for Fire, Police, Ambulance, Coastguard, Mountain Rescue or Cave Rescue. |

To make an **international call** dial 00 followed by the country code, followed by the area code (without the initial 0) followed by the subscriber's number. The codes for dialling directly to other countries are printed at the front of telephone directories and in codebooks.

| | |
|---|---|
| 00 61 | Australia |
| 00 1 | Canada |
| 00 353 | Republic of Ireland |
| 00 64 | New Zealand |
| 00 44 | United Kingdom |
| 00 1 | United States of America |
| 155 | International Operator |
| 155 | International Directory Enquiries (charge for this service). |

**Public Houses** – Pubs may open within the statutory licensing hours: Mondays to Saturdays, 11am to 11pm, and Sundays, 12.30pm to 2.30pm and 6.30pm to 11pm. Young people under 18 years of age are subject to certain restrictions and may be asked for some form of identification.

**Electricity** – The electric current is 240 volts AC (50 HZ); 3-pin flat wall sockets are standard. An adaptor or multiple point plug is required for non-British appliances.

# Shopping and Crafts

Shops in the larger towns are usually open Mondays to Saturdays, 9am to 5.30pm (8pm Wednesdays or Thursdays), Sundays, 10am to 4pm. Supermarkets usually close later than other shops. Some small shops (corner shops in towns) also close very late but others, in country districts, may close at lunchtime. Elsewhere there is all-day closing on Mondays or early closing day (ECD) on Wednesdays or Thursdays (see Michelin Red Guide **Great Britain and Ireland**).

The summer sales in June and July and the winter sales at Christmas and New Year are a popular time for shopping, as prices are reduced on a great range of goods.

Hay-on-Wye has acquired a reputation for **second-hand books**, through Richard Booth, an eccentric and enterprising bookseller, who arrived in Hay in 1961, and was followed by other dealers.

**Craftwork** is a living tradition in Wales; in craft centres all over the country skilled men and women demonstrate their talents and sell their products. Many museums also have demonstrations of traditional crafts. *Wales – A Touring Guide to Crafts* is published by the Wales Tourist Board; local Tourist Information Centres provide information about their own areas. Other bodies providing information on Welsh crafts are:

Dewi Jones of Esgair Moel Mill, Museum of Welsh Life

National Museums and Galleries of Wales

# Notes and Coins

500 Francs featuring
scientists
Pierre and Marie Curie
(1858-1906), (1867-1934)

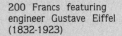

200 Francs featuring
engineer Gustave Eiffel
(1832-1923)

100 Francs featuring
painter Paul Cézanne
(1839-1906)

50 Francs featuring
pilot and writer
Antoine de Saint-Exupéry
(1900-1944)

20 Francs

10 Francs

5 Francs

2 Francs

1 Franc

50 Centimes

20 Centimes

10 Centimes

5 Centimes

# Conversion Tables

## Weights and measures

| | | |
|---|---|---|
| 1 kilogram (kg) | 2.2 pounds (lb) | 2.2 pounds |
| 1 metric ton (tn) | 1.1 tons | 1.1 tons |

*to convert kilograms to pounds, multiply by 2.2*

| | | |
|---|---|---|
| 1 litre (l) | 2.1 pints (pt) | 1.8 pints |
| 1 litre | 0.3 gallon (gal) | 0.2 gallon |

*to convert litres to gallons, multiply by 0.26 (US) or 0.22 (UK)*

| | | |
|---|---|---|
| 1 hectare (ha) | 2.5 acres | 2.5 acres |
| 1 square kilometre (km²) | 0.4 square miles (sq mi) | 0.4 square miles |

*to convert hectares to acres, multiply by 2.4*

| | | |
|---|---|---|
| 1 centimetre (cm) | 0.4 inches (in) | 0.4 inches |
| 1 metre (m) | 3.3 feet (ft) - 39.4 inches - 1.1 yards (yd) | |
| 1 kilometre (km) | 0.6 miles (mi) | 0.6 miles |

*to convert metres to feet, multiply by 3.28 . kilometres to miles, multiply by 0.6*

## Clothing

| Women | | | | | | | Men |
|---|---|---|---|---|---|---|---|
| | 35 | 4 | 2½ | 40 | 7½ | 7 | |
| | 36 | 5 | 3½ | 41 | 8½ | 8 | |
| | 37 | 6 | 4½ | 42 | 9½ | 9 | |
| Shoes | 38 | 7 | 5½ | 43 | 10½ | 10 | Shoes |
| | 39 | 8 | 6½ | 44 | 11½ | 11 | |
| | 40 | 9 | 7½ | 45 | 12½ | 12 | |
| | 41 | 10 | 8½ | 46 | 13½ | 13 | |
| | 36 | 4 | 8 | 46 | 36 | 36 | |
| | 38 | 6 | 10 | 48 | 38 | 38 | |
| Dresses & | 40 | 8 | 12 | 50 | 40 | 40 | Suits |
| Suits | 42 | 12 | 14 | 52 | 42 | 42 | |
| | 44 | 14 | 16 | 54 | 44 | 44 | |
| | 46 | 16 | 18 | 56 | 46 | 48 | |
| | 36 | 08 | 30 | 37 | 14½ | 14,5 | |
| | 38 | 10 | 32 | 38 | 15 | 15 | |
| Blouses & | 40 | 12 | 14 | 39 | 15½ | 15½ | Shirts |
| sweaters | 42 | 14 | 36 | 40 | 15¾ | 15¾ | |
| | 44 | 16 | 38 | 41 | 16 | 16 | |
| | 46 | 18 | 40 | 42 | 16½ | 16½ | |

**Sizes often vary depending on the designer. These equivalents are given for guidance only.**

## Speed

| kph | 10 | 30 | 50 | 70 | 80 | 90 | 100 | 110 | 120 | 130 |
|---|---|---|---|---|---|---|---|---|---|---|
| mph | 6 | 19 | 31 | 43 | 50 | 56 | 62 | 68 | 75 | 81 |

## Temperature

| Celsius (°C) | 0° | 5° | 10° | 15° | 20° | 25° | 30° | 40° | 60° | 80° | 100° |
|---|---|---|---|---|---|---|---|---|---|---|---|
| Fahrenheit (°F) | 32° | 41° | 50° | 59° | 68° | 77° | 86° | 104° | 140° | 176° | 212° |

*To convert Celsius into Fahrenheit, multiply °C by 9, divide by 5, and add 32.*
*To convert Fahrenheit into Celsius, subtract 32 from °F, multiply by 5, and divide by 9.*

**Visual Arts and Crafts**, Arts Council for Wales, 9 Museum Place, Cardiff CF10 3NX ☎ 029 2037 6500; Fax 029 2022 1447; 29 2039 0027 (minicom); information @ccc-acw.org.uk; www.craftinwales.com

**Wales Craft Council**, Henfaes Lane Industrial Estate, Henfaes Lane, Welshpool SY21 7BE; ☎ 01938 555 313; Fax 01938 556 237; crefft.cymru@btinternet.com; www.wales craftcouncil.co.uk

**Fforwm Crefft Cymru**, Snowdon Mill Art & Craft Centre, Snowdon Street, Porthmadog LL49 9DF. ☎ 01766 510 901; Fax 10766 510 913.

The crafts practised include fashion garments, glass-blowing, jewellery, pewter work, pottery, slate work, weaving and wood-turning.

Apart from providing sweet Welsh lamb for the table, the many sheep on the hillsides provide wool which is woven into a variety of **woollen goods** – elegant and fashionable garments for men and women as well as the traditional rugs and blankets. There are mills in most parts of the country.

The **slate** which provides roofs and fences is also made into commemorative plaques and other objects of beauty.

Local glass manufacturers produce **glassware** with typical Welsh designs.

Wooden articles from furniture to a simple salad bowl are hand-turned on the lathe or various types of wood are carved into the elaborate Welsh lovespoons.

---

### Lovespoons

The tradition of carving lovespoons probably dates from the Middle Ages when the spoons were used for eating. They now serve a purely decorative purpose and the handle is highly ornate. The suitor, who fashioned the spoon himself, would spend time and effort to make it elaborate as a measure of his affection. Individual motifs were used to indicate particular intentions: the spoon itself indicated that the suitor would provide for his wife; the wheel that he would work for her; the heart indicated love; the keyhole indicated the provision of a house; the number of links in a chain indicated the number of children hoped for. The maritime symbols – anchors and ships – were probabaly carved by sailors during long sea voyages.

The custom of giving and acceptance of a lovespoon as a symbol of betrothal died out in 19C but in recent years they have again become popular in Wales to commemorate special occasions and among visitors as mementoes of their visit.

---

*FOLLOW THE COUNTRY CODE*
*Guard against all risk of fire*
*Fasten all gates*
*Keep dogs under proper control*
*Keep to the paths across farmland*
*Avoid damaging fences, hedges and walls*
*Leave no litter*
*Safeguard water supplies*
*Protect wildlife, wild plants and trees*
*Go carefully on country roads*
*Respect the life of the countryside*

# Sport and Leisure

Wales is an excellent place for many outdoor sports owing to its long coastline, its many lakes and rivers, and the valleys and hills. Further information on all the activities listed below is available from the Wales Tourist Board *(p 19)* or directly from the organisation concerned. See also the Activities map *(p 15)*.

## Visiting

**Historic Properties** – Many country houses, gardens, historic monuments and ruins are owned or maintained by the following organisations which offer free admission to their members.
The **Great British Heritage Pass** (valid for 7 days, 15 days or one month), which gives access to over 600 properties (country houses, castles and gardens) throughout Great Britain, is available from BTA Offices and Tourist Information Centres.

**CADW** – The organisation, whose name means "To protect", manages 131 ancient monuments, including many castles, in all parts of Wales. Visitors from abroad, who intend to visit more than a small number of CADW properties, should consider becoming members of CADW or of English Heritage, whose members have visiting rights.
**CADW**: Welsh Historic Monuments, Crown Building, Cathays Park, Cardiff CF10 3NQ. ☎ 029 2050 0200; Fax 029 2082 6375; cadw@wales.gsi.gov.uk; www.cadw.wales. gov.uk
**English Heritage**: Customer Services Department, PO Box 9019, London, W1A 0JA. ☎ 020 7973 3434; www.english-heritage.org.uk
CADW offers Explorer passes for free admission to CADW sites:
3-day pass – £9 (1 adult); £16 (2 adults); £21 (family 2A+3C);
7-day pass – £15 (1 adult); £25 (2 adults); £30 (family 2A+3C).

**National Trust** – The National Trust owns and conserves places of historic interest and natural beauty, including coast and countryside properties, throughout both Wales and England. There are reciprocal arrangements between the Trust and similar overseas national trusts (Royal Oak Foundation etc). Non-members of such organisations should consider joining the National Trust if they intend to visit more than a very small number of the Trust properties.
**Head Office**: National Trust, 36 Queen Anne's Gate, London SW1H 9AS. ☎ 02 7222 9251; Fax 020 7222 5097; www.nationaltrust.org.uk (for general information about properties and opening times).
**North Wales Regional Office**: National Trust, Trinity Square, Llandudno, LL30 2DE. ☎ 01492 860 123; Fax 01493 860 233.
**The Royal Oak Foundation** – American public charity affiliated with the National Trust to promote the preservation of the Anglo-American heritage. Royal Oak members automatically receive the rights and privileges of full National Trust members.
**The Royal Oak Foundation**, 285 West Broadway, New York, NY 10013, USA ☎ 00 1 212 966 6565; Fax 00 1 212 966 6619; general@royal-oak.org; www. royal-oak.org

**National Parks** – Wales has three national parks – Snowdonia, the Brecon Beacons and Pembrokeshire Coast – which offer many opportunities for outdoor activities and sports (walking, rambling), and some forests, which are managed with recreation in mind.
**Brecon Beacons National Park**, 7 Glamorgan Street, Brecon LD3 7DP. ☎ 01874 624 437; Fax 01874 622 574; ☎ 01874 623 366.
**Pembrokeshire Coast National Park**, Winch Lane, Haverfordwest SA61 1PY. ☎ 01437 764 636; www.pembrokeshirecoast.org.uk
**Snowdonia National Park Authority**, Penrhyndeudraeth LL48 6LF. ☎ 01766 770 274.
**Council for National Parks**, 246 Lavender Hill, London SW11 1LJ. ☎ 020 7924 4077; Fax 020 7924 5761; www.cnp.org.uk
**Countryside Council for Wales**, Plas Penrhos, Ffordd Penrhos, Bangor LL57 2LQ. ☎ 01248 385 500.
**Forestry Enterprise**, Victoria House, Victoria Terrace, Aberystwyth SY23 2DQ. ☎ 01970 612 367.

**Nature Reserves** – Wales has many nature reserves, some with bird-watching centres, both on the coast and inland where great efforts have been made to re-establish the red kite in its native habitat.

Walking in Snowdonia

K J Richardson/National Trust Photographic Library

**RSPB** (Royal Society for the Protection of Birds), The Lodge, Sandy, Bedfordshire SG19 2DL. ☎ 01767 680 551 Fax 01767 692 365; www.rspb.org.uk
**Wildfowl and Wetlands Trust**, Canolfan Llanelli Centre, Penclacwydd, Llanelli, Dyfed SA14 9SH. ☎ 01554 741 087; www.wwt.org.uk
**Kite Country**, Bryn Aderyn, The Bank, Newtown, Powys SY16 2AB. ☎ 01686 624 143.

**Gardens** – The National Gardens Scheme publishes *Gardens of England and Wales*, an annual guide to private gardens which are open to the public for a limited period in aid of charity.
**National Gardens Scheme**, Hatchlands Park, East Clandon, Guildford, Surrey GU4 7RT. ☎ 01483 211 535; Fax 01483 211 537.

**Tourist Railways** – The many different scenic and tourist lines, some operated by steam engines, are marketed together as **Great Little Trains of Wales** *(see p 19)*. A **Wanderer Ticket** is available valid for unlimited travel during any 8 days within a 15 day period or any 4 days within an 8 day period on all eight **Great Little Trains** – Bala Lake Railway *(see p 85)*, Brecon Mountain Railway *(see p 104)*, Ffestiniog Railway *(see p 234)*, Llanberis Lake Railway *(see p 173)*, Vale of Rheidol Railway *(see p 244)*, Talyllyn Railway *(see p 279)*, Welsh Highland Railway *(see p 235)* and Welshpool and Llanfair Light Railway *(see p 283)*.
An annual free guide to steam railways and museums is published by
**Association of Railway Preservation Societies Ltd**, 7 Robert Close, Potters Bar, Hertfordshire EN6 2DH. ☎/Fax 01707 643 568; www.ukhrail.uel.ac.uk

**Music** – Wales has a long tradition and widespread reputation for music, particularly the human voice, and poetry.

The **Welsh Male Voice Choirs**, of which there are over 60, usually admit members of the public to their rehearsals. A booklet giving rehearsal locations and times, and the names, addresses and telephone numbers of contacts – *Welsh Male Voice Choirs (Corau Meibion Cymru)* – is available from the Wales Tourist Board *(see p 19)* or from local Tourist Information Centres.

The **International Musical Eisteddfod**, held in Llangollen annually in early July (5 days), offers performances by male voice choirs, female choirs, mixed choirs, folk song groups, children's choirs, solo singers and of opera.
**International Musical Eisteddfod Office**, First Floor, Royal International Pavilion, Abbey Road, Llangollen LL20 8FW. ☎ 01978 862 000, Fax 01978 862 002; tickets@international-eisteddfod.co.uk; www.international-eisteddfod.co.uk

The **National Eisteddfod of Wales**, which is held annually in August (9 days), in North Wales and South Wales in alternate years, promotes the Welsh language through a Welsh cultural fair; Welsh dancing, music and poetry recitations in the Bardic tradition take place in the Main Pavilion, while the satellites provide concerts, plays, arts and crafts and science exhibitions.
**National Eisteddfod of Wales**, 40 Parc Ty Glas, Llanishen, Cardiff CF14 5WU. ☎ 029 2076 3777; Fax 029 2076 3737; info@eisteddfod.org.uk; www.eisteddfod.org.uk

**Welsh Language Courses** – Leaflets listing residential Welsh language courses in Wales are available from:
**Welsh Language Board**, Market Chambers, 5-7 St Mary Street, Cardiff CF1 1AT. ☎ 029 2087 8000; 0845 607 6070 (Link-line to Welsh for information about the Welsh language) Fax 029 2087 8001; ymholiadau@bwrdd-yr-iaith.org.uk; www.bwrdd-yr-iaith.org.uk
Most courses for learning Welsh are held between March and September but the following centre operates throughout the year
**Nant Gwrtheyrn Language Centre**, Llithsaen, Pwllheli, Gwynedd, LL53 6PA. ☎ 01758 750 334; Fax 01758 750 335; nantgwr@aol.com; www.marketsite.co.uk/wlc

## Sport

**Rambling** – Wales is a walker's paradise, with a dense network of rights of way and exhilarating mountain and coastal paths. There are two national trails and several waymarked long-distance routes. There are also many trails in nature reserves and forests.
**Ramblers in Wales**, Tŷr Cerddwyr, High Street, Gresford, Wrexham LL12 8PT. ☎ 01978 855 148, Fax 01978 854 445; cerddwyr@wales.ramblers.org.uk; www.ramblers.org.uk
**Ramblers' Association**, 2nd floor, Camelford, 87-90 Albert Embankment, London SE1 7TW. ☎ 020 7339 8500; Fax 0171 7339 8501; www.ramblers.org.uk
**Offa's Dyke Footpath** – This national trail (177mi/285km) runs along the English border from its northern end near Prestatyn to its southern end at Sedbury Cliffs on the River Severn just east of Chepstow; there are information centres in Prestatyn and Knighton.
**Offa's Dyke Association**, West Street, Knighton, Powys. ☎ 01547 528 753.

**Glyn Dŵr Way** – This path (128mi/206km – 8 to 12 days) makes a loop through mid-Wales from Knighton west via Abbey-cym-hir, Llanidloes, Clywedog Reservoir to

Machynlleth, returning east via Llanbrynmair, Llangadfan, Lake Vyrnwy and Maifod to Welshpool. It is designed as a walking route and is therefore not available for use as a bridle or cycle route; it includes long stretches across agricultural land, where dogs must be kept on a lead. The current route was established by Powys County Council during the mid 1970s and is currently managed by Powys County Council in partnership with the Countryside Council for Wales; maintenance work is carried out by landowners, volunteers and contractors. There are railway stations at Knighton and Llangunllo on the Heart of Wales Line and at Machynlleth and

Abseiling and climbing at Porthclais

Welshpool on the Cambrian Line. There are bus services linking Llanidloes, Machynlleth and Welshpool, and a limited bus service in the rural areas. Brochure available from Machynlleth TIC *(see p 203)*.

**Wye Valley Walk** – This path runs beside the river, which, in its lower reaches before it flows into the Severn Estuary, forms the boundary between Wales and England.

**Pembrokeshire Coast Path** – This national trail gives access to the cliffs and beaches of the Pembrokeshire Coast National Park *(see p 223)*.

**Taff Trail** – This path, which doubles as a cycle route, runs from Brecon to Cardiff *(55mi/88km)* along the course of the River Taff, using canal towpaths, disused railways and tram roads to provide a safe and scenic route, which has links with a network of cycle routes, circular walks, bridleways, drives and picnic sites. Information booklet available from the Tourist Information Centre in Cardiff *(see p 117)*.

**Pilgrims' Road** – This path runs along the north coast of the Lleyn Peninsula from Bangor to Aberdaron. Pilgrims set out from Bangor Cathedral and proceeded along the coast to Aberdaron, where they embarked in a boat to cross Bardsey Sound to reach their goal, the monastery on Bardsey Island. As they walked they stopped to pray and worship at some or all of the other 11 churches along the route – Caernarfon, Llanwnda, Llandwrog, Clynnog Fawr, Llanaelhaearn, Pistyll, Nefyn, Edern, Tudweiliog, Penllech and Llangwnnadl.

**Coed Morgannwg Way** – This footpath *(32mi/52km)* runs from Margam Country Park on the shore of Swansea Bay to the Craig-y-Llyn viewpoint beyond the head of the Rhondda Valley.

**Mountain Biking and Climbing** – Centres for hiring and using mountain bikes and quad bikes are fairly numerous.

Snowdonia *(see p 257)* is one of the cradles of British mountaineering where serious climbers spend time in training for their attempts at greater things, such as the conquest of Everest. The Brecon Beacons *(see p 102)* also provide a challenge.

Mountain walkers should bear in mind that temperatures drop rapidly as height is gained, roughly by 2C for every 1 000ft/300m. This, combined with wind-chill, means that summit conditions can be unpleasantly, even dangerously, different from those at the starting point of a climb in the valley bottom.

**National Mountaineering Centre**, Plas y Brenin, Capel Curig. ☎ 01690 720 214; Fax 01690 720 394; info@pyb.co.uk; www.pyb.co.uk

**British Mountaineering Council**, 177-179 Burton Road, West Didsbury, Manchester, M20 2BB. ☎ 0161 445 4747; Fax 0161 445 4500; www.thebmc.co.uk

Golf at Nefyn

**Golf** – Details of the more than 160 golf courses in Wales are given in the Wales Tourist Board's comprehensive brochure *Golfing in Wales*. Many are listed in the **Michelin Red Guide Great Britain and Ireland** and marked on the Activities map *(see p 15)*. Most are privately owned and accept visitors. Municipal courses are usually very heavily used, with long queues at the first tee.

**Royal and Ancient Golf Club of St Andrews**, St Andrews, Fife KY16 9JD. ☎ 01334 472 112; Fax 01334 477 580; www.randa.org

**English Golf Union**, National Golf Centre, The Broadway, Woodhall Spa, Lincolnshire LN10 6PU. ☎ 01526 354 500; Fax 01526 354 020; www.englishgolfunion.org

**English Ladies Golf Association**, Edgbaston Golf Club, Church Road, Birmingham B15 3TB. ☎ 0121 456 2088; Fax 0121 454 5542; office@englishladiesgolf.org

**Cycling** – Much of Wales is ideal mountain biking country, and there are also combined cycling and walking routes like the Taff Trail leading north from Cardiff into the South Wales Valleys. A Cycle Network is being established so that Wales can be crossed by bicycle from north to south and east to west; these routes are part of the National Cycle Network covering the whole of Britain comprising 5 000mi/8 000km of traffic-free routes and traffic-calmed and minor roads. For information apply to **SUSTRANS**, Head Office, 35 King Street, Bristol BS1 4DZ. ☎ 0117 926 8893; 0117 929 0888 (information line); Fax 0117 929 4173; www.sustrans.co.uk

Cycles are available for hire from a number of centres. The Wales Tourist Board brochure *Cycling Wales* gives full details.

Salmon Fishing on the Wye

**Fishing** – Wales offers fishing in the lakes and reservoirs and along the coast. There is also the possibility of deep-sea fishing from a limited number of harbours. The Wye and Usk are famous for salmon fishing; Llyn Brenig is preserved exclusively for fly-fishing.

A leaflet on fishing the reservoirs of Wales, giving information on dates, times, permits, charges and facilities for the disabled, is published by the Welsh Water Authority.

**Welsh Water Authority**, Plas-y-Ffynnon, Cambrian Way, Brecon LD3 7HP. ☎ 01874 623 181, 0800 052 0138 (publications hotline); Fax 01874 624 167; www.hyder.com

**National Federation of Anglers**, Halliday House, Eggington Junction, Derbyshire DE65 6GU. ☎ 01283 734 735; Fax 01283 734 799; www.the-nfa.org.uk

**National Federation of Sea Anglers**, 51a Queen Street, Newton Abbot, Devon TQ12 2QJ. ☎/Fax 01626 334 924; nfsaho@aol.com

**Salmon and Trout Association**, Fishmongers Hall, London Bridge, London EC4R 9EL. ☎ 020 7283 5838; Fax 020 7626 5137; www.salmon-trout.org

**Sailing** – There are many opportunities for sailing at sea off the long and varied coastline of Wales, in the many estuaries and inland on the lakes and reservoirs (dinghy sailing on Bala Lake and Llangorse Lake). Some of the best sailing is to be found off the Lleyn Peninsula. Marinas are shown on the Activities Map *(see p 15)*.

**Welsh Yachting Association**, 8 Llys y Môr, Plas Menai, Llanfairisgair, Caernarfon, LL55 1UE. ☎ 01248 670 738 (9.30-11.30am); www.thewya.freeserve.co.uk

**Canoeing** – Canoeing on Welsh rivers can include white-water experience. Llandysul on the River Teifi, upstream of Newcastle Emlyn, is a popular venue for the National Canoeing Championships. Canoeists also favour the beaches in St Bride's Bay.
**Welsh Canoeing Association**, Canolfan Tryweryn, Frongoch, Bala LL23 7NU. ☎ 01678 521 199; Fax 01678 521 158; welsh.canoeing@virgin.net; www.welsh-canoeing.org.uk

Pony trekking in the Brecon Beacons

**Surfing** – Surfing is popular on a number of west-facing beaches, particularly those in St Bride's Bay and on the Lleyn Peninsula.
**Welsh Surfing Federation**, 29 Sterry Road, Gowerton, Swansea SA4 3BS. ☎ 01729 529 898; Fax 01792 529 897; wsf@ntl.com

**Riding and pony trekking** – This well-developed activity is fully described in the Wales Tourist Board brochure *Discovering Wales on Horseback*.
**Wales Trekking and Riding Association**, 7 Rhosferig Road, Brecon LD3 7NG. ☎ 01874 623 185; Fax 01874 623 775; info@totaltourism.co.uk; www.ridingwales.com

**Horseracing** – There are few racecourses in Wales itself but Chester and Cheltenham are only a short distance over the border in England.
The **flat racing** season at Chepstow runs from late May to mid-September. There is steeplechasing at Chepstow from early October to May and at Bangor-on-Dee from February to May and August to December.
**Chepstow Racecourse**, Chepstow NP16 6BE. ☎ 01291 622 260; Fax 01921 627 061; info@chepstow-racecourse.co.uk; www.chepstow-racecourse.co.uk
**Bangor-on-Dee Races Ltd**, The Racecourse, Bangor-on-Dee, Wrexham LL13 0DA. ☎ 01978 780 323; Fax 01978 780 985. This racecourse is situated in a loop of the River Dee south of Wrexham on B 5069.

Elan Valley Reservoir

# Calendar of Events

**1 March**

**Throughout Wales** . . . . . . . . St David's Day: celebrated all over the country, with special services in St David's Cathedral

**1 May**

**St Fagan's** . . . . . . . . . . . . . . May Day celebrations at the Museum of Welsh Life, St Fagan's, near Cardiff

**May**

**Llangollen** . . . . . . . . . . . . . . Jazz festival

**Wrexham** . . . . . . . . . . . . . . . Arts festival

**Late May-end December**

**Throughout Wales** . . . . . . . . Mid-Wales festival of the Countryside – over 500 events such as birdwatching, guided walks, arts and crafts, sheepdog trials, farm and garden visits

**Late May-early June**

**Hay-on-Wye** . . . . . . . . . . . . . Hay Festival of Literature and the Arts

**Beaumaris** . . . . . . . . . . . . . . Arts festival and regatta, Beaumaris, Anglesey

**Late May-early June**

**Variable location** . . . . . . . . The Urdd National (Welsh League of Youth) Eisteddfod, one of the largest youth festivals in Europe

**July**

**Llanfyllin** . . . . . . . . . . . . . . . Annual Music Festival

**Mid-July**

**Llangollen** . . . . . . . . . . . . . . International Musical *Eisteddfod* (5 days)

**Late July**

**Builth Wells** . . . . . . . . . . . . Royal Welsh Agricultural Show

**August**

**Llanfyllin** . . . . . . . . . . . . . . . Annual Agricultural Show

**August**

**Denbigh** . . . . . . . . . . . . . . . . Denbigh and Flint Show

**Early August**

**Variable location** . . . . . . . . Royal National Eisteddfod of Wales (9 days)

**Mid-August (3 days)**

**Brecon** . . . . . . . . . . . . . . . . . Brecon Jazz Festival – international festival attracting the top names from the world of jazz

**Late August (1 week)**

**Llandrindod Wells** . . . . . . . . Llandrindod Wells Victorian Festival – street theatre, drama, exhibitions, walks, talks and music – all with a Victorian flavour

**Last full week of August**

**Machynlleth** . . . . . . . . . . . . . Arts Festival

**Late August to early September**

**Presteigne** . . . . . . . . . . . . . . Festival of Music and the Arts

**Last full week of September**

**St Asaph** . . . . . . . . . . . . . . . North Wales Music Festival

**Late September**

**Tenby** . . . . . . . . . . . . . . . . . . Tenby Arts Festival

**Late September-early October**

**Cardiff** . . . . . . . . . . . . . . . . . Cardiff Festival

**October**

**Swansea** . . . . . . . . . . . . . . . Swansea Festival of Music and the Arts

*THE GREEN GUIDE*
*Art and architecture; ancient monuments; history; landscape; scenic routes touring programmes; local maps; town plans; site plans*
*A selection of guides for holidays at home and abroad*

# Further Reading

## General

**The Matter of Wales – Epic Views of a Small Country** by Jan Morris (Penguin)

**Wales from the Air** by Chris Musson (Royal Commission on the Ancient and Historical Monuments of Wales)

**Wild Wales** by George Borrow (Century)

**The Journey through Wales and The Description of Wales** by Giraldus Cambrensis (Gerald of Wales) (Penguin)

**Wales – A New Survey** ed by David Thomas (David and Charles)

## Museums

**Getting Yesterday Right** by J Geraint Evans (University of Wales Press)

## History

**A History of Modern Wales 1536-1990** by Philip Jenkins (Longman)

**Wales – A History** by Wynford Vaughan-Thomas (Michael Joseph)

**When Was Wales?** by Gwyn A Williams (Penguin)

**A History of Wales** by John Davies (Penguin)

**Wales in the Early Middle Ages** by Wendy Davies (Leicester University Press)

**Medieval Wales** by David Walker (Cambridge University Press)

**The Revolt of Owain Glyn Dwr** by RR Davies (Oxford University Press)

**Wales 1880-1980 Rebirth of a Nation** by Kenneth O Morgan (Oxford University Press)

**Modern Wales** by Gareth Elwyn Jones (Cambridge University Press)

## Art and architecture

**The Historic Architecture of Wales** by John B Hilling (University of Wales Press)

**Pembrokeshire Architecture** by Michael Fitzgerald (Rosedale)

**The Buildings of Wales** (Penguin)

**Welsh Chapels** by Anthony Jones (Alan Sutton Publishing)

**A Companion Guide to the National Gallery** by Mark Evans and Oliver Fairclough (National Museum of Wales)

**Artists in Snowdonia** by James Bogle (Y Lolfa Cyf, 1990)

**On the Trail of Turner in North and South Wales** by Peter Humphries (CADW 1995)

## Language

**The Welsh Language** by Janet Davies (University of Wales Press)

**A Comprehensive Welsh Grammar** by David A Thorne (Blackwells)

## Fiction, poetry, biography

**Mabinogion** translated by Gwyn and Thomas Jones (Everyman)

**Collected Stories** by Dylan Thomas (Dent Everyman)

**Dylan: From Fern Hill to Milk Wood** by David Rowe (JD Lewis & Sons, Gomer Press, Llandysul, Dyfed

**How Green Was My Valley** by Richard Llewellyn (Penguin)

**Architect Errant** by Clough Williams-Ellis (Portmeirion)

**Clough Williams-Ellis – A Memoir** by Jonas Jones (1996 Poetry of Wales Press Ltd) ISBN 1-85411-166-3

**On the Black Hill** by Bruce Chatwin (Picador)

**Wales: An Anthology** by Alice Thomas Ellis (Fontana)

**Clouds of Time and other stories** by John E Williams (Gwasg Carreg Gwalch)

Glyn Tarell Valley, Brecon Beacons

# Introduction

# Landscape

A mainly mountainous country, Wales also has significant lowland areas and a magnificent coastline (735mi/1 183km). Its mountains, formidable barriers to communication in a few places, are penetrated almost everywhere by river valleys. Wales (8 000sq mi/c 20 000km$^2$) is the smallest of the three countries making up Great Britain. From north to south is about 160mi/260km; although the country's western peninsulas reach far into the Irish Sea, its waist – between Aberystwyth and the English border – is less than 40mi/65km across.

In its Celtic heyday, Wales lay at the heart of an international culture intimately connected via the seaways to the other Celtic lands of Ireland, Cornwall and Brittany. During the country's more recent history, political and economic integration has proved elusive, despite a high degree of linguistic and cultural unity. The development of industry and communications has tended to tie the country ever closer to England; before the 20C there was no capital and even today Cardiff is much easier to reach from many parts of England than from North Wales. The population (2.89 million) is unevenly spread, the majority (more than 60%) living in the industrialised south. Over much of the rest of the country population density is low by Western European standards; this, together with a largely unspoiled countryside, accounts for much of the country's attractiveness for visitors.

**Geology** – The geological foundation is an ancient one and the debt of science to the study of Welsh rocks is reflected in geological nomenclature. Cambria was the Roman name for Wales and the oldest rocks of all, from the **Pre-Cambrian** system, outcrop in **Anglesey**, the **Lleyn Peninsula** and in **Pembrokeshire**. Rocks of **Cambrian** Age form the rugged mountains of the **Rhinog** range and yield the famous slates quarried further north in **Snowdonia** as well as some of the stone from which St David's Cathedral is built. The tribe known as the Ordovices resisted

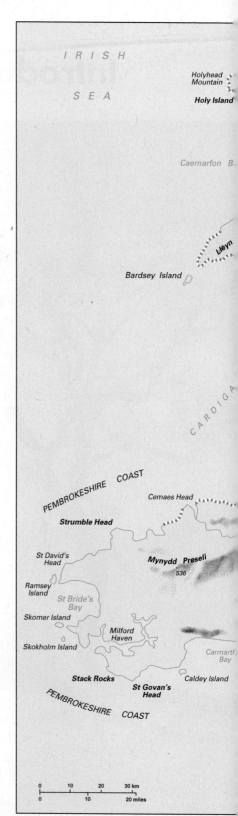

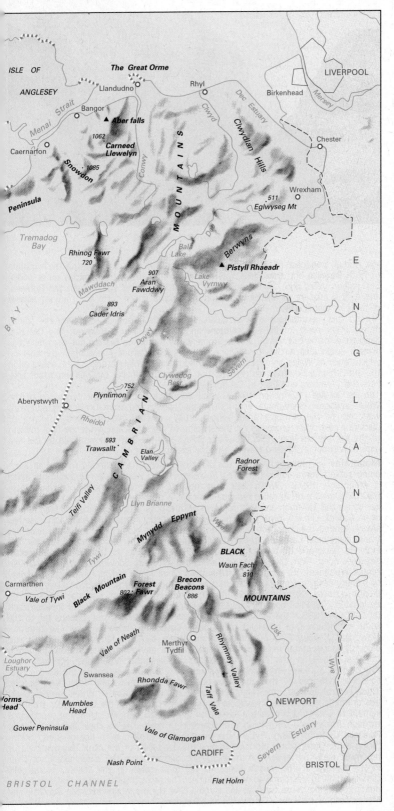

ISLE OF ANGLESEY

LIVERPOOL

The Great Orme

Llandudno

Rhyl

Birkenhead

Bangor

Aber falls

Chester

1062
Carneed Llewelyn

CLWYDIAN Hills

Caernarfon

1085
Snowdon

Peninsula

Menai Strait

Conwy

Clwyd

Dee Estuary

Mersey

MOUNTAINS

Wrexham

511
Eglwyseg Mt

Tremadog Bay

Dee

Rhinog Fawr
720

Bala Lake

Berwyns

Pistyll Rhaeadr

Lake Vyrnwy

Mawddach

907
Aran Fawddwy

893
Cader Idris

Dovey

Severn

Clywedog Resr

Plynlimon
752

CAMBRIAN

Aberystwyth

Rheidol

593
Trawsallt

Elan Valley

Radnor Forest

Teifi Valley

Llyn Brianne

Mynydd Eppynt

BLACK

Waun Fach
810

Carmarthen

Tywi

Vale of Tywi

Black Mountain

Forest Fawr
802

Brecon Beacons
886

MOUNTAINS

Wye

Usk

Loughor Estuary

Vale of Neath

Merthyr Tydfil

Rhymney Valley

Worms Head

Swansea

Rhondda Fawr

Taff Vale

NEWPORT

Mumbles Head

Gower Peninsula

Vale of Glamorgan

Severn Estuary

Wye

Nash Point

CARDIFF

BRISTOL

BRISTOL CHANNEL

Flat Holm

ENGLAND

BAY

39

Rock formation at Cobblers Hole

the Roman conquest of the north, and the volcanic ash which forms the summits of both **Snowdon** and **Cadair Idris** was laid down in the sea of **Ordovician** times (440–500 million years ago). In the southeast it was the Silures who fought the Romans, and it is a mixture of **Silurian** and Ordovician rocks which form the rounded **uplands** of most of **central Wales.**

Around this mountainous core of older rocks to the east and south are the softer, more recent rocks of **Old Red Sandstone** and the **Carboniferous Measures.** The Old Red Sandstone forms the spectacular escarpments of the **Brecon Beacons** but elsewhere has broken down into fertile soils. The rocks of Carboniferous Age contain the coal on which much of Wales' contribution to the Industrial Revolution was based, above all in the once mighty South Wales coalfield but also in the smaller but still important area between Wrexham and Flint in the northeast.

The last **Ice Age** (1.5 million–10 000 years ago) was decisive in the formation of the Welsh landscape; Snowdonia, with its U-shaped valleys and dramatically sculpted *cwms*, was one of the principal areas whose study revealed the profound influence of glaciation and other processes on the shaping of the landscape. With the final melting of the ice, the sea-level rose, drowning valleys such as that now occupied by the fine natural harbour of Milford Haven, a classic example of a *ria*.

**Mountains** – Controversy about the exact definition of a mountain formed an intriguing subject for a comic film (*The Englishman who went up a Hill and came down a Mountain*, 1995); Welsh hills and uplands of modest height (perhaps only 600ft/200m) are often called mountains locally. A high proportion of the land however lies above this elevation and this, together with exposure to the winds and high rainfall of an Atlantic climate, gives much of Wales a decidedly rugged character. Land use has always tended towards pastoralism rather than arable cultivation, and settlement has traditionally been based on scattered farmsteads rather than on nucleated villages. The highland backbone of the country, generally referred to as the **Cambrian Mountains,** stretches north from the uplands of Carmarthenshire into Snowdonia. With its quintessential Welshness, its popularity with visitors of all kinds and its inexhaustible variety of scenery ranging from rocky summits of extreme severity to wooded valleys of great picturesqueness, Snowdonia was inevitably one of the first National Parks to be designated. The Park boundary takes in not only the core ranges around **Snowdon** itself (at 3 560ft/1 085m the highest peak in England and Wales), but extends far to the south to include that equally sublime peak, **Cadair Idris**, brooding over the beautiful Mawddach Estuary. The mountains of mid-Wales lack the fame of Snowdonia and enjoy no special status in terms of National Park or any other protective designation; a proposal made in the 1960s to create a Cambrian Mountains National Park (500sq mi/1 300km$^2$) extending from southern Snowdonia almost to the Brecon Beacons was defeated by the implacable opposition of farmers and other local people. These central uplands, "the remote, beautiful and empty heart of Wales", are certainly less dramatic than either Snowdonia or the Brecon Beacons; the view south from the summit of Cadair Idris reveals a succession of rounded summits stretching southwards through Powys and Ceredigion (Cardiganshire). These rise to their highest point at **Plynlimon** (2 467ft/752m), where the monotony is broken by a line of steep north-facing cliffs. Other scenic incidents include the deep cleft of the Afon Twymyn but, for the most part, the appeal of these uplands derives from the sheer extent of their lonely majesty. Traffic mostly keeps to the main roads in the valleys, occasionally climbing high to overcome some hilly barrier. The most thrilling drives however follow minor roads, like those twisting and turning over the mountains between Staylittle and Machynlleth or between Abergwesyn and Tregaron.

The emptiness of mid-Wales has attracted military use; low-flying jets surprise visitors and sheep alike; to the north of Sennybridge, the moorlands of Mynydd Eppynt echo to artillery fire and are used to test infantrymen to the limits of their endurance. Beyond Mynydd Eppynt rise the scalloped scarps of the **Brecon Beacons** which have been designated a National Park; the ridge-walks, river valleys, caves and waterfalls form a rural playground for the crowded population of South Wales. A hundred thousand pairs of feet a year tread their way up Pen-y-Fan (2 906ft/886m), fewer than the half-million endured by Snowdon but enough to cause severe erosion to the path to the summit.

**Rivers** – Two of Britain's finest rivers, the **Severn** (*Hafren* in Welsh) (220mi/354km long) and the **Wye** *(Gwy)*, have their sources within a short distance of each other on the slopes of Plynlimon, their waters finally mingling in the Bristol Channel. Most of the other rivers, usually copiously filled by the abundant rainfall, have much shorter runs. Their valleys have always formed the principal lines of communication and, in a mountainous country, have provided the sites for settlements. Many are associated with landscapes of distinctive character. For much of its length the lovely **Usk** *(Wysg)* passes through scenes of leafy lushness which have become increasingly rare in an intensively farmed England.

Even the **Vale of Neath**, the focus of early industrial activity, still retains much of the wooded quality so keenly appreciated in the late 18C and early 19C by travellers in search of "picturesque" scenes. The **Teifi**, which forms the boundary between Carmarthenshire and Ceredigion (Cardiganshire), is accompanied along much of its course by the parklands of country houses, whereas the meandering middle reaches of the **Tywi** have a tranquillity quite at variance with the rushing upper courses of many Welsh rivers. In the north, the **Clwyd** has given its name to a prosperous agricultural vale. Tidal water flows inland as far as Llanrwst on the level floor of the **Vale of Conwy**, but the Conwy and its tributaries have a quite different character further upstream, where their waters tumble down steep wooded gorges and crash over spectacular falls.

**Waterfalls** – High rainfall and geological variety make Wales a country of waterfalls. The most concentrated waterfall region is that in the upper part of the **Vale of Neath** and around **Ystradfellte**, where the easily eroded Carboniferous Limestone abuts the much harder Millstone Grit. Here, as well as many of the typical features of "limestone country", such as crags, caverns and underground rivers, there is a whole series of waterfalls of fascinatingly different configuration. The most famous is perhaps **Sgwd yr Eira** (Fall of Snow) with a rocky passageway behind the plunging curtain of water. Inevitably, such spectacular natural attractions are extremely popular with visitors, few more so than the waterfalls in the **Vale of Rheidol** which runs inland from Aberystwyth; at the head of the Vale at Devil's Bridge there is one of the most dramatic examples in Britain of the phenomenon of river capture, where the Mynach flows over a fall (400ft/122m) into the deep wooded ravine of the Rheidol. The mountains of Snowdonia have many waterfalls, one of the highest being **Aber Falls** (200ft/60m) in the north of the National Park, where water pouring off the Carnedd range drops over a sill of hard igneous rock. The highest waterfall in England and Wales is on the easternmost boundary of the northern mountains, at **Pistyll Rhaeadr** (240ft/73m), described by George Borrow as "the grand cataract of North Wales"; the waters plunge over a sandstone precipice at the edge of the lonely Berwyn mountains.

D Noton/National Trust Photographic Library

Winter in the Brecon Beacons

Rhaedr Ddu Falls

**Lakes** – Nature has endowed Wales with many lakes, though the splendid water bodies on the upper reaches of the Rivers **Elan** and Claerwen, which make up the Welsh "Lake District", are entirely artificial, created in the late 19C by the city fathers of far-away Birmingham to supply their citizens with water. A number of other large lakes which stand out in prominent blue on the map of Wales have a similar origin, their benefit to English consumers not always appreciated by the local Welsh whose hamlets and farmsteads were flooded in the process. But few of these reservoirs have failed to become attractions in their own right, especially when their dams are such splendidly monumental pieces of Victorian engineering as the one at **Lake Vyrnwy**. Even more colossal in scale is the modern earth dam of **Llyn Brianne**, supplying Swansea and drowning one of the previously most remote tracts of mid-Wales mountain in the process. Another modern dam, in concrete and the tallest of its kind in Britain, is at **Llyn Clywedog**, intended less for water supply than to regulate the unruly behaviour of the Severn. Natural lakes are many and various. Some, tiny as they are, form an integral part of the high mountain scene; **Llyn Cau**, framed in its half-circle of cliffs reflecting in its sinister dark waters the crags of Cadair Idris, and **Llyn Cwm Llwch** reflecting those of Pen-y-Fan. The larger lakes of Snowdonia add immeasurably to the allure of the landscape; **Llyn Ogwen** seems to intensify the harshness of the glacial trough between the Glyders and the Carneddau, while **Llyn Gwynant** marks the transition from the rugged uplands to the gentler scenery of the valleys. The largest lake in Wales is **Bala Lake** *(Llyn Tegid)* (4mi/6km long). Far to the south, between the Black Mountains and the Brecon Beacons, **Llangorse Lake**, also of glacial origin, has been the scene of exciting archaeological investigations which have revealed the existence of an early medieval artificial island settlement *(crannog)*.

**Coast** – Much of the Welsh coast enjoys protection under various forms of conservation designation. Considerable stretches – unusually for England and Wales – form part of National Parks; the **Snowdonia National Park** has a long stretch of coastline (27mi/44km) where its mountains reach the sea, while spectacular coastal features form the very *raison d'être* of the **Pembrokeshire Coast National Park**. Here are rock stacks, dramatically folded cliffs, intimate inlets, offshore islands, every imaginable kind of beach, as well as the magnificent anchorage of Milford Haven and the quiet estuary of the Daugleddau. Other coastlines of almost equal attraction are official Areas of Outstanding Beauty or Heritage Coasts. They include the whole of the remote and fascinating **Lleyn Peninsula**, most of the island of **Anglesey**, much of the **Cardigan** coast, the **Gower Peninsula**, as well as the sharply eroded limestone cliffs of the **Glamorgan Heritage Coast**. The rivers add their own contribution to the attraction of the coast as they join the sea. South Wales looks out over the glorious expanse of the Severn and the Bristol Channel towards the hills of Somerset and Devon. At low tide the Usk and Taff reach the sea between great tracts of shining mud, though at Cardiff Bay a barrage is due to turn this elemental scene into the tamer one of a controlled lake. The superb **estuaries** of **Loughor** and **Tywi** in the south have counterparts in the north in the sublime scenery of the **Mawddach** and the **Dovey** *(Dyfi)*. Every kind of **beach** occurs along the long Welsh coast, from the secluded coves of Pembrokeshire to the great stretches of sand and dune system of Kenfig and Pembrey in the south, and those of Morfa Harlech stretched out at the foot of the great castle in the north. The whole of the coastline is studded with harbour villages and little towns, all of them once busy with the comings and goings of commercial traffic; some, like Fishguard, function still, others have successfully turned themselves into resorts and pleasure ports.

**Islands** – County-sized **Anglesey** is separated from the mainland by the swirling tidal water of the Menai Strait, seemingly designed by nature to be elegantly bridged by the great structures designed by Telford and Stephenson. Anglesey has its own islands, Puffin Island off Penmon Point in the east, and the much larger **Holy Island** in the west, with the great artificial harbour of Holyhead as well as the bird-rich cliffs dropping into the sea below Holyhead Mountain. **Bardsey Island** off the Lleyn Peninsula and **Caldey Island** near Tenby were important monastic sites (Caldey still is), while Ramsey, Skomer and Skokholm are unsurpassed in their wealth of wildlife.

Sheep and Shepherds, Snowdonia

**Farmland and Forest** – Wales makes little claim to being an agriculturally rich or progressive country. Its farming systems are mainly pastoral, making use of both uplands and valley grasslands to raise large numbers of cattle, and even larger numbers of **sheep**. More than three-quarters of Wales is classified by the European Union as a "less favoured area". Holdings have remained small in extent, and in spite of subsidies, upland farming remains a precarious living. Much of mountain Wales has been losing population for two centuries, the evidence visible in abandoned farmhouses and outbuildings and in unmaintained walls and fences. Other areas like the Vales of Clwyd and Glamorgan, the latter known as the "Garden of Wales", are more favoured; farming is mixed and holdings are larger. Pembrokeshire and the Gower are able to exploit good soils and early spring warmth to produce an early crop of potatoes.

**Forestry** is sometimes seen as an alternative to farming in upland areas, and systematic afforestation has taken place in Wales since the early days of the Forestry Commission founded in 1919. Species are invariably non-native **conifers**, and great tracts of former grass moorland and blanket bog have been converted to forests of spruce, larch and pine, a startling new landscape of variable merit. Some employment has been provided, as well as recreational facilities like picnic and camp sites, but the grandeur and sense of infinite space of many formerly remote areas have been lost. The greatest transformation has perhaps taken place in the chain of uplands reaching southwestwards through Ceredigion (Cardiganshire) and Carmarthenshire, in areas like the vast **Tywi Forest** around Llyn Brianne. The new plantations of **Coed-y-Brenin** have been successfully integrated into the more varied scenery of southern Snowdonia.

**Vegetation and Wildlife** – After the retreat of the ice at the end of the last Ice Age, virtually the whole of Wales was colonised by mixed deciduous woodland, only the mountains over about 2 000ft/600m remaining free of forest. This cover has been steadily removed, mostly by grazing animals, and the soils in the uplands have been so degraded in the process that the forest would be unlikely to regenerate itself even if grazing ceased. Semi-natural fragments of the original woodland remain, in relatively isolated valleys like that of the Rheidol, or in interesting communities on limestone soils in the south which may include rare species like whitebeam or native lime. Hedgerow trees and shrubs still hint at the original forest cover. The commonest native tree is probably still the **oak**; most of the prize specimens coveted by the Royal Navy for its men o' war have long since been felled, and the most frequently encountered oaks are likely to be attractively gnarled and stunted, and, especially in the west, generously coated with lichens and mosses.

Sheltered spots below the rare tops of the highest mountains harbour a number of fascinating alpine species, but the most widespread upland cover is formed by **grass moorland**, with less extensive areas of **heather moor**. In recent years the extent of **blanket bog** with its sphagnum species has been reduced by draining and afforestation with conifers. The rough grazing land *(ffridd)* rising from the smaller fields of the valleys is characterised by bents and fescues, and increasingly invaded by bracken.

The lowlands retain many pockets of fascinating natural vegetation, most of them managed as nature reserves of one type or another. **Cors Caron**, the great raised bog near **Tregaron** is the largest of its kind in the British Isles outside Ireland. Many **estuaries**, like those of the Loughor or the Dovey *(Dyfi)*, are flanked by splendid salt-marshes. **Sand dunes** occur in a number of coastal locations and form a specialised habitat; those at **Kenfig Burrows** support a superb array of orchids. Wildlife in Wales is

43

not significantly different from the rest of Great Britain, though remoteness and low population density favour the survival of wild species. Beavers seem to have been active here longer than elsewhere, and the last Welsh wolf ended his days confined to the moat of Chirk Castle in the late 17C. The spread of conifer forest has led to an increase in the numbers of **pine-martens**, and **polecats** are found too. After teetering on the verge of local extinction, the **red kite** has returned to central Wales.

The greatest glories of Welsh wildlife are to be seen on the coast and around the islands. Grey seals frequent Ramsey Island, dolphins and porpoises Cardigan Bay. There are spectacular colonies of **sea-birds**, gannets on Grassholm, Manx shearwater on Skomer and Skokholm. Guillemots, razorbills and puffins crowd the cliffs of Holy Island, observable by closed-circuit television from the nearby observatory. There are other excellent opportunities for observing wildlife at the Wildfowl and Wetlands Centre on the Loughor estuary near Llanelli, and the Welsh Wildlife Centre on the Teifi just upstream from Cardigan.

**Climate** – Facing westward and consisting largely of uplands, Wales enjoys a climate perhaps best described as fresh. Prevailing Atlantic winds blow in unimpeded from the southwest, bearing moisture which the rising air-stream tends to deposit on the mountains and their surroundings. Rainfall is generally high and increases with elevation; the tip of Snowdon receives an extraordinarily high level of precipitation (160in/4 000mm annually), some of it in the form of snow, though the Welsh mountains generally have less snowfall than their more easterly English counterparts in the Pennines. Local conditions can bring about significant differences, and many Welsh seaside resorts owe their fortune to favourable aspect and shelter. Lying in the lee of Snowdonia, **Llandudno** is no wetter than parts of southeast England.

The country's western position means that year-round temperatures can remain relatively high, especially at sea-level, favouring the growth of exotic plants for gardeners able to provide shelter from the wind.

The reliable winds and exposed uplands of Wales provide many potential sites for wind turbine power stations. Such **wind farms** are encouraged by subsidy from a government committed to generating a proportion of the nation's electricity without the use of fossil fuels. There is however a natural conjunction between suitability of site and environmental importance; many potential sites are within National Parks or other protected areas, and wind farms are opposed in principle by the *Campaign for the Protection of Rural Wales*. Nevertheless, a number have been built on highly visible sites across the country from

Cemmaes Wind Farm

Wales Tourist Board

Jackdaw

Red kite

Razorbill

Puffin

Gannet

Guillemot

JM Labat/PHONE

JM Labat/PHONE

45

# UNITARY AUTHORITIES

1 Anglesey
2 Blaenau Gwent
3 Bridgend
4 Caerphilly
5 Cardiff
6 Carmarthenshire
7 Ceredigion
8 Conwy
9 Denbighshire
10 Flintshire
11 Gwynedd
12 Merthyr Tydfil
13 Monmouthshire
14 Neath Port Talbot
15 Newport
16 Pembrokeshire
17 Powys
18 Rhondda Cynon Taff
19 Swansea
20 Torfaen
21 Vale of Glamorgan
22 Wrexham

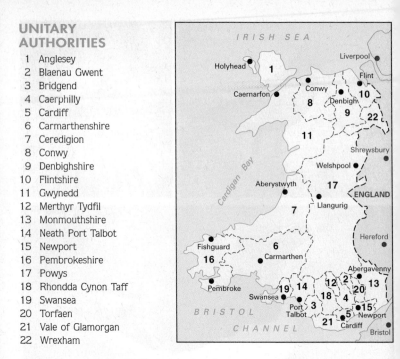

the southeast to Anglesey, and make a dramatic impact with their tall white towers and great blades rotating in a strangely uncoordinated way. The largest power station of this kind, its 103 turbines producing enough electricity for a small town, is the Penrhyddlan and Llidiartywaun wind farm high up in the hills of Powys.

**Towns and Cities** – Ancient Wales had virtually no urban settlements, and many Welsh towns have their origin in the *bastides* planted by the Anglo-Normans. Outside the industrial areas, towns have stayed small if not minuscule, and may have retained the intricate texture more progressive places have lost, with the ancient layout of streets and alleyways intact and with a good variety of buildings of many periods in harmonious proximity. **Seaside resort towns** frequently have a strong Victorian character, best exemplified by **Llandudno** and **Aberystwyth**. Industry has been decisive in Welsh urban development from a very early date. Metalworking marked the landscape of many mountainous areas in Ceredigion (Cardiganshire) and Snowdonia, though its scale remained small as did the settlements in which its workforce lived. The slate quarries of Snowdonia gave rise to **Blaenau Ffestiniog** and **Bethesda**, though the greatest built monument to the industry is probably Penrhyn Castle, the great neo-Norman pile built from the profits of the Penrhyn Quarry. It was in the south that the most dramatic developments took place. Metalworking had begun in the **Merthyr Tydfil** and **Swansea/Neath** areas in Tudor times, and advanced rapidly in the 18C. By the 1880s Merthyr was the biggest town in Wales, albeit with no pretensions to urbanity; **Cardiff**, in the early 19C still one minor Welsh town among many, advanced to prominence first on the products of Merthyr, then as the outlet for the coal extracted from the immensely rich deposits of the South Wales coalfield. Consolidating its capital role in the early 20C by laying out its grandiose Civic Centre, one of the most extravagant exercises ever undertaken in municipal planning, Cardiff remained vulnerable for a long time to the challenge posed by **Swansea**, which has always considered itself a more authentically Welsh city. Utterly distinct from either is the tentacular city represented by **The Valleys**, a landscape as archetypically Welsh as any in the country, albeit at the end of the 20C beset by the problems of the "post-industrial" society. Once entirely dependent on the hundreds of pits sunk into the coal seams, this strange townscape of terraced houses, chapels, miners' institutes and railway lines has the population size and strong character of any more easily recognisable city, even though its constituent parts are separated by the mountains and moorlands rising abruptly between each crowded valley. The almost complete collapse of the coal industry as an employer has been only partly offset by the Welsh Office's assiduous wooing of new industries and offices.

*The length of time given in this guide*
*– for touring allows time to enjoy the views and the scenery*
*– for sightseeing is the average time required for a visit*

# Great Little Trains

**Rise and Decline** – Railways came early to the rapidly industrialising Wales of the early 19C. The first journey on iron rails made by a steam locomotive took place in 1804, when an engine designed by Richard .Trevithick made a short trip at Peny-darren on the Merthyr Tramroad. Three years later, the Oystermouth Railway and Tramroad Company launched the world's first public railway passenger service in 1807 along the shore of Swansea Bay. In the following decades, the railways spread over the whole of Wales, linking inland industries with ports and improving communications between England and Wales and Ireland, then part of the United Kingdom; two of the best engineered lines were Brunel's South Wales Railway (completed 1856) and Stephenson's Chester and Holyhead (completed 1850). In spite of spectacular feats of construction like Stephenson's Britannia Bridge across the Menai Strait to Anglesey, these main lines were easy to build compared with the later lines which extended the system through the more mountainous terrain of rural Wales. Added to the physical difficulty of building these lines were the meagre revenues generated by a thinly populated area with little in the way of industrial traffic. Some lines never made a profit and the last to be constructed tended to be the first to be closed.

**Revival** – The closures of the 1960s affected the railways of Wales particularly severely. Once a more or less complete network, the system is now a mere skeleton. The north and south coasts are still served but only two main lines survive in mid-Wales, both taking passengers through the spectacular scenery; the Cambrian links Shrewsbury with Aberystwyth and Pwllheli, while the "Heart of Wales" runs from Craven Arms to Llanelli.

By way of compensation, something of a renaissance has taken place in the case of a number of minor lines; a good dozen railways of great archaeological and scenic interest, "The Great Little Trains of Wales" *(see p 30)*, have been saved or rebuilt, mostly on the initiative of railway enthusiasts and now form one of Wales' most popular tourist attractions.

Some of these revived railways are venerable in the extreme. The narrow-gauge **Ffestiniog** was built in the 1830s as a horse tramroad to connect the slate quarries of Blaenau Ffestiniog with the sea at Porthmadog; closed in 1946, it has been slowly rebuilt in stages from 1955 onwards, the whole length through the lush Vale of Ffestiniog to the slate tips of Blaenau being reopened to its powerful double-ended steam engines in 1982.

The senior line is generally considered to be the **Talyllyn Railway** of 1866, also narrow-gauge and subjected to the loving attention of enthusiasts since 1951. Its steam trains puff slowly up through the quiet countryside of southern Snowdonia, though never quite reaching the lake after which the line is named.

Owing nothing to enthusiasts and everything to Victorian entrepreneurship, the **Snow-don Mountain Railway** is Britain's only real mountain line. Opened in 1896 and closed only in wartime, it hauls visitors by steam power to the very top of the highest peak in England and Wales.

Wales Tourist Board

Vale of Rheidol Narrow-gauge Train

Not quite so spectacular but still a thrilling experience is a ride aboard the **Vale of Rheidol Railway** (1902), which takes its passengers from the seaside at Aberystwyth up through the forests to the waterfalls at Devil's Bridge.

As its name implies the **Brecon Mountain Railway** runs across the bleak uplands of the Brecon Beacons north of Merthyr Tydfil, whereas the **Welshpool and Llanfair** makes its way through more pastoral countryside. Other narrow-gauge lines include the **Fairbourne and Barmouth**, the **Teifi Valley** and the **Bala Lake**.

The **Llangollen Railway** in the glorious Dee Valley has made a convincing attempt to recreate the atmosphere of the old standard-gauge main line.

While the fate of the surviving rural lines of the national system seems fraught with doubt, the great little railways' future appears assured. In 1995 a generous injection of funds was received from Britain's National Lottery to help rebuild the short-lived **Welsh Highland Railway**; the reopened line is intended to run from the existing terminus at Porthmadog through Snowdonia to Caernarfon.

# The Welsh People

Wales has a population of just under three million, nearly two-thirds of whom live in the industrial conurbations of the south. Smaller towns are strung along the coasts, with a large area of empty mountain and moorland, and scattered rural communities, in the middle.

This pattern of settlement has considerable bearing on the social structure and divisions within Wales. There is, nevertheless, a unifying national feeling and a strong sense of identity that places Wales apart from other nations of the United Kingdom. On a superficial level, it finds its expression in symbols: the **red dragon**, featured on the Welsh flag; the **daffodil** and **leek**, emblems worn on **St David's Day** (1 March) but beneath this surface is a far more complex national life, in which several strands of identity compete and occasionally unite.

**Language** – Perhaps the most apparent cultural division within Wales is that between Welsh-speakers and non-Welsh-speakers. During most of the 20C this corresponded to a great degree with the division between urban and rural Wales. Industrial communities in the south and south-east have tended to become Anglicised, while the farming and fishing communities of north and west Wales have remained predominantly Welsh-speaking. This situation has changed noticeably, though gradually, in the last few decades, as a revival of interest in the Welsh language has spread in the industrial towns, and as bilingual and Welsh-language institutions (such as the Welsh Development Agency, the Welsh Language Board and television and radio channels) have been established in the cities.

A key moment in the struggle for the language's survival came in 1979/80 when central government attempted to go back on a commitment to make the peak hour programmes of the proposed fourth TV channel predominantly Welsh. Mass rallies and the threat by **Dr Gwynfor Evans**, the then President of Plaid Cymru (Welsh Nationalist Party), to undertake a fast to the death were successful; today's peak output of Channel Four (S4C or *Sianel Pedwar Cymru*) in Wales includes many programmes in Welsh, including the popular soap opera *Pobl y Cwm* (People of the Valley). Welsh radio and publishing flourish and, depending on geographical location, much of Welsh education is now in the Welsh language. Most official transactions can be carried out in Welsh and equality of treatment for the Welsh and English languages in the public sector was ensured by the Welsh Language Act 1993. Many place names have reverted to their original Welsh spelling but, where there is any chance of confusion, road signs are bilingual.

At the same time, tourism has had an increasing impact particularly on the north Wales coastal towns, bringing in its wake an influx of English newcomers and encouraging the sale of rural cottages to buyers mainly resident outside Wales.

In the face of these and other threats to the language – it is spoken by only about one in five of the population – Welsh-speakers have frequently adopted a defensive stance, to the exclusion of their English-speaking compatriots. This has been especially evident in the development of Plaid Cymru (see p 71), which until the 1980s concentrated chiefly on the fight to maintain a Welsh-language culture. Much of the opposition to the party within Wales came from industrial towns where it was also seen as a middle-class, agricultural-based movement. Only recently has it tried to broaden its appeal, acknowledging the specifically Welsh identity of Anglicised southern communities.

Wales versus France in 1994

**Anglo-Welsh Culture** – An equally strong national feeling has emerged from English-speaking areas, often existing alongside fervent British and royalist sentiments. It has found its expression in the close life of these communities, which until the 1980s were linked with a common means of employment (the mines or steelworks), in the male voice choirs *(see p 58)* drawing on local membership and in the identification with rugby as a "national" sport, although the Welsh team has not enjoyed much success since its heyday in the 1970s. Meanwhile the capital city, Cardiff, has nurtured its own, separate character, based around the docks, the university, and a multi-ethnic population.

When devolution from Westminster became a possibility in the 1960s and 1970s there was much objection in the north to the prospect of rule by the "socialist" south. Many northern communities felt their Welshness threatened, and in 1979 the Welsh electorate rejected a separate assembly. In 1997, however, there was a narrow majority in favour of a Welsh Assembly *(see p 71)*, which may indicate a merging of Welsh interests and aspirations.

**Folklore** – Folklore is a central element of the Welsh view of Wales and its history. The **Mabinogion**, a group of 11 early medieval tales about the royal Welsh/Brittonic houses, form the most important body of Welsh myth and legend. They evoke a heroic, mysterious past which has played a vital part in the shaping of a Welsh identity. Four connected stories at the heart of *The Mabinogion* relate the adventures of Pwyll, Prince of Dyfed; Branwen, daughter of Llŷr; Manawydan, son of Llŷr; and Math, son of Mathonwy. Other sections tell the stories of Macsen Wledig *(see p 67 and p 56)*, the Dream of Rhonabwy, Lludd and Llefelys and the Arthurian characters Culwch and Olwen. Irish princes and nobles figure largely in the collection, and much of the material is believed to have its roots in historical events. Modern Welsh culture continues to draw on *The Mabinogion* and their imagery, using them as inspiration for art, drama and music.

**Eisteddfod** – No account of Welsh-language culture can ignore the **National Eisteddfod**. This festival-cum-contest-cum-fair is held every August, moving its sites from north to south Wales in alternate years. In a sense it acts as a substitute for permanent arts institutions, providing a stage for instrumentalists, singers, dancers, actors, writers and poets, and including a major exhibition of contemporary fine arts, sculpture and crafts. A multitude of other *eisteddfodau* performs the same function at a local level in schools and halls throughout the country. The **International Music Eisteddfod**, held in Llangollen every year, attracts musical competitors from countries all over the world.

As well as being a focus for the arts, the National *Eisteddfod* is also an occasion for political controversy. This usually centres on language issues – the institution is fiercely guarded as the only national assembly of Welsh-speakers, and moves to introduce English into the proceedings have sparked heated debate; visitors can buy special equipment (like a mobile phone) for translated commentaries. Other issues have highlighted the wide age range of *Eisteddfod* devotees, involving arguments over the availability of alcohol and "fringe" rock concerts organised for the younger generation. The whole spectrum of Welsh-language culture can be witnessed here – from protests and demonstrations on the field *(maes)* to the highly formalised ceremony of chairing the winning bard, conducted before the *Gorsedd* of Bards in their long robes and presided over by the Arch-druid, decked out in white and gold.

**Nonconformity** – Since the Methodist Revival in the 18C *(see p 69)* the Welsh have often been caricatured as tight-lipped, puritanical chapel-goers. The chapel has undeniably been a focal point of Welsh community and family life, and continues to fulfil a significant role in some areas but it is no longer the main cultural and intellectual outlet, and its influence has diminished. Even in the late 20C, however, the legacy of the Methodist temperance drive could still be seen. From 1961 local polls, intended to be held every seven years, gave Welsh counties the chance to decide whether their pubs should open on Sundays. The results established a clear division between the "wet" counties, which voted for Sunday opening, and the "dry", mainly rural and Welsh-speaking. By the time the second poll was held in 1968, the number of "dry" counties had halved. By 1995 only one district – Dwyfor – was still holding out against Sunday opening; now, however, even Dwyfor is "wet".

**Welsh Emigration** – Religious persecution, rural poverty and the decline of customs and language drove hundreds of emigrants out of Wales in the 18C and 19C. In 1796 an attempt was made to establish a Welsh-speaking colony in west Pennsylvania, settled by Quakers fleeing from repression at home. The predominance of American culture and policy doomed this experiment to failure, but Welsh families built a strong Baptist base in the state and maintained links with the homeland.

Rather more success was enjoyed by the group of more than 150 emigrants who in 1865 followed Michael D Jones to the Chubut Valley in **Patagonia** (at the southern extremity of South America). Their aim was to set up a Welsh community free of all English influences and the colony still exists, some of its members speaking a Welsh that has borrowed heavily from Spanish.

Other Welsh families left the country for Africa, Australia, Brazil, Canada and Russia. In most cases the Welsh language did not survive emigration but national pride and customs are still retained in Welsh communities world-wide. St David's Societies celebrate the patron saint's day on every continent, and in the USA Welsh networks are particularly strong, producing newspapers and organising events and exchanges. One of the most stirring ceremonies of the National Eisteddfod is the Expatriates' Day, when groups of Welsh descendants stand to be greeted by the audience as their countries of residence are called out.

**Welsh and English** – The relationship between expatriate Welsh and homeland is chiefly symbolic and sentimental, and does not extend to the Welsh who live elsewhere in Britain, more particularly in England. Generally the Welsh bear an ambivalent attitude towards their nearest neighbours. A 700-year history of English conquest and political and economic ascendancy has fostered resentment, especially towards the wealthy south-east and the London-based government. Since the extension of the electorate in the 19C, Wales has consistently represented the anti-conservative, "radical" wing of politics, whether it be Liberal, Nationalist or Labour, but even under non-conservative administrations the nation has complained of neglect and lack of investment. At the same time, Wales has frequently proved to be an enthusiastic supporter of British, imperial and royal institutions. It seems that for many Welsh patriots a distinct line can be drawn between the concepts of Britishness and Englishness.

Chairing the Bard

The increase of tourism has served to emphasise the sometimes uneasy relations between the English and the Welsh. As in most tourist-based economies, a welcome for increased prosperity and interest is counterbalanced by a fear of the loss of cultural and social integrity. There are many cases of settlers from England becoming immersed in Welsh life and learning the Welsh language, but on the whole contact between the two nations is still marked by a lack of communication and understanding.

# Food and Drink

Although the Welsh food industry has played an important part in the British economy for centuries, the concept of Welsh cuisine has only very recently emerged. In the 1990s promoters have tried to make up for lost time, applying the **Taste of Wales** *(Blas ar Gymru)* accolade to home-grown products and to guesthouses, hotels and restaurants serving fresh local food in new or traditional recipes.

**Seafood** – The long Welsh coastline and its many rivers and lakes provide a wide range of freshwater and sea food, which is now enjoying a gradual revival after a post-war slump. Fish stalls sell fresh catches in Cardiff and Swansea central markets and in smaller ports around Cardigan Bay, and the famous Penclawdd cockles are still gathered on the Gower Peninsula and celebrated in Swansea's September Cockle Festival. Other seafood includes oysters, farmed at Pembroke and Anglesey; whiting, dogfish, crabs and lobsters, hauled in at Milford Haven, and King and Queen scallops from the Anglesey coast. Freshwater delicacies such as salmon and sewin (a pink-skinned sea trout) are fished from the rivers Wye, Dee, Teifi and Usk.

**Laverbread**, lettuce-like seaweed, is a unique Welsh seafood particularly popular in and around Swansea, where it is sold from the market stalls. It is usually served with bacon and can be bought fresh or in tins.

**Meat** – Lamb and beef have been a vital source of income in Wales since the Middle Ages. Until the 19C herds of sheep and cattle were regularly driven hundreds of miles from the Welsh mountains to English markets. The drovers who made these long and dangerous journeys became celebrated members of society and many of their routes can be followed and their resting places, the drovers' inns, visited.

**Welsh lamb** is now marketed all over the world as a lean and natural meat, while beef, traditionally overshadowed by the better-known lamb industry, has begun to profit from new promotion.

**Dairy Products** – A growing interest in old skills and recipes has brought new life to the Welsh dairy industry. **Caerphilly**, perhaps the most famous Welsh cheese, is creamy, white and mild; other cheeses include Llangloffan, which is red and flavoured with garlic, and Y Fenni, a type of cheddar with ale and mustard seed. Cheese-making is largely concentrated in Dyfed, where the shallow valleys and good pasture are ideal for dairy farms.

**Welsh Dishes** – Most traditional Welsh recipes were originally devised for maximum economy and nourishment rather than gastronomic excellence. *Cawl* is a thick broth of meat, vegetables and potatoes, still served as a standard winter meal. *Lobscaws* (pronounced Lobscouse), a stew made with left-overs, was the staple diet of poor Welsh communities in Liverpool in the 19C – hence the name "Scouse" for Liverpudlians.

Bara Brith and Welsh cakes

A mixture of hot milk and bread, sometimes thickened with an egg *(bara-llaeth)* is unlikely to appear on many restaurant menus but a mash of swede and potatoes *(stwnsh rhwdans)* does occasionally make the transition from domestic to professional kitchen.

The **leek** is a popular ingredient in soups and sauces, or combined with potatoes or other vegetables. It is also worn as a national emblem *(see p 51)*.

**Baking** – Old baking recipes are still widely used and are familiar items on café menus. Perhaps the most popular is the Welsh cake, a cross between a biscuit and a currant scone, made like a drop-scone on an iron griddle and eaten, preferably warm, with butter or sugar, according to taste. Methods for baking *bara brith* (which means freckled bread), a rich fruit loaf, vary from cook to cook. Some recipes include spices, some treacle, and some require the fruit mixture to be soaked in tea overnight. A long "cut and come again" cake *(Teisen lap)*, which is less widely available, is made to a traditional Glamorgan recipe using currants and spices such as nutmeg.

**Drinks** – Beer is as popular in Wales as anywhere in Britain, despite (or perhaps because of) the Nonconformist temperance tradition *(see p 50)*. Beer-drinking is a long-established custom in British Legion clubs (set up for ex-servicemen) and sports clubs as well as pubs. Local brews include Felin Foel, made in West Wales, and Brains Beer from Cardiff.

More recent ventures in the drinks industry have included a Welsh brand of whisky, Chwisgi, and Cariad wines, a range of award-winning whites and rosés grown in the Vale of Glamorgan.

### Recipe for Bara Brith

Soak dried fruit (12oz/350g) and candied peel (4oz/110g) in warm water (1 pint/570ml) with mixed spice (half a teaspoon). Then strain and retain the liquor. Sift flour (2lb/900g) and salt (2 teaspoons) and rub in lard (6oz/175g). Cream fresh yeast (1oz/2.75g) with Demarara sugar (8oz/225g) and a few drops of the liquor and add to the flour mixture. Add eggs (2) and enough of the liquor to make a firm dough. Knead well, leave to rise. Knock down; blend in the drained fruit and knead again. Shape into loaves, place in a greased tin and leave to rise in a warm place. Bake at 230°C, 450°F, gas mark 8 for 15min and then at 190°C, 375°F, gas mark 5 for 45min. Allow to stand for 5min and then glaze with honey.

### Recipe for Bara Lawr

Clean some laverbread (1lb/450g) by soaking in sea water for a few hours. Simmer in hot water for several hours until tender. Mix with oatmeal (1lb/450g). Season with salt and pepper. Shape into small cakes, roll in oatmeal and fry in bacon fat.

### Recipe for Welsh Rarebit

Stir together over low heat some melted butter and grated Cheddar cheese (1lb/45g) until the cheese has melted. Add milk or beer (5fl oz/150ml). Season with salt and pepper and mustard and Worcester sauce. Pour the hot mixture over hot buttered toast and brown under the grill. Garnish with parsley.

# The Welsh Language

Welsh is now a living presence in most of the country and the everyday language of half a million people, although it once seemed fated to disappear like its sister languages – Cumbrian and Cornish – and its cousin – Manx, which was spoken in the Isle of Man.

**Welsh Roots** – The Welsh spoken today is a member of the **Celtic** branch of the Indo-European language family which at various times has been spoken over much of Europe, including Gaulish France. The closest living relative of Welsh is the Breton of Brittany, which many Welsh-speakers claim to be able to understand. Scots and Irish Gaelic are more distantly related. Welsh is descended from a mother-tongue called **Brittonic**, the language spoken over most of Britain until the coming of the Anglo-Saxons. A number of English place and landscape names recall this venerable linguistic foundation; they include London, based on a personal name, and York, derived from the Celtic *eburos*, a yew-tree. The Thames shares its ancient root meaning dark water with the Welsh rivers Taff and Teifi, while the generic Celtic word meaning river, as well as passing into Welsh as *afon*, has been used as the name for at least eight English rivers, including Shakespeare's Avon. Dover, together with its river the Dour, is cognate with the Welsh word *dŵr* meaning water.

In Europe in the Dark Ages the invading Germanic people called their adversaries "foreigners" or "Romanised people" and for the Germans, the Italians are still sometimes "die Welschen", while the French-speaking inhabitants of southern Belgium are known as "Walloons". The Anglo-Saxons referred to the British as "Welsh". The Welsh by contrast stressed their togetherness; **Cymry**, their name for themselves, means "fellow-countrymen" or "comrades" while their country is **Cymru** and their language **Cymraeg**.

**The "language of Heaven"** – This particular claim would be difficult to substantiate but Welsh may well claim to be the oldest living language in Europe. The parish church of the little resort of Tywyn has a memorial stone with an inscription in Early Welsh carved around AD 810. Welsh flourished throughout the Middle Ages as the language of royal court and farmstead. Pressure from the English language intensified with Edward I's subjugation of the country in the late 13C, when new towns were peopled with English-speaking burghers. Even before this, tracts of good agricultural land in places like the southern Gower and Pembrokeshire had been settled with English and Flemish colonists. The English character of the towns tended to be diluted as Welsh-speakers moved in from the surrounding countryside, but English advanced elsewhere, slowly conquering the eastern counties. After the Acts of Union in the 16C, the gentry anglicised themselves and Welsh declined in status, becoming, like other minority languages all over Europe, the "patois of the people", kept alive by clergymen and their congregations. A revival began in the late 18C, promoted by scholars and clerics and by the intelligentsia of the large Welsh community in London. The rapid industrialisation of Wales in the 19C brought in many English-speaking immigrants but the general increase in population also added to the number of Welsh-speakers, who totalled nearly a million by 1911. This growth took place despite the anglicisation of education and the employment of the infamous **Welsh Not** used to punish the use of Welsh in the classroom (see p 86). After the First World War numbers began to fall by about 100 000 each decade. By the time of the Census in 1991, 510 920 people over the age of three – just under 19% of the population – claimed a knowledge of Welsh.

**Distribution of Welsh-speakers** – The strongholds of Welsh are commonly held to be in the north and west, and it is indeed in Anglesey, the mountains of the north, the Lleyn Peninsula and in many parts of Cardiganshire and Carmarthenshire that the visitors are most likely to find themselves among obvious Welsh-speakers. In such districts the proportion of Welsh-speakers is high, more than 80% in many places. In terms of absolute numbers, however, most Welsh-speakers live in the towns and resorts along the northern and southern coasts, where they nevertheless form a minority of the population. Part of the recovery of Welsh is associated with a raising of its status; a significant number of people employed in the professions, the media and administration now claim Welsh as their first language, not only in quintessentially Welsh places like Caernarfon but also in Cardiff (see p 48).

**Difference and Similarities** – The language appears at first sight to be formidably different from most other European languages but a closer look reveals affinities (*un*, *dau*, *tri* = one, two, three). Welsh has the advantage over English of being written as it is pronounced. The alphabet has 20 simple letters and eight digraphs (like the unique LL). One confusing feature is mutation, whereby an initial consonant changes in certain circumstances; for example, the towns of Machynlleth and Pwllheli greet their visitors with the traditional "*Croeso!*" road signs but because of mutation these appear as "*Croeso y Fachynlleth!*" and "*Croeso y Bwllheli!*".

A number of words have been borrowed from other languages, mostly from English, but other words like *ffenestr* (window), *pont* (bridge) and *eglwys* (church) from Latin, or like *ffiol* (viol) and *barwn* (baron) from Norman French.

# GLOSSARY OF WELSH WORDS

No visitor to Wales is expected to have a knowledge of Welsh but some familiarity with geographical terms and common signs will enhance the enjoyment of a visit.

## Pronunciation

### CONSONANTS

**b, d, h, l, m, n, p, t** as in English
**c** always like k

**f** like v
**ch** as in Scots loch
**dd** voiced th as in that
**ff** as in fair
**g** as in garden

**ng** as in singing
**ll** difficult for non-native speakers – try ch combined with l
**ph** as in phone
**r** trilled like Scots r
**rh** as in English but with trilled r
**s** as in song
**th** unvoiced th as in thin

### VOWELS can be either long or short (approximations only)

**a** as in hard or fat

**e** as the a in face or self
**i** as in tea or tin
**o** as in ore or pond

**u** like Welsh I in South Wales; more like French u in North Wales
**w** like the oo in moon or cook
**y** like Welsh I in South Wales or like French u in North Wales; sometimes like a in about

Stress is almost always on the penultimate syllable

Abaty – abbey
Aber – mouth of a river
Afon – river
Amgueddfa – museum

Bach, fach – small
Ban – high, height
Bedd – grave
Betws – chapel
Blaen (plural blaenau – head of valley)
Bont – see pont
Brenhines – queen
Brenin – king
Bryn – hill mound
Bwlch – pass

Cadair, cader – seat, stronghold
Caer – fort
Capel – chapel
Carn – rock, mountain
Carreg, craig – rock, crag
Castell – castle
Cefn – ridge
Coch – red
Coed – wood
Cors – bog
Craig – see Carreg
Crib – ridge, arete
Croes – cross
Croeso – welcome
Cwm – combe, valley
Cymraeg – in the Welsh language
Cymreig – Welsh in essence, belonging to Wales
Cymru – Wales

Du – see Ddu
Ddu – black
Dinas – town, fort
Dre, dref – see Tre
Dŵr – water
Dŷ – see Tŷ
Dyffryn – valley

Eglwys – church

Fach – see Bach
Fair – see Mair
Fan – see Ban
Fawr – see Mawr

Felin – see Melin
Ffordd – road, way
Ffridd – enclosed rough grazing land
Ffynnon – well, spring
Frenhines – see Brenhines

Gaer – see Caer
Garn – see Carn
Garreg – see Carreg
Glan – river or water bank
Glyn – glen, valley
Goch – see Coch
Gors – see Cors
Gorsaf reilffordd – railway station
Graig – see Craig
Grib – see Crib
Groes – see Croes
Gwesty – hotel
Gŵr – husband
Gwraig – wife
Gwyn – white

Hafod, hafoty – herdsman's upland summer-dwelling
Hen – old
Hendre – valley (permanent ie winter) dwelling

Isaf – lowest

Llan – church, enclosure
Llwybr cyhoeddus – public footpath
Llyn – lake
Llys – court

Mab – son
Maen – rock
Maes – field
Maes parcio – car park
Mair – Mary
Mawr – big, great
Melin – mill
Merch – daughter
Merthyr – martyr
Morfa – marsh
Moel – bare
Mynydd – mountain

Nant – valley, stream
Newydd – new

Ogof – cave

Pant – valley
Parc – park
Pen – head, top
Penrhyn – promontory
Pentre, pentref – village
Pistyll – waterfall
Plâs – mansion
Pont, bont – bridge
Porth – gate, harbour
Pwll – pool, pond, pit
Pwll nofio – bathing pool

Rhaeadr – waterfall
Rhiw – slope, hill
Rhodfa – promenade
Rhos – moorland

Sarn – causeway
Sir – shire, county
Stryd – street

Tal – end
Tan – end
Theatr – theatre
Traeth – beach
Tre, tref – town
Tŷ – house

Uchaf – highest, uppermost

Y, yr, 'r – the
Yn – in
Ynys – island
Ysbyty – hospital
Ysgol – school

## Phrases

Croeso – Welcome
Croeso i Gymru – Welcome to Wales
Bore da – Good morning
Prynhawn da – Good afternoon
Nos da – Good night
Hwyl – Goodbye
Iechyd da! – Good health!/Cheers!
Diolch yn fawr – Thank you
Dim diolch – No thank you
Os gwelwch yn dda – Please
Esgusodwch fi – Excuse me
Mae'n ddrwg gen i – I am sorry
Sut ydych chi (north Wales) – How are you
Shwmai (south Wales) – How are you
Iawn, diolch – Fine, thank you
Da iawn, diolch – Very well, thank you
Gwyliau hapus – Happy holiday
Tywydd da – Good weather
Lwc dda – Good luck

## Food

Gwely a brecwast – bed and breakfast
Paned o de – cup of tea
Paned o goffi – cup of coffee
Llaeth (south Wales) – milk
Llefrith (north Wales) – milk
Siwgr – sugar
Bara – bread
Bara brith – fruit loaf
Cawl – soup
Cig oen – lamb
Cig eidion – beef
Gwin – wine
Cwrw – beer

# Literature

**Bardic Tradition** – Welsh literary and musical traditions have their roots in Celtic society, where the bard played the role of propagandist, historian and entertainer. By the time of the medieval principalities, poetry was being written in an early version of the Welsh language and used to flatter, encourage or even rebuke the princes and their courts. Bards were highly respected and held a higher status than the storytellers *(cyfarwyddion)*, who created and preserved a more informal body of legend and myth. These stories, part history and part fairy tale, were eventually to be written down as the **Mabinogion** in the 14C and 15C, and relate the histories of Brittonic heroes such as Arthur and Macsen Wledig *(see p 49 and p 67)*. An English version, *The Four Branches of the Mabinogi*, was produced in 1838 by Lady Charlotte Guest, the wife of an industrial magnate.

The earliest written Welsh poetry is generally acknowledged to be that of the 6C bards **Aneirin** and **Taliesin**, who wrote of warriors, heroes and battles in northern Britain. Much of the history of the princes of Powys has been gleaned from the 9C poetry featuring Heledd, Princess of Powys, and Llywarch Hen, a character from northern Britain, transplanted to Powys.

*The Bard* by Thomas Jones

The complex forms developed by these and later poets are still used in Welsh formal verse. By the 14C rhyming couplets of seven-syllabled lines *(cywydd)* had become a vehicle for everyday, often earthy themes, especially in the work of **Dafydd ap Gwilym**, *(see p 265)* who wrote mainly about women and love.

Not all medieval literature produced in Wales was in verse or even in Welsh. **Gerald of Wales**, who accompanied Archbishop Baldwin on a tour through the country in 1188 to rally support for the Crusades, wrote down his observations in Latin; they were collected in two chronicles – *The Story of the Journey through Wales* and *A Description of Wales*, providing a vivid account of 12C Welsh life.

---

### Gerald of Wales

In the attractive figure of Gerald of Wales (c 1146-1223) are combined some of the paradoxical elements in Anglo-Welsh history. In his veins ran both Norman blood and that of the Welsh rulers of the kingdom of Deheubarth; his grandmother was Princess Nest, the "Helen of Wales". He was a scholar and a churchman, known as Giraldus Cambrensis in Latin and as Gerallt Gymroin in Welsh. His overriding ambition, to crown his work for the Welsh church by becoming Bishop of St David's, was frustrated by the reluctance of the English monarch to appoint a Welshman to this important post. Gerald was nevertheless an establishment man, an adviser on Welsh affairs to King John and the tutor of his children. He was born c 1146 on the Pembrokeshire coast in Manorbier Castle *(see p 273)*.

**Bardic Renaissance** – The bardic system fell into decline in the later Middle Ages, to be revived in the 18C through the efforts of a stonemason and antiquarian, **Iolo Morganwg** (Edward Williams, 1747-1846). He renewed interest in the work of Dafydd ap Gwilym, publishing a collection of poetry claimed to be by the medieval bard but which was actually Morganwg's own work. The Convocation of Bards *(Gorsedd)*, a form of honours system for those prominent in the arts, was introduced by Iolo Morganwg and still plays a central role in the **National Eisteddfod** *(see Welsh People)*, although detailed study of his notebooks and documents, conducted after his death, proved that much of his scholarship was the product of his fertile imagination. During this period Welsh culture as a whole drew the attention of scholars and writers, and the societies of Cymmrodorion (1751) and Gwyneddigion (1771) were established by Welshmen living in London, to encourage the study of Welsh literature and history.

To a great extent Welsh poetry has survived as a popular, oral tradition. Although the major literary prizes awarded each year at the **Eisteddfod** are for written work, one of the regular features of the festival is a verbal sparring contest between bards – most of whom are amateurs – and often involves members of the audience.

**Modern Welsh Literature** – From the late medieval period until the Victorian age, most Welsh literature took the form of history or religious verse and instruction; but a resurgence in Welsh-language publishing in the mid to late 19C produced the first popular novels, by writers such as **Daniel Owen** and Gwilym Hiraethog. The Welsh readership was sustained into the 20C by such writers as Kate Roberts, Caradog Pritchard and **T Rowland Hughes**, all of whom wrote about the experiences of urban and rural labouring classes.

A new Welsh radio service, established in the 1930s, gave writers the chance to reach a wider audience. **Saunders Lewis** (1893-1985), co-founder of the Welsh National Party *(see Historical Notes)*, made full use of radio to promote his ideas and his work, which included poetry, drama and prose, as well as journalism and literary criticism. His themes of romantic nationalism drew an enthusiastic following among Welsh-speakers.

Contemporary Welsh-language literature still focuses on the *Eisteddfod* as a market for the arts but many alternative media have emerged since the 1980s. Welsh Television, film and theatre are fostering new generations of writers, who are able to portray a modern Welsh experience, absorbing the influences of English and American culture.

**Welsh Literature in English** – Together with modern Welsh-language literature a new school developed in industrial Wales of work in English about the Welsh experience. Perhaps the most famous figure in Anglo-Welsh literature is **Dylan Thomas** (1914-53), who consciously brought the lyricism and imagery of the Welsh tradition, as well as depictions of small-town Welsh life, into his works – to best effect in his drama for voices, *Under Milk Wood*. Poets such as RS Thomas, Raymond Garlick, Dannie Abse and Harri Webb have carried Anglo-Welsh literature into the 21C and an active publishing industry provides a forum for new writers in a wide range of poetry and prose journals.

*Dylan Thomas* by A Janes

National Museums and Galleries of Wales

*Help us in our constant task of keeping up-to-date*
*Please send us your comments and suggestions*
*Michelin Tyre PLC*
*Travel Publications*
*Green Guides*
*38 Clarendon Road*
*WATFORD*
*Herts WD1 1SX*
*Tel : 01923 415 000*
*Fax : 01923 415 250*

# Music

**Musical Tradition** – In his account of Wales in the 12C **Gerald of Wales** (Giraldus Cambrensis) noted that its people had a great love of and a natural gift for singing in harmony. Long before he made his travels, music had been an integral part of Welsh culture. The *eisteddfod* (literally "sitting") was a musical and literary gathering held for centuries before the first recorded event in 1176; the harp was regularly used to accompany performances of bardic verse. By the 17C and 18C the *eisteddfod* had degenerated into a rowdy, parochial affair but it regained its status and respectability after being taken in hand by Iolo Morganwg. From the 1860s the annual National Eisteddfod became an important showcase for musical performers and composers.

**Folk Music** – Contemporary Welsh compositions in all fields of music still bear the influence of a long folk tradition, despite its struggle for survival during the religious revival in the 18C. As Methodism took hold, music became a vehicle for spreading the gospel, in the **hymns** of William Williams (1717-91) and Ann Griffiths (1776-1805). Many ancient melodies and lyrics were lost and many more were in danger of disappearing during this period, condemned for their impious subject matter. They were saved by the growing academic interest in folk culture and its absorption into the pomp and ceremony of the revived *eisteddfod*. Verses *(penillion)* are still sung in a centuries-old form *(cerdd dant)*, although the verse, sung in counter-melody to a harp or piano accompaniment, is now prepared in advance rather than improvised on the spot, as was the old custom.

*Miners Singing* by Joseph Herman

**Choral Music** – Nonconformity did a great deal to foster a popular choral tradition in Wales, based on chapel services and on community gatherings made "respectable" by the church *(cymanfa ganu)*. Choirs became a feature particularly of mining town life, where there was, and still is, keen rivalry between neighbouring communities for local and national *eisteddfod* honours. Male voice choirs were formed in the south Wales valleys and in north Wales in the mining districts around Wrexham, where three choirs were started by the miners singing as they walked home from the pit. The decline of the coal industry and subsequent migration have reduced their membership but the **Treorchy Male Voice Choir** is one of several that have reached international audiences through their recordings and tours.

**Classical Music** – Welsh classical composers of note have been few and far between. One of the best known, **Joseph Parry** (1841-1903), was made the first Professor of Music at the College of Aberystwyth in 1872, and did much to popularise the study of composition. His opera, *Hywel a Blodwen*, was one of very few major Welsh compositions of the time. Not until the 20C did classical music make any significant impact on Welsh cultural life. **Walford Davies** (1869-1941), Professor of Music at Aberystwyth from 1918 to 1926, played a vigorous role in promoting musical education, and directed the Council of Music in Wales, encouraging orchestral and instrumental activity. In 1946 the **Welsh National Opera** was created, with its base in Cardiff, and singers such as Sir Geraint Evans, Gwyneth Jones and Bryn Terfel have enjoyed world-wide recognition. Modern composers such as William Mathias and Alun Hoddinott have helped create a body of classical work with a recognisably Welsh identity, and in recent years the Welsh capital has been the setting for a major classical singing contest, Cardiff Singer of the World.

**Pop Music** – Youth music in Wales has inevitably followed the lead of Anglo-American pop and rock culture. Welsh-language pop music has, however, been discovering its own voice since the 1960s, when Dafydd Iwan's political ballads became the rallying-cry of young nationalists. In the 1990s Welsh pop opened itself up to a far wider range of cultural influences, drawing on Asian, African, American and Caribbean features and combining them with native folk traditions to carry a distinctively Welsh sound into the 21C.

# Architecture in Wales

There is little which can be considered intrinsically Welsh in the buildings of Wales. Much of the architecture seen throughout the country reflects styles which evolved elsewhere, particularly in England, or sometimes further afield on the Continent. Differences which may be observed are often a matter of degree or emphasis, rather than of total kind. Even so, the Welsh countryside does give its buildings a certain distinctness of character. In part, this stems from the geographical position of Wales, together with its rich cultural and political history but it is nature's stage – the physical landscape – which has always been the dominant factor. Contrasts in the underlying geology, the topography, climate, and the availability of natural resources for construction materials, have all played significant roles.

In Wales, this strong affinity of buildings with the landscape is often unmistakable. It explains why the red sandstone castle of the border sits so well amid a patchwork of brick-earth coloured fields; it emphasises the harmony between the slate-rubble cottage of Snowdonia and the surrounding rugged terrain; and it serves as a reminder that the row of terraced industrial housing in the southern valley was built from the very stones dug alongside more precious iron ore.

**Roman Beginnings** – The Roman legions introduced Classical-style building to this frontier zone of the Empire in the late 1C AD. The Fortress Baths at **Caerleon** (c AD 80) were one of the most prominent architectural showpieces of the new province. At nearby **Caerwent**, the 2C *forum-basilica* complex was a mark of self-government within the civilised Roman world. Small towns and villa-farmsteads gradually emerged on the rich agricultural lands of the south and east, but the decline of Roman military authority in the later 4C severed this Classical building tradition. Evidence of buildings raised in Wales over the next six centuries is scanty in the extreme.

## Middle Ages

For the **Normans** who arrived on the Welsh borders in the late 11C, every emphasis was on the virtues of the new. The conquerors came with a clear preference for stone building, introducing the Romanesque with its thick walls and round-headed arches. Architectural lodges were soon set up in and around the Norman Marcher towns, and Wales came within the sphere of subsequent stylistic developments. Towards the end of the 12C came the first signs of **early Gothic**, characterised by much lighter buildings and by the pointed arch. Almost a century later, the more flamboyant style known as **Decorated** made its appearance. In the later Middle Ages the distinctly **English Perpendicular** style was also to spread into much of Wales.

**Castles and Secular Buildings** – During the hectic years of conquest, Norman castles were frequently raised in earth and timber. At **Chepstow**, however, where the hall-keep dates from 1067-71, there survives perhaps the earliest stone-built castle in the British Isles. Norman Romanesque stone halls and keeps became more prominent throughout the Marches in the 12C, with good examples at **Manorbier** and Ogmore. At **Cardiff**, it was probably Robert of Gloucester (d 1147) who built the majestic polygonal shell keep on top of the huge earthen *motte* which still looks out across the city.

In the first half of the 13C advances in military design were introduced by **William Marshal** (d 1219) and **Hubert de Burgh** (d 1243), both men having extensive experience of warfare in northern France. Marshal's great round tower *(donjon)* at **Pembroke** was highly influential and was mirrored on a smaller scale at **Skenfrith**. These two prominent examples spawned a rash of similar round keeps throughout the southern March, including Bronllys, Caldicot and **Tretower**. **Montgomery** and **White Castle** were to set new trends, particularly in gatehouses of growing sophistication. The grandest and most spectacular of the Marcher castles of this era was **Caerphilly**, begun by "Red Gilbert" de Clare in 1268, an immense "concentric" stronghold (30 acres/12ha) including five twin-towered gatehouses.

The 13C strongholds of the **Welsh princes** tended to be situated in dramatic upland locations; the rocky terrain often giving rise to irregular ground plans. Such was the case at Castell y Bere and **Dolwyddelan**, works of Llywelyn the Great (ab Iorwerth) (d 1240) of Gwynedd. At **Dolbadarn**, in the breathtaking beauty of the Llanberis Pass, Llywelyn's round keep was modelled on those of the south, and at **Criccieth** his twin-towered gatehouse was another English-inspired construction. In the south-west, the princes of Deheubarth built round keeps at Dinefwr and Dryslwyn.

The apogee of castle building in Wales was marked by the chain of immense fortresses constructed by **King Edward I** following his Welsh wars of 1276-77 and 1282-83. In his defeat of Prince Llywelyn the Last *(ap Gruffydd)*, the King hemmed in the ancient kingdom of Gwynedd with some of the mightiest strongholds ever raised in Britain. **Aberystwyth**, **Flint** and **Rhuddlan** were begun after the first war, and the chain was extended with **Caernarfon**, **Conwy** and **Harlech** following the 1282-83 campaign. In 1295, in response to a further Welsh uprising, **Beaumaris** was conceived as the ultimate in concentric defence. The genius behind the design of virtually all these castles was **Master James of St George**, a brilliant military architect brought by Edward from Savoy. Not surprisingly, there are close links between the style of Edward's Welsh castles and those of their architect's homeland.

Caernarfon Castle
1283-1330

Dolbadarn Castle
Early 13C

Chepstow Castle
The Great Tower 1067

Powis Castle
Late 13C

Castell Coch
1875-79

Carew Castle
Begun late 12C

Caerphilly Castle
Begun 1268

Penrhyn Castle
Begun 1821

Illustrations : R. Corbel/MICHELIN

61

Pennant Melangell Church

Castles of the later Middle Ages began to show an emphasis upon gracious living as much as a need for defence. At **Chepstow** and **Kidwelly** this is evident from the late 13C. On a smaller scale, the transition from military stronghold to domestic residence is reflected in the fortified manor house at **Weobley** on the Gower Peninsula. A greater domestic structure of this period is the magnificent palace built in Decorated style by Bishop Henry de Gower (1328-47) in the shadow of his cathedral church at St David's. If one building can sum up the troubled years of the mid to late 15C it is the work of **Sir William Herbert** at Raglan, a vast palace-fortress which echoes the chivalry of its age. Nothing short of exotic in a Welsh context, the inspiration for its design was ultimately French. Its courtyards and surroundings were lavishly landscaped, though only the basic structure remains today of the extensive terraces which helped make Raglan such "a rare and noble sight". Nearby **Tretower Court**, built c 1420 by Herbert's kinsman, **Sir Roger Vaughan**, seems to have been landscaped too, although the turf seats and tunnel arbours of its medieval garden are speculative reconstructions.

**Churches and Monasteries** – Stone-built churches also began to appear in Wales after the arrival of the Normans. Fine **Romanesque** survivals include St Woolos in Newport, St Mary's Priory Church in Chepstow, and the nave of the former Cistercian abbey at Margam. Ewenny Priory is a small gem of West Country Romanesque, c 1116-40, and the nave of St David's Cathedral, begun in the 1180s, was one of the last major buildings raised in this style in the whole of Britain. In the north, the important 12C native Welsh churches at Penmon and Tywyn display strong Romanesque elements. A smaller though no less interesting construction is the little church at Pennant Melangell; in its remote site beneath the Berwyn hills, this delightful place of worship houses the remarkable 12C shrine of St Maracella, founder of an 8C nunnery.

The transition to thinner and lighter early Gothic designs gave rise to the beautiful Llanthony Priory. More developed examples of the early Gothic style include Llandaff Cathedral, the priory church at Brecon, the Cistercian abbey of Valle Crucis, and works in the parish churches at Llanidloes, Llantwit Major, and in St Mary's at Haverfordwest. The finest example of the **Decorated style** in Wales is perhaps the great abbey church at Tintern (c 1270-1310), particularly notable for the quality of its stone window tracery. A new church at Neath Abbey was constructed at much the same time, and the tiny cathedral at St Asaph was rebuilt c 1284-1352.

In the comparatively settled and more prosperous years of the later 15C and early 16C, there was a flurry of church building in many parts of Wales. **Perpendicular** was the predominant style, its vertical lines giving a feeling of increased height. Bangor Cathedral was greatly remodelled c 1471-1532, and St John's Church in Cardiff – which boasts a graceful West Country tower – was built c 1453-73. St Mary's in Tenby was another town church much expanded at this time. The finest group of Perpendicular churches in Wales is to be found in the north-east, centred on those at Gresford, Mold and Wrexham. St Giles' in Wrexham, with its rich pinnacled tower and cathedral-like proportions, is the finest of these but the decorative treatment of All Saints' Church, Gresford and St Mary's, Mold is outstanding. Also in this region is the famous pilgrimage chapel of St Winefride at Holywell with its unusual well chamber in Perpendicular style.

# The Gentry House from Tudor to Georgian Times

From the mid-16C to the 18C Welsh building was dominated by domestic structures. The genesis of the country house can be traced to major conversions of earlier buildings during the Tudor era. The transformations of the castles at Carew and Laugharne into palatial residences by **Sir John Perrot** (d 1592) are good examples of the process. Similarly, at Raglan it was the Third **Earl of Worcester** (d 1589), a leading aristocrat of Elizabethan Wales, who brought the castle up to the standards of his day, complete with a splendid long gallery. Further north, the **Herbert** family bought Powis Castle in 1587 and began the process of turning it into one of the grandest of Welsh stately homes. Elsewhere, the dissolution of the monasteries provided other opportunities. At Neath and Margam, the former Cistercian abbeys provided the basis for Tudor domesticity. Much of Neath survives, if ruinous, and shows a highly imaginative reuse of the monastic structures.

Plas Mawr, Conwy

New building was commonplace too. At Oxwich, for example, the Mansel family raised an extraordinarily large courtyard house overlooking the Gower coast. Towards the end of the 16C, a more radical influence on the development of gentry homes appeared. Gradually, the effects of the **Renaissance** with its formal planning began to take hold. St Fagans Castle, which has a symmetrical E-shaped plan of 1580, is one of the earliest examples. Nearby, at Beaupre, a superb Italianate porch was added to an Elizabethan mansion about 1600. Another late Tudor building with early Renaissance trends is Plas Mawr (c 1576-85), Sir Robert Wynn's wonderful town house in Conwy. The plaster work in its ceilings and chimney-pieces is of the highest quality. The four-square plan of Plas Teg (1610), near Wrexham, in many ways marks the full arrival of the style. Following the **Restoration** of Charles II (1660), later-17C houses reveal more in the way of classic Renaissance features. Tredegar for instance, built c 1670, is a truly lavish country house of the Restoration era. More compact within a town setting at Monmouth is Great Castle House (1673). In the north-east of the country, Erddig was built on a large scale to a very formal plan (c 1683-87); beneath its Victorian veneer, Newton House in Dinefwr Park is another good example of a Restoration gentry home.

New departures in the 18C centred upon refined **Georgian** elegance. At Nanteos, built in 1739, the inspiration was Inigo Jones' **Palladian** style. Later in the century, at Chirk, Richard Myddleton's interiors of 1763-73 were to transform this once-forbidding medieval border fortress. Another fascinating work of this period is the magnificent orangery at Margam (1787-89), designed by Anthony Keck in 1787.

## Chapels

Originally an import from England, the Nonconformist chapel was to become an essentially Welsh vehicle of religious expression. Chapels survive in large numbers; they are sometimes found isolated beside a country road or they can be found frequently in rural villages, but they are virtually omnipresent in the street scene of the valleys in the industrial south. The earliest surviving example is Maes yr Onnen (1696), a converted farmyard barn. The Nonconformist movement gathered strength through the 18C and, in the 19C, it became the major religious force, with a consequent boom in construction. Throughout Wales – spiritually, culturally and architecturally – the chapel became the most important public building. By 1905 there were up to 1 600 examples in the southern valleys alone.

This intense period of building gave rise to a distinctive style of religious architecture, with the façades being particularly characteristic. To begin with, designs were single storey, and the façade arranged along one of the long walls. Growing congregations in the 19C meant that many chapels were rebuilt several times. In some cases a gallery was added on the first floor, though the façade may still be retained on one of the long walls. In the fast growing industrial towns, space was at a premium, and chapels were built at right angles to the road. The architectural emphasis was thus transferred to a gable end, with neo-Classical features becoming the norm. Tabernacl in Pontypridd (now the Pontypridd Historical Centre) is a good example of this type.

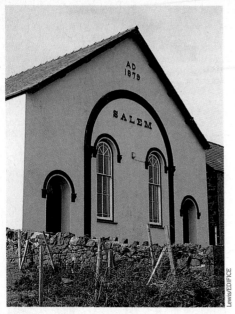

When funds allowed, later chapels included full-blown Classical features, often with projecting porticoes and Corinthian style capitals. Bethesda in Mold (1863) and the English Baptist chapel in Carmarthen (1872) are two very fine examples, whereas the celebrated Tabernacle chapel in Morriston (1873), Swansea, has been called "the great cathedral of Welsh Nonconformity".

## Vernacular Buildings

Buildings of the Welsh countryside were built in traditional ways using traditional materials from the Middle Ages to the industrial centuries. Their general appearance depended on local construction materials. In parts of the extreme west, clay or earth was used for walls. Undressed stone was far more common in much of the north-west, and in regions such as Pembrokeshire and the Vale of Glamorgan in the south

Salem Chapel

and south-west. In the sheltered borders, east of a line from the Conwy in the north to the Usk in the south, the country was a land of timber.

In the borders, the timber-framed **hall house** is one of the earliest survivals of the vernacular tradition. Single-storey examples, heated by a central open fire, can be traced back to the Tudor era. In upland stone areas, the **long house** was once common; the family and cattle were housed under a single roof, divided by a common access passage through the centre of the building.

From the late 16C, the **yeoman's house** with more than one storey began to appear in growing numbers. In border regions and in the more prosperous south, well-made versions of such homes were common by the 17C, but in the west the single-storey dwelling prevailed well into the late 18C.

The form of these houses varied from region to region, and their "typology" is partly determined by the position of the main fireplace. In the stone area of the north-west, fires were set in the end walls, with chimneys at the gables. In the eastern borders, the fireplace was often at the centre of the house, and a "lobby entrance" was created. A third type had the fireplace on one of the long (lateral) walls, often accompanied by a massive projecting chimney.

Throughout Wales, these contrasts can be observed in village and farmstead. Much can also be seen in the marvellous open-air **Museum of Welsh Life** at St Fagans, where vernacular buildings from many parts of Wales have been rebuilt in a parkland setting.

Rhyd-y-car Cottages

# Industrial Buildings

Wales played a key role in the events of the Industrial Revolution. The extraction of coal, copper, lead and slate, and the manufacture of iron, steel and tinplate were especially important. Much of the Welsh landscape was radically transformed. Surviving architectural elements of the age might be found almost anywhere, but as heavy industry has declined once-prevalent features have become increasingly scarce.

Merthyr Tydfil and Blaenavon were major centres of iron production. Merthyr, likened to "the fiery city of Pluto" was probably the largest iron-making town in the world, and it is tragic that so little has been preserved. At Blaenavon, however, where the works were established in 1788, there are the remains of five early blast furnaces and their associated structures. Adjacent are the stone rows of Stack Square, a now rare example of iron industry company housing.

The two principal coalfields of Wales are in the north-east, focused around Wrexham, and in the southern valleys stretching from Pontypool to Kidwelly. The greatest boom in production came from the mid-19C with the opening up of the Rhondda valleys. The Rhondda Heritage Park and Big Pit at Blaenavon are accessible examples of colliery complexes.

Slate quarrying, "the most Welsh of Welsh industries", was centred on Snowdonia. At the Dinorwig Quarry in Llanberis, the workshops of one of the largest quarries survive. Functional they may be but the complex, built in 1870, was also designed to impress; it has the distinct appearance of a colonial British army fort.

What slate was to Gwynedd, so was the tinplate industry to the Swansea region. Unfortunately, most of the equipment and structures have been scrapped but two important centres provide some insight into the processes and architectural history of tinplate manufacture: the Kidwelly Industrial Museum and Aberdulais near Neath. Elsewhere, in north-east Wales, at Greenfield Valley in Holywell, there is another complex of structures associated with non-ferrous industries.

As communications improved in the early 19C with the construction of turnpike roads, canals, and later railways, the difficult terrain of much of the country necessitated the construction of many bridges and tunnels.

The Holyhead road across North Wales built by Thomas Telford is accompanied by a number of fine structures, among them the famous suspension bridges crossing the Conwy and the Menai Strait; his aqueduct at Pont Cysyllte remains one of the most remarkable structures of the Canal Age. In the late 1840s and early 1850s the Conwy and Menai Strait were bridged again, this time to carry the Chester and Holyhead Railway designed by Robert Stephenson; in both cases the line was carried in long tubes in order to reduce the visual impact of the trains, while the Conwy bridge was castellated in an attempt to reconcile it with the great castle whose walls the railway breached. At the very beginning of the 20C the River Usk at Newport was crossed by a most unusual structure, the Transporter Bridge, now one of only two of its type remaining in Britain; it carries vehicles across the river in a small gondola slung from the long steel span joining its two tall towers.

Perhaps the most spectacular engineering structures in Wales are the great dams holding back water supply reservoirs; some are of recent origin, but none surpasses in grandeur the late-19C stone structures in the Elan Valley or at Lake Vyrnwy.

## Historicism in the Victorian Era

The background to 19C architecture is sometimes referred to as the "battle of styles", a period when various historic forms were revived in different ways. From the very turn of the century, Plas Newydd on Anglesey (1795-1806) was a fusion of Classical symmetry with Gothic detailing. Yet more prominent as the century progressed were the sham Gothic "castles", built for the newly-rich entrepreneurs and opportunist industrialists of the age.

The notorious ironmaster William Crawshay commissioned Cyfarthfa Castle in 1825. It overlooked and overawed the workers who toiled at his furnaces in almost medieval conditions. An even richer echo of medieval feudalism was Norman-style Penrhyn, built in 1827-40 for the slate baron George Douglas-Pennant by Thomas Hopper. The monumental "keep" is one of the most extraordinary pieces of building in Wales.

Water Balance Tower, Blaenavon Ironworks

CADW: Welsh Historic Monuments — Crown Copyright

These were, however, small fry when compared to the extravagances lavished on Cardiff Castle and Castell Coch in the later 19C. At these two former medieval strongholds, William Burges and John, Third Marquess of Bute, created the most remarkable mansions of the Victorian era in Wales. Their lavish decoration, brimming with imagery, was the ultimate in romantic escapism from the industrial squalor which made their construction possible.

The style chosen for a number of public buildings in the 19C was that of Greek Revival. The Royal Institution in Swansea (1841) and the Shirehall in Brecon (1842), both now museums, are two of the more successful examples. Later in the century, the University College at Aberystwyth, which began life as a hotel, was a marvellous fantasy in neo-Gothic design.

Variations on the Gothic theme were also extremely popular for the spate of new church building in Victorian Wales. One of the most striking examples is the so-called Marble Church at Bodelwyddan (1860). The splendid south tower and spire at Llandaff Cathedral (1867) are by the well-known architect John Prichard. St Augustine's Church, Penarth (1866), is an outstanding work by William Butterfield, a masterpiece of neo-Gothic polychromatic architecture.

## Twentieth Century

Public buildings represent some of the finest and most easily accessible examples of 20C architecture in Wales.

Cardiff University

As a group, there is little to surpass the outstanding range of structures in the civic centre of Cardiff. There was a different source of inspiration for each, though all represent monumental examples of the neo-Classical style. The Law Courts and City Hall were built in 1901-04, to be followed by the National Museum and Gallery of Wales (1910-27) which was influenced by North American versions of Greek Classical. A little later, in Swansea, the design of the Guildhall (1934) was a watered-down version of Classical styles.

By way of contrast, the monastery on Caldey Island (1910-12) displays elements of both the Art Nouveau and Arts and Crafts movements. Wales also possesses its share of "modernist" structures, buildings which reject all aspects of historicism. As just one intriguing example, a café (1948) on the seafront at Criccieth was designed in concrete and steel by Sir Clough Williams-Ellis, the man responsible for extravagant Portmeirion.

Little of the architecture of the second half of the 20C proclaims any kind of Welsh identity, though the headquarters buildings of the former Gwynedd County Council have been inserted into the historic townscape of Caernarfon with style as well as sensitivity. Concern for the environment is at least as strong in "green" Wales as in any part of Great Britain, and is reflected in the array of earth-friendly structures at the Centre of Alternative Technology in Machynlleth as well as in the ridge-top visitor centre at the Welsh Wildlife Centre near Cardigan.

# Historical Notes

## Prehistory: c 24000 BC to AD 78

**Stone Age** – The headless skeleton of a 25-year-old man provides the earliest evidence of human life in Wales. It was found in Paviland Cave, on the southern Gower Peninsula, where its ritual burial probably took place in about 24000 BC. Cave-dwelling hunters lived in scattered groups along the coast, using tools of flint and bone, until about 10000 BC, when better tool-production and animal-herding techniques spread from the Mediterranean and Atlantic Europe. This later Stone Age era saw the construction of huge stone burial chambers, circles and avenues, some of which still survive; the tombs at **Tinkinswood**, near Cardiff, and **Pentre Ifan** in the Presely Hills are impressive examples.

**Bronze Age** – From about 1800 BC gold, copper and bronze work was introduced into Britain by the Beaker People, named for their practice of burying earthenware pots with their dead in single graves. Stone was still in wide use; during this period the bluestone slabs used to construct Stonehenge in Wiltshire were quarried in the Presely Hills of Pembrokeshire.

**Celtic Tribes** – The Celts first settled in Britain c 1000 BC, having spread from central Europe through the Mediterranean and into Asia Minor. While the Goidelic Celts inhabited Ireland, the Brittonic branch moved into England and Wales, bringing with them sophisticated bronze-working and farming skills. They built villages and wood and earthwork hillforts, grew wheat and barley and made highly decorated tools, weapons and ornaments of bronze and iron. Examples of their metalwork have been found in Llyn Cerrig Bach, a lake on Anglesey, where shields, swords and shackles have been recovered, some bearing the disctinctive swirling Celtic motifs. Religious and political life was administered by an educated elite, the Druids; they worshipped several gods, to whom sacrifices were made, and developed a rich oral tradition of epic poetry and music. Modern Wales can trace its language and elements of its culture back to the Celtic age, which lasted well over a thousand years.

## Wales under the Romans: AD 78 to 5C

Claudius, the Roman Emperor, successfully invaded Britain in AD 43 and by AD 76-78 the western Celtic tribes were under attack. Anglesey, headquarters of the Druids, was conquered in 78, despite the spirited resistance of painted women, who screamed at terrified troops across the Menai Strait. Military bases, linked by long roads, were set up in **Caernarfon** *(Segontium)*, **Chester** *(Deva)*, **Brecon** *(Y Gaer)* and **Caerleon** *(Isca)* to control western territory. On the whole, Celtic life continued undisturbed and many leading families were integrated into Roman society. Some British leaders, such as Magnus Maximus, known in Welsh as Macsen Wledig *(see p 49 and p 56)* were even granted a measure of autonomy.

## Post-Roman Invasions: 5C to 11C

As Roman troops began to withdraw in the 5C, Britain became the target of a series of new invaders. Goidels from Ireland and Picts from Scotland threatened the British Celts from west and north, and Anglo-Saxons swept across the south and east. The Brythons, confined to the western mainland, now began to refer to themselves as *Cymry* (meaning "fellow countrymen") – still the Welsh name for its people; the Anglo-Saxons knew them as "Weleas", or "foreigners" or possibly "the Romanised people".

CADW: Welsh Historic Monuments – Crown Copyright

Roman Amphitheatre, Caerleon

**Missionaries** – With the Irish invaders came Christian missionaries *(sancti)*. Previous attempts to convert the pagan Celts had met with little success: the Roman missionary, St Augustine, apparently offended local chiefs by remaining seated when they were presented to him. The *sancti* had more of an impact and were even granted parcels of land – the *llan* of many Welsh placenames – on which to establish a network of churches and monasteries. One of their number, **David**, born in Pembrokeshire in the mid-5C, became the patron saint of Wales, **David**, *Dewi* in Welsh.

**Welsh Kings** – During the 5C a powerful dynasty was established by Cunedda Wledig in north and west Wales, while other royal houses, possibly of Irish descent, emerged in the southwest. Wales was divided into several principalities, including Gwynedd, Powys, Meirionydd, Ceredigion, Dyfed and Gwent. Each one was a separate political unit, though on the whole they coexisted peacefully. Unity came only with the new threat of the Vikings, the Norsemen, who began their attacks on Britain in the late 8C. By this time three Anglo-Saxon kingdoms had evolved: Wessex in the south, Mercia in the midlands and Northumbria in the north. In 784 Offa, King of Mercia, marked the boundary between his territories and those of the Welsh with a ditch, **Offa's Dyke** (167mi/269km long), which still more or less defines the English-Welsh border.
By the 9C the Vikings had settled in northern Britain and Ireland and on the Isle of Man but they were kept out of Wales by **Rhodri Mawr**, Prince of Powys, who extended his rule through marriage to take in most of the Welsh lands. Nevertheless, while the Anglian (English) kingdoms of the east were developing into a single political power during the 9C and 10C, Wales could not sustain a unified system. The Welsh practice of gavelkind *(cyfran)* – sharing territory between all sons – ensured the division of Rhodri's inheritance into six princedoms, all of which submitted to Alfred, the English king.

**Deheubarth** – Rhodri Mawr's grandson, **Hywel Dda** (Hywel the Good) *(see p 105 and p 177)* built up a new empire, uniting the southern territories into the Kingdom of Deheubarth (south-west Wales) and extending his rule to Gwynedd and Powys. He advocated the policy of living at peace with the English and of paying tribute to the men of Wessex. He too, however, was forced to accept the supremacy of the English throne; he died in 950. His main achievement was to collect and codify the laws and customs of Wales to form a legal system which lasted until the 13C.

## Normans and Welsh Uprisings: 1066 to 1485

Hywel Dda's death was followed by a return to confusion and sporadic internal warfare, leaving the country vulnerable to Norman incursions. William of Normandy, having led his troops to victory against King Harold in 1066, rewarded his closest associates with lands along the Marches (borders) of Wales. The Marcher lords made several inroads into Welsh territory and by the 12C Powys and Gwynedd were cut off from much of the rest of Wales. Norman gains were consolidated with motte-and-bailey castles, first of earth and timber, later rebuilt in stone.

**English Conquest** – In 1194 a descendant of Rhodri Mawr, **Llywelyn the Great** *(ap Iorwerth)*, overran the divided lands of Deheubarth and Powys and declared himself the chief of the princes of Wales. His grandson, **Llywelyn the Last** *(ap Gruffydd)*, known also as *Ein Llyw Olaf* (meaning Our Last Leader) imprisoned his own brothers to avoid dividing the territory and was acknowledged Prince of Wales by Henry III, though still obliged to pay homage to the English king. On the accession of Edward I, however, Llywelyn stopped paying tribute and refused to give homage. Edward seized the opportunity to lead his troops into Wales in 1277 and made rapid advances, building massive fortresses as he progressed. Llywelyn was eventually ambushed and killed and Wales brought firmly under English rule. The Statute of Wales, 1284, created several new counties and Marcher lordships

Llywelyn the Great

and an iron ring of castles was set up to maintain authority, including **Caernarfon**, **Conwy**, **Harlech** and **Beaumaris**. The title "Prince of Wales" was renewed and given to Edward's son, the future Edward II. Several ensuing revolts were put down and led to harsh penalties. During the 14C potential rebels diverted their energies to fight for the king in the Hundred Years War against France, where Welsh longbowmen secured a famous victory at the Battle of Crécy in 1346.

**Glyn Dŵr's Rebellion** – Hit by plague and food shortages and resentful of their overlords, the Welsh rallied to a new leader in the early 15C. **Owain Glyn Dŵr**, a member of the royal lines of Deheubarth and Powys, challenged the crown after losing a minor territorial dispute. He enjoyed early military successes, called parliaments and drew up plans for Welsh universities and a Welsh church, but by 1413 English troops had crushed the revolt and Glyn Dŵr disappeared into hiding.

# Tudors: 1485 to 1603

During the 15C England was torn apart by the Wars of the Roses, a power struggle between the royal houses of Lancaster and York. In 1471 the Lancastrian king Henry VI was murdered and the throne passed to the Yorkists. The Welsh **Tudor** *(Tewdwr)* family had become deeply embroiled in the feud. Lancastrian Henry V's widow, Catherine de Valois, had married Owain Tewdwr of Anglesey, and their grandson, Henry, now became the Lancastrian claimant. After 14 years in exile in Brittany he returned in 1485, hailed by the Welsh as the new leader prophesied by their bards, and defeated Richard III at Bosworth. As Henry VII he ended the civil war by marrying Elizabeth of York and uniting the two houses, and founded the Tudor dynasty that would rule for another 118 years.

**Acts of Union** – Henry's son, Henry VIII, was determined to introduce a uniform political and judicial structure throughout England and Wales. His Acts of Union (1536 and 1543) abolished the Marcher lordships and allowed Welshmen full inheritance rights. A standardised English system of law courts was established and the Welsh language was excluded from all official channels. While covering the Welsh by the same law as the rest of the kingdom, the Acts created an even deeper gulf between the Anglicised gentry and the largely illiterate, Welsh-speaking lower classes. The survival of the language was in great part due to the growing influence of the church and to the publication of a Bible translated into Welsh by **William Morgan** in 1588.

## Social and Industrial Development: 17C to 19C

**Religion and Reformation** – Henry VIII's creation of a Protestant, Anglican church, headed by the king, met with no real opposition in Wales but by the late 17C there was considerable dissatisfaction with church authorities. Most clergymen were badly educated and badly paid; many bishops were non-resident and none spoke Welsh. In the 1730s **Gruffydd Jones** of Llanddowror (1683-1761) set out to reach the illiterate populace through his system of circulating schools, teaching adults and children to read the Bible in Welsh. The bid to win congregations with education was continued by **Thomas Charles** of Bala (1755-1814), who organised Sunday schools and founded the British and Foreign Bible Society, providing cheap Bibles. **Methodism**, which had started as an unconventional movement within the Anglican church, received fervent support in Wales, where it was led by **Howel Harris** of Trefeca (1714-73) and **Daniel Rowland** of Llangeitho (1713-90), both highly emotional, charismatic preachers. In 1811 the Methodists left the Anglican church and for the following 150 years its various Nonconformist offshoots continued to wield a strong influence among the Welsh.

**Industrialisation** – From the late 18C, industrialists began serious exploitation of the mineral wealth of Wales. Slate quarries, copper mines and smelting works appeared in the north and the south, and industrial activity gathered pace during the iron boom of the early 19C. By 1827 Wales was producing half of Britain's iron exports.

Coal, originally mined for iron-smelting, was also in increasing demand, to fire steam trains and ships and to provide domestic fuel. A series of mines sunk in the South Wales valleys transformed the landscape: houses were thrown up in long terraces, eventually to be overshadowed by black slag-heaps. Despite appalling conditions, people flocked to the valleys to find work in the mines and to escape from rural poverty. Close communities were created, with the coal pits as their focus, and the valley towns became the breeding ground for a radical political culture.

Industrial barons reaped vast profits from advances in technology and transport. Railways carried coal from the valleys to new docks built by the Second Marquess of

South Wales Landscape (1948) by Kenneth Rowntree

Banqueting Hall, Cardiff Castle

Bute at Cardiff, which grew to be the biggest coal-shipping port in the world. While coal and slate masters flourished, building extravagant homes such as **Cardiff Castle** and **Penrhyn Castle**, their workers lived on low wages, in dangerous and insanitary conditions. Riots were not uncommon: 20 people were killed in the Merthyr Riots of 1831; 28 died in Newport in 1839 during demonstrations in support of the Chartist movement for electoral and social reform.

Agricultural workers also suffered extreme hardship, exacerbated by depopulation and the imposition of toll charges on roads, discouraging itinerant trade. In the 1840s a spate of attacks on tollgates and houses was carried out by the so-called **Rebecca Rioters** – men dressed in women's clothes who usually operated under cover of night.

## Politics and Education: 1800 to 1920

Political dissent and religious Nonconformity in Wales in the 19C were closely linked in opposition to the Anglican, mainly conservative landowners. Under the 1867 Reform Act industrial workers and tenant farmers were granted the right to vote and returned 23 Liberal members of parliament out of 33 in the 1868 elections. There followed a series of evictions from Tory-owned land which helped speed the introduction of the Secret Ballot Act (1872).

Wales remained predominantly Liberal until the 1920s, its most famous parliamentary representative being **David Lloyd George** (1863-1945), the member for Caernarfon Boroughs. As Chancellor of the Exchequer Lloyd George introduced a programme of social reform, which included the introduction of state pensions, and as Prime Minister he led the government during the First World War.

**Disestablishment** – By the late 19C the Anglican church had become an alien institution to the largely Nonconformist population of Wales. Resentment was particularly focused on the continuing obligation to pay tithes, an ancient Anglican tax. Strength of feeling was such that several violent riots broke out in North Wales, and the growing calls for change eventually led, after several false starts, to the passing of a Disestablishment Bill through parliament in 1914. In 1920 the Anglican church in Wales was disendowed and its money passed to the University, the National Library and Welsh county councils.

**Schools and the Welsh language** – Education in the 18C and the 19C was largely in the hands of the Nonconformist churches. In 1846 three English lawyers were sent as part of a government commission to assess Welsh schools. Their report, known in Wales as "The Treason of the Blue Books", attacked Welsh as a language of slavery and ignorance, and condemned its use by pupils and teachers. Even among the Welsh themselves, use of the language was regarded as a social and economic obstacle, and determined efforts were made to stamp it out. This campaign culminated in the

70

notorious **Welsh Not**, a system of punishment whereby children caught speaking Welsh were obliged to wear around the neck a wooden board, on which the words "Welsh Not" were painted. By 1901 the policy had taken its toll and only 50% of the population still spoke the Welsh language.

Demands for better educational provision had been growing during the 19C and in 1872 the first University College of Wales, funded by public donations, opened in a redundant hotel building in Aberystwyth.

## Growth of National Feeling: 1920 to 1990s

As education became more accessible, new generations emerged of Welsh-speakers, schooled in English and staying in or returning to Wales to find professions. Members of this educated middle class were to play a leading part in the revival of national feeling and identity. Fears that Welsh culture would be lost altogether prompted a vigorous campaign to promote the use of Welsh in schools: one of the most energetic campaigners was **Owen M Edwards** (1858-1920), Chief Inspector of Schools in Wales, who published several Welsh-language magazines and books for children. He also founded Urdd Gobaith Cymru, the Welsh League of Youth which combined Christian and cultural ethics. In 1947 the first Welsh-language primary school was opened, to be followed in 1962 by the first bilingual secondary school, set up in the Anglicised industrial valleys of South Wales.

Political nationalism took on a more defined form after the First World War, and in 1925 the Welsh Nationalist Party was founded by a group of writers and scholars which included the poet and author Saunders Lewis *(see p 57)*. In 1998 it changed its name to **Plaid Cymru** – the Party of Wales. Its appeal was largely to the agricultural, middle classes, and its emphasis lay on the Welsh language and culture. Industrial communities, disillusioned with Liberal government, turned to the growing Labour movement at a time of declining trade and increasing unemployment. **Aneurin Bevan** (1897-1960), an ex-miner who played a leading role in the miners' strike in 1926, was sent to parliament for Ebbw Vale in 1929; as Health Minister in the 1945 Labour government he introduced slum-clearance policies and laid the foundations of the National Health Service.

In the 1960s and 1970s nationalist feeling found a new voice in the **Welsh Language Society** *(Cymdeithas yr Iaith Gymraeg)*, whose followers staged demonstrations and defaced property in the name of the language. Piecemeal changes in the law brought more

*Aneurin Bevan* by Sir David Low (1891-1963)

National Portrait Gallery, London

bilingualism into official life, adding Welsh to road signs, forms and court proceedings. In 1993 a Welsh Language Act stipulated that the Welsh language be treated, as far as is reasonably practicable, on the basis of equality with the English language in the public sector. It also set up the Welsh Language Board *(Bwrdd yr Iaith Gymraeg)*.

## Administration and Economy: 1960s to 1990s

Welsh unemployment was running at twice the UK national average when the **Welsh Office** was established in 1964, giving Wales limited executive powers. This was followed by the creation of the **Welsh Development Agency** (WDA) in 1976, to encourage new economic initiatives. Under the reorganisation of local government in England and Wales in 1974, the 13 Welsh counties were replaced with eight new units, most taking the names of ancient principalities. Another reorganisation of local government in 1997 brought the return of many of the old county divisions.

In the latter part of the 20C there was growing support for a measure of devolution. The first referendum, held in 1979 – for a separate **Welsh Assembly**, without legislative powers – resulted in a majority against.

The 1980s brought radical changes to industrial Wales: by the middle of the decade every coal pit in the Rhondda Valley had been closed. Despite notable success in attracting foreign business to Welsh sites, former mining communities have continued to suffer from high unemployment and social dislocation.

The granting of a Welsh-language television channel – S4C – has encouraged a boom in the Welsh film, TV and animation industries. **Tourism** is another area of economic success but there is widespread concern about its effects on rural society, and especially about the phenomenon of second homes and holiday cottages, which have changed the face of many communities, leaving some virtually deserted outside the tourist season.

In 1997 a second referendum on devolution produced a narrow majority (6 721 – 559 419 pro and 552 698 anti) in favour of the establishment of a **Welsh Assembly**. The parliamentary bill received the Royal Assent in the summer of 1998, making provision for elections to be held on 6 May 1999. The **Welsh Assembly** consists of 60 members, of which 40 are elected from the parliamentary constituencies and 20 from the five EU constituencies. There is simultaneous interpretation in Welsh and English and at present the members meet in Crickhowell House on Cardiff Bay. Discussions are in progress about the construction of a new building, to be designed by the winner of an architectural competition and erected in Cardiff, on a waterfront site looking outwards to the world.

Powis Castle

# ABERAERON ★

Ceredigion – Population 1 493
Michelin Atlas p 24 or Map 403 H 27

This trim little harbour town on the Cardigan coast owes its appeal to the ambitious improvements carried out at the beginning of the 19C by the local landowner. Before this time, Aberaeron had been little more than a fishing village huddled on higher ground a short distance inland away from the narrow coastal plain which suffered frequent flooding and changes of course by the capricious River Aeron.

The Reverend Alban Thomas Jones Gwynne may well have had the advice of John Nash in constructing the stone piers and quays and the two squares around which the new, harmoniously **planned port town** was laid out. Building began in 1807 and proceeded throughout the first half of the 19C, leaving a legacy of fine **terraced houses** whose sobriety of design is set off by well-considered detailing of windows, doors and cornerstones as well as by cheerful colour schemes. The exotic names of some of the houses recall the vessels sailed in by their owners.

Aberaeron's harbour flourished until the early 20C, with a lively coastal trade and considerable shipbuilding activity, mostly of smacks and schooners. The railways eventually killed the coastal trade, though Aberaeron was linked to the national rail network only in 1911. The last steamship set out in 1934 and the last steam train ran in 1963 but the town continues to thrive as a holiday place, the harbour full of pleasure boats and the quaysides of strolling visitors.

**Harbour** – The Harbourmaster's house, overlooking the harbour mouth, was the first building to be erected on the new quayside. Adjacent is an old animal-feed store, now the **Aberaeron Sea Aquarium** ⊙, where displays on the marine life of Cardigan Bay include an insight into the life cycle of the lobster. A local fisherman may be on hand to add a personal touch and visitors can explore the marine ecology of Cardigan Bay – seals, dolphins, porpoises, birds – with a marine naturalist providing a commentary in a jet-powered rigid inflatable boat.

One of the town's two squares enfolds the inner harbour (Pwll Cam). Lines of chestnut trees lend an almost Continental air to the scene. A modern timber footbridge leads towards the grassy banks on the far side of the Aeron where shipbuilding was concentrated in the 19C.

Aberaeron Harbour

## EXCURSIONS

**Llannerchaeron** ⊙ – 2.5mi/4km SE of Aberaeron by A 482.
As is suggested by its name, which means glade by the Aeron, this **gentry house** is prettily sited in a well-wooded vale just inland from Aberaeron. It was designed by **John Nash** in the last decade of the 18C and is unusual in having survived, together with its estate buildings, virtually unaltered.

The five bays of its main façade look out over the now-farmed parkland, while overgrown woodland and shrubbery leads eastward to walled gardens, the model farm and a silted-up lake.

A long-term programme of restoration of the neglected house and grounds has been set under way by the new owner, the National Trust.

**Tourist Information Centre** – The Quay, Aberaeron SA46 0BT ☎ 01545 570 602; Fax 01970 626 566; aberaeronTIC@ceredigion.gov.uk
Church Street, New Quay SA45 9NZ ☎ 01545 560 865; Fax 01970 626 566; newquayTIC@ceredigion.gov.uk

**Beaches** – At Aberaeron South, New Quay and Cwmtudu.

**Craft Centre** – Craftsmen and women can be seen at work in the 18 workshops of the **Aberaeron Craft Centre** ⊙ (behind Holy Trinity Church on A 487).

**Adjacent Sights** – See Aberystwyth, Cardigan, Lampeter, Newcastle Emlyn, Vale of Rheidol, Tregaron.

**New Quay (Ceinewydd)** – 7.5mi/12km SW of Aberaeron by A 487 and B 4342. New Quay, which shares a similar history of coastal trading, fishing and boatbuilding with Aberaeron, had no level land on which to build, and its rows of neat terrace houses are laid out on the slopes which rise abruptly from three beaches and the harbour.

Fishing boats still frequent the harbour, sheltered by the two-tiered stone pier and by New Quay Head which protects the haven from westerly gales.

On the far side of the popular sandy beach is a much smaller pier, which has succeeded the original 'new quay' built in the late 17C, and close by is the modern Lifeboat House.

Dylan Thomas (see p 171) holidayed here; Llareggub in his poem Under Milk Wood may well be based on New Quay.

The **Cardigan Bay Marine Wildlife Centre** ⊙, an interactive information centre, involved in sea watch and research, engages the interest of all ages – sound systems; children's activities; sea charts showing where seabirds, seals and other wildlife can be observed unobtrusively; boat trips to observe **dolphins** in Cardigan Bay and even whales further out to sea.

**Cwmtudu** – 4.5mi/7km SW of New Quay by A 486 and narrow, steep lanes. The main road runs well inland from this part of the spectacular Cardigan coastline, which can be reached only on foot or by car down secret-seeming lanes. Cwmtudu, a secluded cove between the dramatically folded rocks of its headlands, lies at the outlet of a narrow valley whose stream is frequently blocked by shingle to form an attractive freshwater pool. An old lime kiln stands behind the pebble beach.

# ABERGAVENNY ★

(Y-Fenni) Monmouthshire – Population 9 593
Michelin Atlas p 16 or Map 403 L 28

This bustling market town on a glacial mound just above the Usk is overlooked by a number of hills, of which the most distinctive are Sugar Loaf, Blorenge and Skirrid. Once a Roman garrison, then a Norman borough, Abergavenny prospered as early industrial development started in the Clydach Gorge and on the southern fringes of the Brecon Beacons.

The castle is in ruins and the town's defensive walls and gateways have long since disappeared but, although the townscape is a mixture of Georgian, Victorian and modern, older edifices lurk behind many a more recent façade.

A walk around the town centre reveals a number of fine buildings, among them old inns like the black-and-white **Angel** in Cross Street, arcaded and jettied-out shops in **Market Street**, and the old **Cow Inn** in Nevill Street, once the town residence of the owners of Tretower Court (see p 279), and splendidly decorated with dragons and the heads of goats as well as cows. The dominant structure is the copper-clad tower of the **Town Hall** of 1870.

★**St Mary's Church** ⊙ – This large church once served the priory founded by the builder of Abergavenny's castle, Hamelin de Ballon. At the Dissolution it was acquired as their parish church by the townsfolk, who had already been using it more appropriately than the few remaining monks. The old parish church, St John's, became a grammar school, one of the earliest in the country. The present appearance of St Mary's is largely due to the restoration carried out in three phases in the 19C and 20C. The oak choir stalls date from the 14C-15C and there is a Norman font.

★★**Monuments** – The collection of effigies is one of the finest and most extensive in Great Britain, many of the local lords having chosen to be buried in the priory church. After years of neglect, these superb figures are now being restored.

The wooden **figure of a knight** representing Sir John de Hastings (d 1325) is recognised as one of the country's outstanding pieces of medieval sculpture, a product of the court workshop at Westminster.

In the Lewis Chapel are two female effigies in stone – one, the oldest in the church, representing Eva de Braose (d 1256), the other (c 1360) representing an unidentified member of the Hastings family. Also here is the tomb of Dr David Lewis (d 1584), a son of Abergavenny who became the first Principal of Jesus College, Oxford.

---

## Out and About

**Tourist Information Centre** – Swan Meadow, Monmouth Road, Abergavenny NP7 5HH ☎ 01873 857 588; Fax 01873 850 217.

**Adjacent Sights** – See Blaenavon, Brecon, Brecon Beacons, Grosmont, Llanthony Priory, Merthyr Tydfil, Monmouth, Raglan Castle, Tredegar, Tretower, Usk.

## Where to Stay

**Penclawdd Court**, Llanfihangel Crucorney, Abergavenny, NP7 7LB. ☎ 01873 890 719; Fax 01873 890 848. Tudor manor house (3 rm) with medieval origins (Grade I listed) and well-restored features, offering personal service and relaxed ambience.

---

It is, however, the Herbert Chapel which contains the church's greatest glory, three **alabaster tombs**, the work of Midlands craftsmen whose skill enjoyed international recognition. One tomb is that of Sir William ap Thomas (d 1445), the first builder of Raglan Castle, and his wife. Another is that of his son Sir Richard Herbert (d 1469) and his wife. Sir Richard, together with his brother the Earl of Pembroke, had the misfortune to be on the losing side at Edgecote in one of the battles of the Wars of the Roses and both were consequently executed. A third tomb is that of Richard Herbert (d 1510), natural son of Sir William Herbert. There is also the fine post-medieval tomb of Judge Andrew Powell, whose Latin plaque reads "Lately I was a judge; now waiting before a tribunal of a Judge, I am in fear".

Perhaps the most compelling work in the church is the 15C **figure of Jesse**. Nearly all the Jesse Tree, once part of what must have been a truly magnificent reredos, has gone, but this figure of King David's father, with dynamically carved beard and robes, is of extraordinary vigour.

**Abergavenny Castle** ⊘ – The scant remains of the stronghold first established c 1090 by Hamelin de Ballon include the gatehouse, part of the curtain wall and two towers. According to the antiquary Camden, the castle "has been oftner stain'd with the infamy of treachery than any other castle in Wales", and it was certainly the scene of an infamous incident in 1175, when William de Braose and his followers slaughtered a number of Welsh chieftains at the Christmas banquet to which they had been invited. Charles I ordered the castle to be slighted in order to deny its use to the forces of Parliament.

De Ballon's motte, with a fine view of the flood plain of the Usk and the hills beyond, is now occupied by a hunting box of 1819 masquerading as a keep. This houses the local **Museum** ⊘, with displays on the development of the town and its surroundings.

## EXCURSION

**Goytre Wharf Heritage and Activity Centre** – *2mi/3km S of Abergavenny by A 4042 at Llanover.*

In 1810 the Brecknock and Abergavenny Canal Company bought the land at Goytre from a John Sparrow of Staffordshire and built lime kilns and a wharf there. The kilns (renovated) still stand but the only surviving trace of industrial activity is a few lengths of iron, known as "pigs", leaning against the brickwork. Barges can be hired at the wharf and the old Aqueduct Cottage now houses an exhibition of paintings by local artists.

Ceredigion – Population 8 359
Michelin Atlas p 24 or Map 403 H 26

azing resolutely seaward, the gently curving Victorian terraces of this "Welsh
righton" make it one of the most distinctive of the Welsh seaside resorts, held firmly
in the centre of the great arc of Cardigan Bay by the heights to north and south.
berystwyth's history goes back much further than the arrival of the first tourists
owards the end of the 18C. The southern height, Pendinas, is crowned by an Iron
ge hillfort of about 600 BC, while the headland near the twin estuary of the Rheidol
nd Ystwyth carries the remains of a late-13C castle, one of the chain of strongholds
uilt by Edward I to keep the Welsh in check. At first only Englishmen were permitted
o settle in the walled town protected by the castle, but the Welsh soon found ways of
rcumventing this restriction and the population has long been a mixed one.
berystwyth's first wave of popularity came at the end of the 18C, when war with the
rench made foreign travel risky. A second wave followed the building of the railway
n 1864. Since the late 19C, with the foundation of the first University College of
Vales (1872) and the establishment of the National Library (1907), Aberystwyth has
ecome a stronghold of Welshness.

★**The Seafront (Marine Terrace)** (**AX**) – Recently partly repaved and dipping slightly
towards the gravelly beach, the broad promenade is backed by an undulating line
of three- and four-storey pastel-coloured 19C hotels and boarding houses, their
myriad windows reflecting the rays of the sun as it sets over the bay. No recent
intrusions mar the extraordinary homogeneity of this Victorian seaside townscape.
The **Pier**, reputed to be 800ft/243m long at the time of its building in 1865,
has been gnawed at by the sea over the years and is now sadly truncated. The
fulcrum of the seafront is formed by the bandstand, while its northern limit is
marked by the somewhat grim stone façades of Alexandra Hall, once a female
students' hostel.

The rugged slopes of **Constitution Hill** (**AX**) are no longer gardened as intensively as
they were a century ago, and the amusements of Luna Park which occupied the
summit (430ft/132m) have long since been dismantled, but the **Cliff Railway** ⊙ (**AX**)
of 1896 still travels up and down its vertiginous track (778ft/237m long) and the
**Camera Obscura** ⊙ removed in the 1920s has been replaced by a worthy successor
incorporating half a ton of sophisticated optics which give an extraordinary panorama of the town in its spectacular setting of ocean and mountain.

Beyond the pier to the south the promenade is separated from the sea by a high
retaining wall. Above it rise the swelling neo-Gothic façades of Aberystwyth's most
idiosyncratic structure, the "Old" **University College** (**AX U**[1]). It was begun by the
backer of the railway, an over-ambitious entrepreneur named Thomas Savin, who
foresaw a great future in package holidays and began to build a monster hotel
without waiting for his architect to draw up proper plans. The scheme foundered
as the project neared completion and in 1872 Savin was forced to sell the huge
edifice to the newly established **University of Wales** for a fraction of what it had cost
to build. Now used for ceremonial and administrative purposes, the College has a
unique triangular porte-cochère to landward while its prow-like southern tip is
graced with mosaics depicting Archimedes and the emblems of modern science.

Seafront, Aberystwyth

## Out and About

**Tourist Information Centre** – Terrace Road, Aberystwyth SY23 2AG. ☎ 01970 612 125; Fax 01970 626 566; aberystwythTIC@ceredigion.gov.uk

**Arts Centre** – The centre *(see below)* provides a continuous programme of exhibitions, theatre and other performances.

**Beaches** – At Aberystwyth North and South; at Clarach Bay and Borth *(N)* and at Llanrhystud *(S)*.

**Adjacent Sights** – See Aberaeron, Machynlleth, Vale of Rheidol, Strata Florida Abbey, Tregaron, Tywyn.

## Where to Eat

**The Treehouse**, 14 Baker St, SY23 2LJ. ☎ 01970 615 791. Simple café, with plenty of vegetarian choices, serving organic meat and fresh produce, supplied from the shop below.

## Where to Stay

**Sinclair**, 43 Portland St. ☎ 01970 615 158. Victorian terraced house (3 rm), in the town centre, pleasantly furnished and personally run.

**Four Seasons**, 50-54 Portland St. ☎ 01970 612 120. Small, personally run hotel (14 rm), centrally located, with individually decorated bedrooms and its own restaurant.

**Aberystwyth Castle** (AX) – The first castle, a largely timber structure, had bee built in 1110 on the banks of the Ystwyth. Edward I's replacement, one of the firs as well as one of the largest of his Welsh strongholds, began to rise from th promontory near the mouth of the Rheidol in 1277 consisting of two concentri diamonds of walls and towers and with a massive inner gatehouse-cum-keep. I was taken by Owain Glyn Dŵr in 1404, housed French prisoners captured a Agincourt, and was besieged in the Civil War, after which it was blown up; th remaining fragments do indeed lie around the grassy headland as if scattered by mighty explosion. The most substantial remains are those of a wall tower and c the Great Gatehouse facing the town.

**Town Centre** – The approximate line of the walls enclosing the English bastid town on its low rise can be traced in the alignment of King Street, Alfred Place Baker Street, Chalybeate Street, Mill Street and South Road. Great Darkgate Stree leads from the spot once occupied by the town's northern gateway – Great Dar Gate – to the Castle, while Bridge Street, once lined with the town houses of th rural gentry, descends to the three-arched bridge over the Rheidol. To seaward, th river mouth is protected by a pier and mole, and harbours numerous pleasure craft.

In the 19C the town spread north-eastwards beyond the line of the walls. Her streets like North Parade are more spaciously laid out than the narrow thorough fares of the old centre. It was here that the Cambrian Railway found space to buil its terminus in 1864. Its successor, the Great Western, redeveloped the station i lavish English Renaissance style in the inter-war period, leaving a structure far to grandiose for the few trains that still run today.

One of the more striking buildings from the heyday of Aberystwyth is the ebullien stone and terracotta Coliseum Theatre of 1904, now the **Ceredigion Museum** (
(AX M). The displays may not match the flamboyance of artistes like Gracie Field or Maurice Chevalier, who both performed here, but give a good account of th human history of the area, with emphasis on archaeology, the rural scene (with reconstruction of a single-storey cottage), Welsh furniture, and the seafaring o which the town depended before turnpike roads and railways bound it firmly to th rest of Wales, the English Midlands and beyond.

★**National Library of Wales** ⊘ (BX) – This solemn, municipal-looking building i pale stone stands high above the town just below the campus of the Universit College at Penglais. It is one of the United Kingdom's legal deposit libraries, holdin more than 3.5 million printed works, 40 000 manuscripts, 4 million deeds an documents as well as works of art, photographs and audio-visual material. Th Library was established in 1907, and building began in 1911; the latest extensio dates from 1982. It is the pre-eminent research and reference library in Wales an "the treasure house of the Welsh people" .

Dignified interior spaces allow room for temporary exhibitions drawing on th institution's inexhaustible collections as well as material from elsewhere; a larg part of the upper floor is devoted to the Library's **Permanent Exhibition★**. The object on display include such marvels as the first text written in Welsh (reproduction o

# ABERYSTWYTH

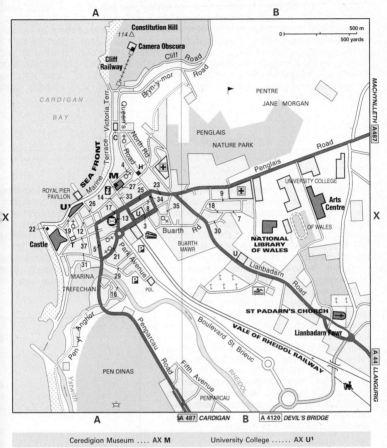

Ceredigion Museum .... AX **M**          University College ...... AX **U¹**

the Surexit Memorandum of the mid-9C), the first map of Wales (from Ortelius' Atlas of 1573), the first Welsh dictionary (1547), a copy of William Morgan's Bible (1588), and the first newspaper in Welsh, the *Seren Gomer* of 1814. There are numerous works of art ranging from topography (Varley's *Conway Castle* of 1808) to portraiture (Richard Wilson's *Captain Walter Griffith*) and pictures by more recent artists like Gwen and Augustus John, Charles Tunnicliffe and Kyffin Williams.

**Arts Centre** ⊙ (**BX**) – The modern buildings of the University step up the steep hillside above the town. At the heart of the campus and flanking a monumental viewing terrace are the recently refurbished buildings of the Arts Centre, the largest in Wales. In addition to a continuous programme of theatre and other performances, the Centre houses major touring exhibitions. There are also changing displays drawn from a very extensive collection of studio pottery, partly assembled by Sydney Greenslade, architect of the National Library and a prodigious collector.

## EXCURSION

**Llanbadarn Fawr** (**BX**) – *1mi/1.5km E of Aberystwyth by A 44*. The name of this village recalls Padarn, a 6C Celtic saint and contemporary of St David, who established a missionary station in what was then a lonely spot overlooking the Rheidol. His monastic church *(clas)* became a centre of learning; some of the 11C and 12C manuscripts produced here by members of the Sulien family have survived, humbler examples of the great Anglo-Irish tradition best represented by the Book of Kells.

★**St Padarn's Church** ⊘ (**BX**) – This large church, cruciform in plan, and with a grea square tower, has a simple dignity which is evocative of its ancient origins, thoug most of the present building dates from the 13C. For centuries it was the paris church of Aberystwyth, which for long bore the name of Llanbadarn Gaerog (walle Llanbadarn). The south door is embellished with slender shafts and graceful capita which recall the fine workmanship of the similar doorway of Strata Florida Abbe *(see p 264)*. In 1988 the **south transept** was transformed with great care into celebration of the evolution of this historically important parish. Fittings and furnish ings like the pitch-pine screen, stained glass and granite altar reflect the best i contemporary craft traditions. The transept contains two stone crosses which onc stood in the churchyard and may be reused pre-Christian standing stones; the large of them, of granite which may have come from the summit of Cadair Idris, ha figures carved into it as well as typically Celtic interlacing, work probably datin from the 10C.

# Isle of ANGLESEY★★

(Ynys Môn) Anglesey – Population 69 149
Michelin Atlas p 32 or Map 403 FGH 23-24

Anglesey, Mother of Wales – *Môn Mam Cymru* – is this island's motto, and man aspects of the heritage of Wales seem to be present here in concentrated form, fron the abundance of prehistoric and early Christian monuments to the high proportion c Welsh-speakers. Like most islands, Anglesey retains a strong individual identity, re inforced rather than diluted by the pair of superb 19C structures – the Menai Bridg and Britannia Bridge – connecting it to the mainland across the Menai Strait. Draw into the mainstream of national life by its position on the strategic route from Londo to Dublin, Anglesey nevertheless retains an air of remoteness over much of it windswept surface, parts of which recall that other Celtic land across the Irish Sea with whitewashed cottages, sedge-sown fields and slow-moving streams.

The island's glory is its coastline, most of it designated as an Area of Outstanding Natural Beauty; much of it is wild and dramatic, like the cliffs of Holyhead Mountain, though in other places rocky headlands shelter delightful coves and bays. The south-west coast is more tranquil, with broad sandy beaches and dune systems like those of Newborough Warren, while the banks of the Menai Strait have an almost Mediterranean atmosphere, with villas embedded in lush vegetation along the cor-niche-like road leading to Beaumaris.

## SIGHTS *in rough clockwise order start-ing from the Menai Bridge*

**Menai Strait** – The channel (15mi/25km long) separating Anglesey from the main-land was once dry land. The divide between two valleys running north-east – south-west was gouged out some 20 000 years ago when the thawing ice sheet covering them released torrents of melting water. As the ice-caps continued to shrink, the sea-level rose, flooding the valleys and making Anglesey an island.

Rip-tides surging up and down the Strait made the ferry crossing a hazardous affair and an undesirable obstruction to the free flow of traffic between London and Dublin via Holyhead, particularly irksome after the Act of Union of 1800. The graceful **Menai Bridge★** designed by Thomas Telford was opened in 1826. The suspension bridge (579ft/176m long) was the first iron struc-ture of its kind in the world, its chains suspended from masonry pylons (153ft/47m high). The meticulous prepa-ration of all the wrought-iron work included heating and soaking in linseed oil, not, as the White Knight told Alice, in wine:

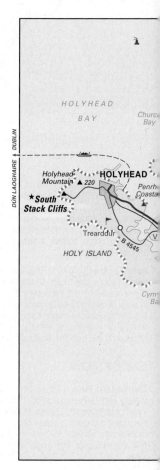

**Tourist Information Centre** – Station Site, Llanfairpwllgwyngyll LL61 5UJ
☎ 01248 713 177; Fax 01248 715 711.

**Beaches** – There are a few beaches on the east coast – Beaumaris, Penmon, Llanddona, Benllech and St David's – and very many all along the west coast.

**Craft Centres** – **Oriel Ynys Môn Craft gallery** *(see below)* and **James Pringle Weavers** *(LlanfairPG)*.

**Adjacent Sights** – See Bangor, Beaumaris, Caernarfon, Holyhead, Llanberis, Plas Newydd, Snowdonia.

> "I heard him then, for I had just
> Completed my design
> To keep the Menai Bridge from rust
> By boiling it in wine."

On the Anglesey bank the great chains were secured by driving tunnels (60ft/18m) into the rock. The actual raising of the first chain was watched by a large crowd, the efforts of the labourers on their capstans encouraged by a fife band. When Telford raised his hat to signal success, two of the workmen were so elated that they somehow managed to clamber across the chain high above the water (590ft/180m).

The **Britannia Bridge** by Robert Stephenson was built a generation later, to carry the Chester and Holyhead Railway. It is an altogether heavier structure, monumentally Egyptian in character, guarded at each end by pairs of lions of distinctly Sphinx-like mien. The twin tracks of the railway were originally led through iron tubes, a method of construction first employed by Stephenson at Conwy, though there were difficulties enough during the period of construction. "The tubes filled my head. I went to bed with them and I got up with them" Stephenson confided to a friend. On 5 March 1850 he hammered the last rivet home and crossed the bridge

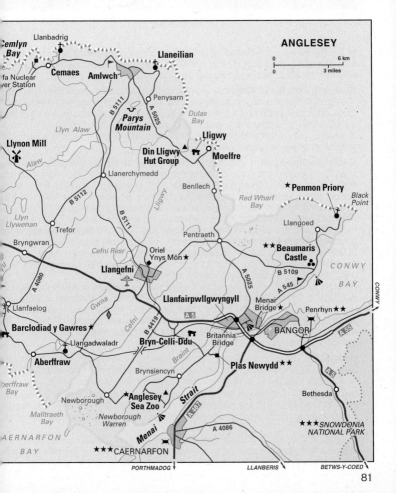

Menai Bridge

(1 513ft/460m long) followed by three trainloads of spectators. The tubular bridge was severely damaged by fire in 1970 and has been reconstructed along more conventional lines, with an additional deck carrying a dual carriageway (A 5).

**Bryn-Celli-Ddu Burial Chamber** – *A 5 and A 4080 W; after 3mi/4.8km turn right*. This passage grave seems to have been built on the site of a late Neolithic henge, a stone circle surrounded by a bank and a ditch. The internal passage, which is lined on one side by a low shelf, leads to a polygonal chamber containing a stone decorated with a spiral design. The finds from the excavations are now in the National Museum in Cardiff *(see p 123)*.

**Llanfairpwllgwyngyll** – This characterless village strung out along the old Holyhead Road leading from the Britannia Bridge was just one of the many places in Wales called Llanfair (meaning St Mary's) until in the 19C a tailor from Menai Bridge struck on the idea of extending its name by several syllables. The trick worked, and, even if its pronunciation and exact meaning (St Mary's Church in the hollow of white hazel near a rapid whirlpool and the Church of St Tysilio near the red cave) are not widely known, everyone has heard of **Llanfairpwllgwyngyllgogerychyrndrobwllllantysiliogogogoch**. What is more, visitors come here in large numbers though all there is to see is the railway station with its cumbersome nameplate and a waiting room sheltering Victorian dummies rather than real passengers, a large coach and car park, and an even larger souvenir complex.

On a rocky mound which served as a hillfort is the **Marquess of Anglesey's Column** ⊘ (112ft/32m high), erected in 1817 by the Noblemen, Gentlemen, Clergy and Freeholders of Anglesey "to testify... high admiration of the heroic conduct of the gallant Marquis of Anglesey *(see p 231)*, in the memorable battle of Waterloo". The reward for climbing its 115 spiral steps is a superlative **view** of the Menai Strait especially the Britannia Bridge in the foreground.

**Llangefni** – The county town of Anglesey stands on the island's longest river, the Cefni, no longer navigable, and on the old road to Holyhead, long since by-passed by Telford's turnpike. The town is at its busiest on market days.

★**Oriel Ynys Môn** ⊘ – Anglesey's fine modern **museum and art gallery** is committed not only to supporting local arts and crafts but also to presenting and explaining the island's strong identity to its visitors, who may well be greeted (in Welsh) by one of the friendly staff.

A series of imaginative displays evoke Anglesey's history, culture and environment. Deep inside a reconstruction of the Neolithic burial chamber of **Barclodiad y Gawres** fire-lit figures may be seen preparing a horrid "witches' brew" . Another scene shows the **royal court of Gwynedd** at Aberffraw with **Llywelyn the Last** *(ap Gruffydd)* sitting uneasily on the throne he was soon to lose. Other displays deal with Anglesey's agriculture, the copper mountain at Amlwch, the rich bird life of the South Stack cliffs and the marine life of the Menai Strait. Emphasis is laid on current issues like the maintenance of Welsh language and identity in the face of contemporary pressures.

There are temporary exhibitions of art as well as a permanent collection, which includes a gift of 300 works by the painter Kyffin Williams whose studio is on the Menai Strait. The centrepiece and the original raison d'être of the museum is a reconstruction of the **studio of Charles Tunnicliffe** (1901-79), where the wildlife and countryside artist worked for 30 years. "No strangers to this fair country", Tunni-cliffe and his wife settled at Malltraeth on the edge of the Cefni estuary in 1947, attracted by its rich bird life. Whereas his early work reveals a passion for the elemental and primeval aspects of traditional life in the countryside, Tunnicliffe as shown here is the master craftsman, meticulous and immensely productive, the illustrator of countless books which indelibly influenced the way in which the British perceive their landscape and the creatures that inhabit it.

★**Anglesey Sea Zoo** ⊘ *– North side of the Menai Strait facing Caernarfon.* Established in what was once a lobster-export business, this is a large, varied and highly entertaining aquarium, which specialises in exhibiting the diverse marine life to be found off the Anglesey coast. As well as conventional fish tanks, the Zoo has ingenious simulations of a number of habitats complete with their denizens. There is a shipwreck, surf crashing on a beach, and a convincing re-creation of the world beneath the pier. A **touch pool**, constantly refreshed by the tide pouring over rocks, allows visitors intimate contact with the more accessible sea creatures such as starfish, whelks and anemones. The most spectacular of the exhibits is the great **Fish Forest**, a huge tank containing 200 000 litres of seawater; a concave window, the largest of its kind in Britain, gives onlookers the sensation of moving among the myriad fish swimming through the fronds of a growing forest of seaweed.

**Newborough Warren** ⊘ *– It is dangerous to venture off the paths on to the mudflats at low tide.* A network of footpaths explores the different habitats of this area, one of the finest dunelands in Wales, which is now a nature reserve, inhabited by a great variety of wildlife. The forest of Corsican pine trees, which is managed for timber, was planted in the mid-20C to stop the dunes from moving; the dunes support an array of plants and insects; the estuaries and freshwater lakes provide feeding and breeding grounds for an abundance of bird life. The history of the dunes is told in the exhibition in the Visitor Centre, housed in the old Pilots' Cottages.

**Aberffraw** – In the early medieval period Anglesey was the island stronghold of the kingdom of Gwynedd, its fertile farmlands helping to sustain the inhabitants of the mountainous mainland. The chief seat of the kingdom was here at Aberffraw, though today's plain little village on the west bank of the River Ffraw gives little hint of the princely pageantry and prestige of a medieval court. Nevertheless, past glories are commemorated in the **Countryside Centre** ⊘, **Llys Llywelyn** (Llywelyn's Court), which occupies some attractive old farm buildings and provides a base for the island's countryside Management Service.

A further reminder of Anglesey's historical importance is the **Cadfan Stone**, set in the north wall of **Llangadwaladr Church** ⊘ on the far side of the river *(1.5mi/2.5km E by A 4080)*. Long before this 12C church was built, the site was the burial ground of the rulers of Gwynedd; Cadfan's qualities are celebrated in the stone's imperious inscription which reads "King Catamanus (= Cadfan), wisest and most renowned of all kings".

★**Barclodiad y Gawres Burial Chamber** ⊘ *– Park in the car park at Cable Bay; 15min there and back on foot.* In a wonderful position on a headland overlooking Cable Bay, this is one of the most evocative late Neolithic monuments in Wales. Beneath the contours of the modern mound is a chamber reached by a passageway and flanked by smaller side chambers, all defined by upright stones, five of which are decorated with spirals, chevrons, zigzags and lozenges, some of the earliest prehistoric art to be seen in Britain. Excavation has revealed evidence of a strange event that took place at some point in the chamber's history; the preparation of a "witches' brew" made up of frog, toad, snake, mouse, hare, eel, wrasse and whiting.

**Holyhead** – *See p 166.*

**Llynon Mill** ⊘ *– W of Llanddeusant.* This tower mill, built in 1775-76, is ready to turn its sails to any favourable wind, especially those that sweep in from the west over the exposed countryside fronting Holyhead Bay. The mill was derelict for 60 years before being restored to working condition and opened to the public in 1984.

**Cemlyn Bay** – *North coast.* The bay is backed by a curving shingle bank and lagoon, a paradise for bird life, in particular for terns, all five British breeding species of which can be seen here.

**Cemaes** – *North coast.* This little resort clustering around its harbour was the chief port of Anglesey's north coast before the rise of Amlwch. Nowadays it stands between the beauty of the Heritage Coast with its splendid cliff walks and the less attractive mass of **Wylfa Nuclear Power Station** ⊙ which presents a welcoming face with extensive landscaping and a lavishly equipped **visitor centre.**
Beyond the promontory enclosing the eastern side of the harbour is another headland, a wonderful site for the tiny parish **church** of **Llanbadrig** ⊙, founded according to legend, by St Patrick in the 5C, and surrounded by its clifftop graveyard. Restoration work in 1884 – red, white and blue glass in the windows, blue glass in the east window, rare sanctuary tiles produced by a glass-making process, mosaic of the Good Shepherd in the niche – was initiated by Lord Stanley of Alderley, who had been a diplomat in the Near East and become a Muslim, and introduced some elements reminiscent of a mosque.

**Amlwch and Parys Mountain** – *North coast.* Of the hills which rise abruptly from the otherwise planed-down surface of Anglesey, Parys Mountain is the most spectacular, less as a work of Nature than of Man. **Copper** was probably worked here in Roman times, but it was in the late 18C that the mountain became the site of the greatest copper mines in the world with Amlwch as their port. Copper was in great demand, not only for domestic utensils, but also to sheathe the hulls of the Royal Navy's battleships. Production was at its zenith in the 1820s, when 9 000t of ore were extracted every year, some of it processed on site, some of it sent to Swansea. The fumes from smelting poisoned vegetation and enabled the vicar of Amlwch to claim damages of £15 a year for "smoke trespass". The Parys seams were however "lean" compared with foreign ores, yielding only 3% of copper, and by the end of the 19C extraction had virtually ceased.
Parys Mountain *(private property; it is dangerous to leave the tracks)* is now a garishly coloured lunar landscape of waste tips and craters, the largest of the latter being the Great Opencast Pit.
In the late-18C to early-19C, according to the Reverend Bingley, **Amlwch** was "a bleak and dismal place" with a population of 6 000 and no fewer than 60 alehouses to slake the miners' thirst.
In the 1790s a cleft in the coast was widened to make a harbour, **Porth Amlwch**, capable of taking 30 craft of up to 100t. The little port retains something of its late-18C appearance and is still used by trawlers and pleasure boats.

**Llaneilian Church** ⊙ – This fine late-15C battlemented church with its buttressed tower and pyramidal spire stands by tradition on the site of a 5C church endowed in honour of St Eilian by the Cambrian Prince Caswallon Law Hir, whose blindness had been cured by the holy man. Inside are a number of remarkable features including a carved oak **screen** with a figure of a skeleton wielding a scythe on the blade of which is inscribed *Colyn angau yw pechod* (The sting of death is sin). The roof beams have a number of charming figures, one of whom is playing the bagpipes. A 14C chapel also dedicated to the saint and built over the site of his cell is reached by a passageway from the chancel.

**Din Lligwy Hut Group** – *20min there and back on foot from roadside lay-by.* The remains of the drystone walls of a settlement of late Roman date are almost entirely surrounded by woodland to the northwest.

**Hen Capel Lligwy** *(short diversion from footpath to hut group)* is another element in the pattern of ancient settlement – the roofless walls of an early-12C chapel stand among the gnarled hawthorn trees of a sheep pasture overlooking Lligwy Bay.

**Lligwy Burial Chamber** – *A 5108 and minor road.* The Neolithic burial chamber raises its massive capstone atop a cleft in the rock and is still protected by now-venerable Ministry of Works iron railings.

**Moelfre** – The lifeboat from this little harbour village has an illustrious history of rescues, though terrible seas stopped it being launched when the Liverpool-bound *Royal Charter* went down in 1859, drowning hundreds and scattering an untold quantity of Australian gold to the waves.

The **Seawatch Centre** ⊙ tells this and other maritime tales, as well as housing a real lifeboat and enabling visitors to observe passing shipping and bird life by remote-control video camera.

# BALA

Its single street attractively lined with trees, Bala stands athwart the long south-west – north-east fault line that has long been an important communication route through the mountains between England and the Cambrian coast. Filling the deep valley to the south-west of the town is the largest natural water body in Wales, Bala Lake *(Llyn Tegid)*, its surface animated by all kinds of water sports enthusiasts in summer.

Bala was founded as an English borough in 1310, in the heart of what was then a thoroughly lawless region. The back lanes running parallel to the High Street mark the limits of the original burgage plots. Described in the 16C by Leyland as "a little poore market" Bala never seems to have enjoyed great prosperity, though for a century or so in the 18C-19C it was famous for its stockings, often knitted in the open air by old and young alike.

By this time its English character had long since faded; as a stronghold of Welshness, Bala witnessed the activities of **Thomas Charles** (1755-1814), and later of **Thomas Edward Ellis** (1859-99). Charles was a great preacher and promoter of Sunday schools, his efforts to distribute Welsh Bibles given enormous encouragement by the famous example of little Mary Jones, who at the age of 16 walked across the mountains to Bala (25mi/40km) in her effort to acquire one. As Liberal MP for Merionethshire, Ellis was an indefatigable fighter for the interests of Wales and was in the forefront of the movement for a National Library. There are statues of both men in the town.

---

**Tourist Information Centre** – Penllyn, Pensarn Road, Bala LL23 7SR
☎/Fax 01678 521 021; bala.tic@gwynedd.gov.uk

**Bala Adventure and Watersports Centre** ⊘ – The centre organises courses (also accommodation) lasting for a few hours or several days, in a range of activities – abseiling, mountain climbing, sailing, white-water rafting, windsurfing.

**Adjacent Sights** – See Betws-y-Coed, Blaenau Ffestiniog, Dolgellau, Llanfyllin, Llangollen, Ruthin, Snowdonia, Lake Vyrnwy.

---

★**Bala Lake (Llyn Tegid)** – This lake was formed in a hollow made by the Dee Valley glacier. Its gloomy waters (4mi/6km long, 140ft/40m deep) are inhabited by a unique sub-species of fish, the *gwyniad*, trapped here since the end of the Ice Age. The winds racing through the long valley between the mountains can make for exciting sailing and windsurfing. Less energetic pursuits are catered for by frequent car parks and picnic areas and by lakeside footpaths.

## EXCURSIONS

**Bala Lake Railway** ⊘ – *0.5mi/1km S of Bala by B 4391, or 6mi/10km to Llanuwchllyn by A 494 and B 4403.* The Llangollen–Bala–Dolgellau railway was closed in 1965. Part of the line has been relaid with narrow-gauge track (2ft/0.6m) from Bala Station to the railway's headquarters at Llanuwchllyn. Little steam locomotives haul tourist trains along the lakeside *(9mi/16km there and back)*.

Bala Lake Railway

**Llyn Celyn** – *4mi/7km NW of Bala by A 4212*. This reservoir (over 2mi/3km long), a rival to Bala Lake in depth, is retained by a dam (2 200ft/670m long). It supplies Merseyside with water and its construction drowned the village of Capel Celyn, together with Hafod Fadog, an early centre of Quaker worship. Liverpool Corporation built a lakeside **chapel** *(2mi/3km further west)* in expiation but it is a melancholy and little-visited place. Periodically released water creates some of the best conditions in Britain for white-water canoeing and rafting on the River Tryweryn below the dam.

**★★Bwlch y Groes** – *11mi/18km S of Bala by A 494, B 4403 and a minor road*. The Pass of the Cross (Bwlch y Groes) is reached by a narrow road which climbs from near the southern end of Bala Lake through the upland farms of Cwm Cynlewyd to the open mountainside. This is the highest road in Wales, offering at the summit magnificent views of the crags of the Arans *(S)*. An equally spectacular prospect opens up as the road begins the steep descent into the upper Dovey (Dyfi) Valley, with noble screes giving way to the lusher enclosed landscape of the valley floor.

# BANGOR
Gwynedd – Population 11 173
Michelin Atlas p 32 or Map 403 H 24
Local map p 261

The wattle fence around a settlement was once known as a "bangor", and the monastery founded here c AD 525 by St Deiniol took its name from the woven enclosure that originally surrounded it. Deiniol became Bishop c AD 546, making Bangor perhaps the oldest territorial diocese in Britain. Hidden from sea-borne marauders by the ridge now occupied by the University, the tiny city languished in obscurity for hundreds of years.

Growth occurred only at the end of the 18C and the beginning of the 19C, when Penrhyn slate started to be shipped out and when the Holyhead Road was completed in 1830. The University came in 1884, and Bangor today is the miniature metropolis for this part of North Wales, a busy place, especially when the 5 000 or so students are in residence.

---

**Tourist Information Centre** – Town Hall, Deiniol Road, Bangor LL57 2RE
☎ 01248 352 786; Fax 01248 362 701; bangor.tic@gwynedd.gov.uk

**Craft Centre** – The **Bangor Museum and Art Gallery** *(see below)* has a well-stocked craft shop.

**Adjacent Sights** – See Anglesey, Beaumaris, Caernarfon, Conwy, Holyhead, Llanberis, Llanrwst, Penrhyn Castle, Snowdonia.

---

**Cathedral** ⊘ – This most modest of cathedral churches is possibly the oldest cathedral foundation (AD 525) in continuous use in Britain. It retains a few fragments of the structure built in the 12C but most of its fabric is 13C–16C, much restored towards the end of the 19C by Sir George Gilbert Scott. The cathedral's discreet location well away from the shore (like St David's) did not save it from repeated depredation by the Vikings in 1073, by King John's soldiers in 1210, during Owain Glyn Dŵr's rebellion in 1402 and from subsequent neglect.

A diminutive buttressed and battlemented belfry of 1532 stands at the western end, while the crossing is marked by a squat tower whose foundations proved to be too insubstantial to support the tall spire proposed by Scott. The interior lacks symmetry, but objects of interest include an oak carving known as the **Mostyn Christ**, a life-size figure of great expressiveness. One modern painting shows the six cathedrals of Wales in their contrasting geographical settings; another, by Brian Thomas, is a touching representation of Christ's encounter with the two people on the road to Emmaus. A "museum corner" has Flemish carvings, stone fragments and misericords.

The area around the cathedral still has a recognisably precinctual character. A **Bible Garden**, laid out in 1962, is filled with plants with Biblical connotations, like the *Cupressus sempervirens* which provided Noah with gopher wood for the Ark. The Bishop's Palace now accommodates local authority offices, and the Canonry houses the Museum and Art Gallery.

**Museum and Art Gallery** ⊘ – This pleasingly old-fashioned museum has a Bangor Room full of local memorabilia, a Welsh kitchen, and a fine collection of 17C–19C furniture from a gentry house near Criccieth. Other furniture includes a splendid

3-tier dresser *(tridarn)* which may date from 1555; its carved inscription reads *Os yw Duw trosom, pwy a all fod i'n herbyn* ("If God is with us who can be against us"). The gallery stages temporary exhibitions.

**University** – In 1880 a committee set up by Gladstone recommended that Wales should have two university colleges. Aberystwyth had been founded in 1872 and Cardiff was opened in 1883 but agitation continued for an institution in the north, supported by the population as a whole, the Penrhyn quarrymen contributing a weekly deduction from their wages. The first students began their studies in 1884 in a converted inn, the Penrhyn Arms.

The main college building on the ridge top, with its two quadrangles and massive tower, is easily the most distinguished structure in Bangor. It was opened in 1911, its architect Henry Hare insisting on open corridors around the cloister-like quadrangles so that conditions "should approach as nearly as may be to an actual outdoor life, plus the warmth necessary to sedentary occupations". Glazing was installed only in the 1950s.

Bangor is a bastion of Welshness, and the University operates a bilingual policy regarding the use of Welsh and English. All official communications are in both languages, and some courses may be studied through the medium of Welsh. About 10% of the students speak Welsh as their first language.

**Pier** ⊙ – Though never managing to turn itself into a resort as such, Bangor shared to some extent in the transformation of the North Wales coast into a holiday region. The recently reopened pier, built in 1896, seems to reach almost to the Anglesey shore of the Menai Strait. It retains nearly all its original features including the procession of charming little kiosks along its entire length (1 550ft/470m). There are fine views of the wooded Strait and of Snowdonia.

# BARMOUTH ★

(Abermaw) Gwynedd – Population 2 306
Michelin Atlas p 32 or Map 403 H 25

This old harbour town enjoys a superlative site at the broad mouth of the Mawddach estuary. The older houses clamber up the rocky slopes which shelter Barmouth from the north, while the more modern buildings of the seaside resort are somehow crammed into the space between the splendid sandy beach and the cliff. The place became popular in Victorian times. Darwin enjoyed staying here, as did Ruskin. Today's crowds fill the beach, the promenade, the amusement arcade, or watch the varied activity around the harbour.

There is a **Lifeboat Museum** ⊙, a small local **museum** ⊙ in an old house called **Tŷ Gwyn**, and, a short distance away, an odd circular **lock-up**, Ty Crwn, in whose constricted space men and women prisoners were somehow separated.

★**Barmouth Bridge** ⊙ – The Cambrian coast railway curves sharply through the town, then straightens out abruptly to cross this extraordinarily long bridge (2 253ft/687m) built on 113 trestles. A double span of lattice girders used to open

M Ivory

Barmouth Bridge

**Tourist Information Centre** – The Old Library, Station Road, Barmouth LL42 1LU ☎ 01341 280 787; Fax 01341 280 787; barmouth.tic@gwynedd.gov.uk

**Beaches** – At Barmouth and Fairbourne.

**Crossing the Mawddach Estuary** – The sandy spit which almost closes the mouth of the Mawddach is linked to Barmouth by **ferry** ⏱ and by railway. This makes possible a trip to Fairbourne, a popular resort with a sandy beach, and a ride on the narrow-gauge **Fairbourne Railway** ⏱, returning to Barmouth by mainline train or on foot using the railway bridge.

**Adjacent Sights** – See Dolgellau, Harlech, Machynlleth, Tywyn.

to allow the passage of larger vessels but only pleasure-craft sail up the Mawddach nowadays. The bridge was opened in 1866. In 1980 it was closed for seven months for repairs costing nearly £2 million, its timber piling having been the subject of the Teredo worm's voracious appetite.

On the upstream side, a **walkway** accompanies the railway, forming a magnificent promenade with incomparable views of the estuary in its mountain setting.

**Dinas Oleu** – Ruskin once declared that the only walk superior to the one from Barmouth to Dolgellau was the one from Dolgellau to Barmouth, but his interest in the place extended further, and included a social experiment involving the letting of cottages to worthy tenants. One of these was the French libertarian Auguste Guyard, a friend of Lamartine, a revolutionary of 1848, then refugee from the Paris siege of 1870. Ruskin had been given the cottages by Fanny Talbot, who in 1895 also presented the National Trust with its very first property, a rugged plot (4 acres/1.5ha) known as Dinas Oleu on the rocky heights above the town. This is linked to Cae Fadog on the adjacent hillside and also to Barmouth's famous **Panorama Walk** which amply justifies its name with its superb views of estuary and mountains.

## EXCURSION

**Llanaber Church** ⏱ – *2mi/3km N of Barmouth by A 496*. Wonderfully sited in a sloping graveyard high above the sea stands this attractive early-13C church, which has a finely detailed south door. In the interior the white walls and coarsely textured stone contrast with the dark flagstones of the floor. The barn-like timber roof of the nave is 16C.

# BARRY

(Y Barri) Vale of Glamorgan – Population 46 368
Michelin Atlas p 16 or Map 403 K 29

Long rows of terraced housing rise over the extensive and little-used docks of this harbour town, in its heyday a rival to Cardiff as a coaling port, but now best known for the amusements and sandy beach of Barry Island.

Up to the mid-19C Barry was no more than a hamlet, and Barry Island a rabbit warren, the former haunt of pirates and smugglers.

The first hotel was built in 1856 by the Crawshay dynasty of ironmasters from Merthyr Tydfil. It was however the coal magnate **David Davies** (1818-90) who was responsible for the explosive growth of the town in the last years of the 19C. Resentful of the Bute stranglehold on coal exports from Cardiff, he and other mine owners filled the channel between Barry Island and the mainland with superbly equipped docks and ran a railway north to the coalfields of the Rhondda. The population swelled from barely 100 in 1881 to 13 000 in 1891, and by 1913 the port was shipping out more coal than Cardiff.

Today the docks make a melancholy sight; shipping movements are infrequent and most of the Barry Railway's quayside sidings (100mi/160km) have been torn up, though the grandiose Port Building of 1898 still stands amid the desolation.

**Barry Island** – The select visitors attracted to the Crawshays' Marine Hotel were eventually joined by day trippers and holidaymakers using the Barry Railway's links to the teeming settlements of the mining valleys, and it is to this clientele that the resort makes its appeal still, with a concentrated array of man-made attractions unsurpassed anywhere else in Wales. Amusement arcades offer the latest in laser technology, the log flume of the **Pleasure Park** ⏱ dominates the skyline, Jolly Pirate Golf can be enjoyed on the expensively refurbished Promenade, and any kind of fast food is instantly available.

**Tourist Information Centre** – The Promenade, The Triangle, Barry Island CF62 5TG ☎ 01446 747 171.

**Boat Trips** – To **Flat Holm Island** ⊘ (5mi/8km offshore), a nature reserve with a resident warden, who gives an introductory talk; the reserve is home for nesting gulls and shelduck and is covered with a profusion of wild flowers in spring.

**Adjacent Sights** – See Cardiff, Cowbridge, Llantrisant, Penarth, Glamorgan Coast, Museum of Welsh Life.

In pride of place on the Promenade stands a spruced-up steam locomotive, rescued from the dockside scrapyard which for many years was the last resting place of many of British Railways' redundant steam engines, and a poignant reminder of Barry's reason for existence.

Two headlands define the attractive sandy beach, Friars' Point to the west still a grassy open expanse, Nell's Point to the east long since given over to the Resort Holiday Centre.

Beyond the **Old Harbour** to the west is **The Knap**, a quieter, more residential area with boating lake and swimming pool, and further west still **Porthkerry Country Park**, a wooded valley running down to a pebble beach.

# BEAUMARIS ★

(Biwmares) Anglesey – Population 2 050
Michelin Atlas p 32 or Map 403 H 24

Founded in the late 13C as one of Edward I's castle towns, Beaumaris thrived first as the chief port and commercial centre for North Wales, and later as the focus of social life for the gentry of Anglesey. The little town has an enviable **setting**, overlooking the Menai Strait which here opens out into a broad and glorious expanse dotted with pleasure-craft; the south shore rises gently to the parklands of Penrhyn Castle, then more dramatically to the mountains of Snowdonia. Of the several locations in Wales which have been compared to the Bay of Naples, this sublime scene is probably the most deserving of the description.

From late Georgian times onward, the town became popular with holidaymakers, growing into a decorous, still small resort, with a **pier**, seafront Green, and cheerfully painted terraces facing the water. The grandest row, **Victoria Terrace**, was built in the 1830s by Joseph Aloysius Hansom, better known as the designer of the cab named after him.

CADW: Welsh Historic Monuments – Crown Copyright

Beaumaris Castle

## Out and About

**Beaches** – In Beaumaris and east at Penmon.

**Adjacent Sights** – See Anglesey, Bangor, Caernarfon, Conwy, Penrhyn Castle, Plas Newydd, Snowdonia.

## Where to Eat

**The Brasserie** (at Ye Olde Bull's Head Inn; *see below*). Modern and informal eating area in the former stables providing all-day eclectic eating; good value.

**The Ship**, LL76 8RJ. *6mi/9km N of Beaumaris by B 5019 and A 5025 to Red Wharf Bay.* ☎ 01248 852 568. Traditional inn, overlooking the sea, with a wide variety of beers and bar food.

## Where to Stay

**Ye Olde Bull's Head Inn**, Castle Street, LL58 8AP. ☎ 01248 810 329, Fax 01248 811 294. An establishment of character and period charm, dating from the 15C, with good individually decorated bedrooms.

**Bishopsgate House**, 54 Castle St, Beaumaris LL58 8BB. ☎ 01248 810 302, Fax 01248 810 166. Georgian house (9 rm), with original character, providing comfortable accommodation and the facilities of a small hotel.

**Hafod**, Amlwch Rd, Benllech, LL74 8SR. *10mi/15km N of Beaumaris by B 5109 and A 5025.* ☎ 01248 853 092. Comfortable Victorian house of great charm with 4 well-furnished bedrooms; good views of the coast.

# SIGHTS

★★**Beaumaris Castle** ⊙ – The castle may lack the drama and presence of the castles at Caernarfon or Conwy but is nevertheless a perfect example of a 13C concentric stronghold, the masterpiece of Edward I's chief military architect, Master James of St George.

The site chosen was low-lying, a *"beau Mareys"* or beautiful marsh, not far from the native Welsh settlement of Llanfaes, whose presumably untrustworthy inhabitants were removed to Newborough at the west end of the Menai Strait. The castle's plan is almost perfectly symmetrical, with a square inner ward defended by walls, six massive round towers, and two formidable twin-towered gatehouses. A many-towered outer ward is hexagonal in shape, protected by a moat and by offset outer gates. It was begun in 1295, with more than 2 000 workmen employed. In 1296 it seems to have been functional as a fortress, though Master James found it necessary to plead in a letter for more resources "And Sirs, for God's sake, be quick with the money for the works". Building continued well into the 14C but Beaumaris was never finished; its towers failed to reach their intended height and the two great gatehouse suites remained uncompleted. In 1403 the castle and its dependent town fell to the supporters of Owain Glyn Dŵr. After their defeat two years later, the town was given the walls its citizens had long petitioned for, though few traces remain today.

The castle is approached by a charming pathway alongside the moat which leads to the **Gate Next The Sea** and the **Dock**, the latter overlooked by the **Gunners' Walk**. Supply by sea was essential if Edward's fortresses were to withstand the expected attack and siege by land forces, and these arrangements enabled the largest medieval vessels to discharge their cargo directly into the castle. Any attacker who had penetrated the outer defences would be exposed to fire from the offset **Barbican** and **South Gatehouse**. This faces the **North Gatehouse** across the Inner Ward, now a broad lawn, but once partly filled with buildings ranged along the east and west walls. The North Gatehouse, only its lower floor complete, was originally intended to resemble its grandiose counterpart at Harlech, designed 12 years earlier by Master James. The massive walls are pierced by passageways and are topped by wall-walks which incorporate no fewer than 16 ingeniously designed latrines. The intermediate tower in the east wall contains the fine vaulted **Chapel** as well as an **exhibition** on Edward's castles which stresses the indebtedness of some of the design features to the castles of Master James' native Savoy. Beyond the North Gatehouse, and again offset from it, is the **Llanfaes Gate**, which once led to the defunct Welsh borough and now gives on to fields of grazing cattle.

**Church of St Mary and St Nicholas** ⊙ – Like St Mary's at Caernarfon, this spacious building served as a garrison church and was built in the early 14C not long after completion of the castle.

Decidedly English rather than Welsh in character, the church has a number of fascinating features, including early-16C **choir stalls** with fine misericords and late-15C alabaster **table tomb** with effigies of William and Elen Bulkeley. The tomb is much defaced with ancient graffiti, currently the subject of academic research.

In the porch is the stone **coffin** of Princess Joan, illegitimate daughter of King John and wife of Llywelyn the Great (ap Iorwerth). The carved cover of the coffin is exuberantly decorated with floral ornament and shows the princess in prayer. The coffin itself served for many years as a horse trough. Coffin, choir stalls and tomb are supposed to have been brought here from the priory at nearby Llanfaes when it was dissolved in 1538.

**Courthouse** ⊘ – The stone-flagged court room, which dates from 1614, was renovated in the 19C and sentence is still passed beneath its hammerbeam roof. An audio tour effectively recreates the atmosphere of past crimes and punishments.

**Gaol** ⊘ – The local prison was built in an appropriately intimidating style in 1829. Its harsh regime is recreated by means of an audio tour which takes in the punishment cell, the treadmill and the condemned cell.

**Museum of Childhood Memories** ⊘ – The nine rooms of a house close to the castle are filled with toys and other items calculated to evoke memories of childhood. Some of the objects go back to Victorian times or even earlier; they range from polyphons, phonographs and that predecessor of film and television, the zoetrope, to tin trains, cars and a clockwork dachshund. Toy savings banks are the subject of a video presentation *(12min)*. Modern memorabilia include plastic Beatles and Miss Piggy in her pink sports car.

## EXCURSION

★**Penmon Priory** – *4mi/7km NE of Beaumaris by B 5109 and minor roads.* Sheltered from the west by a low limestone ridge and looking out across Conwy Bay to the mountains beyond, this is a most evocative grouping of ancient priory, holy well, and splendid stone dovecot.

The traditional founder of the monastery was the 6C Celtic saint, Seiriol, a colleague of St Cybi, but Viking raids destroyed all traces of his establishment. The earliest relics are two fine **crosses**, of late 10C-early 11C date, now in the church. They both have elaborately carved abstract decoration, while the larger cross has a much-eroded panel which may depict the *Temptation of St Anthony*. The cruciform **church** with its sturdy conical tower was built in the middle of the 12C, with a large new chancel added in the 13C, and thoroughly rebuilt in the 19C. The atmosphere of early Christianity seems to pervade the interior, whose plainness is relieved by the richly carved decoration of Norman arches and pillars.

The western range of the monastic buildings has long been converted into a house, the cloister serving as its front garden as well as the approach to the church. The roofless **southern range** is an imposing three-storey high-gabled structure in roughly coursed stone. Its first floor was the monks' dining hall, the second their dormitory.

Close by is the remarkable **dovecot**, a splendid square structure dating from c 1600, capped by a great dome and with niches for a thousand birds.

Set into the low cliffs behind the priory and approached past the monastic fishpond is **St Seiriol's Well**, of uncertain date but traditionally associated with the saint, its healing properties appreciated up to the late 18C. The pool is within a roofed inner chamber built in the 18C with stone seats. The adjacent low walls are unlikely to be the remains of St Seiriol's cell.

# BEDDGELERT

Gwynedd – Population 535
Michelin Atlas p 32 or Map 403 H 24
Local map p 261

Beddgelert stands on the southern flank of the Snowdon massif at the confluence of the River Colwyn and the River Glaslyn, its stone cottages crowding the narrow roads converging on the bridge. The village's farmers and copper miners helped the pioneer tourists of the late 18C find their way around the mountains, and Beddgelert's popularity has increased ever since, aided in no small measure by the appropriation of the ancient legend of Gelert.

**A faithful hound** – The dog Gelert belonged to Prince Llywelyn, who left his baby son in its charge while he went hunting. Returning, he found a blood-soaked hound and no trace of his child. Enraged, he slew the dog, whose dying howl was however answered by the infant's cry. Gelert had hidden the child from a ravening wolf which he had then torn to pieces. Overcome with remorse, Llywelyn never smiled again.

Though the name Beddgelert almost certainly refers to the early Irish Saint Celert, its resonance with the legend of Llywelyn's faithful hound proved of irresistible appeal to the landlord of the Royal Goat, the village's first proper hotel. In 1800 he laid out "Gelert's Grave" in the meadows just south of the village, marking it with monoliths and planting trees, thus creating a tourist attraction which continues to exercise its spell on proportion of the village's many visitors.

**Adjacent Sights** – See Bangor, Betws-y-Coed, Blaenau Ffestiniog, Caernarfon, Criccieth, Lleyn Peninsula, Porthmadog, Portmeirion, Snowdonia.

**Bwthyn Llywelyn (Ty Isaf)** ⊘ – Before the construction of the Royal Goat, travellers had to stay in this former ale house by the bridge over the Colwyn in the centre of the village where, according to one guest, there was "no variety of accommodation" and "the catalogue of negatives is abundant. No butcher's meat, no wheaten bread, no wine, no spirits". The simple early-17C building now houses a National Trust shop and information centre.

★**Aberglaslyn Pass** – Beyond the riverside pastures around Gelert's grave the Glaslyn narrows to enter its gorge, a landscape of "silent wonder... gloom and grandeur" according to the Reverend L Evans. The short-lived Welsh Highland Railway *(see p 235)* rudely pushed its way through the pass in 1922; its abandoned trackbed – including a tunnel – enables walkers to savour the scenic delights of the rocky wooded ravine to the full. The little harbour that once existed just below Pont Aberglaslyn disappeared for ever with the building of the Cob at Porthmadog and the subsequent draining of the levels.

## EXCURSION

**Sygun Copper Mine** ⊘ – *1mi/1.5km NE of Beddgelert by A 498.* Copper may well have been mined around Beddgelert in ancient times, though most activity took place in the 18C and 19C. Above Aberglaslyn, Cwm Bychan is still marked by the pylons of the overhead cableway installed as late as the 1920s to bring ore down the mountain. The Sygun (pronounced Suggin) mine closed in 1903 but is now open as a tourist attraction. It is set in the matchless scenery of the Glaslyn valley above Beddgelert. The underground tour enters the mine by the Deep Adit near the valley floor and provides a realistic impression of what it was like to work by candlelight and of how slow and physically demanding the work was. The guide's explanation of what went on in the warren of adits, shafts and tunnels is supplemented by the reminiscences of ingeniously constructed effigies of old miners. From the exit, which is higher up the mountainside, there is a fine view of the valley.

*The main car parks are shown on the town plans in this guide*

# BETWS-Y-COED ★
Conwy – Population 848
Michelin Atlas p 33 or Map 403 I 24
Local map p 261

The eastern gateway to Snowdonia, Betws-y-Coed, is attractively located at the point where the River Conwy, fed by its rushing tributaries of Llugwy, Lledr and Machno emerges from its narrow and steep-sided mountain valley into the more tranquil agricultural vale leading down to the sea. Miners and lumbermen had long frequented the area but since the late 18C Betws' fortunes have been built on the needs of travellers and tourists. Seen against a romantic background of forested crags, it sombre slate-roofed hotels and houses in local stone still evoke the atmosphere of Victorian mountain resort, though today the majority of its visitors arrive on day trips from the coast. The area around Betws is the most densely wooded part of Snowdonia. Though fine deciduous trees still line the river gorges, most of the woodland is coniferous, planted by the Forestry Commission in the years following the First World War.
Betws-y-Coed lies just within the eastern boundary of the Snowdonia National Park and is a good centre from which to explore.

**A staging post** – The earliest bridge at Betws-y-Coed is **Pont-y-Pair** (Bridge of the Cauldron), firmly anchored in great outcrops of rock in the bed of the Llugwy, with total of 11 arches. It was built in two stages – the first supposedly dating from the late 15C – and the two sections are slightly out of alignment with each other. In 1815 **Thomas Telford** bridged the Conwy at Betws, thus shortening by several miles the recently established turnpike route carrying the Irish mails between London and Holyhead. The great engineer's handsome cast-iron structure, among the first of its kind to be built and inevitably named after the recently won Battle of Waterloo (1815), has spandrels decorated with the emblems (rose, thistle, shamrock and leek) of the four countries which then composed the United Kingdom.

## Out and About

**Tourist Information Centre - Snowdonia National Park Visitor Centre** ⊘ – Royal Oak Stables, Betwy-y-Coed LL24 0AH ☎ 01690 710 426; Fax 01690 710 665.

**Adjacent Sights** – See Bala, Bangor, Blaenau Ffestiniog, Conwy, Llangollen, Llanrwst, Ruthin, Snowdonia.

## Where to Stay

**Pengwern**, LL24 0HF. *1.5mi/2.4km SE by A 5.* ☎ 01690 710 480. Attractive house (4 rm) of Welsh stone with fine views of the Vale of Conwy; communal dining.

**Glyntwrog House**, LL24 0SG. *0.75mi/1.2km SE by A 5.* ☎ 01690 710 930. Pleasant house (4 rm) with mature garden in woodland setting; good bedrooms with en-suite facilities.

**Henllys Old Courthouse**, Old Church Rd, LL24 0AL. ☎ 01690 710 534. Former Magistrates' Court and Police Station (10 rm), with cells converted into bedrooms.

**Bryn Bella**, Llanrwst Rd, LL24 0HD. *1mi/1.6km N by A 5 and A 470.* ☎ 01690 710 627. Simple, good value accommodation (5 rm); good views of the Vale of Conwy.

**Tan-y-Foel Country House**, LL26 0RE. *4mi/6.4km E by A 5 and A 470; on Nebo Rd.* ☎ 01690 710 507; Fax 01690 710 681. Country house (7 rm), in peaceful location with fine views, offering stylish comfort, individual atmosphere and good cuisine.

From here north-westwards the old turnpike road has become the village's main street, lined on one side with villas and hotels. The grandest of the hotels, the *Royal Oak*, preserves in its vestibule the original inn sign painted by the Birmingham artist **David Cox** (1783-1859) who visited Betws every autumn in the 1840s and 1850s and was largely responsible for popularising the place among fellow-artists and their followers.

Cox would have come here by coach, but it was the arrival of the railway in 1868 that made the village accessible to large numbers of people. Exceptionally among Welsh rural railways, the line still exists, its infrequent trains almost empty in winter, but crowded in summer with visitors exploring the rugged valley of the Lledr or on their way to the slate town of Blaenau Ffestiniog.

## SIGHTS

**Church of St Michael** ⊘ – The name Betws-y-Coed signifies "bead-house (or prayer-house) in the woods" and this little 14C-15C church may be the successor to the original "bead-house". It found itself isolated from the rest of the village when the railway was built, and in 1873 was replaced by **St Mary's Church**, a far more imposing structure in sandstone, Cornish serpentine and dark local stone in a central position on the main road through the village.

St Michael's is now used only occasionally but, with its rows of pews facing the pulpit rather than the altar, it remains a rare example of an Anglican place of worship unaffected by the High Church aspirations of the mid-19C. In the chancel is the effigy of Gruffudd ap Dafydd Goch, a knight who served with the Black Prince.

The graveyard flanks the River Conwy, spanned nearby by an elegant little suspension footbridge, seemingly Victorian in character, but in fact dating from the 1930s.

**Conwy Valley Railway Museum** ⊘ – A collection of mostly local railway souvenirs is housed in the museum but the main attraction is the miniature railway whose steam locomotives haul trainloads of excited children around the old goods yard of the railway station.

**Betws-y-Coed Motor Museum** ⊘ – Among the stars in this small private collection of vintage and thoroughbred cars is an immaculate black Bugatti of 1934, an Art Deco icon of an automobile hidden for years in a Dunkirk shed after its Belgian owner had fled the German advance in 1940.

## EXCURSIONS

**Miners' Bridge** – *1mi/1.5km W of Betws-y-Coed by A 5.* Well-worn paths lead through the meadows and woods to this steeply inclined, gangway-like structure which crosses the river on the line of the Roman road known as Sarn Helen.

**Swallow Falls** ⊘ – *2mi/3km W of Betws-y-Coed by A 5.* Hemmed in by steep valley walls clad in beech and oak, the Llugwy makes a fine show of foaming over a series of rocky falls, for long the favourite excursion for visitors to Betws.

**Cae'n-y-Coed** – *2mi/3km W of Betws-y-Coed by A 5; 0.25mi/400m W of Swallow Falls.* Cae'n-y-Coed forms a "Forest Garden", with an arboretum of forestry species from around the world; it is part of the **Gwydir Forest Park** (17 915 acres/7 250ha), which is managed by the Forestry Commission with recreation very much in mind; there is a network of footpaths and cycle trails some of which lead to the little lakes studding the uplands.

**Ugly House (Tŷ Hyll)** ⊙ – *2.5mi/4km W of Betws-y-Coed by A 5.* Overlooking the bridge carrying Telford's highway over the Llugwy, this single-storey cottage built in Cyclopian blocks of stone is popularly supposed to date from the 16C but is much more likely to be one of a series of toll-houses built along the turnpike road in the early 19C. Restored and enhanced by the garden, it is furnished in the style of an 18C-19C Welsh cottage and tells the history of the Snowdonia Society.

**Lledr Valley** – *S and W of Betws-y-Coed by A 470.* Followed by both main road and railway, the valley offers a spectacular transition from the ruggedly romantic scenery of wooded river gorge to expansive upland tracts dominated to the north by the great mass of Moel Siabod.

Tŷ Mawr, Bishop William Morgan's Birthplace

**Tŷ Mawr** ⊙ – *4mi/6km SW of Betws-y-Coed by A 470 and a minor road.* This modest farm dwelling set among conifer plantations up a secluded side valley is the birthplace of Bishop William Morgan (1545-1604), the first translator of the entire Bible into Welsh. A ladder stairway from the ground-floor room leads to bedrooms, in one of which are displayed examples of the Bishop's works. A bridge crosses a stream to outbuildings in which there are further displays, both on Morgan and on the National Trust's vast Ysbyty Estate.

**Dolwyddelan Castle** ⊙ – *7mi/11km SW of Betws-y-Coed by A 470.* Atop its knoll, Dolwyddelan still commands the ancient routeway crossing the high pass from Meirionnydd into the Conwy valley. It was a Welsh stronghold, probably built by Llywelyn the Great (ap Iorwerth) c 1200, and subsequently besieged and captured by Edward I in 1283. The sturdy two-storey keep is intact, though much restored in the 19C. A staircase built within the thickness of its wall leads to roof and battlements, from which there is an outstanding **panorama** of valley and upland.

**Fairy Glen** ⊙ – *1mi/1.5km S of Betws-y-Coed by A 5; 20min there and back on foot by track and steep paths.* Together with the Swallow Falls, this sentimentally named beauty spot in the rocky gorge of the Conwy was an essential destination for Victorian visitors and still retains much of its sylvan charm.

**Conwy Falls** ⊙ – *1.5mi/2.5km SE of Betws-y-Coed by A 5; 40min there and back on foot from car park on steep paths.* A turnstile gives access to the fine beech and oak woodlands fringing the Conwy, whose falls have recently been equipped with an elaborate fish pass to compensate for the disturbance to migration patterns caused by the construction of the road tunnel at the river's mouth.

**Tŷn-y-Coed Farmhouse** ⊙ – *3mi/5km S of Betws-y-Coed by A 5 and B 4406 to Penmachno; from car park at Penmachno Mill 0.5mi/1km on foot beside the river.* Occupied until 1990 by a resident who held steadfastly to traditional ways, the stone farmhouse has been preserved with all its fittings and furniture intact and offers the visitor a unique insight into life as lived by the farming community of these resolutely Welsh uplands.

**Capel Garmon Chambered Tomb** – *3mi/5km E of Betws-y-Coed on minor roads and farm track, then short walk across fields.* This long barrow is most evocatively sited where the pastures of an upland sheep farm give way to boulders, bracken and heather, with views of Snowdonia's peaks ranged in line to the west. The barrow is similar to those of South Wales and the Cotswolds, with "horns" protecting a dummy entrance. The chamber has a central hall with a horseshoe-shaped compartment on either side.

# BLAENAU FFESTINIOG ★

Gwynedd – Population 5 349
Michelin Atlas p 32 or Map 403 I 25
Local map p 261

No place on earth quite resembles this city of slate built into the mountains at the head of the Vale of Ffestiniog. Shining from the frequent rainfall, slate IS the landscape; here the waste from the quarries, which were the local livelihood, is formed everywhere into a glittering chaos of geometric shapes apparently about to engulf the straggling settlements which make up the town. The sombre buildings appear to be made of slate, which also serves as the material for steps, fences, and for the ornaments on sale in souvenir shops. Nowadays slate extraction employs only a fraction of its former labour force but, with two quarries providing trips into the underground world of the slate miner, Blaenau Ffestiniog has to some extent succeeded in reinventing itself as a tourist destination; it is also conveniently located in the valley between the northern and southern peaks of Snowdonia.

## HISTORICAL NOTES

The foundations for Blaenau Ffestiniog's 19C prosperity were laid 500 million years ago, when beds of blue-grey slate were thrust upwards from the floor of the Ordovician sea. Small-scale quarrying for local needs began in the 18C, but it was in the early 19C, with the construction of William Madocks' harbour at **Porthmadog** and the completion of the gravity-powered narrow-gauge **Ffestiniog Railway**, that slate production and export began to boom. Throughout the 19C the demand for roofing slates in Britain and abroad seemed insatiable; at their height, in the 1880s, the Blaenau Ffestiniog mines were producing 139 000t of dressed slate a year and employing more than 4 000 men. Railway companies competed with one another for the lucrative traffic, forcing lines through the difficult mountain terrain. As well as the reopened Ffestiniog, Blaenau still has a mainline railway connection with the outside world via a tunnel beneath the Crimea Pass (nearly 3mi/5km long); it was built by the London and North Western Railway in 1879 and links the area with the resorts of the north coast.

Industrial disputes and the familiar British problem of absentee owners, more interested in profits and dividends than in industrial innovation, led to a steady decline in the town's fortunes. The population of the straggling settlements which make up Blaenau Ffestiniog – Bethania, Glan y Pwll, Maenofferen, Manod, Rhiwbryfdir and Tan-y-grisiau – has declined from more than 12 000 at the end of the 19C to about 5 000 today, and only a handful of workers is still engaged in extracting and splitting slate in the one mine now open to visitors.

## SIGHTS

★ **Llechwedd Slate Caverns** ⊘ – Slate was found at the Llechwedd mine in 1849 and extracted until the 1970s from 16 different levels with some 250 vast chambers linked by 25mi/40km of tunnels. On the surface, visitors can explore a "**Victorian Village**", based on the old settlement of Pentre Llechwedd which somehow managed to coexist with the surface workings of the mine. As well as various shops, the *Miners' Arms* pub, a smithy and workshops, there is an exhibition **Slates to the Sea** which tells the sometimes adventurous story of the slate harbour of Porthmadog and the vessels that were built and sailed from there. One cottage, a survival from the 18C, was the home of the renowned Blind Harpist of Merioneth, David Francis (1865-1929). Also on the surface is the **Slate Mill**, with demonstrations of the seemingly simple but in fact extraordinarily dextrous skill of slate splitting. Slate is still mined here and exported to many parts of the world.

Visitors descend into the **Deep Mine** by a strange stepped vehicle running on a 3ft/900mm track at a gradient of 1:1.8, the steepest passenger railway in Britain. The train stops at Level A, but visitors descend further on foot, eventually reaching Level B, at a depth of 450ft/137m below the summit of the mountain. Here begins a tour of 10 chambers, each with a sophisticated *son et lumière* presentation of aspects of the arduous life and work of those who worked the slate in the heyday of the industry. The tour also passes through a vast lake-filled cavern.

The **Miners' Tramway**, a bone-shaking electric railway, remains on one level, but takes visitors through an equally intriguing series of caverns. Real miners demonstrate some of the wisdom and skills acquired underground and tableaux convincingly recreate the working conditions once encountered.

---

**Tourist Information Centre - Snowdonia National Park Visitor Centre** ⊘ – Unit 3, High Street, Blaenau Ffestiniog LL41 3ES ☎/Fax 01766 830 360.

**Adjacent Sights** – See Abergavenny, Brecon Beacons, Merthyr Tydfil, Newport, Tredegar, Tretower, Usk.

Slate Mine, Blaenau Ffestiniog

G Boutin/EXPLORER

## EXCURSIONS

**Ffestiniog Power Station** ⊘ – *1mi/1.5km SW of Blaenau Ffestiniog by A 469.* Like the more recent and much larger scheme at Dinorwig, this power station operates on the pumped storage principle, with water being pumped to an upper reservoir using cheap off-peak power, then being released to generate electricity when demand is greatest. Ffestiniog, completed in 1963, was Britain's first large-scale power station of this kind. The lower reservoir at **Tan y Grisiau**, close to the Ffestiniog Railway station, was made by throwing a dam (1 800ft/549m) across the River Ystradau, on the banks of which stands the power station itself, two-thirds underground but still the biggest building to be constructed in North Wales in natural stone since Edward I built Caernarfon Castle. A **visitor centre** is located on the approach to the power station.

Higher up the mountain (1 000ft/300m), the upper reservoir, **Llyn Stwlan**, with a dam 800ft/244m long, was based on a pre-existing glacial lake. Access is by means of a vertiginous roadway with several hairpin bends.

**Trawsfynydd Nuclear Power Station** ⊘ – *7mi/11km S of Blaenau Ffestiniog by A 470.* The two monumental reactor buildings loom over the lake from which they drew vast quantities of cooling water when in operation. Trawsfynydd was opened in 1965, the first and last British nuclear power station to be sited inland, and closed down in 1993 in preparation for the process of decommissioning. The lavishly equipped visitor centre remains open, as do the nature trails around the lake, which was first created in 1924 to feed a much more modest venture, the **Maentwrog hydroelectric power station**, whose operational life has recently been extended to the middle of the 21C.

# BLAENAVON
## Torfaen
Michelin Atlas p 16 or Map 403 K 28

Close to this bleak village 1 000ft/300m up on the eastern rim of the South Wales coalfield are two important sites which between them encapsulate much of the region's industrial history.

★**Blaenavon Ironworks** ⊘ – The furnaces and ancillary buildings of this impressive industrial monument are built into the hillside above the village. Production of pig-iron began here in 1789, the year that the Bastille fell, and within a few years Blaenavon was second only to the great Cyfarthfa works at Merthyr Tydfil in terms of output. In the early 19C an extraordinary tram tunnel

**Tourist Information Centre** – Blaenavon Ironworks, Blaenavon ☎ 01495 792 615.

**Adjacent Sights** – See Bala, Beddgelert, Betws-y-Coed, Llanberis, Porthmadog, Portmeirion, Snowdonia.

(1.25mi/2km), the longest in Britain, was bored through the mountain to the north to connect with the Brecon and Abergavenny Canal, enabling the iron to be barged down to the coast at Newport. It was at the Blaenavon works in the late 1870s that **Sidney Gilchrist Thomas** (1850-85) sacrificed his health in the hazardous experiments that enabled phosphoric iron ores to be easily made into steel, a process which immediately and ironically benefited Britain's industrial rivals, the United States and Germany. The short-lived Gilchrist is commemorated by an obelisk in the car park which gives access to the site on the far side of a main road.

The surviving structures of the ironworks are grouped around the open space once occupied by railway lines and the engine house which supplied the blast to the furnaces. Of the four **blast furnaces** built along the retaining wall which forms the western edge of the site, No 2 is the only survivor of the original trio built in 1788-89. One of the 19C furnaces has retained its brick lining intact; on the last day of production the men downed tools before emptying the last load of hot iron; the iron cooled slowly, thus preventing the brickwork from cracking, as was usually the case. Above are the remains of the installations where materials were prepared to be tipped into the tops of the furnaces, while in front are the **cast houses** where the molten iron was led into moulds. The **balance tower** contained a hydraulic lift to hoist materials to the upper level, while **Stack Square**, once dominated by the chimney of the engine house, is a rare and fascinating example of early industrial housing, which is being restored to illustrate various different periods and their social conditions.

**Big Pit** ⊘ – Coal was originally dug from shallow mines in the Blaenavon area to feed the local furnaces but, with the decline of ironworking, coalmining became the principal industry, the fine-quality steam coal firing ships, factories and railways around the world. Big Pit, so-called because of the exceptional size of its shaft, was sunk to its present depth (300ft/90m) in 1880. A century later it was closed but reopened in 1983 as a tourist attraction.

The mine aims to give its visitors an insight into the development of the coal industry in South Wales.

Kitting up at Big Pit

Wales Tourist Board

For most visitors the **underground tour** in the genial company of a former miner is undoubtedly the main attraction. Big Pit is a real mine, and everyone must submit to stringent regulations (no matches, battery-operated watches etc) before donning helmet, cap lamp, battery, and "self-rescuer", and entering the steel cage which lowers parties to the labyrinth of underground workings. Here the rituals, routines and hazards of a miner's working life are explained in vivid detail. The most poignant sight is perhaps the row of stalls which accommodated the mine's ponies, their names (Patch, Tiger, Bounce, Skipper) still painted on the sides of the stalls where they stayed until their working lives were over.

For those reluctant to venture underground, a gallery has been installed on the surface to explain the different methods of cutting coal. It leads up from the chaotic but in fact highly ordered jumble of structures at the pithead to the gleaming white **baths and canteen** perched on a level shelf high above. Before the baths were built in 1939, miners travelled to and from home in their filthy working clothes. The endless rows of lockers and white-tiled shower cubicles are an impressive monument to inter-war ideas of hygiene. Part of the complex contains an extensive **exhibition** on mining life and includes fine examples of the work of photographers like William Edward Jones and James Jarche of the left-wing *Daily Herald*.

From the terrace outside, the extensive **panorama** over the pithead reveals all the components of the Blaenavon landscape: the village clinging to the far slope, the scarred and pitted landforms produced by centuries of hectic industrial activity, now mostly smoothed out by recent reclamation, and the anonymous sheds of the modern industrial estate on the site of the old steelworks.

Below Big Pit is a short stretch of restored railway line, the **Pontypool and Blaenavon Railway** ⊘, on which steam trains are run by enthusiasts.

## EXCURSIONS

**Pontypool** – *6mi/10km S of Blaenavon by A 4043*. The manufacture of tinplate, previously a German monopoly, was introduced to this bustling town in 1730 by Thomas Allgood, who worked for the ironmaster John Hanbury; for many years Pontypool japanned-ware (trays, teapots) was famous. The influence of the town's ironworks was widespread; the first such establishment in America, at Sagus River in Massachusetts, used Pontypool equipment, and the imposing gates of the Governor's Mansion in Williamsburg, Virginia, were exported from here. The area's industrial and social history is recounted in the **Valley Inheritance Museum** ⊙, housed in the fine Georgian stable block of the Hanbury mansion, where outdoor performances are held in the cobbled courtyard in summer.

**Nantyglo Roundhouses** – *4mi/7km W of Blaenavon by B 4248*. These curious round towers, Britain's last castle-type fortifications, were built in 1816 as retreats for the ironmasters, who feared a workers' uprising during the industrial depression which followed the end of the Napoleonic Wars. Built of stone, the towers had fittings of iron, which included flaps for musket holes. The north tower is largely intact but cannot be entered; the south tower is partly ruined.

# BODELWYDDAN ★★
## Denbighshire
### Michelin Atlas p 33 or Map 403 J 24

Two great 19C landmarks – tall church and battlemented castle – make a decisively Victorian impact on the landscape on either side of the North Wales Expressway as it swings inland past St Asaph.

After languishing as a girls' boarding school for many years, the imposing mock-medieval castle in its parkland setting has been transformed into a wonderfully apppropriate home for a superb selection of **19C paintings from the National Portrait Gallery**. The castle's striking skyline of turrets and battlements crowns the rising ground south of the main road. Built in stages in the course of the 19C, the present edifice encases parts of an earlier 16C or early-17C house purchased c 1690 by Sir William Williams, Speaker of the House of Commons, though a house is known to have stood here as early as the mid-15C.

The architect responsible for the major part of the 19C work, carried out c 1830-44, was Joseph Aloysius Hansom, inventor of the Hansom cab. The east front is imposing, the north even more so; it has a niche with the sinister figure of Y Gŵr Hir ("Long Man") as well as a formidable arch, above which rise turrets concealing chimneys from the earlier house. Beyond the twin towers of the gatehouse a curtain wall runs west, turning the corner and leading to new buildings which form part of a hotel.

## TOUR ⊙

**Adjacent Sights** – See Bodnant Gardens, Colwyn Bay, Denbigh, Llanrwst, Rhuddlan, Rhyl, St Asaph.

**Interior** – Great ingenuity has gone into creating a sequence of interiors to complement the fascinating collection of 19C portraits, which are loosely grouped by theme. Atmosphere, rather than academic exactitude has been the aim, with furnishings (many of them select items from the Victoria and Albert Museum) and fittings chosen to give the impression of a sequence of interiors as they might have developed over the years.

The **Entrance Hall** is suffused with the romantic feeling for the Middle Ages so evident in the castle's external appearance; the walls are hung with original weapons and an extraordinary set of fake armour designed in Regency times. There are Williams family portraits and floor tiles bearing their coat of arms of crossed foxes.

A long hallway decorated in the style of the Aesthetic Movement fulfils the painter George Frederic Watts' desire to create a **Hall of Fame** for his contemporaries, with psychologically penetrating portraits of eminent personages from all fields of activity.

The **Billiard Room** has an overtly masculine, sporting atmosphere, with green baize table, leather-upholstered benches, and drawings and watercolours celebrating the life of field, turf and boxing ring.

Portraits of politically and socially progressive figures like Joseph Chamberlain and Lady Dilke dominate the **Dining Room**, where the furniture includes fine pieces by Alfred Waterhouse.

The theme of the **Library** is that of intellectual and scientific life, with pictures of Carlyle, Faraday, Macaulay and other "Victorian National Divinities".

Balancing the masculinity of the Billiard Room is the Late Regency-style **Ladies' Drawing Room** with portraits of women as well as of men, like the dandy Count d'Orsay, known for their enjoyment of female company.

With its 18C mantelpiece and mock-Jacobean stairway the **Staircase Hall** evokes something of the character of the original house.

Beyond lies the splendid vaulted space of the **Drawing Room and Sculpture Gallery** with neo-Classical busts by the Welsh sculptor Gibson.

The rooms on the first floor have extensive displays setting out the context of Victorian portraiture, with sections devoted to artists' careers, the world of art generally and photographic portraiture.

**Grounds** – In 1830-42 the parklands were enclosed by a long limestone wall, and the high brick walls of the kitchen garden were built at the same time. Around 1910 the eminent landscape architect Thomas Mawson "carried out some necessary improvements" to the gardens; more recent landscaping has respected their generally Edwardian character but added an elaborate aviary, an extensive parterre, and a maze. Beyond the southern end of the garden wall is an attractive woodland walk.

**St Margaret's Church** ⊘ – Rising in splendid isolation from the shaven lawns of its graveyard, this sumptuous edifice in pale local limestone was raised in 1860 in memory of Henry, Baron Willoughby de Broke, by his widow, Margaret, a Williams daughter from Bodelwyddan Castle. It is known as the "Marble Church" because of the lavish use of no fewer than 13 different varieties of that material in its interior. The building is the work of a pupil of Sir Charles Barry, John Gibson, who had previously helped in the design of the new House of Commons. There is no doubt about the elegance and impact of the elegant tower and steeple (202ft/62m high) but the interior seems overwhelming in its zealous striving for effect. It is seen at its most dramatic when artificially lit.

Lady Margaret had a new parish created to go with the church, and parts of Bodelwyddan have the character of a Victorian estate village. During the First World War, the area became a vast military transit camp; in 1919 it was the scene of mutinous disturbances among Canadian soldiers impatiently awaiting demobilisation but the young Canadians buried in the church's graveyard were mostly victims not of riot but of the post-war influenza epidemic which proved more lethal than the war itself.

# BODNANT GARDEN ★★
Conwy
Michelin Atlas p 33 or Map 403 I 24 – 8mi/13km S of Conwy by A 55 and A 470

Italianate terraces, a deep romantic dell and magnificent mountain views make Bodnant one of the most appealing late-19C to early-20C gardens in Britain.

The estate called Bodnod on the east bank of the Conwy valley was bought in 1874 by Henry Pochin, an industrial chemist who had made his fortune in Manchester. Pochin gave what had been a typical Georgian house its present, assertive neo-Tudor appearance, then indulged his passion for conifers, planting up the deep Dell with a variety of trees which have become the superb specimens of today. His grandson, the second Lord Aberconway, was a passionate gardener of a different kind; active here until his death in 1953 and in touch with many of the eminent plant hunters of the day, he introduced many rhododendrons, filled up the Dell with moisture-loving plants, and created the series of terraces stepping down from the house with their glorious prospect of Snowdonia. Both Henry and his son Charles were at the centre of horticultural life in Britain, serving as Presidents of the Royal Horticultural Society and in many kindred capacities. Bodnant's place at the forefront of many gardening developments has also been due to the efforts of another dynasty of plantsmen; since 1920 three generations of the Puddle family have supplied the place with its head gardeners.

## TOUR ⊘

A tour of Bodnant normally begins at the lawns around the house, then descends the west-facing terraces. These include the Rose Terrace, with a view of Snowdonia through the branches of a venerable Strawberry Tree, the Croquet Terrace, the Lily Terrace designed around two existing cedars, and the Lower Rose Terrace.

At one extremity of the Canal Terrace is an open-air stage bounded by clipped yews, at the other the **Pin Mill**, brought here from Gloucestershire in 1938 to make one of the most delightful garden buildings imaginable.

**Adjacent Sights** – See Bodelwyddan, Colwyn Bay, Conwy, Llandudno, Llanrwst.

Bodnant Garden

A number of paths, accompanied by a fast-rushing stream, lead steeply downwards into the **Dell**, the deep ravine cut by the little River Hiraethlyn. At the lower end is the rather grand, Italianate Old Mill, while upstream is the calm millpond from which the river escapes in a crashing cascade whose sound fills the valley. From the luxuriant understorey rise the specimen conifers planted by Henry Pochin, many of them well over 100ft/30m tall. Their crowns, and the Dell itself, can be admired from a path running along the upper rim of the valley.

From the millpond a steep path leads up another tiny tributary stream to "The Poem", Pochin's intended mausoleum.

The route continues through extensive shrub borders via a glimpse of parkland to the Round Garden and thence to Bodnant's most famous single feature, the **Laburnum Arch.** This curving tunnel (180ft/55m long) is an almost overwhelming spectacle in late May and early June, when countless golden racemes hang from the metal frames erected a century and more ago.

# BRECON ★

(Aberhonddu) Powys – Population 7 523
Michelin Atlas pp 16 and 25 or Map 403 J 28

Brecon's strategic location, midway on the Roman road west from Gloucester to Carmarthen, was appreciated by the Normans, who built a castle overlooking the confluence of the Usk with the Honddu in 1093. The borough which grew up under the protection of Bernard de Neufmarche's stronghold was defended by 10 towers and four gateways, long since demolished, but the intricate and fascinating street layout of medieval Brecon remains intact. Many of its older houses were rebuilt or given fashionable Georgian façades in the 18C and 19C as the town consolidated its position as the focal point of much of southern mid-Wales.

Brecon remains an important agricultural centre and has a significant military presence too. For much of the year its streets are trodden by tourists, pausing here on the way west – the Romans' route has become the modern highway (A 40) – or using the town as their base for exploration of the Brecon Beacons National Park, whose highest point, Pen-y-Fan, rises half concealed among lesser summits a short distance to the south.

**The Bulwark** – A statue of Wellington stands in this funnel-shaped space which is overlooked, like much of the rest of the town, by the tower (90ft/28m high) of St Mary's Church. It is known as the Buckingham Tower after its builder, the Duke of Buckingham, born in Brecon in 1477; built in red sandstone c 1510-20 and boldly detailed in Perpendicular style, it barely seems to acknowledge the modest and much-restored 14C church to which it is attached.

## Out and About

**Tourist Information Centre** – Cattle Market Car Park, Brecon LD3 9DA ☎ 01874 622 485; Fax 01874 625 256.

**Craft Centre** – **Beacons Crafts** ⊘ *(Bethel Square)* is a cooperative shop formed by local craft producers displaying the selected work of 50 makers.

**Adjacent Sights** – See Brecon Beacons, Builth Wells, Hay-on-Wye, Llandovery, Llanthony Priory, Llanwrtyd Wells, Merthyr Tydfil, Tretower.

## Where to Stay

**Cantre Selyf**, 5 Lion St, Brecon, LD3 7AU. ☎ 01874 622 9044; Fax 01874 622 315. 17C town house (3 rm) with Georgian features and large walled garden; close to museums and famous National Park.

The Bulwark has some of Brecon's grandest Georgian structures, among them the *Wellington Hotel* and the *Brecon & Radnor Express* building. The narrow streets and lanes leading off The Bulwark are full of interest, and demonstrate the town's good fortune in having escaped large-scale redevelopment.

As well as the 18C-19C Guildhall in High Street Inferior, there is the birthplace of the actress Sarah Siddons, numerous narrow-fronted buildings whose Georgian façades conceal much earlier structures, and a few unspoilt Victorian and even Georgian shopfronts.

★**Brecon Cathedral** ⊘ – The "most splendid and dignified church in mid-Wales" (Richard Haslam), once the centrepiece of a Benedictine priory, became the town's parish church at the Dissolution and was elevated to cathedral status in 1923. It stands in well-tree'd surroundings above the Honddu at a discreet distance from the town centre and retains a number of its conventual buildings, one of which, a 16C tithe barn, has been converted into an attractive **heritage centre** ⊘, housing an exhibition which traces the history of the priory and the life of the medieval monks.

The Normans erected a church on this site in 1093, possibly as a replacement for an earlier Celtic place of worship, but the present, somewhat plain building with its sturdy tower was constructed in two main phases, the east end in the 13C in Early English style, the nave and chapels in the 14C in Decorated style. Restoration, including construction of the chancel vaulting, was carried out in the 19C by Sir George Gilbert Scott.

**Interior** – An unbroken vista leads down the full length of the church to the elegant Early English chancel with its outstanding group of five lancet windows. The oldest object in the Cathedral is the large Norman font, carved with grotesque masks and weird beasts. The 30 sockets of a cresset stone, the largest in Britain, once held oil for lighting the church. St Keyne's Chapel has a fine screen and an effigy which may represent the chapel's founder, while the Harvard Chapel holds regimental banners and memorials. There are more fine effigies in the south aisle – one in wood of a 16C lady, another in alabaster of a 17C King's Justice, Sir David Williams, together with his wife.

**Brecknock Museum** ⊘ – The East Gate no longer guards the rise leading to the Bulwark, but this approach to the town centre is still marked by buildings of substance like the splendid mansion of Watton Mount, mid-19C in date but conservatively Georgian in style. Opposite is the fine Doric portico of the old Shire Hall, completed in 1843 and, since the 1970s, the home of the museum collections of the old County of Breconshire. The single most outstanding feature is the Assize Court, in continuous use until 1971 and preserved intact, the power of the law expressed by the superb exedra of Ionic columns as well as by the gaily patterned truncheons on display. There are many objects from the Roman fort of Y Gaer *(3mi/5km W)* and a justly famous, elaborately carved Celtic cross from Neuadd Siarman, Llanynys. The artificial island *(crannog)* on Llangorse Lake inhabited in the 9C-10C is explained, partly with the help of a blackened canoe hewn from the trunk of an oak. Well-conceived displays evoke the traditional life of the countryside as well as its natural history, and there is a large collection of lovespoons. The development of town life in the area is explored by an interactive video projection of 450 old photographs.

**South Wales Borderers and Monmouthshire Regimental Museum** ⊘ – The south-eastern approach to the town centre is formed by The Watton, a long, straight and tree-lined street dominated by an imposing mock-Gothic keep, part of the extensive 19C barracks testifying to Brecon's long association with the army. Next to the keep is the red-brick arsenal of 1805, housing this exceptionally interesting military museum which deals exhaustively with all aspects of the history of these regiments, now united as the Royal Regiment of Wales. The 24th Foot (the South Wales Borderers) covered themselves with glory in the Zulu War of 1879, winning no fewer than 11 Victoria Crosses at the battle of Rorke's Drift. The centrepiece of the museum, not surprisingly, is the Zulu War Room, where, as well as relics like the tattered Union flag which flew above the mission station at Rorke's Drift, there are displays which give an excellent account of the context of the struggle.

**Brecon Castle** – The castle, described as late as 1530 as "very large, strong and well maintained", is now a ruin, though its Great Hall survives as part of the *Castle Hotel*. To the north of the modern road cutting through the castle precinct is the original motte, topped by the Ely Tower, named after the Bishop of Ely imprisoned here during the reign of Richard III (1483-85).

*With this guide,*
*use the appropriate Michelin Maps (scale 1 : 400 000)*
*The common symbols make route planning easier*

# BRECON BEACONS★★

Carmarthenshire, Powys, Rhondda Cynon Taff, Merthyr Tydfil, Monmouthshire
Michelin Atlas pp 15 and 16 or Map 403 J 28

The Brecon Beacons stretch from east to west, a glorious tract of rolling mountain country (40mi/65km) between the crowded industrial valleys of the south and the empty uplands of mid-Wales.

The area, which was designated a **National Park** in 1957, consists of four main blocks, all with the same geological foundation of Old Red Sandstone. The core is formed by the **Brecon Beacons** themselves, which include the highest peaks in South Wales, Corn Du (2 863ft/873m) and Pen-y-Fan (2 906ft/886m), looking northward to the fertile valley of the Usk. To the west is **Fforest Fawr**, a vast rolling upland giving way in the south to fascinating limestone country around Ystradfellte, with its crags and caves, wooded ravines and waterfalls. The **Black Mountain** forms the westernmost block, its lonely centrepiece the remote crags of the Carmarthen Vans (2 460ft/750m). The eastern heights, confusingly named the **Black Mountains**, consist of a spectacular escarpment overlooking the valley of the Wye, behind which long, winding valleys drain southwards towards Abergavenny and the Usk.

Sheep and cattle raising remain the principal land uses of the Park. Grazing by sheep has converted much of the moorland of heather and bilberry into great sweeps of coarse grasses, though the more inaccessible slopes carry a fascinating flora which in places includes rare arctic alpines like purple saxifrage. Afforestation with conifers has compromised the otherwise open appearance of the mountains in many places, and dark plantations of spruce often enfold the many reservoirs, which benefit from the high rainfall (c 100in/2 500mm) to supply the urban areas to the south with water.

The proximity of the Brecon Beacons to large centres of population has made the National Park a favourite destination with day visitors, who outnumber tourists by about two to one. The more popular and accessible places are often crowded, but it is easy to find other spots where relative solitude can be enjoyed.

## EASTERN SECTION – *East of the road (A 470) between Brecon and Merthyr Tydfil*

**★★Pen-y-Fan** – The dramatic north-facing escarpment of the Brecon Beacons is revealed in all its majesty to those who have made the climb to the top of South Wales' highest mountain. The precipitous upper slopes, the deep embayments or cwms, and the U-shaped valleys are the work of glaciers, one of which also created the perfect shape of **Llyn Cwm Llwch**, the lake at the foot of Pen-y-Fan. The structure and colour of the underlying Old Red Sandstone, formed in desert conditions in Devonian times some 395-345 million years ago, gives a delicately ribbed pattern to the steep escarpment. A particularly resistant combination of sandstone and conglomerate caps the summit of both Pen-y-Fan and its near neighbour, Corn Du, creating the effect of paving. Bronze Age people built burial cairns, recently excavated and restored, on both peaks.

The popularity of the path from near *Storey Arms* has led to severe erosion of the moorland grasses, which has been made good in places by the efforts of the National Trust. High above Llyn Cwm Llwch at 2 230ft/701m, an obelisk commemorates Tommy Jones. This unfortunate five-year-old became separated from his family in 1900, while walking in the valley far below, and somehow made his way to this desolate place, where his body was found a month later.

Pen-y-Fan, Brecon Beacons

**Llangorse Lake** – This is the largest natural lake (over 1mi/1.5km long) in South Wales, fringed with reedbeds, alders and willows, and an important habitat for wetland birds. It also attracts campers and caravanners and all kinds of water activities not always compatible with its wildlife. The lake is the site of a fascinating artificial island *(crannog)*, constructed around the 9C AD from layers of stone, earth and brushwood held in place by oaken palisades. The crannog was one of the residences of the king of the Welsh kingdom of Brycheiniog, and was destroyed in the Saxon attack of AD 916. Brecon Museum *(see p 101)* has displays on this fascinating settlement and its history.

**Castell Dinas** – The very fragmentary ruins of this 12C stronghold, which was the highest castle in Great Britain (alt 1 476ft/450m), are contained within the more impressive remains of an Iron-Age **hillfort** with multiple ramparts. The car park is a starting point for a steep walk on the pathways leading to the boggy summit of the Black Mountains, Waun Fach (2 660ft/811m), or, more interestingly, along the spectacular escarpment which looks towards the hills of Radnorshire across the exhilaratingly broad valley of the Wye.

**Talgarth** – This tiny market town, pleasantly Victorian in character, lies on the old routeways between the valleys of the Wye and the Usk. In the churchyard is the tomb of the remarkable **Howel Harris** (1714-73), a charismatic leader of the 18C Methodist Revival who aimed "to agitate the soul to its very foundations". Among his many and varied activities, Harris founded a Utopian community in the nearby hamlet of **Trefeca**; the college which continued his teaching has a small **museum** ⊘ devoted to him.

**Patricio Church** ⊘ – High up on a hillside in a remote valley in the Black Mountains is this secluded little church, dedicated to St Issui, whose shrine was probably housed in the west chapel. The church, which is also known as Patrishow, is of various periods, and was carefully restored at the beginning of the 20C. It has a font (pre-1066) but its great treasure is the beautifully carved **rood screen** and loft made of Irish oak in c 1500. A crude figure of Death with an hourglass, scythe and spade is painted on the west wall of the nave.

★**Penyclawdd Court** ⊘ – *5mi/8km N of Abergavenny near Llanfihangel Crucorney; from A 465 turn left opposite sign to Pantygelli onto minor road and follow signs for Penyclawdd Farm.* This beautifully restored Tudor manor house was built in 1480, extended in the early 17C and passed through several families, including the Cecils and the Herberts (the family of the poet George Herbert). Interesting features include a rare 17C door lintel (most were removed as the average height increased) and a pre-spring bed, made with frame and tautened rope (hence the expression "sleep tight"). A Norman motte with wet and dry moats rises in the grounds; recent herb and knot gardens and a maze have been planted and a terraced garden in Tudor style is planned.

## Out and About

**Tourist Information Centre** – Beaufort Chambers, Beaufort Street, Crickhowell NP8 1AA ☎ 01873 812 105.

**Information Centres** – The best starting point for exploring the Brecon Beacons National Park is the **Brecon Beacons Mountain Centre** *(see below)*, which provides a wide range of information and other facilities. The **Garwnant Forestry Commission Visitor Centre** *(see below)* conducts wayfaring and orienteering courses; there are woodland walks to suit all capacities and cycle routes marked out in the surrounding woodland, as well as special trails for the disabled. The **Craig-y-Nos Country Park** *(see below)* offers lakes, riverside walks, mature woodland and meadows.
Short residential courses providing detailed study and exploration of the Beacons are organised by the **Danywenallt Study Centre**.

**Beacons Bus** ⊘ – The Beacons Bus service, which enables visitors to leave their cars behind and thus avoid congestion in the park, operates in summer on Sundays and bank holidays, between Brecon and other points both within the park and beyond its boundaries.

**Weather Conditions** – Mountain walkers should bear in mind that temperatures drop rapidly as height is gained, roughly by 2 C for every 1 000ft/300m. This, combined with wind-chill, can mean that summit conditions can be unpleasantly, even dangerously, different from those which seemed so encouraging at the starting point of a climb down in the valley. All the usual precautions should be taken before setting out.

**Walking** – This is the dominant recreational activity. Good walking is provided by the foothills and ridges of the **Black Mountains** (south of Hay-on-Wye), the **Taff Trail** (between Brecon and Merthyr Tydfil), the **Usk Valley Walk** along the towpath of the Monmouthshire and Brecon Canal and the Clydach Gorge (including Gilwern). The ascent of **Pen-Y-Fan** from near *Storey Arms* on the main road (A 470) is both popular and relatively easy (climb of only some 1 650ft/500m). Longer but less frequented routes start from the Neuadd reservoir to the southeast (climb of c 3 000ft/900m) or from small parking areas at the head of narrow lanes to the north.

**Pony-trekking** – There are many centres which organise **pony-trekking** for whole or half days.

**Caving** – There are opportunities for caving in the extensive limestone systems in the south-west area of the Park.

**Brecon Mountain Railway** ⊘ – *At Dowlais, 2.5mi/4km north of Merthyr Tydfil.* The old Brecon and Merthyr Railway across the mountains of the Brecon Beacons was one of the highest, most spectacular, and least profitable in Britain. In the severe winter of 1947, a train was stuck in snow near the summit of the line for several days. All services ceased in 1964, but since 1980 a narrow-gauge line has been steadily colonising the old trackbed north from a new station at Pant, and visitors can now enjoy a round trip *(7mi/11km)* into the uplands.

**Monmouthshire and Brecon Canal** ⊘ – There are **narrowboats** for hire at Brecon, at Storehouse Bridge between Llanfrynach and Pencelli, Talybont, Llangynidr and Gilwern *(see also below)*.

**Fishing** – The Wye, Usk and Tywi are famous for their **salmon fishing**. Many reservoirs are stocked with **trout** and there is **coarse fishing** in Llangorse Lake and in the Monmouthshire and Brecon Canal.

**Water Sports** – There is **boating**, **canoeing** and **sailing** on Llangorse Lake, the River Usk and the River Wye.

**Adjacent Sights** – See Abergavenny, Blaenavon, Brecon, Hay-on-Wye, Llandeilo, Llandovery, Llanthony Priory, Merthyr Tydfil.

## Where to Eat

**Nantyffin Cider Mill Inn**, Crickhowell, NP8 1SG. *1.5mi/2.4km W of Crickhowell by A 40.* ☎/Fax 01873 810 775. Converted 16C cider mill; modern and traditional menu; local fish and game; good blackboard specials.

## Where to Stay

**Ty Croesco**, The Dardy, Crickhowell, NP8 1PU. *1.5mi/2.4km W of Crickhowell by A 4077, off Llangynidr rd.* ☎/Fax 01873 810 573. Part of a Victorian workhouse (8 rm) built of Welsh stone, on quiet hillside above the Monmouth and Brecon Canal; spectacular views.

**Glangwryney Court**, Crickhowell, NP8 1ES. *2mi/3.2km S of Crickhowell by A 40.* ☎ 01873 811 288. Family-owned Georgian house (5 rm), spacious garden and personal service.

**Bear**, High St, Crickhowell, NP8 1BW. ☎ 01873 810 408; Fax 01873 811 696. Part 15C former coaching inn (27 rm), well established and friendly, with individually furnished bedrooms.

**Crickhowell** – *6mi/10km W of Abergavenny by A 40.* Despite its small size, Crickhowell has a confident air of urbanity about it; in 1804 Richard Fenton called it "the most cheerful-looking town I ever saw". The townscape has changed little since, and Crickhowell is popular both with residents and with tourists using it as a base from which to explore the Brecon Beacons National Park. The name of the town derives from Crug Hywel, the stronghold of **Hywel Dda** *(see p 68)*, which was built on Table Mountain, dominating the town.

There are two focal points, **Crickhowell Bridge**, one of the finest of several bridges along the Usk, and the **Square**, with a fountain and *The Bear*, a Georgian coaching inn. The bridge was in place in the 15C but was rebuilt in 1706 with cutwaters and, oddly, 12 arches on one side and 13 on the other. Between bridge and square runs the High Street, with good 18C-19C buildings including *The Dragon* with its Venetian window, and then Bridge Street, twisting and falling to the *Bridge End Inn*, once an octagonal toll-house. New Road, an early by-pass for through traffic, leads back north past **St Edmund's Church** (14C), much rebuilt but with fine effigies, including those of members of the Pauncefoot family, lords of Crickhowell Castle, now a few scattered ruins. Along the main road towards Brecon the gateway known as Porth Mawr still stands, though the Herbert mansion it once guarded has disappeared.

**Craig-y-Cilau** – The Carboniferous Limestone which outcrops along the southern edge of the Park also appears high above the Usk near Crickhowell in the form of a majestic amphitheatre of cliffs rising from the lush woodland below. Rare limestone plants abound, including unusual varieties of whitebeam.

Fissures in the cliff face *(experienced cavers only)* lead to an underground network still being explored; its total length has been estimated at 60mi/100km.

**Clydach Gorge** – *3.5mi/6km W of Abergavenny by A 465 (Heads of the Valleys Road) and then along minor roads (signs).* This deep, narrow valley provides a vivid picture of the course of industrial history over some 200 years. Iron-making was a going concern here in the 17C and grew rapidly, as technology advanced and demand increased, but declined in the 19C, unable to overcome the difficulties of this steep terrain; limestone however continued to be quarried. Various trails have been marked out from the Clydach Gorge picnic area, taking in some of the industrial remains, including the Clydach ironworks and lime works, the 19C Llammarch tramroad and the 18C aqueduct of the Brecknock and Abergavenny Canal *(Some steep ascents and descents; visitors should keep to the public footpaths as some areas are potentially dangerous).*

Monmouthshire and Brecon Canal

D Hughes/Robert Harding

**Monmouthshire and Brecon Canal** – The Monmouthshire and Brecon Canal (33mi/53km long), the only British canal entirely within a National Park, runs southeast from its terminal in Brecon to just south of Pontypool. It was completed in 1812 and connected the interior with the coast at Newport and served local collieries, ironworks and limestone quarries, as well as carrying agricultural produce and passengers. Like most such enterprises, its period of prosperity was short. From the mid-19C onwards, its trade went to the railways, and the last commercial toll was collected in 1933.

A new lease of life began in the 1960s when the canal's exceptional recreational potential was realised. A contour canal, winding its way along the lower slopes of the enchanting valley of the Usk and flanking the dramatic scenery of the Brecon Beacons, it has only six locks in its entire length and one section of 22mi/35km is entirely lock-free. Engineering features include lift bridges, the Talybont tunnel and the fine Brynich aqueduct over the Usk. Kingfishers breed on the canal's banks and its waters are well stocked with fish. Some of the old horse-powered tramroads which linked the canal to mines and quarries are now pleasantly graded footpaths. Since 1983 the Monmouthshire and Brecon has been classified as a cruising canal, with narrowboats for hire at a number of locations, including Brecon.

## WESTERN SECTION – *West of the road (A 470) between Brecon and Merthyr Tydfil*

**Brecon Beacons Mountain Centre** ⊙ – *5mi/8 km SW of Brecon by A 470*. This National Park visitor centre, opened in 1966, was the first of its kind in Great Britain, and proved immensely popular from the moment of its inception. The centre stands at a height of 1 100ft/335m on **Mynydd Illtud**, a splendid upland tract with enticing views immediately to the south of the escarpments of Fforest Fawr and the Brecon Beacons themselves.

**Garwnant Forestry Commission Visitor Centre** ⊙ – *6mi/9.5km N of Merthyr Tydfil by A 470 and a long winding side road (brown signs)*. The Visitor Centre, which occupies a picturesque setting next to the Llwyn Onn Reservoir, interprets the natural world of the forests of the Brecon Beacons.

★**Ystradfellte** – *W of Merthyr Tydfil by A 465 and N by minor road. Car parks may be crowded; the pathways have been severely eroded and are potentially dangerous in places, although improvements are under way. Check locally about access to the waterfalls. The caves can be a trap for the unwary and should not be entered.*
The River Mellte flows over a series of fine **waterfalls** downstream from this tiny hamlet in the southern part of Fforest Fawr, first carving itself a miniature, delightfully wooded gorge before disappearing into the gaping maw of **Porth yr Ogof** (50ft/15m wide). This cave, a favourite with potholers, is one of the most extraordinary features of the Carboniferous Limestone country of this part of the Park, swallowing the river until, equally surprisingly, it re-emerges a short distance downstream.
The limit of the soft and permeable limestone and the presence of the harder rocks of the Millstone Grit is marked by the first of the Mellte waterfalls, **Sgwd Clun-gwyn** (White Meadow Fall) about 0.75mi/1km downstream from the river's resurgence. Then come **Sgwd Clun-gwyn Isaf** (Lower White Meadow Fall) and **Sgwd y Pannwr** (Fuller's Fall), while on the Hepste, a tributary of the Mellte, there is **Sgwd yr Eira** (Fall of Snow), where it is possible to walk behind the curtain of water.

★**Dan-yr-Ogof Showcaves** ⊙ – *On A 4067*. The action of water on the Carboniferous Limestone overlying the Old Red Sandstone along the southern margin of the National Park has created some of the most fascinating cave formations open to the public in Britain.
In the upper valley of the River Tawe, the caves were discovered only in 1912, when the Morgan brothers from Abercrave boldly made their way underground, ferrying themselves across a small lake by coracle and reaching a powerful waterfall. Further exploration was carried out in the 1930s and 1960s, and today some of the more spectacular sections of this world beneath the surface has been made accessible, with ingenious lighting effects, tableaux and recorded commentaries. Among the stalactites and stalagmites in the main showcave are intriguing calcite formations like the Fingers, the Frozen Waterfall, the Flitch of Bacon, the Dagger Chamber or the hanging Curtain. In the **Cathedral showcave**, a grotesque figure is known as the Michelin Man. The **Bone Cave** is so called because of the discovery here of human skeletons, some of Bronze Age date.
Outside the caves, the scene is enlivened with a Dinosaur Park presenting an array of life-size replicas of prehistoric creatures, some of which are engaged in eating each other, while a pterodactyl leaps from a crag. There is a geological trail, a reproduction of an Iron Age farm, a museum, a picnic area, a dry-ski slope, and, in the valley below, a shire-horse centre, all helping to make the complex the most popular visitor attraction in the National Park.

**Craig-y-Nos Country Park** ⊘ – *On A 4067*. The 19C mansion house known as Craig-y-Nos (Rock of the Night) has something of a "Scottish Baronial" appearance, due not least to the extensions built at the end of the century for the celebrated Hispano-Italian singer, Adelina Patti, whose ambitions to make the place a miniature Bayreuth included the construction of a theatre. Her iron-and-glass winter garden was moved after her death to a Swansea park, while the grounds she laid out are now a country park, with a small visitor centre containing displays explaining the characteristics of the surrounding limestone country.

★**Black Mountain** – *E of Llandeilo on A 4069. Lake and ridge are accessible only on foot, from the village of Llanddeusant.* Something of the bleak character of this westernmost section of the National Park can be appreciated from the main road (A 4069) between Llangadog and Brynamman which climbs to a height of nearly 1 640ft/500m at Foel Fawr. To the northeast are the slopes leading up to **Carmarthen Fans** *(Bannau Sir Gâr)*, a great pointed ridge with near-vertical walls dropping to two lakes, Llyn y Fan Fawr and **Llyn y Fan Fach**. According to legend, a fairy maiden rising from the waters of the latter helped found a dynasty of healers which lasted from the 13C until the 19C, though she returned to the lake when her husband inadvertently broke her spell.

# BUILTH WELLS
## (Llanfair-ym-Muallt) Powys
### Michelin Atlas p 25 or Map 403 J 27

t a point where several rivers join the Wye, this little castle town in Central Wales njoyed greater strategic importance in the Middle Ages than it does today, though it emains the meeting point of several main roads and provides the site for the ountry's principal agricultural fair, the **Royal Welsh Show**. Of the spa which flourished riefly in the 19C no trace remains, though visitors still come here to enjoy the mbience of the Wye whose banks have been attractively landscaped.

**etrayal and death** – Llywelyn the Last *(ap Gruffydd)*, who in 1260 attacked and estroyed Builth Castle, came to Builth again in the winter of 1282 hoping to enlist ne support of local leaders in his struggle with the English. His ruse of reversing the noes of his horse to confuse his trackers was betrayed by the blacksmith and he was so refused refuge in the castle. Llywelyn was cut down while fleeing along the banks f the Irfon; his head was sent to Edward I and displayed on a spike at the Tower of ondon. He is commemorated by a granite monolith set among oaks in the village of ilmery *(2.5mi/4km W of Builth)*, not far from the spot where he fell.

**Tourist Information Centre** – The Groe Car Park, Builth Wells LD2 3BT ☎ 01982 553 37.

**Craft Centre** – Beside the Rive Wye in an old GWR railway station is **Erwood Station Craft Centre & Gallery** ⊘ *(6mi/8km S by A 470 and (signs) B 4567)*, displaying the work of over 50 craftspeople and artists from Wales.

**Adjacent Sights** – See Brecon, Elan Valley, Hay-on-Wye, Llandovery, Llandrindod Wells, Llanwrtyd Wells, Presteigne, Old Radnor.

**Castle** – A motte-and-bailey stronghold was erected here as early as 1098 as the Normans pushed westward into the heart of Wales but for many years its ownership remained a matter of dispute between the English King, the Welsh princes and the Marcher lords. Following its destruction by Llywelyn the Last in 1260 it was refortified by Edward I between 1277 and 1283 on the same concentric plan as his castles in North Wales. Little masonry remains above ground today, and the main function of the massive earthworks rising up above the town's main street is as a panoramic viewpoint revealing Builth in its setting of river valley and surrounding hills.

*This guide, which is revised regularly, incorporates tourist information provided at the time of going to press Changes are however inevitable owing to improved facilities and fluctuations in the cost of living*

# CAERLEON ROMAN FORTRESS ★★
## Newport
Michelin Atlas p 16 or Map 403 L 29

Together with the other legionary fortresses at Chester (Deva) and Wroxeter (Viroce nium), Caerleon (Isca) controlled the entire system of forts and highways by which the tribes of Wales were held in subjection. Substantial remains of amphitheatre, baths, barracks, and fortress walls testify to the imprint left on Wales by the centuries of Roman occupation, and, even though partly obscured by the later development of the little town of Caerleon, this is one of the most important and evocative Roman sites in Britain.

Isca was the Latinised version of the Celtic name for the River Usk on whose bank the fortress was built c AD 75 to accommodate the **II Augustan Legion**. The Legion had taken part in the invasion of Britain in AD 43 and had then marched into south-eastern Wales in order to subdue the troublesome tribe known as the Silures. Isca, which was close to the mouth of the tidal river, replaced a previous, less accessible base which had been built upstream where the town of Usk now stands. The earth banks which formed the first defences were crowned with a timber palisade, and the first buildings laid out along the standard Roman grid pattern of streets were in timber too; rebuilding, sometimes on the grandest of scales, eventually took place in stone. By the beginning of the 4C AD Isca seems to have been finally abandoned by the Romans, though tradition has it that it evokes here that King Arthur held court.

**Tourist Information Centre** – 5 High Street, Caerleon NP6 1AE ☎/Fax 01633 422 656.

**Adjacent Sights** – See Blaenavon, Caerphilly, Caerwent, Cardiff, Castell Coch, Llancaiach Fawr, Llandaff, Newport, Tredegar, Usk.

★**Fortress Baths** ⊙ – The shell of this extraordinary complex of baths and leisure facilities survived into the Middle Ages. Some of it now lies beneath later buildings, but the long and narrow **swimming pool** (natatio) and part of the **changing room** (apodyterium) and **cold room** (frigidarium) are well displayed beneath the viewing galleries of the splendid new cover building. The audio tour emphasises the central place of the baths in Roman culture and brings to life the Latin slogan venari, lavari, ludere, ridere; occ est vivere (to hunt, to bathe, to gamble, to laugh: these make life worth living). The baths were built soon after Isca's foundation and extended for a considerable distance (360ft/110m); their great vaulted ceiling would have been as dominant in the townscape as any medieval cathedral.

★**Legionary Museum** ⊙ – The well-presented collection of sculpture, mosaics, pottery glass and other artefacts evokes life as lived in the legionary fortress. The most-prized exhibits are the 88 engraved **gemstones** found when the drain of the baths was being excavated. The collection was begun in 1850 as a reaction to the unsupervised plundering of the site of Caerleon which had gone on since the late 18C, and the modern building retains the Classical portico of the edifice erected at that time.

★**Amphitheatre** – The Legion's amphitheatre was built just outside the fortress wall c AD 90, making it contemporary with the Colosseum in Rome. Fully excavated in the 1920s, it is perhaps the finest of its kind in Britain and, although the sand of the arena has been replaced by grass, can still evoke the days when it could provide the entire garrison of 5 000 with the often gruesome spectacles to which they were accustomed. Oval in shape, it consists of massive earth banks reinforced in stone. One of the eight entrances is particularly well preserved and still has the wall of the chamber from which gladiators or wild beasts would emerge. The timber superstructure from which the spectators would have cheered or booed has of course disappeared.

**Barracks** – These are the only remains of legionary barracks in Europe which can still be seen. Located in the south-western angle of the fortress wall, they consist of the base walls of four ranges of buildings, on one of which has the original Roman masonry. Each narrow block had 12 pairs of rooms to accommodate the 80-100 legionaries whose centurion occupied the rather more generously sized rooms at the end. Next to the corner turret of the fortress is the communal latrine.

Tip of a thyrsus in a mosaic fragment, Caerleon Roman Baths

CADW: Welsh Historic Monuments – Crown Copyright

# CAERNARFON ★★★
Gwynedd – Population 9 695
Michelin Atlas p 32 or Map 403 H 24

Welsh through-and-through today, Caernarfon was founded as an English bastide, one of the walled castle towns built to secure Edward I's hold on North Wales. As much a palace as a citadel, its spectacular castle overlooking the Menai Strait was intended to be the focal point of the new principality, a fitting residence for a future Anglo-Norman Prince of Wales. Its ornamentation was correspondingly elaborate, while its grandiose walls and angular towers recall those of Imperial Constantinople.

## Out and About

**Tourist Information Centre** – Oriel Pendeitsh, Castle Street, Caernarfon LL55 1SE ☎ 01286 672 232; Fax 01286 678 209; caernarfon.tic@gwynedd.gov.uk

**Guided Tours** – **Guided tours** of Caernarfon and its district available from Turnstone Tours and Treks *(Waterloo Port)*.

**Caernarfon Audio Trail** is a spoken commentary, in one of six languages, about 63 different sights in and around the walled town of Caernarfon on hire from **Teclyn** *(24 High Street)*; the hand-held device is about the size of a mobile phone.

**Shopping** – **Palace Street** for Welsh crafts, woollens and gifts; also the **Oriel Pendeitsh Gallery** *(Castle Ditch)*. For articles made of slate visit **Inigo Jones Slate Works** *(see below)*. The workshops at **Parc Glynllifon** ⊘ *(6mi/10km S of Caernarfon by A 499)* house a variety of craftsmen and women working in a beautiful parkland setting.

**Cycle Hire** – **Don's Bikes**, 47 Pool Street; ☎ 01286 677 727; **Castle Cycles**, 33 High Street; ☎ 01286 677 400; **Cycle Hire**, 1 Slate Quay; ☎ 01286 676 804.

**Beaches** – At Victoria Dock, at Port Donorwic *(E)* and at Dinas Dinlle *(SW)*.

**Pleasure Boat Cruises** – From Quayside, Slate Quay cruises on the Menai Strait in *Queen of the Sea* and *Snowdon Queen* – Booking Office, ☎ 01286 672 772.

**Sports Facilities** – **Arfon Leisure Centre** *(Bethel Road)* provides badminton, swimming (main pool and learner pool), squash, table tennis, weight training, sauna, steam room, spa baths and sunbeds (equipment for hire); ☎ 01286 676 451.

**Arfon Tennis Centre** *(Bethel Road)* – Tennis (indoor and outdoor courts) and fitness rooms; ☎ 01286 676 945.

**Coed Helen Recreation Park** *(over the footbridge near the Castle)* – Tennis courts, bowling greens, miniature golf, children's play area and picnic area and equipment for hire.

**Walking** – In **South Road Park** *(A 487)*, a wooded park with lake and wildlife.

**Adjacent Sights** – See Anglesey, Bangor, Beaumaris, Beddgelert, Criccieth, Holyhead, Llanberis, Lleyn Peninsula, Plas Newydd, Porthmadog, Snowdonia.

## Where to Eat

**Y Bistro**, 43-45 High St, Llanberis, LL55 4EU. ☎/Fax 01286 871 278. Traditional restaurant, well established and personally run, offering quintessential Welsh cooking with menus written in Welsh.

## Where to Stay

**Ty'n Rhos Country House**, Llanddeiniolen, LL55 3AE. *5.5mi/8.5km NE by A 406 and B 4366; SW of Seion.* ☎ 01248 670 489; Fax 01248 670 079. Small personally run hotel (14 rm) in quiet location with panoramic views; comfortable bedrooms; attention to detail; accomplished Welsh cooking using local produce.

**Isfryn**, 11 Church St, LL55 1SW. ☎ /Fax 01286 675 628. Simple guesthouse (6 rm), close to the Castle and old town, providing good value and tidy accommodation.

**Pengwern**, Saron, LL54 5UH. *3.5mi/5.6km SW by A 487 on Llanfaglan rd.* ☎ /Fax 01286 831 500. Working farm with 3 surprisingly comfortable bedrooms and providing good hearty Welsh farmhouse cooking.

**Bryn Hydryd**, St David's Rd, LL55 1EL. ☎ 01286 673 840. Small, personally run guesthouse (4 rm) with attractive decor and furnishings; good value.

## CAERNARFON

The more modest fortifications of its dependent town are still intact, enclosing gridiron of streets laid out by Edward's surveyors in the last years of the 13C Perhaps more than anywhere else in Wales, historic Caernarfon evokes the lon centuries of Anglo-Welsh intimacy; in 1911, and again in 1969, it was the inevitabl choice for the revived Investiture ceremony of the Prince of Wales.

Caernarfon is the home town of Bryn Terfel, a baritone of international reputation.

## ★★★CASTLE ⊘

Castle and town occupy what was once a short peninsula between the Rivers Seior and Cadnant, the latter long since culverted. The castle, whose walls once ros directly from the estuary of the Seiont and which could easily be supplied by sea defended the southern neck of the peninsula. It had been preceded on this site b a motte-and-bailey stronghold thrown up by Hugh of Avranches, Earl of Cheste c 1090.

The castle's immense scale and unusual architectural treatment can best be appre ciated from the Slate Quay to the south or from Coed Helen on the far bank of th estuary. The great citadel's silhouette is immensely enhanced by the slim turret crowning a number of the towers, the latters' angularity emphasised by the banc of differently coloured and textured stonework. Edward's architect, almost cer tainly the Savoyard **James of St George**, appears to have striven to emulate th outline of the city of Constantinople, captured by Crusaders in 1204, no doubt ¡ an attempt to express the quasi-Imperial aspirations of his master here on th shores of what has been called the "Welsh Bosphorus".

Eleven great towers and massive curtain walls protect the castle interior which divided into two long and narrow upper and lower wards. Building started in 128 and proceeded rapidly. In less than 10 years a complete ring of walls defendin castle and town was ready, though the castle still lacked a wall and tower separating it from the town. In 1294 this allowed the rebels under Madog a Llywelyn not only to sack the town but to take the castle as well and assassinat its sheriff. After this setback, construction proceeded apace and by 1330 wa virtually complete. The castle was garrisoned until Tudor times, its design an layout being sufficiently robust to withstand the sieges of Owain Glyn Dŵr and h French allies in 1403 and 1404. Though its demolition was later ordered, its deca seems to have been slow, and was decisively brought to a halt by the restoratic put in hand by its Deputy Constable, Sir Llewelyn Turner, in the last decades of th 19C.

The castle is entered through the great twin-towered **King's Gate** facing the town ove Castle Ditch, which was once much wider. The gate, and the whole of this side of th castle, form part of the second, post-rebellion, phase of building (1296-1323

Caernarfon Castle

An array of defensive features includes a drawbridge, a series of doors and portcullises, and an inner drawbridge, as well as arrow slits and murder holes. In a canopied niche above the entrance arch is a statue of Edward II, the first "English" Prince of Wales. The inner side of the King's Gate, like a number of other features of the castle, is unfinished, a projected great hall never having been built.

Beyond the remains of the Kitchens and the Well Tower is the **Eagle Tower**, the noblest of the castle's nine towers. It was probably intended as the residence of the King's representative, Sir Otto de Grandison, and its grandeur is accentuated by a trio of tall turrets and numerous carved figures including the much-decayed eagle after which it is named. The basement contains an **exhibition** on the history of Caernarfon, while the former main chamber is used for an ambitious audio-visual presentation. The Eagle Tower was the access point for visitors arriving by sea, though the great Watergate planned to abut it was never built.

Wall-walks lead to the **Queen's Tower**, an imposing home for the military memorabilia of the **Regimental Museum of the Royal Welch Fusiliers** ⊙. The Regiment, which continues to insist on the archaic spelling of its name, served in virtually every part of the world where Britain brought force to bear, and covered itself with glory at Waterloo (1815). It formed a close relationship with the US Marines during the 1900 Boxer Rebellion, and has a Sousa march dedicated to it. The Regimental goat takes part in an annual leek-eating ceremony. Some of the most poignant exhibits are the home-made guns used by Mau Mau rebels during the 1952 Kenyan uprising.

The foundations of the once-magnificent Great Hall fill part of the Lower Ward between the Queen's Tower and the Chamberlain Tower, while all the towers along the castle's southern walls are linked by gloomy wall-passages.

The **Chamberlain Tower** contains the robing chamber used by the Prince of Wales during the 1969 Investiture as well as an exhibition on Edward I's Welsh castles.

The far end of the castle is guarded by the **Queen's Gate**, incomplete on the inside and once connected to the outside world by an immense ramp which has long since disappeared. Displays in the Northeast Tower trace the history of successive Princes of Wales.

## ADDITIONAL SIGHTS

★**Town Walls** ⊙ – Like those at Conwy, the walls of Caernarfon (over 766yd/700m long) are virtually complete. They extend around the medieval bastide on its peninsula and include eight towers and two twin-towered gateways; to landward, the East Gate is linked to the post-medieval town by a stone bridge over Greengate Street, laid out along the course of the former River Cadnant. High Street (*Stryd Fawr* in Welsh) joins East Gate to its seaward equivalent, the West Gate, now the home of the Royal Welsh Yacht Club. A short length of wall-walk is accessible near St Mary's Church, a 13C structure much renovated in the 19C and itself built into the wall.

CADW: Welsh Historic Monuments – Crown Copyright

The straight length of town wall along the quayside is particularly impressive. At the southern end of the wall, the substantial three-storey hotel is completely dwarfed by the Eagle Tower of its giant neighbour, the castle. On the outside of the tower, the arrangements made for the eventual addition of a watergate can clearly be seen.

**Bastide Town** – The architectural character of the town within the walls is now largely 19C and there are no traces of the original dwellings erected on the "burgage plots" (78ft x 59ft/24m x 18m) by the English settlers attracted here by the grant of special privileges. As in all the English bastide towns, the Welsh were unwelcome. A number of 17C and 18C structures remain and the *Black Boy Inn* in Northgate Street is claimed to date from 1522. In Welsh, Northgate Street is called Stryd Pedwar a Chwech, "Four and Six" Street, a reference to the likely charge in shillings and pence a mariner might incur for a night's entertainment when Caernarfon was a thriving port.

### Investiture of the Prince of Wales

Tradition has it that Edward II was born in the Eagle Tower of Caernarfon Castle on the occasion of the second visit of King Edward I and Queen Eleanor in 1284. The King is supposed to have promised the Welsh nobility that he would give them a prince "that was born in Wales and could speak never a word of English" . Whatever the truth of the story, the young man was proclaimed Prince of Wales in 1301, and the title has normally been given to the monarch's first-born son ever since.

The modern Investiture dates only from 1911, vigorously promoted by Lloyd George, who as MP for Caernarfon saw no disadvantage in focusing the nation's attention on his constituency. The castle became the scene of pomp and circumstance, of the kind at which late Imperial Britain so excelled, and the event was repeated in 1969, when Prince Charles was invested with the insignia of the Principality of Wales by his mother, Queen Elizabeth II, watched by a world television audience estimated to number 500 million.

The 19C Classical County Hall is a reminder of Caernarfon's long history as a regional capital but the current seat of administration is in the modern **Pencadlys Gwynedd**, a series of structures inserted with great sensitivity into the existing fabric of the old town, with a slate megalith commemorating the death of Llywelyn the Last *(ap Gruffydd)* in 1282.

A much later Welsh leader, Lloyd George, is remembered in Castle Square; his statue shows this great orator in full cry. Another statue commemorates Sir Hugh Owen, a 19C educationalist.

**Maritime Museum** ⊙ – *Quayside.* The little museum and the restored steam dredger **Seiont II** moored by the quayside evoke Caernarfon's long attachment to the sea. Town and castle were built from materials transported by boat, and for many years the sea remained a principal means of communication. A great surge in population came in the early 19C when a narrow-gauge railway linked the port with inland slate quarries. For a while Caernarfon prospered as a harbour town, even sending emigrant ships to the United States. Today's sea-borne activity is in a much lower key.

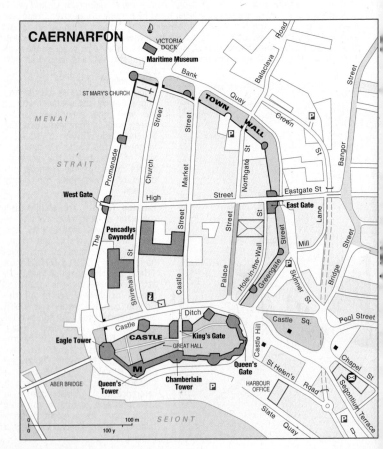

**Segontium Roman Fort** Ⓥ – *About 0.5 mi/0.8km SE of the castle.* Twelve hundred years before Edward I girdled North Wales with his chain of castles, the Romans had secured their hold on this wild land at the periphery of their Empire in a similar way.

After defeating the Ordovices in AD 77, Agricola occupied Anglesey and constructed a series of strongholds connected by new roads. Of these forts the most completely excavated is Segontium, now encircled by the outer suburbs of Caernarfon but then with easy access to the navigable estuary of the River Seiont (after which the Romans named it); nearby are the substantial remains of Hen Waliau, a quayside storehouse.

Segontium was laid out according to the standard Roman plan with symmetrically sited gates and streets; it was first defended by an earth rampart and its buildings were of timber. Later rebuilding was done with locally quarried stone and with the red sandstone from the vicinity of the great legionary fortress at Deva (Chester) which controlled the administration of this part of Britannia. Little remains above foundation level today.

Segontium was occupied until about AD 394, longer than any other Roman settlement in Wales. A few years previously, the Spanish-born adventurer Magnus Maximus had denuded it of troops in support of his bid to usurp the place of the legitimate Emperor; he appears in Welsh legend as Macsen (or Maxen) Wledig in one of the early tales of the *Mabinogion*, while his profile graces some of the coins displayed in the fort's small but fascinating **museum.**

Magnus Maximus is associated in the most tenuous of ways with Caernarfon's parish church, just to the east of the fort and even closer to the site of a temple dedicated to the worship of Mithras. 14C **St Peblig's Church** Ⓥ is named after this early Christian saint, Publicius in Latin, supposedly the offspring of the ambitious commander.

## EXCURSION

**Caernarfon Air World** Ⓥ – *8mi/13km SW.* Now grandly entitled Caernarfon Airport, the old RAF airfield of Llandwrog is laid out on the windswept levels looking south across the sea towards the heights of the Lleyn Peninsula. It was here that the RAF Mountain Rescue Service was formed. An elaborate tableau in the **Air Museum** recalls one of the Service's early exploits, the rescue of Sergeant Pilot Bickerdike in 1943. Flying through cloud at about 3 000ft/900m the unfortunate Sergeant suddenly became aware of sheep all around him. He was lucky enough to survive the ensuing crash-landing on the Snowdonia mountainside. The museum has a number of similar displays as well as several aircraft and countless models.

**Inigo Jones Slate Works** Ⓥ – *6mi/10km S of Caernarfon by A 487.* Through a video visitors learn how slate was mined, delivered by railway (the old trackbed is now a cycle track), unloaded from the wagons, cut to the required shape, polished and engraved by hand and by machine; some of these activities may be seen taking place during a tour of the workshops and visitors may try their hand at calligraphy and at engraving with a hammer and chisel. One section is devoted to the history of the firm.

# CAERPHILLY CASTLE ★★
## (Caerffili) Caerphilly
Michelin Atlas p 16 or Map 403 K 29

This spectacular late-13C castle, standing implacably in its valley setting of great defensive lakes, ranks among the most formidable strongholds of the realm. Its innovative concentric design served as a model for Edward I's castles in North Wales, but the King's triumph in the north in 1282 removed the threat Caerphilly had been intended to counter. It remains as potent a statement of military power as any in British history.

## HISTORICAL NOTES

The Romans built a stronghold here, on the road connecting their major forts at Cardiff and Y Gaer near Brecon. Nearly 1 200 years later, in 1268 **Gilbert de Clare** began work on his castle, which was swiftly completed in spite of its vast extent; Caerphilly was intended to deter **Llywelyn the Last** *(ap Gruffydd)*, the last native Prince of Wales, from any thought of interfering with Norman hegemony in this part of the country. Well aware of the threat it represented, Llywelyn seized the fortress in 1270 when it was only half finished. De Clare regained control by a trick and work proceeded apace, the castle being substantially complete a year later. Llywelyn retired north into the uplands in grim acceptance of this limit set to his ambitions. His defeat and death and the consequent subjugation of the whole country to English control meant that Caerphilly was no longer needed as a frontier fortress, though it continued as the administrative centre for the De Clare estates. It was attacked by Welsh rebels in 1295 but, although the town was burnt down, the castle held out.

# CAERPHILLY CASTLE

In the early 14C the castle's owner was Edward II's favourite, **Hugh le Despenser**, and the King himself sheltered here in the course of the campaign conducted against him by his Queen Isabella and her lover Mortimer. Later generations found the giant stronghold lacking in domestic amenity and preferred more comfortable residences elsewhere. Caerphilly decayed, its stone being plundered for the building of a nearby country house, The Van, and its walls being undermined as the unmaintained lakes dried out. In the Civil War an earthwork was built to the north-west and some deliberate demolition of the castle's defences may have taken place.

The borough of Caerphilly prospered during the Age of Coal, and it was coal money that came to the derelict castle's rescue. As well as pouring their millions into the re-creation of their castles at Cardiff and Castell Coch, the **Bute** family took Caerphilly in hand, protecting the ruins from further damage, removing the houses that had been built up against the walls and carrying out a meticulous programme of restoration. After the castle had passed into State ownership in 1950, the lakes were once more filled with water.

**Tourist Information Centre** – The Twyn, Caerphilly CF83 1JL ☎ 029 2088 0011; Fax 029 2086 0811; tourismpaul@compuserve.com

**Adjacent Sights** – See Blaenavon, Caerleon, Cardiff, Castell Coch, Llancaiach Fawr, Llandaff, Llantrisant, Newport, Rhondda, Tredegar, Museum Of Welsh Life.

## TOUR ⊘

**Outer works** – *Limited parking by the Tourist Information Centre close to the Main Outer Gate; more extensive parking W of the castle (10min walk).*

On a bend in the Rhymne River, Caerphilly is separated from Cardiff and the Glamorgan coast by the abrupt upland of Caerphilly Common. With the removal of the buildings impudently erected against its walls and with water in its lakes once more, the castle has emerged from its entanglement with its once-dependent town and can be seen in all its magnificence. The walk from the western car park enables the sheer extent of the defences to be appreciated. De Clare had been impressed by the artificial lakes at Kenilworth Castle, where he had helped in the siege of Simon de Montfort's forces in 1266. At Caerphilly he ordered some of the most elaborate water engineering of medieval times to be carried out, involving the damming of the marshy valleys of two streams to form two great lakes as well as inner and outer moats. A **hornwork**, an artificial island now known as the West Platform, was created to lend strength to the defences on the west. Beyond this to the north is the site of the **Roman fort** on which the **Civil War earthwork** was raised. No less spectacular than the lakes are the **dams** themselves; the earth platform of the southern dam is reinforced in stone, defended by a tower and a gateway, and has a line of massive buttresses on its outer face. The northern dam also has a gateway, although subsidence has caused the projecting towers to break away from the wall.

Caerphilly Castle

**Outer and Inner Wards** – The castle is approached across its outer moat via the formidable **Main Outer Gate** with its array of defensive features. It served for many years as a prison and now contains extensive displays on the castle's history.

Beyond the inner moat looping round from the south lake is the core of the castle, the concentric prototype for the royal strongholds in the north like Beaumaris. The curtain wall of the outer ward is entered via a relatively modest gatehouse, beyond which is the massive **East Inner Gatehouse** defending the Inner Ward, designed to resist an attacker who might have gained control of the rest of the castle. Its apartments were probably occupied by the castle's constable. Of the corner towers, the **South-east Tower** is the least modified, with original arrow slits and battlements; it leans at an alarming angle, probably the result of subsidence. The splendid **North-west Tower** houses further displays, but the finest structure in the Inner Ward is the **Great Hall**, remodelled by Hugh le Despenser to provide a sumptuous setting for lordly life. Reroofed by the Butes in the 19C, it has magnificent windows in the Decorated style, and one of the corbels seems to have been carved in the likeness of Edward II.

# CAERWENT★

## Monmouthshire
### Michelin Atlas p 16 or Map 403 L 29

Today Caerwent is a small and straggling village, by-passed by the main road, and centred on its 13C church set in a graveyard which looks out across the surrounding fields. All around, however, is evidence of **Venta Silurum** (Market of the Silures), the civil town established by the Romans 9mi/15km to the east of the legionary fortress at Caerleon which had a population of thousands.

The settlement (about 45 acres/c 20ha), the only one of its kind in Wales, was founded c AD 75-80 and may at first have consisted only of timber buildings laid out along the main road between Glevum (Gloucester) and Moridunum (Carmarthen). Later rebuilding took place in stone, and at the start of the 3C AD a conventional grid pattern of streets and building blocks was imposed. Venta was the local capital of the Silures, the tribal occupants of south-eastern Wales, who had caused the Romans much trouble before their final subjugation. Once Romanised, the Silures enjoyed a measure of self-government, as testified by the inscription on the plinth of a statue now placed in the **church porch**, where a small number of other finds are displayed.

**Excavations** – Several excavated sites contrast strangely with the houses and other buildings of the present modest village. Among them is the **Forum-Basilica**, once the focus of social life and administration, and, nearby, a **temple**.

> **Adjacent Sights** – See Caerleon, Caerphilly, Cardiff, Castell Coch, Chepstow, Llancaiach Fawr, Llandaff, Newport, Tintern, Museum of Welsh Life.

A row of **shops** can be seen as well as a **courtyard house**, rebuilt several times over on a progressively more lavish scale. Many of the finds are displayed in Newport Museum *(see p 217)*.

★**Roman Walls** – Caerwent's walls, among the best preserved of any Roman defences in Britain, are the most striking evidence of the Roman presence here. The most impressive section is the southern half, between the sites of the East and West Gates of the town. In places the wall rises almost to its original height and retains its facing stonework. It is punctuated by the remains of six towers.

*To plan a special itinerary :*
*– consult the Map of Touring Programmes which indicates the tourist regions, the recommended routes, the principal towns and main sights*
*– read the descriptions in the Sights section which include Excursions from the main tourist centres*
*Michelin Map no 403 and the Michelin Atlas Great Britain and Ireland indicate scenic routes, places of interest, viewpoints, rivers, forests ...*

# CARDIFF ★★★

## (Caerdydd) Cardiff – Population 279 055
### Michelin Atlas p 16 or Map 403 K 29

Cosmopolitan Cardiff is the Principality's administrative, business and cultural capital as well as the focal point of a vast urban region encompassing much of south Wales. Hardly more than a village at the start of the 19C, and thus accustomed to rapid change, the city looks forward to an increasingly dynamic role in a Europe committed to revitalisation of its regions. Its role as the capital of the Principality has been reinforced by the presence of the Welsh Assembly, first elected in 1999 and eventually to occupy its own building on the revitalised waterfront some time in the third millennium.

## HISTORICAL NOTES

Cardiff grew up under the protection of the Norman castle built on the site of the Roman fort commanding the crossing of the tidal River Taff. It remained just one among Wales' many small harbour towns and trading centres until the end of the 18C, when the iron-masters and colliery owners of the Valleys sought an outlet to the sea for their burgeon-ing enterprises. The Glamorganshire Canal opened in 1798 to Merthyr Tydfil, the Taff Vale Railway to Merthyr and the Rhondda in the 1840s. By the start of the 20C Cardiff was one of the world's great ports, exporting 10.5 million tons of coal annually, and its population had swelled from a mere thousand or two to 182 000.

## CARDIFF

| | |
|---|---|
| Capitol Centre | BZ |
| Castle Street | BZ 9 |
| Cathays Terrace | BY 10 |
| Central Square | BZ 12 |
| Church Street | BZ 14 |
| City Hall Road | BY 15 |
| College Road | BY 20 |
| Corbett Road | BY 21 |

| | |
|---|---|
| Customhouse Street | BZ 23 |
| David Street | BZ 25 |
| Duke Street | BZ 26 |
| Dumfries Place | BY 28 |
| Greyfriars Road | BY 20 |
| Guildford Street | BZ 30 |
| Hayes (The) | BZ 32 |
| High Street | BZ |
| King Edward VII Avenue | BY 36 |
| Mary Ann Street | BZ 39 |
| Moira Terrace | BZ 42 |

| | |
|---|---|
| Nantes (Boulevard de) | AY 44 |
| Penarth Road | BZ 49 |
| Queen Street | BZ |
| Queens Arcade Shopping Centre | BZ 54 |
| St Andrews Place | BY 56 |
| St David's Centre | BZ |
| St John Street | BZ 58 |
| St Mary Street | BZ |
| Station Terrace | BZ 61 |
| Stuttgarter Strasse | BY 62 |
| Working Street | BZ 67 |

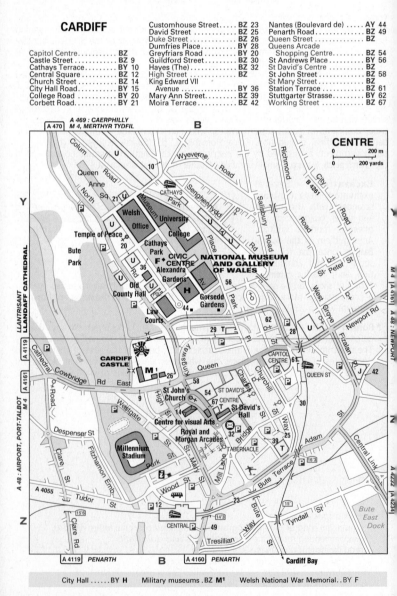

City Hall ......BY **H**     Military museums .BZ **M¹**     Welsh National War Memorial. .BY **F**

## Out and About

**Cardiff Tourist Information Centre** – 16 Wood Street, Cardiff CF10 1ES. ☎ 029 2022 7281; Fax 029 2023 9162. Also **Cardiff Bay Visitor Centre** *(see below)*.

**Sightseeing** – A good way to see the major sights is to board one of the open-top buses for the **Guide Friday Cardiff Bus Tour** ⊘, which circles the city centre, and drop off or reboard at any of the stopping places – Castle Museum, National Museum, Queen Street Station, Pier Head (Maritime Museum), Stuart Street (Techniquest), Mill Lane (shopping), Central Bus Station (TIC).

**Cardiff Card** combines free public transport with free entry to all top attractions in and around Cardiff and discounts on selected restaurants, cafés, craft and gift shops, entertainment venues, car hire and coach tours.

**Shopping** – **Craft in the Bay** ⊘ – *(Bute Street)* Shop window for the work of members of the Makers Guild of Wales – ceramics, glass, textiles, jewellery, wood and basketware. ☎ 01222 756 428.

**Entertainment** – Cardiff has a lively cultural scene, including the Welsh Proms, Welsh National Opera, the Cardiff Singer of the World competition (June), a Festival of Folk Dancing (June) and a Summer Festival (July and August) comprising comedy, street entertainment, children's events, free open-air concerts and fairground fun.

**St David's Hall is** a concert hall (1 900 seats) with bars and restaurants; home of the BBC National Orchestra of Wales (NOW). The Hayes. ☎ 01222 878 444 (Box Office).

**New Theatre** *(Park Place)*, an Edwardian theatre (900 seats), recently restored, puts on performances (three seasons per annum) by the Welsh National Opera Company, and other theatrical productions. ☎ 01222 878 889.

**Cardiff International Arena** *(Mary Ann Street)* is a concert and exhibition venue with bar and restaurant. ☎ 01222 224 488.

The **Sherman Theatre** *(Senghenydd Road)* consists of two modern theatres with programme of drama and cinema and with bar and café. ☎ 01222 230 451, 396 844.

The **Chapter Arts Centre** *(Market Road)* comprises cinemas, theatres, exhibition and workshop spaces, studio and café, presenting contemporary arts, music and culture. ☎ 01222 230 451.

The **Wales Millennium Centre**, funded by a grant from the Millennium Commission and erected on a waterfront site, will be a new arts centre, providing a home for Welsh National Opera and a stage for West End musicals from London; it will also house a cinema with a giant screen.

The **Atlantic Wharf Leisure Village** *(Hemingway Road)* is a themed leisure complex with a multi-screen cinema, bowling arena, restaurants and shops. ☎ 01222 471444.

**Sport** – **Millennium Stadium**, erected on the site of the former **Cardiff Arms Park** stadium, is the new home of the national game – Rugby football.

**Cardiff Ice Rink** *(Hayes Bridge Road)* provides skating for all as well as a venue for ice spectaculars and the home of the Cardiff Devils ice hockey team. ☎ 01222 397 198.

**Adjacent Sights** – See Barry, Caerphilly, Castell Coch, Cowbridge, Glamorgan Coast, Llancaiach Fawr, Llandaff, Llantrisant, Newport, Penarth, Museum of Welsh Life.

## Where to Eat

**Le Cassoulet**, 5 Romilly Cres, Canton, CF11 9NP. ☎/Fax 029 2022 1905. Traditional French neighbourhood restaurant. Seasonal menu; ingredients imported from Toulouse.

**Gilby's**, Old Port Rd, Culverhouse Cross, CF5 6DN. *5mi/8km W by A 4161 and A 48, off A 4050.* ☎ 029 2067 0800; Fax 029 2059 4437. Varied à la carte and good value set menu; seafood specialities; Bib gourmand for quality and moderate pricing.

**Woods Brasserie**, The Pilotage Building, Stuart St, Cardiff Bay, CF10 5BW. *1.5mi/2.4km S by Bute St.* ☎ 029 2049 2400; Fax 029 2048 1998. Modern, busy brasserie with international menu; moderate pricing and Bib gourmand quality.

**Le Gallois**, 6-10 Romilly Cres, CF11 9NR. ☎ 029 2034 1264; Fax 029 223 7911. Modern European cooking; particularly well-priced set lunch; informal ambience – the French name means the Welshman.

**Cutting Edge**, Discovery House, Scott Harbour, CF10 4PJ. ☎ 029 2047 078; Fax 029 2044 0876. Contemporary style and informal ambience offering a modern Mediterranean menu with good wines in the bay area of the city.

## Where to Stay

**Townhouse**, 70 Cathedral Rd, CF11 9LL. ☎ 029 2023 9399; Fax 029 2022 3214. Fully restored neo-Gothic townhouse (6 rm), a short walk to all the city attractions through the Victorian conservation area.

**Annedd Lon**, 157 Cathedral Rd, CF11 9PL. ☎ 029 2022 3349; Fax 029 2064 0885. Traditional B&B (6 rm), friendly and personally run, very well priced, on the north side of the city.

**Lincoln House**, 118 Cathedral Rd, CF11 9LQ. ☎ 029 2039 5558; Fax 029 2023 0537. Victorian house with spacious rooms (18 rm), a short walk from the city centre past the river with views of Bute Gardens.

**Georgian**, 179 Cathedral Rd, CF11 9PK. ☎/Fax 029 2023 2594. Good home comforts (8 rm), well priced and friendly. Just north of the city centre.

**St Mellons**, Castleton, CF3 2XR. *7mi/11km NE by A 48; between Cardiff and Newport.* ☎ 01633 680 355. Spacious garden rooms (4 rm). Well-equipped leisure facilities.

**Angel**, Castle St, CF10 1SZ. ☎ 029 2023 2633; Fax 029 2022 5980. City centre hotel (100 rm), opposite the Castle, convenient for the Millennium Stadium.

**St David's Hotel and Spa**, Havannah St, Cardiff Bay, CF10 5SD. *1.5mi/2.4km S by Bute St.* ☎ 029 2045 445; Fax 029 2048 7056. Hotel (124 rm), contemporary design; modern interior and facilities; panoramic views; comprehensive spa facilities.

This phenomenal growth was due in large part to the vision of the second **Marquess of Bute** (1793-1848) of Cardiff Castle, who invested his fortune in the construction of Bute West Dock, the beginning of the city's modern harbour. The vast wealth this "creator of modern Cardiff" passed on to the Third Marquess (1847-1900) was partly ploughed back into further harbour developments, partly spent on the extraordinary metamorphosis of Cardiff Castle into a dream palace of the Middle Ages. In the 20C the decline of coal and iron has been offset by the city's forceful adoption of other roles, in government and culture – best expressed in the gleaming white palaces of its spacious Civic Centre – and in commerce, visible every day in the teeming life of city centre streets and arcades. Cardiff's focus shifted northwards away from the port, and busy Butetown lost its dynamism, leaving the great structures of the 19C boom like the Coal Exchange and the Pierhead Building without a fitting function. By the 1980s the tide had turned; a Development Corporation is now overseeing the reintegration of the historic waterfront and city centre with an array of ambitious proposals. The catalyst for these is a barrage across the entrance to Cardiff Bay, which has stilled the great tides (40ft/12m) of the Bristol Channel and hidden the mudflats for ever beneath a freshwater lake (500 acres/200ha), a fit setting for such prestige projects as the proposed Opera House for Welsh National Opera and a purpose-built home for the National Assembly for Wales.

## CITY CENTRE

Cardiff's principal axis, lined with a variegated array of 19C and early-20C shops and other buildings, is formed by St Mary Street and High Street. Aligned on the Castle gateway, this was the principal thoroughfare of the medieval town, with long burgage plots of land running away at right angles. This ancient pattern is still apparent in the **arcades** (**BZ**) extending eastwards, which are one of the most attractive features of the city centre; like the bustling **covered market**, these date from the confident days of Victorian commercialism and are lined with specialist shops of all kinds. Both Royal and Morgan Arcades still have original 19C shopfronts.

City Centre Arcade, Cardiff

Wales Tourist Board

Arcades and lanes lead to busy pedestrianised areas centred on Hayes Island, where buses and taxis pick up their passengers by the statue of the city's 19C radical reformer John Batchelor.

Contrasting civic styles are seen in the resolutely modern **St David's Hall** (**BZ**), modelled on the New Philharmonia in Berlin, and the **Centre for Visual Arts** (**BZ**), which was built in 1882 and has been converted into a multi-purpose arts centre.

To the north is the parish **Church of St John** ⊘ (**BZ**), whose elegant Perpendicular tower (130ft/40m) remains a city centre landmark. Inside, the Lady Chapel has an unusual Jacobean monument to two brothers, Sir William Herbert and Sir John Herbert, the latter Chief Secretary to Queen Elizabeth and King James I as well as Ambassador to Denmark, Poland, and to "Henri IV, King of the Gauls". A tiny carving of a non-spherical leather ball, a modest reminder of the Welsh passion for Rugby football, can be seen in the Priory Chapel.

To the east, several city blocks have been redeveloped as the **St David's Centre**, the contemporary equivalent of the 19C arcades. Several of the exits from the Centre connect it with Queen Street, which has also been much redeveloped, although Queen's Chambers, a wonderful Venetian palazzo (c 1877), still stands by the site of the old East Gate.

Between the city centre and the east bank of the River Taff rise four white cantilevered towers suppporting the roof of the gigantic **Millennium Stadium** ⊘, an unavoidable reminder of the place of Rugby football in the life of the Welsh nation, which replaces the former stadium in **Cardiff Arms Park** (**BZ**), originally a piece of marshy land given by the Marquess of Bute for cricket and other games. The first international Rugby game (with Ireland) took place here in 1884. To see the excellent facilities and look down from the top tier of seating, take the guided tour – dressing rooms, press box, TV studio and hospitality boxes; better still go to a match to listen to the Welsh crowd singing and to hear the roar when a try is scored. If you are not a Rugby fan book a seat for one of the many sporting and musical events which take place in the arena; the turf is removed between matches.

## ★★CARDIFF CASTLE ⊘ (BZ)

Deflecting city centre traffic to east and west, the Castle's high curtain wall closes the vista up the High Street and proclaims the long-standing importance of this site, which, fortified by Romans and Normans, became in the 19C a supreme expression of Victorian wealth, confidence and imagination.

The Romans' fort guarded the point where their military road crossed the Taff on its way from the legionary station at Caerleon to Carmarthen. Part of the Roman wall (10ft/3m thick) is visible today, distinguished from later construction by a band of red stone; an impressive section can be inspected at close quarters below ground inside the castle.

The Normans' first castle – a timber structure atop a motte – was stormed by a local Welsh ruler in 1158, and was replaced at the end of the 12C by the superb 12-sided **shell keep** which still dominates the precinct today. In the 13C, **Gilbert de Clare** strengthened the defences further, giving the keep a new gatehouse and building the Black Tower. In the more peaceful conditions of the 15C, living accommodation, including a hall and the Octagon Tower, was built along the west wall of the castle.

In the late 18C the castle became the property of the Bute family, and the process began of converting the castle into a luxurious home. The First Marquess brought in Capability Brown and Henry Holland to "landscape the Grounds and modernise the Lodgings" but it was the Third Marquess and his architect **William Burges** (1827-81), with their shared passion for an idealised Middle Ages, who were responsible for the present fantastic appearance of much of the castle.

Work began in 1867 with the demolition of a row of houses built against the south wall, and continued with construction of the **Clock Tower** at the wall's south-west angle. The external appearance of the tower with its complex skyline, painted statues and heraldic shields gives a bare foretaste of the interior decoration.

**Interior** – The castle was laid out as a series of bachelor apartments with **Winter and Summer Smoking Rooms, Bedroom and Bathroom**. The theme of the extraordinarily ornate decorative scheme is the passing of time, expressed in stained glass, polychrome sculptures, murals and lavish use of colour and gilt in a profusion of detail not quickly absorbed.

A ceiling devil guards the entrance while hounds of Hell bay in the floor, and the eccentric Burges' fondness for parrots finds expression in a door handle. A motto proclaims *Omnia vincit Amor* but, as Bute married in 1872, he can have had only a short time to enjoy these bachelor amenities before the focus of Castle life shifted to the **Nursery**, with its frieze of tales from the Brothers Grimm, Hans Andersen, and the Arabian Nights.

The most startling of all Burges' creations is perhaps the **Arab Room**, built into the 16C Herbert Tower, a reverie in marble and cedarwood of Andalusian ease and luxury, with a ceiling which is a *tour de force* of geometrical complexity.

A similar ceiling graces the **Dining Room**, one of a suite of rooms in the Bute Tower begun in 1872. Vice is defeated by Virtue in the **Sitting Room**, while in the **Bedroom** great play is made with the Marquess' first name, John, and 60 types of marble adorn the **Bathroom** behind its walnut screen.

The tower is capped by the **Roof Garden** with its fountain and peristyle, an evocation of Pompeii or Provence.

In the Beauchamp Tower, elaborate homage is paid in the **Chaucer Room** to the author of the *Canterbury Tales*, while above the **Banqueting Hall** *(illustration – see p 70)* with its great timber ceiling and depictions of episodes from the castle's history is the **Library**, its reading desks equipped with central heating.

Though work continued on the Castle after Burges' death, some of his more grandiose plans like the Grand Entrance Hall were never completed. His whimsical designs for the endearing creatures that gaze down from the **Animal Wall** running along Castle Street were. however, carried out. The wall leads to the lodge to **Bute Park** (**BY**), the Butes' private preserve until 1947.

Bute Park, now part of Cardiff's system of parks and open spaces, the most extensive of any city centre outside London, offers the best view of the castle's romantically medieval skyline of towers and turrets, chimneys and steeples created by Burges and his munificent patron.

The Castle houses two **military museums** (**BZ M¹**) with well-presented displays on the history of the Welch Regiment, founded in 1719, and of the 1st The Queen's Dragoon Guards.

City Hall, Cardiff

# ★CIVIC CENTRE (BY)

The broad avenues, formal layout and grandiose public buildings of Cardiff's Civic Centre constitute an example of Beaux Arts planning more characteristic of Washington DC or Continental capitals than of Great Britain. As the city expanded rapidly in the latter part of the 19C the need became pressing for both open space and for new accommodation for administrative, civic and cultural functions.

The principal attraction for tourists is the splendidly refurbished **National Museum** (**BY**) but the whole precinct is worth exploring as a unique example of late-19C urban design.

**Cathays Park** (**BY**), just to the north-east of the castle, belonged to the Bute family who had laid out a central carriage drive through it, the forerunner of today's King Edward VII Avenue. The park was acquired by the City Council in 1898, and for nearly a century has been slowly filling up with structures designed to maintain the overall harmony of the site, nearly all of them in gleaming white Portland stone.

The overall impression, however, is still that of a park-like precinct with broad roadways, numerous trees, extensive gardens and an array of dignified street furniture, including much sculpture. A wide green space, graced with a *Gorsedd* circle, links the southern part of the precinct to the city centre. From it, that famous North Welshman, Lloyd George, seems to be shaking his fist at the National Museum.

The **City Hall** (**BY H**), less restrained in its design than the Museum, was completed in 1906 and its blend of Baroque more than adequately expresses the pride of a city growing in wealth and confidence. Fierce red dragons on pylons guard the approach, and another much bigger dragon perches on the dome, which itself is upstaged by the elaborately ornamented **clock tower** (194ft/59m high). Welsh heroes in marble grace the stairs, while the Council Chamber rises high into the dome.

The **Law Courts** (**BY**), built in 1904, just to the west of City Hall, play in a minor key, compared to their flamboyant neighbour, and begin a run of buildings along King Edward VII Avenue. A neat little Classical pavilion of 1903/4 houses the University of Wales Registry. **Old County Hall** (**BY**) (1912) has an immensely imperious portico with broad steps and coupled Corinthian columns, while the former Technical College of 1916 is an exercise in severe neo-Grecian style. The **Welsh National Temple of Peace** (**BY**) in the stripped Classical style of the period was completed in 1938 and has an imposing hall in dove-grey marble and a crypt with a Book of Remembrance. The seat of central government in Wales is the **Welsh Office** (**BY**) of 1938, a plain building ornamented with the coats of arms of the then counties and vastly extended to the north by the less harmonious Crown Offices of 1980.

Wales Tourist Board

The spaciousness of the Civic Centre's layout is enhanced by the immaculately maintained flower beds and ornamental trees of **Alexandra Gardens** (**BY**), whose centrepiece is the **Welsh National War Memorial** (**BY F**). This temple-like structure, open to the sky, with its inscriptions in both Welsh and English, was erected in 1928 and adapted in 1949 to honour the dead of the Second World War.

To the east of the Gardens is the long and architecturally somewhat confused façade of **University College** (**BY**).

## ★★★NATIONAL MUSEUM AND GALLERY ⊘ (BY)

The foundation stone of this great national institution occupying the south-eastern corner of Cathays Park was laid in 1912. In gleaming white Portland stone like the other buildings of the Civic Centre, with a dome and with the words *AMGUEDDFA GENEDLAETHOL CYMRU* proudly inscribed above its entrance portal, it is a monumental structure, entirely worthy of the high purpose spelled out for it by its founders "to teach the world about Wales and to teach the Welsh people about their own Fatherland". Of the eight branches of the National Museum, this is by far the most important, a treasure house of art and archaeology, science and natural history, with a reach, particularly in its wonderful painting collections, which goes far beyond the borders of the Principality. A major programme of refurbishment and extension, begun in 1989, has been carried to a triumphant conclusion, not only giving much-needed extra space but enhancing the visitor's appreciation of the grandeur of the calm and dignified interior.

**Main Hall** – Steps of Cornish granite lead into this superlative space, rising 85ft/26m from the extensive marble floor to the inside of the dome. Staircases at either end, lit by secondary domes, lead to the first-floor balconies, which in turn give on to the galleries housing the art collection. Facing the entrance is the figure of an 18C drummer boy, part of the city's Boer War memorial, while an array of museum shops is sited discreetly behind columns and pilasters. A side door near the eastern stairway leads to a two-storey gallery with botanical displays.

★★**Evolution of Wales** – Most of the Museum's ground-floor space is devoted to highly effective, state-of-the-art displays which evoke Wales' 4 600 million-year journey through time, from its original position south of the Equator to its present location. Geological processes are brought vividly to life by means of film and video presentations, while mineral specimens, far from lying inertly in cases, are revealed in all their glittering beauty and intrinsic fascination. Complex and convincing simulations portray ancient landscapes like the Carboniferous forest, basis of the country's former coal wealth, or the Triassic desert with its dinosaur denizens. The universe begins with an appropriately Big Bang, while volcanoes roar and splutter to an audience sitting on a (cool) lava flow, and a mammoth and its calf lumber ponderously around the mouth of an Ice Age cavern. The final gallery presents a scintillating selection of life forms and minerals illustrating the glorious diversity of the natural world, while the variety of Welsh habitats and scenery are the subject of further displays and elaborate simulations; a winter wind blasts through an oakwood, while shoreline and bird-rich cliff are dominated by a wide-jawed basking shark. Beyond, a dimly-lit sea-cavern echoes to the mysterious song of the whales.

★**Pottery and Porcelain** – The museum's collection of 18C porcelain is one of the richest in the world. Work from the great factories of continental Europe, Sèvres, Höchst, Vienna, and above all Meissen, is displayed on the north balcony, complemented by fine pieces from Chelsea, Derby and Worcester opposite. The Joseph Gallery gives a particularly full and fascinating account of the development of ceramics between 1764 and 1922 in the South Wales factories of Swansea, Nantgawr, Glamorgan and Llanelli. One landing showcase has a single superb Vienna bowl (c 1815-17) with colours of great luminosity; another, by contrast, has examples of modern work. More ceramics, along with other decorative art works, are displayed throughout the splendidly refurbished picture galleries in a remarkably effective way.

★★**Art Galleries** – The galleries give a coherent survey of European painting and sculpture from the Renaissance onwards. British, particularly Welsh, art is strongly represented, but the museum's greatest glory is the Davies' collection of late-19C French art, which includes an array of Impressionist and other pictures of rare quality.

**Gallery 1** – Among the French and Italian pictures, the outstanding work is perhaps *Landscape with the Body of Phocion Carried out of Athens* by **Poussin** but there are fine paintings too by **Claude**, Salvator Rosa, Le Nain and Gaspard Dughet.

**Gallery 2** – The British portraits include an endearing picture (c 1625) of *Sir Thomas Mansel and his Wife Jane Hand in Hand* and a somewhat soulful study of 1631 of *Sir Thomas Hammer* by Cornelius Johnson.

**Gallery 3** – This is dominated by a cycle of four tapestries attributed to Rubens which tell the story of Romulus.

# NATIONAL MUSEUM AND GALLERY OF WALES

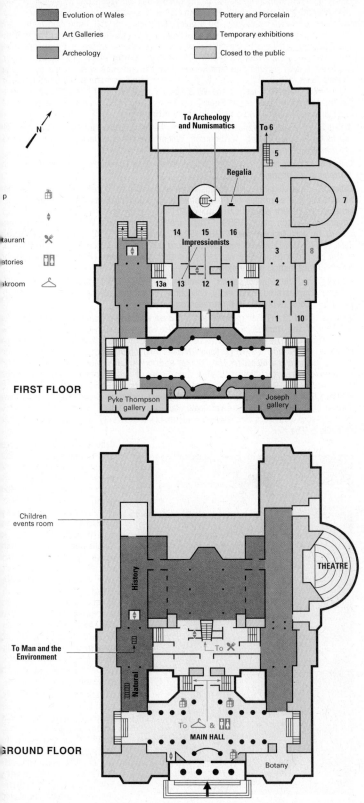

- Evolution of Wales
- Art Galleries
- Archeology
- Pottery and Porcelain
- Temporary exhibitions
- Closed to the public

N

p
aurant
atories
akroom

**To Archeology and Numismatics**

To 6

Regalia

5

4

7

14    15    16
Impressionists

3    8

13a   13   12   11

2    9

1    10

**FIRST FLOOR**

Pyke Thompson gallery

Joseph gallery

Children events room

THEATRE

History

**To Man and the Environment**

To 🍴

Natural

To 🧥 & 🚻

**MAIN HALL**

Botany

**GROUND FLOOR**

Gorsedd Gardens Road

123

**Gallery 4** – Sir Watkin Williams Wynn (1749-89) of Wynnstay in Denbighshire, characteristically munificent 18C patron of the arts, is commemorated her together with two associates, by a splendid Batoni portrait hung above the tabl urns and wine-cooler designed for his London house by Robert Adam. The world the 18C connoisseur and traveller is wonderfully evoked in the array of topograp ical pictures by Sir Watkin's fellow-countryman, **Richard Wilson** (1713-82). Wilsor fascination with picturesque landscapes in Wales and Italy was shared by his pup **Thomas Jones** (1742-1803), who was also responsible for *The Bard*, a highly fancif representation of the last of the Welsh bards about to hurl himself from a storn blasted cliff in the face of his English pursuers. Other 18C works include pictures t Guardi and Canaletto and a typically discomfiting Fuseli.

**Gallery 5** – Here the evolution of the Picturesque tradition in Wales is traced wit works by Copely Fielding, JC Ibbetson, William Daniell and David Cox, with Caerna fon Castle well established as an eminently suitable subject.

**Gallery 6** – **Turner** is the dominant figure here, while Constable is represented by h *Cottage in a Cornfield* (c 1815).

**Gallery 7** – The elegant curve of this room is devoted to British art 1850-1940 an as well as fine examples of Pre-Raphaelite painting by **Burne-Jones**, **Madox Ford** ar others, has superb objects like a marquetry roll-top desk (1862) by JP Seddon and "maiolica" Minton plate (1859). There are tiny, Derain-like Welsh and French lane scapes by **John Dickson Innes** (1887-1914), an associate of the flamboyant **August John** (1878-1961) who is represented here with several striking canvases, though is the more contemplative works by his sister **Gwen John** (1876-1939) which ma leave a more lasting impression.

**Gallery 11** – The Davies sisters, Gwendoline (1882-1951) and Margaret (188 1963), concentrated their early collecting on well-established French artists lik **Millet** and **Corot**, who are well represented here.

★★**Galleries 12 and 13** – These galleries are suffused with the sublime colours of the gre masters of the Impressionist movement, to whom the Davies sisters later turne their attention. The eye is likely to be drawn first of all to the immensely attractiv blue-clad *Parisienne* (1874) by **Renoir**. **Manet**'s *Argenteuil, Boat (study)* is of the sam date, and there is a **Monet** of *The Thames at London*. Later Monets explore the limi of Impressionist technique, among them one of his stunning visions of *Roue Cathedral* (1892-94) and a sequence of *Waterlilies* (c 1905). There are works b **Pissarro**, **Sisley** and **Degas**, some superb **Cézannes** including a majestic *Still Life wi Teapot* (1902-06), and a late **Van Gogh**, *Rain: Auvers* (1890), with rain slicing dow in sharp strokes across fields where sinister black crows fly. Among several bronze by **Rodin** is *The Kiss*.

*La Parisienne* by Renoir

National Museums and Galleries of Wales

**Galleries 14, 15 and 16** – Thes are mainly devoted to 20 British art, which is first se in its European context, wit works by **Vlaminck** and **Mod gliani**, by Central European like **Heckel**, **Jawlensky Kokoschka** and **Max Ernst**, an by Russian Moderns lik **Natalia Goncharova** and **Arch penko**. A direct compariso can be made between Euro pean Surrealism (**Magritte** *Empty Mask* of 1928 an Ernst's *Wood* of 1927) an its paler British counterpar (**Paul Nash**'s *Plage* of 1928 A more robust British trac ition infuses **Eric Gill**'s sculp ture *Mother and Child* o 1910 or **Epstein**'s *Rom* of th same date.

**Gallery 14** – The ceramic include jolly 1920s Chelse pieces by Harry Parr, and i contrast Frank Lloy Wright's cup and saucer fc his Imperial Hotel in Tokyo and a 1921 plate from th State Porcelain Factory Petrograd, proclaimin "Proletarians of the Worlc Unite!".

**Gallery 15** – This gallery has a range of British painting and sculpture between 1930 and 1955 and, as well as sculpture by **Chadwick**, **Hepworth** and **Moore** and paintings by **Nicholson**, **Piper** and **Spencer**, has a good selection of works by Welsh artists or by artists active in Wales. The dominant figure is perhaps **Ceri Richards** (1903-71), whose *White and Dark* (1936) straddles the boundary between painting and sculpture, but there are forceful pictures on mining and work themes by **Josef Herman** (b 1911) and a bold *Farmers, Cwm Nantlle* (1948) by the popular **Kyffin Williams**.

**Gallery 16** – Large canvases by **Bacon**, **Kitaj** and **Allen Jones** set the tone, as does **Michael Andrews'** imposing *The Cathedral, The Southern Faces/Uluru (Ayers Rock)* of 1987.

The spaces to the side of the main galleries contain much of interest, from an array of British glassware benefiting from the brilliantly lit showcases in which it is now displayed, to examples of the japanned ironwork for which Pontypool was famous. The Investiture of the Prince of Wales in 1911 is recalled in a display of **regalia** and by a big painting by E Louis Guillot showing the ceremony being performed in brilliant sunshine.

**Archaeology and Numismatics** – The story of early people in Wales is told in some detail in upper rooms, with displays from the museum's rich archaeological collections supplemented by models and other visual aids.

A Stone Age family's trek across the now impassable Severn is evoked by a cast of the footprints, Britain's oldest, that they left in the tidal mud at Uskmouth. Finely crafted objects include a collar of c 2000 BC and the extraordinary 11C Caergwrle Bowl. An early-1C BC fragment of a bronze bowl is designed in the form of a cat's face, with enamel inlay. Of the same period, but in complete contrast to such sophistication, are the rugged iron firedogs from Capel Garmon, possibly the only ones of their kind in Europe.

A model of the fort at Gelligaer in Caerphilly recalls the Romans' genius for organisation, while serpent bracelets and trumpet brooches testify to their love of luxury.

A fearsome ceremonial sword from the Commandery of the Knights of St John at Slebech in Dyfed introduces thematic displays on medieval Wales, one of which is graced by the enigmatic carved head of a king, taken from the hall of Deganwy Castle. In a spacious, top-lit chamber are some three dozen early Christian monuments (some of which are casts), dominated by the imposing 11C Carew Cross, richly carved in low relief with geometric patterns.

Welsh silver was used in the London mint in Tudor times, and Aberystwyth had a mint for a brief period under Charles I. The well-displayed **coins and medals** are interestingly related to the country's history, and include the Roman ancestors of the old British penny as well as the Welsh pound of 1985 with the motto *Pleidol wyf i'm gwlad* (I support my country), a line from the Welsh National Anthem.

# ★CARDIFF BAY

The historic dockland, typical of many harbour cities which reached their zenith in the 19C, is being renovated by an ambitious programme of conservation and restoration, and the creation of major new cultural and other facilities in a prestigious waterside setting.

Until 1798, when the Glamorganshire Canal was completed, the marshy levels around the muddy estuary of the Taff had been the lonely preserve of grazing animals. The canal was an instant success, handling a steadily growing volume of traffic and attracting workshops and industries to its banks.

Cardiff Bay

Wales Tourist Board

# CARDIFF BAY

Britannia Quay ............ X 2

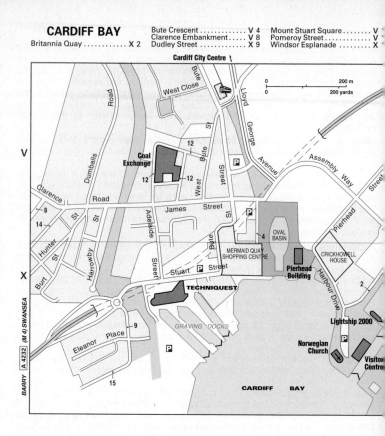

The spectacular rise of the port of Cardiff really began when the **Second Marques** **of Bute** financed the construction of what became Bute West Dock in 1839 an promoted the building of **Butetown**. Although conceived as a residential area, thi 19C New Town came to rival the old city centre, with offices and commercia buildings as well as housing for all classes. As the port prospered, with th construction of ever more capacious docks to the east, moneyed folk moved out t leafy suburbs, replaced by a cosmopolitan population drawn in by the seaway from all quarters of the globe, and the area acquired its unofficial name of Tige Bay. The gardens in the centre of the planned development of **Mount Stuart Squar** were swept away to make room for the huge neo-Renaissance pile of the **Coa Exchange** (**V**), completed in 1886. Millionaires rubbed shoulders on its trading floo in the decades when the world's appetite for Welsh steam coal seemed insatiable after the First World War, coal began to give way to oil; the last deal was struck o the floor of the Exchange in 1958. Only a few of Butetown's 19C buildings hav survived. An impressive boulevard – Lloyd George Avenue – commemorating Wales most celebrated politician *(see p 144)* now links the city centre and the waterside area, where the National Assembly sits in Crickhowell House, pending the construc tion of its own building.

The key to the revitalised waterside is the **barrage** (0.75mi/1km long), stretching from Queen Alexandra Dock in the east to Penarth Head in the west and creating non-tidal freshwater lake (500 acres/200ha) with a waterfront (8mi/13km long which provides a setting for an array of new developments, including shops an restaurants in Mermaid Quay. Some – like the controversial **Opera House** intended t be an inspiring new home for the internationally acclaimed Welsh National Oper company, and a dedicated building for the **National Welsh Assembly** – are still at th planning stage.

Enthusiasm for the new developments is not shared by the defenders of the myria shorebirds, whose rich tidal feeding grounds have been drowned beneath th surface of the new lake.

**Cardiff Bay Visitor Centre** ⊙ (**X**) – The overall vision for the waterside area ca best be appreciated by a visit to the glittering quayside tube which houses th Centre and its enthusiastic presentation of the project.

**Lightship 2000** ⊙ (**X**) – The lightship, resplendent in red paint, was formerly know as Helwick LV14 and last stationed off the Gower Peninsula to warn shipping off th Helwick Swatch, a dangerous sandbank. It has conserved its equipment but has bee refurbished to operate as a floating Christian Centre in Cardiff Bay.

★**Techniquest** ⊙ (**X**) – Beside the old graving docks stands a striking structure of steel and glass. Under its barrel vault it contains 160 hands-on exhibits intended to make the appreciation of scientific principles an enjoyable and stimulating experience. Often thronged with school parties, Techniquest is equally fascinating for adults; it is quite possible to spend the greater part of a day here in enthusiastic interaction. The exhibits, all attractively designed and with clear instructions, range from straightforward demonstrations of hydraulics to more complex laser-aided harmonics and computer animations. In addition, this exciting and innovative institution has a Science Theatre, a Discovery Room for younger children, and a small Planetarium.

**Pierhead Building** (**X**) – In fierce red terracotta and brick and with a wealth of ornamental detail, this wonderfully self-assured landmark in French Gothic style was intended to impress all those arriving in the port. It was completed in 1896 by an associate of William Burges who had assisted in the transformation of Cardiff Castle, and originally housed the offices of the Bute Dock Company. Its dominance of the waterfront is now contested by the impressive St David's Hotel.

**Norwegian Church** ⊙ (**X**) – This endearing little white-boarded structure in "Carpenter's Gothic", the first of its kind to be built (in 1868) outside Norway, was once the social and religious focus of the port's Norwegian community. It was moved to this site and virtually rebuilt with the help of the children's author, **Roald Dahl**, who had been baptised in it. The building is now a café and small exhibition centre.

## EXCURSION

★**Dyffryn Gardens** ⊙ – *8mi/13km W of city centre by A 48 and a minor road from the village of St Nicholas*
Though the Dyffryn estate can be traced back to the late Middle Ages, the present Dyffryn House is a late-19C mansion in French château style now used as a conference centre.
Its extensive grounds are a fine example of the work of the eminent Edwardian landscape architect **Thomas Mawson**, who collaborated with the owner, Reginald Cory, a keen horticulturalist and avid plant collector.
The grounds are rich in exotic trees, mostly grouped in wooded areas which flank expansive central lawns and central canal, and help integrate a fascinating series of enclosures in which Mawson "felt at liberty to indulge in every phase of garden design which the site and my client's catholic views suggested".
Thus there is a Japanese Garden, which is now used as an open-air theatre, a Mediterranean Garden, a Physic Garden and, above all, a colonnaded **Pompeiian Garden**, the fruit of an Italian study tour undertaken by Cory and Mawson. Herbaceous borders extend for more than 300ft/100m, while a walled kitchen garden, dating from c 1600, is a reminder of the antiquity of the site.

# CARDIGAN

(Aberteifi) Ceredigion – Population 3 758
Michelin Atlas p 24 or Map 403 G 27

The former county town of Ceredigion (Cardiganshire) commands the lowest crossing point on the Teifi and has an air of importance out of all proportion to its modest size. The principal axis is formed by the handsome early-18C bridge, the ruined castle on its mound, and by the long, curving High Street which is mainly Victorian in character.
At one time Cardigan was the second most significant port in Wales. Shipbuilding flourished in the 19C when more than 300 vessels were registered here. Most trade was coastal or with Ireland, but emigrant boats carried their human cargoes to Canada and the USA. The coming of railways and silting at the mouth of the estuary ended Cardigan's long history as a port, though formal closure took place only in 1981, and the area downstream from the bridge known as **Castle Pool** still has old warehouses and something of a maritime character.

**Castle** – *Not open to the public.* The Normans' first motte-and-bailey fortress was erected at the downstream end of the convenient mooring known as Castle Pool. Its successor was built at the eastern end of the Pool, overlooking the river at the tip of the spur of land along which the High Street now runs. The present ruins probably date from a rebuilding in stone c 1240. A memorial commemorates the holding here in 1176 of the first recorded *eisteddfod* under the patronage of the Lord Rhys.

**Town Centre** – Short streets run downhill from the High Street ridge, one of them leading to Theatr Mwldan, focal point of the annual Arts Festival. The slope enabled the Victorian architect RJ Withers to insert a **covered market** with bold Moorish arches beneath his neo-Gothic **Guildhall** of 1859. By the river to the east stands Cardigan's big **Church of St Mary**, medieval but with a landmark tower built in the 18C.

## Out and About

**Tourist Information Centre** – Theatr Mwldan, Bath House Road, Cardigan SA43 2JY ☎ 01239 613 230; Fax 01239 613 600; cardiganTIC@ceredigion; .gov.uk

**Beaches** – North at Mwnt, Aberporth, Tre-saith, Penbryn, Llangrannog and Cil Borth.

**Adjacent Sights** – See Aberaeron, Fishguard, Lampeter, Newcastle Emlyn, Pembroke Coast.

## Where to Stay

**Penbontbren Farm**, Glynarthen, SA44 6PE. *9.5mi/15km NE by A 487.* ☎ 01239 810 248; Fax 01239 811 129. Small family-run hotel, situated in secluded valley by River Dulais, specialising in Welsh cooking; 10 rm in converted stables and granary; countryside museum.

**Berwyn**, Cardigan Rd, St Dogmaels, SA43 3HS. *1.5mi/2km W by A 487 and B 4546.* ☎ 01239 613 555. Comfortable guesthouse (3 rm), good home comforts, charming owner; views of the River Teifi and 12C ruins of St Dogmaels' Abbey.

**Gwbert**, Gwbert-on-Sea, SA43 1PP. ☎ 01239 612 638; Fax 01239 621 474. Hotel (15 rm) with modern room amenities for business and leisure guests; on the banks of the River Teifi with views of Cardigan Bay.

**Broniwan**, Rhydlewis, SA44 5PF. *10mi/16km E by A 487 and S by B 4334.* ☎ /Fax 01239 851 261. Grey stone house (3 rm), built for the local doctor in 1867, now a working farm; meals feature home-grown produce; walks around the farm.

# EXCURSIONS

**Cilgerran Castle** ⊘ – *3mi/5km SE by A 478 and a minor road.* Cilgerran's romantic situation on its crag high above the wooded gorge of the Teifi fascinated JMW Turner, who made several studies of the castle in its setting, and the rugged ruin continues to exert its appeal today.

Cilgerran may well have been the home of the adventurous **Nest**, the "Helen of Wales" who deserted it and her husband in 1109 in order to enjoy the favours of her cousin Owain, and later of other lovers. The present stone castle is of a later date, probably the work of William, Earl of Pembroke, in the early 13C.

The drama of the castle's setting is somewhat tamed by the approach past the houses and gardens of the pleasant village of Cilgerran. Beyond the outer ward stand the stronghold's most striking features, two great **drum towers**, four storeys high, together with a formidable gatehouse approached by a drawbridge. The outer walls of the towers have much thicker masonry than the inner sides. The curtain walls along the less vulnerable lip of the gorge were probably added at a later date. As well as Turner, other artists like Richard Wilson found Cilgerran a stimulating subject, and by the end of the 18C the trip by boat up the Teifi had become popular with early tourists.

**Welsh Wildlife Centre** ⊘ – *4mi/7km by A 478, minor road and rough track.* This extensive nature reserve is situated at the point where the Teifi emerges from its steep-sided wooded gorge and broadens out into an area of estuarine marshland. The habitats are exceptionally diverse, not only because of the change in the nature of the river but also because of the presence of old quarry workings, an abandoned railway line and a variety of relief forms carved by glacial meltwater channels.

Footpaths and trails lead the visitor through salt-marsh, areas of slate waste, pools and ponds, woodland, coppice and scrub, water meadows, alder carr (marsh) and river bank. The many species of bird include the rare Cetti's warbler; otters and the occasional seal frequent the river, pursuing the salmon and sewin for which the Teifi is famous. The art of navigating a coracle is sometimes demonstrated on the river.

The outstanding feature of the reserve is the **Visitor Centre**, perched on a ridge of glacial till. As well as containing offices and laboratories, this award-winning three-storey structure has changing displays on the complex ecology of the area, and a café and gallery with superb all-round views. Hailed as heralding the architecture of the 21C, it is an uncompromising edifice in timber and glass, contrasting oddly with features around it like rustic birdtables.

**St Dogmael's Abbey** – *1.5mi/2km W by B 4546.* The slate-roofed houses of the large village of St Dogmael's on the far bank of the Teifi from Cardigan seem to keep to a respectful distance from the ruins of this abbey, possibly marking the outer limits of its ancient precinct. St Dogmael's was founded c 1115, a rare example of a Tironensian establishment, originating from Tiron in western France. The abbey's outline is well defined but only two structures stand to any height – the north transept and the infirmary. Fragments of stonework such as a corbel showing the eagle of St John evoke the richness of the original decorative scheme.

**Ceredigion Heritage Coast** – *Access by side roads branching off N from the A 487.* This splendid stretch of protected coastline runs east-north-eastward from the tiny golfing resort of **Gwbert** on the Teifi estuary to New Quay Head, interrupted only by the town of Aberporth and its RAF station. Nearly all of it remains undeveloped.

There are attractive beaches and fine cliffs but no continuous coastal footpath. Pilgrims for Bardsey Island on the tip of the far-off Lleyn Peninsula used to embark at **Mwnt** with its whitewashed little church and strange pyramidal mount *(mwnt)* projecting seaward. **Aberporth** and adjoining **Tresaith** attract holidaymakers to their sandy beaches and there is a spacious, mostly sandy, beach at **Penbryn**, which the National Trust has kept free of all intrusive facilities. The seafaring village of **Llangranog** is packed tightly into its narrow valley; from this village there are superb cliff walks over the peninsula known as **Ynys-Lochtyn**. Further east still is the little cove of Cwmtudu *(see p 75).*

# CAREW ★

(Caeriw) Pembrokeshire
Michelin Atlas p 14 or Map 403 F 28
6mi/10km W of Tenby by B4318, A477 and A4075

This pleasant little village stands at the crossing of the Carew River, one of the many tidal inlets penetrating deeply into the quiet countryside to the east of Milford Haven. Carew Castle broods over the broad pool that drove the village's tidal mill, the only one still intact in Wales. Nearby is a fine example of a Celtic Cross.

**★ Castle** ⊘ – In this gentle landscape, the slight elevation of the castle site makes for a commanding position, and the defensive ditch guarding the approach to the stronghold was first dug in pre-Nor-

> **Adjacent Sights** – See Haverfordwest, Laugharne, Milford Haven, Pembroke, Pembrokeshire Coast, Tenby.

man times, possibly as far back as the Iron Age. The present substantial ruins succeeded an earth-and-timber castle erected by the lord of Pembroke Castle, Gerald of Windsor, c 1100. Over a period of 400 years beginning in the late 12C, Carew evolved from a simple stone fortress to a palatial Tudor residence.

A small square gatehouse gives access to the outer ward, where the castle's oldest stone structure, the Old Tower, stands next to the modest inner gatehouse. To the north is the outer wall of the Lesser Hall and the projecting semi-octangle of the Chapel Tower. The courtyard seems compact, not least because of the scale and architectural treatment of the structures which enclose it. The Lesser Hall, originally 13C, was refaced by the castle's most flamboyant owner, Sir Rhys ap Thomas (1449-1525) who also provided it with an ornate fireplace. Opposite is the early-14C Great Hall to which Sir Rhys added the oriel window and the elegant three-storey porch which has the arms of Henry VII, Catherine of Aragon, and the Prince of Wales. Sir Rhys, originally a Yorkist who had promised Richard III that Henry Tudor would enter the country only "over my bellie", changed sides, marching with Henry to Bosworth Field in 1485 where he may well have slain Richard. His eventual reward was the Order of the Garter, which he celebrated with a Great Tournament, held here in 1507, perhaps the last as well as one of the most lavish of these medieval events.

The splendid north wing with its rows of mullioned windows was the work of Sir John Perrot, who was granted the castle after Rhys' grandson had been executed for treason. The long gallery was 132ft/40m in length.

Perrot's wing can be appreciated in all its grandeur from the far side of the millpond. Likewise, the massive 14C drum towers flanking the west range are best seen from the outside.

CADW: Welsh Historic Monuments – Crown Copyright

Carew Cross

**Carew Tidal Mill** ⊘ – *Walk from Castle car park (10min) or from National Park c park on north bank of millpond (5min).* The solid-looking four-storey mill buildir standing on the causeway probably dates from the very beginning of the 19C, though mill was present on the site at least as early as Tudor times. Tidal mills had the advar tage over wind and conventional watermills that their period of operation was predic able, varying only with the twice-daily rise and fall of the tide. Open sluices allowed th rising tide to fill the millpond (23 acres/9ha), the stored water then being released c the ebb to drive the pair of millwheels. This would mean frequent night shifts for th miller (one of whom at Carew was an Elizabeth Griffith). The mill worked until 1937 and older local people remember it rumbling and shuddering into the night. An audic visual display gives a full account of the mill's history.

**Carew Cross** – *Close to Castle car park.* The wheel head of this splendid cross is widel known as the aptly chosen symbol of CADW – Welsh Historic Monuments. The Cros (13ft/4m high) commemorates Maredudd ap Edwin, joint ruler of the western Wels kingdom of Deheubarth until his death in battle in 1035. The head and shouldered nec are joined to the shaft and stepped base by a tenon. All sides of the shaft are vigorousl carved with geometric patterning arranged in rectilinear panels.

# CARMARTHEN

(Caerfyrddin) Carmarthenshire – Population 12 247
Michelin Atlas p 15 or Map 403 H 28

Well placed on the rail and road routes to far south-western Wales, the county town c Carmarthen is the market centre for much of this predominantly agricultural region, it daily bustle intensified when the thrice-weekly livestock market is under way.
The town has never hesitated to renew itself but a number of fragments remain of it 2000-year history, literally, in the case of the oak tree associated with Merlin th Enchanter, which was removed to make way for a road-widening scheme and now consists of a few fragments preserved in the Civic Centre.
Under the Romans, Carmarthen, then the tribal capital of the Demetae, became **Moridu num**, the westernmost Roman settlement in Wales, with a large **amphitheatre**, capable c seating up to 5 000 spectators, which is now a public park. The layout of the Roman tow is preserved in the modern street pattern to the east of St Peter's Church.
The Normans preferred to site their **castle** on a rocky knoll directly overlooking th River Tywi; it was sacked by Llywelyn the Great, rebuilt by John Nash and then agai by the County Council in something of the manner of a French château. The 14 twin-towered **gatehouse** survives.
Below the castle, and quite separate from the Welsh borough to the east, an Anglo Norman town grew up; its pleasingly intricate layout of streets and alleyways form the core of the present town centre with the handsome Georgian **Guildhall** as its foca point.

**Carmarthen Museum** ⊘ – *1.5mi/2.5km E of town centre off A 40 in the subur ban village of Abergwili.* The museum is housed in the former palace of the Bishop of St David's, who moved here in 1542, preferring the more central location o Carmarthen to the remote peninsula far to the west. Set in well-tree'd ground above the flood plain of the Tywi, the palace was rebuilt in 1907 but retains som of its original features.
Inside, the exhibits succeed well in reflecting the long past of this predominantl rural area, with displays on the once-important woollen industry and on farming and dairying. Many objects come from Penrhiwbeili Farm, which remained hardl changed from 1790 to 1988. There is jewellery made from the gold mined by th Romans as well as a number of inscribed memorial stones. The Bishops' Chapel car be visited.

---

**Tourist Information Centre** – 11 Lammas Street, Carmarthen SA31 3AQ
☎ 01267 231 557; Fax 01267 221 901; carmarthenTIC@carmarthenshire.
gov.uk

**Craft Centres** – Merlin's Gallery, **Oriel Myrddin** ⊘, *(on the northern edge of the centre, opposite St Peter's Church)* has interesting displays of contem-
porary sculpture, crafts and paintings, many by local artists, arranged on the ground floor of the School of Art. Over 100 makers contribute to the display in **Origin Dyfed Gallery** *(1 St Mary's Street, off Guildhall Square).*
**Gwili Pottery** ⊘ *(3mi/5km N in Pontarsais by A 484 and B 4301)* specialises in hand-thrown and individually decorated ceramics.

**Adjacent Sights** – See Gower Peninsula, Lampeter, Laugharne, Llandeilo, Llanelli, Neath, Newcastle Emlyn, Swansea.

---

## EXCURSIONS

**Llansteffan Castle** – *8mi/13km SW of Carmarthen by B 4312. Car park in village or by beach; 30min on foot there and back, partly up steep hill.* Llansteffan defends the approach to Carmarthen up the tidal Tywi, just as Laugharne Castle commands the estuary of the Taf.

The Norman castle was placed on a site already chosen for its strategic value by the builders of the **Iron-Age promontory fort**, part of whose outline can be traced below the western wall of the castle. The stronghold is entered by the side of the massive, twin-towered **Great Gatehouse**, added c 1280 as part of the additional defences represented by the Lower Ward. Almost as imposing is the North Tower. Grassy slopes lead to the Upper Ward, no longer with its curtain wall, but with a square Inner Gate and the foundations of what would have been a formidable round tower.

The glorious **panorama** over the estuary and the surrounding country confirms the strategic significance of the site. To the north, it is clear how the village of Llansteffan has spread from the original nucleus around the church with its Pembrokeshire-style tower down the slope to its fine sandy beach.

**Gwili Railway** ⊙ – *3mi/5km N of Carmarthen by A 484 and B 4301.* From Carmarthen the Great Western Railway meandered northward through the pretty valley of the River Gwili towards Newcastle Emlyn and Aberystwyth. The line was closed in 1973, but a section (1.5mi/2.5km long) has been reopened by enthusiasts, with steam and, only rarely, diesel passenger-carrying trains.

★**National Botanic Garden of Wales** ⊙ – *8mi/13km E by A 48 or B 4300 and B 4310.* The adaptation of the extensive 18C estate of **Middleton Hall** into a modern botanic garden is an unusual and exciting project. Water is an important element in the design: the main feature of the string of five lakes which are being restored with lakeside walks; a refreshing trickle winding its way down the **Broad Walk** in a pebbled channel; the subject of study in the Water Discovery Centre. The **Great Glasshouse**, a monster oval glass dome, houses a Mediterranean landscape bisected by a ravine – palm trees, cacti and a dragon tree. Among the less usual features are herbaceous borders mulched with Welsh slate, prairie planting, an oval walled garden laid out in the pattern of the DNA double helix, a biomass furnace and a waste-recycling unit. The rare double walled garden awaits restoration. The **old stables** house displays and exhibitions, a restaurant and shop. The house, designed by Samuel Cockerell for Sir William Paxton, was destroyed by fire in 1931; from its site there is a fine **view** of Paxton's Tower and Dryslwyn Castle.

**Paxton's Tower** – *8mi/13km E by B 4300; in Llanarthne turn right opposite the Paxton Arms; then take first left.* This huge triangular structure with its battlemented corner towers is one of the most grandiose follies in Great Britain. It has a magnificent prospect north over the meandering River Tywi; in the middle of the vale, perched on a surprising stump of rock, is the ruin of **Dryslwyn Castle**, scene of a fiercely fought battle in 1287, when 11 000 English successfully besieged Rhys ap Maredudd. The folly was built in 1808 by Samuel Cockerell for Sir William Paxton of Middleton Hall, ostensibly to commemorate Nelson. Other interpretations have suggested Sir William's desire to observe his racehorses on their way to Tenby or his pique at not being elected by the voters of Carmarthen who in consequence were deprived of a promised bridge, as the funds were spent on the folly.

# CASTELL COCH★★
## Cardiff
### Michelin Atlas p 16 or Map 403 K 29 – 5mi/8km NW of Cardiff

The once coal-blackened but increasingly clear Taff approaches Cardiff and the sea through a dramatic wooded gorge, once guarded by the red sandstone castle (Castell Coch = Red Castle) built by Gilbert de Clare in the latter part of the 13C. By the mid-19C De Clare's stronghold had long since crumbled into ruin, and the astonishing silhouette of high walls and conical towers rising through the trees today is the fanciful creation of the coal magnate Lord Bute and his equal in enthusiasm for the Middle Ages, the architect **William Burges** (1827-81).

The Butes' immense fortune had been accumulated through exploitation of coal-rich estates and the far-sighted development of the port of Cardiff. Though continuing to pursue his commercial interests, John, the Third Marquess of Bute (1847-1900), was more interested in immersing himself in the romantic vision he shared with Burges, who, by the late 1860s, was helping him in the transformation of his residence, Cardiff Castle, into something more medieval than the Middle Ages themselves. The ruins of Castell Coch suggested themselves as a "country residence for occasional occupation in the summer", and Burges began work on the imaginative rebuilding of his master's second castle in 1871.

**Adjacent Sights** – See Caerphilly, Cardiff, Cowbridge, Glamorgan Coast, Llancaiach Fawr, Llandaff, Llantrisant, Newport, Rhondda, Museum of Welsh Life.

**Exterior** – Burges' reconstruction stands on the foundations of the original castle, whose sloping walls can best be appreciated from immediately below. Though the architect claimed authenticity for his designs, the exotic outline of his castle with its conical towers and elaborate roof shapes suggests Continental European precedents like the Château de Chillon rather than more local models. Burges took great care to ensure that his drawbridge and portcullis worked and that his murder holes really would direct boiling oil on the heads of any attackers. The polychrome Virgin and Child in its niche over the entrance is a reminder that Bute's mystical approach to religion led him to convert to Roman Catholicism and that Burges' spiritual home was in the High Church.

**Interior** ⊘ – The paved courtyard, with close-up views of the castle's elaborate roofline, steep steps and covered galleries, has served as a most satisfactory set for a number of swashbuckling films.

The glory of the castle, however, lies in its extraordinarily ornate interiors like the **Banqueting Hall**, or the octagonal **Drawing Room** with its starry rib-vault and almost overwhelming profusion of detail showing plants, birds and animals, signs of the Zodiac, the Fates and the Three Ages of Man. By contrast, **Lord Bute's Bedroom** is relatively simple, with stencilled wall patterns and a delightful carved frieze of rabbits and other harmless creatures, but opulence again characterises **Lady Bute's Bedroom**, with its double dome and splendid painted bed, all completed after Burges' death by assistants steeped in his taste and techniques.

The Third Marquess seems seldom to have visited his summer residence, though his interest extended into its wider environment; it was he who planted many of the trees which make such a splendid setting for the castle, though the vineyard he laid out on the slopes to produce Communion wine has now disappeared.

Lady Bute's Bedroom, Castell Coch

CADW: Welsh Historic Monuments – Crown Copyright

*The Practical Information section at the beginning of the guide lists :*
*– information about travel, motoring, accommodation, recreation*
*– local or national organisations providing additional information*
*– calendar of events*
*– admission times and charges for the sights described in the guide*

# CHEPSTOW ★

(Cas-Gwent) Monmouthshire – Population 9 461
Michelin Atlas p 16 or Map 403 L 29

Proclaiming itself the "first historic town in Wales", Chepstow stands on the Monmouthshire-Gloucestershire border, commanding the lower reaches of the tidal Wye just before it flows into the mighty Severn. The strategic importance of the site was recognised by the Norman William Fitz Osbern, the first builder of the splendid castle on its limestone spur high above the great bend of the Wye.

## Out and About

**Tourist Information Centre** – Bridge Street, Chepstow NP16 5EY ☎ 01291 623 772; Fax 01291 628 004; chepstow-tic@tsww.com

**Adjacent Sights** – See Abergavenny, Blaenavon, Caerleon, Caerwent, Monmouth, Newport, Raglan Castle, Tintern Abbey, Usk.

## Where to Eat

**Wye Knot**, 18A The Back. ☎ 01291 622 929. Row of terraced cottages with views at high tide of fishing boats; modern combinations from frequently changing blackboard menu.

**Caldicot Castle** *(see below)* for **medieval banquets** served by candlelight to the sound of singing accompanied by the harp.

## Where to Stay

**Castle View**, 16 Bridge St, NP6 5EZ. ☎ 01291 620 349; Fax 01291 627 397. Hotel (13 rm), built 300 years ago as a private residence; friendly, traditional atmosphere; views of the castle from some rooms.

**George**, Moor St, NP16 5DB. ☎ 01291 625 363; Fax 01291 627 418. Old inn and posting house (14 rm), originally constructed in 1610, at the top of the High St, adjoining the medieval 'port wall' and 16C town gate.

## ★★CASTLE ⊙

The castle is one of the most dramatically sited in Britain, particularly when first seen from the old main road descending to the river. Masonry merges with limestone cliff, making it difficult to distinguish the work of man from that of nature. Fitz Osbern came here in 1067, barely a year after the Norman conquest, erecting the hall keep known as the **Great Tower**, one of the very first stone castles built by the Normans in Britain and modelled on prototypes like Falaise in Normandy. Just over a century later, the castle was inherited by William Marshal, "the flower of chivalry" and builder of the great round keep at Pembroke. He and his sons strengthened Chepstow, rebuilding the walls of the Middle Bailey and adding the Lower and Upper Baileys as well as the Barbican at the furthermost western point of the ridge. The last major additions were those ordered by Roger Bigod III, who held the castle from 1270 to 1306; they included the suites of rooms overlooking the Wye on the north side of the Lower Bailey and the massive tower named after Henry Marten, one of the signatories of Charles I's death warrant, who was held prisoner here for 20 years.

The castle's formidable defences made it one of the few which Owain Glyn Dŵr refrained from attacking; in the Civil War it was held for the King (twice) and surrendered to Parliament (also twice).

**Tour** – The castle is strung out in a series of wards rising towards the high point of the ridge. It is entered from the lowest level, close to the river crossing, through the **Outer Gatehouse**. To the right, domestic accommodation fills the whole of the side of the Lower Bailey, ending in the **Great Hall**. Throughout the castle there are fine views of the great stronghold, set above the river gorge, the first of them from a balcony room in this range of buildings, an addition of Tudor date. To the left of the gatehouse is **Marten's Tower**, four storeys high, built for the personal occupation of Roger Bigod III; this castle within a castle has well-preserved battlements with carved figures as well as a chapel with a finely decorated window. A curtain wall and towers, once the outer face of the castle, protect the Middle Bailey, over which rises the commanding presence of Fitz Osbern's **Great Tower★★**. Roofless, with part of a later third storey disrupting its outline, and with many

Chepstow Castle

later windows, it still speaks eloquently of the first days of Norman rule in Britain and of the conquerors' imported architectural style, with fine chip-carved decoration above its doorway and blind arcading within. An arcaded gallery built directly above the sheer drop to the river leads to the narrow Upper Ward, beyond which is the **Barbican**, reached across a rock-cut ditch which originally formed the castle's outer defences.

## ADDITIONAL SIGHTS

**Chepstow Museum** ⊘ – The local museum occupies the rooms of an exceptionally fine 18C town mansion which once belonged to a prosperous local merchant and apothecary. Its excellent displays give a thorough account of Chepstow's past as a port, shipbuilding centre and market town. In the late 18C-early 19C, the town was the terminus of that early tourist itinerary, the "Wye Tour", its picturesque qualities celebrated in many a print and painting. The port was the main outlet for the timber of the Forest of Dean. Sizeable ships were built at Chepstow until the First World War, when National Shipyard No 1 was sited here, employing thousands of workers, some of whom were housed in a "Garden City" on the western outskirts. Wye salmon are famous, and there is a display of basketwork traps, known as putchers, used to catch them.

**Chepstow Bridge** – The elegant cast-iron bridge was built in 1816 to a design based on the work of John Rennie. It no longer bears the burden of main road traffic owing to the construction of a by-pass to the south, which crosses the Wye next to the railway bridge originally built by Brunel for the South Wales Railway.

**Town Gate and Portwall** – From the late 13C Chepstow was protected by **walls**, which because of the hilly nature of the town site enclosed a large unbuilt area of orchards and open spaces. Several stretches remain. The Town Gate, erected at the same time but much rebuilt, once served as a prison. It stands guard over the upper end of the medieval town, which preserves its intricate street pattern and has suffered relatively little from redevelopment.

**St Mary's Church** ⊘ – Fitz Osbern founded a priory within a short time of starting work on his castle. After the Dissolution the church was neglected; the tower fell in 1700 and there was an unsympathetic restoration in the 19C. Nevertheless, the austere nave remains in service as part of the parish church, and the west tower, built in the early 18C, incorporates a richly decorated Norman doorway.

**Offa's Dyke Long Distance Footpath** – The earthwork, raised by the Mercian ruler, Offa *(see p 169)* and the southern end of the associated long-distance footpath reach the Severn just east of Chepstow at Sedbury Cliffs.

**Wye Valley Walk** – This waymarked walk runs along the Welsh bank of the spectacular gorge of the Wye as far as Monmouth, and then leaves Wales to follow the river upstream as far as Hereford.
The first section of the Walk passes through **Piercefield Park**, now the site of Chepstow Racecourse. In its day this was one of the most famous landscape parks, taking advantage of the dramatic scenery of the lower course of the Wye and enhancing the scene with numerous features such as a Giant's Cave and Druid's Temple, some of which remain along the Walk. After 2.5mi/4km the footpath climbs *(365 steps)* to the splendid viewpoint of the **Wynd Cliff** *(see below)*.

# EXCURSIONS

★**Wynd Cliff** – *2.5mi/4km N by A 466 and a minor road; from car park 20min on foot there and back*. The densely wooded limestone cliffs of the gorge rise here to a height of 800ft/240m. From the giddy **Eagle's Nest viewpoint** at the top of the cliff, the eye ranges over the winding Wye, the great bridges over the Severn, and the English counties beyond.

**Severn Crossing** – One of the most splendid of rivers, the tidal Severn (Hafren in Welsh) was for long a barrier to easy communication between the west of England and South Wales, not least because of its astonishing **tidal range** (up to 46ft/14m).
A **railway tunnel** was built in 1886 between the English shore and Caldicot but, until well into the second half of the 20C, road traffic either went via Gloucester many miles upstream or waited for one of the little **ferries** linking Beachley and Aust.
Bridging the broad estuary presented many problems; the high-energy tidal regime causes fast and unpredictable currents, and the rock foundation is fissured, faulted and water-bearing.
Work finally began on the magnificent road **suspension bridge** ⊙ carrying the M4 motorway in 1961 and it was opened in 1966. It is used by some 50 000 vehicles a day and also by cyclists and pedestrians; tolls are levied on westbound traffic only. The main span is 3 400ft/1 036m in length and the towers are 445ft/146m high. Quite distinct from the main suspension bridge is the more modest but still considerable stayed-girder structure carrying traffic over the Wye.
The capacity of the bridge was soon exceeded, and inconvenience is caused by restrictions placed on its use because of high winds and maintenance operations. Vigorous lobbying, particularly by South Wales industrial and commercial interests, led to studies of alternative additional crossings, including a tunnel. A second bridge was the preferred option. The **Second Severn Crossing** is sited downstream from the suspension bridge so that it does not spoil the magnificent outline of the latter. This new bridge (nearly 3mi/5km long) has as its main span a cable-stayed bridge (1 500ft/450m) approached by viaducts with spans of varying length.

**Caldicot Castle and Country Park** ⊙ – *6mi/10km W of Chepstow by M 4, exit Junction 23 (signs)*. Credit is due to the Victorian barrister and antiquarian, Joseph Cobb, for the survival of this handsome medieval monument. Rejecting the 19C fashion for ivy-clad ruins, he set about the meticulous excavation and restoration of the castle, which was begun by the Normans in the 11C. A stereotaped tour guides visitors around the gritstone tower, which has fine views of the River Severn, and round the Woodstock Tower, which was named after Thomas of Woodstock, who was betrayed by his nephew Richard II and murdered. The gatehouse is particularly impressive; it has fine masonry and a half-timbered upper storey, added by Cobb.

★**Penhow Castle** ⊙ – *7mi/11km W of Chepstow by A 48 or M 4, exit at junction 24*. By the mid-20C this delectable fortified manor house had become little more than an appendage to a farm. Since 1973 it has been restored and refurnished with ingenuity and enthusiasm to give a fascinating insight into the evolution of a squire's residence from crude keep to country house.
Penhow was one of a number of smaller Norman strongholds built in a buffer zone around the mighty castle at Chepstow to warn of any impending Welsh attack. It probably dates from the start of the 12C. The builder of its three-storey **keep** was a member of the Anglo-Norman family, de Saint Maur, who became known as the Seymours and who eventually provided a queen for Henry VIII. The site, a rocky knoll, overlooks what was the main road into South Wales.

Next to the castle, and forming a most attractive group with it, is the little parish **church**, its tower provided with battlements from which archers might shoot back siegers in the back.

By the 13C the castle had been enclosed within a sturdy curtain wall. In the 1480s a fine **Great Hall** with minstrels' gallery was erected above a lower hall. On display are firedogs from Saint Maur on the Loire as well as meat bones chucked carelessly into the moat by medieval trenchermen. In the 1670s a wing was added to the castle in order to provide more comfortable and up-to-date accommodation. Here are rooms whose decor, a modest echo of the grandeur of the great house at Tredegar *(see p 276)*, includes marbled panelling and doorcases with broken pediments; the original panelling in the Carolean Dining Room has been furbished to give a splendid 17C appearance. The story of Penhow is brought into the 19C with the Kitchen and the Victorian Housekeeper's Room.

# CHIRK CASTLE★★

(Castell Y Waun) Denbighshire

Michelin Atlas p 33 or Map 403 K 25

Abutting Offa's Dyke, the intimidating bulk of Chirk Castle looms above the trees of its magnificent parklands within arrow-shot of the English border marked by the River Ceiriog. It was begun in the late 13C by **Roger Mortimer**, who had been granted the lordship of Chirk by Edward I. Since 1595 it has been lived in by the Myddelton family and their descendants. A magnificent sequence of state rooms constitutes one of the finest interiors in Wales.

The castle may have been designed by the King's architect, **Master James of St George**. The original plan was for a rectangular stronghold with curtain walls incorporating half-towers, corner towers, and a south-facing gatehouse. Either the plan was not fully carried out or parts of the castle were subsequently demolished, perhaps during or after the Civil War; the towers do not extend to their full height, and the eastern and western ranges are truncated, with no corner towers. Chirk is nevertheless an awesome sight, its severity only partly relieved by the substitution of mullioned windows for arrow slits.

The lordship of Chirk was no guarantee of good fortune for the castle's early residents. Roger Mortimer may have held sway as Justice of Wales, but fell from favour and died in the Tower of London in 1326. At least five other owners were executed for treason while others perished on the field of battle. Repeatedly held by the Crown, Chirk was granted by Elizabeth I to her favourite, Robert Dudley, Earl of Leicester.

Baroque Gate, Chirk Castle

In 1595 it was purchased by the merchant adventurer, **Thomas Myddelton**, later Lord Mayor of London, whose family claimed descent from the fearsome Ririd Flaidd "The Wolf", a 13C lordling from far-off Merioneth. The Myddel-

> **Adjacent Sights** – See Bala, Erddig, Llanfyllin, Llangollen, Mold, Plas Newydd, Ruthin, Valle Crucis Abbey, Lake Vyrnwy, Wrexham.

tons and their descendants have lived here ever since, save for a lengthy interval between 1911 and 1946, when it was the home of Lord Howard de Walden, an eccentric millionaire with a passion for the Middle Ages and for the arts generally; it was he who employed Eric Gill to carve the war memorial in Chirk village.

## TOUR ⊙

**Interior** – The state rooms open to the public reveal most phases in the Castle's evolution, though by no means in chronological sequence. The **Cromwell Hall** was re-gothicised by **Pugin**, whose work at Chirk between 1845 and 1848 was one of his most important commissions. Above the Hall's oak panelling is mounted an array of arms and armour, while a row of heraldic shields traces the Myddeltons' ancient pedigree. The **Grand Staircase**, in neo-Classical style, was hollowed out of a half-tower in 1777-78; its gallery has a portrait of another Sir Thomas Myddelton, the Parliamentary general who successfully changed sides in the Civil War and was rewarded with a baronetcy for his son.

Both the **State Dining Room** and the **Saloon** show the influence of Robert Adam; the Saloon has a magnificent coffered ceiling with fine plasterwork by Kilminster and mythological cameos by Muls. The **Drawing Room** has a ceiling in similar style. The late-17C **Long Gallery** stretches almost the whole length (100ft/30m) of the east range; its boldly carved oak panelling is the setting for a number of paintings, including one of Charles II, hung between portraits of two Myddelton ladies.

The King's Bedroom occupies a half-tower, there is a much-restored Chapel, while what was the Castle's Great Hall was subdivided in the 16C. On the ground floor of the south range, reached from the courtyard, is the **Servants' Hall**, a dark place redolent of ancient smoke and beer stains. Most evocative of the Castle's early days is **Adam's Tower** in the west range, the great thickness of the walls revealed by immensely deep window recesses. There is a dungeon which housed French prisoners after Agincourt, and the other rooms include the Magistrates' Court, with appealingly crude plasterwork of the early 17C.

**Park and gardens** – A splendid engraving of 1735 shows Chirk set in a large-scale landscape in the Baroque style with terraced lawns, formal gardens, and avenues stretching into the far distance. Most of this formality was swept away when the estate was re-landscaped by William Emes, a follower of Capability Brown. His efforts are reflected in the present park, with its curving lines and clumps of trees, though most of the planting is of later date. Towards the end of the 19C there was a return to more geometrical discipline, when the hedging and topiary of the garden facing the east range was established. Romantic feeling pervades the gardens around the Upper and Lower Lawns; the latter is overlooked by the thatched Hawk House, originally an 18C "green house", rebuilt by Lord Howard de Walden in association with his medievalising enthusiasm for falconry.

One of the great glories of Chirk is the **wrought-iron gates ★** which once guarded the northern forecourt of the castle but which were moved to their present position by the entrance lodge in 1888. A Baroque masterpiece from the ironworks at nearby Bersham, they feature an overthrow of extraordinary elaboration, guarded by a brace of Myddelton wolves.

# COLWYN BAY

(Bae Colwyn) Conwy – Population 29 883
Michelin Atlas p 33 or Map 403 I 24

Backed by wooded hills which dip their feet in its sandy bay, this well-matured late-Victorian and Edwardian resort has little of the brashness that characterises other holiday places along the North Wales coast.

The Chester and Holyhead Railway, which reached here in 1848, was the making of Colwyn, though the resort's development really got under way only in the 1860s and 1870s.

Today's hopes are centred on the Expressway, buried in part beneath the town centre. As well as making the whole of northwest England more accessible, the new road has relieved the centre of the permanent congestion caused by through traffic and helped the town stake its claim as an important shopping centre for the region.

---

**Tourist Information Centre** – Imperial Buildings, Station Square, Princes Drive, Colwyn Bay LL29 8LA ☎ 01492 530 478; Fax 01492 534 789. The Promenade, Rhos-on-Sea LL28 4EP ☎ 011492 548 778.

**Beaches** – At Colwyn Bay and Old Colwyn *(E)*.

**Adjacent Sights** – See Bodelwyddan, Bodnant Gardens, Conwy, Llandudno, Llangollen, Llanrwst, Rhuddlan, Rhyl, St Asaph.

---

**Promenade** – The curving promenade (3mi/5km long) runs from **Rhos-on-Sea** in the west towards the village of Old Colwyn in the east. Rhos (Llandrillo-yn-Rhos) mixes red brick villas and hotels with a few older cottages to create something of the atmosphere of a fishing village.

A pier once stood here, brought in bits from the Isle of Man, and now replaced by a breakwater sheltering a number of sailing dinghies.

On the promenade is the tiny, bunker-like **Chapel of St Trillo** ⊙, reputedly built in the 6C over a holy well.

Eastward, the promenade, complete with its still-extant main pier, is separated from the main built-up area by the railway and the North Wales Expressway.

**Town Centre** – An underpass links the promenade with the railway station, built like most of the centre on the final slopes of the hills. The sculpture gracing a sitting area is in fact a *dolos*, one of thousands of six-ton concrete blocks used to protect the coastal sections of the Expressway.

Station Road slopes upward and away from the station, the upper façades, gables and orièls of its shops more easily appreciated now that it is free of traffic.

Beyond St Paul's Church with its fine tower stretch the leafy suburbs which make Colwyn Bay a favoured place for residence and retirement.

★**Welsh Mountain Zoo** ⊙ – The zoo occupies an incomparable site (37 acres/15ha) high above the town among the woodlands and gardens laid out in the early 20C by the prosperous Manchester surgeon Walter Whitehead.

The zoo, founded in 1963 by the naturalist Robert Jackson, combines serious commitment to conservation and research with great popular appeal. Lions lounge beneath the balcony of the safari restaurant, brown bears lurk in their pit, elephants tread ponderously around their enclosure. As well as such exotic animals, the native fauna is well represented, with red squirrels, polecats and pine-martens, and otters slithering gracefully up and down a chain of pools.

There is a Chimpanzee World and a charming Children's Farm, regular free-flying bird of prey displays, penguin parades and sea-lion training sessions. Away from the animals, a Jungle Adventureland tempts humans into healthy activity.

Walter Whitehead employed the celebrated landscape architect **Thomas Mawson** to design both house and grounds but died when all that had been completed was part of the gardens. They are formal in style but merge with the fine woodlands of pine and oak in the southern part of the site, giving way to more open ground to the north. Here there is a *gorsedd* circle, dating from the National *Eisteddfod* of 1909, as well as a café, built where an observatory once stood. The **view**★ over the bay is magnificent.

# CONWY ★★★

Backed by the many-towered walls of its dependent town, Conwy Castle on its rocky promontory commands the Conwy estuary which for long barred the route westward into the fastness of Snowdonia. A trio of bridges, and, more recently, a boldly planned tunnel, have overcome the obstacle of the river but town and fortress still evoke the time when medieval English kings sought "to embrace and grip the intractable heart of northern Wales".

## HISTORICAL NOTES

The Cistercians were the first to settle on the west bank of the River Conwy, in 1186, though their desire to settle far from the turmoil of the world was not achieved. On several occasions during the following century, the English pursued their quarrels with the Welsh as far as Deganwy, a "crossbow-shot" away on the eastern shore, and in 1245 their soldiery pillaged the monastery. After completing his conquest of Snowdonia in 1283, Edward I determined that English control should be firmly grounded on the west bank of the Conwy; within days of his arrival here from Deganwy work had begun on the new stronghold and walled town, under the supervision of the Crown's great military engineer, **James of St George**. The deployment of immense resources (red sandstone from Chester to supplement the local rock, lead from Flint, iron from Staffordshire...) and the employment of a huge workforce of up to 1 500 craftsmen and labourers ensured swift completion of the great work, which was substantially ready by 1287. The monks, meanwhile, had been moved upriver to Maenan, though their place of worship remained to serve as parish church.

The castle was garrisoned with English soldiers, and the town populated by English immigrants. For hundreds of years it remained a countrified sort of place, with a few streets of buildings backed by gardens, yards and orchards. Even in the 15C the Welsh were still regarded as foreigners, and an attempt was made to sack the "porter of Conwey... for it is no more meet for a Welshman to bear any office in Wales... than it is for a Frenchman to be officer in Calais, or a Scot in Berwick".

By the late 18C the garrison function had long since gone. Instead, Conwy had become a staging post on the way to Holyhead and Dublin, the river crossing an irritation and danger to travellers who had to brave its sometimes perilous waters and the churlishness and extortion of the ferrymen. A bridge was imperative, and was eventually – well into the 19C – provided by the genius of Thomas Telford.

CADW: Welsh Historic Monuments – Crown Copyright

Conwy Castle at night

★★★**Conwy Castle** ⊘(**C**) – Like Caernarfon, Conwy Castle is built on a confined site which made the conventional concentric plan impossible. Instead, it is laid out in linear fashion along the narrow rocky promontory projecting into the estuary. Eight splendid drum towers stud the curtain walls, four protecting a western, **Outer Ward** (**C**), four an eastern, **Inner Ward** (**C**) which contained the royal apartments. Towers and walls were originally rendered white and the towers topped by an array of pinnacles, no doubt lightening somewhat the grim appearance of the massive stronghold.

The castle was originally approached from the east via a watergate, now gone, and from the west by a great ramp which has also disappeared.

Today's visitors enter the castle via an excellent **visitor centre**, thence via a timber bridge and pathway. An entry once guarded by drawbridge and portcullis gives access to the **West Barbican** (**C**), overlooked by two closely spaced towers.

A gate passage leads to the **Outer Ward** (**C**), whose southern wall bows outwards to make the most of the cramped site. Here are the foundations of guard-rooms, kitchens and stables, but there are more substantial remains of the Great Hall, with cellars and three fireplaces. The **Prison Tower** (**C**) has a basement which almost certainly served as the castle dungeon.

The **Inner Ward** (**C S**) is guarded not only by the cross wall separating it from the Outer Ward but also by a cleft cut into the rock. Here too is the castle well (91ft/28m deep). Within the Inner Ward is the suite of **royal apartments** designed by James of St George to accommodate King Edward I and his Queen, Eleanor. There are a few bare hints of past luxury in the remains of fine tracery which once graced the windows of the King's Hall and the East Room, and the **Chapel** (**C N**) too, with its chancel built into the thickness of the tower wall, has remarkable ornamentation. The towers of the Inner Ward have additional turrets which extend their height even further; from the easternmost pair there is a fine **view** of the trio of bridges, as well as down into the **East Barbican** (**C F**). Here a little geometrical garden was laid out for Queen Eleanor, using turf from the nearby water-meadows.

★★**Town Walls** (**AB**) – Edward I's bastide town is still almost wholly enclosed by the circuit of walls built in the same short period as the castle, and, like the castle, designed by **James of St George**. They are the outstanding example left in

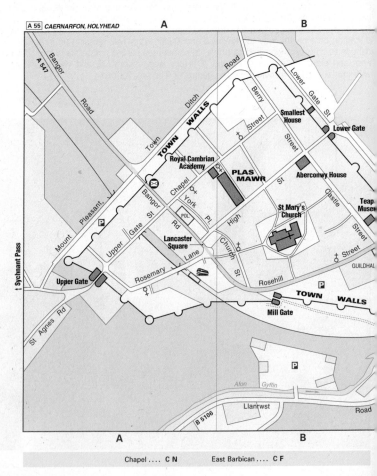

Chapel .... **C N**     East Barbican .... **C F**

Britain of this type of urban fortification, intended to provide an advanced line of the defence of the castle as well as to protect the town itself. They can be viewed from many points in and around the town, while an accessible section of sentry walk (between the **Upper Gate** *(Porth Uchaf)* (**A**) and Berry Street near the quayside) gives fine views over town and castle in their setting.

The walls (1 400yd/1 300m long) are flanked by 21 towers at roughly 55yd/50m intervals and pierced by three twin-towered gates. The hilly nature of the site determined their irregular layout and the consequent shape of the town, whose streets were nevertheless laid out on the grid pattern common to all such planned settlements. The walls were designed to isolate any one section of their length should it fall to an enemy; the swift removal of the simple plank bridges spanning the gap on the inside of the towers would confine any attacker to that part of the wall he had succeeded in scaling. Most of the circuit is in a good state of preservation, in spite of decayed stonework and toppled battlements, though the tower which terminated the spur of wall running out into the river has gone.

Telford breached the wall in two places, in Castle Square to give access to his bridge, and on the north-west side of the town, where the road left for Bangor and where he modified an existing tower to make the "Bangor Arch". Stephenson built a fanciful four-centred arch bridging the gap his railway had made in the walls on the south side of the town.

Close to the **Mill Gate** *(Porth y Felin)* (**B**) is a remarkable example of medieval attention to hygiene, a dozen regularly spaced stone projections, the remains of the garrison's latrines.

**Town Centre** – The focal point is Lancaster Square with a statue of **Llywelyn the Great** *(ap Iorwerth)*. From here the High Street with shops, unusual inter-war cinema (now a bingo hall) and brick-and-terracotta hotel, descends towards the quay, crossing Castle Street, where there is a quirky little museum, **Teapot World** ⊙ (**B**). Though most of the buildings which line the grid of streets are relatively modern, a number of edifices recall the town's long past.

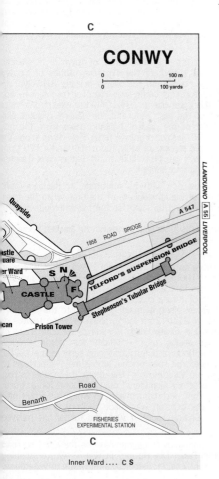

**CONWY**

0 _____ 100 m
0 _____ 100 yards

Quayside

C

A 547

LLANDUDNO A 55 LIVERPOOL

1958 ROAD BRIDGE

TELFORD'S SUSPENSION BRIDGE

Stephenson's Tubular Bridge

astle uare

er Ward

S N

F

CASTLE

can    Prison Tower

Road

Benarth

FISHERIES
EXPERIMENTAL STATION

C

Inner Ward .... **C S**

★★**Plas Mawr** ⊙ (**B**) – Occupying almost the entire frontage of a narrow lane running up from the High Street, this is one of the finest town houses of the Elizabethan period in Britain. H-shaped in plan, laid out around two courtyards and with a gatehouse to the High Street frontage, Plas Mawr was built in the late 16C by Robert Wynne, a true "Elizabethan adventurer" and typical member of one of the great North Wales families who achieved wealth and prominence in Tudor times. With its roughly dressed stonework, mullioned and pedimented windows and crow-stepped gables and dormers, this exuberant building expresses all the vigour of an expansive age. Inside there are elaborate fireplaces and boldly patterned plasterwork.

Plas Mawr was once the home of the **Royal Cambrian Academy** ⊙ (**A**), whose stimulating exhibitions of Welsh art are now shown next door, in a strikingly converted chapel.

**Aberconwy House** ⊙ (**B**) – *Castle Street.* The town's last remaining medieval house stands at the junction of Castle Street and High Street, a prominent location which may reflect the status and prosperity of its original merchant owner. The two lower storeys are of stone, the top floor timber-framed and jettied out on brackets.

The interior has been furnished to reflect the house's changing fortunes. The dining room recalls the late-18C – early-19C merchant-mariner owner, while the great loft is fitted out according to a probate inventory of the mid-17C. A bedroom evokes the period 1850-1910 when the house served as a temperance hotel. Possible removal to the United States was averted when the building was given to the National Trust in 1934.

**St Mary and All Saints' Church** ⊘ (B) – In the centre of town in a spacious graveyard stands what was once the church of the Cistercian Abbey of Conwy completed in 1186. It served as a mausoleum for Welsh princes; Llywelyn the Great was originally buried here before his coffin was removed to Maenan and thence to its final resting place at Llanrwst *(see p 194).* Only the west front, since incorporated into the tower, part of the east wall, and the general ground plan survive from this early church. Most of the present building dates from the late 13C, considerably restored in the 19C. Inside, primitive faces look down from the corbels. There is a splendid 15C carved screen, an early-Tudor font and a 17C floor slab to "Nichs Hookes, Gent, who was ye 41st child of his Father Wm Hookes Esq"; Nicholas went on to sire 27 offspring himself.

**Quayside** (BC) – Overlooking the estuary with its multitude of pleasure-craft, Conwy's quayside still has something of the atmosphere of the time when the town was an important port, not only for fishing but also for the transhipment of slate and other materials from upriver.

Close to the **Lower Gate** *(Porth Isaf)* (B) is a genuine curiosity, the **Smallest House** (B) its shelf of a bedroom reached by trapdoor.

**Conwy Crossing** – Telford's solution – completed 1826 – consisted of a causeway running out from the Deganwy shore to a tiny midstream island, from which an elegant **suspension bridge**★ (C) (327ft/100m long) with lace-like ironwork and slim battlemented towers was flung across to the castle rock. The construction of the causeway determined the alignment of future crossings. In 1848 Robert Stephenson's Chester and Holyhead Railway ran along it, making the leap to the far shore through twin tubes of wrought iron (412ft/126m long), slung between towers of more massive design than Telford's. His **tubular bridge** (C) still carries the trains of the North Wales line, but Telford's bridge, never intended for motor vehicles, showed itself unable to cope with the flood of holiday traffic as early as the 1920s; it was joined in the 1950s by a nondescript road bridge, whose main effect was to funnel the ever-increasing stream of vehicles into the quite inadequate street system of the walled town. No satisfactory alignment could be found for a fourth crossing above ground, and finally, after much controversy, in which the result of a local referendum was overturned, the decision was made to bury it in a tunnel beneath the waters of the estuary. Costly though it was, the tunnel has relieved Conwy of all but local traffic.

**Sychnant Pass** – *1mi/1.5km W of Conwy by the minor road on the left.* The road west suddenly comes to the **Sychnant Pass** ("Dry Ravine" in Welsh) with a stunning **view**★★ down the steep slopes, apparently held together by a minimum of vegetation.

# COWBRIDGE
(Y Bont-Faen) Vale of Glamorgan – Population 6 167
Michelin Atlas p 16 or Map 403 J 29

Set among the rich farmlands of the Vale of Glamorgan, the "Capital of the Vale" consists essentially of a long main street sloping gently upwards in both directions from the early-19C Town Hall. Although founded as a Norman borough, Cowbridge is now largely Georgian in character. Its prosperity depended on its central situation and on its location on the main road westward, the reason for its many inns.

In the mid-19C it survived its own Corporation's wilful diversion of the South Wales Railway away from the town and seems to flourish more than ever now that long-distance traffic has been taken away by motorway (M 4) and by-pass, and visitors are able to browse in its many specialist shops in comfort.

**Adjacent Sights** – See Barry, Caerphilly, Cardiff, Castell Coch, Glamorgan Coast, Llancaiach Fawr, Llandaff, Llantrisant, Margam Park, Penarth, Porthcawl, Museum of Welsh Life.

Among the more famous residents of Cowbridge is Edward Williams, **Iolo Morganwg** *(see p 57)*. His great interest in history and poetry and folklore led him to try to establish himself as a literary figure in London but he failed and settled in Cowbridge, where he kept a shop, opposite the Town Hall *(plaque)*, selling books and groceries.

The **Town Hall** served briefly as a lock-up, and the local **museum** ⊙ is housed in the former cells. Fragments of the Norman town walls remain, including the South Port, the southern gateway, next to **Holy Cross Parish Church** ⊙, a large building with a massive octagonal tower.

## EXCURSION

**Old Beaupré Castle** – *1.5mi/2.5km SE on road to St Athan as far as the lay-by beyond the junction with the road to St Hilary; climb stone stile and cross fields on foot.* Beaupré is a corruption of French *beau-repaire*, and this charming manor house *(partly in ruin and partly in private ownership)* in the tranquil valley of the River Thaw must surely have made a beautiful place of retreat for its medieval and Tudor builders. It was begun c 1300 but its most striking features date from the rebuilding carried out in the 16C. These include the grand **gatehouse** forming the entrance to the Middle Court and, within, the superb three-storey **porch** with superimposed Doric, Ionic and Corinthian columns.

# CRICCIETH
Gwynedd – Population 1 720
Michelin Atlas p 32 or Map 403 H 25

Facing due south across Cardigan Bay, Criccieth has been a family resort since the arrival of the railway in the 1860s. East and West Beaches are separated by a massive outcrop of felsite, on which sits the ruined castle, a native Welsh stronghold and a landmark for miles around.

Criccieth's townscape has a decidedly Victorian flavour, the long terraces of stuccoed boarding houses along the West Beach recalling those of Aberystwyth. The concrete-and-glass beach café is a "progressive" structure by Sir Clough Williams-Ellis, the architect of Portmeirion. Just to the north of the castle there are traces in the street layout of the English borough created after Edward I's conquest of North Wales. On rising ground, beyond the railway line, the town-centre shops line the High Street, a section of the turnpike road laid down in 1807 when it was thought that the London-Dublin traffic might pass this way *en route* for the projected harbour at Porth Dinllaen.

**Criccieth Castle** ⊙ – In the early years of the 13C, **Llywelyn the Great** fortified the hilltop by building a twin-towered gatehouse and square south-eastern tower linked by the curtain wall of the castle's inner

**Adjacent Sights** – See Beddgelert, Harlech, Lleyn Peninsula, Porthmadog, Portmeirion, Pwllheli, Snowdonia.

ward. His grandson more than doubled the size of the stronghold by adding an outer ward also defended by a curtain wall and by two rectangular towers. Once in English hands, the castle fitted well into Edward's strategic plan for maintaining his grip on the North, since it could easily be supplied by sea. Both he and Edward II strengthened the castle but what can be seen today is largely the work of the Welsh. There are splendid all-round **views** from the ruins of coast and mountains, and of Criccieth itself, with the rocky lump of Dinas sticking up among the terraces and echoing the shape of the castle crag.

## EXCURSIONS

*David Lloyd George* by an unknown artist

National Portrait Gallery, London

**Lloyd George Museum** ⊙ – *2mi/3km W by A 497 a Llanystumdwy.* One of Grea Britain's foremost states men of the 20C, **David Lloyd George** (1863-1945), the "Welsh Wizard", wa: brought up in Llanystum dwy by his uncle, the village cobbler.

The purpose-built museum was designed by Sir Clough Williams-Ellis, creator of Portmeirion. As well as reminding visitors of Lloyd George's political career played out on the world stage, it emphasises his debt to, as well as his lifelong affection for, "his race and his village home".

Archive films show fascinat-ing moments in the great man's career, including a drive along the empty *Autobahn* in 1936 en route to a private meeting with Hitler. They end with scenes of his funeral attended by thousands of local mourners.

Adjoining the museum is **Highgate**, the humble home where Lloyd George's widowed mother and her sons were taken in by her brother. A short walk away, among the beech trees on the banks of the rushing River Dwyfor, the boulder on which the youthful rebel used to sit and ponder has been incorporated into his **memorial**, it too the work of Williams-Ellis.

**St Cybi's Well** – *6.5mi/10km NW by A 497, B 4354 and minor roads. 10min on foot there and back from Llangybi churchyard.* The hamlet of Llangybi is lost among the lanes north of the village of Chwilog, an improbable place to find a spa. The curative properties of the waters were attributed to St Cybi, a 6C Cornish saint, but it is doubtful if such a figure ever had any real connection with the area. In the 18C William Price of Rhiwlas was persuaded to erect simple stone buildings over the well-chambers. It is their cottage-like ruins that can be seen today, in the delightful setting of a valley floor beneath wooded slopes.

# DENBIGH ★

(Dinbych) Denbighshire – Population 8 529
Michelin Atlas p 33 or Map 403 J 24

Overlooking the fertile Vale of Clwyd from its hilltop, this old market town is dominated by the ruin of the massive castle begun by Henry de Lacy in 1282.
The natural defences of the summit (468ft/143m) may first have been strengthened by Iron Age people. Dafydd ap Gruffydd, the brother of Llywelyn ap Gruffydd, on whose death he assumed the title of Prince of Wales, held sway from here until his downfall in 1283. The lordship of Denbigh was then granted by Edward I to De Lacy, who immediately set about building his castle together with a walled town to which he granted a charter in 1290.
By the time of the 1294 uprising led by Madog ap Llywelyn, only that part of the castle's defences included in the town walls had been completed, and the Welsh were able to break in. After their ejection, the north and east walls which separate the castle from the town were built to a more rigorous specification, the effect of which can be appreciated today in the far greater thickness and bulk of construction.
Queen Elizabeth I gave the castle to her favourite, Robert Dudley, Earl of Leicester. In 1645 the castle sheltered King Charles I, after his defeat at Rowton Moor, but the following year it was captured by Parliamentary forces and reduced to a ruin.

**★Denbigh Castle** – The approach to the castle leads past the site of the long-since demolished Barbican across a ditch to the **Great Gatehouse**, probably the most massive structure of its kind in Wales. Its trio of

**Adjacent Sights** – See Betws-y-Coed, Bodelwyddan, Bodnant Gardens, Colwyn Bay, Flint, Hawarden, Holywell, Llanrwst, Mold, Rhuddlan, Rhyl, Ruthin, St Asaph.

octagonal towers enclose a grand chamber, originally vaulted, but now open to the sky. High above the entrance arch is a niche containing a statue, probably of Edward I. The grassy expanse of the castle's inner ward is still enclosed by curtain walls, though most of the buildings which were ranged inside, like the Great Hall, have been reduced to foundation level.

There are fine **views** of Denbigh in its dramatic setting, with the Vale bounded by the Clwydian Range to the east and more broken country to the west.

**Old and new town** – The walled town was too high above the plain for convenience and, by the 16C, its citizens had migrated to the lower slopes below the formidable **Burgess Gate**. The old house plots and streets are now mostly grassed over, and the tower of St Hilary's Chapel stands in isolation. A section of the **town walls** ⊙ can be explored; the entrance is close to the roofless, never-completed **Leicester's Church**, begun in 1578 by the Earl of Leicester and probably intended to supplant St Asaph's Cathedral.

The majority of modern Denbigh's streets and alleyways run up and down the steep slopes, although the broad High Street, where the market is held every Wednesday, is laid out on the level. A row of buildings on the north side has a continuous arcade. At the top of Vale Street stands the **County Hall** (1572); it houses the Library and a small **museum** ⊙, with a town model based on Speed's map of 1610.

## EXCURSIONS

**St Marcella's Church, Whitchurch** ⊙ – *Just over 1mi/1.5km E of Denbigh by A 525 and a minor road*. In a rural setting beyond Denbigh's outermost suburbs is the town's parish church, enlarged and remodelled in Perpendicular style in the 15C. The exterior is plain but the double-aisled interior has a number of interesting features beneath its hammerbeam roofs. Corbels are carved to represent angels and animals, and the string courses are enlivened with further creatures, including a fox and a hare as well as a donkey having its tail pulled. There is the imposing tomb of Sir John Salisbury (d 1575), a wall monument to the antiquary Humphrey Llwyd, and a fine brass to Thomas Myddelton (d 1575) with wife, nine sons and seven daughters.

**★St Dyfnog's Church, Llanrhaeadr-yng-Nghinmeirch** ⊙ – *3mi/5km SE of Denbigh by A 525*. Llanrhaeadr – the church by the waterfall – is named after St Dyfnog, a 6C saint who seems to have settled here because of the healing properties of a nearby water source. The donations of medieval pilgrims may have contributed to the ability of a modest country church to fit itself out with some of the finest late medieval stained glass in Wales.

The mostly Perpendicular church is of the double-aisled type, with a tiny tower. The darkness of the interior sets off the luminosity of the Jesse window, but it is worthwhile accustoming one's eyes to the gloom in order to admire the crafts-manship of the roofs; the easternmost bays of the southern aisle have vine carving as well as angels. There is also a splendid Baroque monument to Maurice Jones, gent. (d 1702), of nearby Llanrhaeadr Hall.

The church's glory is the **Jesse Window★★** in which Jesse is shown slumbering, with the genealogical tree of Jesus Christ growing from his chest. Among the total of 23 identifiable figures are Moses, with the Ten Commandments *(left of Jesse)*, Sadoc or Zadok *(right)*, King David in a red garment with gold buttons, carrying a harp *(immediately above)*, and the Madonna and Child *(top centre)*. Directly above the Madonna and Child is the Pelican in her Piety. Tradition has it that the glass was taken down in the Civil War and buried in a trunk to preserve it from the destructive urges of the Parliamentary soldiery. It was certainly removed between 1986 and 1989 to receive the benevolent attentions of the expert restorers of the York Glaziers Trust.

---

### Literary associations

As a child the author Beatrix Potter often stayed with her Aunt and Uncle Burton, whose descendants still live in Gwaeynynog *(W of Denbigh by A 543)*. Many of the illustrations for her book *The Tale of the Flopsy Bunnies* (1909) were drawn in the walled garden of the farm.

A monument by the River Ystrad commemorates the visit of Dr Samuel Johnson, who stayed with the Thrale family during his tour of Wales in 1774.

---

# DOLGELLAU ★

Gwynedd – Population 2 396
Michelin Atlas p 32-3 or Map 403 I 25

On the south bank of the Wynion River, the county town of old Merionethshire ha
long been an important centre for the upland farming community, an importan
market for pedigree mountain sheep and black cattle. From the 18C to the early-19C
it was famous for its cottage industry of cloth-making, but the town's dominant rol
today is as the tourist capital of southern Snowdonia, with access down the beautifu
Mawddach estuary to the coast and to the massive brooding presence of Cadair Idri
just to the south.

The tightly packed buildings in dark stone and slate make a sombre impression bu
give the town a strong and distinctive urban character. There are no monumenta
buildings apart from the 18C **St Mary's Church** ⊙ and the arcaded **market hall** in the littl
square, but the consistent use of materials and the architectural good manners of th
mostly 18C-19C buildings make a stroll around Dolgellau's narrow and winding street
a most satisfying experience.

## Out and About

**Tourist Information Centre**- **Snowdonia National Park Visitor Centre** ⊙ – Ty
Meirioin, Eldon Square, Dolgellau LL40 1PU ☏ 01341 422 888; Fax 01341
422 576.

**Walks and Rides** – The Precipice Walk and the Torrent Walk have delighted
visitors since the 19C; there is a more recent network of footpaths in the Coed
Y Brenin Forest as well as mountain bike routes and hire *(see also below)*.

**Adjacent Sights** – See Bala, Barmouth, Blaenau Ffestiniog, Harlech, Machynlleth, Snowdonia, Tywyn, Lake Vyrnwy.

## Where to Stay

**Abergwynant Hall**, Penmaenpool, LL40 1YF. *3.5mi/5.6km W by A 493.*
☏ 01341 422 160; Fax 01341 422 160. A personally run house (4 rm),
pleasantly set in extensive grounds, providing luxury and tranquillity; communal
dining.

**Ty Isaf Farmhouse**, LL40 2EA. *3.75mi/6km NE at Llanfachreth.* ☏ 01341 423
261. An attractive Welsh longhouse (3 rm) with plenty of period character,
providing good views over the valleys and comparative tranquillity; communal
dining.

**Borthwnog Hall**, LL40 2TT. *5mi/8km W by A 496 Barmouth Rd.* ☏ 01341 430
172; Fax 01341 430 682. Regency style house (3 rm), pleasantly sited on the
Mawddach Estuary, with its own art gallery.

**Cyfannedd Uchaf**, Arthog, LL39 1LX. *7mi/11km SW by A 493 Cregennan Lakes Rd;
turn right at T-junction at end of gated road.* ☏ 01341 250 526. Simple
accommodation (3 rm) in remote location; panoramic view over the Mawddach
Estuary to the mountains.

**Pentre Bach**, Llwyngwril, LL37 2JU. *15mi/24km SW by A 493.* ☏ 01341 250 294;
Fax 0134 250 885. A traditional farmhouse (3 rm) on the coast, dinner available with an emphasis on interesting organic ingredients.

**Llwyndû Farmhouse**, Barmouth, LL42 1RR. *10mi/16km W by A 496.*
☏ 01341 280 144; Fax 01341 281 236. Guesthouse (7 rm) of great character
serving an interesting dinner; sea views.

**George III**, Penmaenpool, LL40 1YD. *2.5mi/4km W by A 470 and A 493.*
☏ 01341 422 525; Fax 01341 423 565. Busy inn (11 rm) with extensive
menu; overlooking the estuary and nature reserve.

**Penrhos Arms**, Cemmaes, SY20 9PR. *15mi/24km SE by A 470.* ☏ 01650 511 423.
A traditional inn (4 rm) with good bedrooms and a reputation for food.

**Minffordd**, Tal-y-Llyn, LL36 9AJ. *8mi/13km S by A470, A 487 and B 4405.*
☏ 01654 761 665; Fax 01654 761 517. A 17C former drovers' inn (6 rm) at
the head of the valley east of Tal-y-Llyn.

**Tyncornel**, Tal-y-Llyn, LL36 9AJ. *8mi/13km S on B 4405.* ☏ 01654 782 282;
Fax 01654 782 679. Traditional hotel (15 rm), renowned for fishing on the
adjacent lake and for fine views of Cader Idris.

**Penmaenuchaf Hall**, Penmaenpool, LL40 1YB. *1.75mi/3km W by A 493.*
☏ 01341 422 129; Fax 01341 422 787. A luxurious personally run country
house with plenty of character, tranquillity, lovely grounds and views.

Dolgellau and Cadair Idris

## EXCURSIONS

★**Precipice Walk** – *3mi/5km NE of Dolgellau by minor roads. Park in National Park car park; 3mi/5km on foot.* A favourite with Dolgellau's visitors since the estate owner laid it out in 1890, this fairly level upland walk makes an excellent introduction to the landscapes of the southern part of the National Park. The path leads at first through woodland but soon emerges on to the open land of Foel Cynwch and follows the contour round this minor massif in an anticlockwise direction. A succession of splendid panoramas opens up, from which the patronisingly worded signboards placed at intervals are unnecessary distractions. First comes Snowdonia proper, followed by the magnificent Coed y Brenin forest, the Rhinog mountains and the lovely valley of the winding Mawddach; finally, and gloriously, rises the great chair or throne of the giant Idris, Cadair Idris. The return is along the banks of Llyn Cynwch, a little lake.

**Torrent Walk** – *3mi/5km E; park in lay-bys on B 4416; 2.5mi/4km on foot.* The walk descends a lane running parallel with the rushing River Clywedog, then returns up the sylvan glen. With its boulders, waterfalls, ferns and mosses, the route was calculated to delight Victorian visitors, though in fact it was laid out much earlier, by Thomas Payne, the designer of the great embankment across the Glaslyn estuary at Porthmadog.

---

### Welsh Gold

In the Middle Ages the mineral rights in the hills around Dolgellau were owned by the monks of **Cymer Abbey** but it was only in the 19C that the area experienced anything like a gold rush. By the First World War the boom was over, in spite of the entrepreneurial efforts of Pritchard Morgan MP, a Monmouth man and Australian migrant who returned to his native country and made a fortune out of the Gwynfynydd mine. The extraction of gold began again in 1981 and for several years the precious metal was made into jewellery bearing the mark AC – Aur Cymru (Welsh Gold) at the Dolgellau workshop *(see also p 170)*.

## Welsh Quakers in Pennsylvania

When George Fox and John ap John, the first Welsh Quaker, made a preaching tour of Wales in 1657, they made a number of converts, drawn from the gentry and the local farmers and tenants. As Quakers believed that it was against the teaching of Jesus to swear oaths, they refused to take the Oath of Allegiance to the Crown and therefore faced imprisonment and eviction from the land. Many of them decided to emigrate to America and purchased 40 000 acres in what later became Pennsylvania, on the understanding, given by William Penn, who had acquired the land in 1861, that the Welsh would have their own territory and live together under their own law, speaking their own Welsh language. In 1682 a group of Quakers set sail from Liverpool in the *Lyon*. Among the hundreds who followed was Rowland Ellis, who named his new residence after his home in Dolgellau; the name, Brynmawr, lives on as the name of the famous women's college. Other Welsh place names took root – Gwynedd, Haverford, Merion and Radnor – and the Quakers worshipped in Welsh in Merion and Gwynedd in Pennsylvania until the mid-18C. William Penn's promise to the Welsh was not realised; the Welsh Tract was divided into two parts and soon lost its Welsh identity. As their dream of a new Wales in America faded, many of the Welsh Quakers returned to the old country *(exhibition in the local Visitor Centre)*.

**Coed y Brenin Forest Park** – *Visitor Centre 9mi/14km N by A 470*. Th vast woodland estate, named the "King's Forest" in honour of the 1937 Silve Jubilee, is one of the Forestry Commission's proudest possessions. Conifers hav been planted a-plenty but the diversity of rock and soil has enabled an unusu variety of species to be used and there is little sense of the regimentation ar gloom of other man-made forests. In many areas the native oak woodland contir ues to thrive. The varied relief is a further asset, with rocky crags and clea streams crashing over waterfalls in deep valleys, and there is a rich wildlif which includes red squirrel and pine-marten, deer and otters, as well as goshaw black grouse and goosander. A network of waymarked footpaths (50mi/80kr radiates out from picnic sites and from the modern **Visitor Centre** ⊘ in the heart c the forest.

**Cymer Abbey** ⊘ – The ruins of the simple abbey church suggest that the abbe was always a modest community; it was founded under the patronage of Meiric nydd in 1108-09 by Cistercian monks who made a living by dairying, hors breeding and even ironworking. The abbey takes its name from its location at th confluence *(cymer)* of two rivers – the Wynion and the Mawddach.

**Penmaenpool** – *2.5mi/4km W by A 493*. Gerard Manley Hopkins invited h readers to "taste the treats of Penmaen Pool" and the point at which th meandering Mawddach is crossed by a rare Victorian wooden toll-bridge (1878) still a most idyllic spot. The riverside inn is no longer separated from the wate by the railway, but a semaphore signal remains as a souvenir of what was once busy holiday line. The **signal box** is now leased to the Royal Society for th Protection of Birds, which has converted it into an **observatory** ⊘ and informatic centre.

# ELAN VALLEY ★★

(Dyffryn Elân) Powys

Michelin Atlas p 25 or Map 403 J 27

A century ago a series of great dams and reservoirs were built high up in mid-Wale in the "green desert" of the Elan and Claerwen Valleys, to supply water to the growir city of Birmingham, over 70mi/113km to the east in the English Midlands. The field and homesteads of a community of some 100 people, together with their church an school, vanished beneath a hundred feet of water. The design of the scheme paid gre attention to its setting in these wild uplands and the catchment area has been manage with great care and sensitivity to protect wildlife and enhance the landscape. The Ela Valley has become a "Lake District" of great appeal where visitors are able to enjo scenic drives, walking and fishing in what was one of the remotest parts of th country. The protective designation (Site of Special Scientific Interest and Nation Nature Reserve) of much of this part of Central Wales emphasises its ecologic importance and visual attractiveness.

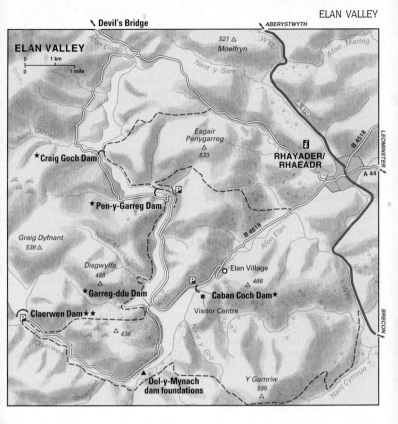

ELAN VALLEY

Devil's Bridge

521 △
Moelfryn

ABERYSTWYTH

0   1 km
0        1 mile

Esgair
Penygarreg
533

RHAYADER/
RHAEADR

★ Craig Goch Dam

LEOMINSTER

B 4518

A 44

★ Pen-y-Garreg Dam

Graig Dyfnant
538 △

B 4518

Disgwylfa
488
△

○ Elan Village

△ 466

★ Garreg-ddu Dam

■ Caban Coch Dam ★

Claerwen Dam ★★

Visitor Centre

△ 436

BRECON

Dol-y-Mynach
dam foundations

Y Gamriw
599
△

## HISTORICAL NOTES

Towards the end of the 19C Birmingham City Council, under the leadership of Joseph Chamberlain, was urgently looking for abundant and reliable sources of fresh water for its expanding industries and close-packed population; the ravages of cholera spread by polluted water supplies earlier in the century had not been forgotten. The Elan area, with its high rainfall, suitably shaped valleys, and impermeable rocks was ideally suited.

Work began on the immense project in 1893. A total of 50 000 navvies were employed, labouring in what for the time were excellent conditions of work; to ensure this, as well as to maintain strict control of the quality of work, Birmingham Corporation preferred to carry out the scheme itself rather than put it in the hands of

**Tourist Information Centre** – Elan Valley Visitor Centre, Rhayader LD6 5HP ☎ 01597 810 898.
The Leisure Centre, North Street, Rhayader LD6 5BU ☎ 01597 810 591.

**Craft Centres** – For pottery visit **Marston Pottery** ⊘ (*Lower Cefn Faes, Rhayader*) and for glassware visit **Welsh Royal Crystal** (*see below*).

**Wildlife Centres** – Some nature reserves provide the opportunity to see the **red kite**, other birds of prey and other wildlife - **Gilfach Farm Longhouse** (*4mi/6km N of Rhayader by A 470 and E by a minor road*); **Gigrin Farm** (*0.5mi/0.8km S of Rhayader by A 470 and E by a minor road*).

**Elan Country Code** – Visitors should observe the following injunctions:
– Do nothing to pollute the water
– Leave all plants and animals for others to enjoy
– Keep dogs under close control
– Take all litter home
– Guard against all risk of fire
– If cycling or driving motor vehicles, keep strictly to the rights of way
– No swimming, boating or camping is allowed

**Adjacent Sights** – See Builth Wells, Llandrindod Wells, Llanidloes, Llanwrtyd Wells, Strata Florida Abbey.

contractors. A superb example of municipal confidence and enterprise, the Birmingham Water Supply Scheme was opened with great pomp on 21 July 1904 in the presence of King Edward VII, Queen Alexandra, and the Lord Mayor.

This was the first phase of the project, consisting of the three dams on the Elan and the base of one of the three planned dams on the Claerwen. When the time came to implement this second phase, advances in technology made it possible for a single dam to perform the work of the projected three. The Claerwen Dam, the largest in the scheme, was completed in 1952. The dams are best seen with water cascading over them, but the Elan Valley is popular at most times of the year and can become congested at times.

**Visitor Centre** ⊘ – The Centre is housed in the original main construction workshop close to the foot of the Caban Coch dam. Its varied displays, including audio-visual programmes, give an account not only of the construction, royal opening and operation of the scheme but also of the history and ecology of the area, marking the contrast in flora and fauna between meadow and woodland and the calm waters of the reservoirs and the fast-flowing mountain streams. There are reminders that Shelley passed some time in the now-submerged country houses of Cwm Elan and Nant Gwyllt, denouncing the poverty and injustice of the social conditions of rural Wales but also penning the lines:

"Woods, to whose depths returns to die
The wounded echo's melody".

The Elan curves past the meadow where the Centre is sited, below the windows of the restaurant, and flows beneath a charming small suspension bridge, now superseded by a stark modern structure giving access to **Elan Village**. This, the successor to the hutments which housed the construction force, has garden city type cottages and a handsome school, now an outdoor pursuits centre.

★**Caban Coch Dam and Reservoir** – The dam, its colossal scale (122ft/37m high and 610ft/186m long) emphasised by rustic masonry and giant-sized coping stones, makes an excellent introduction to the fine engineering works of the scheme as a whole.

Water released from this reservoir (capacity 7 187 million gallons/35 530 megalitres) maintains the flow of the Elan and thence of the Wye, source of much of the water supply of south-east Wales.

★**Garreg-ddu Dam** – *1mi/1.5km upstream.* As Caban Coch is at too low a level for water to run by gravity alone as far as Birmingham, the Garreg-ddu dam impounds water which is taken off at the Foel Tower, a fine example of what has been styled "Birmingham Baroque". From here the water flows along an aqueduct (73mi/117km long) at 2mph/3kph down an apparently shallow gradient (1 in 2 200), which is, however, steep enough to obviate the need for pumping. The dam also serves as a viaduct giving access to the Claerwen Valley.

★★**Dol-y-Mynach and Claerwen Dam and Reservoir** – *4.5mi/7km W of Garreg-ddu.* The road up to the Claerwen dam passes through fine woods of oak, beech and larch, crossing the occasional torrent rushing to the river below. There is a glimpse of the majestic foundations of the never-completed Dol-y-Mynach dam. The boggy terrain upstream is a haven for bird life, which can be observed from a hide. The final approach to the Claerwen dam is across open moorland, enhancing the awesome appearance of the Cyclopean structure, whose bulk can be appreciated both from below (from the main car park) and from the narrow road up to

### Red Kite

The red kite, which was once one of the most familiar birds of prey in Britain, is now one of the rarest. In the Middle Ages it was protected by law as it cleansed the city streets of rubbish by scavenging. In the country, however, where it preyed upon rabbits and poultry, it was trapped or poisoned or shot. So few pairs were left in Wales by 1900 that a number of naturalists, joined in 1905 by the RSPB, sought to prevent the extinction of the red kite, by protecting its nests and offering bounties to farmers who allowed the birds to breed. Owing to careful study of their natural behaviour and judicious assistance in breeding over the intervening years, the kite population in Wales is now able to withstand natural adversities, such as bad weather and a limited food supply. The hanging sessile oakwoods of the Elan Valley are an ideal habitat for nesting and roosting; the large areas of upland sheep pasture, where the sheep are kept out all year round, provide enough dead animals to provide the birds with carrion. Once again this beautiful raptor, with its white head, rusty red body and forked tail can be seen gliding on the thermal currents. Its cry, a high-pitched mewing sound, is most frequently heard during the mating season.

Pen-y-Garreg Dam

viewing platforms on its rim. The dam (184ft/56m high and 1 167ft/355m long) is built in concrete but faced in stone to conform to the aesthetic of the earlier dams; its reservoir (10 626 million gallons/48 300 megalitres) stretches away north-west-wards into the seemingly infinite spaces of the high moorlands, grazed by some of the 40 000 sheep of the Elan estate.

★**Pen-y-Garreg Dam and Reservoir** – *2mi/3.5km N of Garreg-ddu.* This dam, about the same size as Caban Coch, rises from a more intimate setting of conifer forest. It too has a dignified draw-down tower in "Birmingham Baroque". On the far bank of the reservoir (1 332 million gallons/6 055 megalitres), a footpath follows the course of one of the railways used in the construction of the scheme past "Devil's Gulch", a massive crag jutting out into the artificial lake.

★**Craig Goch Dam and Reservoir** – *2mi/3km N of Pen-y-Garreg.* The topmost dam (120ft/36m high and 513ft/156m long) is curved rather than straight like the scheme's other dams. It retains a water body of 2 028 million gallons/9 220 mega-litres.

**Rhayader** – *3mi/5km W of Elan Village by B 4518.* The first town on the Wye, little Rhayader owes its importance to its livestock market and its position on one of the main routes through mid-Wales; it is here that the main Cardiff-Llandudno road joins the Aberystwyth-Oxford road to follow the Wye upstream through its bleak upper valley. Its focal point is the clock tower which replaced a timber-framed Town Hall.
Rhayader is almost always busy with tourists pausing on their way through, or using the town as their base for exploring the neighbouring countryside by car, on foot or on horseback.
The **Rhayader Museum** ⊙ *(East Street, north side, first floor)* evokes local history and way of life through photographs, agricultural implements, poaching equipment and country crafts.

**Welsh Royal Crystal** ⊙ – *Brynberth Industrial Estate, Rhayader.* The company produces full lead crystal made by hand and decorated with traditional motifs as well as Celtic themes. There is a small display of the tools used in glass-blowing and engraving displayed in the entrance hall. On certain days, depending on the production cycle, visitors can watch the craftsmen at work.

**Cwmhir Abbey** – *4mi/6km E of Rhayader by A 44 and a minor road.* The last native Prince of Wales, Llywelyn the Last (d 1282), is commemorated by a handsome tablet, placed in the now ruined 12C Cistercian abbey, where he is thought to be buried. The fact that his grandfather, Llywelyn the Great (1173-1240), was a patron of the abbey may account for the grand scale of the buildings. The abbey never fully recovered from being almost destroyed during Owain Glyn Dŵr's rebellion (1401-02) and was dissolved in 1537 with only three monks in residence. Some of its stone was reused in Llanidloes church.

# ERDDIG★★

Among the most appealing of the National Trust's country houses, Erddig has a fascination due less to its architecture than to the way it evokes the three centuries of life led in it, not only by its masters but by its entire population of servants, skivvies, estate workers and ladies' companions.

## HISTORICAL NOTES

Erddig's first owner and builder was Joshua Edisbury, High Sheriff of Denbighshire, who completed his country residence here on the outskirts of then fashionable Wrexham in the 1680s. The expense bankrupted him; John Meller, the lawyer involved in his bankruptcy proceedings, was the next owner, but in 1733 the estate became the property of the **Yorke** family, in whose hands it remained until 1973.

The Yorkes, invariably named Simon or Philip, seem to have been engaging, mildly eccentric, and to have enjoyed an unusually intimate relationship with those that served them. Nothing was ever thrown away, unusually complete records and accounts were kept, and servants were treated as individuals, more portraits being painted (and later, photographs taken) of them than of the family, and their characteristics and achievements celebrated in whimsical verse. The epitaph of Simon I (d 1767) reads "a very mild, just and benevolent character,… An advantage which Amiable Men have over great Ones", while Philip I, an antiquarian and scholar, was referred to by the sporting writer Nimrod as "the worst horseman I ever saw in the saddle".

By the mid-20C Erddig was in trouble; the family's fortune was depleted and the house was being steadily attacked by subsidence from coal mining. The last Simon sat helplessly in Wellington boots surrounded by buckets and chamber pots to catch the water streaming in through the ruined roof. After his death in 1966, it seemed that demolition was Erddig's inevitable fate. His successor, the last Philip, struggled valiantly for a few more years, then gave house and grounds to the National Trust. After the biggest rescue operation ever undertaken by the Trust, Erddig was opened to the public in 1977.

## TOUR ⊙

**Outbuildings** – Erddig is entered not through the main door but via the extensive outbuildings, "offices" and servants' quarters, which give an excellent idea of the complexity of the domestic economy which sustained the life of a squire's family.

The route from the **Estate Yard** (still in use as the house's maintenance depot) to the Kitchen passes the **Kennel Yard** where the hounds were kept and fed from their own kitchen, the **Lime Yard** and **Saw Mill** (short video film on Erddig's restoration), the coarsely cobbled **Midden yard**, the **Stable Yard** with the family vehicles, the **Brewhouse**, **Bakehouse** and **Laundry Yard** with its hanging linen.

> **Adjacent Sights** – See Chirk Castle, Hawarden, Llangollen, Mold, Plas Newydd, Ruthin, Valle Crucis Abbey, Wrexham.

**Servants' Quarters** – Hare and pheasant lend an authentic atmosphere to the **Kitchen**, where the main meals were prepared, lesser meals like breakfast and tea being prepared in the **Still Room**. The passageway is lined with servants' photographs with captions in verse. **Agent's Office** and **Housekeeper's Room** were the abode of Mr Hughes and Mrs Brown respectively, the last to preside over Erddig's affairs in the early 20C before decline set in. The **Servants' Hall** shows the extent of the Yorkes' interest in those that looked after them; there are two sets of **servants' portraits** with doggerel verses, the first from the 1790s, the second from the 1830s, with bold representations of carpenters, a woodman, a gamekeeper, kitchen man and housemaid, even of a Black coachboy (early 18C). Two long-serving butlers were honoured with hatchment memorials.

**Interior** – Throughout the Yorkes' occupation, Erddig remained mostly furnished with the pieces the family had brought with them in the early 18C. Nor were any significant alterations carried out after John Meller had extended the house by adding wings to the original building. This makes Erddig's rooms almost uncannily evocative; as well as being "a treasure house of 18C furniture, porcelain and glass" (W Condry), it feels as if a member of the Yorke family might appear at any moment, particularly since the National Trust has made every effort to present many of the rooms as they would have been used by the Yorkes at the end of the 19C.

Thus the **Dining Room** with its array of family portraits, has its table laid in accordance with Mrs Beeton's 1901 edition of Household Management, and Louisa Yorke's records of meals eaten and entertainments provided can be seen. The **Saloon** has a metal ceiling; the Yorkes feared fire, and this is one of a number of fire-resistant measures introduced throughout the house. The symmetry of the garden layout can be appreciated from the windows. The **Tapestry Room** has early-18C Soho tapestries, the adjoining **Chinese Room** 18C Chinese painted wall-paper. The **Library** is as it was when used by Philip Yorke II c 1910; the little 17C portraits were drawn to illustrate his ancestor, Philip I's history of the Royal Tribes of Wales published in 1799. As the west-facing Entrance Hall proved draughty in use, the main entrance was moved to the lower ground floor and the hall turned into a **Music Room**; the instruments on display include a 19C Gothick organ. The **Drawing Room** was where the last of the Yorkes, Philip III, made his final stand. Late into the 20C Erddig had no mains water, no gas or electricity; a photograph here shows him reading by a bottled gas flame, whose feeble light was somewhat magnified by an arrangement of reflectors made from 18C silver salvers. In the **Red Bedroom**, the coat of arms was made in cut paper-work by Betty Ratcliffe, for many years the companion of Simon I's widow. Less favoured maids lived in the **Attic Bedrooms**.

The dark-panelled **Long Gallery** is a survival from Erddig's earliest days. The **State Bedroom** has an Oriental flavour; its centrepiece is the State Bed of 1720, which has miraculously recovered from its periodic soaking by rainwater.

Attendance at the **Chapel** was compulsory well into the 20C, the family entering from the Chinese Room, the servants through another door. On the lower ground floor, the **Tribes Room** serves as a **family museum**, the most poignant items being those recalling the varied life of the last Philip, actor with the Arthur Brough players of Folkestone, keen cyclist, Education Corps sergeant in the Second World War, and travel courier on cultural holidays to Spain.

Edward Price, Carpenter

Thomas Rogers, Carpenter

Jane Ebbrel, Spider brusher

Coachboy

★★**Gardens** – Together with Powis Castle, Erddig's gardens bear rare witness to the formal style of landscaping all but swept away in the course of the 18C pursuit of naturalness and informality.

To complement the long façade of no less than 19 bays resulting from his addition of two wings to the house, John Meller extended Joshua Edisbury's small walled garden further eastward. A slight change of level marks the original boundary. The garden is axial in character, the central bay of the house prolonged eastward by a path and then by a **canal** flanked by limes which show signs of having been pleached. The composition is terminated by a wrought-iron screen. On either side of the main axis further rows of pleached limes have been replanted, as have ranks of fruit trees and espaliers, many of them old or rare varieties. Close to the house are mid-19C stalagmitic fountains and early-20C parterres.

The **west front** of the house was not very flatteringly encased in stone in the late 18C to protect it from erosion by wind and rain sweeping in from the west. The conservative Philip I was at pains to protect the layout of the gardens to the east of the house but on the west side he made concessions to fashion, allowing the landscape architect William Emes to remove the gates and screens defining the forecourt and allow Nature to sweep right up to the façade.

**Erddig Country Park** – In part of the extensive grounds, now a country park, there was naturalistic tree planting but Emes' most striking contribution was the **Cup and Saucer**, a circular basin collecting the waters of the Black Brook which then flow out over a cylindrical waterfall, emerging via a tunnel beneath a rusticated arch. The confluence of the brook with the River Clywedog is overlooked by a **Norman castle mound**, while the Saxon earthwork known as **Wat's Dyke** runs through the grounds; no doubt both of these ancient monuments would have had great appeal for the scholarly Philip I.

# FISHGUARD

(Abergwaun) Pembrokeshire – Population 3 128
Michelin Atlas p 14 or Map 403 F 28

Three settlements stand by the shore of Fishguard Bay. **Lower Town** (y Cwm), hemmed in by cliffs at the mouth of the Gwaun valley, is the original fishing village, with seafarers' cottages as well as a small number of fishing boats as well as pleasure-craft. **Fishguard** proper on the clifftop has many of the facilities of a larger town, while on the far, western side of the bay is the village of **Goodwick** together with the railway and modern harbour with its roll-on roll-off ferry service to Ireland.

**Last Invasion of Britain** – An extraordinarily ill-planned and ill-executed expedition brought a motley force of French invaders to a humiliating surrender at Fishguard in 1797. France's hope of bringing Britain to her knees by disembarking an army whose core was composed of 600 convicts led by an elderly American, William Tate, seems far-fetched, especially when a simultaneous invasion of Ireland failed to take place.

The French arrived in Fishguard Bay aboard four men o'war in the early afternoon of 22 February 1797 but retreated eastward when Fishguard fort fired one of its three cannon rounds. The troops were disembarked up the cliffs of **Carregwastad** but spent most of their energy stealing chickens and consuming plundered wine. Similar confusion seems to have reigned on the British side, with squads of volunteers and yeomanry marching and countermarching. Legend has it that the French were dismayed when approached by large numbers of Welshwomen, whom they took to be British grenadiers because of their black hats and red cloaks. One lady, Jemima Nicholas, is supposed to have frightened a dozen Frenchmen into submission with a pitchfork. In the end a surrender was signed in the *Royal Oak Inn* in Fishguard, where memorabilia of this absurd episode may still be seen.

**Transatlantic aspirations** – Fishguard had figured as early as the mid-19C in railway promoters' plans to divert as much of the profitable Irish trade as possible away from the Holyhead route to South Wales, but it was only at the turn of the century that the Great Western Railway set to work to create a fine new harbour below the cliffs at Goodwick. Two million tons of rock were blasted away; a breakwater (2 000ft/600m) and a quay (1 100ft/340m) were constructed, together with a large railway station. All this effort was intended, not just to capture the Irish traffic, but to persuade transatlantic travellers away from Liverpool as the primary port of entry to Britain. For a few years from 1909, great liners like the *Mauretania* and *Lusitania* called, connecting with luxurious express trains that raced their passengers to London in record time. The inconvenience of unloading by tender was never overcome and the service died after the First World War, though the Irish ferries are busy enough and the old *Great Western Hotel* – long since renamed *Fishguard Bay Hotel* – still survives among the trees on the clifftop.

## Out and About

**Tourist Information Centres** – **Town Hall**, The Square, Fishguard SA65 9HA.
☎ 01348 873 484; Fax 01348 875 246.
**Ocean Lab**, The Parrog, Goodwick, Fishguard SA64 0DE – Personal callers only.
**2 Bank Cottages**, Long Street, Newport SA42 0TN ☎/Fax 01239 820 912.

**Craft Centres** – **Fishguard Invasion Centre** ⊙ *(St Mary's Church Hall, Main Street)* displays an **embroidered tapestry** commemorating the French invasion in 1797 and also work by local artists and craftspeople. The **West Wales Arts Centre** ⊙ *(16 West Street)* presents work created within the region and by makers from other parts of Europe. For woollen goods visit **Tregwynt Mill** ⊙ *(SW by A 40 to Letterston and W to Castle Morris and Tregwynt).*

**Beaches** – At Strumble Head *(W)* and at Cwm-yr-eglwys and Newport Sands North *(E).*

**Adjacent Sights** – See Cardigan, Haverfordwest, Newcastle Emlyn, Laugharne, Pembrokeshire Coast, St David's.

## Where to Stay

**Three Main Street**, 3 Main St, SA65 9HG. ☎ 01348 874 275; Fax 01348 874 017. Georgian townhouse (3 rm) just off the market square; informal, friendly style. Unfussy cooking with superb flavours, using lots of local produce, in particular fish, herbs and vegetables; pleasant lighter lunch option also offered.

**Tregynon**, Cwm Gwaun, SA65 9TU. *5.5mi/9km SE by B 4313 and 6mi/10km E by minor road.* ☎ 01239 820 531; Fax 01239 820 808. Rural farmhouse (6 rm) run by the owners, specialising in home-made dishes with the emphasis on local ingredients and vegetarian specialities.

**Heathfield Mansion**, Letterston, SA62 5EG. *5mi/8km S by A 40.* ☎/Fax 01348 840 263. Georgian house (3 rm) with comfortable, individually furnished rooms and peaceful atmosphere, set in 16 acres/6.5ha of pasture and woodland.

**Cnapan**, East St, Newport, SA42 0SY. *7mi/11km E by A 487.* ☎ 01239 820 575; Fax 01239 820 878. Well-established, family-run guesthouse (5 rm), in small town centre, offering home-cooked meals; close to beaches and good walks.

# EXCURSIONS

★**Strumble Head** – *By minor roads W via Goodwick.* **Pen Caer**, the countryside into which the French invasion force stumbled, consists of farmland interspersed with wilder land rising to tors and hillforts like Garn Fawr, whose Iron Age defences are difficult to distinguish from farm walls. The rocky coastline is spectacular and quite unspoiled, culminating in **Strumble Head**, where the promontory with its lighthouse is almost cut off from the mainland. The particular quality of the landscape can also be appreciated from the hamlet of **Llanwnda**, with farmstead, belfried church, a scattering of ancient stones, and fine views seawards.

**Newport** – *7mi/11km E of Fishguard by A 487.* This rather self-consciously trim little town still celebrates the status it enjoyed in medieval times with a Mayor, Lord (or Lady) Marcher and an annual beating of the bounds. The streets below the castle gatehouse *(now a private residence)* still show Norman-planned rectangularity in their layout. The much-decayed quayside at **Parrog** is a reminder of past shipbuilding and trading activity which was carried on despite the dangerous sand bar at the mouth of the estuary of the Nyfer. The **Presely Hills** (Mynydd Preseli) *(see p 226)* rise to the south, reaching a local high point in **Mynydd Carningli** *(1.5mi/2km S by steep footpaths).* Here on the rocky ridgetop is an extraordinary agglomeration of fortifications, terracing and enclosures forming a kind of hill-village which may possibly have been inhabited from Neolithic through to medieval times. It is supposedly the place where the Irish Saint Brynach communed with the angels (Carn Ingli = cairn of the angels).

**Nevern** – *2.5mi/4km E of Fishguard by A 487 and B 4582.* In this quiet village is **St Brynach's Church** ⊙ with a post-Norman tower and, in the churchyard, a superbly carved **Celtic cross** (10C–early-11C), quite the equal of the more famous example at Carew. There are also other outstanding early stones – a beautifully preserved Ogham stone and, nearby, a famous pilgrims' cross. The delightful churchyard is floristically rich, with a recorded 147 species growing among its yew trees, one of which periodically "weeps" a thick, red, blood-like sap.

Pentre Ifan Burial Chamber

**Castell Henllys** ⓥ – *4.5mi/7km W of Newport by A 487 and a minor road.* The density of Iron Age forts in this area suggests a fragmented society struggling for power and terrain. The promontory fort at Castell Henllys has been partly excavated and a thoroughgoing attempt made to recreate the atmosphere of the period by rebuilding three huts and other structures as accurately as possible. On their knoll amid the oakwoods the huts with their conical thatched roofs, lipped entrances and smoky interiors, make an altogether authentic-seeming impression; there are demonstrations of weaving, wood turning and basketmaking, and activities for children.

**Pentre Ifan Burial Chamber** – *4mi/6.5km SE of Newport by A 487 and minor roads.* On a north-facing slope of the Presely Hills (Mynydd Preseli), overlooking the valley of the Nyfer, stands one of the most spectacular megalithic monuments in the country, wondered over and reproduced in drawing and painting from the earliest days of archaeology. It consists of four great upright stones, three of which support a massive capstone. The outline of the burial chamber suggests that this was the burial place of a person or people of considerable importance.

# FLINT
### (Y Flint) Flintshire
Michelin Atlas p 33 or Map 403 K 24

This now entirely industrial Deeside town was the first of Edward I's chain of castles and fortified settlements intended to secure the English hold on North Wales.

**Flint Castle** – Severed from its dependent town by the line of the Chester and Holyhead Railway, the **ruined castle** commands the estuary of the Dee from a low rocky promontory. Building began in 1277 as Edward's northern army pushed its way westwards. The former moat and Outer Bailey precede the Inner Bailey, which is almost a perfect square in plan, with a tower in each corner. This unusual, massive detached keep, the **Great Tower**, probably modelled on the Tour de Constance in the bastide town of Aigues Mortes in southern France, was designed with its own well and surrounded by its own moat, as a last refuge for the garrison should the rest of the castle be captured.

The castle was besieged during Edward's second campaign and again in the Civil War, when its Royalist garrison was reduced to eating its own horses. The Inner Bailey, described by Shakespeare as "the base court where kings grow base", was the scene of Richard II's encounter with the usurper, Bolingbroke.

**Town** – Both castle and town were built with great speed to provide a secure base for Edward's thrust westwards. A workforce of thousands was employed in the initial phases, including hundreds of hardy diggers brought from the far-away Fens of eastern England. Rather than walls, a ditch, bank and palisade enclosed the town, which was laid out on an elongated grid pattern with only one cross street, an arrangement which suited the long burgage plots favoured by medieval surveyors. The town did not grow beyond its walls until the arrival of industry in the 19C, and the ancient street pattern remains.

**Adjacent Sights** – See Denbigh, Hawarden, Holywell, Mold, Rhuddlan, Rhyl, St Asaph.

# GLAMORGAN HERITAGE COAST ★

Vale of Glamorgan
Michelin Atlas pp 15 and 16 or Map 403 J 29

The Vale of Glamorgan faces the Bristol Channel from a splendid stretch of cliffs (13mi/20km) which extend westward from the great power stations at Aberthaw to the little resort of Ogmore-by-Sea. The Heritage Coast, designated in 1972, extends further west to take in the dunes of Merthyr Mawr and Newton Point.
The cliffs (average height 100ft/30m) are composed of alternate layers of Liassic limestones and shales which are continually being eroded by the sea and thus present a constant vertical or overhanging profile. The beach normally consists of a level platform of plates of limestone, sometimes with a band of pebbles at the cliff foot. The great tidal range (up to 50ft/15m) of the Bristol Channel, together with the risk of cliff falls, make the shore a potentially perilous environment.
A number of Iron Age forts, now much eroded, were built along the clifftop, notably at **Summerhouse Point** and **Nash Point**. Rather than looking to the sea, the medieval population settled just inland, farming the rich soils of the Vale and leaving a series of pretty **villages** with houses and churches built from the blue-grey limestone.

---

**Tourist Information Centres** – **Llantwit Major Visitor Centre** ⊙ *(Town Hall)* providing information on the Glamorgan Coast area. **Heritage Coast Visitor Centre** ⊙ *(Southerndown near Ogmore-by-Sea)* presenting displays on the natural history of this unusual coastline.

**Walks** – A **clifftop walk** runs almost the whole length of the coast, giving continually changing views of the Channel and its shipping, and of the coast and hills of Somerset and Devon.

**Beaches** – At a number of places where breaks in the cliff line occur, including **Dunraven Bay**.

**Adjacent Sights** – See Barry, Cardiff, Castell Coch, Llancaiach Fawr, Llandaff, Llantrisant, Margam Park, Penarth, Porthcawl, Swansea, Museum of Welsh Life.

---

**Llantwit Major-Llanilltud Fawr** – This attractive little town is the largest of the settlements fringing the coast, sited, like the others, well inland, and built of the local limestone. The place derives its name from Illtud, a late-5C Celtic saint, founder of the famous monastic college at which, by tradition, St David was educated. The renovated medieval **Town Hall** now houses an Information Centre on the Glamorgan Coast area.
A maze of medieval streets occupies the low rise below which stands **St Illtud's Church** ⊙. This is an extraordinary structure, in effect two churches in one, linked by a slender tower. To the east is the 13C collegiate church, with a splendid wall painting of a big-footed St Christopher, and a Jesse niche. To the west is the original parish church, Norman in date but sited on the foundations of the 6C Celtic church and largely rebuilt in the 15C. It houses a number of effigies as well as a fine collection of **early Christian stones and crosses**, evidence of a school of sculpture which flourished here from the late 9C onwards. Further westward still are the remains of the Galilee Chapel.

**St Donat's Castle** ⊙ – Embedded in woodland roughly midway along the coast is this much-restored castle, now the home of **Atlantic College**, one of a number of international sixth-form institutions which prepare students for the International Baccalaureate Diploma. Restoration of the castle began in the early 20C and was continued by the newspaper magnate Randolph Hearst, who re-roofed the dining hall with a ceiling from a Lincolnshire church. The **gardens** dropping steeply to the shore were first terraced in Tudor times.

---

# GOWER PENINSULA ★★

Swansea
Michelin Atlas p 15 or Map 403 H 29

With its magnificent coastline of dramatic cliffs and sweeping marshlands and its interior of ancient farmland and commons, this peninsula (14mi/22km long) projecting westward into Carmarthen Bay has been called a "microcosm of all that is finest in the Welsh landscape". Its designation in 1957 as Britain's first Area of Outstanding Natural Beauty gave official recognition to its special quality as well as offering it some protection against the spreading suburbs of Swansea at its eastern extremity.
Few contrasts could be greater than that between the formidable rocky ramparts of the Gower's southern coast and the vast expanses of sand dune, salt-marsh and mud which merge into the glittering estuary of the River Loughor to the north. The south shore attracts ramblers to its clifftop paths and myriad families to its glorious sandy

---

## Out and About

**Tourist Information Centres** – **Gower Heritage Centre** ⊙ *(Park Mill; see below)* and **Rhossili National Trust Visitor Centre** ⊙.

**Tide Timetable** – For information about the times of high and low tides consult the display at the Rhossili National Trust Visitor Centre and Old Coastguard Station Visitor Centre or contact the Coastguard ☎ 01792 366 534.

**Beaches** – At Caswell Bay, Port Eynon and Rhossili.

**Exploring On Foot** – There are several good points for leaving the car and taking to the footpaths *(listed in clockwise order from the western outskirts of Swansea)*:

– From the Gower Heritage Centre *(A 4118 – car park)* northwest through deciduous wood to **Park Wood** and the **Giant's Grave**, a prehistoric burial site;

– From Kittle Post Office *(B 4436)* walk south, descending a steep path to an old rocky river bed, where the water can be heard flowing underground;

– From the viewpoint above **Penmaen** *(car park, observation table and picnic site)* walk down to the bay, via stepping stones *(1.5mi/2.5km)*;

– Explore the **Oxwich Bay National Nature Reserve** *(beach car park)* or take the woodland walk to **Oxwich Point**;

– From Pitton car park *(off B 4247)* walk along the cliffs between **Port Eynon** and **Rhossili**;

– Explore the **Whiteford National Nature Reserve** *(car park N of Llanmadog Church)* or walk up to the summit of **Cefn Bryn** for the view and **Arthur's Stone**.

**Worms Head** is accessible by a rocky causeway for only 2hr on either side of low tide.

**Local Specialities** – Sea trout (sewin), cockles (from Crofty on the north coast) and shellfish, laver bread (seaweed), marsh samphire and salt-marsh lamb, mushrooms, gulls' eggs.

**Adjacent Sights** – See Carmarthen, Llanelli, Neath, Port Talbot, Swansea.

---

bays, while surfers ride the curling breakers of westward-facing **Rhossili Bay**, one of the country's most spectacular beaches. The salty grass of the north coast is grazed by sheep and ponies, while its tidal mud provides rich sustenance for a wealth of seabirds *(see p 186)* no longer subjected to such intense competition by the famous cockle-gatherers of Crofty.

## SIGHTS *in clockwise order*

**Bishopston Valley and Pwll Du Bay** – From the medieval church built into the hillside at Bishopston, a walk (1.5mi/2.5km) leads down a narrow, well-tree'd valley to the shingle shore at Pwll Du (Black Pool) Bay.

**Park Mill** – Well placed to catch tourists on the main road to the west of the peninsula is this complex consisting of a restored mill, craft shops and an array of old agricultural implements arranged along the mill leat (900ft/270m).

**Three Cliffs Bay** – *30min on foot there and back from car park near Park Mill or from Southgate village.* At low tide, the stream known as Pennard Pill winds across the sands of this enchanting bay past the feet of the jagged rocks which give the place its name.

Inland, picturesquely perched over the stream and attacked more by drifting sand than by any human enemy, are the ruins of **Pennard Castle**, built at the end of the 13C and abandoned by the start of the 15C. To the east of Southgate, the cliff path leads to **Pwll Du Head** (318ft/97m), the highest point along the coast. More caves have been eroded in the limestone here and have yielded interesting finds; both Minchon Hole and Bacon Hole contained the bones of prehistoric animals, while the former also had relics of Iron Age domestic occupation.

**Oxwich** – The splendid stretch of sand in this bay is backed by dunes and freshwater marshes. Sheltered by trees is the medieval **Church of St Illtyd** ⊙, with a battlemented tower and a chancel ceiling painted in the 1930s by Leslie Young, scene designer for Sadler's Wells.

On the limestone headland above extends the ruin of **Oxwich Castle** ⊙, a splendid 16C courtyard house. The builder of the south range and the gateway with its coat of arms was Sir Rice Mansel, who decamped to Margam c 1540, leaving his son Sir Edward to construct the spectacular six-storey east block, described with minimal exaggeration as a "Tudor skyscraper".

J Cornish/National Trust Photographic Library

Rhossili Beach

**Port Eynon** – The remoteness of the Gower encouraged smuggling. At one point no fewer than eight excise men were stationed at this village of whitewashed cottages to keep illegal imports in check; it is neither they, however, nor their prey who are celebrated in the churchyard by a marble memorial but brave lifeboatmen drowned in 1916. Port Eynon's sandy bay is inevitably hugely popular.

★★**Rhossili** – The approach by road through the farmlands of the western Gower does little to prepare the visitor for the scenic surprises of the peninsula's south-western extremity. To the north, **Rhossili Down**, Gower's highest hill, drops seaward to a grassy platform one field wide, then via a low and shallow cliff to a broad bay curving northward to distant dunes and swept continuously by skeins of surf. To the south, beyond the narrow strips of the village's still-surviving medieval fields, a great sea-snake seems to undulate, raising its rocky head to scan the ocean. This is **Worms Head**, a mile-long limestone spit divided into three sections and accessible on foot for only 2hr 30min either side of low tide, its Anglo-Saxon name *(wurm)* an indication of its serpentine character. To cross the causeway from the mainland, traverse the natural arch known as the Devil's Bridge, and listen to the sea booming beneath the Head is an experience comparable in its sublimity to climbing a high mountain.

Rhossili village was once remote. The railway only ever touched the fringes of the Gower, while Rhossili even lacked a proper road until the early years of the 20C and the inhabitants of the few cottages would make their infrequent journeys to Swansea on foot. The first car seems to have come in 1905; the tiny village now receives half a million visitors a year, its focus no longer the humble church with its saddleback tower but the huge car park.

The **cliff walk** between Tears Point south of Rhossili to Overton and Port Eynon is one of the most exhilarating in Wales. The limestone which forms the majestic headlands is also riddled with fissures and caves. In one – **Paviland Cave** – a famous find was made in 1823, of human bones first named the "Red Lady" because of their red-ochre staining, but later revealed to be the partial skeleton of a young man who lived some 24 000 years ago. Another cave, **Culver Hole**, has been walled in and may be associated with the lost castle of Port Eynon.

**Weobley Castle** ⊘ – In friendly proximity to a farmyard, this compact little castle was more of a fortified manor house than a full-blown fortress. Arranged around a courtyard, its ruins perch on top of the old cliff line of the Gower's north coast. The view across the salt-marshes and the Loughor Estuary to the hills beyond is superb. To the north-west, the sand dunes of Whiteford Burrows stretch out into the estuary, terminated by the now-abandoned lighthouse built in cast iron in 1865.

**Cefn Bryn** – The backbone of the peninsula is a central ridge of Old Red Sandstone, Cefn Bryn (over 600ft/180m), giving broad views over the whole of the peninsula and beyond. Just over 0.25mi/400m north of the minor road running east from Renoldston is the chambered tomb known as **Arthur's Stone**, a massive boulder resting on smaller slabs. At the eastern end of the Gower, shaggy commons border the suburbs of Swansea.

# GROSMONT

(Y Grusmwnt) Monmouthshire

Michelin Atlas p 16 or Map 403 L 28

A compact village like Grosmont is a rarity in this region of scattered farmsteads. The village was originally a medieval borough founded along with the castle above it. The little **Town Hall** in the main street is a somewhat forlorn symbol of former municipal glories. The **Church of St Nicholas** ⊘, with its eight-sided tower, dominant spire and little-used nave, is obviously much too large for the present rural population.

**Three castles fayre** – The "Three castles fayre.... in a goodly ground" (Thomas Churchyard, 1587), which helped consolidate the Norman grip on the southern March, were Grosmont, White Castle and Skenfrith. The "goodly ground" is an apt description of the lovely, lonely farming countryside of northern Monmouthshire, cut by the winding River Monnow and Offa's Dyke Footpath and undisturbed by main roads and modern intrusions.

> **Adjacent Sights** – See Abergavenny, Blaenavon, Brecon, Llanthony Priory, Monmouth, Raglan Castle, Tretower.

**Grosmont Castle** – The castle stands protected by its moat above the Monnow. It owes much of its present appearance to Hubert de Burgh, a distinguished soldier of wildly fluctuating fortunes who was twice lord of the Three Castles in the early 13C, and who built the hall block and improved the defences generally.

A century later, when the Three Castles had passed into the hands of the Earls of Lancaster, and the Welsh threat had been largely overcome, the role of Grosmont changed from fortress to favoured residence and remodelling took place in order to improve the level of comfort. The tall and elegant Gothic chimney dates from this period.

The last time any of the Three Castles saw action was in 1405 when the future Henry V beat off Owain Glyn Dŵr's rebels with great loss of life.

## EXCURSIONS

**White Castle** ⊘ – *7mi/11km S of Grosmont by minor roads.* On its hilltop site, the austere ruin of White Castle stands much as it did in the mid-13C. Like its two companion castles, it almost certainly originated in an earth-and-timber stronghold thrown up in the very first years of the Norman Conquest by the builder of Chepstow Castle, William Fitz Osbern, although it was rebuilt in stone a century later.

It then fell into the hands of the Crown together with Grosmont and Skenfrith, and it was probably the future Edward I, then Lord Edward, who in the 1260s provided it with its splendid array of round towers which so characterise its appearance today. At the same time, the orientation of the castle was reversed; the approach now led through an outer gate and a newly walled outer ward, thence across the deep moat to the great gatehouse with its pair of particularly intimidating towers. The original, southern gateway was replaced with a postern gate, which now provides a delightful, park-like view of the moat and the hornwork beyond.

**Skenfrith** – *7mi/11km SE of Grosmont by B 4347 and B 4521.* Prettily situated by the bridge over the Monnow, Skenfrith consists of a single street winding past its castle and church.

The mainly 13C **St Bridget's Church** ⊘ has a fine squat tower with a two-stage belfry and a huge buttress. The interior has many fascinating features, including a Jacobean pew, a splendid 15C embroidered cope, and the tomb of John Morgan (d 1557), the last Governor of the Three Castles.

**Skenfrith Castle**, plainer even than White Castle, was rebuilt in stone in the early 13C by Hubert de Burgh. Within the high curtain wall with its corner towers is a stern round tower with a battered base, similar in design to the one at Tretower Court *(see p 279)*.

# HARLECH CASTLE ★★

Gwynedd

Michelin Atlas p 32 or Map 403 H 25

Standing four-square on its rock against a spectacular background of sea and mountain, Harlech Castle has inevitably become the very image of a medieval stronghold, its strength the inspiration for the song *Men of Harlech*.

The little town of Harlech lies on the south-west border of the Snowdonia National Park and it is a good base from which to explore the mountains inland.

## HISTORICAL NOTES

In layout similar to Beaumaris, Harlech Castle was one of the "Iron Ring" of fortresses rapidly run up by Edward I to secure his conquest of North Wales. Although its crag overlooking the sea seems a natural site for a stronghold, there is no trace of any earlier fortification, despite a reference to a court at "Harddllech" in the story of Princess Branwen in the *Mabinogion*. The builder of the castle was the redoubtable

160

**Tourist Information Centre** - Snowdonia National Park Visitor Centre ⊘ – Gwyddfor House, High Street, Harlech LL46 2YA ☎/Fax 01766 780 658.

**Beaches** – At Harlech, Llandanwg and Dyffryn Ardudwy.

**Adjacent Sights** – See Bala, Barmouth, Blaenau Ffestiniog, Criccieth, Dolgellau, Lleyn Peninsula, Porthmadog, Portmeirion, Pwllheli, Snowdonia.

**Master James of St George**, Edward's Savoyard architect, who resided here as Constable between 1290 and 1293. In anticipation of attack from landward, the castle was built to be supplied by sea (which reached to the foot of the crag until the 18C) via a watergate. This enabled it to withstand the besieging forces of Madog ap Llywelyn during the revolt of 1294-95, though it fell to Owain Glyn Dŵr in 1404 and briefly became his seat of power before being retaken in 1408 by the future Henry V. The castle demonstrated its importance and the quality of its defences on two more occasions, being the last Lancastrian and the last Royalist stronghold to fall in the Wars of the Roses and the Civil War respectively.

## TOUR ⊘

With its high walls and sextet of massive, outward-facing drum towers, the castle completely dominates the small town of sloping streets gathered around it. Defended more than adequately by cliffs and crags, it was only on the eastern side that it was vulnerable to attack and it is here that the most elaborate fortifications were built. The splendid **gatehouse** is approached across a ditch cut in the rock, originally via a bridge with two towers. An outer gate with twin turrets elegantly corbelled out stands in the outer curtain wall, much of which is in ruins. Beyond the constricted outer ward are the awesome outer towers of the gatehouse and a whole series of obstacles including three doors and portcullises. The gatehouse

Harlech Castle

contained comfortable suites of rooms for the Constable, his high status expressed by the sophisticated architectural treatment of the **courtyard façade**, with its elegant corner turrets and six great windows. The inner ward is made to seem smaller by the scale of its walls; from the sentry-walk there are stupendous **views** over the coastal levels of Morfa Harlech and north to Snowdonia.

Outside the castle, a striking modern (1984) equestrian statue takes as its theme a tragic episode from the *Mabinogion* in which the British king Bendigeidfran lost his nephew Gwern in battle.

## EXCURSIONS

**Ardudwy** – *4mi/7km by A 496*. The coastal plain, known as Ardudwy, stretching south from Harlech is centred on the villages of Llanbedr and Dyffryn Ardudwy.

The coastline has dunes and fine sandy beaches, including **Shell Island** *(Mochras)* with its fascinating deposits of more than 200 kinds of seashell.

The narrow broken plateau inland is dense with evidence of settlement from prehistoric to medieval times, including the tumbled enclosures known as Muriau Gwyddelod ("Irishmen's walls") *(east of and above Harlech)* and Neolithic **burial chambers** at **Cors-y-Gedol** and **Dyffryn Ardudwy**.

**Llyn Cwm Bychan** – *4mi/7km E of Harlech by narrow and steep lanes*. The delightful lake known as **Llyn Cwm Bychan** feeds the equally delightful valley carved by the rushing River Artro. From the car park a mountain path leads to the famous **Roman Steps**, a paved routeway leading up to a pass through the Rhinog range; the steps are in fact medieval in date, probably part of a packhorse trail.

# HAVERFORDWEST

(Hwlffordd) Pembrokeshire – Population 11 099
Michelin Atlas p 14 or Map 403 F 28

Dominated by the ruins of its Norman castle, the old county town of Pembrokeshire still has a townscape marked by the rebuilding that took place in Georgian times, though little remains in today's workaday town of the atmosphere of what, at its height, was called a "little Bath".

Haverfordwest owes its importance to its position at what until the 1970s was the lowest crossing point of the Western Cleddau River. The rebuilding of the castle in stone in the 12C-13C was followed by urban expansion, first in the form of a Flemish settlement around the Church of St Martin, then by a walled and gated town on the river bank below the castle. Trade by sea with France, Spain and Ireland as well as with other British ports made Haverfordwest "the best buylt, the most civill occupied town in South Wales" by Tudor times. The coming of the railway, however, slowly strangled this traffic, although it was not until the 1920s that the last small steamer sailed away down the river. The maritime past is recalled by a few old warehouses and the *Bristol Trader Inn* on the west bank of the river, while the old dock on the east bank has been ignominiously filled in to create a car park.

## Out and About

**Tourist Information Centre** – Old Bridge, Haverfordwest, Pembrokeshire SA61 2EZ. ☎ 01437 763 110; Fax 01437 767 738.

**Adjacent Sights** – See Carew, Fishguard, Laugharne, Milford Haven, Pembroke, Pembrokeshire Coast, St David's, Tenby.

### Where to Eat

**Four Seasons**, Nantgaredig, SA32 7NY. *5mi/8km E of Carmarthen by A 40 and B 4310*. ☎ 01267 290 238. Farmhouse accommodation (6 rm) in relaxed and friendly atmosphere; breakfast served in the farmhouse; modern style of cooking using local produce; small but comprehensive wine shop within the restaurant.

### Where to Stay

**Wilton House**, 6 Quay St, Haverfordwest, SA61 1BG. ☎ 01437 760 033; Fax 01437 760 297. Spacious Georgian accommodation (9 rm) with high ceilings; informal dining; town centre location near shops and craft workshops.

**Lower Haythog Farm**, Spittal, SA62 5QL. *5mi/8km NE of Haverfordwest by B 4329*. ☎ 01437 731 279. Large dairy farm (4 rm) with relaxing conservatory overlooking the garden; creative home-cooked meals prepared by very friendly owner.

**Castle** – The castle was never taken in battle. Its curtain walls and towers are perhaps best enjoyed from below as they brood menacingly over the town. A prison installed here in the early 19C now houses the County Record Office; the County Museum is now housed at Scolton Park *(see below)*.

**St Mary's Church** ⊙ – The stepped buildings of the High Street rise steeply from Castle Square at river level towards the town's principal place of worship. Hemmed in by railings and retaining walls, the large 13C church has much fine carving and a late-15C tie-beam roof.

## EXCURSIONS

**Llys-y-Frân Country Park and Reservoir** ⊙ – *10mi/16km NE of Haverfordwest by A 40, B 4313 or B 4329.* A footpath and cycle trail (8mi/13km) follows the perimeter of this long reservoir (2 310 million gallons/10 500 million litres), built in 1968 to meet the growing needs of Milford Haven's oil terminals and refineries. Its waters provide a home for rainbow and brown trout; a water conservation garden has been laid out near the lake.

**St Michael's Church, Rudbaxton** ⊙ – *4mi/7km N of Haverfordwest by A 40 and minor roads.* In a remote-seeming spot which is in fact only just beyond Haverfordwest's aerodrome, this little early-13C building is the successor to an earlier church granted by Wizo the Fleming to the Knights of St John of Jerusalem. The interior is dominated by the extraordinary **Howard monument★**, which dates from the end of the 17C and occupies virtually the whole of the east wall of the south aisle. Various Howards, all in contemporary dress and vividly coloured, hold skulls in their hands as they stare aloofly over the heads of the congregation.

**★Scolton Museum and Country Park** ⊙ – *4mi/7km N of Haverfordwest by B 4329.* The 19C house known as Scolton Manor has been refurbished to evoke the era at the turn of the 19C-20C. Visitors can wander through the family rooms, servants' parlour and extensive cellars; on the first floor are the nursery and a costume gallery on the theme of "Victorian Vogue". The stable block now houses displays on farriery, carpentry and ironmongery; another outbuilding is devoted to an exhibition on Pembrokeshire railways.
There is a nature trail in the parkland and a visitor centre with exhibits on "green" issues.

**Picton Castle** ⊙ – *5mi/8km E of Haverfordwest by A 40 and minor roads.* Picton, the successor to an earlier castle erected at a strategic point close to the confluence of the Eastern and Western Cleddau rivers, was much rebuilt and added to in the 18C and 19C to transform it into a large and comfortable country house, which is now inhabited by a descendant of the original 13C owner. Tours of the interior offer a glimpse of his art collection, which includes impressive work by members of the family and by Sickert and Sutherland. Craft displays and exhibitions are housed in buildings surrounding the castle courtyard.

**Blackpool Mill** ⊙ – *8mi/13km E of Haverfordwest by A 40, A 4075 and a minor road.* This imposing Georgian corn mill stands on the Eastern Cleddau on the site of an ancient forge. Its machinery has been restored, and "caverns" in the basement contain fearsome replicas of prehistoric beasts as well as a decidedly non-historic dragon.

**Llawhaden Castle** – *9mi/14km E of Haverfordwest by A 40 and minor roads.* The great gatehouse of this ruined castle was the final late-14C addition to what by that time had become a palatial residence rather than a simple stronghold. It still seems to evoke the respect due to its builders, the medieval bishops of St David's, whose extensive estates it protected.

**Narberth** – *10mi/16km E of Haverfordwest by A 40 and B 4314.* This tiny town prides itself on lying astride the **Landsker**, the notional line dividing the Anglicised south of Pembrokeshire from the resolutely Welsh north. All around is unspoiled farming countryside threaded by a network of footpaths. The toytown **Town Hall** (c 1830) with its lock-up is adorned by a cupola. Nearby is the **Wilson Museum** ⊙ displaying local memorabilia and a small but splendidly illustrated exhibition devoted to the *Mabinogion (see p 56)*.

*To find a hotel or restaurant*
*consult the current* **Michelin Red Guide**
*Great Britain and Ireland*

(Penarlâg) Flintshire – Population 1 901
Michelin Atlas pp 33 and 34 or Map 403 K 24

Almost within sight of the city of Chester, Hawarden bestrides the old main road from Cheshire to North Wales. **William Ewart Gladstone** (1809-98) lived at Hawarden Castle and is buried in the parish church; for many years the village was as closely associated with the long-serving Prime Minister as Chartwell is with Churchill or Colombey-les-deux-Églises with de Gaulle.

**Two Castles** – A splendid castle mound, topped by the picturesque ruin of a keep (Hawarden Old Castle), stands in the romantic setting of the well-wooded park-lands laid out in the mid-18C by Sir John Glynne around the country mansion called Broadland Hall. A later Glynne Gothicised the Hall by adding turrets and battlements and changed its name to Hawarden Castle. In 1839 Gladstone married into the family and later made his home there.

> **Adjacent Sights** – See Erddig, Flint, Holywell, Mold, Ruthin, Wrexham.

**St Deiniol's Church** ⊙ – In a secluded setting away from the main road stands the church, which was rebuilt by Sir Gilbert Scott after being burnt out in 1857. In the **Gladstone Memorial Chapel** is the sumptuous Arts and Crafts marble monument to the great Liberal leader. He is shown in recumbent effigy with his wife Catherine, a crucifix between them. The monument, the work of Sir William Richmond, dates from 1906. Slightly earlier is the stained glass of the west window, a fine Nativity by Burne-Jones, designed in 1898, the year of his death and made by the firm of Morris & Co.

**St Deiniol's Library** ⊙ – Close to the church is a building of collegiate character, the only residential library in Britain, which was founded by WE Gladstone "to bring together readers who had no books and books who had no readers". In 1889, at the age of 80, using a wheelbarrow and assisted by his valet and one of his daughters, he transferred 32 000 of his books into two large iron rooms, built to receive them. He endowed the library with £40 000 and the present building (1902), put up after his death, houses not only his extensive book collection but many subsequent purchases.

*For a pleasant and quiet hotel in a convenient location*
*Consult the current edition of the* **Michelin Red Guide** *Great Britain and Ireland*

# HAY-ON-WYE ★

(Y Gelli) Powys – Population 1 407
Michelin Atlas pp 25 and 26 or Map 403 K 27

This little medieval market town on the English border emerged from the sleep of centuries in the 1960s when an eccentric and enterprising bookseller filled fire station, cinema and empty shops with secondhand books. His lead was followed by other dealers, who have made Hay into a magnet for bibliophiles from around the world. The annual Literary Festival attracts many visitors; others use the town as their base for exploring the magnificent landscapes of the Wye Valley and the Black Mountains.

**Town Centre** – Cognate with the French *haie* and the Dutch *Den Haag*, Hay signifies a place surrounded by an enclosure. The town's original nucleus lies just to the southwest, where the parish church – a 19C rebuilding – stands close to the original castle mound of the early 12C. This first Norman fortress was replaced c 1200 by the present **castle** rising over the close-packed streets. It was sacked by Welsh and English in turn, and now consists of keep and gateway and the

> **The Book King**
>
> Since Richard Booth came to Hay in 1961, his book empire has waxed, then waned. The original cinema bookshop is now run by a rival, but Booth's books are still piled high in "The Famous", a labyrinth of a building behind an exuberant Victorian shopfront featuring carved heads of bulls and other beasts. Never slow to promote himself or his adopted cause of rural revival, Booth has remained in the public eye over the years by having himself crowned as the King of Hay, declaring independence from both Wales and Great Britain, and issuing his own, edible banknotes (printed on rice paper).

## Out and About

**Hay-on-Wye Festival** – The Festival of Literature and the Arts *(10 days in late May)* draws on the town's fame as a centre for buying second-hand books; information available from the **Festival Box Office**, Hay-on-Wye HR3 5BX. ☎ 01497 821 299, Fax 01497 821 066; tickets@litfest.co.uk

**Adjacent Sights** – See Builth Wells, Knighton, Llandrindod Wells, Llanwrtyd Wells, Old Radnor, Presteigne, Welshpool.

## Where to Eat

**Old Black Lion**, Lion St, HR3 5AD. ☎ 01497 820 841. 17C coaching inn with local atmosphere and traditional bar meals. Quirky-shaped bedrooms (10 rm); Oliver Cromwell is reputed to have stayed at this inn.

## Where to Stay

**Old Post Office**, Llanigon, HR3 5QA. *2.5mi/4km SW by B 4350.* ☎ 01497 820 008. Charming 17C house (3 rm) with unique character; immaculate style; cosy, personally run.

**Three Cocks**, Three Cocks, LD3 0SL. *5mi/8km SW by B 4350.* ☎ 01497 847 215; Fax 01497 847 339. Part 15C inn; family run and well established; continental cuisine; large selection of Belgian beers.

**Trefecca Fawr**, Talgarth, LL3 0PW. *7.5mi/12km SW by A 4078.* ☎ 01874 712 195. Open Mar-Nov. Medieval Hall (3 rm) with 17C additions, romantic gentry house with antique furnishings, set in gardens in the National Park near the Black Mountains.

**Griffin Inn**, Llyswen, LD3 0UR. *7.5mi/12km W by B 4350 and A 470.* ☎ 01874 754 241; Fax 01874 754 592. Part 15C family run sporting inn (7 rm), comfortable, friendly hostelry with warm ambience; traditional menu using Wye Valley produce.

---

many-gabled Jacobean mansion inserted into the ruins c 1660. The mansion was burnt out in 1977 but has been restored; the ground floor, inevitably so in Hay, is a book shop.

Castle and mansion are built in warm grey stone, as is much of the rest of the town. The overall character of the buildings lining the complex web of streets and alleyways seems Victorian and late Georgian, though in many cases more ancient structures lie hidden behind later façades. The oldest building is a 16C cruck-built hall, now the *Three Tuns* public house. The three town gates have long since disappeared but the triangular outline of the walls can still be traced and some fragments remain to north-east and south-west. The town seems to turn its back on the River Wye, from which it is separated by the course of the 18C horse-drawn tramway and the 19C railway which succeeded it but which was itself closed in the 1960s.

## EXCURSION

★**Hay Bluff** – *4mi/6km S of Hay-on-Wye, mostly on a single track road.* The spectacular north-facing escarpment of the Black Mountains, visible from as far away as the Cotswold Hills (some 50mi/80km to the east) can be appreciated in close-up from the sweeping stretch of open land known as Hay Common or the Allt. The narrow road traverses the common, grazed by wandering sheep and ponies, and winds up to Gospel Pass (1 778ft/542m).

Wales Tourist Board

Bookstalls below the Castle, Hay-on-Wye

---

### Kilvert of Clyro

The area around Hay is indelibly associated with the endearing figure of Francis Kilvert (1857-94), for several years curate of the church in the village of Clyro *(1mi/1.5km NW)*. Kilvert's diaries are among the most widely read in the English language, for their warm humanity, sensitivity to landscape, and above all for the minutely detailed and affectionate picture they give of rural life in Britain in the late 19C.

---

To the west is The Tumpa (2 264ft/690m), to the north-east the solemn mass Hay Bluff (2 221ft/677m), the latter a favourite jumping-off point for hang gliders. Both heights offer incomparable **views** over the Wye Valley and far in central Wales.

# HOLYHEAD

(Caergybi) Anglesey – Population 11 796
Michelin Atlas p 32 or Map 403 G 24

Reached by the great causeway which Thomas Telford built in 1822 to link Angles to Holy Island, Holyhead has long been the main port connecting England and Wal with Ireland, particularly with the capital, Dublin.

## HISTORICAL NOTES

Holyhead harbour is essentially a 19C creation but the port's maritime history go back to the Roman naval base founded here in the late 3C AD in an attempt to contr pirates in the Irish Sea; its walls still stand, forming an enclosure around the paris church, which is dedicated to St Cybi, the Celtic saint who settled here in the 6C. T town's Welsh name, Caergybi – Cybi's Fort – reflects these beginnings.

By the early 17C packet boats were operating on a regular basis between Holyhea and Dublin, despite the need for travellers to cross both the Menai Strait and th channel separating Holy Island from the rest of Anglesey. By the late 18C traffic ha increased dramatically. The construction of Telford's **Holyhead Road** (now A 5) and th Menai Bridge went in parallel with the improvement of the **Inner Harbour**, completed 1821. Steam packets had been introduced in 1817 and the first steam locomoti pulled its boat train into the harbour station in 1850. Between 1845 and 1873 a army of workmen toiled to build the great **breakwater** (nearly 2mi/3km long) to prote the calm water of the **New Harbour**, one of Britain's official ports of refuge, a have where vessels could ride out the fiercest storms.

The completion of the North Wales Expressway (A 55) has encouraged road traffic the expense of rail, and Irish Sea traffic now mostly consists of cars and trucks usir the roll-on roll-off ferries.

Few visitors break their journey here, except when the ferries are stopped by ba weather, but the busy town has something of the allure of all ports. It is also a ba for exploring the magnificent coast of Holy Island which curls around the base Holyhead Mountain.

---

### Out and About

**Tourist Information Centre** – Penrhos Beach Road, Holyhead LL65 2QB. ☎ 01407 762 622.

**Beaches** – At Porth Dafarch, Trearddur Bay and Borth Wen.

**Boat Trips** – Holyhead is only a short sea crossing away from the *craic* and Guinness and Georgian architecture of Dublin.

**Craftwork** – High above the town centre is the **Ucheldre Centre** ⊙, a former convent chapel which has been tastefully converted into an arts and exhibition centre, often with displays of local interest.

**Adjacent Sights** – See Anglesey, Bangor, Beaumaris, Caernarfon, Llanberis, Penrhyn Castle, Plas Newydd, Snowdonia.

### Where to Stay

**Y Hendre**, Porth-y-Felin Rd, LL65 1AH. ☎/Fax 01407 762 929. A comfortable personally run guesthouse with 3 en-suite rooms; 5min drive from the Ferry.

A Williams

Holyhead Harbour

## SIGHTS

**Harbour** – The Inner Harbour and the railway station stand in cosy proximity to the town centre, strung out along the low protective hill immediately to the west. The station approach has a fine cast-iron clock commemorating the visit of the Prince of Wales in 1880. Another royal visit, albeit an involuntary one, is marked by the Doric **Admiralty Arch** (1821), which marks this end of the London-Holyhead Road as the southern end in the capital city is marked by the Marble Arch; it honours George IV, delayed here for several days by a storm in 1821 until persuaded to venture aboard a newfangled steamboat. The great expanse of water sheltered by the breakwater can be appreciated from Beach Road and the Lower Promenade.

The **Maritime Museum** ⓥ is housed in what is believed to be the oldest surviving Lifeboat House (1858) in Wales.

**St Cybi's Church** ⓥ – The sea once lapped at the foot of the rise on which the Romans built their fort. Its walls, with corner towers, still stand to a height of 13ft/4m, a fine example of Roman masonry. At the southern end of the enclosure, the nave of a 14C mortuary chapel served as a school in the 18C. With its squat tower, splendid south porch and battlements, **St Cybi's Church** has an unusual and striking outline. The chancel is 13C but most of the structure dates from the late-15C to early-16C. There is intricate carving on the parapet of the south transept and in the porch.

## EXCURSIONS

★**South Stack Cliffs** – *3mi/5km W of Holyhead by minor roads.* The outskirts of Holyhead give way almost immediately to the rugged landscape of **Holyhead Mountain** (722ft/220m), defended by spectacular cliffs which are deservedly protected as a Heritage Coast. With commanding seaward views, the summit is protected by precipitous slopes and by the massive drystone walls of an **Iron Age fort**. The Romans used this natural vantage point for a watchtower, communicating directly with the fort in Holyhead, and possibly even with their provincial capital at Chester by means of a chain of similar beacons along the North Wales coast. Much later, a 19C signal station was built to the west of the summit to give advance warning to Liverpool shipowners of the approach of their vessels.

On the more hospitable slopes of the mountain, facing southwest, is **Tŷ Mawr**, a group of hut circles of c 1500 BC standing amid the bracken and heather that partly obscures the prehistoric field patterns around them.

To seaward are the magnificent, violently folded **South Stack Cliffs** which are the breeding place of a superb array of seabirds, including guillemots, razorbills and puffins. The birds can be studied from the RSPB Bird Centre on the cliff top but it is worth the time and effort to descend to the island by the steep zigzag path *(400 steps)* and suspension bridge (100ft/30m) and visit the **South Stack Seabird Centre** ⓥ, which is housed in the former lighthouse keepers' accommodation. The **lighthouse** (1809) itself has been open to visitors since 1985, when the light was automated

and the keepers departed *(limited space)*. The birds can also be viewed in liv
close-up from **Ellin's Tower** ⊙, a crenellated summerhouse which has been converte
into a cliff-edge observatory by the RSPB, with a video link to the breeding site
Land birds include ravens and choughs.

**Breakwater Country Park** ⊙ – *2mi/3km W of Holyhead by Newry Beach Roa
and a minor road*. Seven million tons of rock were removed from the norther
flank of Holyhead Mountain to build the great breakwater of Holyhead's Ne
Harbour. The approach to the country park uses the trackbed of the railway whic
transported this huge quantity of material from quarry to construction sit
Beneath the quarry cliffs, the roofless old Crushing Mill has exhibits which tell t
story of this epic effort. Information on local footpaths and country matters
supplied by the museum.

**Trearddur Bay** – *2mi/3km S of Holyhead*. Few contrasts could be greater tha
that between businesslike Holyhead and this informal resort, strung out along
series of delightful rocky coves with sandy beaches.

# HOLYWELL ★

(Treffynnon) Flintshire – Population 8 770
Michelin Atlas p 33 or Map 403 K 24

In a country where belief in the healing powers of sacred waters has become rare, th
spring which issues from the hillside below the little industrial town of Holywe
continues to attract substantial numbers of pilgrims. The Holywell stream, which wa
fed by the spring, never froze and before flowing east into the Dee Estuary its forc
(4 000 gallons per minute) was used to drive various industrial works.

**The story of St Winefride** – A virtuous virgin of the 7C, Winefride (*Gwenfrewi*
Welsh), was wooed by Prince Caradoc. Resisting his advances, she fled towards th
church in which her uncle, St Beuno, was worshipping. Furious, Caradoc hacked o
her head, which rolled down a steep slope. Waters gushed forth from the point
which it came to rest. St Beuno emerged from his church and restored the head
Winefride's shoulders, the join being marked only by a thin white line. Caradoc wa
swallowed up by the ground.
The cult of St Winefride flourished in the Middle Ages but was suppressed at the Refo
mation. Pilgrims nevertheless continued to visit this "blessed fountain of the Faith" (Io
Goch), in spite of the authorities' disfigurement of the shrine and the closure of the loc
inns each year on 3 November, St Winefride's Day. In 1686, James II came here with h
Queen to pray, it is thought, for a Stuart Prince of Wales. Holywell is the only shrine
Britain with an unbroken history of pilgrimage to the present day.

**Adjacent Sights** – See Bodelwyddan, Col-
wyn Bay, Denbigh, Erddig, Flint, Hawarden,
Mold, Rhuddlan, Rhyl, Ruthin, St Asaph,
Wrexham.

**St Winefride's Well** ⊙
The buildings associate
with the spring are attra
tively set into a steep hil
side and are approache
across lawns. The sprin
itself is housed in a we
chamber built in the ver
early 16C in Perpendicula
style by Lady Margare
Beaufort, the mother of Henry VII. The waters, which never freeze, surge up into
star-shaped basin and also fill a rectangular outdoor pool. The surrounding area
honeycombed with mine workings which in 1917 interrupted the natural flow o
the spring, now maintained from a reservoir.

**St Winefride's Chapel** ⊙ – The well chamber forms the basement of St Wine
fride's Chapel, also built by Lady Margaret and recently restored. It has a fir
camberbeam roof and a number of carved corbels.
The nearby parish church, dedicated to St James and much rebuilt in the 18C, ma
be the successor to St Beuno's church.

**Greenfield Valley Heritage Park** – *NE of Holywell town centre; signed from th
road down the valley (B 5121) and from the coast road (A 548). Car park
northern end*. In the 12C a community of Cistercian monks settled at the lower en
of the valley and used the stream to drive a corn mill. Little remains of **Basingwer
Abbey**, except the ruined church (13C) and part of the east and south cloister rang
(12C and 13C).
In the latter half of the 18C many works were established driven by the Holywe
stream; traces of their buildings, wheel pits and water supplies are still visibl
When the goods railway, built in 1869, became a full passenger service in 1912,
was the steepest passenger railway in Great Britain; it closed in 1954 and th
trackbed is now a footpath up the south side of the valley.
The **Abbey Farm Museum** ⊙ was a working farm until 1979; there are displays o
harvesting machinery, carts and harness, a Romany cart and also live sheep, pig
hens and ducks.

# KNIGHTON ★

(Tref-y-Clawdd) Powys – Population 2 851
Michelin Atlas p 25 or Map 403 K 26

is small town on the Herefordshire border began as a Saxon settlement on an easily
fended knoll overlooking the River Teme. The natural defensive qualities of the site
ere reinforced by the alignment along its western end of the great earthwork known
 Offa's Dyke. Around 1100 the Normans built their first castle mound, Bryn-y-
stell, in the valley below but about 80 years later moved their fortress to the
rongpoint on the knoll. Knighton serves as a market centre for the Teme valley and,
ing roughly half way along the long-distance footpath following **Offa's Dyke**, makes a
od base for exploring this part of the border country.

## SIGHTS

**Clock Tower** – The pretentious Clock Tower (1872)
has stood in the steeply
sloping Market Place long
enough for it to have
become the symbol of the
town. To the west, the
Narrows (the local name
for the High Street) rises

> **Tourist Information Centre** – Offa's Dyke
> Centre, West Street, Knighton LD7 1EN
> ☎ 01547 529 424 *(see below)*.
>
> **Adjacent Sights** – See Elan Valley, Llan-
> drindod Wells, Llanidloes, Montgomery,
> Newtown, Old Radnor, Presteigne.

to the "Top of the Town", the summit of the knoll, where the streets respect the
outline of the late-12C Norman castle of which only scanty and inaccessible traces
remain. On the lower ground to the east the street pattern seems to echo the grid
plan probably laid out in the 13C, when the powerful Mortimer family extended
the town and promoted its famous autumn fair. Most buildings in the town centre
have a decidedly Victorian character, a reflection of the prosperity enjoyed after the
opening of the Central Wales Railway in the 1860s. This most rural of British
railways, connecting Shrewsbury to Swansea, surprisingly remains open.

**Offa's Dyke Centre** ⊘ – Housed in a 19C school building, the Centre has displays on
the history of the Dyke and on its use today. The **long-distance footpath** (177mi/285km)
which largely follows the course of Offa's Dyke was painstakingly stitched together
over a long period and was officially opened in 1971. It passes through some of the
most splendid scenery of the borderlands between England and Wales.

**A border barrier from sea to sea** – *"Rex nomine Offa qui vallum magnum inter Britanniam
atque Merciam de mare usque ad mare facere imperavit"* wrote Bishop Asser in the
late 9C, a century after the Mercian king's reign. His statement, that "a king named
Offa... commanded a great bank to be built between the land of the Britons (ie the
Welsh) and Mercia all the way from sea to sea", provides the only evidence we have
that it was indeed Offa, ruler of Mercia throughout the second half of the 8C AD,
who gave orders for the construction of the earthwork that stretches – not without
interruption – from the Severn Estuary to the coast of North Wales.
The Dyke is one of the most impressive monuments in Britain, even in its present
eroded state. Originally it may have stood higher (as much as 40ft/12m), with a
ditch normally on the western side. That it marked the boundary between Offa's

Offa's Dyke, Evenjobb, Powys

powerful Saxon kingdom and the domains of the Welsh princelings seems clear b
whether it was primarily a defensive barrier or simply a demarcation line remai
unclear. Its alignment also presents puzzles; parts of it were obviously surveyed
masterly fashion, running from one viewpoint to another. A zigzag course m
have resulted from sightlines being obscured by woodland. In places the Dyke
absent altogether; was this because there were no territorial disputes with the lo
Welsh, or as a result of natural barriers like floodlands and forests being adequat

## EXCURSIONS

★**Offa's Dyke** – *9.5mi/15.5km NW of Knighton; leaflet available at Offa's Dyke Centre*
The uplands of Clun Forest (just in England) have one of the most spectacular sectio
of the Dyke. The stretch between Springhill Farm and **Llanfair Hill** has been described
"perhaps the most magnificent of all" (CJ Wright). To the south-east the great eart
work can be followed across the moorlands to its highest point (1 408ft/427m).

**Powys County Observatory** ⊘ – *2.5mi/4km SE of Knighton by A 4113, a min
road and rough track.* This recently constructed small observatory high up in t
hills between Knighton and Presteigne has a *camera obscura* and a planetarium
well as a 13in/34cm refracting telescope. There is also a meteorological stati
which images views of the earth's weather from satellite.

# LAMPETER

(Llanbedr Pont Steffan) Ceredigion – Population 1 989
Michelin Atlas p 24 or Map 403 H 27

Described in the 18C as "small and straggling", this little town with its bridge over t
Teifi has origins which go back to a pre-Norman Welsh settlement. The later Angl
Norman castle was much fought over but the town has remained resolutely Welsh
this day, owing its existence as much to its university college as to its role as mark
centre for the surrounding countryside. Mostly Georgian and Victorian in characte
Lampeter seems to have changed little if at all in the post-war period.

The town is folded around **St David's College**, whose core is the single large Tudor-sty
quadrangle standing in attractive grounds. The college was founded in 1822, specifi
ally to provide university education for aspiring young clergymen from Wales who
means precluded study at Oxford or Cambridge. Theology is still important, thou
many other subjects have been added to the curriculum. After much hesitatio
St David's became one of the constituent colleges of the University of Wales in 197
The motte of the castle abuts the quadrangle.

**Adjacent Sights** – See Aberaeron, Cardi-
gan, Elan Valley, Llandovery, Llanwrtyd
Wells, Newcastle Emlyn, Strata Florida
Abbey, Tregaron.

## EXCURSION

**Dolaucothi Gold Mines**
– *9mi/15km SE of Lamp
ter by A 482.* The Roma
operated an important go
mine at Pumsaint ("fi
saints") in the woode
Cothi valley, sending th
precious metal to the Imperial mints at Trier and Lyons. As well as driving stope
deep into the ground, the Romans built reservoirs and lengthy leats to harness th
water power necessary for the "hushing" which liberated the gold from the loc
shales and siltstones. A square-shaped fort was built above the junction of th
Cothi and its western tributary.

The mine was opened up again in the 19C and extraction continued until 1938
when a combination of incompetence, geological problems and lack of investmer
led to closure and clearance. The National Trust has reopened the abandoned sit
bringing in equipment from a Clwyd lead mine to lend verisimilitude, building
visitor centre and running **underground tours** of the early-20C workings. Visitors ca
sometimes pan for gold and there are waymarked walks among the woodlands c
the Trust's extensive Dolaucothi estate.

### Royal Welsh gold

At the Dissolution of the monasteries all mining rights were vested in the
Crown. The Mines Royal Monopoly, formed in 1568, is responsible for
mining gold, silver and copper throughout Wales.

Since a ring of gold from the Gwynfynydd area was made for Queen
Elizabeth II, it has been a tradition that all royal wedding rings are made
from pure Welsh gold.

On the occasion of her 60th birthday in 1986, Queen Elizabeth II was
presented with an ingot of 99% pure Welsh gold, weighing 1 kilogram,
produced by the Gwynfynydd Gold Mine near Dolgellau *(see p 147).*

# LAUGHARNE ★

(Talacharn) Carmarthenshire – Population 1 272
Michelin Atlas p 15 or Map 403 H 28

>t a village, nor a town, Laugharne is a pleasingly decayed township, jealously reserving its ancient Corporation and many rights and privileges as well as medieval rip fields in the adjacent countryside. All traces of its harbour on the estuary of the if have disappeared, and the charming upper part of the township has a good imber of Georgian houses, particularly in King Street. Most visitors come here for e splendid castle ruin, recently reopened after thoroughgoing conservation, or in >mage to Dylan Thomas, whose home and inspiration was the Boat House, over->oking what the writer and poet called the "heron-priested" shore.

## ★Laugharne Castle ⊘ –

With different phases in its construction marked by contrasting red and green sandstone, this splendid high-walled ruin is built on a low bluff overlooking the Strand, where mud, salt-marsh, and a car park have replaced the old harbour.

> **Adjacent Sights** – See Carew, Carmarthen, Fishguard, Haverfordwest, Llanelli, Milford Haven, Newcastle Emlyn, Pembroke, Pembrokeshire Coast, Tenby.

The present structure was begun by the De Brian family in the mid-13C. Reached through a medieval-cum-Tudor **gatehouse**, the diamond-shaped **Outer Ward** is defined by a battlemented garden wall built over what is left of the medieval curtain wall. The whole area was landscaped in the 18C and 19C, and a conscientious attempt has been made to recreate the layout and atmosphere of the **Victorian garden**, into which a timber visitor centre is discreetly set. Great trees further soften the surroundings.

The **Inner Ward** is a particularly picturesque composition, combining elements of the De Brian stronghold with the substantial additions made in the 16C, when Laugharne was turned into a prestigious Tudor residence by the courtier Sir John Perrot. Of the medieval towers, the keep-like **northwest tower** was and still is the most substantial, rising into a superb stone dome whose only equal is at Pembroke. It is flanked by the north range of the Tudor mansion with its fine projecting stair tower. An inner gatehouse, its rugged medieval look civilised by the insertion of Tudor windows, leads to a courtyard with patches of original cobbles, among which were found lead musket balls from the Civil War siege.

Built on the foundations of one of the towers in the outer curtain wall is a **gazebo** giving a fine prospect of the estuary. **Dylan Thomas** wrote his *Portrait of the Artist as a Young Dog* here, and before him the gazebo was used as a writing studio by **Richard Hughes** (1900-76), author of *A High Wind in Jamaica* and of the incomplete epic novel cycle dealing with the rise and fall of Nazi Germany, *The Human Predicament.*

## ★The Boat House ⊘ – Swansea-born **Dylan Thomas** (1914-53) was particularly fond

of Laugharne, declaring that here he "got off the bus and never got on again". He rented accommodation in two other houses in the township before moving with his wife Caitlin to the Boat House in 1949.

Dylan Thomas' Writing Shed

Wales Tourist Board

The white house with its slate roof is in an enviable position, below the lip of the cliff and facing south-eastwards to the saltings and sand dunes around the broad mouth of the Taf. Parts of the interior accommodate a video presentation and other facilities of a heritage centre, but other rooms are laid out much as they would have been in Dylan's time. His voice, declaiming poetry, issues from a wireless set of the period, a reminder of his success as a broadcaster.

A short distance from the house is the poet's "**writing shed**", looking as if he has just left it, with an empty bottle of beer and scrunched up balls of paper written on and thrown angrily on the floor. Dylan Thomas died in New York, his early demise accelerated by his formidable consumption of alcohol. Kingsley Amis thought less of "ranting, canting Dylan the Rhymer, the 'bard' of his native South Wales", than of "disciplined, responsible Thomas, the social chronicler".

The Thomases are buried in the newer part of the graveyard of **St Martin's Church** at the northern end of the township.

Not surprisingly, Laugharne prides itself on being the model for Dylan Thomas' most famous work, the play for voices **Under Milk Wood**, but the claim is vigorously disputed by the harbour town of New Quay *(see p 75)* on the Cardigan coast.

## EXCURSION

**Museum of Speed** ⊙ – *6mi/10km S of Laugharne at Pendine.* Pendine is famous for its great stretch of sandy beach (some 7mi/11km long) where motor aces strove to outdo each other in achieving ever-higher speeds on the near-perfect surface of the sands. The straggling village still has something of the air of the inter-war period when both Sir Malcolm Campbell and the Welshman Parry Thomas broke the record more than once. Parry was killed in 1927 in his attempt to beat the speed (174.8mph/281kph) which Campbell had achieved the previous month. For 40 years his aero-engined machine, the far-from-feminine looking "Babs", lay buried in the dunes. Salvaged and restored, it is now displayed in a new building overlooking the sands; a film and display tell the story of the land speed races. There are exhibits on local beach and sea life.

# LLANBERIS ★

Gwynedd – Population 1 986
Michelin Atlas p 32 or Map 403 H 24
Local map p 261

The starting point for the easiest ascent of Snowdon on foot or by rail, this mountain village has a number of other attractions which make it one of the most popular centres in Snowdonia.

The original settlement was at the hamlet of Nant Peris, at the entrance to the awesome **Pass of Llanberis**, but the modern village has grown up on the south-western shore of Llyn Padarn, a fine stretch of water separated from an upper lake, Llyn Peris, by a narrow isthmus. Copper was extracted in the area at the end of the 18C but Llanberis owes fame and fortune to the immense quantities of slate quarried from the Cambrian rock which makes up the great mass of Elidir Fach (2 565ft/782m) rising from the lakeside.

★**Welsh Slate Museum** ⊙ – Two centuries of quarrying have carved the slate south-western flanks of Elidir Fach into a series of gigantic steps which seem to lead to the very summit of the mountain.

At the foot of the reshaped mountain a handsome range of buildings with corner towers, clock tower and entrance arch is laid out around a courtyard. Here were the repair workshops of the great **Dinorwig Quarry**, whose skilled workforce could make and maintain anything from a cogwheel to a locomotive. The workshops were in daily use until the quarry closed in 1969; they now house the Welsh Slate Museum, a branch of the National Museum. This is a living museum with completely authentic atmosphere, which not only tells the history of this important industry but also carries out repair work for other branches of the museum.

---

**Tourist Information Centre** – 41a High Street, Llanberis LL55 4EU
☎ 01286 870 765; Fax 01286 871 951; llanberis.tic@gwynedd.gov.uk

**Craft Centre** – Unique slate, wrought-iron and wooden products are available in the gift shop at the **Welsh Slate Museum** *(see below)*.

**Adjacent Sights** – See Anglesey, Bangor, Beaumaris, Beddgelert, Blaenau Ffestiniog, Caernarfon, Holyhead, Penrhyn Castle, Plas Newydd, Snowdonia.

The slate industry and its workforce is described in some detail by means of displays and an audio-visual presentation, but the museum's great achievement is its evocation of an age of industry which began in the 18C and only recently came to an end. From 1870 the workshops' machinery was driven by a great **water-wheel** (51ft/15.4m in diameter), one of the largest in the world, tightly encased in its brick housing. The quiet rumble of shafts and pinion wheels transmitting power to the machinery still pervades the southern range of buildings, though the water now turns a more efficient Pelton Wheel installed in 1925. In the **Pattern Loft** patient craftsmen carved the great variety of wooden patterns which their colleagues in the **Foundry** below turned into all manner of items necessary for the running of the quarry, "anything from a bootscraper to a bell, from a window frame to a flywheel". The seemingly effortless skill required to split and dress slates with great precision is demonstrated by experienced quarrymen. The smithy, stores and fitting shop can be seen too, as can the narrow-gauge steam locomotive *Una* which worked in the quarry until the 1960s. Several cottages have been furnished as they would have been in the heyday of slate mining (1860s), at the height of the great strike (Chief Engineer's house in 1901) and when the mine closed (1969). The incline. built (1873-77) to carry slates from the quarry face to the rail link, has been restored to working order.

**Padarn Country Park** ⊙ – The park is laid out along the banks of Llyn Padarn and on the lower oak-clad slopes of Elidir Fach, sharing approach road and car park with the Slate Museum and Llanberis Lake Railway. The Vivian Quarry, part of the Dinorwig enterprise, reaches some 450ft/135m up the mountain and down into a 50ft/15m pit, now flooded. Slate extraction was always a perilous operation. Men worked long hours high up on the exposed mountainside, liable to falls and to slips on greasy wet slate, to injuries caused by sharp fragments and to crushing by machinery. The old **Quarry Hospital**, now the **Visitor Centre**, details these conditions, and also has displays on the local environment.

**Llanberis Lake Railway** ⊙ – The problems of transporting heavy loads of slate to the coast in the early days of quarrying was only partly solved by the use of sleds, boats on Llyn Padarn and packhorses. In 1824 a horse tramway was built, succeeded in 1849 by a steam railway which brought the slate down to purpose-built Port Dinorwic (Y Felinheli) on the Menai Strait. The railway closed in 1961 but its lakeside trackbed has been relaid with narrow-gauge rails along which the little engines which once worked in the quarries pull impressively-long tourist trains.

★**Electric Mountain** ⊙ – The eye-catching modern building serves mainly to intro-duce visitors to the underground mysteries of the **Dinorwig Power Station**, though temporary exhibitions are held on a variety of themes.
A spectacular audio-visual presentation sets out the challenges faced and tri-umphantly met in constructing a pumped storage scheme capable of supplying an area equivalent to the whole of Wales with electricity at 12 seconds' notice. Using cheap, off-peak power, water is pumped from Llyn Peris to an enlarged existing lake, Marchlyn Mawr, high above. When surges in demand occur (typically during commercial breaks in popular television programmes, when the nation dashes to make a cup of tea), the water is released to turn a series of turbines buried deep in the mountain.
The tour of this almost invisible power station (the cables carrying the electricity it generates are buried within the area of the National Park) is an undeniably impressive experience. Minibuses take visitors from the Museum to the carefully designed buildings constructed in local stone around the entrance to the under-ground works on the north-east shore of Llyn Peris, then descend generously wide roadways into the very heart of the mountain. The 10 miles of tunnels and vast cavity to house the turbines involved the excavation of 12 million tonnes of rock; the **Machine Hall** itself is higher than a 16-storey building and could accommodate London's St Paul's Cathedral. Understanding how electricity is generated in what is Europe's largest pumped storage scheme is helped by viewing the components of No 1 Turbine, painted in bright engineering colours, and by a further film show.

★★**Snowdon Mountain Railway** ⊙ – Llanberis is the base station for the narrow-gauge rack-and-pinion railway completed in 1896 to haul passengers to the summit of Snowdon. The only railway of its type in Britain, it is operated by a fleet of sturdy little steam engines based on the prototypes built by the Locomotiv-und Maschinenfabrik of Winterthur in Switzerland, though more recently motive power has also been supplied by diesel locomotives and railcars. By 1995, No 2, *Enid*, built in 1895, had travelled almost a quarter of a million miles (c 400 000km).
The only level section of track is in Llanberis station, where workshops and coaling facilities lend all the atmosphere of a Victorian railway; the rest of the run (4.5mi/7km) is at an average gradient of 1 in 7.8 with a maximum gradient of 1 in 5.5. The locomotives propel the single carriages of each train from the rear, past woodlands and waterfalls initially, then through open sheep country dotted with abandoned farm buildings. A pause is made at Halfway Station to take on water

and allow a descending train to pass. Given clear weather, the mountain views become ever more spectacular as the train chugs higher, past Clogwyn Station to arrive at Summit Station (3 493ft/1 065m above sea-level). After enjoying the incomparable **panorama**★★★ from the summit cairn, passengers can fortify themselves for the descent in the café, the successor to a hotel which itself had been preceded by mountain huts first erected in the 1840s.

Unlike many other railways, the Snowdon Mountain line is so popular that passengers are sometimes turned away, but a token system is operated to reduce the length of time spent queuing. The journey is of course best undertaken in reasonably good weather but the weather is notoriously difficult to predict and may be quite different at the summit. Even during the operating season snow and ice may block the track, and trains may run only as far as one of the lower stations. Whatever the conditions, the opportunity should not be missed to experience this unique railway, a piece of Alpine technology transplanted into the very different environment of the British mountains.

Snowdon Mountain Railway locomotives

**Dolbadarn Castle** – Standing sinister sentinel on its lakeside crag among the storm-blasted mountains, the ruins of Dolbadarn could not fail to become a favourite subject of artists of the Romantic period, foremost among them JMW Turner. The castle's historical associations added to its appeal; not only was it a purely Welsh stronghold, built during the reign of Llywelyn the Great *(ap Iorwerth)* in the first half of the 13C, but it has always been held to be the spot where Llywelyn the Last *(ap Gruffydd)* imprisoned his brother, Owain Goch, for a terrible term of 22 years, after defeating him at the battle of Bryn Derwin in 1255.

The castle's round tower, surrounded by little more than the foundations of curtain wall and other structures, is based on English models which themselves derived from the towers built across northern France by King Philip Augustus (1165-1223).

# LLANCAIACH FAWR MANOR ★
Caerphilly
Michelin Atlas p 16 or Map 403 K 29

Restored and opened to the public, this severe, grey-stone manor house in the Rhymney Valley offers its visitors an entertaining and completely convincing experience of the life led within its walls at the time of the Civil War (1642-48).

The house occupies the site of a medieval dwelling, and was begun in the early 16C for the Pritchard (ap Richard) family. With thick walls (4ft/1.22m), small windows which could not be opened, and narrow, easily defended staircases, it was meant to resist all but the most determined attack, with an east wing capable of being sealed off from the remainder of the house. Improvements made in the 17C included the construction of a grand staircase and the laying out of a formal walled garden. Late-20C improvements have been made with large numbers of visitors in mind, and include the reconstruction of the garden and the provision of an award-winning Visitor Centre most successfully integrated into its historic environment.

Wales Tourist Board

The Kitchen, Llancaiach Fawr Manor

## TOUR ⊘

The **Visitor Centre** goes into great detail about the story of the Pritchard family, dwelling in particular on Colonel Edward Pritchard who benefited from switching sides from King to Parliament in the Civil War.

The house is approached via the two-storey porch, where **servants in mid-17C costume** offer a warm welcome. This, rather than the house's architecture or its somewhat sparse and mostly reconstructed furniture, is what accounts for Llancaiach Fawr's great popularity; the roles of valet, seamstress and footman are played by well-briefed actors able not only to speak in the Welsh-tinged English of the period but also to evoke with great authenticity the life of the house and the area at what was a particularly troubled time, when undisciplined soldiers roamed the neighbourhood in search of provisions and more. The doings of master and mistress are commented on in what is probably a more revealing manner than that of any "official" history, and the staff are well able to field any question likely to be put to them.

The tour moves up through the building from the flagstone paving of the ground floor, with Kitchen and Servants' Hall, to the panelled Great Hall and Parlour, Steward's Apartment (with a peephole for supervision of the servants), to bedchambers, Colonel Pritchard's study, and cheese room. Much is made of bizarre cures, hauntings and the occult (a finely carved pentagram was discovered in the garden).

> **Adjacent Sights** – See Caerphilly, Cardiff, Castell Coch, Cowbridge, Llandaff, Llantrisant, Newport, Museum of Welsh Life.

# LLANDAFF CATHEDRAL★
### Cardiff
Michelin Atlas p 16 or Map 403 K 29 – 2mi/3km NW of Cardiff city centre

Now one of the more refined suburbs of Cardiff, village-like Llandaff with its Green, Bishop's Palace and ancient cathedral was once a borough in its own right.

Its origins go back to the 6C, when the Celtic saint Teilo built a church on the banks of the Taff for the Christian community founded earlier by St Dyfrig. The site was chosen with care, sheltered, like that of St David's Cathedral, from the view of sea-borne raiders. No trace remains of Teilo's church, though a 10C Celtic cross was discovered in 1870 and now stands in the south presbytery aisle.

Today's fine building was begun under the Normans in 1120 by Bishop Urban and added to in the 13C and 14C, while the **Jasper Tower** was built in 1485 as a replacement for the older bell-tower whose ruins can still be seen on the Green.

Cromwell's men treated the Cathedral with their customary lack of respect, while later storms brought down the south-western tower and devastated much of the interior. An early-18C commentator referred to "the poor desolate church of Llandaff", and the situation was hardly remedied by the incongruous Classical church inserted into the ruins by John Wood of Bath in 1734.

Serious restoration began in the 1830s with the removal of Wood's "Italian Temple", extensive rebuilding in an Early Gothic style and the construction of a new south-western tower, named after the architect-in-charge, John Pritchard. An equivalent effort had to be made after the Second World War to make good the extensive damage caused by a German airforce (*Luftwaffe*) landmine in 1941.

**Adjacent Sights** – See Barry, Caerphilly, Cardiff, Castell Coch, Cowbridge, Llancaiach Fawr, Llantrisant, Newport, Penarth, Museum of Welsh Life.

## TOUR ⊙

**Exterior** – Half hidden in its hollow, the Cathedral makes a dramatic impression when approached down the steep slope from the Green. The **Jasper Tower** with its fine Perpendicular pinnacles is matched by **Pritchard's Tower** with its spire (195ft/60m). The cathedral's outline is relatively simple, with no transepts and only the 13C Chapter-house protruding to the south, and the modern (1950s) David Chapel and processional way to the north. The south door is bold Norman work (c 1170), the West Front largely the legacy of Pritchard.

**Interior** – On descending the steps into the nave, the visitor is immediately and theatrically confronted by the extraordinary **Majestas**. This huge aluminium figure of Christ in Majesty, the work of Sir Jacob Epstein, is borne aloft on a cylindrical organ case supported on a parabolic arch of reinforced concrete, the latter intended to represent the screen which would have separated nave and choir in medieval times, though the vista through to the High Altar and Lady Chapel is not obstructed. The organ case also incorporates an array of gilded figures rescued after the 1941 bombing. The work of Bishop Urban is splendidly represented by the beautifully patterned Norman arch leading to the Lady Chapel. Above it is modern stained glass by John Piper. Construction of the 14C arcade to the south was abandoned when the masons realised it would damage the tomb of St Teilo, leaving a strange mixture of rounded, Norman arches and their intended Gothic replacements. The elegant late-13C **Lady Chapel** has recently had its early-20C decorative scheme restored.

St Dyfrig's Chapel has the saint's tomb as well as six panels of the days of the Creation by Edward Burne-Jones in Della Robbia ware. Other 19C decoration includes a Rossetti Triptych in the north aisle and windows by Morris & Co, while the 20C contribution includes the massive font surmounted by a dove.

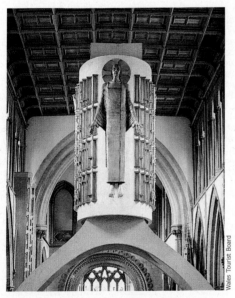

*Majestas* by Sir Jacob Epstein, Llandaff Cathedral

Wales Tourist Board

# LLANDEILO ★

Carmarthenshire – Population 850
Michelin Atlas p 15 or Map 403 I 28

A hilltop site above the Tywi, a magnificent stone bridge, a pleasing assemblage of Georgian and Victorian buildings, and proximity to the ancient parklands of **Dinefwr Castle** give Llandeilo an air of importance out of all proportion to its present diminutive size.

From its bluff, the town overlooks the confluence of the Tywi and Cennen at a point where the main valley narrows and forms a crossing point. The 6C Celtic **Saint Teilo** founded a monastery here, which however was in decline by the 9C. A settlement continued in existence, even outlasting the rival Welsh and English boroughs planted to the west, which had disappeared by about the 15C. The Welsh borough had grown up around Dinefwr Castle, built on another rocky bluff just to the west of Llandeilo.

The name of Dinefwr is one of the most resonant in Wales, for it was the seat of some of the most remarkable and influential of Welsh rulers. Its legendary founder was the 9C Welsh King **Rhodri Mawr**. The princes of Deheubarth resided here, their domain comprising the whole of south-west Wales. The great legislator of the early 10C, **Hywel Dda**, *The Good (see p xxx)*, was associated with Dinefwr, as was the 12C ruler Rhys ap Gruffydd, **the Lord Rhys** (1132-97), under whose stable reign Welsh culture enjoyed something of a Golden Age.

Llandeilo is best approached from the south, across the many-arched **bridge** with its imposing central span (145ft/44m), which in 1848 replaced an earlier more modest structure. The bridge approach climbs the hill towards the town, shouldering aside the older houses which still mark the alignment of the old road. At the top of the hill the highway cuts through the churchyard of the large **Church of St Teilo**, its military-looking tower dating from the 13C but the rest of it a rebuilding by Sir Giles Gilbert Scott in 1850. Other buildings in the town, like the pompous *Cawdor Arms*, reflect the agricultural prosperity of the 18C and early 19C from which the town obviously benefited.

★**Dinefwr Park** ⊘ – *Restoration in progress*. This is one of the finest landscape parks in Wales; it and its two great buildings, **Dinefwr castle** and its more domesticated replacement, **Newtown House**, are the object of conservation.

The **medieval castle** on its rock consists mainly of an angular curtain wall and a massive round keep. After

> **Tourist Information Centre** – Crescent Road Car Park, Llandeilo SA19 6HN ☎ 01558 824 226; Fax 01558 824 252.
>
> **Adjacent Sights** – See Brecon, Brecon Beacons, Carmarthen, Lampeter, Llandovery, Llanelli, Llanwrtyd Wells, Neath, Rhondda, Swansea.

Edward I's Welsh campaigns it became an English royal castle, and in spite of neglect of its defences managed to resist a siege by Owain Glyn Dŵr in 1403. It was abandoned in Tudor times, when one of the dynasty was executed under Henry VII, and a new mansion was built on the site of the present, architecturally undistinguished Newtown House which was erected in 1660, when the family was rehabilitated under the Stuarts; the building was much altered in the late 18C and again in the mid-19C, though the later alterations were never completed. The corner turrets have recently been reinstated and the interior is being reopened progressively as restoration proceeds.

The **park** extends over a tract of attractively irregular countryside which conforms precisely to the dictates of the late-18C taste for the picturesque, not least because it had a ready-made eye-catcher in the ruins of the castle, by then romantically ivy-clad. Lancelot "Capability" Brown came here in 1775 and found that "Nature has been truly bountiful and Art has done no harm", and modestly declined to carry out any major "Improvements", though a number of hilltop clumps of trees are attributed to him and there is a "Brown's Walk".

Deer share the rolling expanses with a herd of White Park cattle, whose ancestors may have been here in the 13C or even earlier. There are remnants of wild woodland as well as more formal clumps of beech, sycamore and oak, and a number of oaks of great age. The unusual variety of natural habitats, including water meadows and an oxbow lake, supports a rich range of wildlife.

## EXCURSIONS

★**Carreg Cennen Castle** ⊘ – *4mi/7km SE of Llandeilo by A 483 and minor roads and on foot across a field*. On its wild and wind-torn crag overlooking the little River Cennen as it tumbles down from the Black Mountain, this ruined fortress rarely fails to stir the imagination.

Prehistoric people frequented the site, Roman objects have been found here, and the lords of Dinefwr had a stronghold on the easily defended limestone spur. Carreg Cennen is however an English castle, built in the late-13C to early-14C by the Giffards, owners of Llandovery Castle, who had been instrumental in putting down the rebellion of Rhys ap Maredudd in 1287. To the south the precipitous drop (295ft/90m) required little more reinforcement than a curtain wall but to the north the defences are formidable, consisting of a round north-west tower, a square north-east tower and an intimidating **central gatehouse** with massive buttressed, half-octagonal towers. In the last phase of construction an elaborate **barbican** was added with a stepped approach ramp, gates and pits to redouble the difficulty of an attack. An outer ward was built at the same time to give extra protection on the eastward, most vulnerable approach. Little remains of its walls and towers, in contrast to those of the inner ward, still proudly crowning the summit.

An intriguing feature of the castle is its **cave**, approached via a vaulted passageway which formed part of the defences.

Carreg Cennen Castle

In spite of all its defensive advantages, Carreg Cennen was taken by Owain Glyn Dŵr in the course of his rebellion (early 15C). In the Wars of the Roses it was held by Lancastrian supporters, considered by the Yorkists to be no more than "rebels and robbers". After their surrender, the castle was demolished by a force of 500 men "to avoid inconveniences like this happening there in time to come".

The farmyard through which the castle is approached has a fascinating collection of old and rare breeds of farm animal as well as an ancient longhouse *(see p 64)*.

**Aberglasney** ⊘ – *5mi/8km E of Llandeilo by A 40 and minor road S*. This estate contains rare examples of early garden features – late-16C to early-17C **gatehouse and cloisters**. The rare **yew tunnel** was formed by creating a series of arches with the branches of a row of yew trees, planted in the 18C. Reconstruction is in progress to restore the formal parterres which were at the centre of the **arcaded walkway** and **parapet walk** in the cloister garden. In the **Upper Walled Garden**, designed by Penelope Hobhouse, ornamentals from all parts of the world enhance the structural planting of classic evergreens known in the 17C. The **kitchen garden** conserves the traditional division into neat quarters edged with box. Underground watercourses are fed into the rectangular Jacobean-style pool, which drains into the **Stream Garden** sloping down into **Pigeon House Wood**.

**Talley Abbey** – *8mi/13km N by B 4302*. Prettily placed in the smiling valley of the Tywi, Llandeilo has the wilderness of the Black Mountain to the east, and to the north the vastness of the lonely uplands, much of them forested, which sweep down south-westwards from central Wales. The remoteness of the region seems crystallised in the poignant ruin of this abbey, unique in Wales in having been founded by the Premonstratensians. An ambitious building plan was never completed and Talley always remained poor. The most striking feature remaining is the crossing tower, parts of the crude masonry still rising to a height of 85ft/26m.

# LLANDOVERY

(Llanymddyfri) Carmarthenshire – Population 2 037
Michelin Atlas p 15 or Map 403 I 28

A small, grey-stone town of character at an important road junction, Llandovery had a Roman fort and a much-disputed Norman castle but its atmosphere perhaps owes more to the days when the cattle drovers paused here on their trek from the grazing grounds of the west to Smithfield Market in London; in the early 19C the town had no fewer than 47 inns. George Borrow, writing in *Wild Wales* (1854) called it "The pleasantest little town in which I have halted in the course of my wanderings".

The site of the Roman Fort is now covered by **St Mary's Church** at Llanfair-ar-y-Bryn just to the north of the town. Fragments of Roman bricks can be seen in the walls. In the churchyard is the grave of **William Williams** (1717-91) from nearby Pantycelyn, composer of countless hymns, many with great lyrical power, among them the immortal *"Guide me O Thou great Jehovah"*.

> **Tourist Information Centre** – Kings Road, Llandovery SA20 0AW ☎/Fax 01550 720 693.
>
> **Adjacent Sights** – See Brecon, Brecon Beacons, Carmarthen, Lampeter, Laugharne, Llandeilo, Llanwrtyd Wells, Merthyr Tydfil.

Only the stump of the castle still crowns the motte.
The **Heritage Centre** ⊘ presents effective audio-visual displays covering Welsh folk legends, local history and the life of the red kite.
The High Street splits to form Market Street and a number of island plots occupied by buildings of some substance like the Market Hall and Town Hall, now occupied by a pleasant **Crafts Centre** ⊘.

## EXCURSION

**Llyn Brianne Dam and Reservoir** – *11mi/17km N by a minor road.* Together with the planting of the vast coniferous **Tywi Forest**, this dam and reservoir have utterly transformed the character of what was one of the remotest parts of upland Wales, as well as making it more easily accessible to visitors.
The dam itself (300ft/90m), which is claimed to be the largest in Europe, seems the work of careless giants, its clay core overlaid with great lumps of rock. A concrete spillway of exceptional crudity leads down to a spectacular outflow fountain. Visitor information is limited to notices prohibiting swimming.
More attractive than this gargantuan engineering is the **scenic road** high above the east bank of the long reservoir. Before linking with the equally fine Abergwesyn-Tregaron mountain road *(see p 198)*, the winding route gives splendid views over the great artificial lake with its highly indented outline and the surrounding dark-green forest.
Downstream from the dam at the junction of the Tywi and Doethi is the RSPB's **Dinas Reserve** ⊘. With its rock crags and ancient oak woodland, the area was one of the last retreats of the red kite before its recent increase in population. A cave is the reputed hiding place of a colourful and much fictionalised 16C character, Twm Siôn Cati, sometimes described as the Welsh Robin Hood.

---

### Drovers' Roads

Wales has a long and thriving agricultural tradition; sheepdog trials and livestock marts are sure places to hear the Welsh language, and drovers' roads can still be traced winding their way through the hills of mid-Wales. In the days before cattle trucks and rail and road transport, cattle, sheep – and even geese – walked to the London markets, fitted with special metal or leather shoes; the geese were made to walk through liquid tar and then grit to protect their webbed feet. At the peak of the trade over 30 000 Welsh Black cattle were driven each year from their Welsh pastures to London. The drovers were entrusted with rents from estates and ship money for the Treasury and returned with the proceeds of the sale. They were respected members of the community, who issued their own bank notes and acted as bank couriers between West Wales and London. The **Bank of the Black Ox**, the drovers' bank, incorporated into Lloyds Bank in 1909, was founded in Llandovery by David Jones, a local farmer's son, in 1799 in a building which is now the *King's Head Inn*. Llandovery still has a thriving cattle mart and the nickname of its Rugby team is The Drovers.

(Llandrindod) Powys – Population 4 943
Michelin Atlas p 25 or Map 403 J 27

This county town and inland resort with its cheerful late Victorian and Edwardian buildings comes as a surprise among the quiet green hills of the former county of Radnorshire. Though the healing properties of its springs had been known "from time immemorial", Llandrindod's heyday began with the arrival of the railway in 1865. By the early 1900s its population had increased more than tenfold but decline set in in the late 1920s. The spa closed in 1971 but reopened a decade later as a centre for complementary medicine. The town is popular as a conference and meeting centre – it is well placed for delegates from all over Wales – and as a touring base for Central Wales.

## HISTORICAL NOTES

The chalybeate springs here had been patronised since the end of the 17C. In 1732 saline and sulphur springs were discovered, and a farmstead was converted into a pump house. The first hotel, where "balls, billiards and regular assemblies varied the pastimes of the gay and fashionable", was opened in 1748 and the Gentleman's Magazine of the same year celebrated Llandrindod's fame by declaring:

Let England boast Bath's crowded springs
Llandrindod happier Cambria sings.

The growing popularity of sea-bathing at the beginning of the 19C and Llandrindod's remoteness held back development but, with the building of the mid-Wales railway line in the 1860s, the town became accessible from the English Midlands and the rapidly expanding towns of South Wales. The local common land was enclosed, enabling a building boom to take place. Hotels, boarding houses and shops were constructed from a wonderful variety of materials – yellow brick, red brick from Ruabon, stone, timber, hung tiles and decorative ironwork. The grand scale of some of the hotels reflects the self-assurance and high expectations of the age.

---

### Out and About

**Tourist Information Centre** – Old Town Hall, Memorial Gardens, Llandrindod LD1 5DL ☎ 01597 822 600.

**Craft Centre** – An interesting Victorian building houses **Porticus** ⊙, a crafts gallery and shop stocking ceramics, glass, knitwear, jewellery, wood and textiles.

**Adjacent Sights** – See Brecon, Builth Wells, Elan Valley, Hay-on-Wye, Knighton, Llanidloes, Llanwrtyd Wells, Newtown, Old Radnor, Presteigne.

### Where to Stay

**Acorn Court**, Chapel Rd, Howey, LD1 5PB. *1.5mi/2.4km S by A 483.* ☎/Fax 01597 823 543. Large, new house (4 rm) with spacious lounge and good home comforts in quiet location a short distance from the Victorian spa town.

**Guidfa House**, Crossgates, LD1 6RF. *3.5mi/5.6km NE by A 483.* ☎ 01597 851 241; Fax 01597 851 875. Georgian home (7 rm) with garden at centre of small village; immaculate rooms and enthusiastic home cooking.

**Ffaldau Country House**, Llandegley, LD1 5UD. *7mi/11km E by A 483 and A 44.* ☎ 01597 851 421. Comfortable, relaxing home (3 rm) with 16C origins – slate flooring, oak beams – set in good cycling and walking country.

---

## SIGHTS

**Rock Park and Spa** ⊙ – The romantic parkland with rushing stream, tall conifers and Lovers' Leap was created and named in 1880, although the chalybeate spring was known as the Well of the Blacksmith's Dingle as early as 1670; it is now dispensed from an outdoor marble fountain given to the public for free perpetual use in 1879. The saline spring was discovered in 1867 and the sulphur and magnesia springs about 20 years later.

Secluded among the trees is the delightful **Pump Room** (1909) in polychrome brick and with cast-iron columns. It now houses a restaurant, where the waters of the saline spring and the magnesium spring may be available, and a small display on the history of the spa illustrated with a slide show in the style of an early silent film *Taking the Waters 1901 (5min)*. The **Centre for Complementary Medicine**, which opened in the 1980s, offering 22 therapies and the services of 12 practitioners, succeeds the treatment available in the 1950s under the National Health Service – saline before breakfast, sulphur morning and afternoon and chalybeate after meals with baths at suitable times during the day; the shortest course was three weeks.

**National Cycling Exhibition** ⊘ – The exhibition is housed in the Tom Norton Automobile Palace, designed by R Wellings Thomas, an early grid-framed steel structure completed in 1911, which operated as a garage until the late 1980s; the roof line is decorated with rampant lions and the side railings *(Princes Avenue)* are in the Art Nouveau style.

The display, which is complemented with enamel advertising signs, consists of over 200 cycles comprising the Tom Norton collection of 26 vintage cycles, the David Higman collection, formerly displayed in Oswestry, and the Raleigh collection of modern bikes which is regularly brought up-to-date with the latest models. The models range from the earliest inventions – Velocipede (1860s), Ariel bicycle (1870), tandem tricycle (c 1879) and penny-farthing (1898) – through more recent conceptions – Sturmey-Archer 3-speed gear, delivery bikes, invalid carriages, mopeds, the BSA paratroop bicycle (1942) and the Kendrick cycle (1937) with two wheels and a basket in front and a single wheel at the rear, made for Tom Norton – to the post-war period – small-wheel Moulton cycle, Chopper cycle (1970), Sinclair C5 (1990), action bikes, mountain bikes, racing cycles, M-Trax Elite ridden by Barry Clarke, National Mountain Bike champion in 1996.

**Radnorshire Museum** ⊘ – The little museum gives an excellent account of the development of the town and contrasts its life with that of the surrounding, utterly rural countryside.

**The Lake** – This artificial body of water with its modern pavilion and shoreline drive is the centrepiece of Llandrindod's remaining stretch of common land. The remains of a small ecclesiastical building, the 12C-13C Capel Maelog, have been removed from a development site and re-erected here.

## EXCURSION

**Cefnllys Church** ⊘ – *About 2mi/3km E by narrow road.* The deep and winding valley of the River Ithon is overlooked by Castell Cefnllys, the hilltop site of both a prehistoric fort and a medieval castle burned down by Owain Glyn Dŵr in 1406. At its foot was a dependent borough, the predecessor of $Llandrindod, of which no trace remains except for the plain little church of St Michael on a slope above the river. This was a favourite picnic spot for Llandrindod's Victorian visitors, reached by the "Shaky Bridge", a primitive and evidently unstable rope suspension bridge, long since replaced.

*The Green Guide – new publications*
  *Hungary, Budapest - Prague – Pacific Northwest – Sicily - USA East – USA West*

# LLANDUDNO ★

Conwy – Population 18 647
Michelin Atlas p 33 or Map 403 I 24

Llandudno is one of the finest examples of a planned seaside resort in Great Britain, with its broad promenade and stuccoed hotels laid out on the isthmus linking the limestone headlands of the Great Orme and the Little Orme. The town owes its elegant appearance to the careful planning undertaken by the local landowners, the prominent Mostyn family, and their architect, Owen Williams. Llandudno is also an excellent urban base for exploring both the North Wales coast and Snowdonia.

## HISTORICAL NOTES

Until the middle years of the 19C, there was little more to Llandudno than a few copper miners' cottages clinging to the slopes of the Great Orme and the occasional fisherman's shack dotted about on the sandy wasteland facing the curving shoreline. Aware both of the need to solve his family's pressing financial problems and of the potential of the sandy wasteland for development as a resort, the Hon E M L Mostyn is supposed to have commissioned Williams to prepare a feasibility study while the pair were sheltering from a sudden downpour in a bathing hut. An early proposal would have made Llandudno the packet station for Ireland, short-circuiting Holyhead.

## Out and About

**Tourist Information Centre** – 1-2 Chapel Street, Llandudno LL30 2YU
☎ 01492 876 413; Fax 01492 872 722.

**Bus Tour** – The **Guide Friday Bus Tour** ⊘ takes in the town centre of Llandudno and Conwy.

**Craft Centres** – The craft shop in the **Oriel Mostyn Art Gallery** *(see below)*, approved by the Crafts Council, offers jewellery, ceramics, glassware and hand-woven textiles.

**Entertainment** – The **Aberconwy Centre** (**BY**) for sports and entertainment and the **North Wales Theatre** (1 500-seats) *(at the western end of the seafront).*

**Beaches** – On the North Shore (dogs permitted).

**Adjacent Sights** – See Bangor, Beaumaris, Bodelwyddan, Bodnant Gardens, Colwyn Bay, Conwy, Llanrwst, Penrhyn Castle, Rhuddlan, Rhyl, Snowdonia.

## Where to Eat

**Martins,** 11 Mostyn Ave, LL30 1YS. ☎ 01492 870 070; Fax 01492 876 661. Traditionally decorated restaurant, serving fresh, good value traditional dishes; with 4 comfortable bedrooms.

**Richard's Bistro,** 7 Church Walks, LL30 2HD. ☎ 01492 877 924. Cosy cellar restaurant, personally run, providing good straightforward cookery.

**Number 1's Bistro,** 1 Old Rd, LL30 2HA. ☎/Fax 01492 875 424. Atmospheric little bistro with blackboard menu of eclectic dishes from around the world.

**Queen's Head,** Glanwydden, LL31 9JP. *2.5mi/4km by A 470 and Goddaeth rd (Penthyn Bay rd).* ☎ 01492 546 570. Very busy out-of-town traditional pub (booking advisable).

**Nikki Ip's,** 57 Station Rd, Deganwy, LL31 9DF. ☎ 01492 596 611. Good Chinese restaurant, personally run, serving authentic dishes; good value.

**Paysanne,** Station Rd, Deganwy, LL31 9EJ. ☎ 01492 582 079; Fax 01492 875 424. Simple little bistro, personally run, with a strong French influence on the atmosphere and cooking.

**Café Niçoise,** 124 Abergele Rd, Colwyn Bay, LL29 7PS. *5mi/8km W by B 5115.* ☎ 01492 531 555. A pleasant little restaurant serving modern food; good value.

## Where to Stay

**Abbey Lodge,** 14 Abbey Rd, LL30 2EA. ☎ 01492 878 042. Comfortable, personally run guesthouse (4 rm) with a high standard of comfort, close to the town centre.

**Lympley Lodge,** Colwyn Rd, Craigside, LL30 3AL. ☎ 01492 549 304. Attractively furnished Victorian house (3 rm), close to the sea yet in a quiet area east of the town, providing a good level of hospitality.

**The Lighthouse,** Marine Drive, Great Orme's Head, LL30 2XD. *1.5mi/2.4km N by Happy Valley Rd.* ☎ 01492 876 819. Old Victorian lighthouse (2 rm), superbly sited on the cliffs of the Great Orme, providing a good standard of bed and breakfast.

**Epperstone,** 15 Abbey Rd, LL30 2EE. ☎ 01492 878 764; Fax 01492 871 223. Traditionally furnished Victorian house (8 rm) with attractively decorated bedrooms; serving dinner.

**Cranberry House,** 12 Abbey Rd, LL30 2EA. ☎ 01492 878 760. Pleasantly furnished townhouse (5 rm), located in the town; ideal base for exploring the area on foot.

**Bryn Derwen,** 34 Abbey Rd, LL30 2EE. ☎ /Fax 01492 876 804. Spacious comfortably appointed small hotel (9 rm), in a quiet residential area; own restaurant.

**Old Rectory,** Llanrwst Rd, Llansanffraid Glan Conwy, LL28 5LF. ☎ 01492 580 611. Well-furnished country house (6 rm) renowned for its cooking; worth a detour.

**St Tudno,** North Parade, LL30 2LP. ☎ 01492 874 441; Fax 01492 860 407. Personally run hotel (18 rm) on the promenade with extensive facilities and well-equipped bedrooms – most with a sea view; good standard of restaurant.

his came to nothing but an Act of Parliament of 1854 gave the Mostyns strict control
er the form development should take, allowing them to set the high architectural and
cial tone which Llandudno has striven to maintain ever since. Commerce was kept away
om the seafront, building heights and road widths were carefully specified , as were the
mensions of rooms and windows. No cellar was to be converted into a separate
welling. Willliams created the sweeping crescent of the Promenade, and *St George's*
otel (1854) was soon joined by others to form a continuous line along the seafront.
he streets behind were laid out in a grid pattern which guided the town's development
ntil it reached the West Shore (1mi/1.5km away).

andudno's heyday came at the end of the 19C, when its population trebled and
uadrupled during the summer season and it succeeded in squaring the circle of
opularity and exclusivity; expensive shops in canopied Mostyn Street served the
ientele of the grand hotels, and entertainment was provided by Prof Beaumont, the
scapologist, and by Signor Ferraria and his Performing Birds.

Seafront and Pier, Llandudno

## ★Seafront (BY)

Owen Williams had no regrets about the generous dimensions of his promenade,
and claimed he would have made it even wider had resources permitted. It is
anchored firmly to the foot of the Great Orme by the seven-storey bulk of the
*Grand Hotel*, breasting the waves like a man-made extension of the headland itself,
and by the **Pier★** (**BX**). The Pavilion, which once seated an audience of 2 000, was
destroyed by fire but the Pier (1 400ft/427m) still protrudes into the sea. It dates
from 1875 and was once compared to "a maharajah's palace floating in a lake"; its
kiosks, ironwork and end pavilion are a delicious confection of exotic, Indo-Gothick
detailing. In contrast to many other piers, but like the town itself, it is in good
shape, and a stroll along its great length is a cheerful experience, not least for the
view of the Promenade in its entirety. The continuous line of pale stucco hotels,
uniquely in Britain, has been preserved intact. Referred to wryly by Clough Williams-Ellis as "Pimlico Palladian", the architecture was already old-fashioned at the
time of building. There are few highlights, rather an impression of restraint and
good manners. The greatest variety is seen at the end nearest the pier, where the
land rises and a few surviving elm trees separate Promenade and hotels, creating
an almost Mediterranean ambience.

## Town Centre

The architectural homogeneity of the seafront gives way to the more diverse
townscape of the shopping streets just inland. Mostyn Street and Lloyd Street still
have many of the charming cast-iron canopies which sheltered Victorian shoppers
from the elements. One of the fiercest defenders of the town's character was Lady
Augusta Mostyn, who founded the **Oriel Mostyn Art Gallery** ⊙ (**BY K**) in Vaughan Street
to house her own collection; reopened in 1979, it is now used for important
temporary exhibitions. Local history from the earliest inhabitants to the present,

## LLANDUDNO and THE GREAT ORME

Augusta Street........... **BY 2**
Chapel Street ........... **AY 3**

Deganwy Avenue ....... **AY 4**
Gloddaeth Street........ **AY 5**
Madoc Street ........... **AY 6**
Maelgwyn Road......... **AY 7**
Mostyn Avenue ......... **BY 12**
Mostyn Broadway....... **BY 13**

Mostyn Street ........... **BY**
North Parade............ **ABX**
Oxford Road............. **BY**
St Mary's Road .......... **AY**
Trinity Street ............ **BY**
Upper Mostyn Street..... **AY**

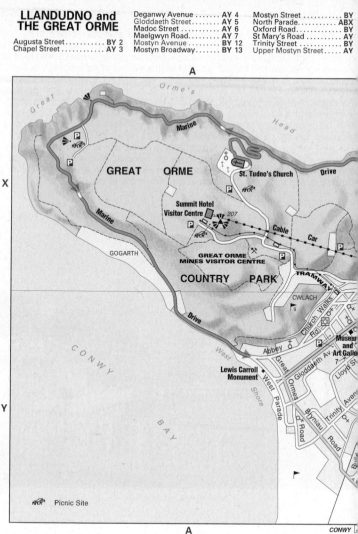

Picnic Site

including "hands-on" displays and a life-size model of the local copper mines in the 19C, can be studied in the **Llandudno Museum and Art Gallery** ⊘ (**AY**) in Gloddaeth Street.

Visitors are sometimes surprised to see Llandudno's lifeboat passing through the streets; the lifeboat station is in Lloyd Street, enabling the vessel to be towed rapidly to the north or the west shore.

**Alice in Wonderland Centre** ⊘ (**BY**) – *Trinity Square*. Animated tableaux celebrate the adventures of *Alice in Wonderland* and *Through the Looking Glass*, inspired by the fact the Alice Liddell and her family took their holidays in Llandudno.

Whether that shy storyteller and devotee of little girls, Charles Dodgson, ever came to Llandudno is still a matter of controversy, but a delightful **statue of the White Rabbit** stands on the West Shore.

---

### Alice in Wonderland and Llandudno

An early visitor to Llandudno was Dean Liddell of Christ Church Oxford, who came for his honeymoon in 1846, later stayed with his family in the house which is now the *St Tudno Hotel*, and then built *Penmorfa*, a permanent holiday home overlooking the West Shore. Here the three Liddell daughters, including Alice, were painted as *The Sisters* against a background of the Great Orme by Sir William Richmond, one of many prominent guests entertained at Penmorfa.

Vaughan Street . . . . . . . . . . . . . . BY 24
Victoria Centre . . . . . . . . . . . . . . BY

Oriel Mostyn Art Gallery  BY<sup>K</sup>

B

## ★The Great Orme

Victorian Llandudno was fortunate in having its own mountain (679ft/207m) rising ruggedly from the very seashore. The limestone headland, a prominent landmark visible along much of the North Wales coast, is a strange mixture of wild nature, long human history, and visitor amenities.

The windy slopes, where sheep wander unchecked, is managed as the **Great Orme Country Park** with footpaths and a nature trail; the **Visitor Centre** ⊙ (**AX**) provides information and displays about the nature reserve, its natural history and wildlife, its local history and geology. Opposite stands the **Summit Hotel** (**AX**), now bereft of battlements and verandas.

The commanding **panorama**★★ made this an inevitable site for one of the semaphore stations which, from the 1820s, relayed shipping information from Holyhead to Liverpool in a matter of minutes.

On the north slope below the summit stands the isolated **St Tudno's Church** ⊙ (**AX**), until the 19C the parish church of Llandudno (the name of the town means "church enclosure of St Tudno"). A notice on the church door urges visitors to "close the outer gate to prevent the sheep getting in".

The Carboniferous limestone of the Great Orme is seamed with metalliferous ores which have been worked since the Bronze Age. Prehistoric miners dug a network of shafts and tunnels up to 1 000ft/300m long into the mountain in search of copper ore, leaving behind thousands of bone tools and stone hammers as evidence of their activity. The first documentary evidence of mining dates from 1692. The last mine closed in the 1850s but the extent of Bronze Age activity makes this perhaps the most important archaeological site of its type in Europe. Some of these extraordinary underground prehistoric workings can be explored in the **Great Orme Mines Visitor Centre**★ ⊙ (**AX**), where there is an imaginative audiovisual presentation.

---

### Access

There is a steep and narrow road to the top for cars and several footpaths for pedestrians.
The **Great Orme Tramway** ⊙★ (**AX**), completed in 1903, gives an exhilarating ride in vintage, cable-hauled tramcars from the west end of the town up to the terminus on the summit.
The **Llandudno Cable-car** ⊙ (**AX**) is a more modern alternative, starting from the west end of the seafront.
The headland is circled by the **Marine Drive** ⊙, a one-way *(anti-clockwise)* scenic road *(4.5mi/7km)* cut into the cliffs in 1878 which offers fine views out to sea; the lighthouse was decommissioned in 1985.

---

*The Practical Information section at the beginning of the guide lists :*
*– information about travel, motoring, accommodation, recreation*
*– local or national organisations providing additional information*
*– calendar of events*
*– admission times and charges for the sights described in the guide*

# LLANELLI

Carmarthenshire – Population 74 698
Michelin Atlas p 15 or Map 403 H 28

For centuries the few inhabitants of what is now the largest town in Carmarthenshire lived from farming and fishing, though by the 16C they had begun, as Leland noted, not only to "digge coales" but to ship them out, first from the banks of the tidal River Loughor at Ysbyty, then from a growing complex of wharves and docks to the south of the present town centre. Coal exports began to decline as early as the mid-19C, but by then Llanelli had become a leading centre of metalworking, especially of the **tinplate** production which has continued until the present day. The town's passion is Rugby football, focused on the fortunes of the home team, the *Scarlets*, whose resounding anthem, *Sospan Fach*, is in fact no more than a ditty about a little saucepan.

Llanelli's rapid industrial growth in the 19C obliterated most traces of its past, and the dominant element in today's townscape consists of variations on the theme of the Victorian terraced house. The busy town centre with its market is mostly pedestrianised and has recently received a much-needed refurbishment.

The **Millennium Coastal Park**, opened in 2000, forms a green belt (14mi/22km), along the seashore, between Machynys (south of Llanelli) and Pembrey, a chain of gardens and woodlands, wetlands and fishing lakes, dunes, quays and harbours, linked by a footpath and cycleway, offering a variety of facilities – water sports centre, outdoor and indoor events areas and an 18-hole golf course.

**Llanelli Museum** ⊙ – *N of the town centre*. The museum is housed in **Parc Howard**, the sombre mansion of a 19C industrialist, which is surrounded by attractive parkland.
On display is an extensive collection of the products of the South Wales Pottery, established in Llanelli in 1840. Paintings include a number of works by JD Innes, born in the town in 1887, but pride of place

goes to mementoes of another local man, **Elwyn Jones** (b 1909), son of a tinplate worker, and later Lord Chancellor.

## EXCURSIONS

**★The Wildfowl and Wetlands Trust, Llanelli** ⊙ – *3mi/5km E of town centre off A 484.* Llanelli tended to turn its back on the splendid stretch of tidal water formed by the estuary of the River Loughor, using it as a site for the now-neglected docks and for industrial plants. Determined attempts are now being made to transform the western part of the area with a promenade and with housing, commercial and leisure developments, but to the east the levels are being returned to Nature, with the levelling of old industries and the establishment in 1991 of this major wildfowl centre, one of eight in Great Britain.
The estuary has international status for the conservation of wildfowl and in particular for wading birds. The area (210 acres/87ha) managed by the Trust consists of a network of lakes and bodies of water and of a magnificent stretch of salt-marsh fronting the estuary. A stylish and spacious **visitor centre** built on the knoll formed by a terminal moraine gives a fine all-round prospect, which ranges from pools just outside its panoramic windows to the Gower coast on the far side of the estuary. The abundance of food in the estuary supports an array of permanent residents and attracts more than 70 000 migrants every year. In addition, exotic birds like Caribbean flamingoes are bred here. A walk through the luxuriantly landscaped site is always a rewarding experience, especially in the company of a guide, while a number of hides provide a prospect both of the lakes and of the levels beyond.

**Pembrey Country Park** ⊙ – *8mi/13km W of Llanelli by A 484.* Facing southwest across Carmarthen Bay is the Pembrey Peninsula, a vast tract of alluvial deposits and sand dunes. Its remoteness attracted military use, first as a gunpowder works in the 1880s, then as a fully-fledged Royal Ordnance factory supplying munitions in both World Wars. From the 1930s the Forestry Commission has been planting up the dunes with conifers. Since the 1965 closure of the factory, virtually a town in its own right, a tract (500 acres/c 200ha) has been turned into an extremely popular country park. Attractions range from horse riding to dry skiing, and from train rides to golf, but the main draw is the magnificent **sandy beach** (8mi/13km).

**★Kidwelly Castle** ⊙ – *9mi/15km NW of Llanelli by A 484 and Kidwelly by-pass.* On its ridge overlooking the limit of tidal water on the River Gwendraeth, Kidwelly (Cydweli) was one of a chain of Norman castles intended to secure the coastal

CADW: Welsh Historic Monuments – Crown Copyright

Kidwelly Castle

route to the west. Roofless, but otherwise well preserved, it conveys a most satisfying impression of a medieval stronghold, especially when its splendid array of walls and towers is viewed from the far bank of the river.

The first fortress, constructed of timber, was built c 1106 by the powerful Bishop of Salisbury, exploiting the cliff-like drop to the river as a natural line of defence on the east and throwing up a great curving bank and ditch on the west. Repeated Welsh attacks stimulated a late-13C rebuilding in stone. A square **inner ward** was erected with round towers at each corner, followed at the beginning of the 14C by a hall and a fine **chapel tower** hanging over the cliff, with windows in a pale stone contrasting with the darker stonework elsewhere. An outer curtain wall with semicircular towers was constructed on Salisbury's earthworks and a massive twin-towered **gatehouse** was begun, though it had not been completed by the time of the Glyn Dŵr rebellion early in the 15C. Finally completed in the early 1410s, it makes an intimidating entrance to the castle today.

**Kidwelly Industrial Museum** ⊘ – *On far side of A 484 from Kidwelly.* The forge at work on this ancient industrial site was replaced by a tinplate manufactory in 1737 which continued in production until 1941. The museum's display of venerable machinery, strung out along the length of the site, explains how Llanelli and the surrounding area gained the name of "Tinopolis".

# LLANFYLLIN

Powys – Population 1 267
Michelin Atlas p 33 or Map 403 K 25

Llanfyllin is an attractive and self-possessed little town with a pleasing mixture of red-brick and timber-framed buildings ranged along its well-kept main street. It shares with Welshpool the distinction of being a native Welsh borough, a planned town laid out in the late 13C by the Prince of Powys on the model of the English new towns being created in the Marches. Llanfyllin is proud of its status, and celebrated the 700th anniversary of its charter in 1993 with great gusto.

The mostly 18C **church** ⊘ is built in the local red brick and is named after St Myllin, a 7C Celtic saint who seems to have been a pioneer of baptism by total immersion. What is reputed to be his **well**, just west of the town, was once used as a cockpit but has recently been restored.

French prisoners were kept in this remote spot during the Napoleonic wars, and one of them, Captain Augerau, decorated the interior of the **Council House** ⊘ with murals showing fanciful mountain scenes.

**Adjacent Sights** – See Bala, Chirk Castle, Dolgellau, Llangollen, Machynlleth, Plas Newydd, Powis Castle, Ruthin, Valle Crucis Abbey, Lake Vyrnwy, Welshpool.

## EXCURSION

★**Pistyll Rhaeadr** – *10mi/16km NW by B 4391, B 4580 and a minor road.* This high waterfall, one of the "seven wonders of Wales", is reached via the pretty village of **Llanrhaeadr-ym-Mochnant** where William Morgan made his famous translation of the Bible into Welsh *(see p 274).*

The area below the falls is a popular picnic spot and camp site. The water which drops a spectacular 240ft/73m originates in the little-visited **Berwyn Mountains** to the west and north, a vast tableland lacking the drama of Snowdonia's mountains, but whose high point at Moel Sych (2 713ft/827m) overlooks east-facing crags and the tiny glacial lake of Llyn Lluncaws.

# LLANGOLLEN ★

Denbighshire – Population 3 267
Michelin Atlas p 33 or Map 403 K 25

Of several river valleys penetrating from the English lowlands deep into the mountains of North Wales, the **Vale of Llangollen**★ has long been considered the most picturesque. The little market town and resort of Llangollen is popular with visitors throughout the year but is best known for its International Musical *Eisteddfod,* held in July, when singers and dancers from dozens of countries fill its streets and perform to packed audiences in the striking Royal International Pavilion.

**A gateway into Wales** – Before breaking out eastward into the English plain, the winding River Dee follows geological fault-lines between the slaty Berwyn Mountains to the south and the magnificent limestone scarp of the Eglwyseg Mountain to the north. The contrast between these stark uplands and the homely, intimate vale with its lush woodlands and verdant pastures seems almost to have been designed with the sensibilities of late-18C and early-19C travellers in mind; in 1798, on his 20th birthday, Hazlitt chose "this enchanted spot" to read from Rousseau's *Nouvelle Héloïse,* and Paul Sandby paused at Llangollen on his extended sketching tour of the North in 1771. Later visitors included Southey, Shelley, Wordsworth and Sir Walter Scott, as well as figures like the Duke of Wellington and his friend Prince Paul Eszterhazy, all of whom were received by the eccentric pair known as the "Ladies of Llangollen" *(see p 231).*

### Out and About

**Llangollen Tourist Information Centre** – Town Hall, Castle Street, Llangollen LL20 5PD Tel 01978 860 828; Fax 01978 861 563.

**Craft Centre** – Y Glassblobbery ⊙ *(15mi/24km W by A 5 and A 494)* offers hand-made ornamental glassware; also contemporary and traditional craftwork. At the **Craft Workshop** ⊙ *(Berwyn lodge, Glynbdyfrdwy; 5mi/8km W of Llangollen)* the building is decorated with the product – large decorative butterflies.

**Dee Valley** – The delightful scenery of the river valley may be explored with the minimum of energy and stress by railway upstream or by canal downstream *(see below).*

**Adjacent Sights** – See Bala, Betws-y-Coed, Chirk Castle, Erddig, Hawarden, Llanfyllin, Mold, Plas Newydd, Ruthin, Valle Crucis Abbey, Lake Vyrnwy, Wrexham.

### Where to Eat

**The Corn Mill**, Dee Lane, LL20 8PN. ☎ 01978 869 5555. Converted corn mill on the banks of the River Dee, pleasant atmosphere and good value for food.

### Where to Stay

**Hillcrest**, Hill St, LL20 8EU. ☎/Fax 01978 860 208. Pleasant furnished guest-house (7 rm), only 2min on foot from the town, providing a good level of comfort and rooms specially modified for elderly guests.

**Oakmere**, Regent St, LL20 8HS. *On A 5.* ☎ 01978 861 126. Spacious town-house (6 rm) with pleasant period charm, garden and parking; only a short distance from the town.

**Gales**, 18 Bridge St, LL20 8PF. ☎ 01978 860 089; Fax 01978 861 313. Busy place (13 rm), of unusual character; small restaurant.

y the time of Hazlitt's musings, the great engineer Thomas Telford had begun work
n the ambitious canal project linking the Mersey, Dee and Severn; a spur to Llangollen
vas built, as well as two of the finest monuments of the Canal Age, the great
queducts at Pont Cysyllte and Chirk. Years later, in 1815, Telford returned to the
rea to build what is still admired as a superb example of highway engineering, the
reat turnpike road across the mountains linking London to Holyhead and thence to
reland, newly joined to Britain by the Act of Union of 1800. Finally the railway
rrived in 1862, eventually linking the industrial cities of Northern England with Bala,
olgellau and the shores of Cardigan Bay, and bringing different kinds and increased
umbers of tourists to Llangollen itself.

**Llangollen Bridge** – Two centuries ago, Llangollen consisted of straggling Bridge
Street to the south and a village green to the north, linked by the bridge known as
one of the "Seven Wonders of Wales". Given an extra span to accommodate the
railway in 1873 and carefully widened in 1969, the four-arched bridge probably
dates from c 1500 but was preceded by an earlier structure supposedly built by the
Bishop of St Asaph in the mid-14C. The Dee here has the character of a wild river,
crashing and foaming over rocky outcrops where willow trees somehow maintain a
precarious hold. The bridge acts as an informal grandstand for spectators
enthralled by the numerous national and international canoe and slalom festivals
held every year. To the north, the land rises steeply to the canal, while to the
south, the town's main shopping street, Castle Street, is part of a modest mid-19C
town planning scheme which directed Llangollen's growth into a grid pattern of
streets to the west.

★ **Llangollen Railway** ⊘ – *North bank*. There is only just room for the curving tracks
and platforms of Llangollen Station between the Dee and the steep slope to the north.
The whistling and hooting of steam and diesel locomotives heard over the roar of the
river contribute to the authentic atmosphere of a mid-20C railway, recreated by the
enthusiasts who have reopened several miles of the old Ruabon-Barmouth line shut in
the 1960s. The regular services, run on what is the only standard-gauge preserved
railway in Wales, are perhaps the best way of exploring the Vale upstream from
Llangollen as far as Glyndyfrdwy; continuation to Corwen is planned.

**Llangollen Wharf** – *North bank*. The Llangollen branch of the Shropshire Union
Canal was built by Telford mainly as a feeder supplying water to the system from
the River Dee but it was used for commercial traffic too. The horse-drawn
passenger service initiated in 1884 has been revived, and a leisurely **barge trip** ⊘ on
the winding waterway along the lower slopes of the Vale is a most relaxing way of
enjoying the varied scenery downstream from Llangollen. Upstream, the towpath
follows the narrowing canal to join the Dee at Telford's **Horseshoe Falls**, a curving
weir of great elegance in a romantic setting.

**Lower Dee Exhibition Centre** ⊘ – *Mill Street; north bank*. Devotees of the
Doctor's adventures will enjoy this collection of **Dr Who memorabilia** – the first
instalment, shown on television in November 1963, the history of the programme
and the costumes worn by the actors who interpreted the role. The Hall of
Monsters is full of grotesque creatures including the menacing Daleks crying
"Exterminate".
In the factory *(lower floor)* one can see various stages in the production of Dr Who
figures and model kits of cars and railway wagons made by Dapoland, Highway
Pioneer and ex-Airfix; also artwork and instructions for Hornby Dublo *(merchandise
available in the shop)*.
The **International Model Railway World** is paradise for all railway enthusiasts; against a
background of video films of steam train journeys, it presents 20 model railway
layouts (10 with hands-on operation), 60 years of railway models, by all the major
manufacturers, and equipment from the Meccano factory which was used to
produce pre- and post-war Hornby Dublo products.

**ECTARC: European Centre for Traditional and Regional Cultures** ⊘ – *Castle
Street*. Originally entitled the European Centre for Folk Studies, this international
organisation exists to promote the regional cultures of Europe, by means of
research, exchanges, performances, conferences and exhibitions. It seems very
much at home in this small Welsh town whose **International Musical Eisteddfod** has
been the forum for so many friendships. The old Baptist Chapel has been imaginatively and sensitively converted to provide a modern auditorium and display space,
where a changing programme of exhibitions celebrates aspects of the Continent's
richly diverse but increasingly threatened local cultures.

**Victorian School and Museum** ⊘ – *Parade Street*. A loving re-creation of the
severe atmosphere of a late-19C schoolroom occupies, appropriately enough, a
Victorian school building of 1868. Here groups of today's children may don
Victorian clothes and sit at desks with inkwells, writing on slates with squeaky
chalk, studying maps of the Indian Empire, and obeying the blackboard's admon-
ition to be "seen and not heard". Other rooms evoke local history and Victorian
domestic life.

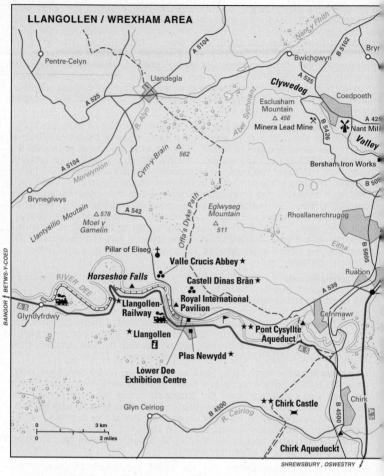

**LLANGOLLEN / WREXHAM AREA**

*(Map showing the Llangollen/Wrexham area with locations including Pentre-Celyn, Llandegla, Bwichgwyn, Clywedog, Coedpoeth, Esclusham Mountain △ 456, Minera Lead Mine, Nant Mill, Valley, Bersham Iron Works, Bryneglwys, Cyrn-y-Brain △ 562, Morwynion, Llantysilio Mountain △ 578, Moel y Gamelin, Eglwyseg Mountain △ 511, Rhosllanerchrugog, Offa's Dyke Path, Pillar of Eliseg, Valle Crucis Abbey ★, Horseshoe Falls, Castell Dinas Brân ★, River Dee, Llangollen Railway, Royal International Pavilion, Glyndyfrdwy, Llangollen, Pont Cysyllte Aqueduct ★★, Cefnmawr, Ruabon, Plas Newydd ★, Lower Dee Exhibition Centre, Glyn Ceiriog, R. Ceiriog, Chirk Castle ★★, Chirk, Chirk Aqueduckt. Scale: 3 km / 2 miles. BANGOR ↑ BETWS-Y-COED. SHREWSBURY, OSWESTRY. Roads: A 5104, A 525, B 5102, B 5426, B 5605, A 539, A 5, B 4500, etc.)*

SHREWSBURY, OSWESTRY

**Royal International Pavilion** ⊘ – *NW of town centre by A 542*. The fabric of its canopy gleaming white against the lush green western outskirts of Llangollen, this extraordinary structure was opened in 1992 primarily to house the events of the International Eisteddfod. Its tensioned PVC-coated polyester is hung from a steel arch (75ft/23m high with a span of 196ft/60m), covering a permanent arena (2 000 seats) which can be extended to shelter an audience of a further 3 000. The monster marquee, a triumph of innovative technology, merges with more conventional structures housing more cultural and leisure facilities – exhibitions, concerts, films shows and conferences.

"Blessed is a World that sings, Gentle are its songs". The motto of the **International Musical Eisteddfod** was coined in 1947, when the festival made its first attempt to link the world with music and friendship, and singers and dancers representing 14 nations found their way to Llangollen. Since then the annual festival, held in July, has welcomed performers from virtually every country in the world. Among them, as a young man, was Luciano Pavarotti but stars are the exception; most

---

### Eisteddfod

The **International Musical Eisteddfod**, held annually in Llangollen, is attended by dancers, singers and players from more than 50 countries (early July); it celebrated its 50th anniversary in 1996. A **National Eisteddfod** has been held every year, alternating between north and south Wales, since 1858 when thousands attended the festival held that year in Llangollen. An eisteddfod (plural eisteddfodau) is a Welsh-language cultural festival, inspired by a competition between bards held in 1789 in Corwen in the Owain Glyndŵr tavern and based on the strong musical tradition which finds expression in the many local choirs; there is one in almost every village and town and many admit visitors to listen to their rehearsals.

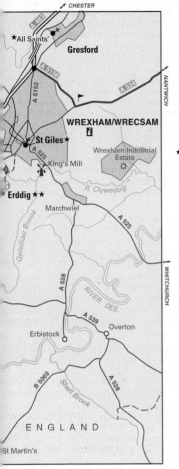

choirs and folklore performers remain anonymous members of troupes, whose bright costumes make a welcome splash of colour in the local townscape. Each July, some 12 000 participants from up to 50 countries make their way here and are somehow found a place in the hotels and private houses of the town and its surroundings, while their performances are watched by crowds totalling 120 000, making this one of the most important events of its kind in the world.

★**Castell Dinas Brân** – *Steep waymarked footpath N of Llangollen.* The stronghold built by a local lord in the mid-13C seems to have had a useful life of only a few years before being burnt down in the course of the First Welsh War of 1277. Its new Anglo-Norman owner found the banks of the Dee at Holt more congenial, and erected his castle there rather than taking up residence on this exposed hilltop some 750ft/c 240m above Llangollen. Since then the rectangular castle, built within the earthen ramparts of an Iron Age fortification, has slowly crumbled away, ignored until the late 18C, when its craggy outline was seen to fulfil all the requirements of a Romantic ruin and it became the most famous landmark in the Vale of Llangollen.

The castle was built of stone quarried from its southern and eastern flanks, leaving a deep defensive ditch, while precipitous slopes protected it from west and north. Fragments of curtain wall, gatehouse, postern gate, keep and apsidal tower survive. Dominating the Vale, the hilltop enjoys wonderful all-round **views**. Beyond the grim scree slopes and limestone buttresses of the Eglwyseg escarpment to the north-east stretches the heather moorland of Ruabon mountain, pitted with the burial mounds and other monuments of its Bronze Age inhabitants.

## EXCURSIONS

**Llangollen Motor Museum** ⊙ – *1mi/1.6km by A 539.* Two forms of transport are combined here in an exhibition which tells the story of British canals and the people who worked on them, while the veteran cars evoke the early days of motoring.

★★**Pont Cysyllte Aqueduct** – *4mi/7km E of Llangollen by A 539.* The official portrait of **Thomas Telford** poses him against the background of this splendid aqueduct which carries the Ellesmere Canal 121ft/37m above the River Dee. The expression on the face of the great engineer is one of confidence and satisfaction, and Pont Cysyllte, built 1795-1810, was indeed a remarkably original achievement. Telford rejected the conventional solution

Llangollen International Musical Eisteddfod

to the problem of crossing a deep valley, a series of locks and a short bridge, in favour of a structure springing directly from the valley's northern rim to the tip of huge embankment on the far side. The canal, together with its towpath, is carried in a cast-iron trough (1 007ft/307m long), supported on four iron arches resting on 18 elegantly tapering stone piers, the upper parts of which are hollow. Alternative recipes are given for the compound used to seal the joints of the piers; lead and flannel boiled in sugar, or lime and oxblood. A stroll along the aqueduct is a vertiginous experience; there is no barrier on the canal side, and the railings along the towpath are in scale with the structure itself, with generous gaps between the uprights. Far below, the Dee follows its picturesque course between wooded banks crossed at just the right point in the composition by a three-arched bridge of 1697. At the northern end of the aqueduct are extensive wharves and basins, laid out in anticipation of the completion of the waterway linking Chester via Wrexham to the Severn at Shrewsbury. In the event the canal, save for the spur to Llangollen terminated here, and never quite enjoyed the commercial success hoped for. But the post-war boom in recreational navigation has revived the fortunes of what in terms of scenery and engineering achievement is one of the most fascinating waterways in the country.

**Chirk Aqueduct** – *7mi/11km SE of Llangollen by A 5*. The barrier of the Ceiriog valley at Chirk was overcome by Telford several years before he tackled the deeper valley of the Dee at Pont Cysyllte. His Chirk Aqueduct is a most imposing structure in its own right, though inevitably overshadowed by the larger structure just to the north. Completed in 1801, the aqueduct is 710ft/215m long and 70ft/21m high. The canal is carried, not in a trough, but over a bed of iron plates between stone walls. Telford later returned to the area to build the single-span road bridge just downstream to carry the Holyhead road, while the aqueduct's visual impact was enhanced in 1848 by the railway viaduct built alongside. To the north, the canal disappears into Chirk Tunnel (1 377ft/420m long), the spoil from which was used to form the massive embankment at Pont Cysyllte.

★**Rug Chapel** ⊙ – *11mi/18km W of Llangollen by A 5 and A 494*. As it was hardly touched by the Victorian restorers, the interior of this wonderfully decorated little chapel retains many of the features characteristic of the "High Church" era of the reign of Charles I. The chapel, unremarkable outside, stands just to the west of the grey-stone town of **Corwen**, where the valley of the Dee opens out and is joined by the River Alwen.

In the 17C the mansion and park of Rug were the property of the colourful figure of **Colonel William Salusbury** (1580-1660), a pious former pirate and stalwart defender of Denbigh Castle against the enemies of the King in the Civil War. The chapel was built in 1637 for the private worship of the Colonel and his family.

Wall painting, Rug Chapel

The **interior**, still medieval in construction, breathes a spirit all of its own. The superb **timber roof** is carved and coloured and ornamented with bosses and a quartet of charming cut-out **angels**, like those which decorate the Gwydir Uchaf Chapel at Llanrwst *(see p 194)*. Strange beasts and monsters appear in the panelled **frieze** which runs the full length of the building, while an altogether different array of creatures appears on the sides of the unusual **benches**. A painting on the north wall is full of symbolism signifying the transience of life and the inevitability of death, the message reinforced by inscriptions in Welsh. The 19C screen in mock-Jacobean style harmonises with the original furnishings.

From Rug an equally unusual building, **Llangar Church** ⊙, can be visited. It was abandoned in the mid-19C but retains its late medieval roof, 18C fittings and fragmentary wall paintings of various dates, including a fearsome figure of Death wielding arrow and hourglass.

# LLANIDLOES ★

Powys – Population 2 616
Michelin Atlas p 25 or Map 403 J 26

The first town on the River Severn, Llanidloes has a quiet charm which seems to owe more to its medieval beginnings as a market centre than to the early 19C, when boom-and-bust in lead and textiles led to Chartist riots and their inevitable suppression. Deprived of its railway in the early 1960s, Llanidloes makes the most of its remoteness from cities and of its proximity to some of the wildest country in Wales; as well as a centre for visitors exploring the lonely uplands around the source of the Severn, the town has attracted many new residents in search of "green" alternatives to conventional consumerism.

## SIGHTS

**Market Hall** – Standing at the crossroads where the four streets of the medieval town plan meet, this delightful timber-framed structure with its open ground floor is the only one of its kind left in Wales. Built c 1600 to replace a medieval market cross, it has been used for a variety of purposes; Quakers met here, and John Wesley preached from the pulpit stone at the north-west corner. In 1839, inspired by Chartism, the workers who had been impoverished by the collapse of the local textile industry assembled here, chasing away magistrates and police, and ruling the town for a week until the arrival of troops from Brecon. At the subsequent trial, 32 Chartists were sentenced and three ringleaders were transported.

The Hall has a rustic look, but some of the buildings around the crossroads lend Llanidloes an air of importance that led the architectural writer Ian Nairn to call the place a "pocket metropolis".

**Tourist Information Centre** – 54 Longbridge Street, Llanidloes, Powys SY18 6EF ☎ 01686 412 605; Fax 01686 413 884.

**Adjacent Sights** – See Elan Valley, Knighton, Llandrindod Wells, Machynlleth, Newtown, Rheidol Valley, Strata Florida Abbey.

**Town Hall** – This is the grandest building, dating from 1908 and financed by the immensely rich Davies family from nearby Llandinam, although its metropolitan pretensions are somewhat undermined by the trees growing in the roadway. The Town Hall houses the little **Llanidloes Museum of Social and Industrial History** ⊙ which tells the story of the town and its surroundings.

**St Idloes' Church** ⊙ – The squat tower dates from the late 14C and has a typical two-stage Montgomeryshire belfry. The interior is remarkable for its incorporation of major elements brought across the mountains from Abbey Cwmhir *(10mi/16km SE by B 4518 and E by a side road)* at the Dissolution, the elegant Early English nave arcade, with stiff-leaf capitals, and the magnificent hammerbeam roof.

## EXCURSIONS

**Hafren Forest** – *7mi/12km W of Llanidloes by minor roads.* The vast man-made Hafren (= Severn) Forest has covered the eastern slopes of the Plynlimon massif with a blanket of lodgepole pine, Norway spruce and Sitka spruce. From the car park at Rhyd y Benwch a number of walks lead into the forest; a short stroll leads along a boardwalk past cascades; another, much more ambitious, extends beyond the upper limit of the forest to the heather and bilberry moor and blanket bog where the Severn has its source.

**★★Dylife Mountain Road** – *20mi/32km NW of Llanidloes by B 4518 and minor roac*
This is one of the most splendid upland drives in Wales, crossing the shoulder o
the Plynlimon massif and descending into the Dovey *(Dyfi)* valley with incomparab
views northwards to Snowdonia.

*For a 4mi/6km detour to Llyn Clywedog reservoir follow signs from B 4518.*

**Llyn Clywedog** – The Clywedog Dam was completed in 1967 primarily in order t
control the Severn's propensity to flood its valley in winter and starve it o
water in summer. It is the tallest concrete dam in Britain (237ft/72m high).
holds back a reservoir (6mi/10km long) of complex and attractive outline
There are scenic look-outs, picnic areas and a sailing club, but one of the mo:
dramatic views, of the dam itself, is from below, where its awesome buttresse
dominate the old **lead** and **barytes mine** at **Bryn Tail**. From the car park there is
path over the footbridge which spans the river to the old western mine worl
ings *(left);* it then follows the line of the old leat downstream through th
wood to the old eastern mine workings.

*Continue on B 4518.*

**Staylittle** – The village name derives from the speed with which the local blacksmith
re-shod travellers' horses.

*1mi/1.5km W of Staylittle turn left.*

After 0.5mi/1km there is an extraordinary plunging **view** into the deep valley of th
River Twymyn, with crags to the left, precipitous slopes to the right and th
**waterfall** (100ft/30m) of **Ffrwd Fawr**.

**Dylife** – Now no more than a hamlet, this place was the scene of intense leac
mining activity in the mid-19C, when 1 200 people lived and worked here. Th
road now crosses a plateau of great bleakness, with views southwards towarc
Lake Glaslyn and the crags which interrupt in places the otherwise smooth cor
tours of the massif. An abrupt descent opens up even more breathtaking view.
northwards. Most travellers pause at the **viewpoint** with its topograph carved i
slate in memory of the immensely popular writer and broadcaster Wynfor
Vaughan-Thomas (1908-87).

*The length of time given in this guide*
*– for touring allows time to enjoy the views and the scenery*
*– for sightseeing is the average time required for a visit*

# LLANRWST

Conwy – Population 3 012
Michelin Atlas p 33 or Map 403 I 24
Local map p 261

Though no longer the only bridging point along the Conwy valley, little Llanrwst sti
wears an air of some importance and serves the urban needs of a wide area. Apar
from the steep and elegant stone bridge which is still sometimes attributed t
Inigo Jones, the place is chiefly notable for its associations with the powerful **Wyn
family**.

**St Grwst Church and Gwydir Chapel** ⊙ – Overlooking the Conwy, the church i
approached via an archway at the end of a narrow street with almshouses endowe
by the Wynns. Inside is a splendid oak **rood screen**, possibly from nearby Maena
Abbey, featuring carvings of the instruments of the Passion and of pigs foragin
for acorns.

With its own door to the churchyard and built to an altogether grander scale is the **Gwydir Chapel**, the Wynns' memorial chapel, dating from 1633. Beneath its fine timber ceiling is an exceptionally interesting array of monuments and other decorative features. They include a massive stone coffin, said to have been that of Llywelyn the Great, an effigy of a knight in armour, magnificent portrait brasses and an exuberant wall monument incorporating every Renaissance feature its designer could think of. The stalls have an assortment of highly idiosyncratic carved heads as finials.

**Craft Centre** – For woollen goods – bedspreads, tweeds, rugs and knitting yarns – produced by a family business visit **Trefriw Woollen Mills** ⊘ (on B 5106 between Betwys-y-Coed and Conwy).

**Adjacent Sights** – See Bala, Betws-y-Coed, Bodelwyddan, Bodnant Gardens, Colwyn Bay, Conwy, Denbigh, Llandudno, Ruthin, St Asaph.

**Gwydir Castle** ⊘ – Descendants of the princes of Gwynedd, the Wynns, once inhabited the bleak castle keep at Dolwyddelan, high up in the Lledr valley, but built these more comfortable but still rugged quarters at the beginning of the 16C. Though extended and altered twice in the 16C and again in the 19C, Gwydir remains one of the finest examples of a fortified manor house in Wales. From here the Wynns exercised their sway over large tracts of North Wales, promoting local industries and improving the navigability of the Conwy.

Rough stone walls, massive fireplaces and a medieval Great Hall (split into an upper and lower floor) recall the remote and mountainous environment from which the family sprang, while other elements – stair tower with Perpendicular (mid-15C) windows and ceiling, grandiose porch, walled garden – evoke the Wynns' successful entry, following the Act of Union in 1536, into the mainstream of English and European courtly life. Sir Richard Wynn was among the group of courtiers who set out for Spain in 1623 to try to arrange a marriage between Charles I and the Spanish Infanta, and some of the first cedars of Lebanon to arrive in Britain were planted in the grounds at Gwydir to mark the event.

In the 1920s, the house was stripped of its furniture and of many of its fittings. The superb panelled Dining Parlour attributed to Inigo Jones, which once languished in the storerooms of New York's Metropolitan Museum, is being reinstated.

**Gwydir Uchaf Chapel** ⊘ – In the woods above the house is a chapel built by Sir Richard Wynn in 1673. Still Gothic in style, it has a ceiling adorned with exuberantly naïve paintings of angels frolicking among clouds.

Painted ceiling, Gwydir Uchaf Chapel

# LLANTHONY PRIORY★★

Monmouthshire

Michelin Atlas pp 16 and 25 or Map 403 K 28

The noble ruin of this Augustinian priory shelters in the Vale of Ewyas, a secluded valley winding up to Gospel Pass on the northern edge of the Black Mountains. Though English Herefordshire lies on the far side of the high moorland ridge to the east, this is one of the remotest, and most delectable, of all the monastic sites in Wales.

## HISTORICAL NOTES

"A world untouched..." This was how artist-craftsman **Eric Gill** (1882-1940) described the idyllic landscape of the Vale of Ewyas, in his time still without a proper road. Gill came here in 1924 with other members of the artistic community he had led in Sussex, in search of a place apart where the creative impulse could flourish in an atmosphere of cooperation and self-sufficiency. The Vale already had a long, if discontinuous tradition of attracting people tired of the temptations of conventional society. Gill and his followers settled at **Capel-y-ffin**, in the abbey founded in 1870 by the charismatic preacher **Father Ignatius**, whose ambition was to infuse new life into British monasticism. Ignatius' abbey was named after Llanthony itself *(4mi/7km down the valley)*, ruined at the Dissolution and abandoned a second time in 1815 by the poet **Walter Savage Landor**, after his romantic attempt to restore it had come to nothing.

Llanthony's legendary origins go back to the time of the Celtic saints, when St David is supposed to have worshipped here and given his name to the place, originally Llanddewi Nant Honddu ("church of David on the River Honddu"). What is certain is that a priory was established here c 1118. Its founder was the Norman Lord of Hereford, William de Lacy, who is said to have been converted to a life of prayer and contemplation when he came across the tranquil Vale in the course of a hunting expedition.

The idyll the Vale appeared to offer did not always prove enduring. Gill's sojourn here lasted only four years, though he often returned. By the time of Father Ignatius' death in 1908, a mere handful of his adherents remained in his abbey, and they soon left. Landor quit the Vale in near despair at his inability to command the cooperation of the local people. Centuries before, Gerald of Wales had described the inhabitants as "barbarous people", who had forced the monks to abandon the Priory c 1135, less than 20 years after its foundation. The community was re-established in the safer surroundings of Gloucester, comfortably within the English border. Eventually, however, the monks returned, tempted by the munificence of De Lacy's descendants, and between 1180 and 1230 built the splendid church whose evocative remains are seen today. The Priory suffered "barbarism" once more in the course of Owain Glyn Dŵr's rebellion, and again some of the monks retreated to Gloucester; by the early 16C, not long before the Dissolution, only four canons were left in the Vale of Ewyas.

---

**Adjacent Sights** – See Abergavenny, Brecon, Grosmont, Hay-on-Wye, Merthyr Tydfil, Monmouth, Raglan Castle, Tretower.

---

## TOUR ⏱

**Priory Ruins** – The priory stands on a level shelf of land a little above the emerald meadows and dark alders which accompany the course of the Honddu. To the northeast, the slopes rising steeply to the high moors are studded with the larches and chestnuts planted by Landor as part of his misconceived scheme to recreate a deer park.

The priory is approached through its cloister, now an open lawn bounded by the remains of the chapter-house to the east and by the surprise of the *Abbey Hotel* to the west, cobbled together from surviving monastic quarters. Vaulted cellars make an atmospheric setting for the hotel's bar, and hardy visitors can lodge in one of the twin west towers.

There are substantial remains of the crossing tower and of the church's east end, but the priory's glory is the arcade on the north side of the nave; eight splendid arches, topped by the ruined triforium, frame views of the tranquil landscape beyond the boundary wall.

**Precinct** – A few traces remain of the complex of buildings and enclosures which once covered an extensive area (40 acres/16ha). Immediately south of the cloister is **St David's Church** ⏱, a small but massively built structure which may have served originally as the priory's infirmary. One of its small windows has modern stained glass showing a dove rising through water, St David's element.

Just beyond the church are the foundations of the monks' dovecot as well as landforms which mark the site of former fishponds.

The outline of the precinct is defined by a stretch of wall, and by banks and ditches, while the 14C western gatehouse is now a barn.

# LLANTRISANT

Rhondda Cynon Taff – Population 9 136
Michelin Atlas p 16 or Map 403 J 29

A rare example in Britain of a true hilltop town, the old borough of Llantrisant commands the strategic point where routes crossing the Vale of Glamorgan from east to west meet those descending from the valleys to the north.

**The Torch-Bearer of Cremation** – Dr William Price (1800-93), who claimed Druidic descent, was a vegetarian, an Unbeliever, a champion of women's rights, and a Chartist supporter who fled to France in a frock after the Newport riot of 1839. He achieved notoriety by illegally cremating the corpse of his baby son at Llantrisant. By the time of his own cremation, and largely thanks to his efforts, this method of disposing of the dead had been accepted, and the ceremony, held on the same site, was celebrated by a crowd of 20 000.

**Royal Mint** – In the expansive 1960s, the area around Llantrisant was thought of as an ideal site for a New Town which would help regenerate the industries of the region. The project was abandoned but housing, industry and other developments have nonetheless spread over the area. The Royal Mint was relocated from London to Llantrisant's business park in 1968 and it is here that all the coinage of the realm is produced.

**Town Centre** – The steep streets and alleyways of the summit are a delight to walk in, and there is a superb panorama over the Vale from the churchyard. The **parish church** ⊘ itself, dedicated to the three saints from whom the

> **Adjacent Sights** – See Caerphilly, Cardiff, Castell Coch, Cowbridge, Glamorgan Coast, Llancaiach Fawr, Llandaff, Rhondda, Museum of Welsh Life.

town derives its name, was much rebuilt in the 16C and again in the 19C. It has an east window attributed to Burne-Jones, with a Crucifixion showing a beardless Christ.

A **statue of Dr William Price** in druidic garb stands in front of the Model House.

**Model House** ⊘ – This imaginatively restored building stands in the Bull Ring on the site of two public houses. Its highly varied past includes use as a rubber glove factory and workhouse. It is now a craft and design centre, the focal point of Llantrisant's attempt to regenerate itself as an attractive tourist town.

There is also a small but fascinating **exhibition** on the Royal Mint, with an interesting emphasis on the increasing sophistication of portraiture.

# LLANWRTYD WELLS

(Llanwrtyd) Powys – Population 649
Michelin Atlas p 25 or Map 403 J 27

Reputedly the smallest town in Great Britain, Llanwrtyd was for many years a popular spa, an inland resort for the crowded industrial population of Swansea and Llanelli. The spas themselves are in an advanced state of decay, but the spruce little town continues to attract visitors, profiting from its position on the south-west–north-east trunk road through the centre of the country, its station on the mid-Wales railway line and its easy access to the uplands all around.

Llanwrtyd's hotels and boarding houses are mostly grouped around the bridge over the Irfon, at the point where the river leaves the uplands to run through a broad vale to its junction with the Wye at Builth Wells.

Hill walking, mountain biking, pony trekking and birdwatching are popular, supplemented by bizarre activities pioneered here in the 1950s like "bog-snorkelling" and a cross-country run in which men compete with horses.

> **Tourist Information Centre** – Ty Barcud, The Square, Llanwrtyd Wells, Powys LD5 4RB. Open Easter-Sep, daily, 10am-1pm and 1-5.30pm; Sep-Easter, daily except Sat, 10am-1pm and 2-4pm. ✆/Fax 01591 610 666; tic@celt.ruralwales.org
>
> **Craft Centre** – The **Cambrian Woollen Mill** (northern outskirts on A 483) produces clothes and accessories, which are on sale in the shop; it was built in the early 19C, when the Welsh woollen industry was booming and is now one of only 14 surviving mills in Wales.
>
> **Adjacent Sights** – See Brecon, Builth Wells, Elan Valley, Lampeter, Llandovery, Llandrindod Wells, Strata Florida Abbey, Tregaron.

To the south-east is the fastness of Mynydd Eppynt, while to the north the Cambrian Mountains form one of the most extensive tracts of wild landscape in all Great Britain. These rugged uplands are home to the rare red kite *(see also p 150)*; the **Tourist Information Centre** *(see below)* has displays about this bird of prey and closed circuit TV coverage of nest activity.

## EXCURSIONS

★**Abergwesyn-Tregaron Mountain Road** – *19mi/32km NW of Llanwrtyd Wells by a steep and mostly single-track minor road to Tregaron.* This road follows the old drovers' route between Ceredigion (Cardiganshire) and central Wales. The road runs northwestward up the leafy valley of the Irfon, past the little **St David's Church** ⊘, built into the hillside. At the hamlet of Abergwesyn the road turns left and climbs through hanging oakwoods to the Irfon's grimly spectacular upper valley where sheep perch on seemingly inaccessible crags. Conifer woods close in at a point where the Devil's Staircase forces all vehicles into the lowest possible gear, followed by a steep drop into the valley of the Tywi and the junction with the Llyn Brianne **scenic road** *(see p 179)*. Something of the former bareness of the mountains remains where one of the loneliest telephone boxes in Britain marks the crossing of the little River Camddwr. After more afforestation, the narrow road begins its long descent to Tregaron *(see p 278)* in the lusher landscapes of lowland Ceredigion.

# LLEYN PENINSULA ★★
### Gwynedd
#### Michelin Atlas p 32 or Map 403 FGH 24-25

Beyond the mountain masses of Snowdonia, defining the northern limit of Cardigan Bay, is this remote peninsula, where the pace of life slows and where Welshness is to be found in some of its purest forms. The hills here are rich in prehistoric remains but it is perhaps the spirit of the Celtic Church and the Middle Ages that is felt most strongly here; there are holy wells and an ancient pilgrimage route – the Saints' Way – trodden by the devout on their way from Bangor to Bardsey Island.

Despite a wonderful, sometimes dramatic coastline, tourism came late to Lleyn. The railway only ever reached as far as Pwllheli, and the attempt to turn Porth Dinllaen into the packet station for Ireland came to nothing. Even today no main road penetrates to the end of the peninsula, and it is only the south coast around Pwllheli that has been much affected by "development". The district was one of the last in Wales to resist the pressure for the Sunday opening of pubs.

## SIGHTS *in clockwise order*

**Criccieth** – *See p 143.*

**Penarth Fawr** ⊘ – *Turn N off A 497 into a minor road.* Built around the mid 15C and modernised c 150 years later, Penarth Fawr is an unusually well-preserved example of a Welsh gentry house, with a spacious hall beneath a splendid timber roof.

**Haven Holiday Park** ⊘ – *Turn S off A 497.* The great array of fun facilities – Sub-Tropical Waterworld, Go-karts, 10-pin bowling, pool tables and crazy golf – attracts day visitors as well as several thousand resident holidaymakers. The enterprise was founded as a Butlin's holiday camp in the 1930s.

---

### Out and About

**Tourist Information Centre** – Min y Don, Station Square, Pwllheli LL53 5HG ☎ 01758 613 000; Fax 01758 701 651; pwllheli.tic@gwynedd. gov.uk

**Beaches** – At Aberdaron and Pwllheli Marina.

**Adjacent Sights** – See Beddgelert, Caernarvon, Criccieth, Porthmadog, Snowdonia.

### Where to Stay

**Neigwl**, Lon Sarn Bach, Abersoch, LL53 7DY. ☎ 01758 712 363. Small personally run hotel (9 rm) with views over the sea; providing good comfort and hospitality – one of the best of its kind anywhere.

**Porth Tocyn**, Bwlchtocyn, Pwllheli, LL53 7BU. *2mi/3km S by coast road.* ☎ 01758 713 303; Fax 01758 713 538. Traditional family-oriented hotel (17 rm) with its own character and charm; attractively located above the sea.

Braich-y-Pwll and Bardsey Island

**Pwllheli** – *At the junction of A 497 and A 499*. The principal town of the Lleyn Peninsula, Pwllheli owes much of its present prosperity as a seaside resort to the giant Butlin's leisure complex to the east.

A borough since the 14C and formerly one of North Wales' most thriving ports, Pwllheli acquired its harbour – perhaps the "salt water pool" which may be the meaning of its name in Welsh – when the sea threw a sandbank across the mouth of the River Erch. The town's maritime role declined with the rise of Porthmadog and with the coming of the railway in 1867, though today the harbour has filled up again, with more than 400 pleasure-craft able to berth in the marina.

Hopes that the place would become a resort to rank with Llandudno remained unfulfilled; at the uttermost end of the Cambrian Railway, Pwllheli never really overcame its remoteness for mass holidaymaking until after the Second World War. The late-19C Promenade with grand hotel and terraced boarding houses still faces southwards over the magnificent prospect of Cardigan Bay, but this West End lacks the animation of the old town, at its best on market day.

**Llanbedrog** – Linked to Pwllheli by a sandy beach is this little resort, sheltered by woods and hills from the west. **Plas Glyn-y-Weddw** ⊘ is an extraordinary neo-Gothic mansion, built as a widow's dower house in 1856. The rooms around the great hall with its gallery, monumental staircase and triple hammerbeam roof are used for changing exhibitions of works by **contemporary Welsh artists**, though there is a semi-permanent collection too.

A famous incident in the story of modern Welsh nationalism took place just to the north of Llanbedrog in 1936. Prevented by vocal and well-organised opposition from setting up bombing ranges at its preferred sites in England, the re-arming RAF came to Pen-y-Berth despite local protests. A clergyman, a teacher, and the writer **Saunders Lewis** set fire to the airfield buildings, then gave themselves up to the police. At Caernarfon court, the defendants were refused permission to plead in Welsh, but the jury failed to convict; at the Old Bailey, however, they received sentences of nine months in prison, thus becoming the first 'martyrs' for Plaid Cymru.

**Abersoch** – The main road (A 499) southwest from Pwllheli ends at this popular little resort, which likes to style itself 'The Welsh Riviera' (*Y Rifiera Gymreig*); on a fine day when the sea sparkles and Abersoch's two sandy bays are full of dinghies and windsurfers the claim does not seem too fanciful. Offshore (about 2mi/3km) are St Tudwal's Islands, the abode of seals and seabirds.

## Butlin's at Pwllheli

Two knights combined to ensure the early success of the Pwllheli holiday camp venture. **Sir Billy Butlin** (1899-1980) – then plain Mr – had started to build one of his popular holiday camps, just before the outbreak of the Second World War put paid to such projects. The Admiralty, however, encouraged him to proceed and used the camp – rechristened *HMS Glendower* – for training, the understanding being that Butlin's would swing into civilian operation as soon as hostilities ceased. Post-war opposition to such a scheme on the edge of Snowdonia National Park was vocal and was crushed only by the somewhat improbable intervention of the patrician figure of **Sir Clough Williams-Ellis** (he too a mere Mr at the time). At a bitterly argued public inquiry, the creator of Portmeirion and prominent preservationist declared himself in favour of "the greatest happiness of the greatest number" ; he poked fun at Pwllheli's hostility to the scheme and at its citizens' fear that "the camp's chalets will be preferred to its own rather grim lodging-houses and the allure of their concrete promenade" . Williams-Ellis's eloquence carried the day, though his subsequent attempts to get Sir Billy to provide the holidaying masses with symphony concerts and painting exhibitions met with only a lukewarm response.

**Llanengan** – The tiny village of Llanengan stands at the foot of the high land running south from Abersoch to form the eastern headland enclosing the long beach of Porth Neigwl, which means Hell's Mouth. **St Engan's Church** ⊘ is a fine double-aisled structure of the 15C-16C with a flagstone floor, a timber roof, held on massive stones, and a splendid screen.

★**Plas-yn-Rhiw** ⊘ – On a steeply sloping site in the shelter of the Lleyn Peninsula's westernmost woodland is this endearing little country house, part Tudor, part Georgian, its **garden** lavishly stocked with plants which thrive in these protected conditions.

The house and garden were rescued in 1939 from two decades of neglect by the Misses Keating, whose love of the place still seems to pervade the modestly furnished interior and the carefully planted compartments of the garden. Eileen, Lorna and Honor worked tirelessly, not only to restore and embellish their home but to conserve the Lleyn countryside, campaigning against the proposal for a nuclear power station, as well as buying land outright whenever the opportunity arose and presenting it, like Plas-yn-Rhiw itself, to the National Trust. Some of Honor's accomplished watercolours showing her fascination with the structure of landscape can be seen in the house.

Apart from the extraordinary variety of plants, the garden is a delight to walk in, with old walls, the remains of old buildings, glimpses of Cardigan Bay, a stream, and a spacious sloping meadow to relieve the wholly pleasurable claustrophobia of the narrow paths and constricting hedges close to the house.

**Aberdaron** – The peninsula's westernmost village looks south across its sandy bay. Just hidden by the headland is Bardsey Island, and for centuries Aberdaron was the last staging post for pilgrims on their way to the island's monastery, many of them finding refuge and

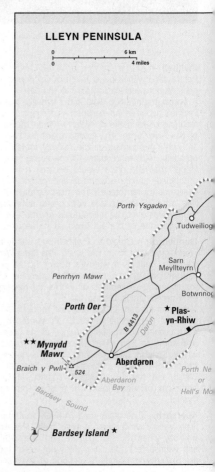

sustenance in the hospice whose site is now occupied by the 17C building known as the Great Kitchen *(Y Gegin Fawr)*. Together with the other cottages, the pair of pubs and the post office, designed by Sir Clough Williams-Ellis, it makes an attractive grouping, rare in this region of scattered farms and homesteads.

Just up the slope stands the **Church of St Hywyn** ⊙, seeming to defy the sea with a west end devoid of all openings save its Norman doorway. It is named after the son of a Breton saint and missionary. The church was almost abandoned to the sea in the 19C in favour of a new building but the outcry was such that it was saved and restored, the unwanted new church being abandoned instead. Between 1967 and 1978 the poet RS Thomas was vicar.

★**Bardsey Island** ⊙ – The Norsemen called this "the island of bards", while the Welsh name *Ynys Enlli* signifies "island of the currents". Both names are appropriate. The bards would have been the inhabitants of the **Celtic monastery**, established here perhaps as early as AD 429, their tranquillity assured (at least until the arrival of the Vikings) by the difficult passage through the tides and rips of Bardsey Sound which separates the island from the tip of the peninsula. A third title – **the isle of 20 000 saints** – refers to the many holy men reputed to be buried on the island. By the 13C the Celtic foundation had been taken over by the Augustinians; Bardsey was sometimes referred to as the "Welsh Rome", its remoteness making three pilgrimages here worth one to Rome itself. Pilgrims for Bardsey Island used to embark not only at Aberdaron but also at **Mwnt** north of Cardigan.

The island consists of a hill, Mynydd Enlli (548ft/167m), whose gentler western slopes are farmed, while an isthmus leads to a peninsula on which stands the lighthouse of 1821. In the 19C about 100 people lived on Bardsey, living from farming, fishing, and the making of lobster pots from willow grown in withy beds. Today's permanent population consists largely of the warden of the National Nature Reserve and a shepherd to tend the mainland sheep sent here to graze. Visitors come here on retreat, attracted by the island's monastic traditions, or to stay at the observatory, enjoying the bird life which as well as choughs includes up to 4 000 breeding pairs of the burrowing Manx shearwater. Seals may be seen offshore.

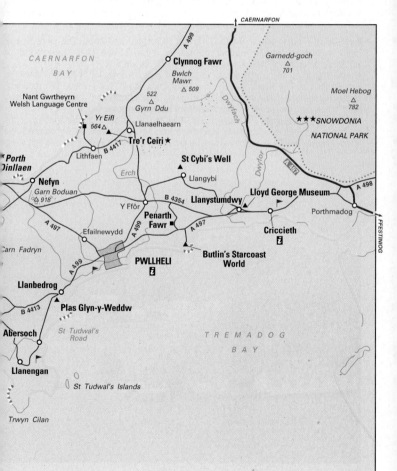

**★★Mynydd Mawr** – Rugged enough to be called a mountain (though only 524ft/160m high), Mynydd Mawr overlooks Bardsey Island (2.5mi/4km away) across the often disturbed waters of Bardsey Sound. It makes a magnificent viewpoint; at its foot to the east the long lines of walled field boundaries suggest an ancient pattern of cultivation, while distant views take in Snowdonia, Cardigan and Caernarfon Bays, and even, in the most favourable conditions, the Wicklow Mountains in Ireland.

**Porth Oer** – The north coast of the peninsula has a number of fine beaches interrupting its cliffs, often only accessible on foot from car parks inland. The splendid sandy beach at Porth Oer is also known as Whistling Sands; its even-grained quartz particles can be induced to give out a note of uniform pitch when squeezed underfoot.

**★Porth Dinllaen** – *National Trust car park outside the golf club entrance; 15min on foot.* The headland jutting northwards into Caernarfon Bay gives a measure of protection to this bay with its sandy beach. Porth Dinllaen has a toytown look; a scatter of houses at the back of the beach, some whitewashed, some in stone, focus on the bright red pub – the *Tŷ Goch Inn.*
In the 18C and 19C Porth Dinllaen's natural advantages made it the focus of more than one attempt to develop it as the main port for the Irish mail. A glance at the map shows straight turnpike roads leading eastwards, forming part of a great highway to London which remained unbuilt, trumped by Telford's Holyhead route. A later proposal to extend the railway westward from Pwllheli met with a similar fate.
The village's tranquillity seems guaranteed following its purchase by the National Trust.

**Nefyn** – There are few signs in this little clifftop resort on the peninsula's northern coast that it was a medieval borough as well as the place chosen by Edward I in 1284 to celebrate his conquest of North Wales (though Edward's Field – *Cae Iorwerth* – is the name given to an area just outside the town). The **Lleyn Historical and Maritime Museum** ⊘, housed in a former church, recalls the maritime history of Nefyn and neighbouring Porth Dinllaen.

**★Tre'r Ceiri** – *Park beside B 4417; 1hr on foot there and back.* The landscape of Lleyn is studded with a number of distinct, often conical hills, the product of volcanic intrusions of the same date as those of Snowdonia.
Above Trefor on the north coast, the trio of peaks known as **Yr Eifl** are rendered into English as The Rivals (though the Welsh meaning is The Forks). The seaward-facing flanks have been much quarried away. The quarrymen's village at Porth y Nant has been revived as the **Nant Gwrtheyrn National Language Centre**.
Dramatically sited atop the easternmost Rival is one of the most fascinating of the country's prehistoric monuments, a fortified Iron Age settlement, known as the Town of the Giants **(Tre'r Ceiri)**. Within a massive enclosing wall with well-defended entrances

Porth Dinllaen

are some 150 round huts, arranged in a series of bands across the width of the settlement. The builders of the huts chose a site whose advantages had been appreciated by their Bronze Age predecessors, who erected a cairn at the higher, eastern end. Unusually, the place continued in occupation well into the Romano-British period.

**Clynnog Fawr** – Still straddling the main road running southwest from Caernarfon, this village was an important stop on the pilgrim route to Bardsey Island. The large and splendid Perpendicular **church** ⊘ is dedicated to St Beuno. Beneath the fine timber roof of the unusually spacious interior are many fascinating features, including 16C choir stalls and screen and a hollowed-out log for pilgrims' offerings. A barrel-vaulted passageway leads to the 16C chapel supposedly built on the site of St Beuno's cell.

# MACHYNLLETH ★

Powys – Population 2 033
Michelin Atlas p 25 or Map 403 I 26

ἱe capital of the lower Dovey valley, this tiny town seems to have retained its tensely Welsh character despite its position at the junction of two major roads. was at Machynlleth in 1404 that Owain Glyn Dŵr was crowned Prince of Wales and ǝre that he held a parliament

ἱe **Dovey** (Dyfi) runs through one of the country's most attractive valleys; few ∍ntrasts could be greater than that between its youthful gorge high in the lonely Aran ⸮ountains and the vast expanses of tidal sand and mud, dune, marsh, fen and bog of ; estuary. The "greener" forms of tourism flourish here, prompted in part by the ∍ll-established Centre for Alternative Technology *(see below)* in the valley of the ∪las, a tributary of the Dovey.

---

**Tourist Information Centres** – Canolfan Owain Glyndŵr, Machynlleth SY20 8EE ☎ 01654 702 401; Fax 01654 703 675.
Corris Craft Centre, Corris, nr Machynlleth SY20 9RF ☎ 01654 761 244; Fax 01654 761 244; corris.tic@gwynedd.gov.uk
Cambrian Terrace, Borth SY24 5HU ☎ 01970 871 174; Fax 01970 626 566; borthTIC@ceredigion.gov.uk

**Craft Centres** – A number of individual makers – woodwork, pottery, leatherwork, toys, candles, jewellery – sell their work in the **Corris Craft Centre** ⊘ *(10mi/16km north by A 487)*. For woollen goods visit the **Meirion Mill Woollen Centre** ⊘ *(30mi/48km south by A 470)*.

**Adjacent Sights** – See Aberystwyth, Barmouth, Elan Valley, Llanidloes, Newtown, Vale of Rheidol, Tywyn.

---

## SIGHTS

★**Celtica** ⊘ – The Victorian mansion known as Plas Machynlleth now houses this ambitious "experience", which uses the most sophisticated audio-visual techniques to evoke the world of the Celts. More conventional displays on an upper floor recall the extent and achievement of the culture of the early Celts, whose history is mostly known through the records of their great opponents, the Greeks and Romans. Visitors can press a button and hear the Lord's Prayer in any one of the modern Celtic languages, either living, like Scots and Irish Gaelic, Breton, or Welsh itself, or in Manx and Cornish, which are being revived. The audio-visual show is designed to be gripping, and succeeds, with small groups being led through a series of tableaux, of which the most striking is that of a Celtic settlement at the moment of return of a raiding party, complete with stolen cattle and the severed heads of their owners. A theatre of eight characters celebrates the unique flavour of the Celtic personality over the ages.

**Owain Glyn Dŵr Centre** ⊘ – This long, low building in rubblestone, a rare example of a late medieval town house, is reputed to stand on the site of Glyn Dŵr's parliament; it contains exhibits on Welsh history and on Glyn Dŵr himself, a figure "not in the roll of common men", who was declared Prince of Wales in 1400, revived the hope of an independent Wales and inspired a national rebellion.

**Museum of Modern Art, Wales (Y Tabernacl)** ⊘ – A former Wesleyan chapel and adjoining buildings have been sensitively converted to house a fascinating semi-permanent collection of 20C Welsh art as well as temporary exhibitions of the work of mostly living artists. Y Tabernacl is also the headquarters of Machynlleth's annual Arts Festival.

**Memorial Clock Tower** – This fantastical Victorian Gothic clock tower was built 1874 at the junction of the town's main thoroughfares, Maengwyn Street ar Penallt Street, to mark the coming of age of Viscount Castlereagh of Plas Machyn leth. The layout of the town around this T-junction may be an indication tha Machynlleth was one of the relatively few native Welsh planned medieval towns.

## EXCURSIONS

### ★★Centre for Alternative Technology ⊘

*3mi/5km N of Machynlleth by A 487*

Since its inception in 1975 a million people have visited this pioneering institutio set up in an old slate quarry, and many of the alternative "green" ideas it promote have entered the mainstream of environmental thinking. The Centre's seriou purposes have in no way inhibited enjoyment, and a sojourn among its earth friendly buildings, luxuriant gardens, wind pumps, ponds and pools cannot fail ti be an intriguing, even exhilarating experience.

Centre for Alternative Technology

*Wales Tourist Board*

Most visitors begin by rid ing up to the main part the site in the wate powered **Cliff Railway**, whic uses the inclined plar (200ft/60m) of the o quarry. The station buil ings, the upper one visib from far away, seem express the ethos of th Centre; generously scale and built in muscular fash ion from locally harveste timber, they proclaim non-traditional but attrac ive and confident aestheti From the **lake** which su plies the railway's wate there is a fine view of th Centre in its setting of hil and mountains whic includes Tarren-y-Gesai the southernmost peak the Snowdonia Nation Park. Between the lake an the **wind turbines** on the f rim of the quarry stretche a kind of exotic park, full of strange structures and unfamiliar plant arrangement inviting careful exploration, though it is quite possible to wander aimlessly and st be stimulated by the highly variegated features on show. A video presentation sho provides orientation.

The various applications of **solar and wind energy** are more than adequately demor strated; the residential staff at the Centre have electricity bills which are a fractio of those outside! Anyone who gardens will be intrigued by the productivity organic plots and the use of natural methods of weed and pest control. Childre will enjoy themselves, not just in the playground provided, but also in the **Mole Hol** deep underground, where giant bugs and beetles can be seen chomping awa among the roots. A light-hearted but informative **Transport Maze** challenges visito to negotiate the complexities and environmental implications of transport choices. The appetising food in the Restaurant demonstrates the virtue of vegetarianis without being patronising, while the Shop has a very wide range of books ar other publications on "green" themes.

### Corris *7.5mi/13km N of Machynlleth by A 487*

Corris, now by-passed by the main road (A 487), is an attractive small village s on a steep slope above the River Dulas.

**King Arthur's Labyrinth** ⊘ – *In the Corris Craft Centre*. The Labyrinth has bee contrived in the caves created by the Braichgoch Slate Quarry, which was worke between the 1830s and 1907 and 1919 and 1971. The underground tour begir in a boat gliding slowly towards a waterfall; it continues on foot through spectac lar caverns where Welsh tales of King Arthur are told with tableaux and stunnir sound and light effects; visitors then reboard the boat.

**Corris Railway Museum** ⊘ – *In Corris village*. The museum was established 1966 in Corris Station to record the history of the line from its inception in 185 as a narrow-gauge horse-drawn operation carrying slate from Corris Uchaf ar

Aberllefenni to the navigable point on the River Dovey (Dyfi), to its closure in 1948 when its rolling stock was sent to the Talyllyn Railway. In 1860 it was linked to the mainline in Machynlleth and in 1870 it converted to steam locomotives; between 1883 and 1930 it carried passengers. A short section of line has been relaid.

## Dovey Estuary – south shore

*30mi/48km SW by A 487 and B 4353*

Between the hills and the broad estuary of the Dovey (Dyfi) is a great expanse of peatbogs, pools and streams, reed-beds and salt-marshes, where grazing sheep are disturbed only by the passing of an occasional train along the single track flanking the riverbank.

**Ynys-hir RSPB Nature Reserve** ⊙ – The reserve is sheltered by woodland and offers a commanding prospect of these undisturbed levels. It has a visitor centre with informative displays on the area's rich wildlife; the Dovey is a haven for wintering birds like widgeon and Greenland white-fronted geese.

**Dyfi Furnace** ⊙ – The massive stone building of this blast furnace was built c 1755, using ore from Cumbria and charcoal from the local woodlands. At the upper level is the building used as a store for the raw materials, which were tipped via the charging platform into the furnace itself. Beyond, among the trees, is the steeply falling stream which was dammed to provide the power which still drives a great water-wheel, though this belongs to a later phase in the building's history as a sawmill.

**Ynyslas Dunes** – This dune system stretches northward from the golf course at the straggling resort of **Borth**, partly closing off the mouth of the Dovey (Dyfi). The dunes are protected as a National Nature Reserve but more obvious are the cars colonising the great sandy beach on the landward side.

# MARGAM PARK ★

Neath Port Talbot

Michelin Atlas p 15 or Map 403 I 29

Comprising the remains of a great Cistercian abbey, the country's longest orangery and a huge and ruined neo-Tudor mansion, the vast domain of Margam is today a country park with a whole array of visitor attractions and an annual programme of events which draws in thousands.

## HISTORICAL NOTES

Numerous early-Christian crosses testify to the existence of a Celtic monastery in the area, but the real history of Margam began when Cistercians from Clairvaux were brought here by the Norman Earl of Gloucester in 1147. Their abbey became the largest and wealthiest in Wales, though by the time of the Dissolution only nine monks remained in residence. Their domain passed into the hands of the Mansels of Penrice and Oxwich, until in the 18C it became the property of the Talbots of Lacock Abbey in Wiltshire.

The "faire and sumptuous" Mansel house was demolished in 1780 and replaced in 1835 by a huge pile designed by Thomas Hopper, the architect of Penrhyn Castle. The Great Orangery was built in 1787 to house the extraordinary collection of citrus trees which seems to have come into the possession of the Mansels by shipwreck or capture about a century earlier.

The Mansels' formal park included a quartet of big fishponds and an avenue, extending almost to the coast, but little of this remained after the Talbots had carried out various "Improvements" which included demolition of the old village of Margam in order to enlarge the kitchen garden. Hopper's great house was requisitioned for military use in the Second World War and never really recovered. Further damage was caused by fire in 1977. The intention of the present owners, the County Council, is to preserve the building in its present state with only partial restoration.

**Margam Castle** ⊙ – Hopper seems to have set out to recreate, with great effort and expense, something of the character of the old Mansel mansion which had accumulated accretions over the centuries. His building is a Tudor-Gothic fantasy of bays, gables, pinnacles and turrets, centred on a great octagonal tower, easier to appreciate as a partial ruin

**Adjacent Sights** – See Glamorgan Coast, Gower Peninsula, Neath, Porthcawl, Port Talbot, Swansea.

perhaps than to live in. The outbuildings house visitor facilities, while the interio
the superb staircase under the tower still intact, has a video show on Margam
history and an odd "Crown Jewels" exhibition.

★**Orangery** – This splendid structure (327ft/100m long) was the work of Anthon
Keck. It is built in Classical style, its succession of round-headed windows termin
ated at either end by pedimented pavilions. It has been adapted for use as
banqueting hall with the judicious insertion of a glass screen to preserve the lor
internal vista.

**Country Park** – The rolling grasslands (800 acres/330ha) extend to a boundar
wall and give way to woodland as the slopes steepen to the north and east. Ther
are waymarked walks, a farm trail, a pets' corner, a mountain bike trail, a
adventure playground and more. High up is an Iron Age hillfort, and, beyond th
boundary, a ruined chapel. Between the Castle on its rise and the abbey ruins an
Orangery lower down are more formal gardens, with terraces, a boating lake an
changing displays of modern sculpture. Giant chess, Fairytale Land, and a hug
maze complete the family-oriented attractions.

**Abbey Church** ⊙ – *Accessible from outside Margam Country Park.* At th
Dissolution, the church was split. The eastern part was left to decay, including th
walls of the 12-sided Chapter House and its elegant central column sprouting a fa
of truncated shafts. The western half, the monks' nave, became the **parish church.**
retains much of the severe character of the typical Cistercian establishment, wit
massive piers inside and round-headed windows and door on the west from
Italianate towers were added in 1810. There are a number of Mansel tombs wit
recumbent effigies, an elaborate canopied 19C Talbot tomb, and stained glass b
William Morris.

**Stones Museum** ⊙ – Housed in the old village school, this is a particular
fascinating collection of early Christian stones dating from the 6C to the 11C.
The oldest is a Roman milestone, reused upside-down in the 6C as a Christia
memorial. The finest is the late-9C–early-10C **Cross of Cynfelyn**, a disc-headed cros
a Glamorgan speciality, with elaborate patterning and crude depictions of St Joh
and the Virgin Mary.

# MERTHYR TYDFIL

(Merthyr Tudful) Merthyr Tydfil – Population 59 317
Michelin Atlas p 16 or Map 403 J 28

High up in the Taff Vale, this bleak town was for many years the "Iron Capital of th
World", sending its products all over the rapidly industrialising 19C globe. As met
manufacture moved elsewhere, coal mining became the principal activity. Now that to
has gone, replaced in part by new light industries. Enough of the early industri
heritage remains, however, to evoke both the vigour and squalor of Merthyr's past.

## HISTORICAL NOTES

In the 16C, as the supply of Wealden timber grew scarce, Sussex ironmasters came t
this remote valley in search of alternative sources of fuel, but the real rise of Merthy
began in the mid-18C when wood was supplanted by coke in the firing of blas
furnaces. As well as coal for coking, the valley offered iron ore, limestone for linin
the furnaces, and water power from the rapidly running Taff.
In 1783 the **Cyfarthfa ironworks** which had been established by Anthony Bacon in 176
was taken over by **Richard Crawshay**, first of a dynasty of immensely rich ironmaster
who later built themselves the huge mock-Gothic residence of **Cyfarthfa Castle**. By th
1840s more than 18 000 people were employed in Merthyr's ironworks and the tow
was the biggest in Wales, a position of pre-eminence it lost only in the 1880
Resentment and radical politics flourished among the hard-pressed workforc
recruited mostly from the rural Welsh but also including English, Irish and a sub
stantial number of Jews. Serious rioting broke out in 1801, 1806 and again in 183
when 20 died in a confrontation with troops; Dic Penderyn, "a martyr of the Wels
working class" as noted on a plaque outside the public library, was hanged in Cardi
for his alleged role in the affray. For many years a garrison had to be stationed her
In 1900 the town returned Keir Hardie to Parliament, Britain's first Labour MP.
The decline of industry seems to have set in early; local supplies of ore ran ou
technological innovation was neglected, the later Crawshays preferred to live in leaf
Berkshire rather than supervise their works directly from their grim castle. On
establishment closed in 1880 and Cyfarthfa, after a brief respite in the First Worl
War, ceased operations in 1919. In 1930 the big Dowlais works fell victim to th
Great Depression, and the ensuing decade saw a rate of unemployment whic
remained at a steady 80%. The very last foundry was shut down by the British Ste
Corporation in 1987. Still smarting from a report of the late 1930s suggesting tha
the town be abandoned and its population settled elsewhere, Merthyr maintains i
pride in the face of adversity.

## Out and About

**Tourist Information Centre** – 14a Cleveland Street, Merthyr Tydfil CF47 8AU ☎ 01685 379 884; Fax 01685 350 043.

**Adjacent Sights** – See Abergavenny, Blaenavon, Brecon, Brecon Beacons, Caerphilly, Cardiff, Llancaiach Fawr, Llantrisant, Rhondda, Tredegar, Tretower.

## Where to Stay

**Nant Ddu Lodge**, Cwm Taf, CF48 2HY. *6mi/9km NW by A 470.* ☎ 01685 379 111; Fax 01685 377 088. Comfortable, colourful rooms (22 rm); busy bar and bistro; spectacular location within the Brecon Beacons National Park; name means black stream.

**Cyfarthfa Castle Museum** ⊙ – The pseudo-medieval stronghold overlooks the valley with the long-abandoned site of the Cyfarthfa ironworks which provided the funds for its construction. The castle was built in 1825 by Richard Lugar for William Crawshay II; it had 72 rooms in which the families of successive "Iron Kings" were able to live a lavish lifestyle. As well as the usual 19C conifers and bedding displays, the extensive grounds (160 acres/67ha) also included an ice-house and a "pinery" for pineapple production; it was the head gardener's boast that he could produce a hundred pineapples for Christmas dinner! The lake, which also supplied water to the works, was liable to leak, and in the end cost as much as the house to construct.

The Crawshays left in 1889. After standing empty for two decades, the building was bought by the Borough Council to house a grammar school and museum. The exhibits on show in the recently restored reception rooms are highly variegated, ranging from stuffed birds and geological specimens to the instruments of the Cyfarthfa brass band and 19C and 20C paintings. The extensive cellars interpret the industrial and social history of Merthyr and its people.

**Ynysfach Iron Heritage Centre** ⊙ – Built in 1836, this dignified structure in contrasting dark and light stone once housed the beam engine which supplied the blast for the adjoining furnaces. Derelict for many years, it now houses a museum which tells the story of iron-making in Merthyr, partly through an excellent audio-visual presentation. Among the objects on display are a number of decorative iron doorstops, including one showing the figure of George Washington.

**Joseph Parry's Cottage** ⊙ – Much of the early housing in Merthyr consisted of "huts and cottages... erected on the spur of the occasion, without plan or design" (John George Wood in 1811), but **Chapel Row** was part of Georgetown, built by the Crawshays to somewhat higher standards in order to encourage company loyalty among the more skilled members of their workforce. The composer **Joseph Parry** (1841-1903) was born at No 4. Generally regarded as Wales' greatest composer, he returned to Merthyr to adjudicate at the 1901 *eisteddfod*. His birthplace has been refurnished in the manner of the mid-19C and the upper floor has a number of exhibits connected with his life.

Outside, in the incongruous surroundings of a modern housing estate, is a short and dry stretch of the **Glamorganshire Canal**, which, until the Taff Vale Railway was built in the 1840s, was constantly congested with barge traffic on its way from the ironworks to the port at Cardiff, a city "made by Merthyr".

**Trevithick's Tunnel** – In 1802, in an attempt to break the Crawshays' monopolistic control of the Glamorganshire Canal, their lifeline to the sea, the other ironmasters of Merthyr combined to build a wagonway down the Taff Vale. It was on this, the **Penydarren Tramroad**, that a steam locomotive, designed by Richard Trevithick, first ran successfully on iron rails. The exploit, carried out on 21 February 1804 in pursuit of a wager, is commemorated by a modern mosaic at the entry to a tunnel just to the south of the town centre.

## EXCURSIONS

**Bute Town** – *5mi/8km E.* High up near the head of the Rhymney Valley are three terraces, built by the Marquess of Bute between 1825 and 1830 to house the workmen from his neighbouring ironworks. Designed in a "robustly Palladian" style (Jeremy Lowe), they may have been based on a plan by James Adam for the village of Lowther in Cumbria. Two of the dwellings now form the fascinating little **Drenewydd Museum** ⊙, furnished appropriately and with informative displays on the social and working lives of their inhabitants.

**Elliot Colliery** ⊘ – *10mi/16km SE by A 465 and A 469.* The old Winding House contains the largest steam engine of its kind in Wales, a Thornhill and Wareham engine, later converted to compressed air and now operated by electricity. The semi-spiral diablo drum enabled one cage to be lowered as the other was raised. A small exhibition charts the history of the local coal industry, particularly Penallta Colliery.

**Ebbw Vale** – *10mi/16km E.* In 1938, with government assistance, one of the most modern steel plants in Europe was sited in this Depression-stricken town at the head of its valley. Respite was relatively short-lived; by 1978 the works had shut. Reclamation of the site began in 1986. One-and-a-half million cubic metres of slag was reshaped, 6 000kg of fertiliser spread and 1.8 million new trees, shrubs and flowers planted, and in 1992 one of Britain's National Garden Festivals was staged in these unlikely surroundings. The core of the **Festival Park** remains, with a **Festival Park Visitor Centre** ⊘, Oriental Pool, Mythical Beast, and Tropical Plant House, centrepiece of what it is hoped will become a dynamic development of new Home Counties-style housing and light industry.

**Aneurin Bevan Memorial** – This group of roughly shaped standing stones erected on the breezy heights above Ebbw Vale commemorates Aneurin Bevan (1897-1960), who was born in Tredegar at the top of the Sirhowy Valley. He represented Ebbw Vale in Parliament for 30 years and was known as an eloquent orator; his lasting legacy is the British National Health Service, which he founded in 1948.

# MILFORD HAVEN

(Aberdaugleddau) Pembrokeshire – Population 13 649
Michelin Atlas p 14 or Map 403 E 28

This splendid waterway was praised by Nelson as being the equal of Trincomalee in Sri Lanka, perhaps the finest natural harbour in the world. From the Bristol Channel, the Haven extends far inland, bringing tidal water up the Western Cleddau River to the old quayside at Haverfordwest and to Canaston Bridge on the Eastern Cleddau. At its entrance by St Ann's Head it is a broad stream (1.25mi/2km wide) and is still quite broad (0.5mi/800m wide) at Pembroke Dock. The strong tides of the Bristol Channel scour its bed, preventing silting and permitting the passage of the largest vessels. Since the 1960s the Haven has become one of Britain's major oil ports, with a clutch of terminals and refineries despite the inclusion of much of its shoreline within the Pembrokeshire National Park.

## HISTORICAL NOTES

Such a superb natural anchorage has naturally had an eventful history. The French disembarked a force here in 1405 to help Owain Glyn Dŵr in his rebellion against the English, but perhaps the most portentous landing was that of Henry Tudor in 1485, en route to Bosworth Field and the English Crown. Most of the settlements around the Haven had some sort of maritime connection, the sheltered beaches and great tidal range obviating the need for the construction of elaborate harbours, while remoteness from centres of authority made smuggling a relatively risk-free activity. After a naval dock was built at the end of the 18C, the need for a proper system of defences was realised, and throughout most of the 19C vast and virtually indestructible forts and barracks were erected around the Haven, or actually in its waters, like the **forts** at **Stack Rock** and **Thorn Island.**

From the middle of the 19C there were high hopes of a great commercial future for the waterway, as well as rivalry between the three towns *(see below),* all of them planned settlements, along its banks. The first railway, built by Brunel, came not to Milford Haven town but to adjoining Neyland, where the great engineer laid out a small new town and quayside from which packets plied to Ireland until diverted to Fishguard in the early 20C. Milford Haven tried desperately to promote itself as a transatlantic port, but had to content itself with landing fish rather than Yankee heiresses at the dock completed in 1888. The Royal Navy dockyard at Pembroke Dock flourished throughout the 19C and especially during the First World War, though in 1926 it was abruptly closed down. During the Second World War the vast expanse of the Haven served as an assembly point for innumerable transatlantic convoys as well as a base for the Sunderland flying boats patrolling the Western Approaches.

**Tourist Information Centre** – 94 Charles Street, Milford Haven SA73 2HL ☎ 01646 690 866; Fax 01646 690 655.
The Guntower, Front Street, Pembroke Dock SA72 6JZ ☎ 01646 622 246; Fax 01646 622 246.

**Adjacent Sights** – See Carew, Haverfordwest, Laugharne, Pembroke, Pembrokeshire Coast, St David's, Tenby.

## THREE PLANNED TOWNS

**Milford Haven Town** – In 1790 the local landowner, Sir William Hamilton, obtained an Act of Parliament "to make and provide Quays, Docks and Piers and other erections and to establish a Market with proper Roads and Avenues thereto". His French planner, a M Barallier, laid out a grid pattern of streets which slowly filled up with houses and shops. Their lack of any architectural distinction is partly compensated for by the town's splendid position on the south-facing slopes overlooking the Haven. The dock, like so many of its kind, now functions mainly as a marina, though fishing boats and other commercial vessels can be seen; there is a small number of historical craft like the bold red Haven lightship.

The **Milford Haven Museum** ⊙, with a full range of well-displayed exhibits on the history of the Haven, has an appropriate home in a late-18C whale oil store.

**Neyland** – Neyland lost its principal *raison d'être*, when the Irish packets were transferred to Fishguard in 1906, and its last commercial maritime link, when the ferry across to Pembroke Dock closed with the opening of the Cleddau Toll bridge in 1975, but its pleasant situation and its 300-berth marina have helped maintain the fortunes of the little town.

**Pembroke Dock** – The Naval Dockyard, relocated here from Milford in 1814, required all the services of a major town. The customary grid pattern was adopted, still very much in evidence today. The Dockyard preserved its privacy with a high wall, within which a number of the original buildings still stand, though their future seems uncertain. For all its fascinating past as a great centre of British naval might, Pembroke Dock is one of the few places in Wales to seem bashful about its heritage, with little to tempt travellers to and from the Irish ferry to linger.

The **Gun Tower** ⊙, rising from the water and reached by a bridge from Pembroke Dock's earliest houses in Front Street, is a tower of the Martello type, though not quite identical to its counterparts along the English Channel coast. Beneath the roof with its swivel-mounted cannon the interior has been restored as closely as possible to its original state, and houses interpretive displays on the Royal Dockyard and on life in the town in the 1850s.

East of Pembroke Dock and Neyland is the **Cleddau Toll Bridge** ⊙, spanning the Haven and giving a wonderful view up- and down-stream. To the east the waterway is rural, with fields and woods sweeping down to the shore, while to the west it is more businesslike, with docks, oil installations, and the tall chimney stack (700ft/213m) of the oil-fired Pembroke power station. Before the opening of the bridge in 1975, road traffic between the north and south shores of the Haven either made a long detour inland or waited for the Neyland-Hobbs Point ferry. A picnic area at the southern end of the bridge allows a more relaxed appreciation of the scene.

## MOLD

(Yr Wyddgrug) Flintshire – Population 9 168
Michelin Atlas pp 33 and 34 or Map 403 K 24

prosperous small market town on the road from Chester to the fertile Vale of wyd, Mold is also an administrative and cultural centre, well known for its modern eatr Clwyd, one of Wales' foremost theatres.

**★St Mary's Church** ⊙ – This large Perpendicular church, one of the finest parish churches in Wales, stands in a commanding position on the slope leading up from the town centre to the parkland site of the Norman motte-and-bailey castle. It was built by Margaret Beaufort in thanksgiving for the victory of her son, Henry Tudor, over Richard III at the Battle of Bosworth in 1485.

**Tourist Information Centre** – Library, Museum & Gallery, Earl Road, Mold CH7 1AP ☎ 01352 759 331.

**Adjacent Sights** – See Denbigh, Erddig, Flint, Hawarden, Holywell, Llangollen, Plas Newydd, Ruthin, St Asaph, Valle Crucis Abbey, Wrexham.

The seven-bay nave is long, low and battlemented, with much carving of animals and other figures along the string course and atop the buttresses. The carving is continued inside, to sumptuous effect, particularly in the nave arcades, where there are numerous references to the insignia of the Stanley family into which Margaret Beaufort had married (eagle's claw, the Three Legs of Man). The tower is an 18C replacement, the chancel a 19C addition by Sir Gilbert Scott, both very much "in keeping". The painter Richard Wilson (1714-82) was partly brought up in Mold and is buried in the churchyard.

**Daniel Owen Museum** ⊙ – A small museum, housed in upstairs rooms in the public library, celebrates another famous son of Mold, the Welsh-language writer Daniel Owen (1836-95), who succeeded in his ambition to write "Not for the wise and learned... but for the common people". His statue stands in the modern square named after him.

# MONMOUTH ★

(Trefynwy) Monmouthshire – Population 8 204
Michelin Atlas p 16 or Map 403 L 28

The old county town of Monmouthshire stands on a neck of land between the W
and its tributary the Monnow, after which the town is named. Though the Roma
had a garrison here, the story of urban Monmouth really began when the Norma
built their castle on a steep rise above the Monnow and established a mark
settlement laid out along a broad street leading downhill to the river crossing. Despi
setbacks caused by repeated flooding and the Black Death when parts of the tov
were abandoned, Monmouth seems to have enjoyed almost continuous prosperi
though its heyday was probably in the 18C; the gentry were joined by the new rich
building fine town houses in order to enjoy the delights of the local social Season. Th
gave the decisive imprint to Monmouth's attractive townscape, though Georgian buil
ing respected the medieval street pattern, still almost intact today.

> **Tourist Information Centre** – Shire Hall,
> Agincourt Square, Monmouth NP5 3DY
> ☎ 01600 713 899; Fax 01600 772 794.
>
> **Adjacent Sights** – See Abergavenny, Blae-
> navon, Brecon, Grosmont, Llanthony Priory,
> Raglan Castle, Tintern Abbey, Usk.

Monmouth is associat
with a number of famo
figures. Of Breton desce
**Geoffrey of Monmou**
(b 1090) was responsib
for the *Historia regnu
Britanniae,* supposedly
translation "from th
ancient British tongue" of
largely mythical history
Britain, which was one
the most popular books
the Middle Ages and is the basis of much of the Arthurian myth. By traditio
**Henry V** was born in Monmouth Castle in 1387.
Admiral **Lord Nelson** made the trip down the Wye in 1802, partly in order to repc
to the Admiralty on the state of that strategic naval resource, the timber of th
nearby Forest of Dean; both he and the town seem to have fallen for each othe
**Charles Stuart Rolls** (1877-1910), who together with Henry Royce founded the fir
which built the world's most prestigious motorcars, was born near the town.
1896, while still an undergraduate, he took three days to drive from Cambridge
Monmouth in the first car ever to be seen in the county.

**Agincourt Square** – The old market square was given this historicising name
1830 in an attempt to raise the town's profile among tourists making the fashio
able picturesque journey down the Wye.

Monnow Bridge

The handsome edifices defining the square include the 17C *King's Head* and *Beaufort Court*, formerly the inn where Nelson stayed, and **Shire Hall** (1724), which has an arcaded ground floor and a less-than-heroic statue of Henry V in a niche.

More convincing is the memorial to Rolls, by Goscombe John; it shows him cloth-capped and gaitered and holding a bi-plane, while panels around the base depict the various exploits of this pioneer motorist and aviator.

**Castle and Great House** – All that really remains of the Castle are the ruins of the Great Tower, built in the late 14C by John of Gaunt in order, it is thought, to provide a fit setting for the birth of his grandson, Henry V.

Within the Castle precinct stands the finely proportioned **Great House**, built (probably of stone from the demolished gatehouse) for the Marquess of Worcester and completed in 1673. It has splendid plaster ceilings beneath its hipped roof and is a fine example of domestic Renaissance architecture, which set the tone for much subsequent building in the town.

One wing contains the neatly laid-out **Regimental Museum** ⊘ which, as well as tracing the rise and decline of the Castle, tells the story of the Royal Monmouthshire Royal Engineers, the senior regiment of the Reserve Army.

**The Nelson Museum** ⊘ – A fine model of Monmouth and much other material bring to life the continuous evolution of the town since Norman times, but most visitors come here for the extensive and fascinating **collection of Nelson memorabilia** built up by Lady Llangattock and subsequently presented to the town. As well as personal effects, letters, ship models, and what was once alleged to be the great man's false eye, there are the swords of the French and Spanish commanders at Trafalgar and Nelson's own fighting sword.

**Monnow Bridge** – The crossing of the Monnow is approached by Monnow Street, whose broad central section accommodated the town's important markets. Here are some of the town's finest Georgian buildings, among them Cornwall House and Chippenham House, though the fabric of many other structures of apparently similar date incorporates much medieval work. The bridge, a 13C replacement of a timber structure, is unique in Britain in retaining its **fortified gatehouse**, and, not surprisingly, has long been one of the emblems of Monmouth, indeed of Wales.

## EXCURSION

**The Kymin** – *2mi/3km E by A 4136 and a steep and narrow lane.* In 1802, accompanied by the Hamiltons, Nelson came up the carriage drive leading to this hilltop in order to admire the little **Naval Temple**, built to honour the architects of Britain's recent victories at sea. The Temple joined another somewhat idiosyncratic structure already erected here, the **Round House**. This had been built in 1796 by local gentlemen as a rural retreat and dining establishment, and was the centre of a small network of pathways and viewpoints. The **views** are superb, taking in not only Monmouth in its immediate setting, but much of this part of the Border country, and the Kymin is justly a favourite stopping place along Offa's Dyke long-distance footpath.

# MONTGOMERY ★

(Trefaldwyn) Powys – Population 1 059
Michelin Atlas p 25 or Map 403 K 26

Apart from main roads and railways, this perfect little town seems hardly to have changed since Georgian times.

Montgomery is a planned settlement, a medieval foundation, which received a Royal Charter in 1227, laid out within the protection of its castle on the ridge high above, in order to consolidate the English hold on the invasion route along the Severn valley into the heart of Wales. The strategic importance of this routeway had long been recognised; the great Iron Age fort of **Ffridd Faldwyn** stands on the ridge a short distance away from the Norman castle, overlooking the crossing of the Severn at Rhydwhiman, close to which the Romans built their strongpoint of **Forden Gaer**.

Shortly after their Conquest of England in 1066, the Normans built a chain of castle mounds along the valley, one of them the work of Roger, a knight from Montgommeri in Normandy. Now known as **Hen Domen** (the Old Mound), this was replaced in the mid-13C by the present castle in its far stronger natural position, though town and castle retained the name of the original founder. Within its walls, which have long since disappeared, the town seems to have flourished, as market town and titular county town, until the last burst of Georgian prosperity, after which it settled into its present charming somnolence.

> **Adjacent Sights** – See Knighton, Llandrindod Wells, Llanidloes, Machynlleth, Newtown, Powis Castle, Welshpool.

## SIGHTS

**Montgomery Castle** – Thoroughly slighted by order of Parliament in 1649 after the Civil War, the castle impresses more from its commanding location than because of its stumpy fragments of stonework. The **view** is extraordinary, commanding the vale of the Severn and stretching far into England. The stronghold was laid out as a series of wards along the narrow spur; the deep ditches were excavated directly into the rock, by miners brought here expressly from the Forest of Dean in Gloucestershire. Even deeper (more than 200ft/60m) is the well.

**St Nicholas' Church** ⊘ – Montgomery's parish church stands in a raised churchyard on the eastern side of the town. It is mainly 13C, with a fine tower added in the early 19C. The nave has a splendid timber roof, and there is a 15C double screen, the eastern section probably brought from Chirbury Priory at the Dissolution. There is a superb early-17C **canopied tomb** of Richard Herbert and his wife; their pious children include the future poet, George Herbert. In the churchyard is a genuine curiosity, the **Robber's Grave**. This is the resting place of John Davies, executed in 1821 while still protesting his innocence of any crime and declaring that no grass would grow on his grave for 100 years. This does indeed seem to have been the case for many years although there is now less bare ground than before.

**Town Hall** – The mostly Georgian buildings ranged along the town's main axis, **Broad Street**, seem to be paying homage to this fine pale-brick building with pediment and clock tower. Built in 1748, it hints at a civic importance that has long since ceased to be, though Montgomery still takes an evident pride in its history; plaques are attached to a number of buildings and it may be the smallest town in Wales to have its own local museum.

**Old Bell Museum** ⊘ – The **museum** ⊘ is housed in a building which dates in parts from the 16C. The exhibits trace local history from the Roman settlement, the site of the original Norman timber castle (c 1070), through civic and social life – brick bread-oven with peles, rake and dough trough (6ft/2m long), clogs and pattens – to Forden Poor House, the Cambrian Railway and the history of the parish church and the neighbouring parish of Llandyssil.

# NEATH

(Castell Nedd) Neath Port Talbot – Population 15 073
Michelin Atlas p 15 or Map 403 I 29

Sited at the point where the attractive Vale of Neath opens out into the sprawl of industries and communication routes around the river mouth, Neath is a busy market town with a not-very-visible but nevertheless venerable past.

The Roman fort of Nidum is buried beneath a main road and the first castle erected by the Normans, also built on the far bank of the river from today's town centre, was soon abandoned. The gatehouse and part of the curtain wall of its replacement now stand guard over the car parks of Neath's modern shopping centre. A great abbey was built close to the first castle, its ruins later colonised by some of the installations which made 18C Neath an early focus of metalworking and other industries. As the tidal river silted up, new docks were built at Briton Ferry to designs by Brunel, while the transport of coal and other materials up and down the Vale was assured by the Neath and Tennant Canals and later by the Vale of Neath Railway.

Within easy reach of Neath are a number of unusually interesting industrial archaeological sites, while the Vale, despite the intensity of its past exploitation, retains much of the original sylvan character which attracted artists in search of picturesque scenery in the 18C and early 19C.

**Tourist Information Centre** – BP Club, Llandarcy, Neath SA10 6HJ ☎ 01792 813 030; Fax 01792 322 451.

**Adjacent Sights** – See Brecon Beacons, Carmarthen, Gower Peninsula, Llandeilo, Llandovery, Llanelli, Margam Park, Porthcawl, Port Talbot, Swansea.

**Neath Museum and Art Gallery** ⊘ – Housed in the 19C galleried concert building known as Gwyn Hall, this is a developing local museum with a range of displays on the evolution of Neath and its surroundings. A warning cry of *Sacsoniad!* – The Saxons are coming! – introduces fascinating finds from Hen Castell, Old Castle, a rare example of a native Welsh royal stronghold, the site of which now lies beneath the great viaduct carrying the motorway (M 4) over the estuarine levels.

**Neath Abbey** – Described by Leland as "the fairest abbey in all Wales", Neath was certainly one of the richest, with an arable estate (5 000 acres/2 025ha) and property interests as far away as Cardiff.

Like Tintern, it conformed to the Cistercian plan of a cruciform church with ancillary buildings arranged around a cloister, though in Neath's case the cloister was on the normal, south side of the church. The ruins are substantial enough to evoke something of the majesty of the medieval abbey but are not enhanced by their situation in an industrial estate.

A fine collection of glazed and decorated **tiles** from the church can be seen in the splendidly rib-vaulted undercroft of the monks' dormitory. Above it rise the skeletal but still imposing walls and windows of the Tudor house built after the Dissolution.

## EXCURSIONS

### Vale of Neath

**Gnoll Estate** ⊙ – *On the NE outskirts of Neath by B 4434.* Gnoll is a rare survival, an 18C landscape. The Mackworth family first harnessed the local streams for industrial purposes – to turn machinery and create fish ponds; they then channelled them to supply ornamental cascades – one in the fashionable French style consisting of stone steps (90ft/27m) descending a hillside and the other less formal in a steep and wooded valley. The works were enhanced with rustic bridges, a mock-medieval tower, a stand of pine trees, a temple and a grotto. Other features to survive include pleasure grounds, terraces, an arboretum, an ice-house and a walled garden with glasshouses and fives court.

★**Aberdulais Falls** ⊙ – *2.5mi/4km NE of the town centre.* After its abandonment as a tinplate works c 1890, this ancient industrial site reverted to near jungle. Since 1981 it has been progressively cleared by the National Trust, and its fascinating history, a palimpsest of industrial archaeology, revealed to its visitors.

The **setting** is highly picturesque, a reminder of the often-rustic landscape in which early industrial activities took place. The famous **falls** roar down through the river-sculpted rock, while mysterious structures stand on the narrow valley floor, hemmed in by steep rocky walls and a luxuriant vegetation seemingly eager to encroach once more.

**Copper** was being smelted here as early as 1584, succeeded by an **ironworks**. By the mid-18C this had given way to a **corn mill**, a favourite subject for romantic painters including Turner. Ironworking revived for a short while (c 1830-40), but the final use of the site was as a **tinplate manufactory**. It is this last phase which was responsible for most of the visible remains like retaining walls and foundations, weir and wheel pit, and tall chimney. A recent innovation has been the installation of a turbine driven by the falls, which supplies power to the site and sells a surplus to the National Grid.

Aberdulais Falls

**Aberdulais Basin** – The tinplate works was served by the Neath and Tennant Canals which meet here in a basin. There is a unique skew bridge and a long **aqueduct** (340ft/104m). A canal towpath leads to a canal depot, known as the Tonna Workshops *(restoration in progress)*.

**Resolven** – *6mi/10km NE of town centre.* The main road (A 465) is accompanied for part of its length by a charming section of the **Neath Canal**. A stretch (4mi/6km long) has been restored and is navigable.
South of Resolven *(turn off B 4434; 30min on foot there and back)* is one of the waterfalls for which the Vale of Neath is famous. Prettily located among mature oak woodland, the **Melincourt Falls** have a spectacular drop (80ft/25m).

**Penscynor Wildlife Park** ⊙ – *3mi/5km NE of town centre off A 465.* A popular family attraction, the close-packed enclosures of this wildlife park occupy a steep hillside down which a spectacular Alpine Slide carries its excited passengers. The park has grown from an enthusiast's parrot collection and there are several species of these bright-hued birds, as well as an amazing array of monkeys and many other animals and birds, some of which can be petted or fed. Serious research and breeding is carried on, and among the institution's achievements was the release into the Brazilian wild of a group of golden lion tamarins threatened with extinction.

**Cefn Coed Colliery Museum** ⊙ – *5mi/8km NE of Neath by A 465 and A 4109.* Coal was being extracted on a small scale from the bleak uplands at the head of the Dulais valley as early as the mid-18C and mining continues here today, albeit using the environmentally contentious open-cast method. Among the woodlands in the lower, narrow part of the valley, Cefn Coed was one of the deepest **anthracite mines** in the world, with seams worked at a depth of more than 2 500ft/800m. The mine closed in 1968, and its pithead now houses extensive displays on the history of mining as well as temporary exhibitions. Visitors can explore a highly atmospheric re-creation of an **underground mining gallery** and admire some of the machinery, epic in scale, essential to the working of the pit. The great black **compressor** gleams wickedly, heavy breathing announces the presence of the massive **winding engine**, and six giant **steam boilers** stand in line, their dimensions outstripping those of any mere locomotive. This display of industrial strength is set off by the pageantry of the miners' banners proclaiming *Workers of the world unite for Peace and Socialism* and by a dainty little double-decker tram, driven by gas, which once plied the streets of Neath between Skewen and Briton Ferry from 1899 to 1920.

# NEWCASTLE EMLYN

(Castell Newydd Emlyn) Carmarthenshire
Population 931
Michelin Atlas p 24 or Map 403 G 27

The Welsh stronghold which gave this tiny town its name was one of only a few to be built in stone. Dating from c 1240, it was named "new" to distinguish it from the "old" castle at nearby Cilgerran. "Plundered and ever since neglected" since its demolition at the end of the Civil War, it consists of stumps of stonework standing picturesquely on a grassy ridge above a loop in the Teifi, an informal public park for the townspeople.
The town itself, at its busiest when the Friday livestock market is in full swing, focuses on the miniature market hall with its disproportionately prominent clock tower.
Owen Edwards had "no words to depict the wealth of beauty in the Teivy Valley", and the tranquil vale of the Teifi both upstream and downstream from Newcastle Emlyn repays unhurried individual exploration, though there are a number of popular attractions as well.

**Tourist Information Centre** – Market Hall, Newcastle Emlyn SA38 9AE ☎/Fax 01239 711 333.

**Craft Centres** – For woollen goods visit the **Museum of the Welsh Woollen Industry** *(see below)*, **Curlew Weavers** ⊙ *(8mi/13km E by B 4571 at Troedyraur, Thydlewis, Llandysul)* and **Rock Mill** ⊙ *(10mi/15km NE by A 475 and B 4459 at Rhydowen).*

**Adjacent Sights** – See Aberaeron, Cardigan, Carmarthen, Fishguard, Haverfordwest, Lampeter, Laugharne, Vale of Rheidol, Tregaron.

Welsh Coracle

## EXCURSIONS

**Cenarth Falls** ⊙ – *3mi/5km W of Newcastle Emlyn by A 484. Car park (paying) on right bank of the Teifi at the northern end of the bridge.* The series of low waterfalls above the 17C two-arched bridge has drawn sightseers for many years and continues to do so. The falls cover a wide area (2 acres/1ha) and present an exhilarating spectacle when the river is in flood. Sheep were made to battle through the water here to prepare their fleeces for shearing.

Salmon were caught from the **coracles** which can still be seen bobbing on the surface of the less agitated stretches of the river. The history of these extraordinary simple and adaptable craft is told with great enthusiasm in the **Coracle Museum ★** ⊙, in the grounds of the ancient **Cenarth Flour Mill** with its working undershot waterwheel.

The coracle originated in Asia but has been used in Britain since at least the Bronze Age. It may even have helped in the recolonisation of the country after the retreat of the ice. More recently, boat people from Vietnam have crossed the South China Sea in coracles, and one was used in the Dalai Lama's escape from Tibet. The museum has many examples of coracles, and a wealth of information on how they were made and used. Old photographs are especially fascinating, particularly those which show the beetle-like appearance of local men carrying coracles on their backs.

**Museum of the Welsh Woollen Industry** ⊙ – *4mi/7km E of Newcastle Emlyn by A 484 and minor road.* The rolling pasturelands rising to either side of the vale of the Teifi are cut by the deep and narrow valleys of swift-flowing streams. The area supplied wool and water-power in abundance for what was the most important Welsh rural industry. In 1921 there were 250 woollen mills in the country, with a notable concentration around **Dre-Fach Felindre**, once known as the "Huddersfield of Wales".

The museum is housed in the Cambrian Mills, built 1902-12 by the Lewis family, who dominated local textile production until the 1970s, by which time the industry had undergone drastic contraction. As a branch of the National Museum, it has exemplary displays on the whole of the history of the industry and the processes involved in turning raw wool into cloth, from sorting, willying, scouring, dyeing, carding, spinning, winding, warping, weaving, to fulling, finishing and napping. Some of the machinery can be seen in use, and the products of the modern industry are for sale in the museum shop. A number of self-guided trails lead visitors beyond the museum walls into the surrounding area which still has many relics of the industry, from teasel gardens to weavers' cottages.

**Teifi Valley Railway** ⊙ – *At Henllan, 4mi/7km E of Newcastle Emlyn by A 484 and B 4334.* The Carmarthen and Cardigan Railway set out from Carmarthen in 1857 but by 1895 it had reached only to Newcastle Emlyn, whereupon it gave up the evidently unequal struggle and settled down to the life of a never-very-profitable branch line. Passenger services were withdrawn in 1952 but in the 1980s a group of enthusiasts relaid the track; today visitors can take a short trip up the Teifi valley, drawn by a centenarian narrow-gauge engine which once worked at the Penrhyn quarries in North Wales.

# NEWPORT

(Casnewydd) Newport – Population 115 522
Michelin Atlas p 16 or Map 403 K 29

The Norman lords of Wentloog appreciated Newport's strategic position as the lowes[t]
crossing point of the tidal River Usk, and began building their castle here in the earl[y]
14C. But Newport remained a modest market town until touched by the Industria[l]
Revolution, when it became the outlet for the coal pits and metal works of the Easter[n]
Valleys as well as an important engineering centre in its own right. What in 1801 wa[s]
a village-sized population of 1 100 had swelled by the start of the 20C to 67 000[.]
Now the third-largest city in Wales, Newport is a thriving shopping and commercia[l]
centre serving a wide region, seeking to repair the damage done by over-enthusiasti[c]
redevelopment in the 1960s and 1970s by more judicious, small-scale civic improve[-]
ments and works of public art.

## "A Savage Storm-swept Night" – The Chartist Uprising of 4 November 1839

The frustration and hopes of Britain's rising working class and small tradespeopl[e]
found expression in the Charter of 1839, with its six-point call for the basic element[s]
of democracy – manhood suffrage, secret ballot, abolition of property qualification[s]
salaried MPs, annual parliaments and equal electoral districts. Gwent was particularl[y]
militant, with up to 25 000 members and sympathisers in the eastern Valleys an[d]
lowland towns like Newport, where radical **John Frost**, a former Mayor, had long bee[n]

## NEWPORT

Allt-yr-yn Avenue ........ **AY** 2
Bellevue Lane ........... **BX** 5
Blewitt Street ........... **AX** 7
Caerau Crescent ........ **AXY** 9
Cambrian Centre ........ **AX**
Capel Street ........... **AY** 10
Clarence Place ........... **AX** 12
Clyffard Crescent ........ **AX** 13

Clytha Park Road ........ **AX** 14
Commercial Street ...... **AXY** 15
Dewsland Park Road ..... **AX** 17
Dock Street ............. **AX** 19
Godfrey Road ........... **AX** 21
Hereford Street ........ **AX** 24
High Street ............ **AX** 26
John Frost Square ....... **AX** 27
Kensington Place ........ **AX** 30
Keynsham Avenue ....... **AY** 32
Kingsway Centre ......... **AX**

Lower Dock Street ...... **AXY** 3[3]
Malpas Road ............. **AX** 3[?]
Newport Bridge ......... **AX** 3[?]
Oakfield Road ........... **AX** 4[?]
Queensway ............ **AX** 4[?]
Summerhill Avenue ..... **AX** 4[?]
Waterloo Road .......... **AY** 5[?]

Museum and Art Gallery . **AX** **M**
Newport Clock ............ **AX** **A**

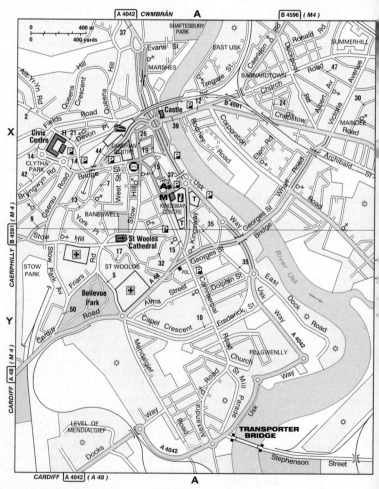

locked in conflict with nearby Tredegar House, whose steward virtually ruled the town. On the "savage storm-swept night" of 4 November 1839 a massive but ill-planned march descended on Newport, fed by columns from Argoed, Nantyglo, Ebbw Vale.... Awaiting the arrival of the insurrectionaries, as they swarmed down the hill from what is now the Cathedral, was a group of special constables and soldiers, holed up in the Westgate Hotel. As the crowd tried to break into the building, the military opened fire, killing perhaps 22 people, though only 10 bodies were recovered. The workers' dream of a "Silurian Republic" which would join with like-minded entities in the rest of Britain was shattered. Repression was harsh; the three leaders, Zephaniah Williams and William Jones as well as Frost were sentenced to be hanged and quartered, though in the event this was commuted to transportation to Tasmania. The Mayor of Newport was knighted and a banquet given for the soldiery.

---

**Tourist Information Centre** – Museum & Art Gallery, John Frost Square, Newport NP20 1PA ☎ 01633 842 962; Fax 01633 222 615; newport-tic@tsww.com
First Services & Lodge, Junction 23A/M4, Magor NP6 3YL ☎ 01633 881 122; Fax 01633 881 985.

**Adjacent Sights** – See Caerleon, Caerphilly, Caerwent, Chepstow, Raglan Castle, Tintern Abbey, Usk.

---

**City Centre** – In spite of the brutalist car parks and insensitively designed commercial buildings which resulted from the over-ambitious redevelopment schemes of the mid-20C, the character of the centre is still predominantly that of a vigorous and self-confident late Victorian commercial and industrial city. Few individual buildings are outstanding, but the pedestrianisation of arteries like Commercial Street highlights the achievement of the turn-of-the-century city fathers in reconciling progress with the creation of good townscape; while ground floors have been adapted to the contemporary retailing requirements, most upper floors are intact, with a wealth of bow windows, oriels and other ornamental features. In recent years, the scene has been enlivened by the addition of a surprising quantity of street sculpture, mosaics and other works of public art; one work at the southern end of Commercial Street recalls **WH Davies**, born in Newport in 1871, author of *The Autobiography of a Super-tramp* and of the lines:

What is this life if, full of care,
We have no time to stand and stare.

At the northern end of the street another more complex tableau commemorates the Chartist uprising of 1839, while John Frost Square, the unfortunate epitome of 1970s replanning, has been given a new focal point in the form of the **Newport Clock** (**AX A**); this triumphal arch (30ft/9m high) in shiny metal, described by its creator as a "cross between a cuckoo clock and an espresso machine", is a contemporary variation on the theme of the animated astronomical clock, which seems to deconstruct itself as the Devil appears in a puff of smoke. An even more prominent modern monument, a bold and brightly coloured abstract sculpture called *Steel Wave*, dominates Town Reach, a short stretch of reclaimed riverbank just south of the Castle.

★**Museum and Art Gallery** ⊘ (**AX M**) – *John Frost Square.* Recently refurbished and housed on several floors in the same modern building as the Public Library, this is one of the major museums and galleries of Wales, with much space given over to well-staged temporary exhibitions.

The art collection's strengths lie in Welsh, particularly local, paintings and drawings, though there are outstanding examples of the work of **English watercolourists**, including Thomas Rowlandson and Richard Dadd. Lack of space means that only part of the collection is on display at any one time. The Iris Fox collection of Wemyss ware and Staffordshire figures can be seen, while entertaining and informative displays based on John Wait's extraordinary **teapot collection** trace the social history of tea drinking, from the introduction of the national drink by Catherine of Braganza in the 1660s to the present day.

The museum's exhibits give a comprehensive and stimulating account of the evolution of Newport in its regional setting. Reminders of prehistoric people's activities along the banks of the Severn include Footprints in the Mud, trodden in the soft silts of the estuary some 6 000 years ago and possibly the earliest preserved footprints in Britain. The importance of the area in Roman times is emphasised, with items of international significance from the nearby civil settlement of Caerwent *(see p 216)*, including a fine but incomplete **mosaic floor** of the Four Seasons; the figures of Summer and Winter survive, together with figures bearing torches

Newport Transporter Bridge

whose size of flame gives further clues as to the progress of the year. The focus of the medieval and later displays is on ecclesiastical, castle, and agricultural life in the surrounding area, then on the growth of Newport in the 19C and its meta-morphosis from a "long, narrow and straggling town" into a teeming port and major industrial city. The Chartist movement is well evoked, and there are any number of objects, models (including a working model of the Transporter Bridge), recreated interiors, photographs and other illustrations which bring to life two centuries of almost continuous change.

**Newport Castle** (**AX**) – Newport's original stronghold, a motte-and-bailey castle on Stow Hill near today's cathedral, was abandoned in the mid-14C when a separate Norman lordship, Wentloog (Gwynllŵg), was carved out of Glamorgan. In its place, Hugh d'Audele began to construct a castle defending the river crossing. His fortress was both strengthened and made more habitable in the early and mid-15C but, after 1521 when its lord, the Third Duke of Buckingham, was beheaded, the building was neglected and by the 18C had fallen into ruin. The *coup de grâce* came when railway and canal promoters drove their schemes through the castle precincts with the utmost ruthlessness and part of the castle became a brewery.

What remains of Newport Castle is, nevertheless, an important civic symbol and a prominent landmark, especially when seen from Newport Bridge; there are sub-stantial remnants of north and south towers, while in the base of the massive central tower is a watergate facing the Usk.

★**Transporter Bridge** ⊘ (**AY**) – By the end of the 19C the industries of Newport had spread to the level lands on the east bank of the Usk, and a need had arisen for a crossing which would be more reliable than the hazardous ferry trip across the fickle Usk river whose tidal range is the greatest in Britain. A conventional bridge having been shown to be impractical, the solution chosen was that of the "transbordeur" patented by French engineer François Arnodin of Châteauneuf-sur-Loire; the towers (242ft/74m high) support a slender span (645ft/197m) giving a clear headway (177ft/54m) for shipping; along the span runs a trolley from which is slung a gondola carrying both people and a small number of vehicles. The bridge is one of only two remaining in Britain.

**St Woolos' (St Gwynllyw's) Cathedral** ⊘ (**AY**) – *Stow Hill.* The first church on this ridgetop site to the south of the town centre was built by a 6C Celtic chieftain, Gwynllyw. His church was plundered by Irish pirates and by the English under Harold Godwinson, then destroyed by Caradoc. The oldest part of the present church is the Galilee Chapel, once the nave of the church as it was rebuilt in the early 11C. This is linked to the spacious mid-12C nave by a splendid doorway with exceptionally bold dogtooth moulding and crudely carved capitals with figures of men and beasts. The church gained cathedral status in 1930 and was given a mock-Perpendicular east end in the 1960s, the most arresting feature of which is a swirling mosaic and a sunburst window by John Piper. The churchyard is dom-inated by the 15C tower. Buried here in unmarked graves are 10 of the Chartists shot dead on 4 November 1839.

On the slopes to the south of the Cathedral is **Bellevue Park** (**BY**), laid out by the eminent early-20C landscape architect Thomas Mawson. The assessors of the design competition he won failed to notice that his scheme had been inadvertently prepared for another site.

**Civic Centre** ⊙ (**AX**) – Though completed as late as 1964, this complex of buildings overlooking the city centre from the north-west is a fine example of the monumental civic architecture of the inter-war period, with a slender clock tower rising over the pantiled roofs of the symmetrically planned flanking wings.

New law courts occupy the space originally intended for a grand circular pool marking the formal approach to the building from the direction of the town.

The main entrance is now from the rear, which should not be a deterrent to viewing the majestic **murals**★ gracing the central hall. These were commissioned in 1960, and carried out by the artist Hans Feibusch; they are perhaps the most ambitious of their kind in Britain, depicting with great verve such events as the coming of the Celts and Romans, Owain Glyn Dŵr's attack on the Castle, the Chartist Riot, the disembarkation of US troops in the Second World War and finally the building of the George Street Bridge in 1964, the most modern crossing of the Usk in Newport.

## EXCURSIONS

**Fourteen Locks Canal Centre** ⊙ – *2mi/3km NW of Newport by B 4591 towards Highcross (signs)*. The small information centre, which traces the industrial origins and decline of the Monmouthshire Canal, also provides sweeping views of the Gwent uplands. Quiet trails follow the now-disused stretch of the canal and its flight of locks and wind away into the surrounding woodlands.

**Cwmcarn Forest Drive and Visitor Centre** ⊙ – *5mi/8km NW of Newport by A 4048*. A woodland drive *(7mi/11km)* winds up from the centre into the mountains above Ebbw Vale and Newport. The best of the picnic sites and viewpoints dotted along the way is the Twmbarlwm Iron Age hilltop settlement, which looks out across the Bristol Channel to England and over the South Wales valleys to the Brecon Beacons.

**Cwmbran** – *5mi/8km N of Newport by A 4042 and A 4051*. The sixth-largest town in Wales, Cwmbran is the only example in the country of the comprehensively planned new towns initiated in Britain after the Second World War. Attempts had been made in the 1930s to counter unemployment by introducing new industries into the area; the success of these efforts caused an acute housing shortage, which the building of Cwmbran, designated as a New Town in 1949, was intended to alleviate. Unexciting architecturally, the town consists of the orthodox mixture of sweeping roads, housing neighbourhoods, industrial estates, and a car-free shopping centre.

# NEWTOWN

(Y Drenewydd) Powys – Population 10 548
Michelin Atlas p 25 or Map 403 K 26

he settlement is aptly named Newtown, as it has enjoyed a succession of new eginnings. In 1279 a native Welsh settlement within the great bend of the Severn as replanned by Roger de Montgomery to serve as a market town. In the early 19C e rapid expansion of hand-looms and textile factories led to hopes of the place ecoming a second Leeds. In the mid-20C planned expansion of industry and housing as promoted by the Mid Wales Development Corporation in order to stem the exodus om this otherwise entirely rural region.

races of De Montgomery's typical medieval grid plan can be distinguished in the street attern but the dominant impression is of the 19C red brick of houses and factories, en, on the outskirts, of the modern residential estates and the 100-plus factories uilt here since the late 1960s.

ewtown has, however, remained relatively small; rivalry with Leeds was never realtic, and the biggest establishment at the end of the 19C was the pioneering ail-order business whose warehouse still dominates today. And the visionary plan of

e 1960s for a linear city nking Newtown with Llanloes *(see p 193)* along the evern valley remained, peraps fortunately, on paper. The ustling town is at its busiest n Tuesdays when the market ls its broad main street; visors may find interest in a trio f unusual little museums.

**Tourist Information Centre** – The Park, Back Lane, Newtown SY16 2PW ☎ 01686 625 580; Fax 01686 610 065.

**Adjacent Sights** – See Knighton, Llanfyllin, Llanidloes, Machynlleth, Montgomery, Powis Castle, Lake Vyrnwy, Welshpool.

## SIGHTS

**Robert Owen Memorial Museum** ⊙ – The reformer **Robert Owen** (1771-185?) was born in Newtown and returned here to die, though his life was spe? elswhere, notably in promoting his Utopian industrial communities at New Lana? in Scotland and New Harmony, Indiana. The museum gives a good account of h? life and his influence on the development of Socialism and the Co-operative mov? ment. Owen's Art Nouveau **memorial tomb** is in the graveyard of the ruined **Church St Mary**. In the 1840s St Mary's was abandoned in favour of the yellow-bri? **St David's** because of the Severn's liability to flood, a situation remedied only by th? recent construction of massive embankments and the building of the Clywed? Dam *(see p 194)* upstream.

**WH Smith Museum** ⊙ – Above the famous newsagents in the town centre wi? its restored façade is a museum telling the story of the firm's evolution, with fin? examples of its Arts and Crafts house style.

**Newtown Textile Museum** ⊙ – On the far side of the bridge over the Severn ? the "inner city" of Newtown, a densely packed grid of streets lined with tall la? Georgian buildings in which the weavers lived and worked, with the looms on th? top floor. The museum occupies some of the original buildings, in which th? lower-storey living quarters have been refurbished.

# PEMBROKE★★

(Penfro) Pembrokeshire – Population 7 230
Michelin Atlas p 14 or Map 403 F 28

The Normans based their operations in south-western Wales on the castle and tow? laid out along a low and narrow limestone spur, once almost surrounded by an inl? from Milford Haven. Their mighty castle still stands, dominated by its great rour? keep and in turn dominating the town which, albeit rebuilt over the centuries, st? retains its ancient street pattern and long burgage plots running down to the vestig? of the medieval walls.

★★**Castle** ⊙ – The castle wa? founded by Roger de Mont? gomery in 1093 and serve? the Normans well, neve? being taken by the Wels? and making an excelle? base for campaigning ? Ireland.
It owes its present form t? the efforts of William Ma? shal, Earl of Pembrok? 1189-1219, and those ? his son, another William. Within the inner ward at the westernmost tip of th? promontory, the first William expressed his power by raising the mighty round kee? (50ft/15m in diameter and 75ft/23m high) with indestructible walls (19ft/6m thic? at the base). This truly monumental structure, based on French practice, an? almost unique in Britain, is crowned by a splendid stone dome, awe-inspiring whe? viewed from below. A lesser tower contains a sinister dungeon, while beneath th? late-13C Great Hall with its Decorated windows is the extraordinary **Wogan Cavern** opening out towards the northern arm of the inlet and probably used as boathouse. Other structures in the inner ward include the remains of the Norma? Hall, probably built at the same time as the Keep, the late-13C–early-14C Count? Court, the Chapel, the Western Hall, and the Horseshoe Gate, the chief entranc? until the outer ward was built.

The great expanse of the outer ward is defended by a curtain wall and a series ? towers, in one of which, by tradition, Henry Tudor, later King Henry VII, was bor? His supposed birthplace is marked with a tableau showing the child with his nurs? and 14-year-old mother, Lady Margaret Beaufort. Additional strength is given b? St Ann's Bastion and, above all, by the great **Gatehouse**, almost a castle within castle, approached by a semicircular barbican. Inside the **Gatehouse Tower** are display? celebrating the role the castle played in English history as "The Seat of Earls" a? well as a fine model clarifying the stages of its construction. In addition there is a? exhibition on the last invasion of mainland Britain in 1797 *(see p 154)*. Th? commanding panorama from the top confirms the wisdom of the Normans' stra? tegic choice of this location.

Having survived all Welsh assaults, the castle fell to Oliver Cromwell after seven-week siege in 1648. His sappers rendered it useless as a fortress by blowin? up the outside-facing walls of the towers. Restoration began in the 1880s an? continued into the early 20C, returning the great stronghold to something like it? medieval appearance.

Pembroke Town and Castle by Richard Wilson

National Museums and Galleries of Wales

**Town Quay** – The town's north gate was demolished in the early 19C but the line of the town wall can be traced eastward along Mill Pond Walk towards the well-preserved three-storey Barnard's Tower and the site of the east gate. The Millpond itself, now closed off by a barrage, once drove a tide mill whose foundations are still in place to the west of the bridge. Until the end of the 18C, when it was overshadowed by Milford and Haverfordwest, Pembroke was the most prosperous town in the region, with a fleet of some 200 ships. A modern seafaring role demanded deeper water than that of a millpond, the 19C railways took away much trade, and the very last coaster cast off from the quayside in 1961.

**Museum of the Home** ⊘ – *No 7 Westgate Hill, opposite the entrance to the castle.* The rooms of the house display a collection of fascinating domestic bygones, whose intrinsic interest is greatly enhanced by their artful arrangement.

This street still has cottages of medieval date and scant traces of the town's west gate.

## EXCURSION

**Lamphey Bishop's Palace** – *2mi/3km E of Pembroke by A 4139.* Even in its ruined state, Lamphey Palace conveys something of the rustic attractiveness which made it the favoured residence of the bishops of St David's. Orchards, vineyards, woodlands and fishponds not only provided the necessities of life but also a reassuring sense of the landed wealth which underpinned the social and political position of these powerful princes of the Church.

The domain was further embellished with gardens and fine buildings, the **Hall** erected by **Bishop Gower** in the early 14C having a similar sophisticated arcaded parapet to its prototype at St David's. Other structures include the remains of two earlier halls, the early-13C Old Hall and the sturdy structure of the hall built by Bishop Carew later that century. The chapel, remodelled in the early 16C, has a fine Perpendicular window with its tracery intact. Once linked to walls defining inner and outer courtyards, the inner gatehouse, also provided with an arcaded parapet, now stands in isolation.

The palace's conversion into the private residence of the Devereux family after the Dissolution lasted only a short while; farm animals then roamed the grounds, until in the 19C the present battlemented western wall was built and the precinct turned into the kitchen garden of nearby Lamphey Court.

**Upton Castle Gardens** ⊘ – *2mi/3km E of Pembroke by A 477.* The gardens, which slope down to a belt of sheltering woodland fringing the Carew Estuary, are at their best in spring and contain many exotic species; most are labelled. From the formal terraces – fishpond, rose gardens and herbaceous borders flanking a swimming pool – a path leads via a covered history corner and along one side of the walled garden to the medieval chapel near the house *(private).* Lovers' Lane leads down through the woodland (15min) to a narrow sea inlet, where birds can be seen at half tide perching on the hummocky rocks, which are draped with green weed.

# PEMBROKESHIRE COAST ★★

Pembrokeshire
Michelin Atlas p 14 or Map 403 EFG 27-28-29

Pembrokeshire is a peninsula divided by bays and by Milford Haven into furth
peninsulas projecting westward towards Ireland and the Atlantic. Together with t
region's diverse geology, this makes for an astonishing variety of coastal scenery. Gre
headlands of hard rock are separated by bays scooped out of softer materials by t
action of the sea, sheltered sandy shores contrast with storm beaches piled high wi
pebbles, while rock stacks and offshore islands offer sanctuary to countless seabirds.

## HISTORICAL NOTES

The area abounds in the dolmens, megaliths and promontory forts of prehistory. On
of the finest burial chambers in Britain, **Pentre Ifan** *(see p 156)*, stands on the slopes
the **Presely Hills** *(Mynydd Preseli)*, a mysterious, brooding upland in the northern, inlar
section of the Park *(see below)* which is considered to be the source of the blueston
from which Stonehenge was built.

Pembrokeshire is even more deeply suffused with the spirit of early Christianity,
wild shores settled by the monks and mystics of the Celtic Church who laid th
spiritual foundations from which the great Cathedral of St David's later rose. Amor
many lesser examples, there are two of the three finest **Celtic crosses** in Wales at Carew
and Nevern.

The Normans quickly consolidated their hold on this part of the country, a steppir
stone to their later operations in Ireland, by building castles and settling the soul
of the area with so many English as well as Flemish immigrants that it has lor
been known as "Little England beyond Wales". A boundary known as the **Landsk**
marked a military and later linguistic frontier between this southern "Englishry" an
the "Welshry", the less fertile northern fastness into which the native Wels
unwillingly retreated. Church architecture still marks the difference between thes
cultural regions, the substantial southern churches having characteristic tall and fort
fied Pembrokeshire towers, the northern churches being of more modest constructio
often with a small belfry rather than a tower.

**Pembrokeshire Coast National Park** – This is the smallest as well as the lea
typical of Great Britain's National Parks, extending not over mountain or hill countr
but over the cliffs and beaches of one of the country's most spectacular and fascinatir
coastlines (180mi/290km).

Stackpole Head

Since its designation in 1952, the National Park's manifold natural attractions have drawn ever-increasing numbers of visitors. Most are holidaymakers, staying for a week or two; in spite of road improvements, Pembrokeshire is still a good distance from South Wales and England, so day trippers are relatively few.

The oil installations, which many thought would destroy the landscape of Milford Haven for ever, have now had 30 years to settle into the scene, and the movements of the supertankers in and out of the Haven have become an attraction in themselves.

Still controversial are the activities of the Army, which was testing its tanks on Castlemartin ranges long before the National Park was created. Gunfire may be disturbing but military occupation keeps out the pressures of intensive farming; uncontaminated by insecticides and herbicides, the ranges are now a refuge for all kinds of wildlife.

## Out and About

**Tourist Information Centre** – The Barbecue, Harbour Car Park, Saundersfoot SA69 9HE ☎ 01834 813 672; Fax 01834 813 673.

**Puffin Shuttle** ⊘ – The Puffin Shuttle service, which helps to ease congestion in the Park by enabling visitors to leave their cars behind, operates every day in summer between St David's and Milford Haven.

**Boat Trips** – From Solva to Ramsey Island *(see also St David's)* by inflatable craft.

**Coastal Footpath** – This footpath runs the whole length of the Park from its south-eastern boundary at Amroth to Poppit Sands near Cardigan in the north, a wonderful experience, if walked from end to end, but equally satisfying if enjoyed in shorter stretches.

**Activities** – Most kinds of seaside activities can be enjoyed in the Park, from surfing, sailing and water-skiing, to sea-angling, birdwatching, or simply sitting on the beach.

**Beaches** – On the south coast at Amroth, Saundersfoot, Freshwater East, Barafundle Bay, Broad Haven, Bosherston, West Angle Bay (see also Tenby); on the west coast at Neyland Marina; Gelliswick, Milford Haven; Dale; Marloes Sands; Martin's Haven; St Bride's Haven; Little Haven, Broad Haven and Nolton Haven *(see also St David's and Fishguard)*.

**Caravan Parks** – There are many caravan parks; their proliferation has been one of the Park planners' greatest problems.

**Craft Centres** – For woollen goods visit **The Woollen Mill** ⊘ *(Middle Mill, Solva)*.

**Adjacent Sights** – See Carew, Fishguard, Haverfordwest, Milford Haven, Pembroke, St David's, Tenby.

## SOUTH COAST

### From Amroth west to Angle

**Colby Woodland Garden** ⊘ – *On the N edge of Amroth by minor roads.* Profits from the local coal pits enabled John Colby to build himself a plain but elegant house to a Nash design in a secluded wooded valley above the coastal village of Amroth.

The garden is at its best from early spring to June, when the extensive collection of rhododendrons and azaleas assembled in the early 20C blaze their bright colours against the green background of the valley trees.

**Saundersfoot** – Saundersfoot began as an outlet for the high-quality coal extracted from the now-defunct Pembrokeshire coalfield; pleasure-craft rather than colliers now fill its harbour. The little resort is at the centre of the National Park's most popular and urbanised stretch of coastline, extending north-east towards Amroth and south to Tenby.

★★**Tenby** – *See p 271.*

★**Caldey Island** – *See p 273.*

**Manorbier Castle** – *See p 273.*

**Bosherston** – Below the village church with its churchyard cross is a late-18C–early-19C landscape whose lushness is in complete contrast to the wild coastline to the west, with sheltered leafy valleys containing freshwater pools whose surface turns white in early summer with the flowers of countless lilies.

**★St Govan's Chapel** – *Access by steps from the clifftop; sometimes restricted by firing on Castlemartin ranges.* Few sites could be more evocative of the saintly isolation of certain early Christians than this cell-like chapel huddling in the cliff face of the savage coastline, though the structure seems to date from the 11C rather than the Dark Ages. Chased by pirates to the edge of the cliff, Govan was saved by the rocks opening up, then closing over him. He stayed here until his death in AD 586.

**★Stack Rocks** – *Access sometimes restricted by firing on Castlemartin ranges.* Together with the natural arch known as the Green Bridge of Wales, these rock pillars standing just out to sea are among the most spectacular sights of the National Park, every available surface covered by countless seabirds during the nesting season *(April-August)*.

**Angle** – Close to the tip of the peninsula closing off the southern entrance to Milford Haven, this attractive street village with its colour-washed cottages still has traces of ancient strip fields outlined by later enclosures.

**Thorn Island** – Offshore from the tip of the peninsula near West Angle Bay lies Thorn Island, crowned by a fort, built in 1854, which is now privately owned and run as an hotel; visitors are attracted by the sailing, diving and windsurfing, and to see the dolphins and whales and the birds which nest on nearby Skomer and Skokholm *(see below)*.

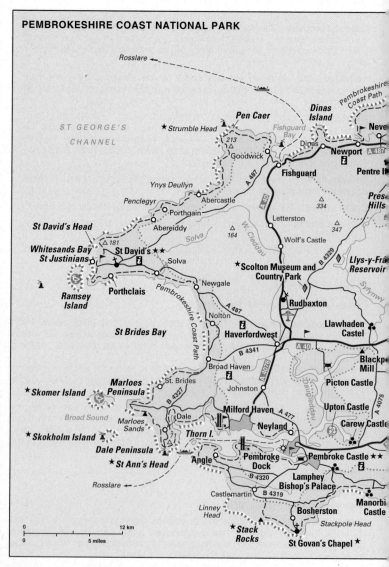

PEMBROKESHIRE COAST NATIONAL PARK

### Sea Empress

Disaster threatened the Pembrokeshire coast in February 1996 when the *Sea Empress*, a Liberian-registered oil tanker, went aground off St Ann's Head at the entrance to Milford Haven and spilled more than 72 000t of oil into the sea. As a southerly wind was blowing, much of the oil drifted away from the shore but, even so, 125mi/200km of coastline were affected by the pollution. If the oil spill had occurred during the breeding season for birds and the spawning season for fish, the effects would have been more serious. By May most signs of the pollution had been eradicated and the beaches were ready to receive the summer visitors.

## DAUGLEDDAU

This is the name given to the least-known section of the National Park, the quiet landscape around the tidal inlets reaching inland from Milford Haven *(see p 208)* to Carew *(see p 129)* and Haverfordwest *(see p 162)*. Woods and parkland run down to the high-tide mark at many points along the course of the two Cleddau rivers, the Cresswell and Carew. Old villages stand by the shore, some of them with an interesting maritime history including the shipping of coal from the long-abandoned Pembrokeshire coalfield. Castles, some like Upton *(see p 221)* and Benton *(not open to the public)*, guard the waterways, which no longer carry commercial traffic but are used by pleasure-craft based at Broad Tar, Lawrenny and other moorings.

## WEST COAST

### From St Ann's Head north to St David's

**Dale Peninsula** – The village of **Dale**, fronting on to its shingle beach and sheltered bay, is a popular yachting centre. The Victorian fort at Dale Point is now a field studies centre.

★**St Ann's Head** with its lighthouse is the best vantage point from which to view supertankers on their way in and out of Milford Haven *(car park about 0.75mi/1km from the Head)*. It was at Mill Bay, just to the north, that Henry Tudor landed in 1485 at the start of his march to Bosworth Field. Close to the lighthouse, a dramatic cleft in the cliff is known as Cobblers Hole, the ruddy hue of the Old Red Sandstone contrasting with the bright greens and blues of grass and sea.

**Marloes Peninsula** – The treeless windswept landscape of the Dale and Marloes peninsulas is nevertheless very fertile, producing some of Pembrokeshire's famous crop of early potatoes. The beautiful stretch of **Marloes Sands** *(about 0.5mi/800m on foot from National Trust car park)* is pierced by jagged stumps of rock and guarded at the western end by the equally rugged Gateholm, an island at high tide.

★**Skomer Island and Skokholm Island** ⊘ – As their names suggest, both these islands were once the lurking place of Viking raiders, though Skomer has extensive remains of the fields and dwellings of the Iron Age people settled there a full millennium before the coming of the Norsemen. As befits their outstanding wildlife interest, both islands are now owned and managed by the Dyfed Wildlife Trust.

With its rugged coastline, Skomer (1.16sq mi/3km²) has been aptly described as a paradise for bird-watchers and enjoys protection under both British and European conservation legislation. It is the most important **seabird breeding site** in southern Britain, with puffins, guillemots, razorbills, fulmars, kittiwakes and various species of gull. Vast numbers of nocturnal Manx shearwaters make their burrows in the crumbly soil. Among other species there are also a few choughs and peregrine falcons.

Wales Tourist Board

St Govan's Chapel

The waters around t[...] island form a Mari[...] Nature Reserve, and ha[...]bour the second-largest c[...]ony of **grey seals** in Wale[...] Farming ceased on Skom[...] not long after the Seco[...] World War, and in ea[...] summer its plateau surfa[...] has a near-continuous c[...]ver of bluebells and r[...] campion.

Skokholm, much smalle[...] (240 acres/97ha), with [...] similar range of bird sp[...]cies, was the site in 19[...] of Britain's first bird c[...]servatory.

**St Brides Bay** – A numb[...] of coastal settlements fa[...] west across the bro[...] expanse of the bay. Lit[...] **Haven** is hemmed in [...] cliffs, while the expanding village of **Broad Haven** has a spacious sandy beach. Noll[...] **Haven** too has a sandy shore as well as remains of the installations once used in t[...] export of coal. **Newgale** is famous for its sands, its surf and its great storm beach [...] banked-up shingle (17ft/5m high) which threatens to overwhelm the coastal roa[...] The source of the multicoloured pebbles on the beach is the line of magnifice[...] cliffs which mark the northern limit of St Brides Bay. It is here that St Carad[...] lived as a hermit on a diet of fish; he was buried in St David's Cathedral. **Solva** is[...] long and deep inlet, a ria like that of Milford Haven *(see p 265)*, which makes [...] perfect little harbour for this sophisticated sailing village.

## NORTH COAST

### From St David's northeast to Cemaes Head

The main road from St David's *(see p 252)* to Fishguard *(see p 154)* runs w[...] inland, leaving much of this stretch of coast in pleasant isolation, though there a[...] substantial traces of former quarrying activity at **Abereiddy**, where a "blue lagoo[...] takes on the colour of the slate which used to be exported, and at the harbour [...] **Porthgain**, where stone and slate were quarried and bricks made.

★**Strumble Head and Pen Caer** – *See p 155.*

**Dinas Island** – Now permanently connected to the mainland by a narrow neck [...] land that was once a glacial meltwater channel, the island divides Fishguard B[...] from Newport Bay, offering superb views in all directions.

**Newport and Nevern** – *See p 155.*

Between Newport Bay and Cemaes Head is one of the most spectacular and lone[...] stretches of the National Park's cliff scenery. Access to the shore is rare, thoug[...] there is an inlet at the little cove at **Cwibwr** where there is a memorial to the writ[...] Wynford Vaughan-Thomas who made a gift of the bay to the National Trust. Th[...] coastal path leads north-east past the rocky cove at Pwllygranant, then up to th[...] top of the viciously contorted and colourful crags of **Pen-yr-Afr** ("Goat's Head"), [...] splendid place to be on a clear day, when the view extends from St David's Head [...] the south-west to far-off Snowdonia in the north.

## PRESELY HILLS (MYNYDD PRESELI)

The boundary of the National Park loops inland to include this mysterious upland, [...] series of massifs extending from Dinas Mountain (Mynydd Dinas) in the west to th[...] village of Crymych in the east (about 15mi/24km). The lovely wooded valley of th[...] **Gwaun** separates the western part of the area from the Presely Hills proper, whic[...] rise to the highest point in **Foel Cwmcerwyn** (1 760ft/536m). As well as the famou[...] burial chamber *(cromlech)* of **Pentre Ifan**★ *(see p 156)* and the hilltop settlement [...] **Carningli** *(see p 155)*, many other prehistoric sites stud the moorlands which ar[...] also marked by dramatic jagged projections of cairns or tors.

The nearly level walk across the top of Mynydd Preseli on an ancient trackwa[...] which once formed a route linking England with Ireland is an exhilarating experi[...]ence. One of the finest panoramas, from the cairn on **Cerrig Lladron** (1 535ft/468m[...] is accessible from Bwlch-Gwynt *(30min on foot there and back)* on the roa[...] between Haverfordwest and Cardigan (B 4329).

# PENARTH

Vale of Glamorgan – Population 20 448
Michelin Atlas p 16 or Map 403 K 29

Penarth Head overlooks Cardiff Bay from the west. At its foot, soon to be joined to the eastern side of the bay by the barrage, is an extensive marina, successor to the docks built in the mid-19C as part of the expansion of the coal exporting facilities in Cardiff. No more than a village at that time, Penarth grew rapidly, less as a harbour town than as an exclusive resort and residential area, with pier, promenade, and the mansions of millionaires.

**The Esplanade** – Recently refurbished, this attractive seaside promenade overlooking the pebbly beach was first laid out in 1883. From it the **pier** of 1894 extends into the Bristol Channel, minus the concert hall at its tip but still with a fine landward pavilion in Anglo-Indian style. The Esplanade is backed by characterful Edwardian buildings, a magnificent pub which was once the public baths, the Yacht Club, and the pretty Italian Gardens.

**Tourist Information Centre** – The Pier, The Esplanade, Penarth CF64 3AY ☎ 029 2070 8849.

**Beaches** – At Penarth Marina.

**Adjacent Sights** – See Barry, Cardiff, Castell Coch, Cowbridge, Glamorgan Coast, Llancaiach Fawr, Llandaff, Llantrisant, Museum of Welsh Life.

**Town Centre** – Penarth's curving suburban streets eventually lead to the town centre, which is linked to the seafront by Alexandra Gardens, one of the town's many parks. Windsor Arcade was built in 1898 very much on the same lines as the arcades of Cardiff city centre. The **Turner House Gallery** ⊘, a building of glaring red brick and terracotta, once housed the collection of James Pyke Thompson, but is now part of the National Gallery and stages changing exhibitions. From the start it opened on Sundays, in accordance with Thompson's desire to diffuse culture among the masses.

**St Augustine's Church** ⊘ – Built in 1866 as a replacement for the infinitely more modest medieval parish church which preceded it, St Augustine's is the work of William Butterfield (1814-1900), a master of neo-Gothic polychromatic architecture. The saddleback tower of the old church on this prominent site (230ft/70m above sea-level) had acted as an important landmark for mariners, and Butterfield repeated this feature, on a grander scale, in the new building. The austere exterior in grey limestone belies the exuberant use in the interior of materials in contrasting colours and patterns.

**Lavernock Point** – A clifftop walk leads south from the Esplanade to this headland. In 1897, the first radio message to be transmitted across water was sent from the island of Flat Holm (3mi/5km offshore) and received on Lavernock Point by Guglielmo Marconi.

## EXCURSION

**Cosmeston Medieval Village** ⊘ – *1.5mi/2.5km south of Penarth, off B 4267.* The nature trails and picnic areas of **Cosmeston Lakes Country Park** have been laid out around flooded quarry workings. From the visitor centre a boardwalk leads to a fascinating reconstruction of a real medieval settlement still undergoing archaeological investigation.
Of Norman origin, the village was given its name by the De Costentin family from the Cotentin peninsula in Normandy. It seems to have flourished until the middle of the 14C, when its demise was probably brought about by the Black Death. After excavation a number of buildings have been reconstructed in as authentic a way as possible, using the local limestone, timber and thatch, and already enable the visitor to experience something of the atmosphere of a 14C Norman-Welsh village, an impression helped by the convincingly costumed "inhabitants" and by domestic animals of breeds similar to those of medieval times. As well as cottages, a farmstead, a barn and a pigsty, there is a bakehouse where bread is sometimes baked. Other buildings will be added as excavations proceed, and an attempt has already been made to recreate medieval gardens.

*Respect the life of the countryside*
*Drive carefully on country roads*
*Protect wildlife, plants and trees*

# PENRHYN CASTLE★★

## Gwynedd
Michelin Atlas p 32 or Map 403 H 24

This huge country house disguised as a Norman castle is one of the 19C's most ambitious attempts to recreate the spirit of the Middle Ages. The castle's picturesque outline of towers, curtain walls and massive keep rises above the trees of the great park occupying the peninsula ("penrhyn") protruding into the Menai Strait just east of Bangor.

The man responsible for this fantastic building complex was George Hay Dawkins Pennant (1763-1840), heir to two fortunes, one based on Jamaican sugar plantations, the other on the highly productive Penrhyn slate quarries just inland. The quarries had been developed and linked by tramway to a purpose-built harbour at the north western corner of the park by Richard Pennant, First Baron Penrhyn and notable late-18C "Improver", who had also transformed the estate's ancient hall house into a castellated Gothick mansion. This edifice was incorporated into George Dawkins Pennant's new castle, begun c 1821 and completed about 13 years later. The architect was Thomas Hopper, who blended architectural motifs spanning three centuries of medieval development to produce an entirely convincing if highly imaginative interpretation of a medieval stronghold. The building occupies an area of one acre/nearly half a hectare, and has a frontage of 600ft/more than 180m. More than any comparable 19C structure, Penrhyn seems ready to withstand a siege, with a keep (124ft/38m high), based on that at Castle Hedingham in Essex, a high curtain wall and four massive towers complete with murder holes.

---

**Adjacent Sights** – See Anglesey, Bangor, Beaumaris, Betws-y-Coed, Bodnant Gardens, Conwy, Holyhead, Llanberis, Llanrwst, Plas Newydd, Snowdonia.

## TOUR ⊙

**Interior** – The main rooms of the castle surpass even its exterior in their exuberant late Georgian reinterpretation of the Middle Ages. Hopper excelled himself not only in his mastery of such imperious spaces as the **Grand Hall** but in his attention to detail. Much of the furniture is his but the most skilled craftsmen were used to carve the woodwork of panelling and ceiling or chisel the stonework of corbel and capital. The National Trust has been at great pains to recreate the carpets, wallpapers and stencilling which contributed so much to the richness of the original decorative scheme.

The intimate passageway of the Entrance Gallery gives little hint of the vastness of the **Grand Hall**. Described by one visitor as "about as homely as a... railway terminus", it does indeed form a kind of interchange between keep and main part of the building, and would have been at its best when filled with guests and servants and other castle denizens hurrying along its side passageway and upper gallery. Its clustered columns, round-headed arches and rich Norman mouldings set the tone for the rest of the interior, as does Hopper's octagonal tilt-top table.

The **Library**, marginally more intimate, incorporates part of the original medieval house, while the **Drawing Room** occupies the position of the former great hall.

The Library, Penrhyn Castle

The **Ebony Room** has furniture made both of real ebony and of ebonised woods. Here is the first major painting from the castle's **collection of Old Masters** which became the most important of its kind in North Wales; from the studio of Dieric Bouts, it represents the *Virgin and Child with St Luke*.

The Grand Staircase is another tour de force by Hopper, rising to a skylight reminiscent of a rose window. The fantastic carving of grotesque heads and human hands must have provoked many a Gothick shudder, to which anthropomorphic lamp brackets added an extra touch of horror.

The **State Bedroom** has a Norman four-poster bed (pure invention by Hopper) and a stately dressing room and WC.

In the gallery and passageway, pictures of Port Penrhyn and Jamaica are reminders of how all the ostentation was financed.

A suite of rooms in the **Keep** includes a great tombstone-like bed of slate, NOT slept in by Queen Victoria when she stayed here in 1859, though the Prince of Wales apparently made use of the brass bed specially bought for him in 1894. The India Room is misnamed, its delightful hand-painted wallpaper being Chinese.

The **Chapel** continues the remorseless Norman theme, less amusing in this starker ecclesiastical setting. In the aisles of the Grand Hall there is remarkable stained glass, the work of Thomas Willement, who captured the character of medieval glass with great fidelity.

Together with the **Breakfast Room**, the **Dining Room**, with a wonderful carved coffer ceiling, was designed to show off the picture collection, which includes paintings by Rembrandt, Canaletto, Jan Steen, Van de Velde and Guardi. Henry Thomson's portrait of Richard Pennant shows this "Improver" pointing to a map of the mountain road he built into Snowdonia, which became the basis of Telford's later Holyhead route.

**Outbuildings** – Beyond the extensive domestic quarters are equally extensive outbuildings which included brewhouse, soup kitchen and ice-house. The stables have been used to house the **Industrial Railway Museum**, featuring locomotives and rolling stock from the Penrhyn and Dinorwic quarries as well as steam engines from other industries. *Fire Queen* (1848) belongs to an early generation of such machines, with big driving wheels and no protection whatsoever for the crew.

**Grounds** – By the late 19C the Penrhyn Estate extended over a great area (72 000 acres/29 140ha) of Caernarfonshire; they included more than 600 farms, as well as the enormous quarries which at their height were yielding profits (at today's values) of £4 million annually. Progressive forestry was practised over the estate as a whole, while in the park itself exotic conifers were added to the existing native oaks and other trees. A staff of 30 helped the long-serving head gardener Walter Speed (c 1835-1921) produce grapes, nectarines, figs, peaches and pineapples.

The castle's strategic position on the route to Holyhead and Dublin resulted in many members of the Irish Ascendancy staying here, while trees were planted by the occasional royal visitor, like Queen Victoria (a Sierra redwood in 1859) or the Queen of Romania (a Caucasian fir in 1890).

The **park** is of the most expansive kind, tree-studded sweeps of grass coming right up to the castle walls without any intermediate terracing, very much in the (by the 1820s) old-fashioned manner of Capability Brown. Formality is to be found down the slopes, in the **walled garden** named after an early-20C Lady Penrhyn, where there are many unusual plants.

The chapel which served the original house was made into a garden feature in the late 18C; its ruin, with gravestones of family dogs, stands atop a rise.

The park is guarded by a long wall of rubble topped with Penrhyn slate coping stones and entered by an impressive gatehouse. Near the tip of the promontory, Richard Pennant built a sea bath with heated water. On the quayside of his harbour at **Port Penrhyn**, on the edge of the built-up area of Bangor, is a famous circular 12-seater gentlemen's lavatory resembling a dovecot.

# PLAS NEWYDD ★★
### Anglesey
Michelin Atlas p 32 or Map 403 H 24

In the late 18C the original hall house on the Anglesey shore of the Menai Strait was transformed into a palatial country residence by the Earl of Uxbridge. The severe, grey stone exterior conceals rooms of the greatest interest, one of them decorated with the Plas Newydd mural, the masterpiece of the inter-war artist Rex Whistler (1905-44).

**Setting** – The Plas Newydd estate includes 1.5mi/2.5km of the Menai coastline. The house is sited on a shelf of land cut into the slope sweeping down to this noble stretch of water, with the whole of Snowdonia as an incomparable backdrop. The splendour of the situation was enhanced at the very end of the 18C by the landscape designer **Humphry Repton**, who added trees which have now reached their full magnificence. Visitors can savour this splendid setting to the full as they approach the house via a long and curving path leading downhill from the National Trust's shop and café in the former Dairy. The path also reveals a fine example of one of Anglesey's many Neolithic monuments, a cromlech, seen against the background of the extensive stable buildings. The waterside is defined by a battlemented wall with bastions and a jetty while later additions to the grounds include an Italianate garden and extensive plantings of rhododendrons.

> **Boat Trip** ⊘ – From the jetty directly in front of the house (by the 3 cannons) the *Snowdon Queen* makes a return trip *(40min)* northwest as far as the Britannia Bridge; commentary on the landmarks on the shore of the .Menai Straits, one of the most scenic and romantic waterways in Europe.
>
> **Adjacent Sights** – See Anglesey, Bangor, Beaumaris, Caernarvon, Holyhead, Llanberis, Penrhyn Castle, Snowdonia.

## TOUR ⊘

Tentative "improvements" were made to the house in the course of the 18C but it was the Earl of Uxbridge's employment of **James Wyatt** and Joseph Potter in the 1790s that gave the house its present overall character, a comfortable synthesis of the neo-Classical and Gothick styles. Some further remodelling took place in the 1930s. In the ownership of the National Trust since 1976, Plas Newydd contains a wealth of furniture, paintings and portraits. Entry is via the galleried and vaulted **Gothick Hall**, which gives a foretaste of the adjacent **Music Room**, successor to the original Great Hall and one of the finest interiors in Wyatt's cool reinterpretation of medieval style, though the execution of his plans was by Potter. In 1832, aged 13, the future Queen Victoria is supposed to have "danced the gallop" here and "stayed up till near nine".

**Lady Anglesey's bedroom** *(first floor)* is the creation of one of the leading designers of the 1930s, Sibyl Colefax, while **Lord Anglesey's quarters**, with flying tester bedstead, reflect his axiom that "every bathroom should have a bedroom".

In the red and white **Octagon Room** *(ground floor)* the informal taste of the Angleseys in the 1930s is seen again. The **Saloon** too was refurnished at this time, though it is dominated by huge pastoral scenes painted by the late 18C-early 19C Flemish artist Ommeganck. A mahogany architect's table is used to display drawings of the Menai bridges.

The **Rex Whistler Room** is preceded by an exhibition of the graceful and witty work of this tragically short-lived artist, who was killed in action shortly after D-Day in 1944. The displays include book illustrations, stage designs, rebuses and reversible faces. Among the larger pictures is one of Plas Newydd with the Marquess of Anglesey and his bicycle, and a canvas entitled *Girl with Red Rose*, a portrait of Lady Caroline Paget with whom Whistler was in love. All these delights fade however in comparison with the **Rex Whistler Mural** (58ft/18m) stretching along the wall of the **dining room**. The talented Whistler was a welcome guest in country

Detail of mural by Rex Whistler

house circles, and had already decorated a number of interiors as well as the restaurant of the Tate Gallery. His Plas Newydd mural, "whimsy carried to extremes", extends along the whole of one wall and shows a visionary landscape of city, coast and mountains in which architectural features like Windsor Castle co-exist with numerous family and personal references. A cigarette burns where spectacles have been dropped and a book left unread, while a soulful Whistler himself poses with a broom. Neptune has abandoned his crown and trident and left a trail of watery footprints leading towards the dining table.

The **Cavalry Museum** *(in the former servants' quarters)* displays one of the very first articulated wooden legs, the property of the **First Marquess of Anglesey**, Field Marshal Henry William (Bayly) Paget, Second Earl of Uxbridge (1768-1854), a larger-than-life figure, who was undoubtedly the most famous owner of Plas Newydd.

Considered to be *"le plus beau garçon d'Angleterre"*, he kept his looks into old age, marrying twice and siring 18 children. A hero of Waterloo, he suffered the loss of a leg through grapeshot, which evinced from him the deathless remark to the Duke of Wellington *"By God, sir, I've lost my leg!"*, to which the Duke responded, before getting on with the business in hand, *"By God, sir, so you have!"*. The Marquess's courage is commemorated by the great column overlooking the Britannia Bridge.

Here too are mementoes of another and rather different Marquess of Anglesey. Nicknamed "Toppy" by his friends, the **Fifth Marquess** (1875-1905) indulged his taste for drama by converting the chapel into a theatre and organising elaborate productions of which he was invariably the lavishly costumed star. His extravagance threatened the family fortune despite the disposal of many of Plas Newydd's treasures in the course of a 40-day auction in 1904. He died in hiding from his creditors in Monte Carlo.

# PLAS NEWYDD★

## Denbighshire
Michelin Atlas p 33 or Map 403 K 25 – Local map see p 254

is highly individual black-and-white house on the slopes just to the south of ngollen was for 50 years the home of by far the most famous residents of the ighbourhood, an extraordinary couple of Irish cousins, known as the Ladies of ngollen.

**dies of Llangollen** – The long relationship between **Lady Eleanor Butler** and **Sarah nsonby** caught the imagination of Regency society, which regarded their "model of rfect friendship" with a mixture of curiosity and affection. The couple, both from e upper reaches of Anglo-Irish society, first met when the orphaned Sarah, in her rly teens, was languishing in boarding school. Spinster Eleanor, 16 years Sarah's nior, later came under pressure from her family to become a nun, while Sarah had deal with the unwelcome attentions of her male guardian. A first attempt to elope, sguised as men, was frustrated but eventually, in 1778, the pair were able to leave eland. Finding the Vale of Llangollen "the beautifullest country in the world", they set house here with the ostensible aim of leading a "life of sweet and delicious tirement", though there is little evidence that they made any serious effort to elude e fame which their relationship, their mannish dress and their general sociability ought them. Eminent visitors were welcomed and an extensive correspondence aintained, which kept them in touch with "the tattle and scandal of the world". The ign of the uncrowned Queens of Llangollen lasted for half a century; Lady Eleanor ed in 1829, aged 90, and Sarah followed her partner to the grave in Llangollen urchyard two years later.

## TOUR ⏱

**House** – The Ladies were enthused by the Gothicising spirit of their age. The house, which had been an unpretentious three-bay stone cottage, was extended and fitted out

> **Adjacent Sights** – See Bala, Betws-y-Coed, Chirk Castle, Erddig, Llanfyllin, Llangollen, Ruthin, Valley Crucis Abbey, Lake Vyrnwy, Wrexham.

with pointed windows, stained glass, and above all, old **oak carving**. Visitors were encouraged to contribute fragments, and the effect, particularly in the porch, the entrance vestibule and stairs, is that of an oaky grotto.

Other rooms include the Library, evocative of the Ladies' bookishness and with the only authentic portrait of them, the State Bedchamber to accommodate their frequent visitors, and the Ladies' own Bedchamber, no longer containing their "Capital Four-Post Bedstead" which was auctioned off in 1832.

A later owner, General Yorke, promoted the cult of the Ladies and added much oak himself, as well as the external timbering, though the extension he built was subsequently demolished.

Wales Tourist Board

Exuberance in oak, Plas Newydd

**Gardens** – The Ladies' passions extended to gardening, and in their day the grounds were a model of "picturesque" taste, with rustic pathways leading to the deep and ferny dell of the River Cyflymen. The Gorsedd circle on the lawn was added at the beginning of the 20C; together with tall beech trees, topiary and distant view of Castell Dinas Brân *(north of Llangollen – see p 191)*, it conveys an image of Romantic seclusion of which the Ladies might well have approved, though suburban houses lie just beyond the boundary.

# PORTHCAWL

Bridgend – Population 16 099
Michelin Atlas p 15 and Map 403 I 29

With crowded caravan parks focused on the Coney Beach amusement park and a more genteel west end whose tone is set by Rest Bay and the Royal Porthcawl golf links, Porthcawl epitomises the contrasts to be found in many Welsh seaside resorts.

The town's rise began in the early 19C when a tramroad was built to link the expanding iron and coal industries in the valleys to the north to a new harbour at Pwll Cawl. Features from this era – like the big stone shed on the quayside, or the lighthouse and the short section of tramway on the breakwater – can still be seen but the port of Porthcawl never really flourished, and was killed off at the turn of the century by the far bigger docks at Barry *(see p 88)* and Port Talbot *(see p 238)*.

The resort's late-Victorian and Edwardian streets focus on the curving **Promenade**, laid out in 1887 and recently refurbished with great elan. The most conspicuous activity today is surfing.

**Newton** – The villages of Nottage and Newton were the nuclei from which Porthcawl grew. Once a little port in its own right, Newton has an attractive village green on which stands the mainly 15C **Church of St John the Baptist** ⊘ whose battlemented tower has a saddleback roof. Inside is a stone pulpit, crudely carved, with beardless Christ.

**Tourist Information Centre** – Old Police Station, John Street, Porthcawl CF3 3DT ☎ 01656 786 639 or 782 211.
McArthur Glen Design Outlet Village, The Derwen, Bridgend CF32 9SU ☎ 01656 654 906; Fax 01656 646 523.

**Beaches** – At Rest Bay.

**Adjacent Sights** – See Cowbridge, Glamorgan Coast, Gower Peninsula, Laugharne, Margam Park, Neath, Port Talbot, Swansea.

## EXCURSIONS

**Kenfig** – *3mi/5km N of Porthcawl.* A medieval borough of some substance was overwhelmed by the violent storms which plagued the South Wales coast in the 15C. The town now lies buried beneath the extensive **sand dunes** known as **Kenfig Burrows**, with only the stump of its castle visible. To the north, the horizon is dominated by the industrial installations of Port Talbot.
The dunes are a **nature reserve** ⊙ of international significance, with a large fresh-water pool, breeding and migrant birds, dragonflies and damselflies, and over 600 flowering plants including fen orchids. There are boardwalks, bird hides and a visitor centre.

**Cefn Cribwr Ironworks** – *1mi/1.6km NE of Porthcawl by A 4229 and A 428; in Pyle turn right onto B 4281.* Industrial archaeology and nature are combined on a trail that leads through the Waun Cimla Country Park to the remains of the 18C iron-works developed by John Bedford, a Midlands entrepreneur. The coke ovens and charge house were abandoned in the 19C and now stand in romantic ruin among the undergrowth; panels explain their original purpose. The trail continues along the dis-used railway track that once carried coal and minerals from Caerau to Porthcawl.

**Merthyr Mawr** – *7mi/11km E of Porthcawl by A 4106, A 48 and minor roads.* The picturesque thatched cottages of this out-of-the-way village were built and the little church rebuilt in the mid-19C by the local landowner, who succeeded perfectly in creating a tranquil and timeless effect. Beyond the village are the evocative remains of Candleston Castle, a fortified manor house. It guards the approach to **Merthyr Mawr Warren**, a vast tract (600 acres/250ha) of mountainous sand dunes resting on a ridge (200ft/60m) of limestone, which makes it the second-highest such system in Europe, with a rich variety of wildlife.

**Bridgend** – *6mi/10km E of Porthcawl by A 4106.* Undistinguished architecturally, busy Bridgend is the urban centre for much of the western Vale of Glamorgan and the valley of Ogwr Fawr to the north.
Its origins go back to the early 11C when a trio of Norman castles was built to guard the Vale against Welsh incursions from the west. Bridgend's stronghold, now a ruin, was named **Newcastle**. Its **gateway** is a fine example of Norman decorative work.
The more extensive, mostly 14C, remains of **Coity Castle** can be seen in the village of Coity *(2mi/3km NE of Porthcawl).*

**Bryngarw Country Park** ⊙ – *6mi/10km NE of Porthcawl by A 4229, M 4 (E) to Junction 36, A 4061 and A 4065.* The focal point of this park (113 acres/46ha) is an unpretentious 18C house, built by Morgan Popkin Traherne and recently con-verted into a hotel and restaurant. Trails lead through woodland to a Japanese garden, planted by a later Traherne, and along the fast-flowing Garw (Rough River), known as Black River in the days when valley industries polluted its waters.

**Ewenny Priory Church** ⊙ – *8mi/12km E of Porthcawl by A 4106 and A 48 and S by B 4265 and a minor road.* This Norman priory retains its church and the defensive walls of its precinct in a setting of manor house and farmyard. Never in the forefront of ecclesiastical life, the church escaped the zeal of 19C restorers and remains a fine example of untouched Norman architecture.
The priory's defences seem to have been built more for show than for function, though they are imposing enough, with towers and gatehouses; the great central tower of the church is battlemented. The church was built between 1116 and 1120, while the priory itself was founded in 1141 as a cell of the great Benedictine abbey of Gloucester; the austere splendour of the church's architecture may be due to the influence of the Gloucester masons. The nave with its massive circular piers has always served as the parish church, but it is the **east end** *(separate entrance)* with round-arched windows and ceiling where the finest Norman work is concentrated.

**Ogmore Castle** – *10mi/16km E of Porthcawl by A 4106, A 48, B 4265 and B 4524.* This was the third of the castles built by the Normans to guard the western approaches to the Vale of Glamorgan. The most prominent feature of the ruins is the west wall of the keep (40ft/12m high). A roofless 14C building may have been the manorial courthouse. Ogmore is visited less for its archaeological interest than for its attractive setting on the Ogmore River, overlooking the meadows which are linked by a fine set of stepping stones.

# PORTHMADOG
Gwynedd – Population 1 675
Michelin Atlas p 32 or Map 403 H 25
Local map p 261

Porthmadog recalls the name of its founder, **William Madocks** (1773-1828), as well as echoing that of Prince Madog, legendary discoverer of America, who is supposed to have set sail from the estuary here in the 12C three centuries before Columbus. It reached its peak of maritime activity in the decade 1850 to 1860. In season it is a busy place, its long High Street crowded with holiday traffic making its way around the southern rim of Snowdonia, its harbour full of pleasure craft. A plume of steam announces the approach of a train along the ruler-straight embankment known as the **Cob**, for Porthmadog is the terminus of Wales' foremost narrow-gauge railway.

---

**Tourist Information Centre** – Station Yard, Porthmadog LL49 9HW
☎ 01766 512 981; porthmadog.tic@gwynedd.gov.uk

**Craft Centres** – **Snowdon Mill Art and Craft Centre** ⊘ *(signed from town centre)* is a cooperative run by makers. For woollen goods visit **Brynkir Woollen Mill** ⊘ *(3.5mi/5km by A 487)*.

**Adjacent Sights** – See Beddgelert, Blaenau Ffestiniog, Caernarfon, Criccieth, Harlech, Lleyn Peninsula, Portmeirion, Pwllheli, Snowdonia.

---

**Porthmadog Maritime Museum** ⊘ – *Quayside*. An old slate shed houses the exhibits which trace the development of the harbour in the 1820s, the transition from sail to steam in the 1880s, and the *Western Ocean Yachts*, which contributed largely to the town's 19C prosperity; they were built in Porthmadog between 1860 and 1913, to carry slate to Germany and saltfish to Newfoundland and Labrador. There are displays of shipboard tools, sailing rigs and navigation instruments.

★★**Ffestiniog Railway** ⊘ – William Madocks built the Cob in 1811 in order to turn the broad estuary of the Glaslyn into profitable farmland. He thereby provided a convenient route by which a horse-powered tramway could bring its wagons loaded with slate from the Ffestiniog mines directly to the waiting sea-going ships in the harbour. Riding in "dandy-carts" on the downward journey, the horses hauled the empty wagons back up the line from 1836 until 1863, when the company acquired

Crossing the Cob, Ffestiniog Railway

its first steam locomotives. By the 1920s, the Ffestiniog was making as much money from tourists as from slate, indulging in publicity which exaggerated the Alpine character of the indubitably scenic Vale of Ffestiniog. The Second World War killed both the slate and the tourist trade. The line was closed in 1946 but, thanks to the efforts of dedicated enthusiasts, the section across the Cob was reopened in 1955 and finally reached Blaenau Ffestiniog again in 1982.

The terminus of the Ffestiniog Railway, **Porthmadog Harbour station**, has an air of importance which the mainline station at the other end of town has lost altogether. Though largely built by volunteer labour, the line is run professionally, with automated signalling and crossings. Long trains wait in the station, perhaps headed by one of the ingenious double-ended Fairlie locomotives which enabled the railway to haul exceptionally heavy slate trains on what is only a narrow-gauge line (2ft/600mm). The extensive station buildings include a small **Museum**; its star exhibit, apart from an O-4-0 tank engine, is a railway hearse.

The ride across the Cob is exhilarating enough but better still is the journey ever higher through the wonderful woodlands of the **Vale of Ffestiniog**. **Plas Halt** gives access to the magnificent grounds of **Plas Tan-y-Bwlch** ⊘ *(see below)*.

Near Dduallt the line reaches open mountain country and gains height by the only **rail spiral** in Britain. The barrier created by the construction of the **Tan-y-Grisiau power station** and reservoir has been triumphantly overcome, and, 13.5mi/22km after leaving Porthmadog, the line carries its passengers into what was its heartland and *raison d'être*, the slate town of **Blaenau Ffestiniog★**.

**Welsh Highland Railway** ⊘ – Porthmadog has a second "Great Little Railway", part of the short-lived narrow-gauge line linking Porthmadog, Beddgelert and Caernarfon, which opened in the 1920s and closed soon after. Here visitors can see a station and depot, and ride a train *(45min)* on the short section of line which has been reconstructed. There are plans to reopen much more of the original line, providing public transport for inhabitants and tourists alike.

## EXCURSIONS

**Tremadog** – *1.25mi/2km N by A 487*. Before entering on the great enterprise of closing off the Glaslyn estuary with the Cob, William Madocks founded this urbane little settlement as a staging post on the prospective London–Ireland route via the never-to-be-built harbour at Porth Dinllaen *(see p 202)*. Its sombre stone buildings, their sobriety relieved by plenty of white paint, cluster in orderly fashion around a generously scaled market place. This was the birthplace of TE Lawrence, Lawrence of Arabia.

**Plas Tan-y-Bwlch** ⊘ – *7mi/11km E of Porthmadog by A 496; turn left (sign) to car park*. The house *(private)*, which dates from the Tudor to the Victorian period and is the residential study centre of the Snowdonia National Park, overlooks a singular and magnificent garden laid out in the "picturesque" style on the steeply sloping north bank of the River Dwyryd. It was begun in 1789 by William Oakeley who created a water garden among the natural fissured rocks and enlarged the huge terraces which provide views of the Vale of Ffestiniog. The planting includes rhododendron, magnolia and imports from Chile; among the parkland trees are the Western Red and Himalayan Cedar as well as native oaks.

*FOLLOW THE COUNTRY CODE*
*Guard against all risk of fire*
*Fasten all gates*
*Keep dogs under proper control*
*Keep to the paths across farmland*
*Avoid damaging fences, hedges and walls*
*Leave no litter*
*Safeguard water supplies*
*Protect wildlife, wild plants and trees*
*Go carefully on country roads*
*Respect the life of the countryside*

# PORTMEIRION★★★
## Gwynedd
### Michelin Atlas p 32 or Map 403 H 25

A leading luminary in the movement to conserve the environment, the architect **Si Clough Williams-Ellis** (1883-1978) devoted much of a long lifetime to creating his own idea of the perfect environment, the dream village of Portmeirion, a serious ye inimitably playful attempt to show "that one could develop a very beautiful site without defiling it, and given sufficient loving care, one could even improve on wha God had provided".

Portmeirion is almost impossible to categorise. It functions as a tourist village, accommodating overnight guests in its hotel and in many of the buildings around the site Day visitors come in large numbers, browsing among the books, Portmeirion pottery and other tasteful souvenirs on sale in several shops, patronising the café and ice cream parlour but mostly just enjoying the sensations of being in a place which is unique.

The village owes much to its site, a short and steep-sided valley running down through woods to the sweeping sands of the estuary of the River Dwyryd, but much more to the spirit of its creator. Sir Clough embraced modernity, building the occasional "progressive" structure such as the concrete-and-glass beach café at nearby Criccieth *(see p 143)*, but seems to have revelled more in the Baroque and Rococo, with its love of colour, theatricality, visual virtuosity, and of life as celebration and festival. The result, at Portmeirion, is akin to the sparkling fantasies of Mediterranean landscape and architecture conjured up in the murals painted at Plas Newydd by Rex Whistler *(see p 230)*.

Portmeirion

## TOUR ⊙

The approach to the village is via a long drive with trees and shrubs arranged to heighten a sense of anticipation. Even the car park, laid out on an irregular pattern and densely planted, reveals the hand of a master landscaper. The sense of arrival is further enhanced by passing through more woodland, then through the archways of **Gatehouse** and **Bridge House**. The eye has already been deceived by Sir Clough's illusionism and use of false perspective into thinking that these arches are much larger than they really are. The Gatehouse's mural by the Austrian artist Hans Feilbusch is only one of many decorative delights with which the village is embellished.

The **Belvedere Lookout** reveals the glorious setting of estuary and mountain, its scale in such contrast to the intimacy and intricacy of the village. At **Battery Square**, the full richness of Portmeirion begins to tell. Here are some of the earliest buildings on the site, dating from the late 1920s and early 1930s.

Beyond, dominating the Citadel area, is the **Campanile** (80ft/24m high) but looking much taller, drawing the eye skywards, then allowing it to fall to the **Piazza**, which forms the green heart of the village, the best place in which to sit and soak up the architectural wizardry on display all around. The skyline to the left of Bridge House is broken by the **Pantheon**, its dome originally made from plywood, its supports from rolled cardboard, while a nearby turret is crowned by a cupola fashioned from an upturned pig-swill boiler. Sir Clough's ambitions frequently outran his means and such expedients were common.

Below the Pantheon is the 18C **Bristol Colonnade**, rescued from that city following bomb damage, and mischievously decorated with a small bust of Sir Clough by Welsh sculptor Jonah Jones. Uphill, beyond the other delightful structures scattered along the valley rim, is a miniature **Triumphal Arch**. The Piazza is defined at its lower end by a **Gothick Pavilion**, at its upper end by the **Gloriette**, built, like much of the village, for "no useful purpose save that of looking both handsome and jolly". What seem to be jolly statues atop its flanking pillars are no more than cut-outs.

Beyond the buildings flanking the Piazza is the most substantial example of Sir Clough's magpie nature and his desire to rescue "fallen buildings", the **Town Hall**, built from fragments of a demolished Jacobean mansion.

The main path leads downwards towards the **Hotel** and the shoreline, with its **Stone Boat** moored by the quayside. Further on still are a **Camera Obscura** and **Lighthouse**.

**Portmeirion Peninsula** – Portmeirion is built on a peninsula with the now-forgotten and rather inauspicious name of Aber Iâ – Frozen Estuary.

In the 1840s, an ancestor of Sir Clough built the mock-medieval **Castell Deudraeth**. All traces of its predecessor, a real Welsh castle, were later erased "lest the ruins should become known and attract visitors to the place".

Caton Haig, a collector and breeder of famous **rhododendrons**, who was a tenant under Sir Osmond Williams, planted an extensive **woodland garden** known as the **Gwyllt**, through which Sir Clough threaded a network of footpaths (20mi/32km).

## EXCURSIONS

**Plas Brondanw** ⊙ – *4mi NE of Portmeirion by A 487; in Penrhyndeudraeth turn left to Garreg; after passing the Brondanw Arms turn right (sign) at fortified arch; 2min on foot from car park (left) to garden entrance.*

The **garden** of Sir Clough Williams-Ellis' own home, set on the steep bank of a narrow river, is composed of terraces decorated with topiary work and divided in places by pleached hedges into smaller compartments. The house *(private)* was rebuilt in 1953 after a fire. On the opposite side of the road, a path leads uphill *(10min on foot)*, to a **waterfall** which flows down a steep rock face into a basin; the path continues across a field to a **folly** built in the form of a ruined tower.

### Portmeirion on film

The unusual and varied architectural styles of Portmeirion make it an ideal film set. One of the earliest films shot here was *Kipps* (1941) based on the novel by HG Wells.

The most famous is **The Prisoner** (1966-67), a TV series starring Patrick McGoohan, produced by Everyman Films for ITC, which has spawned an appreciation society and of which videocassettes are on sale in the Prisoner Shop and Information Centre.

Portmeirion has also featured in *Doctor Who*, *Citizen Smith*, *Brideshead Revisited*, *Under Suspicion* and episodes of *Bread* and *Sorry!*.

# PORT TALBOT

Playing Vesuvius in the fanciful comparison of Swansea Bay with the Bay of Naple
the cooling towers, chimneys and smoky pall of Port Talbot dominate the easter
shore of this splendid coastal crescent with its backing of hills and mountains.

Now one of the largest towns in Wales, Port Talbot is descended from **Aberavon** whic
claimed to be the only borough of native Welsh origin in the south of the countr
Metals were being worked here in the early 18C. In 1834 a floating dock was built t
serve the growing iron and copper industries in Cwm Afan to the northeast, and give
the name Port Talbot after Christopher Rice Talbot of nearby Margam Park *(see
205)*, who financed it. The port was extended at the end of the 19C, mainly for th
export of coal. In 1972 a deep-water harbour was added to take the bulk ore-carrier
supplying the vast **steelworks** built after the Second World War.

No traveller heading westward out of the Vale of Glamorgan can fail to become awar
of Port Talbot. Squeezed into the narrow strip of land between the shore and abruptl
rising hills, the main railway line and motorway are forced into intimate contact wit
the town. The steelworks stretch for nearly 5mi/8km, accompanied by a number c
more recent industrial plants. The industrial picture is completed to the west b
extensive chemical works, while the housing estates, in which most of Port Talbot
population live sprawl between the small town centre and **Aberavon Sands**, which ar
backed by a promenade.

## Cricket at sea

In 1993 a brief cricket match was held about seven miles offshore from Port
Talbot on a sandbank. The match lasted for about an hour and a half, long
enough for each team to have an innings of about 13 overs. A batsman who hit
the ball into the water scored six but was also declared out. The match was
staged to raised money for charity. The sandbank, known as the Scarweather
Sands, is exposed very seldom – about once every five years – at exceptionally
low tides.

## EXCURSION

**Afan Argoed Countryside Centre and Welsh Miners' Museum** ⊙ *– 6mi/10km
NE of Port Talbot by A 4107.* Once busy with metalworking and coal mining, th
deeply incised valley of the Afan has undergone dramatic transformation since th
closing of its last deep pit in 1970. Although the valley is one of the shortest i
South Wales – a mere 12mi/19km from its head at Bwlch yr Afan to the sea a
Port Talbot – it was the scene of some of the most intense industrial activity in th
country, its isolation remedied by the construction of railway tunnels linking it t
Neath, the Vale of Glamorgan, and, most spectacularly, to the Rhondda via th
longest bore (10 329ft/3 148m) in Wales.

Systematic **afforestatio**
began in the late 1930
and has not only clad th
once wild and open upland
with the country's mos
extensive man-made fores
– **Coed Morgannwg** – but ha
softened the scars of indus
try in the valley itself. Th

> **Adjacent Sights** – See Glamorgan Coast,
> Gower Peninsula, Llanelli, Margam Park,
> Neath, Porthcawl, Swansea.

most imposing industrial monument is the **Pont Fawr Aqueduct** at Pontrhydyfen, a
massive four-arched structure of 1827, which was used not only for water supply
but for navigation and to carry a railway.

The modern **visitor centre** in the Afan Forest Park offers good views over the new
landscapes of the valley. It is also the half-way point along the trail known as the
**Coed Morgannwg Way** (32mi/43km). This footpath runs from the lush parklands o
Margam in the south to the superb viewpoint of Craig-y-Llyn beyond the head o
the Rhondda Valley.

Most visitors come here to experience the **Welsh Miners' Museum**. Set up on loca
initiative, this tells the often-poignant social and human story of the valley's mining
communities with documentary material, reconstructions of how families lived and
worked, and with mining equipment displayed in its new and leafy setting.

*With this guide
use the appropriate Michelin Maps (scale 1 : 400 000)
The common symbols make planning easier*

# POWIS CASTLE ★★★

Powys

Michelin Map p 25 or Map 403 K 26

One of Wales' grandest residences, this superb building in warm red stone stands atop its ridge, buttressed by its Baroque terraced gardens, among the few to have survived anywhere in Great Britain.

## HISTORICAL NOTES

The origins of the castle are obscure, though it almost certainly began as a timber fortification of the rulers of the medieval principality of Powys. By the end of the 13C century it had been rebuilt in stone and had taken on much of its present appearance. It was at this time that its lord, **Gruffudd ap Gwynwynwyn**, was obliged by Edward I to renounce his royal titles and accept the title of Baron de la Pole (= Pool or Powis). In 1587 the castle passed into the hands of **Sir Edward Herbert**, son of the Earl of Pembroke, who was responsible for much of the remodelling of the interior including the building of the Long Gallery. In 1688 his descendant, the Catholic Marquess of Powis, went into exile in France with James II, and lived at St Germain-en-Laye.

In 1722 the castle was returned to the family, into which **Edward Clive**, son of **Clive of India**, later married. In 1804 Clive was granted the title of Earl of Powis, and spent much of his huge fortune in restoring the neglected castle and filling it with fine paintings and furniture as well as with the family's unsurpassed private collection of Indian artefacts. It was at this time that Sir Robert Smirke was employed to romanticise the castle's outline. At the beginning of the 20C another eminent architect, **F Bodley**, undertook major alterations, while the Fourth Earl's wife embellished the gardens. In 1952 Powis Castle was given to the National Trust.

## TOUR ⊘

**Exterior** – The sandstone castle, known justifiably in Welsh as Y Castell Coch ("The Red Castle") enjoys a magnificent position on the

> **Adjacent Sights** – See Llanfyllin, Machynlleth, Montgomery, Newtown, Lake Vyrnwy, Welshpool.

gritstone ridge which rises grandly over extensive parklands. Seen from the lower ridge to the southeast, its outline, with chimneys, battlements and regular window patterning, is unmistakable. The castle's core is arranged around a small inner court. The principal entrance up to the late 18C was the East Gate facing towards Welshpool, but the main approach today is from the west, through a narrow medieval gateway and on to the great **forecourt** with its splendid Baroque lead statue of Fame. To the left is the Ballroom Range, originally the castle's curtain wall; to the right a breathtaking prospect of the gardens and park and the Severn Vale. The west entrance is dominated by the bulky twin towers of the keep.

**Interior** – This comprises what is often considered to be the finest suite of rooms in Wales.

**Ground Floor** – An appropriately grandiose beginning is provided by the **Great Staircase** (c 1675-85), probably the work of William Winde who had built the family's London house. The *grisaille* wall paintings of the lower hall seem pale in comparison with the ceiling, painted by Verrio in imitation of *The Triumph of Venice* by Veronese. Verrio's pupil Gerard Lanscroon was responsible for the wall paintings.

To the left of the staircase is a private dining room with a Brussels tapestry, while to the right is the much larger **Dining Room**, possibly on the site of the medieval great hall, with numerous family portraits by Romney and Reynolds among others. The room's Elizabethan atmosphere is almost entirely due to Bodley's skill in designing authentic-seeming panelling and plasterwork.

**First Floor** – Rows of books climb high on the tall walls of the **Library**, the paintings even higher. The ceiling painting is by Lanscroon, the delicate **miniature** of **Lord Herbert of Cherbury** by Isaac Oliver (d 1617). It shows the subject resting pensively in a landscape not wholly unlike that to be seen through the windows of several of the rooms on this floor.

The **Oak Drawing Room** was the centrepiece of Sir Edward Herbert's late-16C scheme of improvements, though again the splendid plasterwork and linenfold panelling is the work of Bodley. There is an unmistakable portrait of Charles II by Kneller and a Bellotto of the River Adige at Verona, bought by Clive of India in 1771.

The **Gateway Room** serves as a family museum.

The **State Bedroom**, an "extraordinary and extravagant casket of a room" (R Haslam), is unique in Britain in having the Versailles arrangement of a balustrade protecting the bed area from the crowd attending the levee of its eminent occupant.

The magnificent T-shaped **Long Gallery** is the only one of Sir Edward Herbert
rooms to remain intact; above its *trompe l'œil* wainscoting is an array of Herber
coats of arms and a fine plaster ceiling. The splendid items of furniture include gi
console tables bearing sculptures, one of which is a rare Roman marble of th
1C BC of a snarling **Cat** and writhing **Snake**.

Leading from the gallery are the State Bathroom, the Walcot Room with a be
made — possibly by Bodley — of crudely carved 17C panels, and the Galler
Room with fine examples of Empire furniture. The Duke's Room with Brusse
tapestries and the Lower Tower Bedroom are contained within the castle's west
ern towers.

The **Blue Drawing Room** with more Brussels tapestries, panelling of about 1660, an
a ceiling by Lanscroon, has remained unaltered since the start of the 18C.

At the foot of the servants' staircase, the Billiard Room has an amazing array c
traditionally stuffed and mounted birds.

E Pelham/National Trust Photographic Library

The Tipu's Tent

**Ballroom Range** — These rooms bear the stamp of the Clive family, the Ballroom itsel
being originally hung with Clive of India's picture collection. *Lord Clive Receiving th
Grant of the Diwani from the Great Mogul* by Benjamin West is full of fancifu
pageantry, its impact equalled by that of the superb Tournai tapestry showing
Venetian embassy to Cairo. The most extraordinary object, in the **Tent Room**, is the
reconstruction of part of **Tipu Sahib's tent**.

Beyond the Ballroom is the **Clive Museum**, recently fitted out with a masterly se
of **showcases**, designed entirely in the spirit of British India, in which is displaye
the fascinating **Clive Collection** of Indian and Far Eastern works of art, arms and
armour.

**Gardens** — The dramatically terraced gardens are the finest example in Britain of a
kind of landscaping that was all but obliterated in the 18C by fashionable enthusi
asm for the informal style which took Nature, rather than architecture, as it
model.

The designer of the gardens and their exact date are unknown but they are
characteristic of the taste of the late 17C. The sojourn of the exiled Marquess o
Powis in France must have influenced their layout; in the mid-18C the antiquary
Thomas Pennant refers to the family's penchant for copying "the wretched taste o
St Germain-en-Laye" but the real inspiration must be the great Renaissance garden:
of Italy, where villas and their surroundings were boldly laid out on the steepest o
slopes.

The southeast-facing terraces, three in number, run for about 200yd/180m below the windows of the castle. The **Top Terrace** has the giant **yews** which have grown wildly beyond the bounds originally set for them, when they would have been regularly trimmed into formal, compact shapes. The most massive outbreak of yew is at the northern end of the terrace, a monstrous, strangely textured hedge which drops ponderously down the lower terraces and completely dwarfs Hercules' valiant attack on a hydra; this fine sculpture is one of several at Powis which came from the workshop of the Fleming John van Nost.

Van Nost's shepherds and shepherdesses animate the balustrade of the **Aviary Terrace**, accompanied by a jolly bagpiper. The aviary once occupied the vaulted room built into the back wall of the terrace.

The **Orangery** which gives its name to the next terrace has a fine doorway moved here by Bodley from the inner gateway of the castle; it commands a broad space presided over by the figure of Pan. Below the balustraded wall is the Apple Slope, once planted up as an orchard, then beyond, in total contrast to the intricacy of the terraces, the vast and level space of the **Great Lawn**. No trace is left of the water gardens whose elaborate layout so disgusted Pennant, though their centrepiece was probably the statue of Fame which now graces the castle forecourt.

Undulating walls of box lead from the Orangery Terrace to the **Formal Garden** laid out in the early 20C by the Fourth Earl's wife, who was also responsible for the decorative planting which so enlivens the terraces.

Beyond the Great Lawn a lesser ridge rises, providing the classic viewpoint from which to admire the castle and terraces as well as giving glimpses of the harmonious countryside of the Severn Vale. The woody ridge, known as the **Wilderness**, continues westwards to the informal Garden Pool.

**Park** – The extensive parklands of Powis run northwards to Welshpool and melt into the woodlands of the wider countryside to the west. Visitors to the castle must drive through part of the park, whose sweeping slopes and great trees are in such contrast to the controlled, architectural character of the castle gardens. This part of Montgomeryshire has long been famous for its wonderful trees; Admiral Rodney insisted on Powis oaks for the Royal Navy, and at the beginning of the 20C the largest tree in Britain grew in the park here, an oak with a girth of nearly 32ft/10m.

# PRESTEIGNE

(Tref-y-Clawdd) Powys – Population 1 815
Michelin Atlas p 25 or Map 403 K 27

This little town, situated right on the Herefordshire border, formed here by the River Lugg, seems altogether English in character, though from the 16C to the 19C it was the county town of Radnorshire.

Its original name – Presthemede – probably derives from a group of Saxon priests who built a small church by the Lugg in the 10C or early 11C. During its first 400 years it was ravaged on several occasions – by Gruffyd ap Llywelyn in 1052, by Llywelyn the Great in 1213 and by Owain Glyn Dŵr in 1402. In 1482 it became a market town and owed much of its prosperity to its situation on the London-Aberystwyth road; when this was rerouted in the early 19C via Knighton, Presteigne began a genteel decline, accelerated after 1899 by the removal of county functions to Llandrindod Wells.

Evidence of the former importance of Presteigne includes the large parish church, a number of fine **inns** and a pretentious Venetian Gothic **Market Hall** (1865). The overall character of the streets is Georgian but behind many a street front is an older, perhaps 17C, structure.

**Tourist Information Centre** – Shire Hall, Presteigne LD8 2AD ☎ 01544 260 650; Fax 01544 260 652.

**Annual Festivals** – The **Presteigne Festival of Classical Music** offers one week of classic and new music, interspersed with talks and walks *(5 days centred on August bank holiday)*; information from the **Presteigne Festival Box Office**, Presteigne, Powys, Wales; the Irish Folk Festival and the Sheet Music Festival are held in July; information about all festivals from the Tourist Information Office.

**Adjacent Sights** – See Builth Wells, Hay-on-Wye, Knighton, Llandrindod Wells, Llanidloes, Montgomery, Newtown, Old Radnor.

**Judge's Lodging** ⊙ – The former **Shire Hall**, an elegant Georgian building with a imposing portico, and the rooms, where the judge lodged during the court hearings, have been restored to their Victorian state and furnished with contemporary items, many found in the attic and cellars. The audio tour *(40min)* guides visitor through 14 rooms on three floors and provides a realistic evocation of the localit at that period on the eve of the Assizes; the tour ends with a trial taking place i the courtroom.

Other rooms house the local **museum** displays, which identify the local flora an fauna and trace the history of Radnorshire from the Stone and Bronze Age through Celts and Romans to the medieval period when the Mortimers held sway The most remarkable exhibits are based on the contents of the Ironmonger's sho owned by Charles Newell. Though continuing to trade profitably into his 90s Mr Newell seems never to have cleared out old stock – ramrod worms, salmo spears, pastry jiggers, shovel heads, gun nipple keys and a humane mousetrap.

**St Andrew's Church** ⊙ – This church, which is one of the finest in the old count of Radnorshire, dates mainly from the 13C-15C, although it incorporates frag ments of earlier Saxon and Norman churches in the north aisle. The tapestry date from the early 16C and represents Christ's entry into Jerusalem. The chance (1460) is in the Perpendicular style with a Tudor panelled roof. The church has ring of eight bells and a rare carillon (1726) controlled by the clock mechanism t play tunes on the eight bells at 9 and 3 o'clock. Since 1565 the curfew bell ha been rung every evening.

# Old RADNOR
## (Pencraig) Powys
Michelin Atlas pp 25 and 26 or Map 403 K 27

Today Old Radnor, which was replaced in the 13C by the planned settlement of New Radnor, is hardly more than a hamlet but it has kept a parish church of unusual siz and beauty.

**★St Stephen's Church** ⊙ – The church stands in a round graveyard high u (840ft/256m) on the slopes of Old Radnor Hill with fine views north-west to Radno Forest. The present 15C and early-16C building i Perpendicular style wa preceded by a Norma structure which itself prob ably replaced an ancien Welsh foundation. Th tower, visible from fa away, has battlements an

> **Adjacent Sights** – See Builth Wells, Hay-on-Wye, Knighton, Llandrindod Wells, Presteigne.

arrowslits and provision for a beacon to be lit above its stair-turret.

Inside, a massive boulder of dolerite was roughly hewn into shape to serve as font, possibly as long ago as the 8C. Its crude workmanship is in total contrast to the church's great treasure, the late-15C **screen** running right across the nave and aisles, the work of Gloucestershire craftsmen; its delicate carving is unequalled i Wales, though its gilding and colouring were removed when the church wa restored in the 19C. Equally exquisite workmanship can be seen in the decoratio of the **organ case**, dating from the early 16C and the oldest in Britain. At the eastern end of the north aisle is a naïve portrayal in 15C stained glass o St Catherine holding her wheel. An array of 18C memorials commemorates mem bers of the local Lewis family, though their most famous scion is remembered no here but in New Radnor.

**New Radnor** – *3mi/5km W of Old Radnor.* Laid out in the mid-13C on a characteristic grid pattern, New Radnor was one of several planned towns in the Marches which failed to meet their founders' expectations. In spite of its market privileges, New Radnor never grew into a proper town; some of the streets shown in Speed's plan of 1611 have disappeared, and even at that time there were mor empty plots of land than houses. The little church, completely rebuilt in the 19C stands on the abrupt slope leading up to the huge motte, which was once crowned by the stone castle sacked by Owain Glyn Dŵr in the early 15C. From the tumble earthworks, the outline of the sad little town's long-neglected defences can just be traced in the layout of fields and hedges.

The entrance to New Radnor is marked by a surprisingly tall neo-Gothic monumen to Sir George Cornewall Lewis Bt (1806-63), scholar and politician, born in Londo but considered to be "Radnorshire's most distinguished son".

**Radnor Forest** – *W of Old Radnor by A 44.* New Radnor serves as a base fo walkers and birdwatchers exploring this great tract of open upland, which rises to 2 166ft/660m and is really forested (with recent plantations of conifers) only on its northern flank.

In one of the valleys which penetrate deep into the massif is **Water-Break-its-Neck**, waterfall (80ft/25m) *(signed from A 44 about 1.5mi/2.5km southwest of New Radnor).*

# RAGLAN CASTLE ★
## Monmouthshire
### Michelin Atlas p 16 or Map 403 L 28

"With Raglan... the long era of castle-building in Wales comes to a magnificent end" (John Hilling). The substantial ruins of this great late-medieval stronghold, crowning a rise above the modern Monmouth-Abergavenny road, exemplify the taste, wealth and sophistication of its 15C and later owners, concerned as much with ostentation and luxury as with defence. Fine stonework, the remains of sumptuous decoration and the traces of what were some of the finest gardens in Britain evoke the expansive way of life lived by its early owners.

Raglan Castle

A Williams, Guildford

## TOUR ⊘

**Yellow Tower of Gwent** – The castle occupies the site of a modest manor house which itself may have been erected on a castle mound of Norman date.

Work was begun in the 1430s by William ap Thomas, a member of the minor Welsh gentry, and continued by his son, William Herbert, one of the first Welshmen to be elevated to the ranks of the English gentry as the Earl of Pembroke. Both men had campaigned in France, and much of the castle, like its machicolations, bears the imprint of French architectural practice. It was the first William who built the "Tower of great bredth", whose pale Redbrook sandstone caused it to be named the Yellow Tower of Gwent. Though its interior is rudely exposed and without the topmost of its five storeys, it is still the castle's single most imposing feature. Originally approached by a drawbridge, its later role was as a redoubt which could be held if the rest of the stronghold had fallen. Close by is the South Gate, once the original entrance to the castle.

The main approach is now through the twin-towered **Great Gatehouse**, built around the 1460s by William Herbert, with fine stonework and elaborate machicolations ornamented with gargoyles. To the north is the more massive **Closet**

**Adjacent Sights** – See Abergavenny, Blaenavon, Caerleon, Caerwent, Grosmont, Monmouth, Tintern Abbey, Usk.

**Tower**, which once had a prison in its basement, while beyond the gate passage is the first of the castle's two courtyards, the **Pitched Stone Court**, whose Tudor cobbling conceals an even older layer of stone pitching. Dividing this courtyard from the Fountain Court is the **Hall**, the finest of all the castle's living quarters, built in the middle of the 16C and once covered with a superb hammerbeam roof of Irish oak. High up, part of an elaborate Renaissance fireplace stands where once the **Long Gallery** ran. The **Fountain Court** was named for the "pleasant marble fountain

in the midst thereof... continually running with clear water" which seems to hav
stood until the 18C; the courtyard is bounded by living apartments which wer
reached by an ornate Grand Stair.

**Gardens** – The gardens, which were laid out between 1549 and 1628, seem to hav
matched or even surpassed the magnificence of the castle's architecture. Though a
detailed features like the elaborate "water parterre" have been lost, the structure o
this ambitious Tudor landscape remains, in the massive turf-covered terraces to th
north-west and in the spacious raised lawns to the south-west. One of these was
bowling green on which Charles I tested his skill against a local champion.

In 1646 Royalist Raglan was besieged. Its fall marked the virtual end of the Civ
War and the end of its own glory. It was reduced to a ruin, some of its materia
being carried off to help repair the bridge at Bristol.

# Vale of RHEIDOL ★
## Ceredigion
Michelin Atlas p 24 or Map 403 I 26

The landscape in this valley was probably shaped by volcanic forces. The compresse
silts which form the local rocks may have been heaved into their present position b
ancient volcanoes but the falls and chasms are the result of the phenomenon known a
river capture. Rheidol and Mynach, its tributary, originally flowed roughly southward
but a shorter stream, flowing westward to the coast, cut back into the course of th
Rheidol in the uplands and "captured" their waters, so that the Rheidol now describe
a dramatic right-angled bend and falls precipitously into the bed of its new partner.

★★**Vale of Rheidol Railway** ⊘ *(See town plan of Aberystwyth p 79 –* **AB X***)* – "I thin
I may safely predict that the Vale of Rheidol Light Railway Company will be i
existence in a flourishin
condition ... long after th
Cambrian Railway is dea
and buried." The Compan
Chairman's prophecy o
1903 came true; the Cam
brian disappeared in 192
but steam locomotives sti
haul packed trainloads o
tourists through the spectacular Vale of Rheidol between Aberystwyth and Devil'
Bridge.

> **Adjacent Sights** – See Aberaeron, Aberyst-
> wyth, Elan Valley, Lampeter, Llanidloes,
> Llanwrtyd Wells, Machynlleth, Tregaron.

The narrow-gauge line (35.5in/600mm and 11.5mi/19km long) was completed i
1902. Its original purpose was to serve the lead mines and timber interests of th
Vale and surrounding uplands, hitherto dependent on poor roads and packhorses
but goods traffic soon took second place to tourism.

No standard-gauge track could possibly have performed the contortions necessar
to adapt the line to the steep sides of the glaciated valley and to overcome th
change in level (480ft/146m) in the final stretch (4mi/6km) between Aberffrw
and Devil's Bridge. This section is a true mountain railway; locomotives No 7 *Owai
Glyndwr* or No 9 *Prince of Wales* have to work hard to beat gradients of up to 1 i
48. In places the train runs along a rocky ledge, elsewhere tunnelling through
green vault of ferns, birch and ancient oakwood, with glimpses of the Vale fa
below, before arriving at the Devil's Bridge terminus.

**Rheidol Power Station** ⊘ – *9mi/15km E of Aberystwyth by A 44 and minor roac
The Rheidol rises 2 000ft/600m up near mid-Wales' highest summit, Plynlimon
The river's descent near Devil's Bridge is abrupt (1 000ft/300m in 6mi/10km)
Combined with a sizeable catchment and abundant rainfall, ideal conditions exist fo
the generation of hydroelectric power. The scheme was implemented from 1957 to
1961. The workings of the power station are explained in the **visitor centre**.

A **scenic drive** gives views of the upland reservoirs at Nant-y-Moch and Dinas bu
most visitors make for the lower valley, where the stone-built, creeper-clad mai
power station is located, its turbine fed via an underground pipeline from Dinas
the water enters the power station at its terminal velocity (c 130mph/210kph).

There is a **trout farm** supplying fish for the reservoirs and, on the adjoinin
reservoir, a fish ladder and a weir with ingenious arrangements to encourag
salmon to continue their upstream migration.

**Nant-yr-Arian Forest Centre** ⊘ – *10mi/16km E of Aberystwyth by A 44.* Th
largely man-made Rheidol Forest extends far across the uplands northward from
the road (A 44) towards Machynlleth. The Forestry Commission's modern **visito
centre** commands wonderful views southward down the deep Melinddŵr valley and
is the starting point for a number of woodland walks.

**Llywernog Silver-lead Mine** ⊘ – *11mi/18km E of Aberystwyth by A 44.* Th
geological map of this part of Wales shows dozens of lodes of silver-lead ore
running in a south-west to north-east direction and the desolation of the upland
scenery is intensified by the leats, shafts, waste tips and general impedimenta o

some 130 abandoned mines, most spectacularly at Cwmystwyth to the east of Devil's Bridge. The ore may have first been worked in pre-Roman times, while the Romans themselves used lead extensively for pipes, coffins and medals. As building construction became more sophisticated from about the 11C, lead was mined again more or less continuously until decline began towards the end of the 19C. The lack of local labour in the sparsely inhabited uplands was overcome by immigration; Germans came in the Middle Ages, convicts in the 17C, and tin-miners from Cornwall and Devon in the 19C, the last bringing their Wesleyan version of Nonconformity with them.

The old workings at Llywernog are being restored, to bring to life the whole story of this previously somewhat neglected chapter in Welsh industrial history. The handsome Main Building in contrasting dark slate and pale brick contains reconstituted underground scenes and a *California of Wales* exhibition, while a trail leads around the extensive site with its processing sheds, water-wheels, narrow-gauge tramway equipment and machinery of all kinds. Underground workings can be explored and visitors can pan for silver and fool's gold.

★**Devil's Bridge Waterfalls** ⊙ – The waterfalls on the River Mynach plunging into the deep wooded chasm at the head of the Vale of Rheidol attracted Romantic tourists like Wordsworth, who came here in 1824. George Borrow, who visited 30 years later, thought the place had "all the appearance of an extinct volcano".

The first bridge across the gully carved out by the Mynach may have been built by the monks of Strata Florida Abbey *(see p 264)*. Its attribution to the Devil is based on the story of an old crone and her cow, which had strayed to the far side.

Thinking to outwit the old lady, Old Nick offered to build an instant bridge provided he could have the soul of the first living being to use it. But the crone turned the tables on him by sending over her dog before crossing herself to retrieve the cow.

Above the simple stone arch of this medieval bridge are two successors, one dating from about 1708 and the other an iron structure built at the beginning of the 20C, when the Vale of Rheidol Railway began to bring large numbers of visitors to what had become one of the most famous sights in Wales.

The waterfalls in their setting of moss-grown rock and wonderful oak woodland are fenced off and must be approached through turnstiles.

A short descent to the east leads to what George Borrow described as "a horrid seething pot or cauldron", a cavity worn by the Mynach from which it escapes through a "gloomy volcanic slit" to fall in a series of spectacular cascades to the Rheidol far below. The cascades can be viewed close to from the longer path to the west, which includes a steep drop known as Jacob's Ladder and an almost equally steep climb back up to the level of the road. From this path the lesser falls on the Rheidol can also be seen.

Devil's Bridge Waterfalls

Wales Tourist Board

# The RHONDDA

Rhondda Cynon Taff
Michelin Atlas p 16 or Map 403 J 28-29

At their peak just before the First World War, the mines of the Rhondda Fawr and Rhondda Fach valleys were producing nearly 10 million tons of coal a year. More than 50 pits supported a workforce of some 50 000 miners, living with their families in the terraced houses which cling to the steep valley sides in an almost continuous line from Pontypridd to the valleys' end. Once a synonym for coal and the close-knit community dependent on it, the Rhondda lost its last pit in 1990.

## HISTORICAL NOTES

Prehistoric people had kept out of the densely wooded and swampy valleys, preferring to range over the sandstone plateau which rises to a height of 2 000ft/600m. Even in 1807, Malkin the antiquary enthused over "such scenes of untouched nature, as the imagination would find it difficult to surpass" as he explored the "Glamorgan Alps", and as late as the 1840s another traveller exclaimed over "the air... aromatic with wild flowers and mountain plants". Even at the start of the 19C, when the first small-scale extraction of coal began, the population was still small and scattered in farmsteads and occasional clusters of labourers' cottages. But with the arrival of the railway in 1856, the technical ability to sink deep mines, and the industrialising world's insatiable appetite for fuel, the Rhondda's coal boom began. In 1861 the population still numbered only 4 000; by 1871 it had increased to 17 000 and by 1921 to the extraordinary total of 163 000. Only just over half of the inhabitants were of local origin; many were immigrants from England, Scotland, Ireland, even from Spain and Italy.

The Rhondda bred more than its share of working-class leaders. The tireless **AJ Cook** (1884-1931) worked in the Lewis Merthyr colliery, now a Heritage Park, before becoming General Secretary of the Miners' Federation of Great Britain in 1924 and playing the leading role in the General Strike of 1926 and the subsequent year-long lockout. For more than two decades after the Second World War the National Union of Mineworkers was run by Rhondda men, Arthur Horner from Maerdy, the place once known as Little Moscow because of its politics, and Will Paynter from Cymmer.

**Pontypridd** – Pontypridd, which stands at the southern outlet of the Rhondda into the Taff Vale, is a market town of some substance with industrial traditions of its own, of which the most important was the manufacture of all the Royal Navy's anchor chains. The Taff is crossed by a famous and elegant 18C **bridge**, built in stone by William Edwards who remained undeterred by the collapse of his two previous attempts.

> **Tourist Information Centre** – Historical and Cultural Centre, Bridge Street, Pontypridd CF37 4PE ☎ 01443 409 512; Fax 01443 485 565.
>
> **Adjacent Sights** – See Brecon Beacons, Caerphilly, Cardiff, Castell Coch, Llancaiach Fawr, Llandaff, Llantrisant, Merthyr Tydfil, Tredegar, Museum of Welsh Life.

Two fine chapels stand by the bridgehead on the western bank, one converted into a doctors' surgery. The other, formerly the Tabernacl, houses, in its unusually grand interior, the **Pontypridd Historical Centre** ⊙ which tells the story of the town and its people. The musical traditions of the area are celebrated with tributes to local men such as Evan and James James, who composed the Welsh National Anthem "*Mae hen wlad fy nhadau*", Tom Jones, the popular singer and cabaret performer, and Sir Geraint Evans, genial opera singer, shown here in high good humour and swaddled in padding as he prepares himself for the role of Verdi's Falstaff. There is also a fascinating model of Pontypridd railway station, which was the pride of the former Taff Vale Railway and still has the longest platforms in Britain; at its zenith, it would handle 11 000 passengers and 500 trains a day.

**★Rhondda Heritage Park** ⊙ – That icon of British industrial might, the pithead winding gear, has virtually disappeared from today's landscape. But the one which served the Lewis Merthyr mine at Trehafod until its closure in 1983 has been preserved, centrepiece of an ambitious and still developing attempt to tell the story of the Rhondda and its people in as vivid a way as possible.

A tour of the Heritage Park begins at the **Visitor Centre**, which has a mall of reconstructed shops and space for exhibitions. On permanent display is a growing collection of artwork with a mining theme, including stark linocuts by Paul Piech, atmospheric watercolours by Valerie Ganz, and a poignant canvas by David Carpanini showing the artist as a *Tourist of Our Past*. Beyond the Centre are the pithead buildings, dominated by an immensely tall brick chimney. Pithead paraphernalia lends authenticity and includes trucks *(drams)* of the coal brought up on the last day of working of various mines. The tour, which is expertly and humorously led by a former miner, does not descend into the mine until a vivid multi-media presentation in the **Trefor Winding House** has recounted the history of the Rhondda up

246

Wales Tourist Board

The Rhondda Heritage Park

to the nationalisation of the coal industry in 1947. Once equipped with safety helmet, the visitor is let down in the cage to **Pit Bottom**, where the underground world of the miner of the 1950s is brought to life with great – sometimes almost frightening! – verisimilitude. A trip aboard an underground train regains the surface with surprising speed. Once recovered, the visitor can discover more about what life was like in the mining communities, in the **Bertie Winding House** where the show concentrates on disasters and stirring events like the Tonypandy Riots of 1910, or in the **Fan House**, which examines the role of women.

**Tonypandy** – Confrontation between strikers, police and troops turned into a riot at Tonypandy in 1910, in which a miner was killed and shops looted. Winston Churchill, then Home Secretary, was held responsible for the provocative deployment of mounted troops, though his initial response had been a cautious one. A bronze **sculpture** of a miner, his wife and child stands by the roadside.

**Rhigos Gateway** – The Rhondda Fawr valley remained a cul-de-sac until the inter-war period, when connecting roads over the passes linking to other valleys were built as a measure of unemployment relief.
One of these highways leads west to **Bwlch y Clawdd** from where there are magnificent **views** of the valley.
Another climbs north to the Rhigos Gateway, with equally fine **views** of lowering sandstone bluffs and waterfalls, recalling a long-distant past and a reminder that the Rhondda existed before the reign of King Coal and will doubtless outlive him.
Nearby is **Hen Dre'r Mynydd**, a cluster of collapsed drystone enclosures of unknown date which served as summer shelter for shepherds and their flocks.

# RHUDDLAN CASTLE★★

Denbighshire
Michelin Atlas p 33 or Map 403 J 24

Even deprived of their battlements, the stout towers of Rhuddlan Castle still stand confidently on the low rise above the Clwyd, the river diverted by Edward I's engineers to enable his new fortress to be supplied directly from the sea.

## HISTORICAL NOTES

Rhuddlan was the second of the great castles, after Flint, to be built in the course of Edward I's subjugation of North Wales, but invaders had been this way before.
The Saxons had founded a settlement here. In 1073 the Norman known as Robert of Rhuddlan had thrown up a **castle mound**, known as **Twthill**, still prominent on its site just to the south of the later stronghold; it was accompanied by a planned town of which some earthworks remain.
The fordability of the Clwyd was the principal determinant of the castle's location, but the river had to be led into a new bed to conform to the plans of Edward's architect, the Savoyard James of St George. For three years from 1277 onwards, diggers from

Rhuddlan Castle

the Fens and elsewhere laboured to excavate the new channel (2mi/3km long) as the castle walls took shape on the slope above. In 1282 Rhuddlan formed the main base of operations for the attack on Snowdonia. A **bastide town** (minus walls) was laid out, its outline still evident in the street pattern of the small modern town.

It was at Rhuddlan that the **Statute of Wales**, sometimes also known as the Statute of Rhuddlan, was issued in 1284. It was described by some as the "first colonial constitution" and regarded by others as a charter protecting the "rights and privileges of the Welsh". It regulated Welsh affairs right up until the Tudor Acts of Union in 1536 and 1543. By tradition, it was while spelling out their place in the new dispensation to the Welsh nobility assembled at Rhuddlan that Edward heard of the birth of his son at Caernarfon; seizing the moment, he named the infant as their prince "born in Wales and could speak never a word of English".

**Ruins** ⊙ – The most prominent part of the castle ruins is the **West Gatehouse**. This was one of two gatehouses guarding the castle's inner ward, diamond-shaped in plan, and with single towers at the other two corners.

The only trace remaining of such substantial timber structures as the Queen's Hall and King's Hall are foundations, beam holes and roof creases. Edward's first wife, Queen Eleanor, had a garden made in the courtyard, laid with 6 000 turves and with seats around a fishpond surrounding the well.

The lower towers and walls of the outer ward descended to the river, where there was a dock. A dry moat ran round the remainder of the walls.

> **Adjacent Sights** – See Bodelwyddan, Colwyn Bay, Holywell, Rhyl, St Asaph.

*Where to eat ? ... Where to stay ? ...*

*Consult :*
*– the Michelin Red Guide Greater London*
*– the Michelin Red Guide Great Britain and Ireland*
*They contain :*
*– general hotel information*
*– a selection of good restaurants*
*– a selection of pleasant, quiet, secluded hotels*
*The Green Guide Great Britain*
*The Red Guide Great Britain and Ireland*
*The Michelin Map no 986 Great Britain and Ireland*
*Three publications that complement each other perfectly*

(Y Rhyl) Denbighshire – Population 24 909
Michelin Atlas p 33 or Map 403 J 24

t the beginning of the 19C what is now a popular resort was no more than a
ollection of fishermen's huts at the point where the Clwyd finds its way to the sea
hrough a broad belt of marshland. Development began in earnest after 1848 when
he railway arrived, and Rhyl soon joined the ranks of the other watering places of the
orth coast, with a promenade, pier, winter garden, respectable terraces of hotels and
oarding houses, and a medley of churches and chapels, including St Thomas' by Sir
ilbert Scott with its landmark steeple. Pier and winter garden have gone, accommo-
ation is now mostly in flatlets and caravans, and bingo halls and amusement arcades
tud the townscape.
he town is, however, committed to reversing what had been perceived as a decline
nd has invested heavily in new facilities to cater for the more sophisticated demands
nade nowadays by its traditional Merseyside and Lancashire clientele.

**Promenade** – Rhyl's Promenade (2mi/3km long)
overlooks a sandy beach
which at low tide seems to
extend to the horizon. At
its western end, fishing
boats mingle with recre-
ational craft at the mouth
of the Clwyd.

A stroll eastwards brings
the visitor into tempting
contact with one attraction
after another – Ocean
Beach Amusement Park,
Activity Centre for teen-
agers, Waterpark, Sky-
tower (240ft/73m), pad-

**Tourist Information Centre** – Rhyl Children's Village, West Parade, Rhyl LL18 1HZ
☎ 01745 355 068; Fax 01745 3442
255.
Offa's Dyke Centre, Central Beach, Prestatyn LL19 7EY ☎ 01745 889 092.

**Parking** – There is an underground car
park beneath the Promenade.

**Adjacent Sights** – See Bodelwyddan,
Colwyn Bay, Holywell, Rhuddlan, St Asaph.

dling pools and a Children's Village. A sparkling new focal point has been created in
the open-air Events Arena (capacity 8 000) which is sheltered from sea breezes. It
is flanked to the west by the big blue barn of the **Sea Life Aquarium** ⊙, one of
several in Britain, which reveals the secrets of maritime life by a judicious combination of instruction and entertainment, the latter inevitably featuring the horrors of
shark attack.
Beyond the lifeboat station to the east is the resort's ambitious attempt to counter
the pull of more clement coastlines, the Sun Centre. This enormous structure of
steel lattice, glass and bronze-tinted PVC houses a bewildering variety of water
experiences, from conventional family pool to dragon slide and tropical storm, all
of which can be observed from an overhead monorail.
Further east still is the newest of Rhyl's three theatres, the New Pavilion
(1 000 seats).

**Museum and Arts Centre** ⊙ – *Church Street*. As well as offering space for
temporary exhibitions, this new building also provides reminders of how Rhyl's
masses of visitors managed to enjoy themselves in the past; part of the museum
has been laid out like the old pier, with a panoramic mural depicting the Promenade in the late 19C.

## EXCURSION

**Prestatyn** – *4mi/6km E by A 548*. Prestatyn is Rhyl writ smaller and marginally
more dignified. The centre seems withdrawn from the sea at the foot of the
northernmost rise of the Clwydian Range, and the town is as much a place of
retirement as a place for holidays.
In the 1930s the seafront attracted one of Britain's first holiday camps but the
dominant feature on the promenade is now the Nova Entertainment Centre, an
assemblage of pastel-coloured structures (including a big conservatory) built into
the sea wall and housing pools, bars, a restaurant and fitness centre.
Nearby is the **Offa's Dyke Interpretive Centre** ⊙ which provides information of every
sort about the long-distance footpath which follows Offa's Dyke (*see p 169*). It
seems that the Mercian ruler failed to extend the earthwork to the water's edge;
nevertheless, the pillar here marks the official northern terminus of the dyke,
which runs south (124mi/200km) through the Welsh Marches to the Severn.

*THE GREEN GUIDE*
*Art and architecture; ancient monuments; history; landscape; scenic routes*
*touring programmes; local maps; town plans; site plans*
*A selection of guides for holidays at home and abroad*

# RUTHIN

(Rhuthun) Denbighshire – Population 5 029
Michelin Atlas p 33 or Map J 24

The market and castle town of Ruthin dominates the southern, upper end of the Va'
of Clwyd as Denbigh dominates the north. Its hilltop site is less dramatic, but th
townscape of the main street and market place extending along the ridge top betwee
parish church and castle is attractively varied.

Ruthin

**St Peter's Church** ⊙ – The churchyard is guarded by fine early-18C wrought-iror
gates, the work of the Bersham *(see p 285)* craftsmen who fashioned the ever
more splendid examples at Chirk Castle. Originally founded in 1284 as a collegiate
church, St Peter's has the double nave typical of the area, which may reflect its
dual function from 1310 onward as parish church. With its tall 19C steeple the
church forms the centrepiece of a small and delightful precinct consisting of old
18C grammar school, 19C **almshouses** and the much-altered building known as the
Old Cloisters, part of the 14C college.

The earliest part of the church is the present north aisle, to which the south aisle
was added in the 14C. Both have camberbeam roofs, that of the north aisle being
particularly elaborately carved. Since 1663 the church has lacked a chancel, which
was demolished to provide building material for the Town Hall.

Among the monuments is a crudely carved and painted bust of Ruthin-born Dr
Gabriel Goodman (1528-1601), Dean of Westminster and benefactor of his native
town, who was responsible for the re-establishment of the college after the
Dissolution.

**St Peter's Square** – The Town Hall, on its island site in the centre of
the square, was demolished in its turn and replaced by an elaborate stone
structure of 1883, combining the functions of clock tower, drinking fountain
and horse trough. Among the generally well-mannered three-storey buildings are
the very grand red-brick *Georgian Castle Hotel* and its incongruous neighbour,
the *Myddelton Arms*, known as the *Eyes of Ruthin* because of the multiple
dormers staring out from its cat-slide roof. The neatly restored Old Court
House (1401) is now a bank, as is the former Exmewe House, home of another local man made good, Thomas Exmewe (c 1468-1529), Lord Mayor of
London 1517-18. Outside is a limestone boulder, supposedly an Arthurian execution stone.

**Nantclwyd House** ⏱ – *Stryd y Castell*. Behind the porch with its columns and projecting upper room is a 15C cruck hall house, with features of many subsequent periods. This palimpsest of a building will eventually make a fine home for a local museum.

**Ruthin Castle** – Reginald de Grey's late-13C stronghold was laid waste after the Civil War, but in the early and mid-19C an extensive mock castle was built within the precinct still enclosed by substantial remains of the original walls and towers. The design was by Henry Clutton and William Burges, the enthusiastic medievaliser of Cardiff Castle. In the late 19C and early 20C the castle was the seat of the extravagant George Cornwallis West, second husband of the actress Mrs Patrick Campbell. It is now a hotel.

# ST ASAPH

(Llanelwy) Denbighshire – Population 3 399
Michelin Atlas p 33 or Map 403 J 24

The city of St Asaph consists of little more than the single street climbing from the five-arched bridge over the River Elwy to the low rise on which stands the smallest of Britain's cathedrals.

## ★CATHEDRAL ⏱

The simplicity of the square-towered edifice seems to proclaim its affinity with the Celtic monastery founded here in AD 560 by St Kentigern, also known as St Mungo, Bishop of Strathclyde, and led later by his successor, St Asaph.
The present building was begun in the early 13C but its history is one of frequent destruction followed by restoration and further building. Its present appearance is in part due to the extensive restoration carried out by Sir Gilbert Scott in the second half of the 19C. The cathedral has survived several attempts to transfer the diocese to other locations, in the late 13C to Rhuddlan, in the 16C to Denbigh, and later to Bangor. In the post-Reformation period it was a great centre of Welsh learning.

In the churchyard stands a memorial, erected in 1888, to two local men, William Salesbury and Bishop William Morgan (1545-1604), for their work in translating the Bible into Welsh.

**Adjacent Sights** – See Bodelwyddan, Colwyn Bay, Denbigh, Flint, Holywell, Llanrwst, Mold, Rhuddlan, Rhyl, Ruthin.

## Welsh translation of the Bible

The see of St Asaph played a prominent part in the translation of the Bible and Prayer book into Welsh. In 1533 an Act of Parliament was passed ordering the five bishops in Wales and Hereford to provide Welsh translations of the Bible and the Book of Common Prayer by St David's Day 1567; no funds were provided but one bishop responded, the Bishop of St David's, Richard Davies (1501-81), who was born in the Conwy Valley.

He undertook the translation of the the the Book of Common Prayer (1559) and invited William Salesbury, who lived most of his life in Llanrwst *(see p 194)* to be responsible for the major part of the New Testament, which was translated from the Greek, and Thomas Huet, Precentor of St David's, to undertake the Book of Revelation. In his preface to the New Testament Bishop Richard compared Protestantism with the purity of the early Celtic Church. The printing in London was supervised by Salesbury and the work was published in 1567. It provided a basis for the translation into Welsh of the entire Bible, which was completed in 1588 by William Morgan (c 1545-1604), Bishop of St Asaph, who was born near Betws-y-Coed *(see p 194)*. This monumental achievement was revised by his successor, Bishop Parry, in 1620.

**Interior** – Despite its relatively small dimensions, the interior conveys an atmosphere of great spaciousness and calm, and achieves the dignity and presence appropriate to a cathedral. There is much bare stone and little ornamentation; the nave arcades have no capitals, though there are medieval carved corbels supporting the timber roof of the nave. In the choir are late-15C canopied stalls, the only ones of their kind in Wales. Bishop Morgan is buried beneath the throne and his Bible and other literary treasures are displayed in an alcove by the Chantry Chapel.

*Some hotels have their own tennis court, swimming pool, private beach or garden*
*Consult the current edition of the Michelin Red Guide* **Great Britain and Ireland**

# ST DAVID'S ★★

(Tyddewi) Pembrokeshire – Population 1 959
Michelin Atlas p 14 or Map 403 E 28

On its far western peninsula, this tiniest of British cities exerts the same pull on today's visitors as it did on the medieval pilgrims making their way to the shrine of St David, the patron saint of Wales.

**Dewi Sant** – Tradition has it that St David (AD c 462-520) was born during a thunderstorm on the windswept clifftop where a chapel was subsequently dedicated to his mother, St Non *(see below)*. The monastery he founded was located a little further inland, in the marshy valley through which the little River Alun makes its way to the sea, and it is here, on a drier shelf of land just above the stream, that today's superb cathedral stands.

The wildness and remoteness of the spot suited the demands of monastic life. David himself practised an asceticism even more strict than that of his monks, drenching himself in cold water to still the urgings of the flesh, hence his name "David the Waterman", although it may refer to his refusal to touch alcohol. His monastery may have enjoyed the seclusion of its inland valley site but its peninsula setting put it in contact with the ancient seaways linking Britain, the Continent and Ireland, making it accessible to the pilgrims who thronged to what became the saint's shrine. This openness to the ocean also made the monastery vulnerable to attack from less benign seafarers; after a series of Viking raids in the 10C and 11C, the site was abandoned.

## CATHEDRAL CLOSE

The pastoral setting of Palace and Cathedral in their hollow, with farmland beyond and within the protection of the close wall, is uniquely evocative of the religious life of the Middle Ages, even though none of the clergy residences are older than the 18C. The presence of orchards and grazing land within the precinct can easily be imagined, while the little tower built at the point where the Alun leaves the close probably controlled the flow of water to adjacent fishponds.

## Out and About

**Tourist Information Centre** – National Park Visitor Centre, The Grove, St David's SA62 6NW ☎ 01437 720 392; Fax 01437 720 099.

**Beaches** – At Aber Eiddi and Whitesand Bay *(north)*; at Caerfai Bay and Newgale *(south)*.

**Boat Trips** ⊘ – There are excursions by conventional or inflatable boat to see the wildlife around and on **Ramsey Island** *(see below)* and also white-water specials *(1hr)* in jet-powered rigid inflatable boats through Ramsey Sound.

**Adjacent Sights** – See Fishguard, Haverfordwest, Milford Haven, Pembrokeshire Coast.

## Where to Eat

**Morgan's Brasserie**, 20 Nun St, SA62 6NT. ☎/Fax 01437 720 508. Well run town house with an imaginative blackboard menu; emphasis on fresh local seafood.

**Harbour Lights**, Porthgain, SA62 5BW. *7.5mi/12km NE by A 487 and Llanrian rd.* ☎ 01348 831 549; Fax 01348 831 193. Friendly, informal and busy ambience (booking advised) (light lunch only); set price evening meal; largely seafood; located within a gallery.

## Where to Stay

**The Waterings**, Anchor Drive, SA62 6QH. *0.25mi/0.5km E by A 487.* ☎ 01437 720 876. Spacious accommodation (5 rm) in a sheltered courtyard; modern style; set in tranquil landscaped grounds, a short walk from the town centre.

**St Nons**, Catherine St, SA62 6RJ. *0.25mi/0.5km SW on Porthclais rd.* ☎ 01437 720 239; Fax 01437 721 839. Simple hotel (20 rm) with modern amenities; informal Mediterranean dining style.

**Y Gorian**, 77 Nun St, SA62 6NU. ☎ 01437 720 837; Fax 01437 721 148. Comfortable accommodation (5 rm) with all amenities; warm and hospitable host; guest lounge with panoramic views towards Whitesand Bay.

★★**St David's Cathedral** ⊘ – The unique appeal of the finest church in Wales is due partly to the way in which it suddenly reveals itself to the visitor. Seen from Tower Gate (Porth y Twr) which forms the entrance to the precinct from the city, the great building of finely textured and coloured stone seems to fill the valley, its centrepiece the tall tower which helps to draw the contribution of different building periods into a harmonious whole.

**Interior** – Almost the sole trace of the earlier cathedral is the Celtic Abraham stone, now built into the wall of the south transept. The present building was begun c 1180 by the third Norman Bishop of St David's, Peter de Leia, perhaps aided by Gerald of Wales *(Giraldus Cambrensis)*. Peter de Leia was responsible for the grand rounded arcades of the **nave**, which are combined in characteristic Transitional style with the pointed arches of the triforium. The collapse of the tower in 1220, an earthquake in 1248, and subsequent settlement on the sloping site has left the westernmost pillars leaning disconcertingly outwards, while the floor of the building rises a full 14ft/3.5m upwards from west to east. No heavy stone vaults could hold in these conditions, and the nave is covered with a magnificently-carpentered 16C **ceiling** of Irish oak, its flatness more than compensated for by rich carving of arches, pendants, and motifs like the Green Man and dolphins. The remaining Norman arch supporting the tower is partly obscured by the splendid 14C **screen** or pulpitum. This was part of the building programme in Decorated style initiated by the Cathedral's other great builder, **Henry de Gower**, Bishop from 1328 to 1347, who also increased the height of the aisles throughout, added new windows, built the central stage of the tower and gave the south door its two-storey porch. The screen contains his **tomb (1)**.

Further rebuildings and additions took place in the 15C and 16C, including the provision of the choir stalls with their exceptionally appealing **misericords**. They include further examples of the Green Man, an array of curious beasts, and an obviously unwell passenger aboard a ship upon a stormy sea.

On the north side of the presbytery is what was once considered to be the bare shrine of **St David**, built in 1275 but desecrated at the Reformation; close to it is the table tomb of **Edmund Tudor (2)**, father of Henry VII. To the east of the high altar **(3)**, the fan-vaulted early-16C **Holy Trinity Chapel (4)** has a wall recess with an oak reliquary containing bones which were found during a Victorian restoration and were claimed by the Dean of St David's, William Williams, as those of St David and of his confessor, Justinian; carbon dating proved the bones to be 11C or 12C and the medical evidence suggests they belonged to St Caradog, who lived on fish on Newgale beach *(see p 226)* and was buried in St David's. The **Lady Chapel** has medieval bosses, as does the 14C **St Thomas Becket's Chapel** (**5**), including one depicting the face of Christ.

During the course of the 19C and 20C the cathedral was completely restored, early work being carried out with caution and ingenuity by Sir George Gilbert Scott, who completely rebuilt the tower without taking it down and reconstructed the west front, giving it something like its original, Transitional appearance.

**\*Bishop's Palace** ⊙ – The palace of the Bishops of St David's lies on the far bank of the Alun, proclaiming, even in ruin, the power, wealth and taste of these ecclesiastical magnates.

The first bishops seem to have concentrated their efforts on the construction of the Cathedral, and the earliest buildings on the site, the west range, have a plainness and modesty which contrast with the grandeur of the later structures.

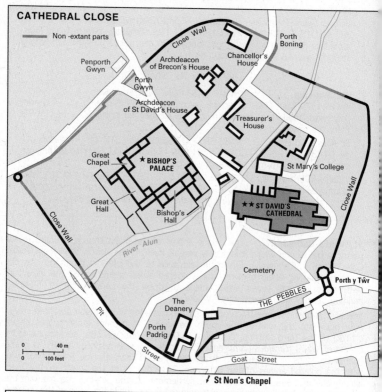

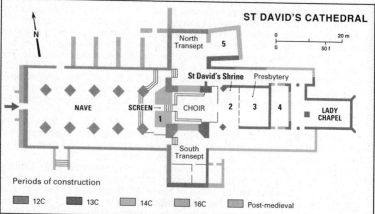

Bishop's Palace, St David's

Improvements and additions were probably carried out under the stimulus of King Edward I's pilgrimage here in 1284, but the decisive imprint is that of Bishop Henry de Gower, who not only built on an ambitious scale but unified the whole ensemble with the wonderfully ornate **arcaded parapet**. This is perhaps the Palace's most striking single feature, a hint of Mediterranean luxuriance given by its chequerboard patterning and enrichment with finely carved corbels. The Palace courtyard is entered through a gateway whose primary purpose seems to have been aesthetic rather than defensive.

On the far, southern side of the courtyard is Gower's splendid **Great Hall**, raised to first-floor level, like all the principal rooms, on a series of vaults. Approached via an ornate porch, it has fine traceried windows and a majestic, deeply-set wheel window in its gable. After being entertained in the Hall, the more privileged of the Bishop's guests would have retired to the Solar to the west, though its partition wall has long since disappeared. Beyond the skew doorway is the **Great Chapel**, an earlier structure with an elaborately carved piscina and a stubby spire.

Gower had earlier converted the east range into a series of private apartments, including the Bishop's Hall, Solar and private Chapel. A fine Kitchen was then added, linked by a passageway to the Great Hall.

The grandeur of Gower's establishment reflected the wealth of the diocese, which was one of the greatest landowners in medieval Wales. The see also benefited from the offerings of the many pilgrims who flocked to St David's, mindful that two pilgrimages made here were equal to one ever to Rome. But even by the 14C and 15C financial decline had set in, causing ever more difficulty in maintaining such an extensive building complex. During the episcopate of the first Protestant Bishop, William Barlow (1536-48), the chief residence of the Bishops was moved to Abergwili just outside Carmarthen. The Palace at St David's fell into ruin, accelerated, it was mischievously alleged, by Barlow's selling its lead roofing to provide dowries for his five daughters!

## CITY CENTRE

St David's usually has a busy air, which evokes faint traces of the atmosphere of medieval pilgrimages, and has more facilities than might be expected. The life of the little city turns around the 14C preaching or market **cross** standing in a small open space just uphill from the Tower Gate.

Those wanting to learn more about the life of the sea breaking on the cliffs only a short distance away should visit the **Oceanarium** ⊘.

## EXCURSIONS

**St Non's Chapel** – *0.75mi/1km S of St David's.* The traditional birthplace of St David is marked by the ruin of what was one of several pilgrimage chapels scattered around the area, satellites of the great cathedral. The small rectangular building on its site sloping down to the sea has proved difficult to date; it has served as a dwelling house, a vegetable garden and a repository for rocks collected from the surrounding fields. The nearby holy well has retained something of its potency; an arch was built over it in the 18C and its present state is due to its restoration, by the Roman Catholic Church in 1951.

**Porthclais** – *1mi/1.5km SW of St David's*. At this point the River Alun runs into a narrow tidal inlet which was once an active little harbour, as the lime kilns on the quayside testify. It was here, according to the *Mabinogion*, that the great boar *Twrch Trwyth* swam ashore from Ireland after its encounter with King Arthur and his knights; it carried between its ears three golden objects which Culwch had to obtain before he could marry Olwen; it was defeated by Culwch after devastating the surrounding countryside.

Westward from St David's extends a true *finis terrae*, a salty, weatherbeaten tract of rock and cliff, where bracken and heather are barely kept at bay by hedgebanks around the small fields.

**St Justinians** – *2mi/3km W of St David's*. There is a precipitous drop to the tiny cove almost filled by the **St David's Lifeboat Station**.

**Ramsey Island** – This island nature reserve is the domain of wild flowers and red deer, of porpoises and the largest breeding colony of Atlantic grey seals on the Welsh coast, and of countless seabirds – peregrines, choughs, ravens, guillemots, razorbills, kittiwakes and fulmars. It lies on the far side of Ramsey Sound, through which tides can rip at 8 knots, foaming angrily against the rocks known as the Bitches.

**Whitesands Bay** – *2.5mi/4km NW of St David's*. The bay has a splendid west-facing sandy beach, popular with surfers. From here a breezy walk to **St David's Head** can be enjoyed, taking in the site from which St Patrick is supposed to have embarked for Ireland, Iron-Age fortifications, hut circles and field systems and the cromlech known as Coetan Arthur.

**St David's Head** – *N of Whitesands Bay*. From this headland, and from the miniature mountain of **Carn Llidi** (595ft/181m), there are magnificent **views**, which in exceptional conditions can encompass both Snowdonia and the mountains of Waterford and Wicklow in Ireland.

# SNOWDONIA ★★★

**(Eryri) Gwynedd and Conwy**
Michelin Atlas p 32-33 or Map 403 H-I 24-25

The vast and mountainous area of North Wales takes its name from its highest peak, Snowdon (3 560ft/1 085m), which, in the opinion of many, is the most beautiful mountain in England and Wales. The approach to this heartland is guarded by other mountain ramparts like Cadair Idris overlooking the Mawddach and Dysynni valleys far to the south. Virtually identical to the ancient kingdom of Gwynedd, Snowdonia was a seat of rebellion which had to be secured for England by a chain of mighty castles. It is still a stronghold of Welshness. Until the 16C the area stayed remote, roamed by wolves and bears. The economy remained tied to the meagre yields of upland agriculture, until the quickening pace of life in the 18C and early 19C brought both industry – in the form of mineral and slate extraction – and tourists in search of "picturesque and sublime" scenery.

**Snowdonia National Park** – The second largest National Park in England and Wales, which was established in 1951, extends over the greater part of the mountainous area. Its name in Welsh, *Eryri*, means Place of Eagles, although there are no eagles now. With its unrivalled combination of glorious mountain ranges and a splendid coastline, Snowdonia depends on tourism for much of its livelihood. Most visitors come for the day, from resorts on the north coast or from Snowdonia's own coastline on Cardigan Bay but climbers and serious walkers prefer to stay in one of the small towns or villages within the Park.

**The Mountains** – Snowdonia's geology is varied and complex. The oldest rocks, from the Cambrian period of c 600 million years ago, form the resistant and rugged Rhinog range. Cadair Idris, the Aran and Arenig mountains, as well as Snowdon itself owe their origin to outbursts of volcanic activity in Ordovician times, while the slate rocks which have contributed so much to the appearance and economy of parts of Snowdonia were formed as a result of the Silurian earth movements, which also gave the Scottish mountains their basic structure.

The decisive force which shaped the surface of the landscape seen today was the **ice**, which advanced and receded across the area for a period lasting some 70 000 years and which beat its final retreat only some 10 000 years ago. The slopes of both Snowdon and Cadair Idris were sculpted by glaciers into spectacular *cwms* separated by almost razor-sharp ridges, their depths filled with the glacial **lakes** that are one of the glories of the Park.

**The Valleys** – The mountain blocks are divided by valleys, many of which were ground into characteristic U-shapes by the action of the glaciers, leaving the hanging valleys typical of this kind of country, a phenomenon developed to perfection in the Pass of Llanberis and the Nant Ffrancon valley. The rivers form many attractive stretches; the Conwy and its tributaries around Betws-y-Coed are marked by a series of waterfalls, while the defile of the Glaslyn at Aberglaslyn is one of the famous sights of Snowdonia.

The northern and southern peaks are separated by the lush landscapes of the **Vale of Ffestiniog** beside the River Dwyryd. Here is situated **Plas Tan-y-Bwlch**, the residential study centre of the Snowdonia National Park, set in magnificent and picturesque grounds *(see p 235)*. It can be reached by the road or the Blaenau-Ffestiniog Railway. The slate quarries and waste tips of Blaenau Ffestiniog were tactfully excluded from the National Park when its boundaries were being drawn.

Slate Fencing, Llanffestiniog

## NORTHERN SNOWDONIA

This is Snowdonia proper, centred on Snowdon itself, but including other ranges like the Carneddau and the Glyders, as well as outstanding individual peaks like shapely Moel Hebog (2 566ft/782m) and sharply pointed Cnicht (2 264ft/690m) rising on either side of the Pass of Aberglaslyn.

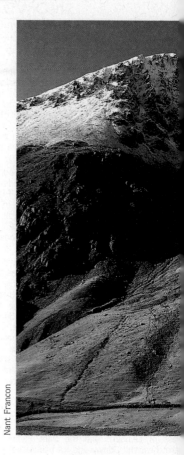

Nant Francon

***Snowdon** – The Great Mound (Yr Wyddfa) is the Welsh name for Snowdon, the "snowy height" marvelled at by the early Anglo-Saxons who no doubt first saw the wintry mountain from the relative safety of the sea.

Snowdon has been compared in shape to a starfish or Catherine wheel. From the summit, a series of ridges extends outwards, precipitous cwms dividing one from another. In places the ridges rise to form subordinate peaks like Moel Eilio to the northwest or Yr Aran to the south.

As is to be expected, the **panorama** from the summit, in clear conditions, is outstanding, encompassing most of North Wales and perhaps reaching to the Isle of Man, the Lake District, and even the Wicklow Mountains in Ireland.

**Paths to the summit** – The highest mountain south of the Scottish border inevitably attracts numerous admirers and would-be conquerors.

The **Snowdon Mountain Railway★★** (see p 173) is rarely short of passengers, as it climbs doggedly up the long ridge from Llanberis but the footpaths to the summit are also well trodden.

Parallel with the railway up the north face runs the **Llanberis Path** (5mi/8km) which is generally considered to be the most popular footpath to the top, if not the most exciting.

Another relatively easy path is the **Snowdon Ranger Path**, which approaches the summit from the west above Llyn Dwellyn (A 4085) and can be combined with the Rhyd Ddu Path for the descent.

Perhaps the most rewarding approach to the summit is via the **Pyg Track**, which climbs up the east face starting at a relatively high point (1 168ft/356m) from the large car park at Pen-y-Pass (A 4086) near the southern end of the Pass of Llanberis; it gives a fine vista down the whole length of the pass towards Anglesey and ends with a strenuous zigzag haul to the summit. The descent can be varied from the bottom of the zigzag by branching off down the **Miners Track**, which drops abruptly to Llyn Glaslyn and then more gently to Llyn Llydaw with old copper workings much in evidence along the way.

The **Watkin Path**, up the south face starting from Pont Bethania (A 498) in the Nant Gwynant valley, is perhaps the most arduous of the Snowdon paths, since it involves a long climb (3 300ft/over 1 000m), virtually the whole height of the mountain. By way of compensation, the lengthy climb passes fine waterfalls, the rock where the 84-year-old Gladstone spoke in defence of the rights of small nations, and the waste tips and structures abandoned long ago by the slate quarries which once ate away at the mountain. The views of the great embayment formed by Snowdon, Yr Aran and Craig-ddu are superb.

Far more of a challenge than any of these walks is the famous **Snowdon Horseshoe**, an airy ridge-top scramble which takes those with no fear of heights around the great crescent enclosing Llyn Glaslyn and Llyn Llydaw. This exhilarating excursion begins at Pen-y-Pass, proceeds at snail's pace along the razor-sharp ridge of **Crib Goch**, takes in the summit of Snowdon and returns along the ridge top leading to Y Lliwedd.

R O Eames/National Trust Photographic Library

Only in a few places is it possible for more passive observers to get an overall view of the mountain, though the range can easily be circumnavigated on main roads. One of the **grandest vistas** opens up for motorists driving west along the road (A 4086) from Capel Curig; another can be enjoyed from a lay-by off the road (A 498) near the head of the Nant Gwynant valley.

**Carnedd Range** – This block of mountains fills a vast area between the sea, the Vale of Conwy and the Nant Ffrancon valley. **Carnedd Llewelyn** (3 485ft/1 064m) and **Carnedd Dafydd** (3 423ft/1 044m) are the second and third highest mountains in Snowdonia, part of a spine of mostly rounded grassy summits running north-south with subsidiary ridges branching off and enclosing lakes, most of which are now used as reservoirs. The streams fed by these lakes run eastward to the Conwy, their final steep sections forming waterfalls in places. It is, however, to the north that one of Wales' most spectacular falls is found, Rhaeadr Fawr or **Aber Falls** (200ft/60m), at the point where the River Goch crashes over a barrier formed by hard igneous rock.

Just outside the National Park boundary to the north, the great rock buttress of **Penmaenmawr** projects into Conwy Bay, for centuries a formidable barrier to travellers along the coast, now overcome by the railway and the road (A 55). Made of quartz dolerite, the headland has been gnawed away for years for roadstone, the quarry operations contributing adversely to the allure of the little resort of Penmaenmawr, which was once a favourite with Gladstone.

Away from the coast, the Carneddau have a brooding, solitary atmosphere. No roads penetrate the interior of the massif, though the Roman highway from Canovium (Caerhun) to Segontium just outside Caernarfon crossed the pass at Bwlch y Ddeufaen, a route followed by today's bunched powerlines. Some idea of the grandeur of these mountains can be gained from the Iron-Age fort of **Pen-y-Gaer**, superbly located high above the Vale of Conwy and reached by a steep minor lane from the road (B 5106) near Dolgarrog.

**The Glyders and Nant Ffrancon** – The south-west rim of the Carnedd range drops abruptly to **Nant Ffrancon**, the spectacular U-shaped valley which, with its cwms, rock bars, moraines and perched rocks, provided 19C British geologists with conclusive evidence about the effects of glaciation on landforms. The floor of the lower valley was once filled by a lake, whose disappearance has left a flat surface across which the River Ogwen meanders. At the exit from the valley are the huge **Penrhyn Quarries**; below them lies their dependent town of **Bethesda**, like Blaenau Ffestiniog built on and out of slate.

The valley has long provided a route of some kind through the mountains, described in the 18C as "the most dreadful horse path in Wales". Telford improved the situation, his splendidly engineered Holyhead road still the basis of today's highway (A5). The arch of the old packhorse bridge can still be seen beneath the later bridge below **Ogwen Cottage**. Here, at the western end of the gloomy waters of **Llyn Ogwen**, is a youth hostel and mountain rescue post, the starting point for climbers and walkers on their way up the dramatically gouged northern flanks of the Glyder range. Britain's first National Nature Reserve, **Cwm Idwal★**, "a monument to ice", was designated here in 1954, to protect the crags and cliffs around the great cleft of the **Devil's Kitchen**, the glacial lake of **Llyn Idwal**, and the arctic-alpine flora, which makes a glorious late-spring and early-summer display, at least in those areas inaccessible to sheep. The rocks here present the kind of challenge which made them a training ground for the ascent of far higher peaks.

Some of the finest walks in Snowdonia make use of the different approaches to the summits here, which include Y Garn (3 104ft/946m), **Glyder Fawr** (3 279ft/999m) and **Glyder Fach** (3 262ft/994m), where the frost-shattered rocks are piled into strange formations like the Cantilever and the **Castle of the Winds**. **Tryfan** (3 010ft/915m) is

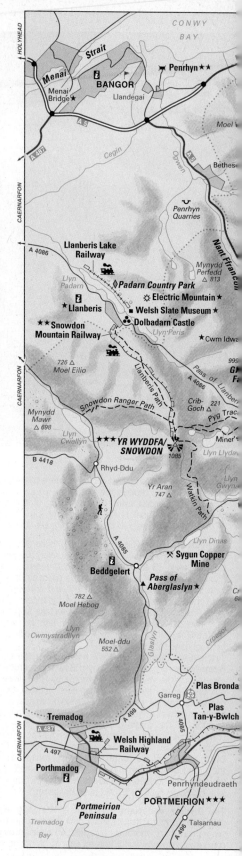

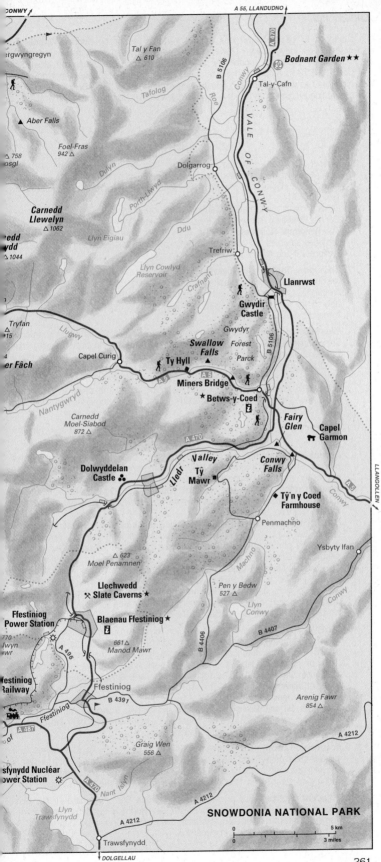

CONWY

Tal y Fan
△ 610

Bodnant Garden ★★

B 5106

A 470

Tal-y-Cafn

ergwyngregyn

Tafolog

Aber Falls

Foel-Fras
942 △

△ 758

osgl

Roe

Conwy

Dolgarrog

V
A
L
E

O
F

C
O
N
W
Y

Carnedd
Llewelyn
△ 1062

Dulyn

Porth-Llwyd

edd
ydd
△ 1044

Llyn Eigiau

Ddu

Trefriw

Llyn Cowlyd
Reservoir

Crafnant

Llanrwst

Gwydir
Castle

Tryfan
△
15

Llugwy

Gwydyr
Forest
Parck

B 5106

er Fâch

Capel Curig

Swallow
Falls △

Tŷ Hyll

A 5

A 5

Miners Bridge △

Betws-y-Coed ★
i

Fairy
Glen

Capel
Garmon

Nantygwryd

Carnedd
Moel-Siabod
872 △

A 470

Valley

Conwy
Falls △

Conwy

A 5

LLANGOLLEN

Dolwyddelan
Castle

Lledr

Tŷ
Mawr

Tŷ'n y Coed
Farmhouse

Penmachno

Machno

Ysbyty Ifan

△ 623
Moel Penamnen

Pen y Bedw
527 △

Llyn
Conwy

Conwy

Llechwedd
Slate Caverns ★

Ffestiniog
Power Station

Blaenau Ffestiniog ★
i

B 4406

B 4407

770
lwyn
awr

A 496

661 △
Manod Mawr

festiniog
Railway

Ffestiniog

Arenig Fawr
854 △

B 439 7

of

A 487

Ffestiniog

A 4212

sfynydd Nucléar
ower Station

A 470

Nant Islyn

Graig Wen
556 △

Llyn
Trawsfynydd

A 4212

A 4212

SNOWDONIA NATIONAL PARK

0                    5 km

0              3 miles

Trawsfynydd

supposed to be the only peak in Wales which cannot be climbed without using one's hands. Beyond Llyn Ogwen to the east, the road (A 5) leads to **Capel Curig** overlooked from the south by the beautiful elongated shape of Moel Siabod (2 861ft/872m). Capel Curig is famous, less for the Celtic holy man who gave the place his name than for **Plas y Brenin**, long-established as a school for the mastery of mountaineering technique, now the official National Mountain Centre.

## Out and About

**Visitor Centres** – Information Centres run by the Snowdonia National Park Authority are situated in Betws-y-Coed *(see p 92)*, Blaenau Ffestiniog *(see p 95)*, Dolgellau *(see p 146)*, Harlech *(see p 160)* and Aberdovey *(see p 280)*.
Other Tourist Information Centres are located in Bala, Barmouth, Conwy, Corris, Llanberis *(see p 172)*, Porthmadog and Tywyn.
The **Residential Study Centre** at Plas Tan-y-Bwlch *(see p 235)* near Porthmadog provides courses on a great variety of activities related to the natural features of the National Park.

**Snowdon Sherpa Bus Service** ⊙ – The service, which helps to ease congestion in the Park by enabling visitors to leave their cars behind, operates throughout the year but more frequently in summer. Timetables are available from the Snowdonia National Park Information Centres and Tourist Information Centres.

**Weather Conditions** – A 24hr **weather forecast** is available on Mountaincall Snowdonia ☎ 0891 500 449. Mountain walkers should bear in mind that temperatures drop rapidly as height is gained, roughly by 2 C for every 1 000ft/300m. This, combined with wind-chill, can mean that summit conditions can be unpleasantly, even dangerously, different from those which seemed so encouraging at the starting point of a climb down in the valley. The upper sections can be treacherous in wet or icy conditions and snow can fall in Snowdonia not only in winter but at any time of the year.

**Emergency** – In the case of injury telephone ☎ 999 and ask for the police.

**Ascent of Snowdon** – Climbing to the summit of Snowdon or any other peak in Snowdonia requires exactly the same precautions and equipment as any other mountain walk and should not be undertaken lightly. There is a **mountain rescue post** at the western end of Llyn Ogwen. Information on appropriate equipment is available from the Snowdonia National Park Information Centres *(see above)*.
Most of the different **paths or tracks leading to the summit** are described in the text below. Lurking beneath the summit is a café, successor to a hotel, much decried by purists, but a welcome source of hot drinks and other refreshments nevertheless.
The **National Mountain Centre** ⊙, at Plas-y-Brenin near Capel Curig *(west of Betwys-y-Coed by A 5)*, offers expert tuition to individuals and groups in various aspects of mountaineering (abseiling, rock climbing. ice climbing, indoor climbing, orienteering, skiing) and canoeing (white water, kayak). ☎ 01690 720 280; Fax 01690 720 394.

**Other Activities** – Snowdonia is popular for many outdoor activities, such as walking, climbing, cycling and water sports. As most of the area incorporated within the National Park is privately owned, there is no automatic right of access to land in the Park. Legal rights of way are shown on Ordnance Survey maps. The following sites are open to the public – Bala Lake for **water sports**; Coed-y-Brenin Forest Park and Gwydir Forest Park for **walking** and **mountain biking**.
**Rhiw Goch Ski and Mountain Bike Centre** *(Bronaber, Trawsfynydd)* – Nursery slopes and mist system; hire of mountain bikes of all sizes; off-road network of cycle tracks in Coed-y-Brenin Forest Park.

**Accommodation** – There are hotels and guesthouses in the towns and villages *(see pp 92 and 146)*, B & B accommodation in many of the farms and villages, and a youth hostel at the western end of Llyn Ogwen. People wishing to camp must first obtain the permission of the landowner.

**Adjacent Sights** – See Anglesey, Bala, Bangor, Barmouth, Beaumaris, Beddgelert, Betws-y-Coed, Blaenau Ffestiniog, Bodnant Gardens, Caernarvon, Conwy, Criccieth, Dolgellau, Harlech, Llanberis, Llandudno, Llanrwst. Penrhyn Castle, Porthmadog, Portmeirion.

# SOUTHERN SNOWDONIA

The National Park extends southwards beyond Cadair Idris to overlook the mouth of the Dovey *(Dyfi)*, one of the three splendid estuaries which penetrate the mountains and add greatly to their appeal. Between the outlets of the rivers is a fine coastline, in part formed by the lower ranges of the mountains themselves, which are traversed by corniche-like main roads, and in part consisting of coastal flats and sand dunes with fine west-facing beaches, a unique feature in a British National Park. Inland, apart from Cadair Idris and perhaps the Rhinogs, the mountains are less visited than northern Snowdonia, and walks of great solitude and splendour are still possible.

★**Cadair Idris** – Although the great "Chair (or Throne) of Idris" (2 928ft/892m) is just the third-highest peak in Snowdonia, its majestic presence is surpassed only by Snowdon itself. Cadair Idris dominates the country to the south of Dolgellau, though its character is best appreciated from some distance away, such as the **Precipice Walk** *(see p 147)* or close to. A drive along the minor road from Dolgellau to the exquisite little **Cregennen Lakes** reveals something of the mountain's grandeur, and it is also possible to ascend from this northern side.

The finest approach to Cadair Idris on foot, though not the easiest, is undoubtedly by the **Minffordd Path**, which begins on the south-eastern flank of the mountain, just north of Tal-y-llyn Lake. A steep climb through ancient oak woods leads across rugged open country to one of the most awe-inspiring sights in Snowdonia, **Llyn Cau**, its dark waters held in a great cauldron of cliffs. This was the scene that the painter **Richard Wilson**, quite unnecessarily, sought to improve upon in his famous picture of 1774, by reordering the various elements of the composition and adding a precipice. The climb to the summit slowly ascends the rim of the cauldron, the reward being a superb **panorama** over the valley of the Mawddach towards Snowdon to the north and to the rolling heights of mid-Wales to the south. The return is by the same route.

**Rhinog Range** – The Rhinogs, the most rugged of mountains, their rocky, ankle-twisting slopes somewhat softened by a dense coat of bilberry and heather, form an implacable but not impenetrable barrier between the coast of Cardigan Bay to the west and the interior. The principal peaks are **Rhinog Fawr** (2 362ft/720m) and **Rhinog Fach** (2 333ft/711m), both of which can be approached by minor roads leading up through the prettily wooded valleys of Ardudwy, the ancient name given to the long-settled country between sea and mountain. One road leads to **Llyn Cwm Bychan**, part of an old route through the uplands which includes the so-called Roman Steps *(see p 162)*. Another road runs up Cwm Nantcol towards **Bwlch Drws Ardudwy**, the spectacular pass between Rhinogs Fach and Fawr. To the south, ridges descend towards the Mawddach estuary, one of them ending in the crags over looking Barmouth *(see p 87)*, others sheltering wooded valleys like the one running down to Bontddu, where

Morfa Bychan

W R Davis/National Trust Photographic Library

the Romans mined gold. To the east is softer country, a spacious sweeping uplan
bounded by Llyn Trawsfynydd with its nuclear power station and partly filled by th
Forestry Commission's vast and splendid Coed y Brenin — the King's Fore
*(see p 148).*

**Arenig and Aran Ranges** — **Arenig Fawr** (2 800ft/854m) and **Arenig Fac**
(2 264ft/689m) stand sentinel over the approach from central Snowdonia to the grea
artificial lake of Llyn Celyn. The former presents a fine set of crags but is easi
ascended; according to one of Britain's most experienced mountain writer
WA Poucher, it is "higher and more shapely" than the latter which is "of no interest t
the climber".

Forestry plantations and grassy slopes conceal the true majesty of the **Arans** fro
the Bala-Dolgellau road. These lonely summits are best seen from the east, where
trio of mountain roads climb up to a high pass at **Bwlch y Groes**★★ *(see p 86).*
sinister line of crags rises to **Aran Fawddwy** (2 970ft/907m), the second-highest pea
in Snowdonia, best reached on foot from the end of the minor road running u
Cwm Cywarch.

# STRATA FLORIDA ABBEY ★
## Ceredigion
Michelin Atlas p 24 or Map 403 I 27
15mi/24km SE of Aberystwyth by B 4340 and a minor road

Here, as elsewhere in Wales, the Cistercians chose a remote and beautiful spot fc
their monastery. The abbey **ruins** stand at a point where the valley of the Teifi leave
the uplands and broadens out, still bounded by graceful, part-wooded hills.

The Abbey of the Flower
Vale *(Strata Florida)* wa
founded in 1164 an
shortly afterward cam
under the patronage c
Rhys ap Gruffudd (d 1197
a genial princeling who re
stored the fortunes of th
south-western kingdor

> **Adjacent Sights** — See Aberaeron, Aberyst-
> wyth, Elan Valley, Lampeter, Llanidloes,
> Llanwrtyd Wells, Vale of Rheidol, Tregaron.

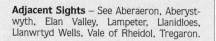

known as Deheubarth. The abbey soon eclipsed Llanbadarn both as a centre of learn
ing and as a tomb-church for the rulers of Deheubarth. In the early years of the 13
its economy flourished, based on great flocks of sheep which roamed the uplan
pastures. Later in the century it suffered in the course of Edward I's campaigns an
the church was burnt down after being struck by lightning in 1286. Like most abbey:
it declined gently in the course of the 14C and 15C, and by the time of the Dissolutio
the community consisted of a meagre band of seven monks and their abbot.

CADW: Welsh Historic Monuments – Crown Copyright

Detail of West Doorway, Strata Florida

## TOUR ⊙

In few places do the ruin
rise much over head-heigh
it is the setting rather tha
the architecture which im
presses.

The entrance to the abbe
the superb archway of it
great **West Door**★, is, how
ever, happily almost com
pletely intact. This is
wonderful synthesis of th
Romanesque with th
native Celtic spirit, with fiv
bands of roll moulding
sweeping right round th
semicircular opening, whil
a sixth terminates at th
springing in subtle spira
scrolls. All are boun
together by straps wit
similar scrolls.

The internal layout of th
abbey church was unusua
in that the nave wa
divided from the aisles b
stone screens. In the 14
the abbey was lavishl
retiled and some of th

surviving tiles have been relaid in the chapels of the south transept; motifs include a griffin, birds, a fleur-de-lys, and a lissom youth looking in a mirror, perhaps an allegory of vanity.

To the south, the **abbey garth** is closely bounded by a farmhouse which may incorporate parts of the monks' refectory. Beyond the wall to the north is the modest **parish church**. The poet Dafydd ap Gwilym *(see p 56)* is buried in its extensive graveyard, the spot marked by a venerable yew. Nearby is a diminutive gravestone noting that a left leg and part of a thigh were "cut off and interr'd here June the 18th, 1756"; this loss of limb failed to deter Henry Hughes, a cooper, from later emigrating to America.

# SWANSEA ★

(Abertawe) Swansea – Population 181 906
Michelin Atlas p 15 or Map 403 I 29

city of strong and varied personality, Swansea is the unrivalled capital of south-west Wales, with a commercial centre rebuilt after wartime bombing, a revitalised maritime quarter, a university and a dramatic setting on the splendid sweep of its great bay. The uplands of central Wales come rolling almost to the waterfront, the city has its own seaside resort of The Mumbles, and to the west are the cliffs, beaches and unspoilt countryside of the Gower Peninsula, Britain's first officially designated Area of Outstanding Natural Beauty (AONB).

## SWANSEA

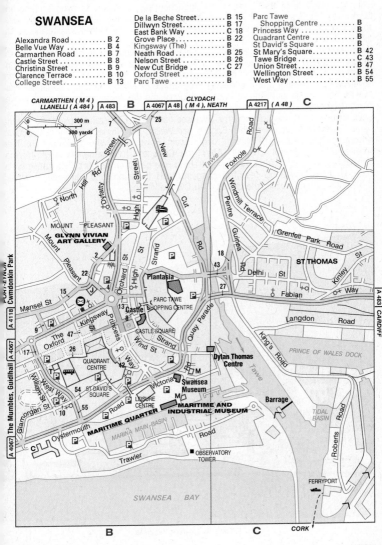

Cultural life is at least as vibrant as that of the capital, Cardiff. Once a focal point
the Industrial Revolution, the city has cleared away the dereliction left by centuries of
reckless industrial development and is proud of its heritage of parks, gardens ar
other green spaces.

Swansea's more salubrious suburbs extend westwards. They include Edwardian U
lands, where **Dylan Thomas** was born and passed his early years in what he called "th
lovely, ugly town", often musing in Cwmdonkin Park where there is a memorial t
him.

The challenge this posed was defined, then triumphantly met, in a massive operatic
of regeneration, known as the Lower Swansea Valley Project. The vast tracts
derelict land have been replaced by a new landscape of broad roadways, open space
new industries and leisure facilities.

## HISTORICAL NOTES

The most vivid aspect of Swansea's past was its industry which from an early dat
began to make use of the area's abundant and shallow coal seams. Metalworkin
began in the Neath area in Tudor times but its centre of gravity shifted in the 18C t
the banks of the tidal Tawe, which offered a better anchorage for boats bringing
the ores which were then smelted using the easily worked local coal. Copper was firs
smelted in the Lower Swansea Valley in 1717, lead in 1755; zinc was produced on
large scale from the 1840s, as was tinplate; Wilhelm Siemens began making steel o
the open-hearth method in 1869. The environmental impact of all this activity wa
acute even in the early days, with severe air pollution causing woodland destruction o
a large scale, though visitors and artists found the hellish landscape of the Lowe
Swansea Valley with its forest of fuming chimneys a source of wonderment an
fascination. Decline set in at the turn of the century; by the 1950s the valley was
sorry picture of decay and environmental degradation, the biggest wasteland in th
whole of industrial Britain.

Swansea was more than a cradle of industry. Even as metalworking was enriching th
(mostly English) entrepreneurs, the town had high hopes of its becoming a secon
Brighton. At the beginning of the 19C assembly rooms were built, the foreshore wa
developed for bathing and a glittering programme of events filled the social calenda
at least for a while, until the advance of industry and the development of docks prove
more decisive in defining the city's character.

Even before the coming of industry, Swansea had been a substantial place. Its origina
name, Sweyn's Island, is neither English nor Welsh, but Norse, possibly in commem
oration of the 10C-11C Danish King, Swein Forkbeard, who is known to hav
frequented the Bristol Channel. After the Conquest it became an Anglo-Norma
borough with a castle, a market and a trading role based on its port. The native Wels
seem to have stored up resentment against this intrusion, and the town was ver
thoroughly sacked during the Owain Glyn Dŵr rebellion.

Maritime Quarter, Swansea

## Out and About

**Tourist Information Centre** – Plymouth Street, Swansea SA1 3QG 01792 468 321; Fax 01792 464 602; swantrsm@cableol.co.uk
Oystermouth Square, Mumbles SA3 4DQ ☎ 01792 361 302; Fax 01792 363 392.

**Entertainment** – The lively **cultural life** of Swansea includes regular concerts by international orchestras and soloists in the **Brangwyn Hall** (Box Office ☎ 01792 302 489), opera and ballet and touring productions in the **Grand Theatre** (Box Office ☎ 01792 475 715), a variety of productions in the smaller theatres – **Dylan Thomas Theatre** (☎ 01792 473 238), the **Taliesin Theatre** (Box Office ☎ 01792 296 883) and the **Cwmtawe Theatre** (Box Office ☎ 01792 830 111) and **Penyrheol Theatre** (Box Office ☎ 01792 897 039).

**Festivals** – The most popular of the local festivals are the **Swansea Summer Show** (August), **Swansea Festival of Music** (Autumn), the **Margam Festival** (July-August) and the **Llanelli Festival** (September-October), the **Gower Festival** of small concerts in the churches of the area (July); except in summer visitors may attend the rehearsals of the famous **male voice choirs**.

**Craftwork** – The **Lovespoon Gallery** ⊙ *(Mumbles Road, Oystermouth)* offers a wide range of lovespoons in different designs and types of wood, also varying sizes and prices. For woollen goods visit the **Maritime and Industrial Museum** *(see below)* and see the machinery from the Neath **Abbey Woollen Mill** in action.

**Indoor Activities** – The Swansea Leisure Centre provides for many such – swimming (water slide and diving tank), roller skating, squash, badminton, trampoline, volleyball, martial arts, table tennis, bowling, sauna, steam room, sunbeds.

**Outdoor Activities** – These make the most of the natural elements – sea and wind – canoeing, sailing, surfing (Bay Caswell and Langland Bay or Llangennith for the Atlantic rollers), windsurfing (Oxwich, Port Eynon), water-skiing (Swansea Bay, Oxwich Bay), hang-gliding and parascending (Rhossili Bay). Good beach at Swansea Marina.

**Adjacent Sights** – See Brecon Beacons, Carmarthen, Gower Peninsula, Llandeilo, Llanelli, Margam Park, Neath, Port Talbot.

## Where to Eat

**Hansons**, Pilot House Wharf, Trawler Rd, Swansea Marina, SA1 1UN. ☎ 01792 466 200. Friendly and informal ambience. blackboard menu; simple fresh cooking – some fusion influences – superb fish; good value set lunch; located at the end of the marina where trawlers tie up.

**L'Amuse**, 93 Newton Rd, The Mumbles, SA3 4BN. ☎ 01792 366 006; Fax 01792 368 090. Well established neighbourhood bistro, with well priced menu, offering authentic cooking, using top quality Welsh and French produce.

## Where to Stay

**Beaumont**, 72-73 Walter Rd, SA1 4QA. ☎ 01792 643 956; Fax 01792 643 044. Traditional style hotel (16 rm) with simple comforts, accommodating business and cultural visitors to the city.

**Hillcrest House**, 1 Higher Lane, The Mumbles, SA3 4NS. ☎ 01792 363 700; Fax 01792 363 768. Small hotel (7 rm) privately owned; rooms themed subtly around countries; close to the beaches of the Gower.

**Fairyhill**, Reynoldston, Llandrhidian, SA3 1BS. ☎ 01792 390 139; Fax 01792 391 358. 18C country house (8 rm); individually appointed rooms; attentive service with genuine hospitality; outstanding wines and imaginative cooking – Welsh and modern.

# ★MARITIME QUARTER (B)

A succession of docks was built throughout the 19C to cater for what seemed like an ever-expanding influx of shipping, bringing in ores from Cornwall and beyond and taking out the coal from the 200 or so pits around the city. Today, the commercial docks, including the car ferry to Cork, are all to the east of the Tawe, now controlled by a **new barrage** (C) and lock. On the far bank, close to the city centre, the South Dock was built in 1859, occupying the once-fashionable area known as the Burrows and putting paid to Swansea's aspirations as a resort.

The wheel has now come full-circle; closed in 1969, the dock has been saved from dereliction and transformed into the sparkling centrepiece of what the city proudly calls its Maritime Quarter, with an array of new housing, a marina for 600 boats, restaurants, a theatre, a gallery, a luxury hotel and a fine museum. The whole area has been enriched with public art, which ranges from an engaging statue of **Dylan Thomas** on the quayside to quizzical sculptures on a maritime theme along the new promenade facing Swansea Bay.

★**Maritime and Industrial Museum** ⊘ (**B**) – Housed in the former Coast Line warehouse, this is an important museum, a stimulating starting point for any appreciation of Swansea and its setting. The emphasis is on the city's long-standing connection with the sea, on industry and on transport.

The ground floor gives an imaginative and comprehensive account of the evolution of industry and of the thoroughgoing way in which its legacy of dereliction has been tackled. There is a large number of stationary engines and transport exhibits, ranging from that archetypal Welsh mode of transport on water, the coracle, to the reconstructed interior of a mid-20C garage.

The upper floor has a vivid tableau of the traditional activity of cockle-gathering, several small craft, and many models and pictures on a maritime theme. There is plenty of space for temporary exhibitions. The machinery from the nearby Neath Abbey Woollen Mill has been installed here and can be seen in action.

In the separate Tramshed stands a doubledecker tram, once the property of the Swansea Tramways & Improvement Co, together with the cab of the last tram to run on the Mumbles Railway *(see p 270)*.

Not shut away in a shed, but floating in their natural element by the quayside, are a number of historic vessels, including the tugboat *Canning*.

**Swansea Museum** ⊘ (**B**) – In the angle between the South Dock and the River Tawe, a little network of streets is all that is left of the area once known as the Burrows.

Among the Regency houses and pompous public buildings of the Victorian era stands a splendid Ionic structure, a temple to culture which was the earliest museum in Wales. Built in 1841 by the Royal Institution of Wales, it is a striking symbol of Swansea's aspirations to civic leadership. The Cabinet of Curiosities gallery *(first floor)* is laid out along Victorian lines, presenting a hotch-potch of items with no discernible theme. A Greek jug made in 700 BC sits next to a 1930s toaster; a 19C Welsh kitchen is recreated next to a millinery display

*Wayward Wind* by David Carpanini

A reconstructed Egyptian tomb and a collection of local ceramics are among the items displayed in the other galleries of the museum, which is gradually modernising the presentation of its wide range of exhibits.

**Dylan Thomas Centre** ⊘ (**BC**) – *Somerset Place*. The former Guildhall, a colonnaded Georgian building overlooking the marina, has been transformed into the **National Literature Centre for Wales**, which houses a theatre, exhibition galleries and a meeting room for writers and artists. A permanent, though changing, exhibition explores the life and friendships of **Dylan Thomas** through photographs, letters and film. New and second-hand works are on sale in the bookshop-cum-café.

## CITY CENTRE

Swansea's commercial heart is crammed into the narrow strip of land between the shoreline and the abruptly rising slopes just to the north, now covered with suburban housing.

The centre, severely battered by the enemy bombing in 1941, makes few claims to obvious historical or architectural interest but pulses with vigorous life, especially around the famous covered Market with its fabulous range of fresh foods. The modern retail centres of The Quadrant and St David's pick up the theme of crowded shopping under cover. Close by is the Grand Theatre, still with its auditorium of 1897.

Princess Way and Kingsway reflect post-war planners' none-too-successful attempts to dignify the city centre with grandiose boulevards but Castle Square is currently being expensively restyled and landscaped to make it a more fitting focal point.

The first fortress erected by the Normans has disappeared and the fragments of **castle** (**B**) visible today were the work of Henry de Gower, Bishop of St David's 1328-47. The castle has a similar arcaded parapet to that of Gower's Palace at St David's. The castle was sacked by Owain Glyn Dŵr, then later served as a debtors' prison. Part of it became the newspaper offices where Dylan Thomas worked as a cub reporter; when the paper moved out in the late 1950s the castle itself narrowly escaped being sacked again, this time by the city council.

Below the castle the land falls quite steeply to the Strand, a curving street marking the old course of the Tawe, which was led into the New Cut some distance to the east when the 19C North Dock was built. Repeating the curve of the Strand is Wind Street, with a pleasing mixture of Georgian, Victorian and other buildings which give some flavour of the commercial city in its 19C heyday. The North Dock has been replaced in its turn by a complex of shopping and leisure facilities known as Parc Tawe.

★**Glynn Vivian Art Gallery** ⊘ (**B**) – This airy yet intimate gallery was opened in 1911 to house the art collections donated to the city by Glynn Vivian (1835-1910), a member of the wealthy dynasty who had made Swansea the copper capital of the world. The collections reflect not only this eccentric younger son's extensive travels in Europe, but also the pre-eminence of the famous Swansea (later Cambrian) Pottery in the late 18C-early 19C.

In addition, a sufficient number of Welsh artists are represented to make the gallery one of the few places to convey an adequate impression of the nation's relatively minor but still fascinating contribution to the visual arts in modern times. Pre-eminent is Ceri Richards (1903-71) who, while obviously influenced by artists like Picasso and Matisse, also dwelt on specifically local themes like the landscape of the Gower Peninsula, his father's tinplate mill, or the poetry of Dylan Thomas. Thomas makes an appearance in sketches by the virtuoso draughtsman Alfred Janes and there is a portrait of his wife, Caitlin, by Augustus John. Jack Jones (1922-93), sometimes referred to as the "Welsh Lowry", is represented by a pair of industrial landscapes. Evan Walters (1893-1951) painted fine studies of working subjects like his cheerful *Cockle Woman* (c 1935) and his *Welsh Miner* (1926-30), before turning to more progressive techniques in later life. The atmosphere of the South Wales mining valleys has rarely been more sharply portrayed than by David Carpanini (b 1946), while the country's hospitality to and impact on foreign-born artists is revealed in canvases by Ernest Neuschul (1895-1968) and Josef Herman (b 1911).

The gallery has a modern extension and an attractive sculpture garden.

**Plantasia** ⊘ (**B**) – Conceived as a replacement for old glasshouses in the city's botanical gardens, this extraordinary structure seems to have landed from a different planet among the mega-shops and leisure malls of Parc Tawe. It is however firmly held in place, not least by the large amount of compost (1 500m$^3$/52 970cu ft) supporting its exotic array of plant life. Within its glass and white-metal envelope are three computer-controlled and completely-convincing artificial habitats – a tropical zone, a rainforest and a desert. The amazing array of plants is supplemented by the birds, butterflies, fish and reptiles that would coexist with them in the wild.

## SWANSEA BAY

To the west of the mouth of the Tawe, the splendid shoreline curves round in a tightening crescent that ends in the rock islands of Mumbles Head and is accompanied for its entire length by a chain of parks and other green spaces. The main highway, almost always busy with traffic, parallels a cycleway laid out along the promenade which replaced the much-mourned **Mumbles Railway**. This famous and fascinating line, claimed to have been the first passenger railway in the world, extended from its dockside station all along the seafront to Mumbles Pier and seemed for many years an irreplaceable part of city life. It was built in 1804 and carried passengers from 1807 onwards until, underfunded and with outworn rolling stock, it was closed in 1960.

At weekends or on fine evenings the exodus from the city intensifies as the population flocks westward for the fresher air of the Mumbles or of the Gower Peninsula just beyond. The prospect of sea, city and hills has sometimes been compared to the Bay of Naples, a hyperbole forgivable on a summer evening when the Bristol Channel tides have covered the extensive mudflats. A modern County Hall has taken advantage of the view, and those able to afford it have always resided in this part of the city, well to windward of the source of their wealth, the pollution-producing enterprises lining the Tawe to the east of the city.

**Guildhall** ⊙ – Just inland from Mumbles Road, this civic palace in Portland stone is an exercise in the stripped Classical architecture of the inter-war period, not set among equals like Cardiff's City Hall but surrounded by modest houses. The apparent coolness of its character is offset by a delight in the detail of windows

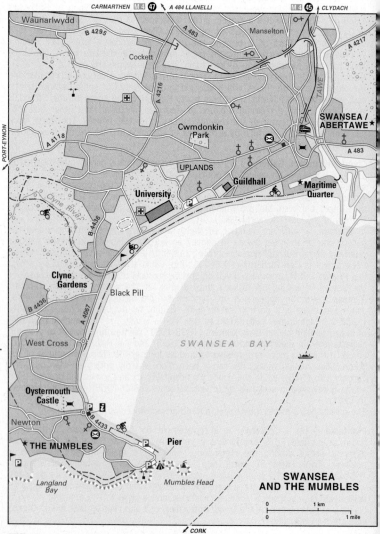

SWANSEA AND THE MUMBLES

doors, lamps and the stone medallions along the cornice, and even more so by the sumptuousness of its interior.

The high point is **Brangwyn Hall**, a much-used venue for concerts and other events, named in honour of the Anglo-Welsh artist Sir Frank Brangwyn (1867-1956), who painted the magnificent **British Empire Panels★** that enliven its otherwise somewhat stark interior. Originally destined for the House of Lords, the 16 panels swarm with people and animals in a setting of exotic vegetation, and are perhaps a celebration less of Imperial grandeur than of life itself in all its fecundity of forms and colour.

**University** – Part of the University of Wales, this is a densely built-up campus establishment, occupying part of Singleton Park, once the domain of Swansea's copper kings, the Vivian family.

**Clyne Gardens** ⊙ – The Clyne Valley Country Park follows the little Clyne River inland, using the trackbed of an old railway line as a cycle path cutting across the neck of the Gower Peninsula. The gardens (50 acres/20ha) once belonged to the Vivians, and their mansion, Clyne Castle, was the meeting place of royalty and statesmen. In the 1920s and 1930s its fine woodlands were planted up with a spectacular profusion of azaleas and rhododendrons.

**★The Mumbles** – Mumbles has a multiple personality. Its 13C castle has looked down on oystermen, mansion-dwellers and sedate Victorian holidaymakers as well as today's yachtsmen and other water sports enthusiasts. The difficult approach to Swansea Bay is guarded both by the lighthouse and by the famous Mumbles lifeboat.

The Mumbles has become the city's favourite suburb, both for commuting residents and for the weekend revellers who throng the pubs and restaurants crowded along the waterfront road. Bathers nowadays prefer the smaller bays at Langland and Caswell to the west of Mumbles Head.

**Waterfront** – The footpath and cycleway from Swansea city centre lead visitors to the slipway used by the yacht clubs, overlooked by a popular modern café. At high tide the scene is always busy with people messing around in boats, while at any state of the tide this is one of the best places from which to absorb the splendid panorama over the Bay. Closer to Mumbles Head with its small Victorian fort is the **Pier**, now deserted by pleasure steamers as well as by the Mumbles Railway but still patronised by fishermen and idlers. The lifeboat house with its characteristic red roof stands just alongside.

**Oystermouth Castle** ⊙ – Atop its knoll and with much of its masonry still intact, the ruined castle makes an imposing sight when approached across the parkland above Oystermouth village. It is a mid-13C rebuilding of an earlier Norman stronghold destroyed by the Welsh, with a gateway, keep, curtain walls and a chapel wing with exceptionally fine window tracery added in the 14C. From the wall-walks are some of the best views of the Bay.

# TENBY★★

(Dinbych-y-Pysgod) Pembrokeshire – Population 4 808
Michelin Atlas p 14 or Map 403 F 28

This little harbour town, medieval then Georgian, combines many of the ingredients of a seaside resort in a compact and pleasing pattern.

Tenby's Welsh name means "little fort of the fishes" and the settlement began as a native Welsh stronghold atop the limestone promontory of Castle Hill. Of the Norman fort which succeeded it there remain a number of fragments, some of which have been adapted to house the local museum. There are more substantial remains of the walls built to protect the Norman town from Welsh resentment.

Vessels from Tenby traded with Ireland, France, Portugal and Spain, as well as across the Bristol Channel, but by the 18C the port had declined and the town languished in squalor and decay.

## English mathematician

Tenby was the birthplace of Robert Recorde (1510-58), who introduced algebra to England. He was the foremost English mathematician of his age and the first to write on astronomy and other scientific subjects in the English language. He was a Fellow of All Souls College in Oxford and later taught in Cambridge, where he took a medical degree. He became physician to Edward VI and to Queen Mary I. He died in prison in London and there is a memorial tablet to him in Tenby Church.

Tenby

Rescue came towards the end of the century in the person of Sir William Paxton of Middleton Hall *(see p 131)*, who exploited Napoleon's closure of the Continent to British travellers by promoting Tenby as a fashionable watering-place, with baths, assembly rooms and lodging houses. Rows of elegant Georgian houses in pastel colours rise up above the bay. Today Tenby still flourishes as a holiday destination thanks to its own charm, its central position in south Pembrokeshire and, not least, the superabundance of caravan parks in its hinterland.

## SIGHTS

**★★Harbour and Seafront** – An almost too-perfect composition is formed by the jetty, old warehouses backed by massive retaining walls, Fishermen's Chapel, and the broken semicircle of pastel-coloured Georgian and Regency houses climbing gently to the clifftop.
Beyond the pleasure craft and fishing boats grounded within the harbour at low tide stretch the splendid sands of **North Beach**, interrupted by jagged rock outcrops. The red-roofed lifeboat station stands out to sea from Castle Hill, on the far side of which are more fine stretches of sand, **Castle Beach** and **South Beach**. A Victorian fort (1869), one of several built to protect Milford Haven, is visible on St Catherine's Island.

**Museum** ⊘ – As well as permanent and rotating displays on the history and natural history of Tenby and its surroundings, the museum has a number of paintings by artists associated with the town, particularly **Augustus John** and his sister, **Gwen**, who spent their childhood here. There are also mementoes of the farcical French invasion of Pembrokeshire in 1797 *(see p 154)* as well as cannon balls from the siege of 1644. An outside wall is covered with a superbly bold **mural** celebrating the sea by Jonah Jones (b 1919).

**Tudor Merchant's House** ⊘ – This late-15C town house is the sole surviving example of many such buildings erected in Tenby's heyday as a busy port. Restored in exemplary fashion, and ruggedly picturesque outside, its interior has been furnished with the help of the National Museum to evoke various periods in the house's long history before it passed into the possession of the National Trust in 1937. Many pieces are of exceptional interest, like the mid-18C food cupboards, unique to Wales, or the late-17C–early-18C Welsh oak armchair, described as "the most satisfying example of chair design on public display in Wales". Other evidence of long occupation is provided by the latrine tower extending to all floors, the cesspit of which has revealed intimate details of the diet of long-dead residents.

**St Mary's Church** ⊘ – With its tall spire (152ft/46m) rising over the town centre, St Mary's is one of the largest parish churches in Wales. It was begun in the 13C but was much modified and enlarged in the 15C, when the nave arcades were built and the chancel given its stepped approach to the sanctuary. The chancel also has a fine wagon roof, with a multitude of bosses carved in grotesque and humorous designs, including a mermaid.

## Out and About

**Tourist Information Centre** – The Croft, Tenby SA70 8AP ☎ 01834 842 402; Fax 01834 845 439.

**Excursions by boat** – To Caldey Island *(see below)*.

**Carriage rides** ⊘ – Rides in a horse-drawn carriage *(30min)* round the town centre from the churchyard.

**Beaches** – North Beach (in the harbour) and South Beach *(W of the headland)*.

**Adjacent Sights** – See Carew, Haverfordwest, Laugharne, Milford Haven, Pembroke, Pembrokeshire Coast.

## Where to Stay

**Broadmead**, Haywood Lane, SA70 8DA. *0.75mi/1km NW*. Well established, well appointed hotel (20 rm) with individually designed bedrooms; conservatory overlooking south-facing gardens.

**Waterwynch House**, Narberth Rd, Waterwynch Bay, SA70 8TJ. *2mi/3km N by A 478*. ☎ 01834 842 464; Fax 01834 845 076. Family-owned hotel (14 rm), built in 1820 by the artist Charles Norris, set in a secluded valley on the shores of Carmarthen Bay.

**Penally Abbey**, Penally, SA70 7PY. *2mi/3km SW by A 4139*. ☎ 01834 843 033; Fax 01834 844 714. Gothic style stone-built country house (12 rm), personally managed by the owners; individually styled rooms with period furnishing; views over Tenby golf course and Carmarthen Bay.

The numerous **memorials** naturally reflect the social history of the town; they include the elaborate tombs of late-15C merchants, a splendid early-17C wall monument to the wife of Thomas ap Rees, and an early-19C tablet commemorating Peggy Davies, a "Bathing Woman" whose "good humour, respectful attentions, Gratitude, made her employers – Friends". The cadaver of a late-15C cleric strikes a less jolly note.

**Town Walls** – The layout of the town reveals how the Normans' habitual grid of streets could be seriously distorted by a site as pleasingly irregular as that of Tenby. The seaward line of walls has disappeared but to the south-west, together with a number of towers, they run in an almost ruler-straight line and are virtually intact and enhanced by tree planting. They represent a 15C reconstruction of the defences originally built in the 13C. The south-west gate is a semicircular barbican, known as the Five Arches from the openings made in it in the 19C.

## EXCURSIONS

★**Caldey Island** ⊘ – *2mi/3km S of Tenby by boat*. This monastic island lies just off the coast *(only 0.5mi/1km)* south of Giltar Point. There was a Celtic monastery here in the 6C, of which no trace remains. In 1136 Caldey was granted to the Benedictines, already settled at St Dogmael's near Cardigan. At the Dissolution only one monk was to be found on the island; in 1906 the Benedictines returned but gave way to the present Cistercian community in the 1920s.

Caldey's seclusion and its deep religious roots enhance the special character common to all islands. The walk from the jetty leads through dunes and woodland to a "village green". Here, as well as a terrace of whitewashed cottages, timeless-looking but built only in 1953, is the post office, a *jeu d'esprit* of a building with dormers and projecting roof. Inside is a small number of displays on the island's history. Caldey perfumes are sold in the nearby shop.

The dominant structure is the modern **monastery**, an oddly placeless assemblage of buildings with pale-rendered walls under red-tiled roofs. To the west is the little **St David's Church**, much rebuilt but on pre-Norman foundations.

A farm track climbs southward to the clifftop **lighthouse** with its brace of keepers' cottages, passing on the way Caldey's farmyard, which abuts the Old Priory, the most complete set of monastic buildings in Wales. The centrepiece is the little 13C **Church of St Illtud**, with pebble floor, Ogam stone, and a spire well out of true. Around the compact courtyard stand gatehouse, guest lodgings, refectory, prior's quarters and monks' dormitory; just outside is the monastic fishpond.

**Manorbier Castle** ⊘ – *6mi/10km W of Tenby by A 4139 and B 4585*. The great churchman known as **Gerald of Wales** *(see p 57)*, who was born in this secluded seaside castle c 1146, described Manorbier as "the most delectable spot in Wales", praising in lyrical terms its setting of orchards, vineyards, fishponds and hazel woods.

The present castle was mostly built after Gerald's time. It is approached from a car park laid out on what was once an inlet connecting the stronghold to the sea. A partly excavated ditch is crossed to the sturdy little gatehouse, flanked by the partly ruinous Old Tower. The curtain walls are strengthened to north and south by substantial round towers. Within the attractively gardened inner ward is the modern house built by JR Cobb, who restored the castle in the late 19C; at the far end are remains of the chapel and the hall block.

Though much of the surrounding area is swamped in shrubby growth, and the sandy beach is crowded in the season, something remains of Manorbier's medieval allure. As well as the remains of a mill there is a fine dovecot with a corbelled roof. On the hillside opposite stands the 12C **Church of St James the Great** ⊘ with a fine Pembrokeshire tower, a cavernous interior, and an excellent view of the castle on its sandstone spur.

# TINTERN ABBEY★★
## Monmouthshire
### Michelin Atlas p 16 or Map 403 L 28

The Cistercians came to this remote and lovely location amid the woods of the winding Wye in 1131, and the picturesque ruins of their great abbey still stand, a magnet for visitors ever since the first tourists floated down the river in search of sublime and romantic scenery in the late 18C.

Its roof gone, its glass smashed, its walls obliterated by ivy, the abbey church nevertheless remains essentially intact and, although the greater part of its extensive out-buildings have been reduced to stubs of walls, Tintern still conveys a powerful impression of the architectural splendour which accompanied the severities of monastic life.

**Norman Foundation** – Tintern was the first Cistercian abbey to be established in Wales, a daughter house of the abbey at L'Aumone in Normandy, whose monks were invited here by Walter Fitz Richard de Clare of Chepstow Castle (see p 133). The lords of Chepstow were to continue as benefactors of the abbey, the greatest of them being Roger Bigod III who was responsible for the lavish rebuilding of the abbey church in the late 13C. By the time of the Dissolution, Tintern was the wealthiest abbey in Wales, a complex of buildings extending over much of the narrow strip of flat land between the river and the steep wooded slopes.

### Out and About

**Adjacent Sights** – See Abergavenny, Blaenavon, Caerleon, Caerwent, Chepstow, Monmouth, Newport, Raglan Castle, Usk.

### Where to Eat

**Parva Farmhouse**, Tintern, NP16 6SQ. *8mi/13km N by A 466*. South-facing stone farmhouse (9 rm), re-built in the mid-17C, on the northern edge of Tintern; traditional cooking and warm hospitality provided by the owners.

**Romantic Tintern** – In the mid-18C the abbey ruins were taken in hand by the Duke of Beaufort, who tidied and turfed the interior, thus making it ready for the tourists who were soon to arrive.

Among the first was the Revd William Gilpin, one of the foremost promoters of "Picturesque" sensibility, who, in his *Observations on the River Wye* (1782), suggested that the ruins might benefit from the judicious use of a mallet to knock them into even more attractively irregular shape. Equipped with his book, parties of visitors would descend the river from Ross to Chepstow in boats provided by local innkeepers, who by special arrangement would also provide a torchlight tour of the abbey ruins by night.

The elegiac atmosphere sought by such visitors was captured by the artist **JMW Turner** (1755-1851) who made a number of studies of the ruins in the course of the 1790s. Tintern occupied a special place in the heart of **William Wordsworth** (1770-1850), who came here twice, in 1793 and again in 1798, composing his famous *Lines Written a Few Miles above Tintern Abbey* which recall:

> ... these steep and lofty cliffs,
> Which on a wild secluded scene impress
> Thoughts of more deep seclusion....

**Abbey Ruins** ⊘ – Souvenir shops and car and coach parks attest to Tintern's longstanding popularity. Entry is via discreetly designed modern buildings flanking the riverside car park, and most visitors will be drawn first to the majestic **abbey church**, built, unusually, to the south of the cloister and its surrounding buildings. With its high walls crowned by the four great gables of nave, transepts and sanctuary, this is the structure raised by the munificence of Roger Bigod between 1269 and 1301 to replace the far more modest 12C Norman church whose outline is marked on the floor of the nave.

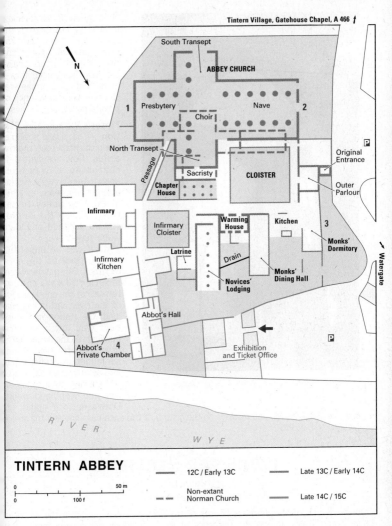

Tintern Village, Gatehouse Chapel, A 466

N

ABBEY CHURCH
South Transept

Presbytery       1        Nave        2

Choir

North Transept

Passage

Sacristy

Chapter House

CLOISTER

Original Entrance

Outer Parlour

Infirmary

Infirmary Cloister

Warming House

Kitchen

Latrine

Drain

Novices' Lodging

Monks' Dining Hall

Monks' Dormitory        3

Infirmary Kitchen

Abbot's Hall

Abbot's Private Chamber        4

Exhibition and Ticket Office

Watergate

R I V E R   W Y E

## TINTERN ABBEY

0 — 50 m
0 — 100 f

— 12C / Early 13C
- - Non-extant Norman Church

— Late 13C / Early 14C
— Late 14C / 15C

All the screens and subdivisions which reflected the complexities of monastic ritual have long since disappeared, and the eye is led directly to the far end of the building, where the **east window** (1), bare of all tracery and with but a single central mullion, links the abbey with its gloriously wooded setting. Columns, shafts and pointed arches in Decorated style still evoke something of the confidence and expansiveness of the late 13C, but it is the great, seven-light **west window** (2) which is the most splendid surviving single feature. In the presbytery, massive upturned roof bosses are reminders of the weight and substance of the stone vaults which disappeared at the Dissolution.

Bigod's late-13C rebuilding of the abbey church had been preceded earlier in the century by reconstruction of the accommodation around the **cloisters.**

Along the north side are substantial remains of the monks' dining hall, flanked by **kitchen** to the west and **warming house** to the east. Still partly vaulted, this last structure housed the abbey's only permanent winter fire, where monks might recover from the chilling effects of protracted worship in otherwise stone-cold surroundings. The western range of the cloister contained the quarters of the lay brothers; to the east are the remains of the chapter-house, novices' lodging and monks' dormitory. The foundations of the latrine block are visible, once flushed by the drain which runs roughly west-east across the whole site; its alignment may have forced the reversal of the traditional Cistercian siting of church to the north and cloister to the south, to maximise natural light and warmth.

The abbey precinct (27 acres/11ha) extended over an area larger than that of most medieval Welsh towns. To the east of the main cloister, a secondary cloister developed, dominated by the infirmary and by the abbot's quarters (4), both of which were added to and improved in the course of the 14C and 15C.

Crossing and East Window, Tintern Abbey

CADW: Welsh Historic Monuments – Crown Copyright

To the west of the complex there are foundations of the guest house, the arch of the watergate leading to the river; the gatehouse chapel has been converted into a house and parts of the precinctual wall now enclose private gardens.

**Tintern Village and Station** – The village straggles along the main road and riverside. Now residential in character, it was once known for its wire works established as early as 1566 in the side valley to the west, where the Angidy stream supplied abundant water power.

Tintern was an important passing place on the now-defunct Chepstow-Monmouth railway, though because of the configuration of the river and lack of flat land, the station had to be built well upstream. The buildings of the **Old Station** ○ have been preserved, and its surroundings transformed into an attractive picnic area and starting point for riverside and woodland walks. Drawn up in a siding, old coaches house a shop and displays on the history of this once-busy line and the area it served.

# TREDEGAR HOUSE★★
## Newport
### Michelin Atlas p 16 or Map 403 K 29

Tredegar is one of the grandest houses of the post-Civil War period in the whole of England and Wales. It was the residence of the enormously rich **Morgan** family until death duties reduced their inheritance.

After 20 years of attrition caused by its use as a school, it passed into public ownership and is now the jewel in Newport's civic crown. As the process of sensitive restoration continues, Tredegar has recovered its spirit, and is now as fascinating inside as out. Its well-tree'd grounds have become a popular country park.

**From Monmouthshire to Monte Carlo** – The Morgans of Tredegar began their rise as a Monmouthshire gentry family in the late 15C, their fortunes gaining a great boost through their support of Henry Tudor in his bid for the English throne in 1485. The oldest surviving part of Tredegar House, the stone-built south-west wing, dates from this time.

In the expansive times following the end of the Civil War the house was almost completely rebuilt between 1664 and 1672 on a new and altogether lavish scale, reflecting the wealth and prestige the family had acquired through enterprise and judicious marriages. Their income of perhaps £4 000 pa was hardly equalled in Wales at that time, and it was later claimed that a man could walk from Newport to Cardiff without stepping off Morgan land. In the 18C and 19C, investment in works like the Monmouthshire and Brecon Canal and the Sirhowey to Newport tramroad brought further returns; the tolls collected from the tramroad traffic passing through the estate led to its being known as the Golden Mile. The Morgans, who were elevated to the peerage in 1859, were largely responsible for the development of modern Newport's docks and town centre. By the 20C, lifestyle seems to have taken over from investment; it was the expenditure of capital rather than income that enabled a Morgan yacht to cruise the oceans, and the last resident, eccentric Evan Morgan, to throw sensationally scandalous parties for a glittering set of international celebrities. His successor, John Morgan, fled to the tax haven of Monte Carlo to live off the proceeds of the sale in 1951 of the house and most of its contents.

# TOUR ⊘

**Exterior** – Tredegar was a great estate, virtually self-sufficient, with home farm, brewhouse, mill, bakehouse (now gone), and a great

**Adjacent Sights** – See Abergavenny, Blaenavon, Brecon Beacons, Caerphilly, Merthyr Tydfil, Rhondda, Tretower.

barn (255ft/78m long), now split in two. The house, built in newly fashionable red brick rather than in stone, is approached through some of these outbuildings and across a courtyard, with entry via a new side hall made in the northeast wing in the 19C.

The more imposing **entrance** is the original one, facing north-west across the Middle Court; it has a broken pediment with lion and griffin carried on twisted columns entwined with laurel leaves. The long two-storey façades are terminated by pavilions at either end, and surmounted by a roof pierced by dormers and with a ridgeline that has been subsequently lowered. Dressings in Bath stone embellish the windows. The house has traditionally been attributed to Inigo Jones but the architectural treatment, inside and out, is quite straightforward, with none of his verve.

**Interior** – Even more than the exterior, the stately interiors still recall the power and luxury enjoyed by the Morgan dynasty. Although nearly all the original furniture and fittings were dispersed, some have been recovered and other items have been replaced with substitutes from sources such as the Victoria and Albert Museum, enabling the rooms to evoke the atmosphere of varying epochs in the house's history. There are numerous pictures as well as portraits of many of the Morgans.

The 17C **New Parlour** with its dark oak panelling is presented as a Victorian dining room, displaying the Tredegar Salt. The sparsely furnished **New Hall**, which was entered from the main doorway, has a fascinating array of vigorously painted 17C representations of kings, queens and sibyls.

Nothing in the **Brown Room**, designed in the reign of Charles I, distracts from the extraordinarily exuberant **carving** enriching panelling and doorways; *putti* swarm up pilasters, strange beasts mingle with foliage, and odd faces peer out at the visitor; could it really be Charles I in the guise of a mischievous bewhiskered mouse?

The **Gilt Room** is even more striking; painted figures and landscapes on the darkened walls set off the generous gilding, while the chimney-piece has all the pomp of an Italian Baroque altarpiece. The oval ceiling painting is original.

Approached via the cavernous **Great Staircase**, the first floor has a **Best Chamber** painted in the authentic "drab" of the 17C, while the **King's Room** is furnished to evoke the "Indian Summer" of Tredegar in the 1930s, when Evan Morgan entertained his guests with a menagerie of animals including Alice the bear and Somerset the boxing kangaroo. His bust, carved by Prince Birabongse, the Siamese racing driver, stands in a corner of the room. Evan's second wife, Princess Olga, occupied the Red and Blue Rooms adjacent.

The **Master's Bedchamber** contains a superb bed (c 1720) and gives on to the **Cedar Closet**, its exquisitely scented wood much prized at the time.

The **Bathroom** (1905) was very advanced for its date with bidet and multi-directional shower.

The stairs leading to the servants' quarters have a number of cartoons by **Low** of some of the famous figures who frequented Tredegar – George Bernard Shaw, HG Wells, a languid Aldous Huxley.... **Below Stairs** gives an excellent picture of life as lived by the small and highly hierarchical army of servants, always ready to respond to the summons of the many bells hanging in Bells Passage.

North Front, Tredegar House

The **Great Kitchen** is equipped on an almost industrial scale. The **Still Room** has an array of copper jelly moulds requiring constant cleaning. The **Housekeeper's Room** expresses its occupant's status with its spaciousness and modest luxury. The **Servants' Hall** with its long refectory table occupies a wing of the medieval house and gives on to the gloomy courtyard.

★**Grounds** – Several layers of landscaping are represented at Tredegar. To the north-east are the fine specimen trees beloved of the Victorians, set in the sweeping **late-18C parkland** which was originally intended to envelop the house entirely in the manner of Capability Brown.

Fortunately this plan was never fully implemented and the immediate surroundings of the house retain much of the **late 17C-early 18C formal layout**, with its emphasis on buildings and rectangular enclosures in orderly relationship with one another. The centrepiece is the magnificent **stable building**★, designed in the same grand manner as the house itself; its walls have half-height pilasters reflecting the spacing of the stalls within the building.

The stables are linked to the house by the Stable Court and Middle Court, between them the superbly showy ironwork of the **gates** made by the Edney gatesmiths of Bristol and erected in 1718.

The cobblestone and gravel patterns of both courts are laid out in distorted geometrical perspective which is corrected when viewed, as it was meant to be from the upper floors of the house.

South-west of the house is a series of enclosures defined by tall brick walls. The **Orangery Garden** has the original, centrally heated building designed to preserve throughout the winter months that essential 18C status symbol, a collection of citrus trees. It houses a permanent **garden exhibition**. The geometrically patterned **parterres** discovered by recent excavation have been splendidly recreated, using the original materials of coal dust, crushed seashells and coloured earths.

The **Cedar Garden**, the backdrop to views from many of the state rooms, is the largest of the enclosures; it has a poignant hedged monument to *Sir Briggs*, the horse which carried Captain Godfrey Morgan at the Charge of the Light Brigade in 1854.

An oak avenue carries the eye north-westwards from the main entrance of the house; once focused on an Iron Age hillfort, it is now interrupted by the traffic speeding by on the motorway (M 4).

# TREGARON

Ceredigion – Population 1 177
Michelin Atlas p 24 or Map 403 I 27

Tregaron's square used to resound with the lowing of countless cattle as the drovers prepared for the crossing of the Elenydd, the vast upland tract to the east, which has also been called "The Great Desert of Wales", separating Ceredigion (Cardiganshire) from the rest of the Principality.

In the post-war period there was an echo of the commotion caused by the drovers and their charges, when pony-trekking became a popular activity and riders assembled in large numbers in the square. The black-and-white *Talbot Hotel* is a survivor of the 20 or more inns which served the drovers at the turn of the century.

In the square is the statue of a local man, Henry Richard, who as MP for Merthyr Tydfil brought Welsh problems to the attention of a wider world and was consequently nicknamed "The Member for Wales".

The much-restored **Church of St Caron** stands in a circular churchyard, which follows the outline of the enclosure set out by this Celtic saint in the 6C.

The drovers' route east across the mountains to Abergwesyn and Llanwrtyd Wells is a spectacular drive *(see p 198)*.

**Craftwork** – The **Welsh Gold Centre** ⊙ specialises in designs inspired by Welsh legends and mythology and Celtic heritage; see jewellery being made.

**Adjacent Sights** – See Aberaeron, Aberystwyth, Lampeter, Llandovery, Llanwrtyd Wells, Vale of Rheidol, Strata Florida Abbey.

## EXCURSION

**Tregaron Bog (Cors Caron)** ⊙ – *2.5mi/4km N by B 4343.* The flat expanse of this National Nature Reserve (4sq mi/10km²) forms a fascinating contrast with both the hill country to the east and the rolling, enclosed farmland to the west.

Cors Caron is a raised bog, the result of the colonisation of a post-glacial lake bed by a succession consisting first of reed-beds, then of shrubs and trees, and finally of peat bog. More than 160 species of bird have been recorded here, including more than 40 breeding species. The famous red kite can sometimes be seen. A nature trail along an old railway line leads to a tower from which this unusual landscape can be observed.

# TRETOWER COURT AND CASTLE

(Tretŵr) Powys

Michelin Atlas p 16 or Map 403 K 28

9mi/15km W of Abergavenny by A 40 and A 479

etween them, the castle and court at Tretower illustrate the transition that took place from the rugged strongholds of Norman times to the more expansive domestic arrangements of the later Middle Ages.

## TOUR ⊘

**Castle** – The castle, now approached across grazed farmland, was built towards the end of the 11C by a follower of Bernard de Neufmarche of Brecon in

> **Adjacent Sights** – See Abergavenny, Blaenavon, Brecon, Brecon Beacons, Grosmont, Llanthony Priory, Merthyr Tydfil, Tredegar.

order to control the route leading from the Usk to the Wye Valley. The early timber castle was rebuilt in stone in the middle of the 12C in the form of a shell keep. Following partial destruction by the Welsh, a massive, three-storey **round tower** was rather incongruously inserted at the beginning of the 13C into what remained of the shell keep. This remains the major feature of the castle today, dominating the peaceful surroundings of the flat valley site.

**Tretower Court** – The round tower seems to have found little favour as a residence and was probably abandoned about 100 years after it was built in favour of the first section of Tretower Court, the **north range**, with a central hall reaching up into the roof.

In the 15C Sir Roger Vaughan, a kinsman of Sir William Herbert of Raglan Castle, rebuilt and extended the Court, adding the **west range** with its fine timber work and inserting an upper floor into the hall. Later in the century the courtyard was completely walled round and provided with a gatehouse and wall-walk. Minor remodelling took place in the 17C; at the end of the 18C this fine example of late medieval building became a farm.

Tretower Court admirably exposes the anatomy of late medieval construction. An equally admirable attempt to add greater atmosphere to the place is being made by the development, in as authentic a way as possible, of a late medieval **garden**, entered by an opening in the south wall of the courtyard. The layout of the garden, based not on archaeological site evidence but on study of what was then a thoroughly international art form, incorporates many of the features depicted in contemporary paintings and manuscripts – arbours, turf benches, a flowery mead, a fountain and fruit trees.

# TYWYN

Gwynedd – Population 3 028

Michelin Atlas p 24 or Map 403 H 26

Between the estuaries and sand bars of the Dysynni to the north and the Dovey (Dyfi) to the south is Tywyn with its two sites – the modest modern family resort facing a long stretch (6mi/10km) of sandy beach and the older core lying a mile inland.

**Old Tywyn** – The focus is a small square with a pair of big hotels and a confident Assembly Rooms (1897), now a cinema. Here too is the ancient **Church of St Cadfan** ⊘, mostly of Norman date. Cadfan was a Christian missionary from Brittany, who founded a monastery here early in the 6C; dating from the 8C, the so-called Cadfan Stone in the church bears an inscription whose interpretation is disputed, but which is almost certainly the earliest example of written Welsh.

★**Talyllyn Railway** ⊘ – This narrow-gauge line, originally opened in 1866 and closed in 1950, was the first to receive the loving attentions of railway preservation enthusiasts, among them the Reverend Awdry, writer and prolific creator of steam locomotives with human characteristics, notably Thomas the Tank Engine. When the preservationists took over in 1951, the track, according to one account, was held together only by the grass that had grown through the sleepers.

The trains chuff their way through pretty valley scenery, crossing an imposing brick-and-stone viaduct, depositing sightseers at the Dolgoch Falls *(see below)*, and terminating in the forest at Nant Gwernol (about 8mi/13km inland). Because this is the most senior of preserved lines, its **museum** ⊘ at Tywyn has much railway material which might not otherwise have found a home.

## EXCURSIONS

**Dolgoch Falls** ⊘ – *5mi/8km NE of Tywyn by A 493 and B 4405 or by Talyllyn Railway to Dolgoch Falls station; 1hr on foot return or 15min for main falls only.* The Dolgoch stream drops from its hanging valley high above the River Fathew via a trio of falls. The leafy surroundings of the falls have been a popular excursion spot since it was given to the public in 1902 by its then owner.

**Castell y Bere** – *8mi/13km NE of Tywyn by A 493 and minor roads.* In a remote valley leading into the mountain fastness of Cadair Idris, this castle ruin evokes that distant age before English domination when Llywelyn the Great was able to style himself Prince of North Wales.

One of the relatively small number of native Welsh castles, Castell y Bere was built in 1221 in the form of an elongated triangle along the top of a rock spur rising from the valley floor. With its characteristically Welsh D-shaped towers and elaborate entrance, it was intended to secure Llywelyn's southern border, more in the face of his turbulent fellow princes than against the English. Nevertheless, it was fated to fall to the forces of Edward I, who, after taking it in 1283, set about repairing its defences, only to abandon both castle and incipient English borough shortly afterwards, leaving Castell y Bere to its centuries of melancholy solitude.

**Tal-y-Llyn Church** ⊙ – *11mi NE of Tywyn by A 493 and B 4405.* A typical small Welsh **church** stands at the southern end of Tal-y-Llyn Lake. At the east end, above the altar, is a **tester**, a curved wooden ceiling, divided into 48 panels, arranged in four rows of 12 and decorated alternately with red or white roses, a form of decoration which was popular at the end of the Wars of the Roses in the late 15C, when this building replaced an earlier timber structure. The wooden roof beams are secured with projecting wooden pegs. The altar rails and the vestry screen in the south transept were part of a gallery built at the west end in 1765. Stone lych gates with pitched roofs mark the two entrances to the churchyard.

**Aberdovey (Aberdyfi)** – *5mi/8km S of Tywyn by A 493.* Aberdovey, a cheerful place of brightly coloured boarding houses and a timber pier, looks south from the foot of abruptly rising hills over the relatively narrow mouth of the estuary to the Cardigan shore opposite.

The main road east runs along the shore of the wide estuary of the Dovey (Dyfi), accompanied by the railway, which, at Dovey Junction just upstream, has a rarity of a station with no access other than by train.

# USK

(Brynbuga) Monmouthshire – Population 2 187
Michelin Atlas p 16 or Map 403 L 28

A bridge town on the river of the same name, little Usk was originally the Roman legionary fort of Burrium, which lost its importance when the II Augustan Legion moved downstream to Caerleon. Later, the site's strategic importance was appreciated by the Normans, who built a castle here. Now in ruins, though its gatehouse is inhabited, the castle was the scene of a bloody massacre of Welsh prisoners in 1405 during the Owain Glyn Dŵr uprising. The attractiveness of the town's streets and two squares was much enhanced when most through traffic was transferred to the dual-carriageway Newport-Monmouth road.

**Adjacent Sights** – See Abergavenny, Blaenavon, Brecon Beacons, Caerleon, Caerwent, Chepstow, Monmouth, Newport, Raglan Castle, Tintern Abbey.

**Usk Rural Life Museum** ⊘ – Housed in a malt barn whose origins may go back to the 15C, the museum has a fascinating and almost overwhelming collection of every kind of object to do with the life of the countryside, as lived from the early 19C until quite recently. The rustically elegant forms of seemingly timeless wooden farm wagons contrast with the thrusting crudity of a primitive Sanderson tractor of 1916. Every traditional craft is represented, echoed in the names of many an English-speaking family: Carpenter, Miller, Cooper, Sawyer, Thatcher.

**St Mary's Priory Church** ⊘ – Now without the chancel and transepts removed after the Dissolution, St Mary's was the church of a Benedictine priory for nuns founded in the 12C by Richard de Clare. It has a massive Norman tower, a fine 15C rood screen partly recoloured in the 19C, an organ with splendid trumpet pipes, and the oldest extant brass memorial in Welsh, commemorating the medieval chronicler, Adam of Usk (c 1270).

# VALLE CRUCIS ABBEY★

## Denbighshire

Michelin Atlas p 33 or Map 403 K 25 – 2mi/3km N of Llangollen by A 542

The substantial ruins of this abbey are set in a wild and until recently quite unspoiled valley, a characteristic location for the Cistercians who came here in 1201.

Valle Crucis was the last of the 14 Cistercian monasteries in Wales but became one of its richest. Its founder, buried here on his death in 1236, was Madog ap Gruffudd Maelor, an ancestor of Owain Glyn Dŵr and ally of Llywelyn the Great. In its heyday the abbey was a centre of learning and literature, associated with the poets Iolo Goch and Guto'r Glyn. By the end of the 15C the abbots had acquired a taste for good living; the last but one of their number brought disgrace on the Order through shady property deals and was imprisoned in the Tower of London. By the time of the Dissolution, the community had been reduced to a mere six monks.

In the years that followed, the abbey was robbed for its stone and lead, while parts were converted into dwelling houses and farm buildings. Restoration began as early as the mid-19C, when archaeological investigations began and Sir Gilbert Scott repaired the abbey's most distinctive feature, its splendid west front.

Valle Crucis Abbey and Dinas Brân

Firmly set on the valley floor, the abbey ruins are first seen against a background of steep and shaggy slopes rising above the little River Eglwyseg. The stream supplied fresh water and fed one of the essential components of the monastic economy, the fishpond, which still remains, the only one of its kind in Wales.

> **Adjacent Sights** – See Bala, Chirk Castle, Erddig, Hawarden, Llanfyllin, Llangollen, Mold, Plas Newydd, Ruthin, Lake Vyrnwy, Wrexham.

## TOUR ⊙

Both east and west fronts of the abbey are largely intact. The **west front** belongs to the first phase of building in the early 13C but windows and elaborately carved doorway were inserted somewhat later, while the gable and the rose window with its delicate tracery date from the mid-14C. The east end is characterised by a striking series of flattened buttresses framing the windows. The south transept is also well preserved.

Attached to it is the restored east range which served for many years as a farmhouse. Here are a number of fine interiors including a splendidly vaulted **Chapter House**, the **Monks' Dormitory** and the **Abbots' quarters**, the latter provided with fireplaces, a sure sign of luxurious living. Laid out in the Dormitory are a number of **sepulchral slabs**, including a particularly vigorously carved example commemorating Madog ap Gruffydd (d 1306), great-grandson of the founder.

A short distance to the north of the Abbey stands the **Pillar of Eliseg**, the lower part of a 9C cross with much-eroded lettering proclaiming the glories of the ancient rulers of Powys.

# Lake VYRNWY ★

Powys

Michelin Atlas p 33 or Map 403 J 25

Fed by streams draining from the remote high country on the borders of Powys and Gwynedd, the waters of this great reservoir are held back by the first large masonry dam to be built in Britain.

In the late 19C, the valley community of Llanwddyn, a village of several dozen houses, had to give way to the imperatives of water supply for the thirsty city of Liverpool. Completed between 1881 and 1888, Lake Vrynwy supplies Liverpool with water via a conduit (68mi/110km long).

**Visitor Centre** ⊙ – A multi-media display tells the tale of the area in the words of Wddyn the Wise, a holy recluse who by tradition dwelt in a cell by a local waterfall.

> **Tourist Information Centre** – Unit 2, Vyrnwy Craft Workshops, Lake Vyrnwy SY10 OLY ☎ 01691 870 346.
>
> **Adjacent Sights** – See Bala, Chirk Castle, Dolgellau, Llanfyllin, Llangollen, Machynlleth, Plas Newydd, Valle Crucis Abbey.

**Shore Drive** – A road (11mi/18km long) encircles the lake, which occupies a valley given its shape by glacial action. The dam (84ft/26m high), which is guarded by a quartet of pavilions at either end, is faced in coarsely-worked masonry which emphasises its heroic scale. It is at its most spectacular when water is released, not through a spillway at the side, but down the face of the dam.

The **Straining Tower**, attached to the north bank by a bridge, is a fanciful structure which, together with the extensive plantings of spruce and fir, gives the lake and its surroundings something of the romantically Germanic atmosphere so much appreciated by the late Victorians.

From the start, the lake was seen as a positive addition to the landscape, and a **hotel** was provided for the convenience of the sportsmen attracted to the area. Fishing continues, while other visitors are catered for with craft workshops, nature trails and birdwatching hides, and boating on the lake.

*The Practical Information section at the beginning of the guide lists :*
*– information about travel, motoring, accommodation, recreation*
*– local or national organisations providing additional information*
*– calendar of events*
*– admission times and charges for the sights described in the guide*

In 1947 the Tudor mansion known as St Fagans Castle and some of its grounds (100 acres/42ha) were made available to the nation by the Earl of Plymouth. An important open-air museum of vernacular buildings has been established on the site and is now one of the country's most visited tourist attractions.

The museum is devoted to the serious study and conservation of Welsh folk culture and aims to show how Welsh people lived and worked from the 16C-17C onwards. At its heart is the array of more than 30 traditional structures from all parts of Wales, rescued from demolition and re-erected here.

The Castle itself serves as a complementary exhibit, a reminder of the social and economic interdependence of gentry and common people. Great efforts have gone into giving the museum a lived-in atmosphere; the trades and crafts once practised in many of the buildings are still carried on in them; traditional breeds of farm animal roam the hedged or fenced enclosures dividing up the parkland, and events and festivals are held throughout the year.

## TOUR ⊙

**Adjacent Sights** – See Barry, Caerphilly, Cardiff, Castell Coch, Cowbridge, Glamorgan Coast, Llancaiach Fawr, Llandaff, Llantrisant, Penarth, Rhondda.

**Galleries** – The museum presents a somewhat intimidating face to the outside world, in the shape of the long and low modern edifice housing service facilities and galleries. The galleries themselves are spacious and allow the wealth of objects on display to be appreciated fully.

The array of implements in the **Agriculture Gallery** helps trace the development of farming techniques in a land which environmental conditions often made difficult to work and remind the visitor of the importance of livestock farming in a mountainous country.

The **Costume Gallery** is dimly lit in order to preserve the fragile evidence of how the Welsh have dressed since the beginning of the 18C.

The **Gallery of Material Culture** has an extraordinary accumulation of instruments and artefacts relating to all aspects of daily life, from tools, toys, games, guns and swords, to musical instruments, kitchen implements, Welsh dressers and love spoons (see p 28).

**Open-air Section** – The museum's collection of old buildings is still growing, and space is available for further structures. The buildings are dispersed over the extensive site, some arranged in interesting groupings, others related to their own carefully devised and authentic-seeming context of garden, yard or forecourt. The materials of walls and roofs reflect the diversity of Welsh landscapes; coarse stonework is exposed to magnificently bold effect in **Y Garreg Fawr** farmhouse (1544) but is often rendered, as are the walls of **Nantwallter Cottage** (1770), made of clom, a form of cob composed of clay, gravel and straw.

Wood-turning at the Museum of Welsh Life

The 17C black-and-white **Abernodwydd farmhouse** from Powys tells of close link with English traditions of timber construction. Furnishings have been chosen t evoke a particular period, not always that of the time when the building was fir: erected.

The primary theme is that of farming, with fascinating examples of how accommo dation for both people and animals has evolved since all lived together in th **Hendre'r-ywydd Uchaf longhouse** (1508), from Llangynhafal in north-east Wales, to th **Llwyn-yr-Eos farmstead** (1820), still on its original site on the banks of the River E and eloquent testimony to the rationality and relative comfort of Georgian time: Other farmhouses include **Kennixton** (early 17C) from the Gower peninsula, painte red to discourage evil spirits, and there are labourers' cottages, barns and corbelled drystone pigsty resembling the *trulli* of southern Italy. There are barn and a hayshed, the **Melin Bompren cornmill** (working) and, more unusually, a little m which reduced the prickly sprigs of gorse to palatable horse fodder.

Examples of enterprises serving the rural economy include a **sawmill**, a **woollen mill**, **tannery** and a working **bakery**, while among community buildings are an 18C **Unitaria chapel**, a **Victorian school**, a tiny **post office**, the well-stocked **Gwalia Stores**, and, th largest edifice on site, the **Oakdale Workmen's Institute** (1916), the equivalent of modern leisure centre. A 17C thatched circular **cockpit** from the *Hawk and Buck Inn* in Denbigh recalls the crueller pleasures of an earlier age.

A **tollhouse** is furnished in the style of 1843, a year which saw the destruction c many tollgates by the Rebecca Rioters.

The **Rhyd-y-car cottages** *(illustration see p 64)* make up one of the most evocativ exhibits. Built c 1800 in Merthyr Tydfil by the ironmaster Richard Crawshay t house his workers, they have been meticulously furnished to represent six differen periods from 1805 to 1985, enabling interesting comparisons to be made. Vege table gardens and outhouses complete this fascinating picture.

Overlooking one of the fishponds of St Fagans Castle is a **boathouse** with a uniqu collection of coracles and fishing implements of all kinds, some legitimate, some like salmon poachers' paraphernalia, ingenious but illegal.

**St Fagans Castle** – This many-gabled, cream-painted mansion was built in 158( on the E-shaped plan typical of English houses of the period, on the site of Norman motte and bailey protecting the western approaches to Cardiff. Its immedi ate surroundings include the sequence of ancient fishponds which are overlooke by the 19C terraces of the attractively mature **formal gardens**, with walls, clippe hedges, parterres, Lebanon cedars, lime avenue and herb garden.

The workaday themes of the rest of the museum are continued in some of th Castle's outbuildings, where there is a cider mill, a turner, a cooper and a clo maker.

The interior is furnished in the style of the 19C but retains many earlier features like vigorously carved overmantels. The **Long Gallery**, used by the family for exercise and amusement on rainy days, was the first of its kind to be built in Wales.

*Michelin Maps, Red Guides and Green Guides are complementary publications - to be used together*

# WELSHPOOL ★

(Y Trallwng) Powys – Population 5 900
Michelin Atlas p 25 or Map 403 K 26

The market town of Welshpool stands in the deep valley of the Lledan Brook close to its confluence with the Severn. In touch with the English lowlands as well as with the Welsh interior, it has long been the focal point of communication routes; two roads lead westward, one via Llanfair Caereinion to Dolgellau and southern Snowdonia, the other via Newtown to Machynlleth. The Montgomeryshire Canal arrived in 1797, the mainline railway in 1860, the narrow-gauge line to Llanfair Caereinion in 1903.

Together with Llanfyllin, the town is one of the two planned boroughs laid out in the mid-13C by Gruffudd ap Gwynwynwyn, Prince of Powys. **Pool Street**, divided into Broad, High and Mount Streets, formed the principal axis of the medieval town, running from the central crossroads and curving gently to climb the ridge whose prolongation southwards made an excellent defensive site for Powis Castle *(see p 239)*. The character of the street is attractively mixed, mainly Georgian and Victorian but with some obviously older buildings and a pleasing variety of mater ials, including brick, timber framing and the local grey-green sandstone. The street would be periodically filled with the bleating of countless sheep, brought to what was (and still is) the biggest one-day **sheep market** in Europe, though the market itself has long been removed to a less cramped site.

## SIGHTS

**Town Centre** – The dominant building is the Town Hall (1874), an incongruous structure in French Renaissance style.
Almost equally incongruous is the massive mid-19C **Christ Church**, built on the slopes to the west of Mount Street, "an alarming neo-Norman elephant" (E Beazley).

The much rebuilt and restored medieval parish **Church of St Mary** ⊘ is also in a peripheral position to the town centre, its churchyard high above Church Bank as it curves away from the town. The glacial boulder in the churchyard is said to be the Abbot's chair from Strata Marcella.

**Powysland Museum and Montgomery Canal Centre** ⊘ – Housed in a restored warehouse with a great awning overhanging the canal, this is one of the most fascinating local museums in Wales, with an intriguing array of exhibits presented in exemplary fashion. The collections are based on those of the Powysland Club established in 1867, which at one point were seriously considered as a possible core collection for the proposed National Museum. All aspects of the locality are dealt with, from impeccably arranged archaeological artefacts onwards.
There are wonderfully patterned tiles from the medieval abbey of Strata Marcella and every kind of object once found in local shops, though the mutton-bone guillotine made by Napoleonic prisoners of war was presumably never for sale. Hung by the stairway is the gleaming nameplate of the Great Western Railway's Castle Class locomotive *Powis Castle*.
The little canal basin is bounded by cottage-like buildings in red brick which once served as stores, shops and offices. The **Shropshire Union Canal** once reached towards the heart of mid-Wales, connecting Newtown with the waterways of the English Midlands. Long neglected, it is now undergoing restoration, and narrowboats ply sections of the canal close to Welshpool.

**Welshpool and Llanfair Light Railway** ⊘ – This narrow-gauge steam-operated railway line climbs and twists on its way (8mi/13km) through the hills and valleys west of Welshpool to the tiny country town of **Llanfair Caereinion.**
The line was one of a number of cheaply built light railways constructed at the turn of the 20C to improve communications with remote country districts. The Welshpool and Llanfair was completed in 1903, just in time to meet the competition from road traffic, and never prospered. Passenger trains stopped running in 1931, goods trains in 1956. The service, now entirely tourist-oriented, was fully restored in 1981, with steam engines hauling trains up the steep gradient from the newly built station at the western end of town. Development within the town itself has meant that the urban section of the line snaking past backyards and across roads can never be linked to the main line with its magnificent neo-Tudor **station.**

## EXCURSIONS

**Sarn-y-Bryn-Caled Timber Circle** – *1.5mi/2.5km S of Welshpool.* For some years, aerial photography had hinted at the existence of a prehistoric ritual and funerary complex on the flood plain of the Severn to the south of Welshpool. Archaeological excavation undertaken in the early 1990s as the Welshpool by-pass was being built confirmed the existence of a double timber circle built c 2100 BC, one of a number of possible prototype henges for the far more famous but untypical Stonehenge. The site now lies beneath the by-pass but there are explanatory panels in the car park of the evolving **nature reserve** based on the gravel pit used in the construction of the road.

**Berriew** – *5mi/8km SW of Welshpool by A 483.* Berriew prides itself on its frequent wins in the Best Kept Village competition, and it is certainly a pretty place, with a number of timber-framed cottages and houses around its circular churchyard.
Other pretty things can be seen in the **Andrew Logan Museum of Sculpture** ⊘. The founder of the "Alternative Miss World Competition" has been described as the "Wizard of Odd", and the plain shed whose interior has been transformed by the London-based artist's kaleidoscopic creations might equally well be described as a "cathedral of camp".

(Wrecsam) Wrexham – Population 40 614
Michelin Atlas p 33 or Map 403 L 24
Local map see p 190

This busy town, the largest in North Wales, stands at the centre of a sprawling distri
which grew up around the local industries of coal and iron. Wrexham seems to hav
flourished at most periods of its existence.

Beginning as a village, it exploited its position between lowlands to the east an
mountainous country to the west, becoming an important market town in the Midd
Ages. The mineral-rich uplands enhanced its prosperity in the 18C and 19C, b
enthusiasm for industrial progress led to desertion by the gentry who had hithert
made Wrexham the focus of their social activity. Not one of their town mansion
remains; of the fine country houses, which once stood in a more or less complete rin
around the town, Erddig alone survives, recently rescued from mining subsidence.

Wrexham still has its magnificent parish church, one of the "Seven Wonders of Wales
after much ill-advised demolition the town centre is well cared for and efforts ar
being made to open up the fascinating industrial heritage of the hinterland.

★**St Giles' Church** ⊙ – The
church's dominant feature
is its splendid three-stage
tower (136ft/42m high). It
is a highly ornate structure,
crowned by four corner
turrets of differing heights
and by 16 minor pinnacles;
nearly all of the total of
30 niches still contain
sculpted figures of saints.
The tower was completed
in 1506, the last stage of a

**Tourist Information Centre** – Lambpit
Street, Wrexham LL11 1WN ☎ 01978
292 015; Fax 01978 292 467; tic@wrex-
ham.gov.uk

**Adjacent Sights** – See Chirk Castle, Erddig, Hawarden, Llangollen, Mold, Plas
Newydd, Ruthin, Valle Crucis Abbey.

15C rebuilding in Perpendicular style following a fire in 1463 which had gutted th
previous edifice.

The harmonious **interior** has a fine timber roof, decorated with figures of angels sing
ing or playing instruments. There are traces of a 15C wall painting of the Last Judge
ment over the chancel arch; beyond is an unusual polygonal apse. Carved corbel
include figures of a mermaid, a man with toothache, and a sow suckling her young;
particularly grotesque figure in the clergy vestry may represent Gluttony.

The most striking monument is one by Roubiliac to Mary Myddelton (d 1747) o
nearby Chirk Castle (see p 136); it shows an angel sounding the Last Trump while
the rejuvenated lady rises from her shattered sarcophagus.

The church stands in its pleasant graveyard only a short distance from the High
Street. The approach is through a fine set of early-18C wrought-iron gates, mad
at Bersham by the same craftsmen who fashioned the even more elaborate gate
for Chirk Castle.

In the churchyard is the tomb of **Elihu Yale** (1648-1721), benefactor of Yale
University, with its famous inscription:

> Born in America, in Europe bred,
> In Africa travell'd, and in Asia wed,
> Where long he liv'd and thriv'd;
> in London dead.

Elihu Yale's family had originally come from Bryn Eglwys and he himself maintained
a home in Wrexham in later life. In 1901 the graduates of Yale University paid for
the restoration of St Giles' porch; in the 1920s a reproduction of the church's
tower was erected on the Yale campus.

**County Borough Museum** ⊙ – Regent Street. The modest display (extension
planned) illustrates the social and industrial history of the area with exhibits o
Ruabon brick and terracotta and a reconstructed porch lined with majolica tiles
there are interactive displays for children.

## EXCURSIONS

**Clywedog Valley** – Hurrying down its attractively wooded valley, the busy little
River Clywedog once supplied water and power for a variety of enterprises, one o
which, John Wilkinson's Bersham Ironworks, played a significant role in the early
years of the Industrial Revolution. 1986 saw the closure of the last coal mine. The
sights, some of them still in the course of archaeological excavation, are linked by a
trail (8mi/13km).

**Minera Lead Mine** ⊙ – 6mi/10km W of Wrexham by A 525 and B 5426 (sign Bersham
Heritage Centre). The name Minera comes from the Latin for ore and, while it is
possible that the Romans exploited the lead ores here, the first hard evidence for
lead mining dates from the Middle Ages. Minera's boom years came in the 18C and
19C, when galleries and shafts were sunk deep into the mountain.

The scene today is one of fragmentary remains of this intense activity; the most impressive structure is the restored Cornish Beam Engine House *(34 steps to the top)*. Just below it is a small **visitor centre**, which traces the history of lead mining, explains mining techniques and the uses of lead and zinc; visitors can handle mineral samples.

**Nant Mill** ⊘ – *2mi/3km E of Minera by B 5426 and a minor road*. In a leafy setting by the Clywedog an old corn mill has been converted into a **visitor centre** with displays on the ecology and local history of the area which are especially appealing to children. The footpath downstream follows an old wagonway, once used to haul limestone from Minera to the Bersham Ironworks, and crosses an impressive section of Offa's Dyke *(see p 169)*.

**Bersham Ironworks** ⊘ – *2mi/3km SW of Wrexham by B 5099 and a minor road*. A blast furnace was at work here as early as the 17C but it was in 1721 that a new owner, Charles Lloyd, began using coke instead of charcoal to smelt iron, a process initiated in 1709 by his friend, Abraham Darby of Coalbrookedale. By the middle of the 18C the works had been taken over by the Wilkinson family, whose most prominent member became known as John "Iron Mad" Wilkinson. In the 1770s, his boring machine, first used for producing highly accurate cannon barrels, was employed in making the cylinders for James Watt's new steam engines. At the height of their success, the Bersham Ironworks formed an advanced industrial complex employing hundreds of workers, but decline set in when Wilkinson founded a new ironworks at nearby Brymbo in 1795.

A **Heritage Centre** ⊘ in a Victorian school introduces the site as well as other local industries. Nearby are the cabin-like Bunkers Hill cottages built by Wilkinson for his workforce c 1785, while the surviving buildings of the ironworks, saved from demolition by their reuse as farm buildings for many years, lie beyond the Wrexham by-pass. They include the Mill (which served as a foundry), a newly exposed blast furnace and coking ovens, and an octagonal structure which was probably the cannon foundry. The cannon themselves were test-fired into a ballistics bank on the far side of the stream.

The surroundings, with church, barge-boarded cottages, bridge and stream, more tranquil now than 200 years ago, nevertheless evoke the rustic setting in which much of Britain's Industrial Revolution took place.

The trail continues downstream, passing a working dairy farm and Erddig Hall *(see p 152)* before terminating at King's Mill, where the "Miller's Tale" evokes the life and work of an 18C corn mill.

**Gresford** – *3mi/5km N of Wrexham by B 5445*. This attractive village with its duckpond and almshouses has one of the finest parish churches in Wales.

★ **All Saints' Church** ⊘ – The church was rebuilt in Perpendicular style in the late 15C and is consequently exceptionally harmonious in appearance. It is set in a churchyard with old yews and tastefully rearranged tombstones. The pinnacled tower, not completed until the 16C, is particularly impressive, while the exterior generally is rich in the carving of string course, corbels and gargoyles, the latter ready to spout water from a variety of orifices.

The airy **interior** has elaborate camberbeam roofs with figures of angels and numerous bosses. There is a fine set of screens, but the glory of the church is its stained glass, despite damage caused by over-zealous cleaning.

Among the saints filling the east window of the north aisle is St Apollonia, the patron saint of sufferers from toothache, holding a tooth in pincers, while the equivalent window in the south aisle shows the execution of John the Baptist, with a cruel-looking Salome waiting with her charger.

An unusual monument is that to John Trevor (d 1589); his effigy reclines within a three-arched structure, his middle parts covered by the Welsh inscription filling the centre arch.

A recent painting commemorates the Great Disaster at Gresford Colliery in 1934, when 266 miners perished. News of the disaster was first communicated locally by the silence of the miners returning from the pit, as they usually sang while walking home.

Close to the east window in the north aisle is a niche containing a modern statue of the *Virgin and Child*. It is thought that Gresford's beauty and elaboration may have been due to its being a place of pilgrimage and that this niche may have contained the object of veneration.

# World Heritage List

In 1972 the United Nations Educational, Scientific and Cultural Organization (UNESCO) adopted a Convention for the preservation of cultural and natural sites. To date, more than 150 States Parties have signed this international agreement, which has listed over 500 sites "of outstanding universal value" on the World Heritage List. Each year a committee of representatives from 21 countries, assisted by technical organizations (ICOMOS – International Council on Monuments and Sites; IUCN – International Union for Conservation of Nature and Natural Resources; ICCROM – International Centre for the Study of the Preservation and Restoration of Cultural Property, the Rome Centre), evaluates the proposals for new sites to be included on the list, which grows longer as new nominations are accepted and more countries sign the Convention. To be considered, a site must be nominated by the country in which it is located.

The protected cultural heritage may be monuments (buildings, sculptures, archeological structures etc) with unique historical, artistic or scientific features; groups of buildings (such as religious communities, ancient cities); or sites (human settlements, examples of exceptional landscapes, cultural landscapes) which are the combined works of man and nature of exceptional beauty. Natural sites may be a testimony to the stages of the earth's geological history or to the development of human cultures and creative genius or represent significant ongoing ecological processes, contain superlative natural phenomena or provide a habitat for threatened species.

Signatories of the Convention pledge to co-operate to preserve and protect these sites around the world as a common heritage to be shared by all humanity.

Some of the most well-known places which the World Heritage Committee has inscribed include: Australia's Great Barrier Reef (1981), the Canadian Rocky Mountain Parks (1984), The Great Wall of China (1987), the Statue of Liberty (1984), the Kremlin (1990), Mont-Saint-Michel and its Bay (Great Britain and Ireland, 1979), Durham Castle and Cathedral (1986).

### UNESCO World Heritage sites included in this guide are:

**Beaumaris Castle**

**Caernarfon Castle and town walls**

**Conwy Castle and town walls**

**Harlech Castle**

# Admission Times and Charges

As admission times and charges are liable to alteration, the information printed below – valid for 2000 – is for guidance only. Where it has not been possible to obtain up-to-date information, the admission times and charges from the previous edition of the guide are printed in italics.

⊙ – Every sight for which times and charges are listed below is indicated by the symbol ⊙ after the title in the Sights section.

Order – The information is listed in the same order as in the Sights section of the guide.

Facilities for the disabled – ᐊ (ᐊ) mean full or partial access for wheelchairs. As the range of possible facilities is great (for impaired mobility, sight and hearing), readers are advised to telephone in advance to check what is available.

Dates – Dates given are inclusive. The term weekend means Saturday and Sunday. The term holidays means bank and public holidays, when shops, museums and other monuments may be closed or may vary their times of admission. The term school holidays refers to the breaks between terms at Christmas, Easter and during the summer months and also to the short mid-term breaks (one week), which are usually in February and October. See PRACTICAL INFORMATION.

Admission times – Ticket offices usually shut 30min before closing time; only exceptions are mentioned below. Some places issue timed tickets owing to limited space and facilities.

Charge – The charge given is for an individual adult. Reductions may be available for families, children, students, senior citizens (old-age pensioners) and the unemployed; it may be necessary to provide proof of identity and status. Large parties should apply in advance as many places offer special rates for group bookings and some have special days for group visits.

Foreign languages – Where foreign languages are mentioned, an English language version is also available.

Abbreviations – EH = English Heritage
CADW = Welsh Historic Monuments
HS = Historic Scotland
NACF = National Art Collections Fund
RSPB = Royal Society for the Protection of Birds
YOC = Young Ornithologists' Club (junior section of the RSPB)
NT = The National Trust (for England, Wales and Northern Ireland)
NTS = The National Trust for Scotland
NTJ = The National Trust for Jersey
NTG = The National Trust for Guernsey

There are reciprocal arrangements among the NT, NTS, NTJ, NTG and the Royal Oak Foundation in the USA.

# A

## ABERAERON

**Aberaeron Craft Centre** – ᐊ Open daily, 10am-6pm (4pm winter). Model railway and village. Parking. Licensed restaurant. ☎ 01545 570 075; crafts@dircon.co.uk; www.crafts.dircon.co.uk

**Aberaeron Sea Aquarium** – ᐊ Open Apr-Oct, daily, 10am-5pm. £3.50, £2.00 (senior citizen), £7.50 (family 2A+2C), £1.50 (child). Parking on Quay. Information available. ☎ 01545 570 142; Fax 01545 570 160.

**Coastal Voyages** – ᐊ Operate daily (tide and weather permitting) from outside Aberaeron Sea Aquarium. 1 hour trip £10, £7 (child under 14); 2 hour trip £17, £10 (child under 14). Commentary and information provided by crew/marine ecologist. ☎ 01545 570 142; Fax 01545 570 160.

**Llanerchaeron (NT)** – Restoration in progress. Parkland: Open all year, sunrise-sunset. Home farm, gardens and grounds: Open Apr-Oct, Thurs-Sun and bank holiday Mon, 11am-5pm. House: Times available by telephone. £2, £1 (child). Guided tour Thur, July-Aug, 90p. ☎ 01545 570 200.

**Cardigan Bay Marine Wildlife Centre** – Open Apr-Sept, daily, 9.30am-5pm. Donation welcome. Boat trips in Cardigan Bay (2hr-£8; 4hr-£16 and 8hr-£35) and to the Irish coast (5-day; £40 per day for the boat only). Gift shop. ☎/Fax 01545 560 032.

**St Mary's Church** – Open daily, 10am (2pm Sun) to 4pm; sometimes closed betwee noon and 2pm. Services: Sun, 8am, 9.30am (1st Sunday), 11am, 6pm; Wed, 10a Tues, Thur-Fri, 7pm. Key available from the Vicarage. Information available (Dutc French, German, Italian, Spanish, Welsh). Parking. ☎ 01873 853 168 (Vicarage www.stmarys-priory.org

**Abergavenny Museum** – (&) Open Mar-Oct, Mon-Sat, 11am-1pm and 2pm-5pr Sun, 2pm-5pm; Nov-Feb, Mon-Sat, 11am-1pm and 2pm-4pm. £1, 75p (concessior no charge (child). Picnic area. ☎ 01873 854 282; Fax 01873 736 004.

**Cliff Railway** – & Operates on demand Easter-Oct, 10am-5pm (6pm July-Aug Return £2, £5.80 (family 2A+2C), £1 (child). Guide book available. Children's pla area. Café. Gift shop. ☎ 01970 617 642; Fax 01970 617 642.

**Camera Obscura** – (&) Open Mar-Oct, daily, 10am-5pm (6pm, mid-Jul to mid-Sep No charge. Children's play area. ☎/Fax 01970 617 642.

**Ceredigion Museum** – & Open all year, Mon-Sat, 10am-5pm. No charg ☎ 01970 633 088; Fax 01970 633 084.

**National Library of Wales** – & Open all year, Mon-Sat, 9.30am-6pm (5pm Sat during main exhibitions, 10am-5pm. Closed bank holidays and first full week in Oc No charge. Parking. Refreshments (Mon-Sat). ☎ 01970 632 800; Fax 01970 61 709; holi@llgc.org.uk; www.llgc.org.uk

**Aberystwyth Arts Centre** – & Open daily, Mon-Sat, 9am-8pm. Concert hall. Theatr Studio. Cinema. Bookshop. Galleries. Café. ☎ 01970 622 882 or 623 323; Fa 01970 622 883; lla@aber.ac.uk; www.aber.ac.uk/artscentre

**St Padarn's Church** – Open daily, sunrise-sunset. Leaflet. Guide book (Welsh ☎ 01970 623 368.

**Marquess of Anglesey's Column** – Open daily, 9am-5pm. Guide book. Refreshments picnic tables. Shop. Parking. ☎ 01248 714 393.

**Oriel Ynys Mon** – & Open Tues-Sun and bank holiday Mon, 10.30am-5pm. Museur £2.25, £5.50 (family), £1.25 (concession); Art Gallery no charge. Guide book and tex (English/Welsh). Café. Shop. Phone in advance for wheelchairs. ☎ 01248 724 444 Fax 01248 750 282.

**Anglesey Sea Zoo** – & Open Mar-Oct, daily, 10am-6pm (5pm last admission) otherwise, telephone for details. £5.50, £19.95 (family 2A+3C), £4.50 (child), £ (senior citizen), season tickets available. Adventure playground. Water games. Parking Coffee shop. Gift shop. ☎ 01248 430 411; Fax 01248 430 213. fishandfun@ seazoo.demon.co.uk; www.nwi.co.uk/seazoo

**Newborough Warren** – (&) Open July to early-Sept, daily, 10am-8pm. Parking £2 ☎ 01248 716 422 (Warden).

**Llys Llywelyn Countryside Centre** – Open Whitsun to early-Sep, Tues-Sun and ban holiday Mon, 11am (1pm Sun) to 5pm. No charge. ☎ 01407 840 845; Fax 0140 840 846.

**Llangadwaladr Church** – Services: Sun, 11.15am. Church guide. Key available from the Rector or Church Wardens (appointment may be necessary); enquire locally a Hermon.

**Barclodiad Y Gawres Burial Chamber** – Key from Countryside Centre, Llys Llywelyr (see above). ☎ 01407 840 845/6.

**Llynon Mill** – Open Jul-Sept, daily except Mon, 11am (1pm Sun) to 5pm. No charge Parking. Tearoom. ☎ 01407 730 797.

**Wylfa Power Station** – & Guided tour (90min; Welsh) Apr-Oct, daily, 10am-5pm Nov-Mar, daily, 11am-4pm. Closed 25 Dec-4 Jan. Booking essential. No charge Parking. Refreshments. Facilities for the disabled; telephone in advance. ☎ 0140 711 400; Fax 01407 711 202.

**Llanbadrig Church** – & Open usually end-May to Sept, daily, 10am-12noon 2pm-4pm. Services: May-Sept, 4th Sunday in the month, 10am (Welsh), 11.15am (English). Key available by telephoning. Brochure. Guide boards in Dutch, French German. Parking. ☎ 01407 710 356, 01407 711 171.

**Llaneilian Church** – Open May-Sep, daily, 10am-4pm. Services: Sun, 9.30am (Holy Communion; Gospel in Welsh). ☎ 01407 830 349 (Warden).

**Seawatch Centre** – & Open Easter-Sept, Tues-Sat, 11am-5pm, Sun, 1pm-5pm. No charge. Parking. ☎ 01248 410 277.

## ALA

**ala Adventure and Watersports Centre** – The centre organises courses (also commodation) lasting for a few hours or several days, in a range of activities – seiling, mountain climbing, sailing, white-water rafting, windsurfing. ☎/Fax 01678 21 59; 01678 521 600 (bookings); balawatersports@compuserve.com; www.bala ventureandwatersportscentre.co.uk; www.whitewaterrafting.co.uk

**ala Lake Railway** – Operates July and Aug, daily, from Llanuwchllyn at 11.15am, 2.50pm, 2.25pm, 4pm, from Bala at 11.50am, 1.25pm, 3pm, 4.35pm; mid-Apr, ay, June and Sept, daily except Mon and Fri, at same times as above. Duration: ngle 25min; return Llanuwchllyn-Bala-Llanuwchllyn 1hr, Bala-Llanuwchllyn-Bala 1hr 0min including stop at Llanuwchllyn to take on coal and water. Single £3.80, £2 hild); return £6.50, £3 (child); £14 (family 2A+1C: each additional child, £1). ☎/Fax 01678 540 666.

## ANGOR

**angor Cathedral** – ♿ Open Sun-Fri, 8am-5.30pm, Sat, 9am-12.30pm. Services: un, 8am, 9.45am (Welsh), 11am, 3.15pm, 5pm (Welsh). Leaflet (French, German, panish, Welsh). ☎ 01248 370 693 (Deanery); Fax 01248 352 466.

**angor Museum and Art Gallery** – (♿) Open Tues-Fri, 12.30pm (10.30am Sat) to .30pm. Wheelchair access to ground floor only. ☎ 01248 353 368; Fax 01248 370 49; patwest@gwynedd.gov.uk

**angor Pier** – ♿ Open all year, 8.30am-sunset. Closed 24-25 and 31 Dec. 25p, 10p hild). Parking 50p. Children's play area. Restaurant. Shop. ☎ 01248 352 421, 1248 354 608; Fax 01248 371 090.

## ARMOUTH

**armouth – Fairbourne Ferry** – Operates (weather permitting) on demand. £1.50, 1 (child). ☎ 01341 250 362; Fax 01341 250 240.

**airbourne Railway** – Operates Apr to late-Sept, daily, 10.30am-5.05pm; also Easter 3 days). Return £4.30, £12.40 (family 2A+3C), £2.75 (child), £3.80 (concession). ature Centre: Open daily, 11am-4.30pm (last admission). £1, 50p (child). Parking. earoom at Fairbourne; café at Porth Penrhyn. ☎ 01341 250 362; Fax 01341 250 40.

**NLI Museum** – Open Apr-Sept, daily, 10.30am-4.30pm. No charge. Parking nearby.

**y Gwyn Museum** – Open May-Sept, daily, 10am-5pm. No charge.

**armouth Bridge** – Open all year, daily. Toll payable Apr-Sept, daily, 8.30am-9pm. 0p, 25p (child); 10p (cycle). Parking. ☎ 01341 280 243.

### xcursion

**lanaber Church** – Open daily, 9am-6pm. Services: Sun, 11.30am. ☎ 01341 280 16.

## ARRY

**lat Holm Project** – Operates regular crossings from Barry Harbour depending on he time of the tide. Return £9, £5 (child 5-16). For short visits (3-4hr including uided tour) or for a longer stay. Self-catering accommodation available. ☎ 01446 47 661; Fax 01446 739 629; flatholmproject@btinternet.com; www.cardiff.gov.uk

**arry Island Pleasure Park** – Open (weather permitting) Whitsun to early-Nov, daily, pm-10pm; Mar-Whitsun, Sat, Sun only. £5 for a book of tickets for the rides. Café. ight spot. Gift shop. ☎ 01446 732 844; Fax 01446 721 186.

## BEAUMARIS

**Beaumaris Castle (CADW)** – (♿) Open Apr-Oct, daily, 9.30-6.30pm; late-Oct to nd-Mar, Mon-Sat, 9.30am (11am Sun) to 4pm. Closed 1 Jan, 24-26 Dec. £2.20, 6.10 (family), £1.70 (concession). ☎ 01248 810 361. '

**Church of St Mary and St Nicolas** – Open daily, sunrise-sunset. Services: 2nd and th Sunday of the month, 8am, 10am (Welsh); 1st and 3rd Sunday of the month, 11am (English); Wed, 11am (English).

**Beaumaris Court House** – Open Easter to late-Sep, daily, 10.30am-5pm. Joint ticket 3.50, £10 (family 2A+2C), £2.50 (concession); court house only £1.50, £1 (concession); gaol only £2.75, £7 (family), £1.75 (child). Guided tour of gaol by appointment. ☎ 01248 811 691 (court), 01248 810 921 (gaol).

**Beaumaris Gaol** – As for Court House.

**Museum of Childhood Memories** – Open Apr-Nov, daily, 10.30am-5.30pm; Sun, noon-5pm; last admission 1hr before closing. £3.00, £8.50 (family 2A+2C), 1.75 (child), £2.50 (concession). ☎ 01248 712 498; Fax 01248 712 498; www.nwi.co.uk/museumofchildhood

## BEDDGELERT

**Bwthyn Llywelyn (Llywelyn Cottage) (NT)** – &. Open Apr-Oct, daily, 11am-5pm. No charge. ☎ 01766 890 293; Fax 01766 890 545.

*Excursion*

**Sygun Copper Mine** – Guided tour daily, 10am (11am Sun) to 5pm (4pm Sat). £4.75, £3 (child), £4 (senior citizen). Hard hat provided; warm clothing and flat-sole shoes recommended; three flights of steps from lower to middle and middle to top level. ☎ 01766 510 100; Fax 01766 510 102; sygunmine@cs.com

## BETWS-Y-COED

**Snowdonia National Park Visitor Centre** – &. Open Easter-Oct, daily, 10am-6pm; Nov-Easter, daily, 9.30am-1pm and 2pm-4.30pm. Closed 1 Jan, 25 and 26 Dec. No charge. Brochure (French, German, Welsh). Parking. ☎ 01690 710 426; Fax 01690 710 665.

**Church of St Michael** – Key available from the Conwy Valley Railway Museum (see below). ☎ 01690 710 333; fosm@jonric.force9.co.uk

**Conwy Valley Railway Museum** – &. Open Easter to end-Oct, daily 10.15am-5.30pm (6pm public hols); Nov-Mar, Sat-Sun and public hols 10.15am-4.30pm. Museum £1; Steam Railway 75p. Audio Guide. Parking. Refreshments. Museum shop. ☎ 01690 710 568; Fax 011690 710 132.

**Motor Museum** – &. Open Easter-Oct, daily, 10am-6pm. £1.50, £1 (child). ☎ 01690 710 760.

*Excursions*

**Swallow Falls** – (&.) Open all year. Turnstile £1. Parking. Viewing platforms. Ramps.

**Ugly House (Ty Hyll)** – Open Mar-Sept, daily, 10am-5pm. 70p, no charge (child member). ☎ 01960 720 287.

**Ty Mawr (NT)** – (&.) Open late-Mar to late-Sep, Thur-Sun and bank holiday Mon midday-5pm; Oct, Sun, Thur, Fri, midday-4pm. £2, £5 (family 2A+2C), £1 (child). Wheelchair access to ground floor only. ☎ 01690 760 213.

**Dolwyddelan Castle (CADW)** – Open Apr to late-Oct, daily, 9.30am-6.30pm; late-Oct to end-Mar, daily, 9.30am (2pm Sun) to 4pm. Closed 1 Jan and 24-26 Dec. £1.70, £4.60 (family 2A+3C), £1.20 (concession). ☎ 01690 760 366.

**Fairy Glen** – Open all year, daily, 9am-sunset (3pm Oct-Mar). 50p. Parking. Picnic tables. ☎ 01690 710 225.

**Conwy Falls** – Open all year. 50p. Woodland trails to waterfalls (9 acres). Restaurant; café (closed 25 Dec). peter.armstrong@conwyfalls.freeserve.co.uk

**Ty'n-y-Coed (NT)** – Open Apr-Oct, Thur, Fri, Sun, midday-5pm (4pm Oct). £2, £5 (family 2A+3C), £1 (child). Parking. ☎ 01690 760 229.

## BLAENAU FFESTINIOG

**Snowdonia National Park Visitor Centre** – Open Easter-Oct, daily, 10am-1pm and 2pm-6pm. ☎ 01766 830 360.

**Llechwedd Slate Caverns** – (&.) Open all year, daily, 10am-5.15pm (last admission 4.15pm Oct-Feb). Closed 1 Jan, 25 and 26 Dec. £6.95, £4.80 (child). Audio guide (French, German, Welsh). No dogs. Parking. Licensed restaurant; café; Victorian pub; Shop. Partial wheelchair access to tramway tour and most surface attractions. ☎ 01766 830 306; Fax 831 260; llechwedd@aol.com; www.llechwedd.co.uk

*Excursions*

**Ffestiniog Power Station** – Open Easter week, daily, 10am-4pm; mid-July to Aug, daily, 10.30am-4.30pm; May to mid-July and Sept to late-Oct, daily except Sat 11am-3pm. £2.75, £7.25 (family 2A+2C), £1.50 (child), £2 (concession). Guided tour available. Brochure (Welsh, French, German). ☎ 01766 830 310; Fax 01766 833 472; roberts.b@fhc.co.uk; www.fhc.co.uk

**Trawsfynydd Power Station** – (&.) Visitor Centre: Open Mar to end-Oct, daily, 9.30am-4.30pm. No charge. Guided tour of power station (charge) at 10am, 11am, 1.30pm and 2.30pm. Leaflet available (Dutch, French, German). ☎ 01766 540 622; Fax 01766 540 619.

## BLAENAVON

**Blaenavon Ironworks (CADW)** – &. Open Apr-Oct, daily, 9.30am (10am Sat, Sun) to 4.30pm (5pm Sat). £1.50, £4 (family 2A+3C), £1 (concession). ☎ 01495 792 615.

**Big Pit** – &. Open early-Mar to end-Nov, daily, 9.30am-5pm (3.30pm last admission); Dec-Feb, subject to closure, phone for details and times. £5.75, £17 (family 2A+2C), £3.95 (child). Underground tour (1hr; child under 5 not admitted) 10am-3.30 pm, at frequent intervals. Site guide (French). Parking. Licensed cafeteria, tearoom; picnic areas. Shop. Ramps; underground tour for the disabled by prior arrangement only. ☎ 01495 790 311; Fax: 01495 792 618.

**nty Pool and Blaenavon Railway** – (占) Operates Easter to late-Sept, week-
ds and bank holiday Mon, 11.30am-4.30pm, every 30min. All day ticket £2.20,
.50 (family), £1.10 (child). Special events at Christmas, Easter and May Day
nk holiday; telephone for details. Parking. Refreshments on train. ☎ 01495
92 263.

## xcursion

**alley Inheritance Museum** – 占 Open Jan-Dec, daily, 10am (2pm Sun) to 5pm.
.20, £2.40 (family 2A+2C), 60p (concession). Parking. Coffee shop; picnic area.
ft shop. ☎ 01495 752 036; Fax 01495 752 043.

## ODELWYDDAN

**odelwyddan Castle** – 占 House: Open Apr-Oct, daily except Fri, 11am to 5pm;
ov-Mar, daily except Fri and Mon, 11am to 4pm; last admission 1hr before closing.
ardens: Open same dates as above, 10am (11am in winter) to 4pm. £4, £10 (family,
A+2C), £2.50 (child), £3.50 (senior). Grounds only: £1, £2.50. Audio guide, guide
ook, leaflet (French, German, Welsh), braille guide. Gift shop. ☎ 01745 584 060;
ax 01745 584 563.

**t Margaret's (Marble) Church** – 占 Open daily, 9am-5pm (later in summer).
ervices: Sun, 11am and 6pm (5pm in winter); Wed, 10am. Ramps. ☎ 01745 583
34.

## ODNANT GARDEN

**odnant Garden (NT)** – 占 Open mid-Mar to Oct, daily, 10am-5pm. £5, £2.50
hild). Plant sales (not NT). Parking. Refreshments; picnics in car park. Steep garden
ith many steps; wheelchairs available. ☎ 01492 650 460; Fax 01492 650
48.

## RECON

**eacons Crafts** – Open Mon-Sat, 10am-5.30pm. ☎ 01874 625 706.

**recon Cathedral** – 占 Open all year, daily, 8am-6pm. Services: Sun, 8am (Holy
ommunion), 11am (Matins or Sung Eucharist), 3.30pm; Fri, 5.45pm (Choral Even-
ong); Wed, 11am (Holy Communion).

**eritage Centre:** Open Mar-Dec, Mon-Sat, 10.30am-4.30pm. Guided tour by
ppointment. Leaflet (Danish, Dutch, French, German, Italian, Spanish, Welsh). Park-
g. Restaurant. Shop. ☎ 01874 625 222.

**recknock Museum** – 占 Open all year, Mon-Fri, 10am-5pm, Sat, 10am-1pm and
pm-5pm (4pm Nov-Feb); also Apr-Sept, Sun, noon-5pm. Closed Good Friday, 24 Dec
o 1 Jan. £1, 50p (concession), no charge (child). Brochure (English, Welsh). Limited
arking. Lift to all floors, 2 stair lifts, access at rear of building. ☎ 01874 624 121;
ax 01874 611 281; brecknock.museum@powys.gov.uk

**outh Wales Borderers and Monmouthshire Regimental** – 占 Open Apr-Sept,
aily, 9am-5pm; Oct-Mar, Mon-Fri, 9am-5pm. Closed Christmas and New Year. Guided
ur (1hr) and access to archives by appointment. ☎ 01874 613 310; Fax 01874
13 275; swb@rrw.org.uk; www.rrw.org.uk

## RECON BEACONS

**eacons Bus** – Operates late-May to late-Sept, Sun and bank hols. Between Brecon
nd many points within and beyond the park boundaries – National Park Visitor
entre, Swansea, Bridgend, Merthyr, Cardiff (with trailer for 24 bikes max), Risca,
wmbran, Abergavenny, Hay-on-Wye. Hail and ride within the park; otherwise official
tops only. ☎ 01874 624 437 (National Park); 01874 622 485 (Brecon TIC).

**recon Mountain Railway** – 占 Open Apr-Oct. Return £6.20, £3.10 (child); family
cket available. ☎ 01685 722 988; Fax 01685 384 854; www.breconmountain
ailway.co.uk

**Monmouthshire and Brecon Canal Trips** – 占 Operate from Brecon Mar-Oct, Wed,
at and Sun, at 3pm; public hols, at midday and 3pm; extra trips in summer. £5, £3
child). Commentary. Parking. Refreshments. Wheelchair lift. ☎ 07831 685 222
Dragonfly Cruises); info@dragonfly.bizland.com

**Monmouthshire and Brecon Canal Trips (2)** – Operate from Storehouse Bridge,
alybont, Llangynidr and Gilwern. ☎ 01873 486 382 (Water Folk Craft); 01873
30001 (Castle Narrow Boats).

**Howell Harris Museum** – (占) Open by appointment usually all year, daily, 9am-4pm.
losed Easter, weekends in Jan, Feb, Dec; also 24-26 Dec. Parking. Refreshments by
rrangement. ☎ 01874 711 423; Fax 01874 712 212; trefeca@surfaid.org

**atricio Church** – Open daily. Services: 1st and 3rd Sun of the month, 11.30am;
Rogation Sunday, 11am. See notice-board for other services. Leaflet (French, German).
☎ 01873 810 348.

**Penyclawdd Court** – Open Apr-Sept, Thurs-Sun, 2pm-5pm (4pm last admission). £. £2 (child, concession). Refreshments by arrangement; Tudor feasts and other event. Accommodation. ☎ 01873 890 719; Fax 01873 890 848.

**Mountain Centre** – ♿ Open daily, 9.30am to 5pm (6pm Jul-Aug; 5.30pm weekend Apr, May, Jun, Sep; 4pm Nov-Feb). Closed 25 Dec. Parking (pay and display). Te. room. ☎ 01874 623 366; Fax 01874 624 515.

**Garwnant Forestry Commission Visitor Centre** – Open Mar-Dec, 10.30am-5p. (6pm June-Aug). Leaflet on walks, trails. Parking £1. Cycles for hire. Playgroun. Café; picnic site. Gift shop. ☎ 01685 723 060.

**Dan-yr-Ogof Caves** – Open Easter-Oct, 10am-3pm (last admission). £7.50, £4 (child. Parking. Coffee shop, under-cover picnic areas. Craft shop. Unsuitable for wheelchair. ☎ 01639 730 284; Fax 01639 730 293; info@showcaves.co.uk; www. showcaves.co.uk

**Craig-y-Nos Country Park** – ♿ Open May-Aug, daily, 10am-6pm (7pm Fri-Sun, b. Sat-Sun in May); Mar, Apr, Sep, Oct, daily, 10am-5pm (6pm Sat-Sun); Nov-Feb, dail. 10am-4pm (4.30pm Sat-Sun). No charge. Parking (pay and display). ☎ 01639 73. 395.

🚹 The Groe Car Park – LD2 3BT – ☎ 01982 553 3C

**Erwood Station Craft Centre & Gallery** – Open mid-Feb to Dec, daily, 9am-6p. (5pm autumn and winter). Refreshments; picnic area. ☎/Fax 01982 560 67. alan@erwood-station.co.uk; www.erwood-station.co.uk

# C

## CAERLEON

**Caerleon Roman Fortress Baths (CADW)** – ♿ Open Apr to late-Oct, dail. 9.30am-5pm; late-Oct to end-Mar, daily except Fri, 9.30am (1pm Sun) to 5pm. Close. 1 Jan, 24-26 Dec. £2, £5.50 (family 2A+3C), £1.50 (concession); joint ticket wit. Roman Legionary Museum £3.30, £8.10 (family 2A+3C), £2 (concession). ☎ 0163. 422 518.

**Roman Legionary Museum** – ♿ Open daily, 10am (2pm Sun) to 5pm. Closed 1 Jar. 24-26 and 31 Dec. £2.10; joint ticket with Roman Fortress £3.30, £2 (student), n. charge (concession). ☎ 01633 423 134; Fax 01633 422 869.

## CAERNARFON

**Parc Glynllifon** – (♿) Park: Open daily, 9am-5pm. Visitor Centre and tearoom. Easter-Sept, daily, 10am-5pm. Craft workshops: Open usually Easter-Sept, Sun-Thu. 11am-4pm; each workshop keeps its own hours. Parking £1.50. ☎ 01286 830 222.

**Caernarfon Castle (CADW)** – Open early-Apr to late-Oct, daily, 9.30am-6.30pm. late-Oct to end-Mar, daily, 9.30am (11am Sun) to 4pm. Closed 1 Jan, 24-26 Dec. £4.20, £11.60 (family 2A+3C), £3.20 (concession). ☎ 01286 677 617.

**Regimental Museum of the Royal Welch Fusiliers** – Open as for Caernarfon Castl. (see above). No charge. ☎ 029 2067 3362.

**Town Walls** – Key available from Caernarfon Castle. No charge. ☎ 01286 677 617.

**Maritime Museum** – ♿ Open spring bank holiday to mid-Sept, daily, 11am-4pm. £1. no charge (child). Parking. ☎ 01286 675 269.

**Segontium Roman Fort (CADW)** – (♿) Open daily, 10am (2pm Sun) to 5pm (4pr. Oct-Mar). £1.25, no charge (concession). Parking. ☎ 01286 675 625.

**St Peblig's Church** – ♿ Open by appointment. Services (Welsh only): Sun, 10am. 6pm, Fri, 8.30am. ☎ 01286 674 181; Fax 01286 673 750.

### Excursions

**Caernarfon Air World** – ♿ Museum: Open Apr-Oct, daily, 9.30am-5.30pm; Nov-Mar. Sat-Sun. £4.50, £11 (family 2A+2C), £2.50 (child). Guided tour (Welsh available). Pleasure flights: all year, daily (weather permitting); phone in advance. Restaurant. coffee shop. ☎ 01286 830 800; Fax 01286 830 280.

**Inigo Jones Slate Works** – Open Easter-Sept, Mon-Fri, 9am (10am Sat-Sun and. bank hols) to 5pm; Oct-Easter, daily except Sun, 9am-5pm (midday Sat). Workshop. Open Mon-Fri, 9am-4.30pm (3.30pm Fri); last tour 4pm. £2.50, £2 (concession). ☎ 01286 830 242; Fax 01286 831 247; inigojones@netwales.co.uk

## CAERPHILLY

**Caerphilly Castle (CADW)** – Open daily, 9.30am (11am Sun, Nov-Mar) to 6pm (5pm. Apr, May, Oct; 4pm Nov-Mar). Closed 1 Jan, 24-26 Dec. £2.50, £7 (family 2A+3C). £2 (concession). ☎ 029 2088 3143.

**Guide Friday Bus Tour** – Operates mid-Apr to late-Oct, daily, every 10-15min (less frequently in winter). £7, £16.50 (family 2A+4C), £2.50 (child), £5.50 (student/senior). Ticket valid all day and for discounts at many major attractions, retailers and restaurants. ☎ 029 2038 4291 or 01789 284 466; info@guidefriday.com; www.guidefriday.com

**Craft in the Bay** – Open daily, 10am-5pm. ☎ 029 2048 4611; Fax 029 2049 136.

**St John's Church** – Open daily, 9.30am-6.30pm. Services: Sun, 8am, 11am, 6pm; Mon, Tues, Wed, 10am; Thurs, 11am; Fri, midday; Sat, 8.30am. ☎ 029 2022 0375 (vicarage); 029 2039 5231 (church).

**Millennium Stadium** – ♿ Guided tour (1hr) daily, 10am-6pm (5pm Sun), every hour on the hour. Closed 1 Jan, Good Friday, 24-26 Dec, 31 Dec. Booking essential. £5, £15 (family 2A+2C), £2.50 (child 5-16), £3 (student/senior). ☎ 0990 582 582.

**Cardiff Castle** – Castle Green, Roman Wall and Norman Keep: Open all year, daily, 9.30am-6pm (4.30pm Nov to end-Feb). Closed 1 Jan, 25-26 Dec.
Guided tour (1hr functions permitting) or short tour (30min): Mar-Oct, daily, 10am-5pm (last tour), every 20min; Nov-Feb, Mon-Fri, at 10.30am, 11.45am, 12.45pm, 2pm, 3.15pm, Sat-Sun, at 10.30am, 11.45am, 12.15pm, 1.30pm, 2pm (possible 2.30pm and 3.15pm).
Castle Green, Roman Wall, Norman Keep and Military Museum £2.50, £1.50 (child); Guided tour (including Castle Green, Roman Wall, Norman Keep and Military Museum) £5, £3 (child); Short tour (including Castle Green, Roman Wall, Norman Keep and Military Museum) £3, £1.80 (child).
Brochure (French, German, Italian, Japanese, Spanish, Welsh). Tea room. Gift shop. ☎ 02920 878 100; Fax 02920 878 100; cardiffcastle@cardiff.gov.uk

**Welch Regiment Museum** – Open daily except Tues, 10am-6pm (4.30pm Nov-Mar). Closed 1 Jan and 25-26 Dec. ☎ 02920 229 367.

**Queen's Dragoon Guards Museum** – (♿) Open daily except Fri, 10am-6pm (4.30pm Nov-Feb). Closed 1 Jan, 25-26 Dec. Shop. Wheelchair access to the Guards Museum only. ☎ 02920 222 253; Fax 02920 781 384.

**National Museum & Gallery** – ♿ Open Tues-Sun and most bank holiday Mon, 10am-5pm. £4.50, no charge (concession). Audio guide and brochure. Refreshments. ☎ 029 2039 7951; Fax 029 2037 3219.

**Cardiff Bay Visitor Centre** – ♿ Open daily, 9.30am (10.30am weekends and bank hols) to 5pm (6.30pm May-Sept). Closed 24-26 Dec. No charge. Leaflet of Cardiff (Dutch, French, German, Japanese, Spanish, Welsh). ☎ 029 2046 3833; Fax 029 2048 6650.

**Lightship 2000** – Open daily, 10am (2pm Sun) to 5pm. Donation welcome. Guided tour available. Coffee shop. ☎ 029 2048 7609; 029 2070 0611 (Chaplain).

**Techniquest** – ♿ Open Mon-Fri, 9.30am-4.30pm, Sat-Sun and bank hols, 10.30am-5pm. £5.50, £15.75 (family 2A+3C), £3.80 (concession), no charge (child under 5). Guide books (French, German). Café. Shop. ☎ 029 2047 5475; Fax 029 2048 2517; gen@tquest.org.uk; www.techniquest.org

**Norwegian Church Centre** – Open daily, 10am-4pm. No charge. Coffee shop. ☎ 029 2045 4899; Fax 029 2049 5122; norwegian.church@talk21.com

## Excursion

**Dyffryn House and Gardens** – ♿ Open all year, daily, 10am-sunset. Apr-Oct £3, £2 (child under 16); Nov-Mar, no charge. ☎ 029 2059 3328. Garden tour available. Visitor centre. Shop.

## CARDIGAN

### Excursions

**Cilgerran Castle (CADW)** – ♿ Open Apr to late-Oct, daily, 9.30am-6.30pm; late-Oct to end-Mar, daily, 9.30am-4pm. £2, £1.50 (concession), £5.50 (family 2A+3C). ☎ 01239 615 007.

**Welsh Wildlife Centre** – ♿ Open daily, 10.30am-5pm. Visitor Centre: Open Easter-Nov, daily. £2.50, £6.50 (family 2A+2C), £1.75 (concession). Parking. Restaurant; Café. Shop. Lift and flat surfaced paths. ☎ 01239 621 600; Fax 01239 613 211.

## CAREW

**Carew Castle** – ♿ Open Easter-Oct, daily, 10am-5pm. Castle and mill £2.75, concession available; castle or mill only £1.90. Guided tour (1hr). Leaflet (Welsh). Wheelchair access to the ground floor. ☎ 01646 651 782, 651 657; Fax 01646 651 782.

**Carew Tidal Mill** – (♿) Open Easter-Oct, daily, 10am-5pm. Prices as for Carew Castle (see above). Audio-visual presentation. Leaflet (Welsh). Picnic site. Wheelchair access to the ground floor. ☎ 01646 651 782.

**Oriel Myrddin** – Open daily except Sun, 10.30am-4.45pm. ☎ 01267 222 77 Fax 01267 220 599.

**Gwili Pottery** – Open Mon-Sat, 9am-5pm, Sun, check by phone. ☎ 01267 253 44 gwilipottery@hotmail.com; www.gwili.co.uk

**Carmarthen Museum** – (&) Open Mon-Sat, 10am-4.30pm. Closed 1 Jan and 2 Dec. No charge. Parking. ☎ 01267 231 691; Fax 01267 223 830.

**Gwili Railway** – Open Aug, daily, 11.15am-4pm (5 departures); Apr-Oct and De certain days only. £4, £10 (family 2A+3C), £2.50 (concession). Parking. Picnic are refreshments on the train and at Bronwydd. Shop. ☎ 01267 230 66 gwili@talk21.com; www.gwili-railway.co.uk

**National Botanic Garden of Wales** – & Open daily, 10am to 6pm (5.30pm Sep-Oc 4.30pm Nov to mid-Apr). £6.50, £16 (family 2A+4C), £3 (child 5-16), £5 (conce sion). Parking. Cafeteria; covered and open-air picnic areas. ☎ 01558 668 76 Fax 01558 668 933; www.gardenofwales.org.uk

**Castell Coch (CADW)** – Open daily, 9.30am (11am Sun, late-Oct to end-Mar) t 6.30pm (5pm end-Mar to end-May; 4pm late-Oct to end-Mar). Closed 1 Jan, 24-2 Dec. £2.50, £7 (family 2A+3C), £2 (concession). ☎ 029 2081 0101.

**Chepstow Castle (CADW)** – (&) Open daily, 9.30am (11am Sun, late-Oct t end-Mar) to 5pm (6pm Jun-Sep; 4pm late-Oct to end-Mar). Closed 24-26 Dec. £ £8 (family 2A+3C), £2 (concession). Wheelchair access to ground floor onl ☎ 01291 624 065.

**Chepstow Museum** – (&) Open Jul-Sept, daily, 10.30am (2pm Sun) to 5.30pm Oct-June, 11am (2pm Sun) to 5pm. Closed 1pm-2pm. ☎ 01291 625 98 Fax 01291 635 005; chepstowmuseum@monmouthshire.gov.uk

**St Mary's Church** – Open daily, 8.15am-5pm. Services: Sun, 8am, 10am, 6.30pm Wed, 10.15am; Holy days, 7pm.

**Severn Bridge** – Toll (westbound traffic only) £4.20 (cars), £8.50 (lorries and var up to 3.5 tons). £12.70 (heavy goods vehicles). ☎ 01454 632 436; www severnbridge.co.uk

**Caldicot Castle and Country Park** – Open Mar-Oct, daily, 10.30am (1.30pm Sun) t 5pm. £1.50, 85p (concession). Play areas in park. Parking; large chessboard. Tearoor (daily, 11am (2pm Sun) to 4.30pm); picnic areas; medieval banquets. Shop. ☎ 0129 420 241, 01291 424 447 (medieval banquet); Fax 01291 435 094; calmus monmouthshire.gov.uk

**Penhow Castle** – (&) Open Aug, daily, 10am-5.15pm (last admission); Good Frida to end-Jul and Sept, Wed-Sun, daily, 10am-5.15pm (last admission); Oct-Easter, Wed 10am-4pm, Sun (sometimes), 1pm-4pm. Audio tour available (French, German Welsh). Evening candlelit tour by arrangement. Christmas tour (mid-Nov to early-Jan) Overnight accommodation by arrangement. ☎ 01633 400 800; Fax 01633 400 99

**Chirk Castle (NT)** – & Castle: Open Apr-Nov, Wed-Sun and bank hols, noon-5p (4pm Oct). Gardens: As for castle, 11am-6pm (5pm Oct). Castle and gardens £5 £12.50 (family 2A+2C), £2.50 (child); gardens only £2.80, £1.40 (child). Hous guide (Dutch, French, German, Spanish, Welsh). Parking 200yds/180m from castle courtesy coach from car park-castle. Licensed tearoom. Wheelchairs, stairclimbe ☎ 0691 774 701; Fax 0691 774 706.

**Chapel of St Trillo** – Open Easter-Oct, daily. Services: Fri, 8am (Holy Communion) ☎ 01492 548 878 (Vicar).

**Welsh Mountain Zoo** – & Open daily, 9.30am-5pm (4pm Nov-Feb). £6.25, £17.7 (family 2A+2C), £4.15 (child), £5.15 (concession); no charge (blind and wheelchair bound). Parking. Refreshments. ☎ 01492 532 938; Fax 01492 530 498 welshmountainzoo@enterprise.net; www.welshmountainzoo.org

**Boat Trips** – Operate Easter to mid-Oct, daily, 11.15am-4.15pm, every 30min. £3 £2 (child). Booking for parties only; places available when full capacity not required b party. Commentary. Refreshments on board. ☎ 07775 610 990 or 01492 592 284

**Conwy Castle (CADW)** – Open daily, 9.30am-5pm (6pm late May-Sept; 4pm Nov-en Mar). Closed 1 Jan, 24-26 Dec. £3.50, £2.50 (concession), £9.50 (family 2A+3C) ☎ 01492 592 358.

**Teapot World Museum and Shop** – Open Easter-Oct, daily, 10am (11am Sun) to 5.30pm. ☎ 01492 596 533, ✆/Fax 01492 593 429; paulgibbs.teapot@btinternet. com; www.teapotworld.co.uk

**Plas Mawr (CADW)** – ♿ Open Easter-Oct, Tue-Sun and bank holiday Sat-Mon, 9.30am-5pm (6pm late-May to early-Sep; 4pm Oct). £4, £11 (family 2A+3C), £3 (concession). ☎ 01492 580 167.

**Royal Cambrian Academy** – (♿) Open all year, daily except Mon, 11am-5pm, Sun 2pm-4.30pm. £1, no charge (child), 50p (concession). Wheelchair access to ground floor only. ✆/Fax 01492 593 413; rac@nol.co.uk; www.rcaconwy.org

**Aberconwy House (NT)** – Open late-Mar to Oct, daily except Tue, 11am-5pm. £2, £5 (family), £1 (child). ☎ 01492 592 246.

**St Mary and All Saints Church** – Open in summer whenever steward is present; key available at the Vicarage. Services: Sun, 8am, 11am; Wed, 11am. Leaflet. ☎ 01492 593 402.

## COWBRIDGE

**Cowbridge Museum** – (♿) Open first Sat in every month, 11am-4pm. 50p, 20p (concession). Parking at rear. ☎ 01446 775 139.

**Holy Cross Church** – Open daily, 8.30am. Services: Sun, 8am, 10.45am, 6.30pm. If locked, key available from Parish Office, in the Church. ✆/Fax 01446 772 302.

## CRICCIETH

**Criccieth Castle (CADW)** – Site: Open all year. Visitor Centre: Open Apr-Sept, daily, 10am-6pm. Closed 1 Jan, 24-26 Dec. £2.20, £6.10 (family 2A+3C), £1.70 (concession). ☎ 01766 522 227.

## Excursion

**Lloyd George Museum** – (♿) Open July-Sept, daily, 10am-5pm; June, Mon-Sat and bank holiday Sun, 10am-5pm; Apr-May, Mon-Fri, 10am-5pm; Oct, Mon-Fri, 11am-4.30pm. £3, £7 (family), £2 (concession). Guided tour (1hr; English, Welsh). Leaflet (French, German). Guide book (English, Welsh). Parking. Picnic area. Shop. Wheelchair access to Museum and to ground floor of Highgate Cottage and Shoemaker's Workshop. ☎ 01766 522 071.

# D

## DENBIGH

**Denbigh Town Walls** – Key available from the Museum or Library; for times see Denbigh Museum below.

**Denbigh Museum** – (♿) Open daily, 9.30am (10.30 Thur, 9am Sat) to 5pm (7pm Mon, Wed; 1pm Sat). Closed bank holidays, Good Friday and Easter Monday. Parking nearby. ☎ 01745 816 313; Fax 01745 816 427.

**St Marcella' Church, Whitchurch** – Open Apr-Oct, first Saturday in the month, 10am-noon. Services: most Sun, 9.30am. Leaflet (Welsh). ☎ 01745 812 970.

**St Dyfnog's Church, Llanrhaeder-yng-Nghinmeirch** – Open all year, daily, during daylight hours. Services: Sun, 8.30am, 11.15am. Guide book; brochure on Jesse window. ☎ 01745 890 250.

## DOLGELLAU

**St Mary's Church** – Open daily, 9am-5pm. Services: Sun, 8am, 10am, Mon-Fri, 8.30am, 5pm, Thurs, 10.30am. Leaflet (Welsh). ☎ 01341 422 225; Fax 01341 422 225; carl@meirionnydd.freeserve.co.uk; www.geocities.com/stmarys–dol

**Snowdonia National Park Visitor Centre** – Open daily, 10am-6pm. ☎ 01341 422 888; Fax 01341 422 576.

**Coed y Brenin Forest Park** – (♿) Open Easter-Oct, daily, 10am-5pm (approx); Nov-Easter, Sat-Sun, 11am-4pm. Leaflet (Welsh). Mountain bike hire. 3 mountain bike routes – Expert route (22mi/35kms; 2-4hr); Sport Route (14mi/22km; 1hr 30mn-2hr); Fun Route (18mi/11km; 30min-2hr). Parking £2 (long stay), 50p (short stay). Café; riverside picnic place. ☎ 01341 440 666 (Visitor Centre), 01341 422 289 (Forest District Office).

**Cymer Abbey (CADW)** – Open daily, 9.30am-6pm (4pm late-Oct to end-Mar). Closed 1 Jan, 24-26 Dec. £1.20, £3.10 (family 2A+3C), 70p (concession). ☎ 01341 422 854.

**Penmaenpool Observatory** – Open Easter week and Whitsun to early-Sept, daily, 11am-5pm; Easter-Whitsun, weekends only, midday-4pm. No charge. Parking. ☎ 01341 422 071.

# E

## ELAN VALLEY

**Marston Pottery** – Open daily, 10am-5pm approx. ☎/Fax 01597 810 875 philrogers@ntlword.com

**Gilfach Farm** – Open July-Aug, Thur-Mon, 10am-5pm; Apr-June and Sept, Fri-Su and bank holiday Mon, 10am-5pm. £1.50, £1 (concession), no charge (child) ☎ 01597 870 301; Fax 01597 823 298.

**Gigrin Farm – Kite Country Interpretive Centre** – & Open mid-Oct to mid-Ap daily, 10am-8pm. Birds of prey feeding time: 2pm. £2.50, £1 (child), £2 (senior) ☎ 01597 810 243.

**Elan Valley Visitor Centre** – & Open Easter-late Oct, daily, 10am-5.30pm. N charge. Parking £1. Café. ☎ 01597 810 898, 810 880.

**Rhayader Museum** – Open mid-July to Sept, Mon, Wed, Fri, 2pm-5pm, Sat, 10am midday and 2pm-5pm; Whitsun to mid-July, Fri, 2pm-5pm, Sat, 10am-midday an 2pm-5pm; Easter and Whitsun, Mon, Tues, 2pm-5pm, Sat, 10am-midday an 2pm-5pm. Donation welcome. ☎ 01597 810 052.

**Welsh Royal Crystal** – Shop: Open daily, 9am (9.30am Sun) to 5pm. Cutting an engraving demonstrations: Mon-Fri, 9am-12.30pm and 1.30pm-4.30pm. Close 1 Jan, 25-26 Dec. Self guided tours £1. Guided tours by appointment only £1.5C Factory shop. Café. Parking. ☎ 01597 811 005; Fax 01597 811 129; sales@ welshcrystal.co.uk

## ERDDIG

**Erddig (NT)** – (&) Country Park: Open daily, sunrise-sunset. House: Open Mar-Nov, Sat-Wed and Good Fri, midday-5pm (4pm Oct-Nov). Gardens: Open Mar-Nov, Sat-Wed, 11am (10am Jul-Aug) to 6pm (5pm Oct-Nov); last admission to house 1hr before closing. House, outbuildings and gardens £6, £15.00 (family 2A+3C), £3 (child); house (excluding family rooms), outbuildings and gardens £4, £10 (family 2A+3C), £2 (child). Leaflet (French, German, Welsh, Dutch). Parking. Licensed restaurant; refreshments. Plant sales, NT shop. Access to the house difficult for wheelchairs; boarded walk in the country park. ☎ 01978 355 314; Fax/Infoline 01978 313 333 erddig@smtp.ntrust.org.uk

The Kitchen, Erddig

# F

## FISHGUARD

**Fishguard Invasion Centre** – & Open Apr-Oct, daily, 10am (2pm Sun) to 5pm Nov-Mar, daily, 11am (Sun 2pm) to 4pm. £1.50, 50p (child 8-16). Parking behin Town Hall. ☎ 01348 874 997; Fax 01348 872 402; www.ecommerce.ac.uk/fish/

**West Wales Arts Centre** – (&) Open Mon-Sat, 10am-5.30pm; Sun, check by phone ☎ 01348 873 867 or 874 540; Fax 01348 873 867; westwalesarts@btconnect com; http://home.btconnect.com/WEST-WALES-ARTS/

**Tregwynt Mill** – Open Mon-Fri, 9.30am-5.30pm; also in summer, Sat-Sun, shorte hours. ☎ 01348 891 225; mail order 01348 891 644; Fax 01348 891 694 info@melintregwynt.com.uk

**St Brynach's Church, Nevern** – Open daily. Services: Sun, 11am. ☎ 01239 82C 427.

**stell Henllys** – (&) Open Apr-Oct, daily, 10am-5pm. £2.70, £7.10 (family 2A+3C), .80 (concession). Guided tour available. Guide book (Welsh for children). Leaflet elsh). Exhibition; information panels. Parking; 5min on foot from ticket office to e. Refreshments. Gift shop. Partial access for wheelchairs to site; ramp to shop. /Fax 01239 891 319.

## G

## LAMORGAN COAST

**antwit Major Visitor Centre** – Open daily, Mon-Fri, 9am-1pm and 2pm-4pm, Sat d bank hols, 10am-1.30pm and 2pm-6pm, Sun, 1.30pm-6pm. ☎ /Fax 01446 796 6.

**amorgan Heritage Coast Visitor Centre** – & Open all year (except Christmas), n-Fri, 9am-5pm, weekends and public holidays, 1pm-5pm when possible; when sed a message is left advising when open. Parking. Slipway to beach. ☎ 01656 0 157; Fax 01656 880 931; heritagecoast@highways.valeofglamorgan.gov.uk

**Illtud's Church** – Open during daylight hours. Services: Sun, 10am, 6pm; week-ys, see church notice board. Brochure. Guided tour available. ☎ 01446 792 324; x 01446 795 551; ksmallton@compuserve.com

**Donat's Castle** – (&) Guided tour Jun-Jul, Mon-Fri, at 2.30pm. Castle and rdens and audio-visual presentation £3.50. ☎ 01446 799 027; Fax 01446 795 7.

## OWER

**wer Heritage Centre Park Mill** – & Open all year, daily, 10am-6pm. Closed 25 c. £2.80, £7.80 (family), £1.80 (concession). Guided tour. Guide book. Leaflet elsh). Parking. Tea shop; coffee shop. ☎ 01792 371 206; Fax 01792 371 471; ww.gowerheritagecentre.com

**ossili Visitor Centre** – Open late-Mar to Oct, daily, 10.30am-5.30pm; Nov-ristmas, Wed-Sun, 11am-4pm; Feb-March, weekends only, 11am-4pm. No charge. eelchair access to ground floor and shop. Worms Head: Accessible 2hr either side low tide. ☎ 01792 390 707.

**Illtyd's Church** – Open in summer, most days. Services: Sun, 9.30am (Holy mmunion), 6pm (during August).

**wich Castle (CADW)** – Open May-Sept, daily, 10am-5pm. £2, £5.50 (family +3C), £1.50 (concession). ☎ 01792 390 359.

**eobley Castle (CADW)** – Open Apr to late-Oct, daily, 9.30am-6pm; late-Oct to d-Mar, 9.30am-5pm. £2, £5.50 (family 2A+3C), £1.50 (concession).

## ROSMONT

**Nicholas's Church** – Open 6am-6pm (sunset Oct-Apr). Services: Sun, 11am (Holy mmunion); 1st and 3rd Sunday of the month, 6pm (Evensong). Guide book. Post rds.

**hite Castle (CADW)** – Open Easter-Sept, daily, 10am-5pm. £2, £5.60 (family +3C), £1.50 (concession). ☎ 01600 780 380.

**Bridget's Church** – Open usually daily, 9am-9pm (sunset Oct-Apr). Services: 1st d 3rd Sun of each month, 9.30am (Holy Communion); also Mar-Nov, 2nd and 4th n, 8.15am (Holy Communion). Guide book. Post cards.

## H

## ARLECH

**owdonia National Park Visitor Centre** – & Open Easter-Oct, daily, 10am-1pm d 2pm-6pm; July-Aug, 10am-6pm. ☎/Fax: 01766 780 658.

**rlech Castle (CADW)** – Open Apr-Oct, daily, 9.30am-6pm (5pm Oct); Nov to d-Mar, Mon-Sat, 9.30am (11am Sun) to 4pm. Closed 1 Jan, 24-26 Dec. £3, £8 mily 2A+3C), £2 (concession). ☎ 01766 780 552.

## AVERFORDWEST

**Mary's Church** – Open daily, 7.30am-5pm. Services: Sun, 8.30am (Holy Euchar-), 11.15am (Holy Eucharist or Matins). Leaflet (German). ☎ 01437 763 170 ectory).

## Excursions

**Llys-y-Fran Country Park and Reservoir** – & Open daily, 8am (later in winter)
sunset. Cafeteria (mid-Mar to end-Oct and winter weekends, 8am-5.30pm). Sh
(mid-Mar to end-Oct, 8am-5.30pm). Cycle permits £1; mountain bike hire. Fishi
tackle for sale or hire; fly fishing tuition available; fishing facilities for the disable
☎ 01437 532 694, 532 273; 532 732 (Ranger Unit – fishing enquiries).

**St Michael's Church, Rudbaxton** – Open weekdays. Services: Sun, at 10a
☎ 1437 762 625.

**Scolton Country Park** – Open Apr-Sept, daily, 10am-5.45pm; Oct-Mar, dai
9am-4.30pm.

**Picton Castle** – & Castle: Guided tour Apr-Sept, Sun afternoons, Tues-Fri afternoon
Grounds: Open Apr-Oct, Tues-Sun, 10.30am-5pm. House and grounds £4, £3.!
(senior), £1 (child). Grounds only £2.75, £2.50 (senior), £1 (child). Parking. Ca
Shop. ☎/Fax 01437 751 326; pct@pictoncastle.freeserve.co.uk; www.pictoncast
freeserve.co.uk

**Blackpool Mill** – Open Apr-Oct, daily, 11am-6pm. Café; tearoom. Shop. ☎ 014
541 233; Fax 01437 541 233.

**Wilson Museum** – (&) Open Apr-Oct, daily except Sun, 10.30am-4.30pm (1pm Sa
otherwise by appointment. £1, 50p (concession). Bookshop. ☎ 01834 861 719.

## HAWARDEN

**St Deiniol's Church** – Services: Sun, 8am (Holy Communion), 10am (Holy Comm
nion); 3rd Sunday in the month, 6pm (3.30pm in winter) (Evensong), Thurs, 10.:
(Holy Communion). ☎ 01244 520 091.

**St Deinol's Library** – & Open only to registered readers. Guided tour for groups
appointment. B&B available. ☎ 01244 532 350; Fax 01244 520 643; deini
visitors@btinternet.com; www.stdeiniols.chester.ac.uk

## HAY-ON-WYE

**Hay-on-Wye Festival** – The Festival of Literature and the Arts (10 days in late Ma
draws on the town's fame as a centre for buying second-hand books; informati
available from the Festival Box Office, Hay-on-Wye HR3 5BX. ☎ 01497 821 2ς
Fax 01497 821 066; tickets@litfest.co.uk

## HOLYHEAD

**Ucheldre Centre** – (&) Open daily, 10am (2pm Sun) to 5pm and certain evenin
for special events. Parking. Licensed restaurant. Ramps in buildings and groun
☎ 01407 763 361; Fax 01407 763 341.

**Maritime Museum** – Open Easter-Sep, daily except Mon, 1pm-5pm. £2, £5 (fam
2A+2C), £1 (concession). Parking. Teabar. Shop. ☎ 01407 769 745.

Holyhead Harbour

**Cybi's Church** – (♿) Open June-Sept, Mon-Sat, 11am-3pm. Services: Sun, ).30am, 6pm. Leaflet. History and information brochure 20p. Ramps. ☎ 01407 ³3 001; john.nice@talk21.com

**⊃uth Stack Seabird Centre (RSPB)** – Open Easter-Sept, daily, 11am-5pm (4pm last ⁻ket issued). Tickets available from South Stack Kitchen on cliff-top; £2, £1.50 ⊃ncession). 400 steps down to lighthouse and centre on the island. Parking. ⌐ 01407 704 973; www.rspb.org.uk

**⌐lin's Tower** – Open Easter to mid-Sept, 11am-5pm. No charge. Guided tour along ⁻ffs available from first Sunday in May, every Sunday, 2pm. Refreshments at South ⁼ack Kitchen. ☎ 01407 764 973; southstack@interramp.co.uk; www.rspb.org.uk/ ⌐mru/defaults.htm

**⁻eakwater Country Park** – (♿) Footpaths: Open all year, daily, 8am-8pm (5.30pm ⁻nter). Country museum and nature kiosk: Open July-Sept. Leaflet (Welsh). Guided ⌐ur by appointment. Parking. Refreshments (June-Sept). ☎ 01407 760 530.

## ⌐OLYWELL

**Winefride's Well** – ♿ Open Apr-Sept, daily, 9am-5.15pm (5.30pm Sun; 4.30pm ⁼t); Oct-Mar, daily, 10am-4pm. 20p, 10p (child). Guided tour on request. ☎ 01352 ⌐3 054.

**⁼ Winefride's Chapel (CADW)** – Key available from St Winefride's Well (see above); ⁻posit of £5 reimbursed on return of the key.

**⊃bey Farm Museum** – ♿ Open Easter-Oct, daily, 10am-5pm. £2.25, £1.25p ⊃ncession), no charge (child under 5). Bilingual guide. Tape trail. Café. Shop. ⌐ 01352 714 172; Fax 01352 714 791; www.marketsite.co.uk/greenfld

## ⁼FRMT**

## ⁼NIGHTON

**⁻ffa's Dyke Centre** – ♿ Open Easter-Oct, daily, 9am-5.30pm; Nov-Easter, Mon-Fri, ⁐m-5pm. No charge. Parking. ☎ 01547 528 753; oda@offasdyke.demon.co.uk; ⌐ww.offa.demon.co.uk/offa

### ⁻xcursion

**⊃wys County Observatory** – ♿ Open by arrangement. Parking. ☎/Fax 01547 520 ⌐47; starlink@eidosnet.co.uk; http://pages.eidosnet.co.uk/starlink

## ⁼AMPETER

### ⁻xcursion

**⊃olaucothi Gold Mines (NT)** – (♿) Site: Open Easter to mid-Sept, daily, 10am-5pm ⁐st tour). Underground tour (1hr): unsuitable for the infirm or under 5; hillside ⁐lking, stout footwear recommended; helmets with lights provided. Site £2.60, ⁼.50 (family 2A+3C), £1.30 (child). Underground tour £3.60, £14.50 (family ⁐A+3C), £1.80 (child); £2.60 (NT member), £6.50 (NT member's family), £1.30 (NT ⁻ember's child). Exhibitions; gold panning. Tearoom. Shop. Wheelchair access to ⁻ception, exhibition centre and mine yard. ☎ 01558 650 359, 650 707.

## ⁼AUGHARNE

**⁐augharne Castle (CADW)** – ♿ Open May-Sept, daily, 10am-5pm. £2, £1.50 (con- ⁻ssion), £5.50 (family). ☎ 01994 427 906.

**⁼he Boathouse** – Open Apr-Oct, daily, 10am-5pm; Nov-Mar, daily, 10.30am-3pm. ⁼.75, £1.75 (concession), £1 (child over 7). Audio-visual presentation (25min). ⊃ookshop. Tearoom. ☎ 01994 427 420.

**⁐useum of Speed, Pendine** – Open Easter holidays and Spring bank holiday to Sept, ⁐ily, 10am-1pm and 1.30pm-5pm; end of Easter holidays to Spring bank holiday and ⁼t, Fri-Mon, 10am-1pm and 1.30pm-5pm. Closed Nov-Easter. No charge. Parking. ⌐ 01994 453 488.

## ⁼LANBERIS

**⁐elsh Slate Museum** – ♿ Open Easter-Oct, daily, 10am-5pm; Nov-Mar, Sun-Fri. ⁼.50, £2 (concession). 3-D audio-visual show (Welsh, French, German). Children's ⁐ay area. Café; picnic areas. Shop. ☎ 01286 870 630; Fax 01286 871 906; ⁻smpost@btconnect.com; www.nmgw.ac.uk

**Padarn Country Park** – (&) Park: Open all year, daily except 25 Dec. Car park: Op
all year, daily except 25 Dec, 9am-7pm (6pm Easter to Spring bank holiday; 5p
mid-Sep to Easter). Trail leaflet. Trail for less able. Woodland walks. Railway. Wat
sports centre. Boat trips. Craft workshop. Café; picnic areas. ☎/Fax 01286 870 89
padarncountrypark@gwynedd.gov.uk

**Llanberis Lake Railway** – (&) Open Apr-Sept, daily; Oct, Mon-Thurs; Mar, certa
days; min 4 departures per day. £4.20, £2.50 (child), family rate available. Ca
Shop. Wheelchair access to train. ☎/Fax 01286 870 549; llr@lake-railwa
freeserve.co.uk; www.lake-railway.freeserve.co.uk

**Electric Mountain** – (&) Guided tour Easter-Oct, daily, 9.30am-5.30pm; Oct-Chris
mas, daily, 10.30am-4.30pm; Jan-Easter, Fri-Sun, 10.30am-4.30pm; last admissi
1hr before closing. Booking essential. Underground tour: £5, £12 (family 2A+2(
£2.50 (child), £3.75 (concession). No charge for Visitor Centre. Multi-media sho
(Welsh). Parking. Café; tea garden. Art galleries. ☎ 01286 870 636; Fax 01286 8
331; info@electricmountain.co.uk; www.electricmountain.so.uk

**Snowdon Mountain Railway** – & Operates (weather permitting) mid-Mar to earl
Nov, daily, 9am/9.30am-5pm (earlier when demand is slack; 3.30pm Sat), eve
30min. Before mid/late-May and after mid-Oct (when summit rarely accessible
train) trains terminate at Clogwyn or Rocky Valley (penultimate and ante-penultima
stop). Duration: 2hr 30min including 30min at summit. Return £15.80, £11.
(child); £42 (family 2A+2C at 9am, 9.30am and 10am in peak season only); sing
£11.30, £8.10 (child); reduced fares when trains terminate at Clogwyn or Roc
Valley. Brochure (Dutch, French, German, Italian, Russian, Spanish, Welsh). Parkin
Café; snack bar. Gift shop (station). Licensed bar; cafeteria (summit). Ramp
☎ 01286 870 223; Fax 01286 872 518; www.snowdonrailway.force9.co.uk

**Llancaiach Fawr Manor** – & Annual programme of events: telephone for detai
Closed late-Dec to early-Jan. £4.50, £12 (family 2A+2C), £3 (concession). Guide
tour available. Parking. Refreshments. ☎ 01443 412 248.

**Llandaff Cathedral** – Open daily, 7am-7pm. Services: Sun, 8am, 9am, 11a
(Sung Eucharist), 12.15pm (Said Eucharist), 3.30pm (Sung Evensong), 6.30p
(Parish Evensong). Guided tour: details by telephone from the Dean's office. Parkin
Restaurant: Open daily, 10am-3pm. ☎ 029 2056 4554.

**Dinefwr Park** – (&) Newton House (NT): 1 Apr to end-Oct, daily except Tues a
Wed, 11am-5pm. Park: Open as for Newton House; also in winter during daylig
hours. House and Park: £3, £7.50 (family), £1.50 (child); park only: £2, £1 (chil
£5 (family)! Tearoom. Boardwalk (600m) through a bog wood to the millpond dar
Braille guide. ☎ 01558 823 902; Fax 01558 822 036; dinefwr@ntrust.co.uk

**Carreg Cennen Castle (CADW)** – Open daily, 9.30am-7.30pm (sunset, Oct-Mar
Closed 25 Dec. £2.50, £2 (concession), £7 (family 2A+3C). ☎ 01558 822 291.

**Aberglasney** – Open Apr-Oct, daily, 9.30am-6pm (5pm last admission). Guided to
at 11.30am and 2.30pm. £3.95, £9.85 (family 2A+2C), £1.95 (child), £3.4
(senior), £1.45 (disabled). Café. Tel/Fax 01558 668 998; info@aberglasney.or
www.aberglasney.org

**Llandovery Heritage Centre** – & Open daily, 10am-1pm and 2pm-5pm. Donatio
welcome. ☎ 01550 721 228.

**Llandovery Craft Centre** – & Open Mon-Sat, 10am-5pm. No charge. Caf
☎ 01550 721 452.

Excursion

**Dinas Reserve Visitor Centre (RSPB)** – Parking £1 per car. ☎ 01550 760 22
gwenffrwd@interramp.co.uk

**Porticus** – Open Mon-Sat, 10.30am-5pm (early closing Wed). ☎ 01597 823 989.

**Rock Park and Spa** – & Open all year, daily, 9.30am-6.30pm. Parking. ☎ 0159
829 267.

**National Cycling Collection** – Open all year, daily, 10am-4pm. £2.50, £1 (child), £
(concession). Leaflet. Parking. ☎ 01597 825 531.

**Radnorshire Museum** – (&) Open Apr-Sept, daily except Mon, 10am-1pm an
2pm-5pm; Oct-Mar, daily except Sun, Mon and Sat afternoons, 10am-1pm an
2pm-5pm. £1, no charge (child under 16). No parking. Ramp to ground floor onl
☎ 01597 824 513.

Excursion

**St Michael's Church, Cefnllys** – Open daily. Services: 1st Sunday of each month, 3pm. ☎ 01597 822 043.

## LLANDUDNO

**Guide Friday Bus Tour** – Operates late-May to late-Sept, daily (except 10 June to 15 July, weekends only). £6, £13 (family 2A+4C), £5 (child), £1 (student/senior). ☎ 01492 876 606; Fax 01244 347 457; info@guidefriday.com; www.guidefriday. com

**Oriel Mostyn Art Gallery** – ♿ Open Mon-Sat, 10am-5pm. Closed 1 Jan, 25-26 Dec. ☎ 01492 879 201, 870 875; Fax 01492 878 869; www.mostyn.org

**Llandudno Museum** – (♿) Open Easter-Oct, Tues-Sat, 10.30am-1pm and 2-5pm; Sun, 2.15pm-5pm. Nov-Easter, Tues-Sat, 1.30pm-4.30pm. Closed Christmas. £1.50, £3.50 (family 2A+3C), 75p (child), £1.20 (concession). ☎ 01492 876 517.

**Alice in Wonderland Centre** – ♿ Open daily, from 10am. Closed Christmas, New Year and Sundays in winter. Audio guide (Dutch, French, Japanese, Russian). Transcript (German, Hebrew, Italian, Welsh). Shop. Accompanied wheelchair-users welcome. ☎/Fax 01492 860 082; alice@wonderland.co.uk; www.wonderland.co.uk

**Great Orme Tramway** – ♿ Open Apr-Sept, daily, 10am-6pm. Wheelchairs carried empty on tram platform. ☎ 01492 574 234, 01492 876 749; Fax 01942 860 821.

**Llandudno Cable-car** – Open (weather permitting) Easter to first week in Oct, 10am-5pm (summer), 10am-1pm and 2pm-4.20pm (winter). Return £5, £2.60 (child); single £4.50, £2.30 (child). ☎ 01492 877 205.

**Marine Drive** – Scenic Toll road (4mi/6.4km – one way – danger of falling rocks). £2 (vehicle); £1.50 (motor cycle); no charge (pedestrians and cyclists). No coaches.

**Great Orme Visitor Centre** – Open Mar to end-Oct, daily, 9am-5.30pm. No charge. Way-marked walks and Nature Trail. Wildlife gift shop. Large print, braille booklets and audio tape guides available for blind and visually impaired people (£10 deposit). ☎ 01492 874 151 (Warden's Office), 01492 870 097 (summit complex).

**St Tudno's Church, Great Orme** – Open Easter to late-Oct, daily. Services: last Sunday in May to last Sunday in Sept, 11am. ☎ 01492 878 209 (Churchwarden); 01492 876 624 (Rector).

**Great Orme Mines Visitor Centre** – (♿) Open Feb to end-Oct, daily, 10am-5pm. £4.40, £12 (family 2A+2C), £2.80 (child). Tour available (1hr). Audio visual presentation. Parking. Refreshments. ☎/Fax 01492 870 447; gomines@greatorme.freeserve. co.uk; www.greatorme.freeserve.co.uk

## LLANELLI

**Parc Howard Museum and Art Gallery** – Open Mon-Fri, 11am-1pm and 2pm-6pm (4pm Oct-Mar), Sat-Sun, 2pm-6pm (4pm Oct-Mar). Closed 1 Jan, 25-26 Dec. No charge. Refreshments (weekends and school holidays). ☎ 01554 772 029.

Excursions

**Wildfowl and Wetlands Trust** – ♿ Open daily, 9.30am-5pm (4pm Oct-Mar). Closed 24-25 Dec. £5.10, £13 (family 2A+2C), £3 (child). Guide book, brochure, leaflet (Welsh). Parking. Restaurant. Shop. ☎/Fax 01554 741 087; wwtllanelli@aol.com

**Pembrey Country Park** – Open daily, sunrise-sunset. July-Aug, per car £5; Apr-June, Sept £3; Oct-Mar £1. Adventure playground. Miniature railway. Cycle route. Dry ski slope and toboggan run. Equestrian centre. Orienteering. Pitch and putt. Visitor Centre. Parking. Restaurant. Shop. ☎ 01554 833 913; Fax: 01554 835 498.

**Kidwelly Castle (CADW)** – ♿ Open Apr to late-Oct, daily, 9.30am-6.30pm; late-Oct to end-Mar, daily, 9.30am (11am Sun) to 4pm. Closed 1 Jan, 24-26 Dec. £2.20, £6.10 (family 2A+3C), £1.70 (concession). Parking. Ramps. ☎/Fax 01554 890 104.

**Kidwelly Industrial Museum** – ♿ Open June-Aug, daily and May Day and Spring Bank holidays, 10am (2pm Sat-Sun) to 5pm. No charge. Leaflet. Guided tour by appointment all year. Parking. Refreshments. ☎ 01554 891 078; 01554 891 084 (Museum Trust Secretary).

## LLANFYLLIN

**St Myllin's Church** – Open daily, 9am-4pm. Services: Sun, 9.30am, 6.30pm, Thurs, 10am. Leaflet. Access for the disabled, if arranged in advance. ☎ 01691 648 306.

**Council House Murals** – *Open by appointment only.* ☎ *01691 648 244 (adjoining chemist's shop).*

Angel, Rug Chapel

## LLANGOLLEN

**Y Glassblobbery** – Open Easter-Oct, Wed-Sun (also Tue after bank hols) 10.30am-5pm; also Jul-Aug, daily; Nov-Easter, by appointment. Evening talks by appointment. ☎/Fax 01490 460 440; tplustotalise.co.uk

**Craft Workshop** – Open daily, 10am-6pm (5pm winter). ☎ 01490 430 300.

**Llangollen Railway** – ⅄ Operates May to end-Oct, Mon-Fri, at 11am, 1pm, 3pm; Sat, at 11am, 12.40pm, 2.20pm, 4pm; Sun from 11am-4pm (hourly); Sept-Oct Sat-Sun, 10.45am, 12.30pm, 2.15pm, 4pm. Return £7.50, £18 (family 2A+2C) £3.80 (child), £5.50 (concession). Joint rail and canal trips on certain days. Special events for enthusiasts and families. Refreshments. ☎ 01978 860 951 (24hr Talking Timetable), 01978 860 979 (enquiries); office@llanrail.freeserve.co.uk www.joyces.demon.co.uk/llangollen

**Thomas Telford Aqueduct Trips** – Open Easter-Oct, daily (sometimes closed Oct Thur-Fri, except in school holidays); Mar, weeknds only. ☎ 01978 860 702; sue@ horsedrawnboats.co.uk; www.horsedrawnboats.co.uk

**Llangollen Canal Cruises** – Operate Easter-Oct, daily, frequent departures; Mar weekends only. Horse-drawn passenger boat trips (45min return); cruise to the Horseshoe Falls (2hr return). ☎ 01978 860 702; sue@horsedrawnboats.co.uk www.horsedrawnboats.co.uk

**Llangollen Canal Cruises** – Operate daily, day and evening. Dinner cruises on restaurant boat (12-52 people). ☎ 01978 823 215 (Ribbon Plate Restaurant Boats).

**Lower Dee Exhibition Centre** – Open daily, 10am-5pm. Closed 1 Jan, 25-26 Dec Doctor Who Experience £5.75, £15.50 (family 2A+2C), £3.50 (child); Model Railway Exhibition £4.75, £13.50 (family 2A+2C), £3.75 (child); both attractions: £9 £24.95 (family 2A+2C), £6 (child). Coffee shop. No access for wheelchairs ☎ 01978 860 584.

**ETARC European Centre for Traditional and Regional Cultures** – ⅄ Office: Open Mon-Fri, 9am-5pm. Exhibitions: phone for times. Shop. ☎ 01978 861 514; Fax 01978681 804; ectarc@aol.com

**Victorian School and Museum** – Open Apr-Oct, daily. £1.40, 95p (child), £1.15 (senior citizen). ☎ 01978 860 794.

**Royal International Pavilion** – ⅄ Open (functions permitting) Mon-Fri, 9am-5pm weekends for special events. Café-bar. ☎ 01978 860 111; Fax: 01978 860 046 enquiries@royal-pavilion.co.uk; www.royal-pavilion.co.uk

**Llangollen Motor Museum** – Open Mar-Oct, daily except Mon, 10am-5pm. £2 ☎ 01978 860 324.

**Rug Chapel (CADW)** – ⅄ Open May-Sept, Wed-Sun and bank holiday weekends 10am-5pm. £2, £5.50 (family 2A+3C), £1.50 (concession). ☎ 01490 412 025.

**Llangar Church (CADW)** – Access arranged through custodian at Rug Chapel ☎ 01490 412 025.

## LANIDLOES

**Lanidloes Social and Industrial History Museum** – (♿) Open all year, Mon-Fri, 10am-1pm and 2pm-5pm (4.30pm Fri); Apr-Sept, Sat-Sun, 10am-5pm; Oct-Mar, Sat, 10am-1pm. £1, 50p (senior), no charge (child). ☎ 01597 824 513.

**St Idloes' Church** – ♿ Open Mon-Sat, 9am-6pm (5pm winter). Services: Sun, 8am, 11am, 6pm. Information sheet (French, German). ☎/Fax 01686 412 370 (Vicar); dennis@stidloes.freeserve.co.uk

## LANRWST

**Trefriw Woollen Mill** – Open Mon-Sat, 9.30am (10am Sat) to 5.30pm (5pm winter); also July-Aug, Sun, 2-5pm. Tearoom. ☎/Fax 01492 640 462.

**St Grwst Church and Gwydir Chapel** – Open May-Sept, Tues-Fri, 10am-4pm; Oct-Apr, by appointment. Services: Sun, 9am (Welsh), 11am (English), 6pm (2nd Sun of month), Wed, 10.30am (English). ☎ 01492 640 191 (enquiries) or 01492 641 172 (Verger).

**Gwydir Castle** – ♿ Open Mar-Oct, Sun-Fri, 10am-5pm; otherwise limited opening hours. £3, £1.50 (child). Parking. Refreshments by arrangement. ☎ 01492 641 687; www.gwydir-castle.co.uk

**Gwydir Uchaf Chapel (CADW)** – Open Mon-Thur, 10am-5pm (4.30pm Fri). Key available from Forest Enterprise Office (adjacent to Chapel), 8am-closing time; key also available from Gywydir Castle at weekends. ☎ 01492 412 025.

## LANTHONY

**Lanthony Priory** – Open daily, 9am-6pm. Parking. Licensed premises: Closed Nov-Easter, midweek (except at Christmas). ☎ 01873 890 487.

**St Davids Church** – Open daily. Services: Sun, 8.30am. Guide book. Access for the disabled by appointment. ☎ 01873 890 349.

## LANTRISANT

**Parish Church** – Open by appointment. Key available from the Vicarage. Services: Sun, 8.30am, 9.30am (10am 1st Sun of the month), 6pm, Wed, 9.30am. ☎ 01443 223 356 or 237 913; Fax 01443 230 631.

**Model House** – ♿ Open Tue-Sun and bank hols, 10am-5pm. No charge. Access for wheelchairs. ☎ 01443 237 758; Fax 01443 224 718.

## LANWRTYD WELLS

**Cambrian Woollen Mill** – ♿ Open Mon-Fri, 9am-5pm (4pm Fri). ☎ 01591 610 173; Fax 01591 610 314; info@cambrianwool.softnet.co.uk

**St David's Church** – Open daily. Services: May-Aug, every other Fri, 6.30pm (Holy Eucharist). Guide. ☎ 01591 610 231 (Vicarage).

## LEYN PENINSULA

**Penarth Fawr** – ♿ Open Apr-Oct, daily, 9.30am-6.30pm, Nov-Mar, daily, 9.30am (2pm Sun and public hols) to 4pm. No charge. Tea shop. Parking. ☎ 01766 810 880.

Play-yn-Rhiw

**Haven Holiday Park** – (&) Open Mar-Oct, daily, 10am-10pm; Mar, Sat-Sun; la admission 3pm. £3, £10 (family). Boating lake. Adventure play areas. Indoor an outdoor swimming pools. Parking. Restaurant. ☎ 01758 612 112.

**Plas Glyn-y-Weddw Gallery, Llanbedrog** – (&) Open daily except Tues, 11am-5pr £2, £5 (family 2A+2C), £1 (concession). Parking. Shop. Tearoom. ☎ 01758 74 763; Fax 01758 740 232.

**St Engan's Church, Llanengan** – Key available from the Rectory in Abersoc ☎ 01758 712 871 (Rectory).

**Plas-yn-Rhiw (NT)** – (&) Open late-Mar to mid-May, daily except Tues-Wed; mid-Ma to Sept, daily except Tues; Oct, Sat-Sun, midday-5pm (4.30pm last admission). Hou and garden: £3.20, £8 (family 2A+3C), £1.60 (child). Garden only: £2, £1 (child Guided tour by appointment (except during July-Aug). Woodland walk. Picnic area. N shop. Parking (no coaches). Braille guides available. ☎ 01758 780 219.

**St Hywyn's Church, Aberdaron** – & Open weekdays, 9.30am-5pm (later in sum mer). Services: Sun, 11am (Holy Communion). Information about Bardsey Island ar the Bardsey pilgrimage. ☎ 01758 760 278 (Warden).

**Bardsey Island** – *Ferry from Porth Meudwy (weather permitting) Sun-Fri; advanc booking essential. £20 per person. Information on boats and accommodation availab from Bardsey Island Trust, Coed Anna Nanhoron, Pwllheli, Gwynedd LL53 8PI* ☎ *01758 730 740 (Bardsey Island Trust) or 01766 522 624 (Boatman).*

**Lleyn Historical and Maritime Museum** – Open early-July to mid-Sept, Mon-Sa 10.30am-4.30pm, Sun, 2pm-4pm. Donation welcome. ☎ 01758 720 270 (Secre tary); amgueddfeyddmuseums@gwynedd.gov.uk

**St Beuno's Church, Clynnog Fawr** – Open Good Friday to Nov. Services: June-Oc Sun, 11.15am (English); Nov-May, 1st, 3rd and 5th Sunday in the month, 11.15ar (English). Guided tour by appointment. Leaflet. Exhibitions. ☎ 01286 660 54 (Canon Thomas).

# M

## MACHYNLLETH

**Corris Craft Centre** – Open daily, 10am-6pm (4pm in winter). Children's play area Restaurant; picnic area. ☎ 01654 761 584; Fax 01654 761 575.

**Meirion Mill** – & Open Mar-Oct, daily, 10am (10.30am Sun) to 5pm; Nov-Feb Wed-Sun, 10.30am-4pm (4.30pm Sat-Sun). Closed 1 Jan, 25-26 Dec. Parking. Coffee shop. ☎ 01650 531 311; Fax 01650 531 447; vs@meirionmill.co.uk

**Celtica** – & Open daily, 10am-6pm. £4.95, £13.75 (family), £3.80 (concession Audio visual (French, German, Welsh). Tearoom. Bookshop; gift shop. ☎ 01654 70 702; Fax 01654 703 604; bryn@celtica.wales.com; www.celtica.wales.com

**Owain Glyndŵr Centre** – (&) Open Easter to early-Oct, daily except Sun, 10am-5pr otherwise by arrangement. Interpretive Centre and Brass Rubbing Centre. No charge Guide (Welsh). ☎ 01654 702 827.

**Museum of Modern Art, Wales - Y Tabernacl** – Open daily except Sun, 10am-4pm Closed Christmas week. No charge. Lift, ramp, induction loop in the auditorium ☎ 01654 703 355; Fax 01654 702 160; momawales@tabernac.dircon.co.uk www.tabernac.dircon.co.uk

**Centre for Alternative Technology** – & Open daily, 10am-5.30pm (4pm winter) Closed at Christmas and New Year. £5.90, £16.25 (family), £2.90 (child). ☎ 0165 702 400; Fax 01654 702 782; help@catinfo.demon.co.uk; www.cat.org.uk

**King Arthur's Labyrinth** – Guided tour (45 min), Apr-Oct, daily, 10am-5pm. £4.40 £3.10 (child), £3.90 (senior). Warm clothes and sturdy shoes recommended. Parking Refreshments. ☎ 01654 761 584; Fax 01654 761 575. king.arthurs.labyrinth@ corris-wales.co.uk

**Corris Railway Museum** – Open Easter to Sept and bank holiday weekends; furthe details from the local Tourist Information Office. ☎ 01654 761 303. www corris.co.uk

**Ynysh-hir Nature Reserve (RSPB)** – (&) Open daily, 9am-9pm. Visitor Centre Apr-Oct, daily, 9am-5pm; Nov-Mar, weekends only, 10am-4pm. £3, £1 (child), n charge (RSPB and YOC members). Nature trails. 7 Birdwatching hides. Informatio leaflet with trail guide (Welsh). Parking. Picnic tables. Wheelchair access to parts o the reserve. ☎ 01654 781 265; Fax 01654 781 328.

**Dyfi Furnace (CADW)** – Open May-Sept, daily, 9.30am-6.30pm. Closed 1 Jan, 24-2€ Dec. £1.50, £4 (family 2A+3C). ☎ 01654 781 368 (Key holder).

## MARGAM

**Margam Castle and Grounds** – Open Apr-Sept, daily, 10am-4pm; Oct-Mar, grounds only, Wed-Sun, 10am-4pm (3pm last admission). £3.85, £11.85 (family), £2.85 (child). Parking. Coffee shop. ☎01639 881 635; Fax 01639 895 896.

**Margam Abbey Church** – Open Easter to late-Sept, daily, 11.30am-4.30pm. Services: Sun, 8.30am (Eucharist), 11am (Eucharist), 3pm (Evensong); Wed, 10am (Eucharist). Key available from Parish Office Margam Abbey (open Wed-Sun). ☎ 01639 871 184; Fax 01639 871 179.

**Stones Museum (CADW)** – (♿) Open Wed-Sun, 10am-4pm; also Apr-Sept, Tues. Closed 1 Jan, 24-26 Dec. £2, £1.50 (concession), £5 (family 2A+3C). ☎ 029 2050 0200.

## MERTHYR TYDFIL

**Cyfarthfa Castle Museum** – ♿ Open Apr-Sept, daily, 10am-5.30pm; Oct-Mar, Tues-Fri, 10am (midday, Sat-Sun) to 4pm. £1.80, £1 (concession). Parking. Victorian tearoom. Lift. ☎/Fax 01685 723 112.

**Ynysfach Iron Heritage Centre** – Open only by appointment through Cyfarthfa Castle Museum (see above) and the Tourist Information Centre. Parking. Coffee shop. ☎ 01685 723 112 (Cyfarthfa Castle Museum).

**Joseph Parry's Cottage** – (♿) Open Apr-Sept, Thurs-Sun, 2pm-5pm. 60p, 50p (concession). Wheelchair access to ground floor only. ☎ 01685 723 112 (Cyfarthfa Castle Museum).

**Drenewydd Museum (Bute Town)** – (♿) Open Sat-Sun, 2pm-5pm. Parking. Refreshments; picnic area. Shop. ☎ 01685 843 039.

**Elliot Colliery Winding House** – Open Easter to Oct, Sat-Sun and bank hols, 2-5pm. £1, 60p (concession). ☎/Fax 01443 822 666.

**Festival Park Visitor Centre** – (♿) Open sunrise-sunset. Shopping Centre: Open Mon-Sat, 9.30am-5.30pm (7pm Thurs), Sun, 11am-5pm. Parking. Refreshments. ☎ 01495 350 010; Fax 01495 307 363.

## MILFORD HAVEN

**Milford Haven Museum** – ♿ Open Easter-Oct, Mon-Sat, 11am-5pm, Sun, midday-5pm; bank and school holiday Sun, midday-6pm. Shop. Wheelchair available. ☎ 01646 694 496.

**Pembroke Dock Gun Tower** – (♿) Open mid-July to Aug, daily, 10am-5pm; Apr to mid-July and Sept-Oct, daily except Sun, 10am-5pm. No charge. Video (12min). Wheelchair access to main floor. ☎/Fax: 01646 622 246.

**Cleddau Toll Bridge** – Open all year. 75p (car); 75p (caravan); 35p (motor cycle). ☎ 01646 683 517.

## MOLD

**St Mary's Parish Church** – Open July-Sept, Wed, 10pm-4pm. Services: Sun, 8am, 9.30am, 11am, 6.30pm; Wed, 11am; other days, 8am. ☎ 01352 752 960.

**Daniel Owen Museum** – Open Mon (except bank hols) to Sat, 9.30am-7pm (5.30pm Wed; 12.30pm Sat). ☎01352 754 791.

## MONMOUTH

**Castle and Regimental Museum** – ♿ Open Apr-Oct, daily, 2pm-5pm; Nov-Mar, weekends, 2pm-4pm. No charge. ☎ 01600 772 175.

**Nelson Museum** – (♿) Open Mon-Sat, 10am-1pm and 2pm-5pm; Sun, 2pm-5pm. ☎ 01600 713 519; nelsonmuseum@monmouthshire.gov.uk

## MONTGOMERY

**St Nicolas Church** – ♿ Open daily, 8.30am-6.30pm. Services: Sun, 9.30am, 6.30pm, Wed, 11am, daily, 8.30am, 6pm. Induction loop. ☎/Fax 01686 668 243; ahirst@avnet.co.uk; www.avnet.co.uk/ahirst/

**Old Bell Museum** – Open Apr-Sept, Sat and bank hols, 10.30am-5pm; Sun, Wed, Thurs, Fri, 1.30pm-5pm; also Mon-Tues, Aug. £1, 25p (child). Parking. ☎ 01686 668 313.

# N

**Neath Museum and Art Gallery** – ⓖ Open Tues-Sat, 10am-4pm. No charge. Lift. ☎ 01639 645 726.

## Excursions

**Gnoll Estate** – Open daily, 8am-8pm (4.30pm Sept-Mar). Visitor Centre : Open daily, 10am-7pm. Café. No charge. Tel 01639 635 808 (Warden).

**Aberdulais Falls (NT)** – (ⓖ) Open Apr-Nov, daily, 10am-5pm (11am-6pm Sat-Sun and bank hols); Mar, Sat-Sun, 11am-4pm. £2.80, £7 (family 2A+2C), £1.40 (child). Guided tour July-Aug, daily. Audio tour. Parking. Dogs on lead. Refreshments (summer, weekends and holiday Mon). Wheelchair access; lift to falls. ☎ 01639 636 674; qaboff@smtp.ntrust.org.uk

**Penscynor Wildlife Park** – ⓖ Open Easter-Oct, daily, 10am-6pm. £5, £15 (family 2A +4C), £3 (child). Parking. Ramps and slopes. ☎ 01639 642 189; Fax 01639 635 152.

**Cefn Coed Colliery Museum** – ⓖ Open Apr-Oct, daily, 10.30am-4.30pm. £3, £6 (family 2A+2C), £1.50p (concession); Monday no charge. Parking (100yds/100m). ☎ 01639 750 556; Fax 750 556.

**Curlew Weavers** – ⓖ Open Mon-Fri except bank hols, 9.30am-5pm. Closed Christmas. Demonstrations. Parking. ☎ 01239 851 357; Fax 01239 851 357; CWeavers@fsbdial.co.uk

**Rock Mill** – Open Mon-Fri, 10am-5pm (Nov-Mar, mill closed). ☎ 01559 362 356.

**Cenarth Falls Car Park** – Car park: Open all year. £1.30.

**Coracle Museum** – ⓖ Open Easter-Oct, daily except Sat, 10.30am-5.30pm; otherwise by appointment. ⓖ 01239 710 980; ☎/Fax 01239 710 980; martin fowler@btconnect.com; www.coraclecentre.co.uk

**Museum of the Welsh Woollen Industry** – (ⓖ) Open Apr-Sept, Mon-Sat, 10am-5pm; Oct-Mar, Mon-Fri, 10am-5pm. Closed 1 Jan, 24-26 Dec. 50p, no charge (concession). Guided tour (1hr) at 11am and 2pm or by appointment. Guide book and leaflet (Welsh). Parking. Café. Wheelchair access to ground floor only. ☎ 01559 370 929; Fax 01559 371 592.

**Teifi Valley Railway** – ⓖ Open Apr-Oct, Sun-Fri (also some days in Dec), 10.30am-5pm. £5, £3 (child), £4 (concession). Walks. Crazy golf. Miniature railway. Café. Shop. ☎/Fax 01559 371 077.

**Newport Museum and Art Gallery** – ⓖ Open Mon-Thur, 9.30am-5pm (4.30pm Fri; 4pm Sat). No charge. Information centre. Shop. ☎ 01633 840 064; Fax 01633 222 615.

**Newport Transporter Bridge** – Open Mon-Sat, 8am-6pm; Sun, public hols, 1pm-5pm. 50p (vehicle), no charge (pedestrian). Limited parking. ☎ 01633 232 602.

**St Woolos Cathedral** – ⓖ Open daily, 9am-6pm. Services: Sun, 8am, 10.30am (choral), 6.30pm (choral), Wed, 7pm (boys' voices), Fri, 7pm (full choir); term-time, weekday (sung services). Guide book. ☎ 01633 263 338 (Deanery); 01633 212 077 (Cathedral Administrator).

**Civic Centre** – ⓖ Open by appointment only, daily, 8.30am-7pm. Leaflet available (charge). Parking. ☎ 01633 232 000.

## Excursions

**Fourteen Locks Canal Centre** – Open Apr-Oct, Thu-Mon, 10.30am-5.30pm. ☎ 01633 894 802 (summer) and 01633 838 838, ext 2664 (winter).

**Cwmcarn Forest Drive and Visitor Centre** – Drive: Open Easter-Sep.; daily, 11am-7pm (6pm Sep): Oct, Sat-Sun, 11am-5pm. £2.50 (car); £12 (season ticket). Visitor Centre: Mar-Sep, daily, 11am (10am Mon) to 5pm (6pm Fri-Sun); Oct-Feb, Sat-Sun, 10am-4.30pm. ☎ 01495 272 001 (Warden).

**Robert Owen Memorial Museum** – ⓖ Open Mon-Fri, 9.30am-noon and 2pm-3.30pm; Sat, 9.30am-11.30am. Closed Good Friday and Christmas week. No charge. Guided tour by arrangement. Video film (23min). Publications and souvenirs. Parking within walking distance. Stair-climber for front steps. ☎/Fax 01686 626 345; johnd@robert-owen.midwales.com; http://robert-owen.midwales.com

**W H Smith Museum** – Open Mon-Sat, 9am-5.30pm. Closed public hols (except Good Fri). No charge. Leaflet. Public car park nearby. ☎ 01686 626 280.

**Newtown Textile Museum** – Open May-Sept, Tues-Sat and bank holiday Mon, 2pm-5pm. No charge. Leaflet (Welsh). Parking (short term) in town. ☎ 01686 622 024.

# P

**Pembroke Castle** – ♿ Open daily, 10am (9.30am Apr-Sept) to 5pm (6pm Apr-Sept; 4pm Nov-Feb). Closed 1 Jan, 24-26 Dec. £3, £8 (family 2A+2C), £2 (concession). Guided tour (1hr) summer, daily except Sat, 50p. Brochure (French, German, Italian, Welsh). Refreshments (in summer). ☎ 01646 681 510; Fax 01646 622 260.

**Museum of the Home** – Open May-Sept, Mon-Thur, 11am-5pm. £1.20. ☎ 01646 681 200.

**Upton Castle Gardens** – Open Apr-Oct, Sun-Fri, 10am-5pm. £1.20, £3 (family 2A+3C), 60p (child). Tel 01646 651 782 (Carew Castle).

## PEMBROKESHIRE COAST

**Puffin Shuttle** – Operates late-May to late-Sept, daily, 9am-6.30pm approx. Hail and ride service between St David's and Milford Haven stopping at points not more than 6.5mi/10.5km apart which give access to the coast path by road or footpath. ☎ 01437 764 636 (National Park Authority); 01437 764 551, ext 5227 (Pembrokeshire Council); 01348 840 270 (Summerdale Coaches).

**Solva Woollen Mill** – Open Mon-Fri, 9.30am-5.30pm; also Easter-Sept, Sat, 9.30am-5.30pm, Sun, 2pm-5.30pm. ☎ 01437 721 112; enquiries@solvawoollenmill.co.uk; www.solvawoollenmill.co.uk

**Colby Woodland Garden (NT)** – (♿) Open Apr-Nov, daily, 10am-5pm. Walled garden: Apr-Oct, daily, 11am-5pm. £2.80, £7 (family), £1.40 (child). Guided walks with the gardener-in-charge. Events programme. Family Fun activity days. Shakespeare in the meadow. Safari fun pack for children. Parking. Tearoom; picnic area. Shop. Braille guide available. ☎ 01834 811 885 or 01558 831 771.

**Skomer Island Ferry** – Operates from Martinshaven (weather permitting) Apr-Oct, Tues-Sun and bank holiday Mon, at 10am, 11am, noon. Island closes for 4 days in early June for bird count. £6, £5 (child). Parking at West Hook Farm (charge) or Martinshaven (charge). ☎ 01437 765 462.

**Skomer Island National Nature Reserve** – Open Apr-Oct, Tues-Sun and bank holiday Mon. Landing fee, £6, £5 (senior citizen), £3 (students), no charge (child under 16). Ferries at 10am, 11am, 12noon; £6, £5 (child/concession), no charge (child u 5). Closed first Sun-Wed in June. ☎ 01437 765 462; Fax 01437 767 163 (Wildlife Trust West Wales).

**Skomer Island** – No pets. For information on accommodation on Skomer Island ☎ 01437 765 462 (Wildlife Trust West Wales).

**Skokholm Island Ferry** – Operates Apr to end-Sept, for overnight visits only. Guided walks: June and Aug, Mon; advance booking. ☎ 01437 765 462.

## PENARTH

**Turner House Gallery** – (♿) Open (only during exhibitions) Tues-Sun, 10am-5pm; telephone to check. £1.25, no charge (concession); Sun no charge. Leaflet (Welsh). Wheelchair access to ground floor only. ☎ 029 2070 8870.

**St Augustine's Church** – Open June-Aug, daily, 2pm-5pm. Services: daily except Tues and Sat. ☎ 029 2070 9463.

**Cosmeston Medieval Village** – ♿ Open Apr-Sept, daily, 11am-5pm; Oct-Mar, 11am-4pm. Guided tour. Audio tour (French, German, Welsh). Nature trails, wetland walks. Parking. Restaurant, picnic area. ☎ 029 2070 1678; Fax 029 2070 8686; sltham@valeofglamorgan.gov.uk

## PENRHYN

**Penrhyn Castle (NT)** – (♿) Open late-Mar to Nov, daily except Tues, noon (11am July-Aug) to 5pm. Grounds and stable block exhibitions same months and days, 11am (10am July-Aug) to 5pm. £5, £12.50 (family 2A+2C), £2.50 (child); grounds and stableblock only £3.50, £2 (child). Audio tour £1. Industrial Railway Museum. Adventure playground. Parking (200m). Licensed tearoom; picnicking in grounds. Shop. Wheelchair available; access to ground floor; induction loop audio tour; Braille guide. ☎ 01248 353 084 or 371 337 (information); 01248 371 337 (special events); Fax 01248 371 281.

Chamber Pot, Penrhyn Castle

M Caldwell/National Trust Photographic Library

## PLAS NEWYDD (ANGLESEY)

**Snowdon Queen** – Operates daily except Thur and Fri (weather and demand permitting). £3.50, £10 (family 2A+2C). ☎ 01248 670 131 or 01248 671 156 or 07970 038 27.

**Plas Newydd (NT)** – & Open Apr-Oct, daily except Thur and Fri, midday (11am garden) to 5pm. Rhododendron garden: Open Apr to early-June. £4.50, £11 (family 2A+2C), £2.25 (child). Garden only: £2.30, £1.25. Guide books. Brochure. Short guide (Dutch, French, German, Spanish, Welsh). Guided garden walks. Woodland walk giving access to marine walk on the Menai Strait. Concerts, open-air jazz; theatre. Festival week. Family fun days. Children's adventure playground. No dogs. Parking. Licensed tearoom, picnic area. Ramps to ground floor; wheelchair available; stair climber access to first floor. ☎ 01248 714 795; Fax 01248 713 673; ppnmsn@smtp.ntrust.org.uk

## PLAS NEWYDD (DENBIGHSHIRE)

**Plas Newydd (Llangollen)** – (&) Open Apr-Nov, daily except Thur and Fri, 11am-5.30pm (noon-5pm house). £4.50, £11 (family), £2.25 (child); gardens only £2.50, £1.25 (child). Guide book (French, German, Spanish, Welsh). Parking (7min on foot from house; minibus provided); limited parking close to house. Tearoom. Wheelchair access to ground floor and grounds. ☎ 01248 715 272; www.ntrust.org.uk

## PORTHCAWL

**St John Baptist Church, Newton** – Open summer, 2pm-5pm. Services: Sun, 8.30am, 11am, 6pm; Tues, 10.30am; Fri, 10.30am. When locked key available from the Rectory, 64 Victoria Avenue, Porthcawl. ☎ 01656 782 042 or 782 573; philipmasson@hotmail.com

### Excursions

**Kenfig National Nature Reserve** – & Open daily except 25 Dec, 2pm (10am Sat-Sun) to 4.30pm. No charge. Free parking. ☎ 01656 743 386; Fax 01656 745 940.

**Bryngarw Country Park** – Visitor Centre: Open May-Aug, daily, 11am-6pm; Sep-Apr, Sat-Sun, 2-4pm. £2 per car (May-Aug, Sat-Sun and Bank Hol Mon; school hols, Mon-Fri). ☎ 01656 725 155 (Warden).

**Ewenny Priory** – Open usually during the day. Service: Sun, 9.30am.

## PORTHMADOG

**Snowdon Mill Art & Craft Centre** – Open Easter-Sept, 9.30am-5pm; also Jul-Aug, bank hols and weekends, times by telephone; Oct-Easter, 10am-4pm. Closed 25 Dec to first Mon after New Year. ☎ 01766 510 910; Fax 01766 510 913; craft@snowdon-mill.co.uk; www.snowdon-mill.co.uk

**Brynkir Woollen Mill** – Shop: Open Mon-Fri, 8.30am-4.30pm (4pm Fri); check winter and mill opening times by phone. Closed public hols. Parking. Wheelchair access to mill. ☎ 01766 530 236.

**Maritime Museum** – & Open Easter week and Spring bank holiday Mon to Sept, daily, 11am-5pm. £1.00, £2.50 (family), 50p (concession). No parking. ☎ 01766 513 736, 01766 512 864.

**Ffestiniog Railway** – & Operates late-Mar to early-Nov, daily, 9am-5pm; late-Nov to early-Mar, certain days, 9am-5pm. Porthmadog – Blaenau Ffestiniog – Porthmadog (2hr 15min). Maximum £13.80; no charge (child accompanied by an adult). Parking. Refreshments. ☎ 01766 512 340 (for timetable); Fax 01766 514 995; info@festival.demon.co.uk; www.festival.co.uk

**Welsh Highland Railway** – & Operates Easter-Sept (also one week in Oct), daily, at 10.30am, 11.30am, 12.30pm, 2pm, 3pm, 4pm. Return £2, £6 (family 2A+2C), 1.25p (child), £1.75 (concession). Café. Shop. Parking. ☎ 01766 513 402; www.whr.co.uk

**Plas Tan-y-Bwlch** – Open daily, 10am-sunset. £2.50, £5 (family). Guided tour (1hr) by arrangement with the administrator. Guide book and brochure (Welsh). Parking. Most of the gardens on a steep slope; inaccessible to wheelchairs. ☎ 01766 590 324; plas@eryri-npa.gov.uk

## PORTMEIRION

**Portmeirion** – (&) Open daily, 9.30am-5.30pm. £4.50. Brochure (Welsh). Audio visual presentation. Audio tour. Parking. Refreshments. ☎ 01766 770 000; Fax 01766 771 331.

**Plas Brondanw** – (&) Open daily, 9am-5pm. £1.50, 25p (child). Leaflet. Parking. ☎ 01766 770 484; 07880 766 741.

**fan Argoed Countryside Centre** – &  Open Apr-Sept, daily, 10.30am-5pm (6pm ⸱eekends), Oct-Mar, 10.30am-4pm, (5pm weekends). Forest walks. Cycle trails; cycle ⸱re. Caravan park and camping. Parking (charge in summer). Café. Wheelchairs ⸱ailable; trandom bikes for less-able adults; tricycles for less-able children; improved ⸱ccess for wheelchairs to woodland garden from Rhyslyn car park. ☎ 01639 850 ⸱64; Fax 01639 850 446.

Powis Castle

## POWIS

**Powis Castle (NT)** – Castle: Open July-Aug, daily except Mon, 1pm-5pm; Apr-July and Sept-Oct, daily except Mon-Tues, 1pm-5pm. Garden: Open same days as the castle, 11am-6pm. £7.50, £18.75 (family), £3.75 (child); garden only £5.00, £12.50 (family), £2.50 (child). Guide book (Dutch, French, German, Spanish, Welsh). No dogs. Parking. Licensed restaurant. ☎ 01938 554 338, Fax 01938 554 336.

## PRESTEIGNE

**Judge's Lodging** – (&) Open Mar-Oct, daily, 10am-6pm, Nov-Dec, Wed-Sun, 10am-4pm. £3.75, £2.75 (concession), £11 (family). Audio tour. Audio transcripts (French, German, Welsh). Local history exhibition (Welsh). Wheelchair access to ground floor only.

☎ 01544 260 650/1; Fax 01544 260 652.

**St Andrew's Church** – Open daily. Services: Sun, 11am.

# R

## RADNOR

**St Stephen's Church, Old Radnor** – Open daily, 10am-7pm. Services: 1st Sunday of ⸱he month, 6.30pm; 3rd Sunday, 6pm; 2nd and 4th Sunday, 11.30am. When closed ⸱ey available from Mrs G Hughes, Lower House, Burlingjobb (☎ 01544 230 428).

## RAGLAN

**Raglan Castle (CADW)** – Open Apr-May and Oct, daily, 9.30am-5pm; Jun-Sept, ⸱.30am-6.30pm, Nov to end-Mar, Mon-Sat, 9.30am (11am Sun) to 4pm. Closed ⸱4-26 Dec. £2.40, £6.70 (family 2A+3C), £1.90 (concession). ☎ 01291 690 228.

## Vale of RHEIDOL

**Vale of Rheidol Light Railway** – Operates late-July to Aug, Mon-Thurs, 4 trains per ⸱ay, Fri, Sat and Sun, 2 trains per day; Apr, May, June, Sept and Oct, 2 trains per day ⸱some exceptions). Single journey (approx 12mi) 1hr, return journey 3hrs (including ⸱ hr stop at Devil's Bridge). Return £10.50, £1.50 (for 1st and 2nd child), £5.25 (for ⸱rd and subsequent child). Parking. Café at Devil's Bridge. ☎ 01970 625 819; Fax ⸱1970 623 769; www.rheidolrailway.co.uk

**Rheidol Power Station** – (&) Open Apr-Oct, daily, 10am-4.30pm. Guided tour ⸱40min) available. No charge. Parking. Refreshments. ☎ 01970 880 667; Fax 01970 ⸱80 670.

**Nant-yr-Arian Forest Centre** – &  Open 10am to 5pm (4.30pm winter). No charge. ⸱eaflet 50p. Parking £1. Red kite feeding in winter. Access-for-all walk. Mountain bike ⸱oute. Children's play area. Picnic areas. Shop. ☎ 01970 890 694.

Vale of RHEIDOL

**Llywernog Silver-Lead Mine** – Open mid-Mar to Oct, 10am-6pm; also during school holidays in Feb. £4.95, £14 (family), £2.95 (child), £3.95 (senior citizen/students). Guide sheet available (French, Welsh). Parking. Tearoom; picnic area. Mine shop. ☎ 01970 890 620; Fax 01545 570 823.

**Devil's Bridge Waterfalls** – Open Apr-Oct, daily, 10am-5pm (5.30pm weekends, public hols, 9.30am-7pm; Nov-Mar, any time (entrance through turnstiles). Summer £2.20, £1.10 (child); winter £2. Parking. Refreshments. Gift shop. ☎/Fax 01970 890 233.

## RHONDDA

**Pontypridd Historical Centre** – & Open Mon-Sat, 10am-5pm. 25p, 15p (child). Craft shop. Bookshop. ☎ 01443 409 512.

**Rhondda Heritage Park** – & Open Apr-Sept, daily, 10am-6pm; Oct-Apr, daily except Mon, 10am-6pm. Closed 25-26 Dec. Guided tour 10am-4.30pm (last tour). Under ground tour: A Shift in Time. Audio-visual presentation (French, German, Italian, Japanese, Spanish, Welsh). Leaflet (French, German, Italian, Japanese, Spanish, Welsh). Guide book (Welsh). Children's giant play area. Free parking. Coffee shop; licensed restaurant. Ramps, lifts. ☎ 01443 682 036; Fax: 01443 687 420.

## RHUDDLAN

**Rhuddlan Castle (CADW)** – Open May-Sept, daily, 10am-5pm. £1.70, £4.60 (family 2A+3C), £1.20 (concession).

## RHYL

**Sea-Life Aquarium** – & Open all year, daily except 25 Dec, 10am-5pm (later in summer), in winter telephone to check times. £4.99, £3.99 (concession/child over 4); ticket valid all day. Children's outdoor play area. Refreshments. ☎ 01745 344 660; Fax 01745 332 991.

**Museum and Arts Centre** – & Open Mon-Fri, 10am-5pm; Sat, 9.30am-12.30pm. Closed most public hols. No charge. Café. ☎ 01745 353 814; Fax: 01745 331 438.

**Offa's Dyke Interpretive Centre** – & Open Easter-Sept, daily, 10.30am-1pm and 1.30pm-5pm. No charge. Parking (charge). ☎ 01745 889 092.

## RUTHIN

**Ruthin Craft Centre** – Open Spring bank holiday to Sept, daily, 10am-5.30pm; Oct to Spring bank holiday, daily, 10am (midday Sun) to 5pm. Closed 1 Jan, 25-26 Dec. ☎ 01824 704 774 (administration), 703 992 (tourist information); Fax 01824 702 060.

**St Peter's Church** – Open Apr-Sept, 9am-5pm. Services: Sun, 8am, 10.30am, 6.15pm. Key available from the Cloisters, School Road. ☎ 01824 702 068.

**Nantclwyd House** – Closed indefinitely. ☎ 01824 703 992.

# S

## ST ASAPH

**St Asaph Cathedral** – & Open daily, 8am-6pm (4pm winter), Sun, 12.30pm-3pm and 4.30pm-6pm. No charge. Guided tour (1hr). Fact sheet (French, German). Parking. Braille guide. ☎ 01745 583 429, 583 597.

## ST DAVID'S

**Thousand Islands Expeditions** – Operate from St Justinian's or Whitesand Bay according to season. Booking Office in Cross Square, St David's. Trip round Ramsey Island and into sea-caves (2hr) £20, £10 (child under 14). Jet-powered white-water rafting unsuitable for children (1hr) £20. Trip to Ramsey Island by conventional boat: landing (all-day) £10, £5 (child); landing and around (3hr on the island and 1hr 30min cruising) £18, £9 (child); around only £10, £6 (child). Puffin Watch (with RSPB guide) April to end-July, £12. Sunset Shearwater Watch (with RSPB guide) May to end-July, £12. ☎ 01437 721 686, Freephone 0800 163 621; Fax 01437 720 747; www.tiex.co.uk

**Voyage of Discovery** – Operates daily according to demand and the time of year from the Lifeboat Station in St Justinian around Ramsey Island (1hr 30min; no landing). Booking office at 1 High Street, St David's. Conventional boat £10, £6 (child); inflatable £12, £7 (child), £34 (family 2A+2C). ☎ 01437 720 285.

**St David's Cathedral** – & Open daily, 7.30am (12.15pm Sun) to 6pm. Donation £2, £1 (concession). Guided tour (1hr 30min) early-July to late-Aug, Mon, Wed, Thurs, at 10.45am. Guided tour £3, £1.20 (child under 16). Brochure (Welsh, French, German). Parking. ☎ 01437 720 691; Fax 01437 721 885; www.stdavidscathedral.org.uk

**Bishop's Palace (CADW)** – (&) Open May to early-Oct, daily, 9.30am-6.30pm; Mar to early-May and Oct, daily, 9.30am-5pm; late-Oct to end-Mar, Mon-Sat, 9.30am-4pm, Sun, midday-2pm. £2, £5.50 (family 2A+3C), £1.50 (concession). ☎ 0437 720 517.

**Oceanarium** – (&) Open Apr-Sept, daily, 10am-5pm (6pm or later in school holidays); Oct-Mar, 10.30am-4pm. £3, £9 (family 2A+2C), £1.80 (child 3-16). Refreshments; picnic area. Gift shop. Wheelchair access to ground floor. ☎ 01437 720 453; www.sealife.demon.co.uk

## SNOWDONIA

**Snowdon Sherpa Bus Network** – Operates June-Oct; limited service in winter. Timetables available. ☎ 01766 770 274 (Snowdonia National Park Information Centre).

**National Mountain Centre** – Open mid-July to early-Sept, daily, 9.30am-5.30pm; courses (2hr) at 9.30am, midday and 3pm in abseiling, climbing, canoeing (participants must be able to swim; change of clothes advisable) and skiing (long trousers, long sleeves and gloves); £7.50 per course. Booking available. Equipment provided. ☎ 01690 720 214, Fax 01690 720 394; info@pyb.co.uk; www.pyb.co.uk

Shattered Rocks, The Glyders

K J Richardson/National Trust Photographic Library

## STRATA FLORIDA ABBEY

**Strata Florida Abbey (CADW)** – Open May-Sept, daily, 10am-5pm. £1.70, £4.60 (family 2A+3C), £1.20 (concession). ☎ 01974 831 261.

## SWANSEA

**Lovespoon Gallery** – Open daily except Sun, 10am-5.30pm. ☎ 01792 360 132.

**Maritime and Industrial Museum** – & Open Tues-Sun and bank holiday Mon, 10am-5pm. Historic vessels and tramshed: Open Apr-Sept. Closed 1 Jan, 25-26 Dec. No charge. Parking nearby. Café. Gift shop. ☎ 01792 650 351 or 470 371; swansea.maritime.museum@business.ntl.com; www.swansea.gov.uk

**Swansea Museum** – Open all year, Tues-Sun and bank holidays, 10am-5pm. No charge. Parking. Free guide (English, Welsh). ☎ 01792 653 763; Fax 01792 652 585.

**Dylan Thomas Centre** – & Open Tues-Sun, 10am-5pm (4.30pm last admission). Bookshop. Gift shop. Parking. Restaurant and bar. Wheelchair access and lift. ☎ 01792 463 980.

*Landore Viaduct* by Jack Jones

**Glynn Vivian Art Gallery** – (♿) Open Tues-Sun and bank holiday Mon, 10am-5pm. No charge. Shop. Wheelchair access to ground floor only. ☎ 01792 651 738 and 655 006; Fax 01792 651 713.

**Plantasia** – ♿ Open daily (except Mon, Oct-Jun), 10am-5pm (4.30pm last admission) £2.30, £1.60 (concession), Guide (Welsh). Gift shop. Plant trails. ☎01792 474 555; Fax 01792 652 588; www.plantasia.org

**Brangwyn Hall** – ♿ Open (private functions permitting) Mon-Fri, 9am-5pm; phone to check. Closed 1 Jan, bank holidays, 25-27 Dec. ☎ 01792 635 489.

**Clyne Gardens** – Open daily, 8.30am-sunset. No charge. ☎ 01792 401 737 or 635 444.

**Oystermouth Castle** – Open Easter-Sept, daily, 11am-5pm. £1, 80p (child). Pay-and-display parking nearby. ☎ 01792 368 732.

# T

## TENBY

**Tenby Carriage rides** – Operate from the parish church (30min approx; 8 max). £2, £1.50 (child).

**Tenby Museum and Art Gallery** – Open all year, Mon-Fri, 10am-5pm; also Apr to end-Oct, Sat-Sun. Admission charge. ☎/Fax 01834 842 809; tenbymuseum@hotmail.com

**Tudor Merchant's House (NT)** – Open Apr-Sept, daily (except Wed), 10am (1pm Sun) to 5pm; Oct, daily except Wed and Sat, 10am (midday Sun) to 3pm. £1.80, 90p (child). ☎ 01834 842 279 (during season), 01558 822 800 (during office hours).

**St Mary's Church** – Open daily, 9am-5pm. Services: see notice in main porch.

### Excursions

**Caldey Island Ferry** – (♿) Operates (weather permitting) Easter-Oct, Mon-Fri, from 10am, every 20-30min; also June-Aug, Sat, from 10.45am. Time 20-30min. £7, £3 (child). Access for the disabled easier at high tide. ☎ 01834 844 453 (John Cattini).

**Manorbier Castle** – ♿ Open Easter-Sept, 10.30am-5.30pm. £2, £1 (child), £1.50 (senior). Parking. ☎ 01834 871 317 or 01834 871 394.

**St James's Church, Manorbier** – Open Easter-Oct, daily, 9.30am-6pm. Services: Sun, as shown on the notice board.

## NTERN

**ntern Abbey (CADW)** – ♿ Open daily, 9.30am (11am Sun, late-Oct to Mar) to 5pm pm Jun-Sep; 4pm late-Oct to Mar). Closed 24-26 Dec. £2.40, £6.70 (family +3C), £1.90 (concession). ☎ 01291 689 251.

**ntern Old Station** – ♿ Open Apr-Oct, daily, 10.30am-5.30pm. Audio-visual pro-amme. Camp site for walkers, cyclists and canoeists (no vehicle entry). Refresh-ents; picnic and barbecue area. ☎/Fax 01291 689 566.

## REDEGAR

**edegar House** – (♿) Open Easter to Sept, Wed-Sun and bank hols, 11.30am-4pm st admission). House and garden £4.75, £12.95 (family), £2.25 (child), £3.65 oncession). Audio guide for formal gardens £2. Country House tour (1 hr). Guide ok. Special events all year and at Halloween and Christmas. Children's playground. ating. Parking £1. Restaurant, picnic area. Craft shops. Gift shop. Wheelchair access ground floor only; wheelchairs available. ☎ 01633 815 880 (opening times); Fax 633 815 895.

## REGARON

**elsh Gold Centre** – (♿) Open Mon-Sat, 9.30am-5.30pm; also June-Sept, Sun, am-6pm. Closed 1 Mar. Ramp for wheelchairs. ☎01794 298 415; Fax 01974 298 90.

**egaron Bog (Cors Caron)** – ♿ Open all year. No charge. Permits required from arden for walks (except on the Old Railway Line). Parking. ☎ 01974 298 480 Warden); pculyer@ccw.gov.uk; www.ccw.gov.uk

## RETOWER

**etower Court and Castle (CADW)** – ♿ Open Mar-Oct, daily, 10am-5pm (6pm d-May to Sept; 4pm Mar to early-Apr). £2.20, £6.10 (family 2A+3C), £1.70 oncession). ☎ 01874 730 279.

## YWYN

**owdonia National Park Visitor Centre** – Open Easter-Oct, daily, 10am-1pm and m-6pm. ☎ 01654 767 321.

**t Cadfan's Church** – Open daily, 9am-sunset. Services: Sunday, 11am, 6pm; 2nd and h Sunday of the month, 8am (Eucharist), 11am, 6pm. Guided tours and history of Cadfan: Easter-mid Oct, Mon, 10am-midday. ☎ 01654 710 295; martinriley@ synet.co.uk

**alyllyn Railway** – ♿ Operates from Tywyn Wharf June-Nov, daily, 10am-4pm; Apr, ay and 26 Dec-1 Jan, 11am-2.30pm; also Sun, from 1 Mar, 11am-2pm. Return hr 30min)/All-day Rover £9, £2 (child); cheapest single £1.50 (concessions avail-le); 8-day Run-about-Ticket £20, £10 (child); Narrow Gauge Wanderer Ticket valid r unlimited travel on all eight «Great Little Trains» during any 8 days within a 5-day period or any 4 days within any 8-day period. Leaflet (Danish, Dutch, French, nnish, German, Japanese, Norwegian, Swedish). ☎ 01654 710 472; Fax 01654 11 755; enquiries@talyllyn.co.uk; www.talyllyn.co.uk

## xcursions

**olgoch Falls** – Open all year. Donation welcome. 300yds from hotel and car park to st falls; full circuit 45min. Parking.

**t Mary's Church** – ♿ Open sunrise-sunset. Services: Christmas Day, 10.30am ucharist). Ramp; no steps. ☎ 01654 782 268.

## U

## SK

**sk Rural Life Museum** – (♿) Open Apr-Oct, daily, 10am (2pm Sat-Sun) to 5pm; ov-Mar, telephone for times. Wheelchair access to lower levels of museum only. ☎ 01291 673 777.

**riory Church of St Mary** – Open weekends and bank hols. Services: Sun, 8am, 0am, 6pm (summer), 4pm (winter). ☎ 01291 672 653.

*he key on page 9 explains*
*e abbreviations and symbols used on the maps and plans*

# V

**Valle Crucis Abbey (CADW)** – (&) Open May-Sept, daily, 10am-5pm. £2, £5.⸱ (family 2A+3C), £1.50 (concession). ☎ 01978 860 326.

**Lake Vyrnwy Visitor Centre** – (&) Open Apr-25 Dec, daily, 10.30am-5.30p (sunset in winter); Jan-Mar, Sat-Sun, 10.30am-4.30pm. No charge. Leaflet (Welsh Parking. ☎ 01691 870 278; Fax 01691 870 313.

# W

**Welsh Life, Museum of** – (&) Open daily, 10am-5pm. Closed 24-26 Dec. Ap Oct £5.50, no charge (concession); Oct-Mar £4.50, no charge (concessio Guide book (Dutch, French, German, Japanese, Welsh). Parking. Refreshment ☎ (029) 2057 3500; Fax (029) 2057 3490; post.awc@btconnect.com; www.nmg ac.uk/mwl/

**St Mary's Church** – Open in summer at advertised times. Key available at t Vicarage on presentation of proof of identity. Services: Sun, 8am, 11am, 6.30p Guide book. Wheelchair access difficult. ☎ 01938 553 164.

**Powysland Museum and Montgomery Canal Centre** – & Open May-Sept, da except Wed, 11am-1pm and 2pm-5pm; Oct-Apr, Mon, Tues, Thurs and Fri, 11am-1p and 2pm-5pm, Sat, 2pm-5pm. £1, 50p (concessions), no charge (child under 1€ Parking for disabled visitors only. ☎ 01938 554 656.

**Welshpool and Llanfair Light Railway** – & Open Easter to mid-Oct. Retu £7.90, first child accompanying adult £1, other children £4 each. Informati sheet (Dutch, French, German). Tearoom. Shop. ☎ 01938 810 441; Fax 0193 810 861.

**Andrew Logan Museum of Sculpture** – & Open Jun-Aug, Wed-Sun, midday-6pm Easter, May, Sept and Oct, weekends and bank holiday Mon, 12pm-6pm. £2, £ (concession). Tearoom; coffee bar. Gift shop. ☎ 01686 640 689; Fax 01686 6⸱ 764; info@andrewlogan.com; www.andrewlogan.com

**St Giles' Church** – & Open Apr-Oct, Mon-Fri, 10am-4pm. No steps. ☎ 01978 3⸱ 808; Fax 01978 313 375.

**County Borough Museum** – Open daily, 10.30am-5pm (3pm Sat). No charg ☎ 01978 317 970; Fax 01978 317 982; museum@wrexham.gov.uk

**Minera Lead Mine** – & Open Easter-Sept, weekends and bank holidays, midday-5p (4.30pm last admission). No charge. Country park: Open daily. ☎ 01978 753 4( (mine); 751 320 (country park).

**Nant Mill** – & Open Easter-Aug, daily, 10am-4.30pm; Sept-Easter, Sat-Su 10am-4.30pm. No charge. Brochure available. ☎ 01978 752 772.

**Bersham Ironworks** – Open Easter-Sept, weekends and bank holidays, mi day-4.30pm (last admission). No charge. Parking. ☎ 01978 261 529; Fax 0197 361 703.

**Bersham Heritage Centre** – Open daily, 10am-4.30pm (3.30pm; Oct-Easter). N charge. Parking.

**All Saints Church** – Open Apr-Sept, daily, 10.30am-4pm. Services: Sun, 8am, 11a (Holy Communion), 6pm (Evensong). 1st Sun of the month, 10am (Welsh); 2nd S⸱ of the month, 10am (family service); 3rd Sun of the month, 10am (family comm nion). When locked ☎ 01978 852 140 (Mrs Davis). ☎ 01978 852 236; Fax 0197 856 630; suepcc@hotmail.com; http://members.aol.com/allstgres